THE PAPERS OF

WOODROW WILSON

VOLUME 10
1896-1898

SPONSORED BY THE WOODROW WILSON
FOUNDATION
AND PRINCETON UNIVERSITY

THE PAPERS OF
WOODROW WILSON

ARTHUR S. LINK, *EDITOR*

JOHN WELLS DAVIDSON AND DAVID W. HIRST

ASSOCIATE EDITORS

JOHN E. LITTLE, *ASSISTANT EDITOR*

JEAN MACLACHLAN, *CONTRIBUTING EDITOR*

M. HALSEY THOMAS, *CONSULTING EDITOR*

Volume 10 · 1896-1898

PRINCETON, NEW JERSEY

PRINCETON UNIVERSITY PRESS

1971

INTRODUCTION

THIS tenth volume of *The Papers of Woodrow Wilson*, covering the period from September 1896 to September 1898, opens on a high note with Wilson's delivery on October 21, 1896, of his Sesquicentennial address, "Princeton in the Nation's Service," certainly the outstanding speech of his academic career and one of the noblest of his lifetime. By the close of the volume, in the summer of 1898, no other professor in the University was, in President Patton's words, as highly favored as Wilson.

The intervening two years saw Wilson making significant advances in several fields. In the fall of 1896, he opened a campaign to enrich the quality of teaching in the University in general and his own field of interest in particular. Concern about developing the History Department led him to a protracted attempt to recruit for Princeton the rising young historians at the University of Wisconsin, Frederick Jackson Turner and Charles Homer Haskins. A wealth of correspondence enables one to follow the shifting stages of negotiation and to measure the depth of Wilson's chagrin when the plan was ultimately frustrated.

Wilson's own academic fortunes rose further, however, when he was named McCormick Professor of Jurisprudence and Politics in 1897 and reorganized his teaching program. Indications of fresh academic contributions are found in the lecture notes for his course, Elements of Politics, printed in full in this volume. Simultaneously, he participated in the work of the newly formed Committee on University Affairs, whose labors culminated in an exhaustive and illuminating report, also included in this volume.

Stimulated by the success of the Sesquicentennial oration, which echoed far beyond the Princeton campus, Wilson's fame as a speaker brought him heavy obligations on the alumni circuit and as a public lecturer. To his weeks of absence from Princeton in the winters of 1897 and 1898 in order to continue his annual lecture series at the Johns Hopkins, we owe more of the intimate correspondence between Wilson and his wife that affords such remarkable insight into the Wilson family's affections and preoccupations. Moreover, the series of these letters in February and March 1898 shows Wilson hammering out, day by day, his Donovan lectures on Bagehot and Maine, just prior to their delivery.

That same March, the offer of the Chairmanship of the Faculty and a law professorship at the University of Virginia brought the matter of Wilson's permanent relationship to Princeton to a head. Alarmed by the prospect of losing him, a number of influential Princeton trustees, spearheaded by Cornelius Cuyler Cuyler of New York, closed ranks to provide a material guarantee that he remain in Princeton. The rallying of forces, the earnest pleas that he concede to the arrangement, and the agreement itself are all found in the closing pages of the volume. Sure of himself now, Wilson believed that twenty years of apprentice work lay behind him and that "quiet hours, continuous thought and uninterrupted labour" lay ahead.

The number of news reports of Wilson's addresses has increased substantially in this volume and will continue to grow in future volumes; hence this seems an appropriate time to describe our method in selecting them. In every case, we examine all reports in all extant newspapers and other publications. From among these, we select for inclusion what is deemed to be the fullest report, adding in footnotes significant and interesting portions of additional text found in the reports that are not published. When it seems useful to do so, we print parallel reports of the same address. We have tried to include at least one report of all of Wilson's public speeches, not only in order to make the documentary record as complete as possible, but also because these reports are often our best source of Wilson's reactions to the political and diplomatic events and developments of his time.

Readers are again reminded that *The Papers of Woodrow Wilson* is a continuing series; that persons, institutions, and events that figure prominently in earlier volumes are not reidentified in subsequent ones; and that the Index to each volume gives cross references to fullest earlier identifications. Readers are also reminded that it is our practice to print texts *verbatim et literatim*, repairing words and phrases only when necessary for clarity or ease of reading, and that we make silent corrections only of obvious typographical errors in typed copies.

We are grateful to Mrs. Bryant Putney for continued excellent copyediting and other assistance, to Miss Marjorie Sirlouis and Colonel James B. Rothnie, U.S.A., Ret., for deciphering Wilson's shorthand; to Dr. Herbert Aptheker for furnishing copies of letters from William Edward Burghardt Du Bois to Wilson, from the Du Bois Papers in his possession; and to Professor Ray A. Billington of the Huntington Library for continuing to supply information about Wilson materials in the several collections of the Papers of Frederick Jackson Turner.

THE EDITORS

Princeton, New Jersey
October 28, 1970

CONTENTS

ILLUSTRATIONS

Following page 294

TEXT ILLUSTRATIONS

ABBREVIATIONS

ALI	autograph letter initialed
ALS	autograph letter(s) signed
EAW	Ellen Axson Wilson
EAWhwL	Ellen Axson Wilson handwritten letter
enc(s).	enclosed, enclosure(s)
env.	envelope
hw	handwriting or handwritten
hwS	handwritten signed
L	letter
PCL	printed copy of letter
S	signed
sh	shorthand
T	typed
TCL	typed copy of letter
tel.	telegram
TLS	typed letter signed
WW	Woodrow Wilson
WWhw	Woodrow Wilson handwriting or handwritten
WWS	Woodrow Wilson signed
WWsh	Woodrow Wilson shorthand
WWT	Woodrow Wilson typed
WWTLS	Woodrow Wilson typed letter signed

ABBREVIATIONS FOR COLLECTIONS AND LIBRARIES

Following the National Union Catalog of the Library of Congress

DLC	Library of Congress
LNHT	Howard-Tilton Memorial Library of Tulane University
MdBJ	The Johns Hopkins University Library
MH	Harvard University Library
NjP	Princeton University Library
NjR	Rutgers University Library
NN	New York Public Library
PPAmP	American Philosophical Society, Philadelphia
RSB Coll., DLC	Ray Stannard Baker Collection of Wilsoniana, Library of Congress
ScU	University of South Carolina Library
ViU	University of Virginia Library
ViW	College of William and Mary Library
WC, NjP	Woodrow Wilson Collection, Princeton University
WHi	State Historical Society of Wisconsin, Madison
WP, DLC	Woodrow Wilson Papers, Library of Congress

SYMBOLS

[Oct. 8, 1896]	publication date of a published writing; also date of document when date is not part of text
[*Oct. 21, 1896*]	latest composition date of a published writing
[[Aug. 5, 1897]]	delivery date of a speech if publication date differs

THE PAPERS OF

WOODROW WILSON

VOLUME 10

1896-1898

THE PAPERS OF
WOODROW WILSON

To Richard Watson Gilder[1]

My dear Mr. Gilder,   Princeton, Sept. 10, 1896.

Your suggestion about the Blennerhassett document[2] sounds very attractive, but of course I cannot form any definite judgment upon it without more explicit information about the character of the paper.

I shall try to get to N. Y. soon to have a look at it if you will let me. I will of course drop you another line beforehand.

It doesn't look now as if I should have much time this winter for occasional essays, but of course one never knows what he can do until he knows the subject suggested.[3]

Very sincerely yours,   Woodrow Wilson

EAWhwL, WWS (WW Coll., NjR).
    [1] Editor of the *Century Magazine* of New York since 1881.
    [2] Nothing is known about this document by or relating to Harman Blennerhassett. Perhaps it came from the collection referred to in Therese Blennerhassett-Adams, "The True Story of Harman Blennerhassett," *Century Magazine*, LXII (July 1901), 351-56.
    [3] This letter was written by Mrs. Wilson because Wilson, having suffered a small stroke in May 1896, was still unable to use his right hand freely. See WW to Harper and Brothers, May 27, 1896, n. 2, Vol. 9.

To Harper and Brothers

My dear Sirs,   Princeton, New Jersey, 14 September, 1896.

The proofs[1] you were kind enough to send me last week reached me immediately after my arrival from Europe, and I found so many things waiting to be done at once that I have not been able to complete my examination of them as soon as I wished and intended. I send them back to-day, however, with the necessary revision, and trust that the delay has not caused you serious inconvenience.

I was greatly surprised to find the pages cast without illustrations. Is it possible that you mean to print the book without the illustrations that accompanied the articles in the Magazine? I sincerely hope not. Mr. Pyle's drawings, particularly, added so much to their value that they will be sadly missed, and I had hoped to see the text even more fully illustrated than before.[2]

I must beg you to indulge me in the matter of hyphens. You

will find that I have marked out a great many in the proofs. We are in danger of Germanizing our printing by using them so much; and I have a very decided preference in the matter.

I have been strongly advised by my friends not to add anything to the chapter on the Revolution, which I had intended to expand a little; and I shall, therefore, send you the copy for the rest of the book at once.*

Very sincerely Yours,   Woodrow Wilson

* I send Chaps. VI., and VII. to-day, and should like to see proofs before the pages are cast.

WWTLS (Berg Coll., NN).
    1 Of Wilson's *George Washington*, issued by Harper and Brothers in December 1896.
    2 Most of Howard Pyle's illustrations for Wilson's articles in *Harper's Magazine* were used in the book. They were tipped in.

Two Letters from Harper and Brothers

Dear Sir: New York City   Sept. 28. 1896.

We send you today, by express, prepaid, complete cast proofs of "George Washington."

In response to your inquiry, we beg leave to say that the numbering of the pages is as it will appear when the book is printed. The illustrations will not be folioed, but will appear in the list of illustrations as facing page so and so.

Very truly yours,   Harper & Brothers.   per a.

Dear Sir: New York City   Oct. 2. 1896.

Your letter of yesterday is at hand. In reply we regret to say that the foreman of the composing room misunderstood his instructions, and had the second half of "George Washington" cast without first submitting proofs to you. We shall have another set of proofs pulled of that portion of the work and forward them to you tomorrow. Please to mark such corrections as you wish to make and we will have the plates altered accordingly. The proofs which you have of the first part were taken before your corrections were made. The corrections have since been made, and proofs of the corrected pages will be sent to you.

Yours very truly   Harper & Brothers.   per a.

ALS (WP, DLC).

A News Report

[Oct. 8, 1896]

HALL MASS MEETING.

The meeting under the auspices of Whig and Clio Halls to acquaint new students with the aims and methods of the two Societies, was held yesterday at 1.30 in Murray Hall. [John Musser] Frame '97 presided and introduced the speakers. Prof. Wilson and R. M. McElroy '96 represented Whig, Prof. Bliss Perry and Alexander McGaffin '94, Clio. Prof. Wilson spoke of the necessity of Hall training. The Halls are Democratic institutions and student organizations. The men who do not engage actively in Hall work, lose much of what they ought to get out of the college course, and forget the duty they owe both to themselves and to society in general. Prof. Perry dwelt more especially on the traditions and historic life of the Halls, and upon the distinct advantage for perfecting an all around development. Because of the diversity of college life there is a necessity of a unifying principle in our intellectual life and this need is only to be supplied through the agency of our literary societies. . . .

Printed in the *Daily Princetonian*, Oct. 8, 1896; one editorial heading omitted.

To Francis Henry Smith[1]

Princeton, New Jersey,

My dear Professor Smith,   13 October, 1896.

I am sincerely glad to learn that you are to be at our Celebration;[2] I am only sorry that I did not know of it before choosing and inviting my guests. Will you not write at once to Prof. Andrew F. West, University Hall, Princeton, of your official delegation; and to Prof. Wm. Libbey, at the same address, with reference to accommodation? We should all feel very badly to see a representative of the University of Virginia ill provided for.

Your questions are easily answered; and I am wholly glad to serve you in the matter. The day on which addresses are to be presented from other institutions is Tuesday, the twenty-first, in the afternoon at three o'clock. But that is the least interesting day of the three, and I sincerely hope you will be able to be here throughout the Celebration.

It is very much hoped that all representatives will wear the academic costume; and we feel quite sure that most of them will; but it is by no means our idea to force the adoption of the cap and gown, and the form is in no sense obligatory.

I hope that you will pardon this mechanical way of writing. I have been threatened of late with "writer's cramp," and dare not for the present use the pen.

It was a real pleasure to hear from you and I shall look forward to greeting you next week with genuine satisfaction.

Most sincerely Yours,   Woodrow Wilson

WWTLS (Tucker-Harrison-Smith Coll., ViU).
1 Professor of Natural Philosophy at the University of Virginia.
2 The Sesquicentennial of the College of New Jersey.

From the Minutes of the Princeton Faculty

5 5′ P.M., Wednesday, October 14, 1896.

The Faculty met. The Dean[1] presided in the absence of the President.[2] . . .

Letters were read from Lord Kelvin, Professor of Natural Philosophy in the University of Glasgow, Scotland, in acknowledgement of the congratulations of the Faculty of the College upon the Celebration of the Semi-Centennial of his appointment as Professor in the University and of the attendance of Professor Woodrow Wilson as the representative of the Faculty at the Celebration. . . .[3]

"Minutes of the Faculty, 1895-1902," bound minute book (University Archives, NjP).
1 James Ormsbee Murray.
2 Francis Landey Patton.
3 See WW to EAW, June 17, 1896, n. 1, Vol. 9.

A Newspaper Report of an Address
at the Brooklyn Institute

[Oct. 15, 1896]

IDEALS OF DEMOCRACY.

Professor Woodrow Wilson, LL.D., of Princeton college, spoke before the members of the Brooklyn Institute of Arts and Sciences in Association hall last night on "The True Grandeur of the Republic."[1] Dr. Wilson was introduced to the audience by John A. Taylor, president of the department of political science, and among those who occupied seats on the platform were Dr. Thomas J. Backus, Felix Campbell, John Winslow, Professor William Cranston Lawton, the Rev. J. C. Ager, Jacob C. Dettmer, Charles P. Abbey, Dr. P. W. Ray and Dr. Robert Ormiston.

The address of the evening was devoted to an analysis of the meaning and ideals of Democratic government—an apropos theme in view of the approaching presidential election. That the audience appreciated this fact was evident by its frequent applause of the lecturer's hits; for, although recent politics was religiously avoided, there was occasional apt characterization and satirical reference which Dr. Wilson's hearers took as directed to present conditions.

"Government is old," said Professor Wilson, "old as love and loyalty and intelligence, and we know its history. It is a singular fact that invent as fast as we may in other departments of activity we rarely if ever invent anything new in government. Since the Germanic tribes gave us the principle of representation practically nothing has been added save as to the forms of government. Those who planned our constitution were aware that they were not inventing a new kind of rule. They simply sought to Americanize the English government, casting aside the old narrow monarchical ideas and at the same time, by a system of checks and balances, preventing the too hasty will of the people from finding expression in legislature, executive or judiciary. We have in a measure undone their work. Year by year we have sought to bring government nearer the public. Our presidential candidates are nominated by party conventions; our state legislatures are electing senators more and more, in accordance with the popular will expressed at the polls, and we are daily growing more uneasy if the successful candidate for the presidency does not receive a majority of the people's ballots. Ours, however, is not the first government in which public opinion has been a potent factor; public opinion has always ruled. The people are the source of authority under our government, it is true, but the authority itself is not lodged in their hands. The people have no originating power. They have not even an alternative choice. They must accept or reject the issues presented to them by conventions and other bodies.

"What we really mean when we say that the people govern themselves is that they freely consent to be governed on condition that a certain part of them do the governing. The ideal Democratic government is that in which the processes of government are best; where self selection for leadership and influence is most encouraged, and where strength, knowledge and originality are heartened to display themselves and compete for the best prizes. A self reliant, self mastered, self elevated man like Lincoln is no more a man of the people than Washington was a man of the people. He has come out from the people; has separated himself from the mass of unknown men by reason of excellency and knowledge; has raised himself above the common level of others and constituted himself a master spirit among men holding the credentials of rulership.

"The freedom of a Democratic form of government consists in the undictated choice by the people of the things they will accept and the men they will follow. A democracy need not always accept and always like the things it is told to accept. It makes adult choice. Conceive it mechanically and it is a great sensitive registering machine. We study to play on it; we make it register our best impressions. This, it seems to me, is an infinitely more vital, more stimulating way to conceive democracy than to imagine the people what they are not—our masters. If they are, indeed, sovereigns why, then, we must conform in all things, must be patient and humble under the tyranny of our next door neighbor, must repress our individuality, endeavor to catch the common thought, the cant phrases, and repeat them continually. But if we live in a nation that waits to be led and which has sovereign liberty to follow even us what an incentive we have to be sincere, to press our claims, to mend our lives to suit the station we would achieve.

"This is an age of labor, and those who labor, as Mr. Bagehot has said, have no time to form opinions. Chain a man to a ledger and take something off his salary every time he leaves it and you can't expect that he will form reasoned opinions about the silver question or the Behring sea controversy or the Venezuelan boundary. I believe in the people; I believe in their honesty, sincerity and sagacity, but I do not believe in them as my governors. They are rather the stuff out of which the leading minds come and the fabric of government is made.

"The advantage of Democracy is not an advantage of structure. Monarchical nations have a quickness and readiness to move in great emergencies which our form of government can hardly boast of. The advantage of Democracy lies in the opportunity it affords to the private man. His opportunity is limited only by himself. How we cheat ourselves by living in submission to public opinion when we might make it! In this controversy of opinions a man has to fight his ground; but what man expects to do otherwise? There is dust and heat in the arena, but he is prepared for that. A free nation loves a bold man. It uses slaves only for lack of better men when there is work to be done. It is well that institutions are slowly changed and that ideas prevail slowly among the great masses of men. We do not want a country that is continually setting up altars to unknown gods. Progress is a march, not a scamper. It is achieved by the orderly advance required the more incisive strokes of Woodrow Wilson, professor of jurisprudence in Princeton, to carry the learned men clear out of their reserve. He seemed to gather almost as much keen enjoyment from some of his sorties as did those who sat smiling back at him from the depths of their official gowns.

The day begun [began] with the meeting of the visiting delegates and faculty and trustees in Marquand Chapel. There instructions were given regarding the formation of the parade, which once more led to Alexander Hall, where the regular exercises were held. The long procession was headed by President Patton and Dr. Charles E. Green, and between them walked Governor Griggs, of New Jersey, who presided at the morning session. Dr. Green prefaced the session with a further announcement of names of institutions from which letters of congratulation had been received, and then presented Governor Griggs, who rose in his place to respond to the greeting that the audience bestowed upon him. He made no allusion of a personal character, and simply introduced the Rev. Dr. Van Dyke to read the ode. Dr. Van Dyke was present as the representative of the Cliosophic Society, and the poem was of his own writing. Throughout the reading he was attentively followed, and at suggestive places was frequently interrupted by applause. . . .

As the next speaker, the orator of the day, Governor Griggs presented Professor Woodrow Wilson, with the conclusion of whose splendid address the session came to an end. His subject was "Princeton in the Nation's Service." . . .[2]

Printed in the *New York Tribune*, Oct. 22, 1896; editorial headings omitted.

[1] Alexander Hall was indeed packed on October 22, the third day of the Sesquicentennial, as President Patton announced in his address that henceforth the College of New Jersey would be known as Princeton University. The exercises continued with the conferring of honorary degrees and concluded with an address by President Cleveland.

[2] Here follow brief extracts from Wilson's address.

A Commemorative Address[1]

[Oct. 21, 1896]

PRINCETON IN THE NATION'S SERVICE

We pause to look back upon our past today, not as an old man grown reminiscent, but as a prudent man still in his youth and lusty prime and at the threshold of new tasks, who would remind

[1] The text printed below is that of the only extant manuscript of "Princeton in the Nation's Service." The manuscript vividly reveals the difficulties under which Wilson worked at this time because of his small stroke. Working perhaps from an earlier draft, Wilson began typing the address with his left hand on his Hammond typewriter and completed eleven pages. He could type no more,

himself of his origin and lineage, recall the pledges of his youth,
assess as at a turning in his life the duties of his station.

We look back only a little way to our birth; but the brief space
is quick with movement and incident enough to crowd a great
tract of time. Turn back only one hundred and fifty years, and
you are deep within quiet colony times, before the French and
Indian war or thought of separation from England. But a great
war is at hand. Forces long pent up and local presently spread
themselves at large upon the continent, and the whole scene is
altered. The brief plot runs with a strange force and haste:—
First a quiet group of peaceful colonies, very placid and common-
place and dull, to all seeming, in their patient working out of a
slow development; Then, of a sudden, a hot fire of revolution, a
quick release of power, as if of forces long pent up, but set free
at last in the generous heat of the new day; the mighty processes
of a great migration, the vast spaces of a waiting continent filled
almost suddenly with hosts bred to the spirit of conquest; a con-
stant making and renewing of governments, a stupendous growth,
a perilous expansion. Such days of youth and nation-making
must surely count double the slower days of maturity and cal-
culated change, as the Spring counts double the sober fruitage
of the Summer.

Princeton was founded upon the very eve of the stirring
changes which put the revolutionary drama on the stage,—not to
breed politicians, but to give young men such training as, it
might be hoped, would fit them handsomely for the pulpit and
for the grave duties of citizens and neighbours. A small group
of Presbyterian ministers took the initiative in its foundation.
They acted without ecclesiastical authority, as if under obligation
to society rather than to the church. They had no more vision
of what was to come upon the country than their fellow colonists
had; they knew only that the pulpits of the middle and southern
colonies lacked properly equipped men and all the youth in those

---

and the remainder of the manuscript (pages 12-32) was typed on a different
machine, undoubtedly by other hands. There are numerous handwritten emendations and insertions by Wilson and his wife, including one paragraph written
by Wilson with his left hand. The manuscript also bears many linear markings.
At some time before delivery, Wilson concluded that his address was much too
long and marked the sections which he would read. The portions that he omitted
are printed in italics.

It is possible that Wilson spoke from a printed copy made from his manuscript, for the latter bears the printer's instructions, "Don't set," at two of the
sections that Wilson had denoted for deletion.

The text of "Princeton in the Nation's Service" as Wilson delivered it appeared in the *New York Evening Post*, October 21, 1896, and in the *Daily Princetonian*, October 22 and 23, 1896. The complete version of the address was first
printed, with a few changes in the text printed below, in the New York *Forum*,
XXII (December 1896), 447-66. The address was reprinted many times.

parts ready means of access to the higher sort of schooling. They thought the discipline at Yale a little less than liberal and the training offered as a substitute in some quarters a good deal less than thorough. They wanted "a seminary of true religion and good literature" which should be after their own model and among their own people.

It was not a sectarian school they wished. They were acting as citizens, not as clergymen, and the charter they obtained said never a word about creed or doctrine; but they gave religion the first place in their programe, which belonged to it of right, and confided the formation of their college to the Rev. Jonathan Dickinson, one of their own number, a man of such mastery as they could trust. *Their school was first of all merely a little group of students gathered about Mr. Dickinson in Elizabethtown. Its master died the very year his labours began; and it was necessary to induce the Rev. Aaron Burr, one of the trustees, to take the college under his own charge at Newark. It was the charm and power of that memorable young pastor and teacher which carried it forward to a final establishment. Within ten years many friends had been made, substantial sums of money secured, a new and more liberal charter obtained, and a permanent home found at Princeton. And then its second president died, while still in his prime, and the succession was handed on to other leader's of like quality.*

It was the men, rather than their measures, as usual, that had made the college vital from the first and put it in a sure way to succeed. The charter was liberal and very broad ideas determined the policy of the young school. There were laymen upon its board of trustees as well as clergymen,—not all Presbyterians, but all lovers of progress and men known in the colony: no one was more thoroughly the friend of the new venture than Governor Belcher the representative of the crown. But the life of the college was in the men who administered it and spoke in its class rooms, a notable line of thinkers and orators. There had not been many men more to be regarded in debate or in counsel in that day than Jonathan Dickinson; and Aaron Burr was such a man as others turn to and follow with an admiration and trust they might be at a loss to explain, so instinctive is it, and inevitable—a man with a touch of sweet majesty in his presence, and a grace and spirit in his manner which more than made amends for his small and slender figure; the unmistakable fire of eloquence in him when he spoke and the fine quality of sincerity. Piety seemed with him only a crowning grace.

For a few brief weeks after Burr was dead Jonathan Edwards, whom all the world knows, was president in his stead; but death came quickly and left the college only his name. Another orator succeeded him, Samuel Davies, brought out of Virginia, famous out of all proportion to his years, you might think, until you heard him speak and knew the charm, the utterance, and the character that made him great. He too was presently taken by the quick way of death, though the college had had him but a little while, and Samuel Finley had presided in his stead, with a wise sagacity and quiet gift of leadership, for all too short a time, and was gone, when John Witherspoon came to reign in the little academic kingdom for twenty six years. It was by that time the year 1768. Mr. Dickinson had drawn that little group of students about him under the first charter only twenty-one years ago; the college had been firmly seated in Princeton only these twelve years in which it had seen Burr and Edwards and Davies and Finley die, and had found it not a little hard to live so long in the face of its losses and the uneasy movements of the time. It had been brought to Princeton in the very midst of the French and Indian war, when the country was in doubt who should possess the continent. The deep excitement of the Stamp Act agitation had come, with all its sinister threats of embroilment and disaffection, while yet it was in its infancy and first effort to live. It was impossible it should obtain proper endowment or any right and equable development in such a season. It ought by every ordinary rule of life, to have been quite snuffed out in the thick and troubled air of the time. New Jersey did not, like Virginia and Massachusetts, easily form her purpose in that day of anxious doubt. She was mixed of many warring elements, as New York also was, and suffered a turbulence of spirit that did not very kindly breed "true religion and good literature."

But your thorough Presbyterian is not subject to the ordinary laws of life,—is of too stubborn a fibre, too unrelaxing a purpose, to suffer mere inconvenience to bring defeat. Difficulty bred effort, rather; and Doctor Witherspoon found an institution ready to his hand that had come already in that quickening time to a sort of crude maturity. It was no small proof of its self-possession and self-knowledge that those who watched over it had chosen that very time of crisis to put a man like John Witherspoon at the head of its administration, a man so compounded of statesman and scholar, Calvinist, Scotsman, and orator that it must ever be a sore puzzle where to place or rank him,—whether among great divines, great teachers, or great statesmen. He seems to be all these and to defy classification, so big is he, so various, so prodigal of gifts. His vitality entered like a tonic into the college, kept it alive in that time of peril,—made it as individual and inextinguishable a force as he himself was, alike in scholarship and in public affairs.

It has never been natural, it has seldom been possible, in this country for learning to seek a place apart and hold aloof from affairs. It is only when society is old, long settled to its ways, confident in habit, and without self-questioning upon any vital point of conduct, that study can affect seclusion and despise the passing interests of the day. America has never yet had a season of leisured quiet in which students could seek a life apart without sharp rigours of conscience, or college instructors easily forget that they were training citizens as well as drilling pupils; and Princeton is not likely to forget that sharp schooling of her youth, when she first learned the lesson of public service. She shall not easily get John Witherspoon out of her constitution.

It was a piece of providential good fortune that brought such a man to Princeton at such a time. He was a man of the sort other men follow and take counsel of gladly and as if they found in him the full expression of what is best in themselves. Not because he was always wise, but because he showed always so fine an ardour for whatever was worth while and of the better part of man's spirit; because he uttered his thought with an inevitable glow of eloquence; because of his irresistable charm and individual power. The lively wit of the man, besides, struck always upon the matter of his thought like a ray of light, compelling men to receive what he said or else seem themselves opaque and laughable. A certain straightforward vigour in his way of saying things gave his style an almost irresistable power of entering into men's convictions. A hearty honesty showed itself in all that he did and won men's allegiance upon the instant. They loved him even when they had the hardihood to disagree with him.

He came to the college in 1768, and ruled it till he died, in 1794. In the very middle of his term as head of the college the Revolution came, to draw men's minds imperatively off from everything but war and politics, and he turned with all the force and frankness of his nature to the public tasks of the great struggle, assisted in the making of a new constitution for the State; became her spokesman in the Continental Congress; would have pressed her on, if he could, to utter a declaration of independence of her own before the Congress had acted; voted for and signed the great Declaration with hearty good will when it came; acted for the country in matters alike of war and of finance; stood forth in the sight of all the people a great advocate and orator, deeming himself forward in the service of God when most engaged in the service of men and of liberty. There were but broken sessions of the college meanwhile. Each army in its turn drove out the little group of students who clung to the place. The college building became now a military hospital and again a barracks for the troops,—for a little while, upon a memorable day in 1777, a sort of stronghold. New Jersey's open counties became for a time the revolutionary battleground and field of manoeuvre. Swept through from end to end by the rush of armies, the State seemed the chief seat of the war; and Princeton a central point of strategy. The dramatic winter of 1776-77 no Princeton man could ever forget, lived he never so long,—that winter which saw a year of despair turned suddenly into a year of hope. In July there had been bonfires and boisterous rejoicings in the college yard and in the village street at the news of the Declaration of Independence,—for, though the rest of the country might doubt and stand timid for a little to see the bold thing done, Doctor Witherspoon's pupils were in spirits to know the fight was to be fought to a finish. Then suddenly the end had seemed to come. Before the year was out Washington was in the place, beaten and in full retreat, only three thousand men at his back, abandoned by his generals, deserted by his troops, hardly daring to stop till he had put the unbridged Delaware between himself and his enemy. The British came close at his heels and the town was theirs until Washington came back again, the third day of the new year, early in the morning, and gave his view halloo yonder upon the hill, as if he were in the hunting field again. Then there was fighting in the very streets, and cannon planted against the walls of Old North [Nassau Hall] herself. 'Twas not likely any Princeton man would forget those days when the whole face of the war was changed and New Jersey was shaken of the burden of the fighting. There was almost always something doing at the place when the soldiers were out, for the strenuous Scotsman who had the college at his heart never left it for long at a time, for all he was so intent upon the public business. It was haphazard and piece-meal work, no doubt, but there was the spirit and the resolution of the Revolution itself in what was done,—the spirit of Witherspoon. It was not as if someone else had been master. Doctor Witherspoon could have pupils at will. He was so much else besides schoolmaster and preceptor, was so great a figure in the people's eye, went about so like an accepted leader, generously lending a general character to a great cause, that he could bid men act and know that they would heed him.

The time as well as his own genious enabled him to put a distinctive stamp upon his pupils. There was close contact between master and pupils in that day of beginnings. *There were not often more than a hundred students in attendance at the college, and the President, for at any rate half their course, was himself their chief instructor. There were two or three tutors to whom the instruction of the lower classes was entrusted; Mr. Houston was professor of mathematics and natural philosophy, and Dr. Smith professor of moral philosophy and divinity; but the President set the pace. It was he who gave range and spirit to the course of study.* He lectured upon taste and style as well as upon abstract questions of philosophy, and upon politics as a science of government and of public duty as little to be forgotten as religion itself in any well considered plan of life. He had found the college ready to serve such purpose when he came, because of the stamp Burr and Davies and Finley had put upon it. They had one and all consciously set themselves to make the college a place where young men's minds should be rendered fit for affairs, for the public ministry of the bench and the senate as well as of the pulpit. It was in Finley's day, but just now gone by, that the college had sent out such men as William Paterson, Luther Martin, and Oliver Ellsworth. Witherspoon but gave quickened life to the old spirit and method of the place where there had been drill from the first in public speech and public spirit.

And the Revolution, when it came, seemed but an object-lesson in his scheme of life. It was not simply fighting that was done at Princeton. The little town became for a season the centre of politics too; once and again the legislature of the State sat in the college Hall, and its revolutionary Council of Safety. Soldiers and public men whose names the war was making known to every man frequented the quiet place, and racy talk ran high in the jolly tavern where hung the sign of Hudibras. Finally, the federal Congress itself sought the place and filled the college hall with a new scene, sitting a whole season there to do its business,—its President a trustee of the college. A commencement day came which saw both Washington and Witherspoon on the platform together,—the two men, it was said, who could not be matched for striking presence in all the country,—and the young salutatorian turned to the country's leader to say what it was in the hearts of all to utter. The sum of the town's excitement was made up when, upon that notable day of October in the year

1783 news of peace came to that secluded hall, to add a crowning touch of gladness to the gay and brilliant company met to receive with formal welcome the Minister Plenipotentiary but just come from the Netherlands, Washington moving amongst them the hero whom the news enthroned.

It was no single stamp or character that the college gave its pupils. James Madison, Philip Freneau, Aaron Burr, and Harry Lee had come from it almost at a single birth, between 1771 and 1773:—James Madison, the philosophical statesman, subtly compounded of learning and practical sagacity; Philip Freneau, the careless poet and reckless pamphleteer of a party; Aaron Burr, with genius enough to have made him immortal and unschooled passion enough to have made him infamous; "Lighthorse Harry" Lee, a Rupert in battle, a boy in counsel, highstrung, audacious, wilful, lovable, a figure for romance. These men were types of the spirit of which the college was full: the spirit of free individual development which found its perfect expression in the president himself.

It has been said that Mr. Madison's style in writing is like Dr. Witherspoon's, albeit not so apt a weapon for the quick thrust and instant parry; and it is recalled that Madison returned to Princeton after his graduation and lingered yet another year in study with his master. But in fact his style is no more like Witherspoon's than Harry Lee's way of fighting was. No doubt there was the same firmness of touch, the same philosophical breadth, the same range of topic and finished force of argument in Dr. Witherspoon's essays upon public questions that are to be found in Madison's papers in the Federalist; but Dr. Witherspoon fought, too, with the same overcoming dash that made men know Harry Lee in the field, albeit with different weapons and upon another arena.

Whatever we may say of these matters, however, one thing is certain: Princeton sent upon the public stage an extraordinary number of men of notable quality in those days; became herself for a time in some visible sort the academic centre of the Revolution; fitted, among the rest, the man in whom the country was one day to recognize the chief author of the federal constitution. Princetonians are never tired of telling how many public men graduated from Princeton in Witherspoon's time[:] twenty Senators, twenty-three Representatives, thirteen Governors, three judges of the Supreme Court of the Union, one Vice President, and a President; all within a space of scarcely twenty years, and from a college which seldom had more than a hundred students. Nine Princeton men sat in the Constitutional Convention of 1787 and, though but six of them were Witherspoon's pupils, there was no other college that had there so many as six, and the redoubtable Doctor might have claimed all nine as his in spirit and capacity. Madison guided the convention through the critical stages of its anxious work, with a tact, a gentle quietness, an art of leading without insisting, ruling without commanding,— an authority, not of tone or emphasis, but of apt suggestion, —such as Dr. Witherspoon could never have exercised. Princeton men fathered both the Virginia plan which was adopted, and the New Jersey plan which was rejected: and Princeton men advocated the compromises without which no plan could have won acceptance. The strenuous Scotsman's earnest desire and prayer to God to see a government set over the nation that should last was realized as even he might not have been bold enough to hope. No man had ever better right to rejoice in his pupils.

It would be absurd to pretend that we can distinguish Princeton's touch and method in the Revolution or her distinctive handiwork in the constitution of the Union. We can show nothing more of historical fact than that her own President took a great place of leadership in that time of change, and became one of the first figures of the age; that the college which he led and to which he gave his spirit contributed more than her share of public men to the making of the nation, outranked her elder rivals in the roll-call of the constitutional convention, and seemed for a little a seminary of statesmen rather than a quiet seat of academic learning. What takes our admiration and engages our fancy in looking back to that time is the generous union then established in the college between the life of philosophy and the life of the state.

It moves her sons very deeply to find Princeton to have been from the first what they know her to have been in their own day: a school of duty. The revolutionary days are gone, and you shall not find upon her rolls another group of names given to public life that can equal her muster in the days of the Revolution and the formation of the government. But her rolls read since the old days, if you know but a little of the quiet life of scattered neighborhoods, like a roster of trustees, a list of the silent men who carry the honorable burdens of business and of social obligation,—of such names as keep credit and confidence in heart. They suggest a soil full of the old seed and ready, should the air of the time move shrewdly upon it as in the old days, to spring once more into the old harvest. The various, boisterous strength of the young men of affairs who went out with Witherspoon's touch upon them, is obviously not of the average breed of any place, but the special fruitage of an exceptional time. Later generations inevitably reverted to the elder type of Patterson [Paterson] and Ellsworth, the type of sound learning and stout character, without bold impulse added or any uneasy hope to change the world. It has been Princeton's work, in all ordinary seasons, not to change but to strengthen society, to give, not yeast, but bread for the raising.

It is in this wise Princeton has come into our own hands; and today we stand as those who would count this force for the future. The men who made Princeton are dead; those who shall keep it and better it still live: they are even ourselves. Shall we not ask, ere we go forward, what gave the place its spirit and its air of duty? "We are now men, and must accept in the highest spirit the same transcendent destiny; and not pinched in a corner, not cowards fleeing before a revolution, but redeemers and benefactors, pious aspirants to be noble clay plastic under the Almighty effort, let us advance and advance on chaos and the dark!"²

No one who looks into the life of the Institution shall find it easy to say what gave it its spirit and kept it in its character the generations through; but some things lie obvious to the view in Princeton's case. She has always been a school of religion and no one of her sons, who has really lived her life, has escaped that steadying touch which has made her a school of duty. Religion, conceive it but liberally enough, is the true salt wherewith to keep both duty and learning sweet against the taint of time and change; and it is a noble thing to have conceived it thus liberally, as Princeton's founders did. *Churches, among us, as all the world knows, are free and voluntary societies, separated to be nurseries of belief, not suffered to become instruments of rule; and those who serve them can be free citizens, as well as faithful churchmen. The men who founded Princeton were pastors, not ecclesiastics. Their ideal was the service of congregations and communities, not the service of a church.* Duty with them was a practical thing, concerned with righteousness in this world, as well as with salvation in the next. There is nothing that gives such pith to public service as religion. A God of truth is no mean prompter to the enlightened service of mankind; and character formed, as if in his eye, has always a fibre and sanction such as you shall not easily obtain for the ordinary man from the mild promptings of philosophy.

This, I cannot doubt, is the reason why Princeton formed

² From the third paragraph of Emerson's essay, "Self-Reliance," as it appeared in *Essays* (Boston, 1841), p. 39.

practical men, whom the world could trust to do its daily work like men of honor. There were men in Dr. Witherspoon's day who doubted him the right preceptor for those who sought the ministry of the church, seeing him "as high a son of liberty as any man in America," and turned agitator rather than preacher, and he drew about him, as troubles thickened, young politicians rather than candidates for the pulpit. But it is noteworthy that observing men in far Virginia sent their sons to be with Dr. Witherspoon, because they saw intrigue and the taint of infidelity coming upon their own College of William and Mary, Mr. Madison among the rest; and that young Madison went home to read theology with earnest system ere he went out to the tasks of his life. He had no thought of becoming a minister, but his master at Princeton had taken possession of his mind and had enabled him to see what knowledge was profitable.

The world has long thought that it detected in the academic life some lack of sympathy with itself, some disdain of the homely tasks which make the gross globe inhabitable,—not a little proud aloofness and lofty superiority, as if education always softened the hands and alienated the heart. It must be admitted that books are a great relief from the haggling of the market, libraries a very welcome refuge from the strife of commerce. We feel no anxiety about ages that are passed; old books draw us pleasantly off from responsibility, remind us nowhere of what there is to do. We can easily hold the service of mankind at arms length while we read and make scholars of ourselves, but we shall be very uneasy, the while, if the right mandates of religion are let in upon us and made part of our thought. The quiet scholar has his proper breeding and truth must be searched out and held aloft for men to see for its own sake by such as will not leave off their sacred task until death takes them away. But not many pupils of a College are to be investigators: they are to be citizens and the world's servants in every field of practical endeavor, and in their instruction the College must use learning as a vehicle of spirit, interpreting literature as the voice of humanity,—must enlighten, guide, and hearten its sons, that it may make men of them. If it give them no vision of the true God, it has given them no certain motive to practise the wise lessons they have learned.

It is noteworthy how often God-fearing men have been forward in those revolutions which have vindicated rights, and how seldom in those which have wrought a work of destruction. There was a spirit of practical piety in the revolutionary doctrines which Dr. Witherspoon taught. No man, particularly no young man, who heard him could doubt his cause a righteous cause or deem religion aught but a prompter in it. Revolution was not to be distinguished from duty in Princeton. Duty becomes the more noble when thus conceived the "stern daughter of the voice of God"; and that voice must ever seem near and in the midst of life if it be made to sound dominant from the first in all thought of men and the world. It has not been by accident, therefore, that Princeton men have been inclined to public life. A strong sense of duty is a fretful thing in confinement, and will not easily consent to be kept at home clapped up within a narrow round. The University in our day is no longer inclined to stand aloof from the practical world, and, surely, it ought never to have had the disposition to do so. It is the business of a University to impart to the rank and file of the men whom it trains the right thought of the world, the thought which it has tested and established, the principles which have stood through the seasons and become at length part of the immemorial wisdom of the race. The object of education is not merely to draw out the powers of the individual mind: it is rather its right object to draw all minds to a proper adjustment to the physical and social world in which they are to have their life and their development: to enlighten, strengthen and make fit. The business of the world is not individual success, but its own betterment, strengthening, and growth in spiritual insight— "So teach us to number our days, that we may apply our hearts unto wisdom" is its right prayer and aspiration.

It was not a work of destruction which Princeton helped forward even in that day of storm which came at the revolution, but a work of preservation. The American revolution wrought a radical work of change in the world: it created a new nation and a new polity; but it was a work of conservation after all, as fundamentally conservative as the revolution of 1688 or the extortion of Magna Charta. A change of allegiance and the erection of a new nation in the West were its inevitable results but not its objects. Its object was the preservation of a body of liberties, to keep the natural course of English development in America clear of impediment. It was meant, not in rebellion, but in self-defense. If it brought change, it was the change of maturity, the fulfilment of destiny, the appropriate fruitage of wholesome and steady growth. It was part of English liberty that America should be free. The thought of our Revolution was as quick and vital in the minds of Chatham and of Burke as in the minds of Otis and Henry and Washington. There is nothing so conservative of life as growth: when that stops, decay sets in and the end comes on apace. Progress is life, for the body politic as for the body natural. To stand still is to court death.

Here, then, if you will but look, you have the law of conservatism disclosed: it is a law of progress. But not all change is progress, not all growth is the manifestation of life. Let one part of the body be in haste to outgrow the rest and you have malignant disease, the threat of death. The growth that is a manifestation of life is equable, draws its springs gently out of the old fountains of strength, builds upon old tissue, covets the old airs that have blown upon it time out of mind in the past. Colleges ought surely to be the best nurseries of such life, the best schools of the progress which conserves. Unschooled men have only their habits to remind them of the past, only their desires and their instinctive judgments of what is right to guide them into the future: the College should serve the state as its organ of recollection, its seat of vital memory. It should give the country men who know the probabilities of failure and success, who can separate the tendencies which are permanent from the tendencies which are of the moment merely, who can distinguish promises from threats, knowing the life men have lived, the hopes they have tested, and the principles they have proved.

This College gave the country at least a handful of such men, in its infancy, and its president for leader. The blood of John Knox ran in Witherspoon's veins. The great drift and movement of English liberty from Magna Charta down was in all his teachings; his pupils knew as well as Burke did that to argue the Americans out of their liberties would be to falsify their pedigree. "In order to prove that the Americans have no right to their liberties," Burke cried, "we are every day endeavoring to subvert the maxims which preserve the whole spirit of our own";[3] the very antiquarians of the law stood ready with their proof that the Colonies could not be taxed by Parliament. This Revolution, at any rate, was a keeping of faith with the past. To stand for it was to be like Hampden, a champion of law though he withstood the king. It was to emulate the example of the very men who had founded the government then for a little while grown so tyrannous and forgetful of its great traditions. This was the compulsion of life, not of passion, and College Halls were a better school of revolution than Colonial assemblies.

Provided, of course, they were guided by such a spirit as Witherspoon's. Nothing is easier than to falsify the past. Lifeless instruction will do it. If you rob it of vitality, stiffen it with pedantry, sophisticate it with argument, chill it with unsym-

---

[3] From Edmund Burke, "Speech on Moving His Resolutions for Conciliation with the Colonies, March 22, 1775," in *The Works of the Right Honorable Edmund Burke*, 5th edn. (12 vols., Boston, 1877), II, 130.

pathetic comment, you render it as dead as any academic exercise. The safest way in all ordinary seasons is to let it speak for itself: resort to its records, listen to its poets and to its masters in the humbler art of prose. Your real and proper object, after all, is not to expound, but to realize it, consort with it, and make your spirit kin with it, so that you may never shake the sense of obligation off. In short, I believe that the catholic study of the world's literature as a record of spirit is the right preparation for leadership in the world's affairs, if you undertake it like a man and not like a pedant.

Age is marked in the case of every people just as it is marked in the case of every work of art, into which enters the example of the masters, the taste of long generations of men, the thought that has matured, the achievement that has come with assurance. The child's crude drawing shares the primitive youth of the first hieroglyphics; but a little reading, a few lessons from some modern master, a little time in the old world's galleries set the lad forward a thousand years and more, make his drawing as old as art itself. The art of thinking is as old, and it is the University's function to impart it in all its length: the stiff and difficult stuffs of fact and experience, of prejudice and affection, in which the hard art is to work its will, and the long and tedious combinations of cause and effect out of which it is to build up its results. How else will you avoid a ceaseless round of error? The world's memory must be kept alive, or we shall never see an end of its old mistakes. We are in danger to lose our identity and become infantile in every generation. That is the real menace under which we cower everywhere in this age of change. The old world trembles to see its proletariat in the saddle; we stand dismayed to find ourselves growing no older, always as young as the information of our most numerous voters. The danger does not lie in the fact that the masses whom we have enfranchised seek to work any iniquity upon us, for their aim, take it in the large, is to make a righteous polity. The peril lies in this, that the past is discredited among them, because they played no choosing part in it. It was their enemy, they say, and they will not learn of it. They wish to break with it for ever: its lessons are tainted to their taste.

In America, especially, we run perpetually this risk of newness. Righteously enough, it is in part a consequence of boasting. To enhance our credit for originality we boasted for long that our Institutions were one and all our own inventions; and the pleasing error was so got into the common air by persistent discharges of oratory, that every man's atmosphere became surcharged with it, and it seems now quite too late to dislodge it. Three thousand miles of sea, moreover, roll between us and the elder part of the world. We are isolated here. We cannot see other nations in detail, and looked at in the large, they do not seem like ourselves. Our problems, we say, are our own, and we will take our own way of solving them. Nothing seems audacious among us, for our case seems to us to stand singular and without parallel. We run in a free field, without recollection of failure, without heed of example.

This danger is nearer to us now than it was in days of armed revolution. The men whom Madison led in the making of the Constitution were men who regarded the past. They had flung off from the mother country, not to get a new liberty, but to preserve an old, not to break a Constitution, but to keep it. It was the glory of the Convention of 1787 that it made choice in the making of the government of principles which Englishmen everywhere had tested, and of an organization of which in every part Americans themselves had somewhere made trial. In every essential part they built out of old stuffs whose grain and fibre they knew.

> *" 'Tis not in battles that from youth we train*
> *The Governor who must be wise and good,*
> *And temper with the sternness of the brain*
> *Thoughts motherly, and meek as womanhood.*
> *Wisdom doth live with children round her knees:*
> *Books, leisure, perfect freedom, and the talk*
> *Man holds with week-day man in the hourly walk*
> *Of the mind's business: these are the degrees*
> *By which true Sway doth mount; this is the stalk*
> *True Power does grow on; and her rights are these."*[4]

The men who framed the government were not radicals. They trimmed old growths, and were not forgetful of the old principles of husbandry.

It is plain that it is the duty of an institution of learning set in the midst of a free population and amidst signs of social change, not merely to implant a sense of duty, but to illuminate duty by every lesson that can be drawn out of the past. It is not a dogmatic process. I know of no book in which the lessons of the past are set down. I do not know of any man whom the world could trust to write such a book. But it somehow comes about that the man who has travelled in the realms of thought brings lessons

---

[4] From William Wordsworth, "I grieved for Buonaparté. . . ."

home with him which make him grave and wise beyond his fellows, and thoughtful with the thoughtfulness of a true man of the world.

He is not a true man of the world who knows only the present fashoin [fashion] *of it. In good breeding there is always the fine savor of generations of gentlemen, a tradition of courtesy, the perfect knowledge of long practice. The world of affairs is so old, no man can know it who knows only that little last segment of it which we call the present. We have a special name for the man who observes only the present fashions of the world: and it is a less honorable name than that which we use to designate the grave and thoughtful gentlemen who keep so steadily to the practises that have made the world wise and at ease these hundreds of years. We cannot pretend to have formed the world, and we are not destined to reform it. We cannot even mend it and set it forward by the reasonable measure of a single generation's work if we forget the old processes or lose our mastery over them. We should have scant capital to trade on were we to throw away the wisdom we have inherited and seek our fortunes with the slender stock we have ourselves accumulated.*

This, it seems to me, is the real, the prevalent argument for holding every man we can to the intimate study of the ancient classics. *Latin and Greek no doubt have a grammatical and syntactical habit which challenges the mind that would master it to a severer exercise of analytical power than the easy-going synthesis of any modern tongue demands; but substitutes in kind may be found for that drill. What you cannot find a substitute for is the classics as literature; and there can be no first-hand contact with that literature if you will not master the grammar and the syntax which convey its subtle power. Your enlightenment depends on the company you keep. You do not know the world until you know the men who have possessed it and tried its ways before ever you were given your brief run upon it. And there is no sanity comparable with that which is schooled in the thoughts that will keep. It is such a schooling that we get from the world's literature. The books have disappeared which were not genuine,—which spoke things which, if they were worth saying at all, were not worth hearing more than once, as well as the books which spoke permanent things clumsily and without the gift of interpretation. The kind air which blows from age to age has disposed of them like vagrant leaves. There was sap in them for a little, but now they are gone, we do not know where.* All literature that has lasted has this claim upon us: that it is not dead; but we cannot be quite so sure of any as we are of the ancient literature that still lives, because none has lived so long. It holds a sort of leadership in the aristocracy of natural selection.

Read it, moreover, and you shall find another proof of vitality in it, more significant still. You shall recognise its thoughts, and even its fancies, as your long-time familiars,—shall recognise them as the thoughts that have begotten a vast deal of your own literature. *We read the classics and exclaim in our vanity: "How modern! it might have been written yesterday." Would it not be more true, as well as more instructive, to exclaim concerning our own ideas: "How ancient! they have been true these thousand years"?* It is the general air of the world a man gets when he reads the classics, the thinking which depends upon no time but only upon human nature, which seems full of the voices of the human spirit, quick with the power which moves ever upon the face of affairs. "What Plato has thought, he may think; what a saint has felt, he may feel; what at any time has befallen any man, he can understand." *There is the spirit of a race in Greek literature, the spirit of quite another people in the books of Virgil and Horace and Tacitus, but in all a mirror of the world, the old passion of the soul, the old hope that keeps so new, the informing memory, the persistent forecast.*

It has always seemed to me an odd thing, and a thing against nature, that the literary man, the man whose citizenship and freedom are of the world of thought, should ever have been deemed an unsafe man in affairs; and yet I suppose there is not always injustice in the judgment. It is a peculiarly pleasant and beguiling comradeship, the company of authors. Not many men when once they are deep in it will leave its engaging talk of things gone by to find their practical duties in the present. But you are not making an undergraduate a man of letters when you keep him four short years, at odd, or even at stated, hours in the company of authors. You shall have done much if you make him feel free among them.

This argument for enlightenment holds scarcely less good, of course, in behalf of the study of modern literature and especially the literature of your own race and country. You should not belittle culture by esteeming it a thing of ornament and accomplishment rather than a power. A cultured mind is a mind quit of its awkwardness, eased of all impediment and illusion, made quick and athletic in the acceptable exercise of power. It is a mind at once informed and just,—a mind habituated to choose its course with knowledge, and filled with full assurance, like one who knows the world and can live in it without either unreasonable hope or unwarranted fear. It cannot complain, it cannot trifle, it cannot despair. Leave pessimism to the uncultured, who do not know reasonable hope; leave fantastic hopes to the uncultured, who do not know the reasonableness of failure. Show that your mind has lived in the world ere now; has taken council with the elder dead who still live, as well as with the ephemeral living who cannot pass their graves. Help men, but do not delude them.

I believe, of course, that there is another way of preparing young men to be wise. I need not tell you that I believe in full, explicit instruction in history and in politics, in the experiences of peoples and the fortunes of governments, in the whole story of what men have attempted and what they have accomplished through all the changes both of form and purpose in their organization of their common life. Many minds will receive and heed this systematic instruction which have no ears for the voice that is in the printed page of literature. *But, just as it is one thing to sit here in republican America and hear a credible professor tell of the soil of allegiance in which the British monarchy grows, and quite another to live where her Majesty is Queen and hear common men bless her with full confession and loyalty, so it is one thing to hear of systems of government in histories and treatises and quite another to feel them in the pulses of the poets and prose writers who have lived under them.*

It used to be taken for granted—did it not?—that colleges would be found always on the conservative side in politics (except on the question of free trade), but in this latter day a great deal has taken place which goes far towards discrediting the presumption. The college in our day lives very near indeed to the affairs of the world. It is a place of the latest experiments; its laboratories are brisk with the spirit of discovery; its lecture rooms resound with the discussion of new theories of life and novel programs of reform. There is no radical like your learned radical, bred in the schools; and thoughts of revolution have in our times been harbored in Universities as naturally as they were once nourished among the Encyclopedists. It is the scientific spirit of the age that has wrought the change. I stand with my hat off at very mention of the great men who have made our age an age of knowledge. No man more heartily admires, more gladly welcomes, more approvingly reckons the gain and the enlightenment that have come to the world through the extraordinary advances in physical science which this great age has witnessed. He would be a barbarian, and a lover of darkness who should grudge that great study any part of its triumph. But I am a student of society and should deem myself unworthy of the comradeship of great men of science should I not speak the plain truth with regard to what I see happening under my own eyes. I have no laboratory but the world of books and men in which I live; but I am much mistaken if the scientific spirit of the age is not doing us a great disservice, working in us a certain great degeneracy. Science has bred in us a spirit of experiment and a contempt for the past. It has made us credulous of quick improvement, hopeful of discovering panaceas, confident of success in every new thing.

I wish to be as explicit as carefully chosen words will enable me to be upon a matter so critical, so radical as this. I have no indictment against what science has done: I have only a warning to utter against the atmosphere which has stolen from laboratories into lecture rooms and into the general air of the world at large. Science,—our science,—is new. It is a child of the nineteenth century. It has transformed the world and owes little debt of obligation to any past age. It has driven mystery out of the Universe; it has made malleable stuff of the hard world, and laid it out in its elements upon the table of every class room. Its own masters have known its limitations: they have stopped short at the confines of the physical Universe, have declined to reckon with spirit or with the stuffs of the mind, have eschewed sense and confined themselves to sensation. But their work has been so stupendous that all other men of all other studies have been set staring at their methods, imitating their ways of thought, ogling their results. We look in our study of the classics now-a-days more at the phenomena of language than at the movement of spirit; we suppose the world which is invisible to be unreal; we doubt the efficacy of feeling and exaggerate the efficacy of knowledge; we speak of society as an organism, and believe that we can contrive for it a new environment which will change the very nature of its constituent parts; worst of all, we believe in the present and in the future more than in the past, and deem the newest theory of society the likeliest. This is the disservice scientific study has done us: it has given us agnosticism in the realm of philosophy, scientific anarchism in the field of politics. It has made the legislator confident that he can create and the philosopher sure that God cannot. Past experience is discredited and the laws of matter are supposed to apply to spirit and the make-up of society.

Let me say, this is not the fault of the scientist: he has done his work with an intelligence and success which cannot be too much admired. It is the work of the noxious, intoxicating gas which has somehow got into the lungs of the rest of us from out the crevices of his workshop,—a gas, it would seem, which forms only in the outer air, and where men do not know the right use of their lungs. I should tremble to see social reform led by men who had breathed it: I should fear nothing better than utter destruction from a revolution conceived and led in the scientific spirit. *Science has not changed the laws of social growth or betterment. Science has not changed the nature of society, has not made history a whit easier to understand, or human nature a whit easier to reform. It has won for us a great liberty in the physical world, a liberty from superstitious fear and from disease, a freedom to use nature as a familiar servant; but it has not freed us from ourselves. It has not purged us of passion or disposed us to virtue. It has not made us less covetous or less ambitious or less self-indulgent. On the contrary, it may be suspected of having enhanced our passions by making wealth so quick to come, and so fickle to stay. It has wrought such instant, incredible improvement in all the physical setting of our life, that we have grown the more impatient of the unreformed condition of the part it has not touched or bettered, and we want to get at our spirits and reconstruct them in like radical fashoin* [fashion] *by like processes of experiment. We have broken with the past and have come into a new world.*

Do you wonder, then, that I ask for the old drill, the old memory of times gone by, the old schooling in precedent and tradition, the old keeping of faith with the past, as a preparation for leadership in the days of social change? We have not given science too big a place in our education; but we have made a perilous mistake in giving it too great a preponderance in method in every other branch of study. We must make the humanities human again; must recall what manner of men we are; must turn back once more to the region of practicable ideals.

Of course, when all is said, it is not learning but the spirit of service that will give a college place in the public annals of the nation. It is indispensable, it seems to me, if it is to do its right service, that the air of affairs should be admitted to all its class rooms. I do not mean the air of party politics but the air of the world's transactions, the consciousness of the solidarity of the race, the sense of the duty of man towards man, of the presence of men in every problem, of the significance of truth for guidance as well as for knowledge, of the potency of ideas, of the promise and the hope that shine in the face of all knowledge. There is laid upon us the compulsion of the national life. We dare not keep aloof and closet ourselves while a nation comes to its maturity. The days of glad expansion are gone. Our life grows tense and difficult; our resource for the future lies in careful thought, providence, and a wise economy; and the school must be of the nation. I have had sight of the perfect place of learning in my thought: a free place, and a various, where no man could be and not know with how great a destiny knowledge had come into the world:—itself a little world; but not perplexed, living with a singleness of aim not known without: the home of sagacious men, hard-headed and with a will to know, debaters of the world's questions every day and used to the rough ways of democracy; and yet a place removed—calm Science seated there, recluse, ascetic, like a nun, not knowing that the world passes, not caring, if the truth but come in answer to her prayer; and Literature, walking within her open doors in quiet chambers with men of olden time, storied walls about her, and calm voices infinitely sweet; here "magic casements, opening on the foam of perilous seas, in fairy lands forlorn," to which you may withdraw and use your youth for pleasure; there windows open straight upon the street, where many stand and talk intent upon the world of men and business. A place where ideals are kept in heart in an air they can breathe; but no fool's paradise. A place where to hear the truth about the past and hold debate about the affairs of the present, with knowledge and without passion; like the world in having all men's life at heart, a place for men and all that concerns them; but unlike the world in its self-possession, its thorough way of talk, its care to know more than the moment brings to light; slow to take excitement, its air pure and wholesome with a breath of faith: every eye within it bright in the clear day and quick to look toward heaven for the confirmation of its hope. Who shall show us the way to this place?

WWT, WWhw, EAWhw, and T MS. (WC, NjP).

From the Diary of Horace Elisha Scudder

1896 Wednesday 21 October

We met again at Marquand chapel and marched over to Alexander Hall. Van Dyke recited with fine delivery an academic ode and Wilson's address was most admirable, a well considered historical discourse closing with a strong plea for the humanities in the college course. There was hardly time to go for luncheon, as we had been invited, to Professor [Charles Woodruff] Shields, so we lunched here & . . . hurried to the foot ball game between Princeton & U. Va.[1] . . . Then came dinner at Dean Murray's. . . . Later, when the torch light procession formed and began to pass a number of persons came in and we watched the pageant from windows and piazzas. Then with D. C. Gilman and others I made my way through the crowd to the stand in front of Nassau Hall where the President of the United States reviewed the procession. The cheers were hearty, many of the transparencies were amusing and the fireworks were as beautiful as any I ever saw, such superb bursts of rockets with stars falling through golden rain. The illumination too of Nassau Hall was singularly beautiful, the old building and all its windows being outlined with orange electric lights. So back to the Deans and then to the Wilsons[2] where I was the first to arrive.

Bound diary (H. E. Scudder Papers, MH).
    [1] Princeton defeated the University of Virginia, 48 to 0.
    [2] Scudder, a guest of the Wilsons during the Sesquicentennial, was awarded a Litt.D. degree on October 22.

From Silas Weir Mitchell[1]

Dear Mr. Wilson—   Princeton   Wednesday [Oct. 21, 1896]

I seize a moment of leisure to assure you of the great pleasure with which I listened to your very able & original address. I do not remember to have heard its equal. It was strong & competent in argument—delightfully humourous—full of noble appeal & with here & there a starry gleam of poetic statement. I really enjoyed it & hope to renew my satisfaction when it is in print. I do not think I lost a word of it.

Believe me very thankfully yours   Weir Mitchell

ALS (WP, DLC).
    [1] Born in Philadelphia on February 15, 1829. A.B., University of Pennsylvania as of Class of 1848; M.D., Jefferson Medical College, 1850. Prominent physiologist and neurologist, he wrote many articles in these and other fields. He was also a man of letters, the author of several volumes of poetry and numerous psychological novels and historical romances. Long-time trustee of the University of Pennsylvania. Received the LL.D. at the Sesquicentennial of Princeton University. Died January 4, 1914.

From Stockton Axson

My dear Brother Woodrow: Brooklyn, N.Y.   Oct 22, 1896

By piecing together extracts published in various papers yesterday afternoon and this morning, I am enabled to get some idea of the noble address which you delivered yesterday, and I want to congratulate you on it. It must have required some genuine courage to speak so plainly to the scientific fellows (or rather to the fellows who seek to misapply scientific principles) as you did, for on such an occasion it must be easier to say the graceful, amiable thing than the downright true thing. I admire your courage and I hope that this note is only one of many expressions of gratitude from people who, like myself, feel how necessary it is that such things should be said with force and power. Unless we believe that the world really is going to the devil in a canter we must believe that there are many people who sometimes pause to think a moment and who consequently will appreciate the wisdom of the advice which you have given us. I hope that the oration will be published entire in some permanent form, for it seems to me that it deserves a place in our standard American literature, both for its matter and its manner.

I hope that Sister explained to you why I failed to see you when you were in Brooklyn.[1] My interior arrangements selected that afternoon and evening for such violent gyrations that I was reduced to a state of collapse and could only lie on my lounge and writhe with pain. Also on the following Saturday I was too far gone to make the journey to Princeton to hear Professor Dowden's lecture,[2] a circumstance that I regretted very much.

The fact is that my spirit is about broken and my courage almost gone. I am however in the care of famous experts in New York who can save me if anybody can I suppose, though they find it very hard work to even bring me into such a normal condition as to be able to tell exactly where the seat of the trouble lies. I suspect that it lies everywhere, all through me.

But I see that I am likely to write a dreary letter if I continue. And this was not my purpose, but rather to thank you for your worthy defense of that which is best in human life and society.

My best love to all.

Affectionately yours　　Stockton Axson

ALS (WP, DLC).

[1] When Wilson spoke at the Brooklyn Institute of Arts and Sciences on October 14.

[2] Edward Dowden, Professor of Rhetoric and English Literature at Trinity College, Dublin. He lectured on "The French Revolution and English Literature" in Alexander Hall on six successive days beginning October 12.

From William Brenton Greene, Jr.[1]

My dear Dr. Wilson:　　　　　　　　　Princeton. Oct. 22nd, 1896.

May I try to tell you how much I appreciate your oration of yesterday? To say that for grace of delivery, for purity of style, for true interpretation of the past, for philosophic insight into the present, for breadth of conception as to the future, for moral and religious purpose and power, it was worthy of the occasion is the highest praise; but it is also the only just praise.

Not merely every alumnus, but every scholar, every patriot, every christian, the world over, you have put under an obligation to you that could not be fully discharged.

These words, coming from me, may seem to you presumptuous. If so, I must suffer in your estimation; for though I have slept over them & am of an only too cold temperament, I can not keep them back.

Sincerely yours,   W. Brenton Greene, Jr.

ALS (WP, DLC).
1 Stuart Professor of the Relation of Philosophy and Science to the Christian Religion at Princeton Theological Seminary since 1892.

From John Davidson[1]

My dear friend   New York, Oct. 22nd 1896

I *heard* your magnificent oration! *I was proud of you!* A thousand congratulations.

I must have a copy of it when it is printed.

Yours very truly   John Davidson

ALS (WP, DLC).
1 Real estate broker of Elizabeth, N.J., and New York, and father of Jenny Davidson Hibben. Davidson had helped the Wilsons make arrangements to finance the construction of their home in 1895.

To Silas Weir Mitchell

My dear Dr. Mitchell,   Princeton, 25th October, 1896.

Your generous appreciation of my address has heartened me more than I can say. I wanted very much to say to you in person how it had cheered and fortified me, but was prevented by the hurrying engagements of the Celebration. I know of no one whose praise I would rather have than yours, and I hold the doctrines of my address with so deep a conviction that to be told that I expressed them adequately gives me the keenest pleasure. "The form of sound doctrine" seems to me of the utmost consequence. "The impassioned expression which is in the countenance of all science," "the breath of the finer spirit of all knowledge," the education and enfranchisement of the spirit, seem to me the real stuff alike of culture and of intellectual power; and I only wish I could have given such a view of the truth as it would be impossible to forget:—for a man has such an audience only once in a lifetime.

Most sincerely yours,   Woodrow Wilson

Printed in Anna Robeson Burr, *Weir Mitchell: His Life and Letters* (New York, 1929), pp. 241-42.

From Thomas Raynesford Lounsbury[1]

My dear Professor Wilson: New Haven, Oct. 25, 1896

I have been engaged this morning in writing letters, & as two or three have been addressed to Princeton, I thought it would be no harm to add one more to their number. The Princeton Sesquicentennial was throughout the best managed & most successful celebration I have ever known, & the perfection of every detail down to the minutest point has impressed me most strongly. But while everything was good, I must sincerely say that the crowning success of the three days was your oration. Of course, I do not purpose to abandon my Iago-like powers of finding fault with it in one or two places, for like that interesting & amiable character, "I am nothing if not critical"; & if the Archangel Gabriel should blow the finest music on his trumpet, I have the comfortable consciousness that I could succeed in finding somewhere a discordant note. But that does not prevent me from expressing my great admiration for it as a whole: & this was intensified by the bungling efforts of Remsen[2] the night of the banquet to take exception to portions of it;[3] for the only impression I got from his criticism was of his personal ability to reduce tediousness to an exact science, of which he would be the foremost professor.[4] If for no other reason I think my trip to Princeton would have well repaid me, in that I heard your oration & made your personal acquaintance, had there been nothing else.

You will pardon me under the circumstances for dropping formalities & sending you this little bit of a love-letter.

Sincerely yours   T. R. Lounsbury

ALS (WP, DLC).

[1] Professor of English at Yale University and Librarian of the Sheffield Scientific School. He received the L.H.D. degree at the Sesquicentennial.

[2] Ira Remsen, Professor of Chemistry at, and soon to be President of, The Johns Hopkins University. He received an LL.D. at the Sesquicentennial.

[3] The banquet was given in the Casino, a large university building, during the evening of October 22 by the alumni and faculty in honor of the delegates. Remsen responded to the toast, "The Physical Sciences." No report of his remarks seems ever to have been published.

[4] For another account of the banquet, see EAW to Mary E. Hoyt, Oct. 27, 1896.

To Edward Dowden

                                 Princeton, New Jersey,
My dear Professor Dowden,   27 October, 1896

It was a deep disappointment to me that I did not have a final word of parting with you. You had gone from the President's luncheon before I could find you in the crowd; and I was kept away from the banquet on Thursday night by a sick headache, brought on by the accumulated excitements of the Celebration.

I feel, in looking back upon the whole affair, that its chief reward for me was the relation, may I not say of friendship, into which it brought me with you and Mrs. Dowden,—and I know that Mrs. Wilson feels just as I do about it. I heard of your very handsome, your very generous references to my address in your speech at the banquet. You must, surely, have been speaking rather as a friend than as a critic; but, however you may have been prompted, it gives me the keenest pleasure to have won, if only for the moment, your critical approval.

I hope that you realize the feeling of personal debt, of personal enjoyment, may I not say of personal affection which your visit to Princeton created. We shall not hereafter feel that you live very far from us; and Mrs. Wilson and I shall wish always to feel that we have added Mrs. Dowden and you to the number of our friends.

Most cordially and sincerely Yours,   Woodrow Wilson[1]

ALS (Edward Dowden Correspondence, University of Dublin).
[1] Insofar as is known, this is the first letter that Wilson wrote with his right hand following his slight stroke in 1896.

To Howard Pyle

My dear Mr. Pyle,   Princeton, Oct. 27, 1896.

My friend Mrs. Conover, of this place, is President of the Mt. Vernon Ass.,[1] and has charge of the matter of refurnishing Washington's house in respect of such articles as carpets and the like. She has asked me if I thought it too great an imposition upon you to ask the loan of your knowledge of the furnishings of Washington's time, and I, knowing your good-nature, have volunteered to write to you in her stead.

Will you not be kind enough to advise me what sort of carpet ought to be bought, both as to pattern and stuff for the main rooms of the house; and will you not allow me to ask, with apologies for the impertinence, whether you had any special model or authority in your mind when you drew the carpet in your striking picture of Washington's interview with Mary Phillipse, in my "Harper" articles?[2] The carpet seems an Eastern one. Would Mrs. Conover be justified in buying one of that kind?

If you can without inconvenience answer these questions, you will be doing a real service to a very noble, interesting and enlightened woman.

I havn't before had a chance to express to you my very heartfelt admiration for your noble series of illustrations for my "Washington." They dignify and illuminate the work in every way.

I am using another hand to write this because my own has been threatened with writer's cramp.

With much regards,

Most sincerely yours,   Woodrow Wilson

EAWhwL, WWS (deCoppet Coll., NjP).
    [1] Helen Field (Mrs. Francis Stevens) Conover was the Vice-Regent for New Jersey of the Mount Vernon Ladies' Association of the Union. Wilson was mistaken about her title; there was no "President" of the Association. Its officers at this time were a Regent, Justine Van Rensselaer (Mrs. Howard) Townsend, and Vice-Regents for each state.
    [2] *Harper's Magazine*, xcII (March 1896), 572.

Ellen Axson Wilson to Mary Eloise Hoyt

My dear Minnie,   Princeton, Oct. 27/96

I hasten to answer your letter, which came today.[1] The silk under-garment is here and shall be sent at once; the other things, after the most careful search, cannot be found. You evidently did not leave them here.

Madge's[2] bicycle proved quite satisfactory,—at least as long as she was here. I have not heard from it since. It was bought at O'Neill's in New York and cost $48.00. He keeps them no longer, but Ed[3] says Wanamaker's is, he thinks, the same thing and at practically the same price. It is called the "Continental"

We are just through with our great celebration, you know;— the grandest thing of the sort, everyone says, that America has ever seen. It was the most brilliant, *dazzling*, success from first to last. And *such* an ovation as Woodrow received! I never imagined anything like it. And think of *so* delighting *such* an audience, the most distinguished, everyone says, that has ever been assembled in America;—famous men from all parts of Europe. They declared there had been "nothing to equal it since Burke"; with scores of other compliments equally great. Mr. Dowden was the most enthusiastic of all. His after-dinner speech at the banquet was simply one long expression of his delight with it. He was one of those that compared him with Burke. (I was in the ladies gallery, and heard it all!) As for the Princeton men some of them simply fell on his neck and wept for joy. They say that those who could not get at Woodrow were shaking each others hands and congratulating each other in a perfect frenzy of delight that Princeton had so covered herself with glory before the visitors. And that of course is what makes it such a sweet triumph; it was not a selfish success, it all redounded to the honour of Princeton before the assembled academic world. How I wish you could have heard it; of course you can read it later, but then he delivered it so superbly.

The poem was beautiful too;—though one of the guests said that the orator was more of a poet than the poet!

Excuse this *very* hasty scawl. With a heart full of love to you & the dear ones in Rome.

Your ever fond cousin   Ellen

ALS (in possession of William D. Hoyt, Jr.).
   1 It is missing.
   2 Margaret Randolph Axson, Ellen's younger sister.
   3 Edward William Axson, younger brother of Ellen.

From Henry Newell Hoxie[1]

My Dear Sir;   Haverford, 10/30/96

I was so greatly uplifted by your Oration at the Sesquicentennial Celebration at Princeton on the 21st inst. that I make bold to ask you if it is published as yet in permanent form, and where I can get it.

I have it in the Philada. Public Ledger of the 22nd inst.

I think you may take sincere happiness in the success of your effort on that occasion—splendid as it was.

The bright & stirring outline of the college history, and more especially for me, your critically correct estimate of our isolation as a country or nation from the higher civilizing influences of Europe; your references to the worth of the classic literatures which as I read them the next day on my return train home made me resolve to go back to my Phaedo and other great writers of the past (which I have since done with real joy.)—all these and other parts of your utterances on that occasion,—conservative and thus wisely progressive,—make me wish to have your Oration in a more portable form,—if I can secure it.

Perhaps a record of the entire celebration will be printed,[2] and if so, you would kindly inform me. Any expense attending a copy I will gladly remit to you, if you could send me one, and will kindly mention it. It would please me much to have your autograph on your oration.

Very truly yours,   Henry N. Hoxie

ALS (WP, DLC) with WWhw notation on env.: "Ans."
   1 A teacher at the Haverford School, a college preparatory school.
   2 It was indeed—under the title, *Memorial Book of the Sesquicentennial Celebration of the Founding of the College of New Jersey and of the Ceremonies Inaugurating Princeton University* (New York, 1898).

A Bibliography on Cabinet Government[1]

[c. Nov. 1, 1896]

BIBLIOGRAPHY of the PRINCETON-HARVARD DEBATE.
(Dec. 18, 1896.)

Resolved: That assuming the adoption of adequate constitutional amendments, the United States should institute a system of responsible cabinet government.

Princeton, affirmative.

Harvard, negative.

Brookings and Ringwalt. Briefs for debate. N. Y. 1896. (contains brief and bibliography).

Bagehot. English constitution. Lond. 1872, also Hartford 1889-91 (Works)

Boutmy. English constitution. Lond. 1891.

Bourinot. Parliamentary government in Canada. (Amer. Hist. Assoc. Rept. for 1893 in U.S. 52 Cong. 1 Sess. Misc. Doc. Vol. 5 No. 173)

Bryce. American Commonwealth. Lond. 1888, also N.Y. 1893-95 Vol. 1, Chap. 15, 16 and 25.

Burgess. Political Science &c. Bost. 1890-91 Vol. 2 PP. 11-16, 17-21, 32-40.

Dupriez. Les Ministres d'Europe et d'Amerique. Paris 1892-93. Vol. 1., pp. 1-200 (England.) Vol. 2. pp. 1-169 (United States.)

Gladstone. Kin beyond the Sea. *In his* Gleanings. Vol. 1.

Follett. The Speaker of the House. N.Y. 1896.

Grimke. Works. Columbus 1871. Vol. 2, Chap. 6.

Hare. American constitutional Law. Bost. 1889. Vol. 1, Lect. 10.

Hamilton. The Federalist. Chap. 51.

Helps. Thoughts upon Government. Lond. 1872.

Lowell. Essays on government. Bost. 1892.

      " Governments and parties in continental Europe. Bost. 1896.

Lefroy. The British vs the American system of national government. 1891.

Lalor. Encyclopedia of Political Science. 1882-84. "*Ministry.*"

Landon. Constitutional history of the U. S. Bost. 1889.

McCulloch. Men and measures. N. Y. 1888, Chap. 30.

Sidgwick. Elements of politics. Lond. 1891, Chap. 22.

Strauss. Origin of republican form of government. N. Y. 1887

Stickney. True Republic. N. Y. 1879.

Wilson. Congressional government. Bost. 1885

      " An old master &c. N. Y. 1893 Essay No. 5.

Gneist. History of the English constitution. Tr. by Ashworth. 1886. Vol. 2, Chap. 44 Seq.

Periodicals.

Annals American Acad. Pol. & Soc. Sci. Vol. 2, p. 289; vol. 3, pp. 1, 306 (Snow)
Atlantic Monthly. Vol. 57, p. 512; V. 65, p. 766; V. 67, p. 580.
Blackwood. Vol. 146, p. 276.
Contemporary Review. Vol. 48, p. 864.
Forum. Vol. 5, p. 591.
Nation. Vol. 12, p. 101; Vol. 34, p. 318; Vol. 6, p. 66.
Nineteenth Century. Vol. 23, p. 297, 441.
North American Review. Vol. 118, p. 1, 127, 179; Vol. 131, p. 383.
International Review. Vol. 4, p. 230.
Columbia College studies in Polit. Sci. Vol. 5, No. 2.
Revue des deux Mondes. Vol. 77, p. 626.

WWT MS. (WP, DLC).
[1] The *Daily Princetonian*, October 29, 1896, announced that the committee on arrangements for the Princeton-Harvard debate had agreed upon the question, "Resolved, that assuming the adoption of adequate constitutional amendments, the United States should adopt a system of responsible cabinet government." Since Wilson, according to the *Princeton Press*, December 19, 1896, had suggested the question, it seems likely that he supplied this bibliography to the preliminary Princeton debaters within a few days of the committee's meeting. For further developments, see the news item printed at November 19, 1896.

To Frederick Jackson Turner

My dear Turner,   Princeton, Nov. 5, 1896.

As you may have seen in the papers recently, Princeton has just obtained an increase of endowment. Not much of it has been left free by the donors to be used as we please, but it seems reasonably certain that out of what has been left free, a chair of American history will, among other things, be added;[1] and I am going to take the liberty of asking you, point blank, whether you *would* consider a call to such a chair here, for a salary of (say) $3400. The work of the chair would be altogether with the upper classes and graduates, and amidst such an environment of free study and quiet living as cannot, I confidently believe, be matched on the continent. I am asking this question entirely on my own responsibility. I have, of course been consulted about what is to be done, and shall be throughout, but I have not been authorized to make overtures to you or anyone else; I am simply taking this means of making my advice very definite.

There is no place in the country where a man is more freely allowed to do his own work in his own way than at Princeton; the spirit of American history dwells here from of old; and far and away the largest sums recently given us have been given for the development of our too meagre library. I hope therefore that you will give this matter your most serious consideration, unofficial though this letter may be. I have told you before how much I desired you for a colleague and now I wish to give substantial proof of the purpose. You need have no fear that should you come here your work as an historian would be any less separate from mine.

I am not using my own hand because of a threat of writer's cramp.

Most cordially & sincerely yrs.   Woodrow Wilson

EAWhwL, WWS (photostat in F. J. Turner Papers, MH).
 [1] At the meeting of the Princeton Board of Trustees on December 10, 1896, the Committee on Endowment reported that subscriptions to the Sesquicentennial Endowment Fund through October 22, 1896, totaled $1,358,351.23. Of this amount, approximately $342,415 was unrestricted and hence might have been used in part to support a chair of American history. However, there was no subscription specifically intended for the support of American history, or, for that matter, of history in general. "Minutes of the Trustees of the College of New Jersey and Princeton University, 1894-98," bound minute book (University Archives, NjP), pp. 417-23.

From Waterman Thomas Hewett[1]

Dear Professor Wilson: Ithaca, 7 Nov. 1896.

I wish to thank you for the sound words expressing that upon which all education is based, which you uttered on the occasion of the recent celebration at Princeton. They were nobly spoken and on an impressive occasion where they must have much weight.

I have just returned after an absence of some months in Europe. In my absence action was taken here which I deeply regret by which the bachelor of arts degree was hereafter to be conferred for any studies and all studies. The question has come up before but has always been decisively defeated. It may be said that on this occasion this action was accomplished only by the votes of the technical men. As the university has been reorganized such action in the Faculty of Arts and Sciences alone would be impossible.[2]

Thanking you for what you said and the way in which you said it, I am   Most sincerely yours   W. T. Hewett.

ALS (WP, DLC) with WWhw notation on env.: "Ans. 11 Nov. '96."
1 Professor of the German Language and Literature at Cornell.
2 The faculty of the Department of Arts and Sciences at Cornell had dropped
the Latin and Greek requirement for the Bachelor of Arts degree and eliminated
the degrees of Bachelor of Science and Bachelor of Philosophy. This action
set off a bitter counterattack by classicists throughout the country. See Morris
Bishop, *A History of Cornell* (Ithaca, N.Y., 1962), pp. 324-25.

An Announcement

[Nov. 7, 1896]

Sunday, Nov. 8. . . . 5 p.m. Services in Marquand Chapel, [to
be] conducted by Prof. Woodrow Wilson.

Printed in the *Daily Princetonian*, Nov. 7, 1896.

Notes for a Chapel Talk

Sunday, 8 Nov., 1896
Rom. VII., 6, last clause
*"That we should serve in newness of spirit, and not in the oldness of
the letter."*
Not *disobedient* to the law, *but disburdened* of it: free of all law by
change of attitude toward it.
Spirit and power. We have prayed for an intellectual awakening in
Princeton that she may be a University indeed: we ought to pray
for a spiritual awakening that she may be a power indeed.
The Oxford Movement.
"Newness of spirit" = 1) *Spontaneity* instead of *routine.* No real
power in anything (e.g. writing) done
by rote.
2) *A sort of self-pleasing vigour* instead of
painful effort.
3) *A wholesome naturalness* that is without
cant or canting thought.
Vigour of faith a concomitant of all right thinking and feeling, *the
fresh and individual air of the mind.*
The change *illustrated in our own college life,* where the things of
truth and honesty are becoming not so much matters of law as of
spirit.
*Things seen in the fine revealing light of faith are the real verities
of life.*

WWhw MS. (WP, DLC).

From Frederick Jackson Turner

My dear Wilson: Madison Wisconsin Nov. 8, 1896
Nothing could have come to me as a greater surprise than your
enquiry. I will not deny that it gave me very great pleasure to

receive this evidence of your interest and confidence in me. Princeton is a college that any man might be proud to be connected with, and to have you as a colleague would give me even more personal satisfaction. What my reply would be in case of official overtures, would depend upon the outcome of some more or less opposing considerations, and since you have given me your confidence in the matter, I shall ask you to consider some of these questions with me and aid me by your advise. I want to be entirely frank with you and so I shall risk fatiguing you with a pretty full statement of my own state of mind.

I have been reasonably successful in my work here. When I came from Johns Hopkins the work was conducted by Professor [William Francis] Allen and myself, and the elective classes did not number more than 50 students. Of course the kind of teaching that Allen did was of a grade of scholarship beyond anything that we have been able to reach. But since then our teaching force has increased so that we have now: [Charles Homer] Haskins, Professor of Institutional History; [Victor] Coffin, Asst. Professor of Modern European History; [Orin Grant] Libby, Instructor; and a teaching fellow. The aggregate attendance on our history classes—including some large freshmen required work—is about 600. I have about 175 elective students myself, including eight or ten graduate students. Of course I do not mistake "bigness for greatness," but knowing as I do that my work is regarded as far from being "a snap," I cannot do other than regard this as one test of success here. My salary is $2500, which I increase to $2800 by teaching in the summer school here for six weeks. I have a library—State Historical—which, in its newspapers and periodicals, government documents, local history, and documentary material on the Mississippi Valley, ranks with the four or five best in the country. This library is about to go into a fire proof and impressive building on the University grounds in two or three years: the foundation is now up. We shall have three historical seminary rooms there, in which all our classes will meet, with free access to books & papers, and with abundant apparatus for lecturing.

I have made for myself a field of study in Western history, and if nothing unforeseen happens, I ought to grow more influential in this field as I grow older. There is an abundant opportunity for investigation here, and my library and myself have become in a way adjusted to this problem. There are so few students in this field that it would be a matter for regret to have them diminished even by one.

Madison is beautiful. I have a home by the lake recently built, and very pleasant. Of course it could be disposed of, without loss, but it is pleasant, and I should dislike to pull up stakes without pretty definite knowledge of the future home.

Haskins is a colleague after my own heart; I should leave him with real regret. My parents live some forty miles away, and are growing old. My wife's people live in Chicago, but as my wife's sister is about to move to Holyoke, Mass., they might be near us by frequent visits. Finally, I have lived most of my life in the West and I like it.

These are the considerations that constitute the cake of custom, and the conservative tendencies in my problem.

On the other hand, Princeton is a noble old University, with evidences that her vigor is augmenting rather than declining. I should doubtless gain by the contact with Eastern men and ideals, and a new sort of students. I should be near to the centers of literary activity in the East. My wife has close friends in New York City, and I should rejoice in companionship with you, and your friends.

I think I could find opportunity for reconstructive work on the Middle region and the back country of the South, quite equal to my Western field; and I should like to infiltrate some of my Western interpretation of our national development into an American history course in the East.

Of the library facilities at Princeton, in American history, I know nothing; and I must ask you for more information upon opportunities for investigation there. Where do you do your American history work?

Are the students in earnest in their work?

What chances are there for graduate development?

How many hours of teaching would be expected?

Is any religious test applied to professors? Of course I am no radical, or propagandist, but my sympathies are in the Unitarian direction; I have never been accused of lack of sympathy with the other religious movements in my historical work, however.

What is the winter climate of Princeton? Here I am rendered unhappy for weeks at a time in the winter, by colds of a catarrhal character, and my physician tells me that unless I have a change of climate, I am likely to become "hard of hearing" as a result, in the course of time. Such a possibility as this has often made me declare that if I ever got a call to the seaboard I should accept it; but I might get out of the frying pan into the fire. Baltimore freed me from any such trouble; but that was farther south. My wife, also, has hay fever, and I wish she might be within reach of the Maine coast, or the Eastern mountains, for the summer.

Here we are so far that travelling is an impossibility on our salary.

What the relative financial gain at Princeton would be I do not know. Madison is not a cheap place to live in, as rents are high; but I suppose provisions and so on are far higher at Princeton, and desirable homes not easy to get. Can you assist me with information on this financial question? My family is not an *inex*pensive joy, for the three little children need a nurse, and altogether I have found it almost impossible to make both ends meet here. Would there be likelihood of increase of salary there? What are the normal salaries?

What would be my official relationship to other historical professors? Is there any such system of graduation as in Chicago?

What about schools for the children? Is society there so organized that there is exclusiveness. We are not dependent on our social relations; in fact my wife and myself do not care much for a great deal of that life; but here we have most pleasant associations in that respect; and I know that in some Eastern cities the "old comers" and the "new comers" are still at odds as they were in the primitive days.

Now, I should not have asked so many questions, nor made so tiresome a recital of my situation here, if I were not giving the matter very serious consideration, and if I were not anxious to decide wisely for us all.

I may add that I am not entirely contented with the policy of President [Charles Kendall] Adams here. I do not look for much progress while he and some of the Regents pursue their present policy. He is not likely to press any vigorous educational ideals; and there are not the most cordial relations existing between the faculty and him.

Mrs Turner joins with me in kindest regards.

I wish we could talk the whole situation over with you, for I rely very much on your good judgment. Confidentially, I may tell you, also, that I have received intimations similar to, though not so definite as yours, from members of the faculty of four other prominent Universities within the past year, so the problem of my remaining here is one that I may have to settle before long, even if your enquiry proves to be another evidence of your friendship and does not result in an official call.

In any case, let me tell you again how much I value your friendship.   Yours cordially   Frederick J. Turner

ALS (WP, DLC) with WWhw notation on env.: "Ans. 16 [15]/96."

To Houghton, Mifflin and Company

My dear Sirs,   Princeton, New Jersey, 10 November, 1896.

Please accept my thanks for your very thoughtful kindness in sending me so promptly a copy of my Essays.[1] The appearance of the book is most pleasing and satisfactory, and altogether a beautiful piece of workmanship.

I would gladly avail myself of your kind offer to mail copies of the book to such addresses as I might furnish; but I should like to inscribe a line or two in each copy that I give away; and shall ask you to send me the eleven copies now at my disposal by express, if you will.

In looking critically at the title page of the book, it strikes me that the E in the word OTHER ("and other essays") is from the wrong font, and not like the E in essays. Am I not right?[2]

Very sincerely Yours,   Woodrow Wilson

TCL (RSB Coll., DLC).
[1] *Mere Literature and Other Essays.*
[2] Wilson was right. The error was corrected in the next printing.

From Stockton Axson

Brooklyn, N. Y.

My dear Brother Woodrow: November 10, 1896

How can I tell you of the mixed emotions of surprise, love and gratitude which surge upon me as I open the volume "Mere Literature" just received and find that you have done me the honor to dedicate it to me![1] As it has all happened within the past two minutes I shall not dare to try to express all that I feel, for if I did I should "slop over" I know. It gives me an additional reason for wanting to get well in order that I may try to live to be a little worthy of the beautiful dignity of those dedicatory words. And as for having my name connected with such literature—well that is more than I had ever hoped for!

But best of all is it to have such an expression of your love. Not that I really needed such a testimonial to be assured of it, but love bears many forms of repetition—and I like this form. Thank you again and again.

I was just preparing to drop a line to Ed when your package was handed to me. In reply to a note from him I was going to say that I hardly dare to invest in a Yale-Princeton football ticket unless they are pretty cheap, for the chances are that I shall be unable to attend the game—I have to guard so carefully against fatigue now. Will you tell him that I should like a ticket if he

MERE LITERATURE

AND OTHER ESSAYS

BY

WOODROW WILSON.

BOSTON AND NEW YORK
HOUGHTON, MIFFLIN AND COMPANY
The Riverside Press, Cambridge
1896

The title page of the first printing of "Mere Literature"

doesn't have to pay more than a dollar and a half for it. I am afraid these tickets are selling at a higher price.

I am making a hard fight to keep at work. I see the doctors everyday and am leaving it for them to say when I have reached the danger point. It is a rough struggle, but I think I can say truly that with the exception of the *physical* melancholy—a thing over which I have no control—I am much easier in my mind than I was. This simply means that I am reconciled to the possibility of giving up regular intellectual work. Having attained to this the rest doesnt seem so hard. I think something will turn up. In the meantime I am still at work.

With best love for all and renewed thanks

Very affectionately yours   Stockton Axson

ALS (WP, DLC).
  1 See WW to EAW, June 19, 1896, Vol. 9.

From Edward Dowden

Buona Vista, Killiney,
My dear Professor Wilson   Co. Dublin, Nov. 10, 1896.
I do feel indeed that Mrs. Dowden & I have true friends in Princeton in Mrs. Wilson & you. If ever we should be in America once more, we could hardly help turning aside from any other road to have the happiness of meeting you both again. But it is more likely that you & Mrs. Wilson will be somewhere within range of Dublin. If so, remember that we want you to be occupants of a room in this house, from which you could see something of the country about the Wicklow lakes & hills.

What I said about your address was, I need not say, what I felt; but it was also what so many other persons thought & felt that I had no peculiar possession in it. The address seemed to many of us as wise in its spirit & idea as it was admirable in expression.

Our homeward voyage was moderately good—no great gales, but some cold head winds. We had a table to ourselves—Princeton delegates—with pleasant additions of Professor Darcy Thompson of Dundee (returning from a Commission on the subject of Seals, with many photographs) & a Dundee barrister. Mrs. J. J. Thomson[1] was only once at table; my wife proved a better sailor. Then, on arriving, came a load of arrears of work.

At first during our little time in America I was rather overwhelmed by the material aspects of life & then I seemed to see something of the spirit and character which lay behind these.

I came back with such a feeling towards America—of confidence in what is best in her life & character, as I could not have acquired from books. Toward which, you made no small contribution.

Give my most cordial remembrance to Mrs. Wilson, & believe me   Most sincerely yours   Edward Dowden

ALS (WP, DLC).
[1] Rose Elizabeth Paget Thomson, wife of Joseph John Thomson, Cavendish Professor of Experimental Physics at Cambridge University.

To Waterman Thomas Hewett

My dear Prof. Hewett,   Princeton, N. J., Nov. 11, 1896

Allow me to thank you very warmly for your kind letter of Nov. 7th. Nothing of recent years has gratified me more than the almost universal approval of the views expressed in my address. I knew the attitude of the Faculty of Arts at Cornell on the subject of requiring the classics for the Bachelor of Arts degree, and felt sure, when I heard of the recent action in the matter, that it must have been a victory won by the sheer numbers of the technical men. It is deplorable and Philistine so to empoverish the arts degree; but we must live to fight another day. I believe the fortunes of the day can be turned in favour of the classics, if we are only stubborn, tactful, and eloquent enough. To my surprise and satisfaction, I find the plain men, whose sons we are teaching, very largely in favour of the old drill, and "practical men" beginning to notice the failure of the technical schools to fulfil their first promise.

Pardon my not writing with my own hand. I have been threatened with writers cramp.

Let me thank you again for your letter, and believe me
                    Most sincerely yours,   Woodrow Wilson

EAWhwL, WWS (WC, NjP).

To Charles William Kent

My dear Charlie,   Princeton, Nov. 11, 1896.

I am obliged to get Mrs. Wilson to write for me because I have been threatened with writer's cramp.

I hunted Mr. McNair up just as soon as I could, and had the pleasure to find that he had already determined to accept the University's invitation.[1]

Your new scheme for religious work interests me very much,

and I shall expect it to be crowned with a very high sort of success.

It was very pleasant to see your handwriting again, and I can certainly reciprocate your wish, that we might have more frequent opportunities to see each other upon a footing of intimacy, as in the old days. There is nothing so hard to put up with in America as its distances. They cruelly curtail intimacies, and make friends foreign to each other for sheer lack of opportunities to meet.

I took a bicycle trip in Great Britain this summer, and had the pleasure on the return voyage of having Mr. Jourolman of Knoxville[2] as a fellow passenger; he is certainly a most cultivated and delightful gentleman; I feel that I have found a valuable friend in him. He had many pleasant things to say of you.

Please give my warm love to Heath Dabney, and beg him to write to me. Give my warmest regard to Mrs. Kent, and to Prof & Mrs. Smith,[3] and believe me, my dear fellow,

> Your affectionate friend,   Woodrow Wilson

EAWhwL, WWS (Tucker-Harrison-Smith Coll., ViU).
[1] Kent, in a missing letter, had inquired about William Irving McNair, a student at Princeton Theological Seminary, 1895-96, who had been offered the secretaryship of the Young Men's Christian Association at the University of Virginia.
[2] Leon Jourolmon, a lawyer. See L. Jourolmon to WW, Nov. 20, 1896.
[3] Professor and Mrs. Francis Henry Smith, Kent's parents-in-law.

To Frederick Jackson Turner

My dear Turner,   Princeton, N.J., Nov. 15/96.

The implication of your letter, (if I read it right,) that you will be favourably inclined towards a call from Princeton has given me the deepest gratification; and I shall try to return an answer as full, as confidential, and as satisfactory, as your own.

I confess that I should feel not a little guilty should I be instrumental in drawing you away from your chosen study of westward development, and I must tell you, at the outset, that the weakest part of Princeton is her library. We have just gotten a noble gift for a library building of the newest and amplest sort;[1] and we have very well-founded hopes indeed that we shall be able to go steadily forward with considerable purchases of books from year to year until our equipment on that side is of the first order; but for the present we have little enough material for original work. The library numbers over 100,000 vols., but there has never been a department of American history here, and nobody has ever paid any especial attention to developing the library on that side. I am constantly being surprised at finding rather rare and out of the way books in it, which I did not expect to find, and at not finding standard books which I supposed would be in any library. Upon the establishment of a chair of American history there will of course, I take it for granted, be a special appropriation for the purchase of the books most needed; and there would unquestionably follow a steady growth. Fortunately, we have such libraries as the Lenox just at hand in New York, whose directors spend almost everything they have in purchase of the rarest materials of our history; and so one can afford to wait upon the development here, and can rejoice in being personally in charge of it.

I do not see that it would be necessary for you to quit your present field of study. Undoubtedly, the history of "the Middle region and the back country of the South" not only needs, but is crying out for reconstruction, and that work seems to me as rich in possibilities as any; but it seems to me that it is but a part of the same story whose western end you have been scrutinizing, and that the two fields could very well be made one. But you, of course, are a better judge of that matter than I am.

As for the earnestness of the students here in their work, we, of course, have a great many men, the sons of men of means, who are college students only because their fathers and grandfathers were, and who take their work with a very easy conscience; but a majority of the undergraduates are serious fellows, and really have a notion of scholarship. They are quick to give attention, and to accord their thorough liking to any instructor whom they deem liberal-minded and capable. Anyone who takes their attention can get some of them to work as much as he wishes,—as many as he will find time to handle individually. We have a few graduate students now, and shall have many more as soon as we shall provide special instruction for them. We hope to make such special provision very soon, and I confidantly expect such a development in that matter, slow though it may be, as will quite satisfy us.

We have none of us been overtaxed with teaching here, and I don't think there is any likelihood that we shall be. Six to eight hours a week, I should say, was the maximum. I have, so far, had only four hours a week, our courses being two hours per week courses; but we shall very probably make them three hours a week in the near future, and in that case I shall have at least six hours a week of lectures; but I do not expect to have more. The undergraduate history classes here are apt to be so large that lecturing is the only possible method of instruction.

I think I can justly commend our winter climate. It is subject to rapid changes here, as everywhere else near the coast, and we have a good deal of rain, but Princeton lies high upon the foothills, and is as healthful and salubrious a place as ever I had the fortune to live in. It's a happy compromise between New Eng. and Baltimore. It is a much easier place, I should say, to keep one's health in than Balt.,—less damp, very little colder when it is cold, not so relaxing when it is warm, and as nearly without malaria as any place on the ordinary levels.

As for the cost of living here, it is rather high; an average rental for the sort of house you would want would be—say—$500.00, servants' wages are from $12.00 to $16.00 a month. The staple dry groceries are about the same here as everywhere; prime meat is 18 cts to 20 cts a pound, butter 30 cts to 40 cts, milk 5 to 8 a qt. The normal salary for a full professor is what I named in my last letter, $3400. There is, I should say, a fair prospect of an increase to $4000. Some of our full professors get less than $3400, and no one at the present writing gets more than $3500. There is a movement just now to increase the salaries of half a dozen of the most prominent men in the faculty to $4000, and I should say that continued success was likely to ensure the latter amount.

There is no system of gradation among the professors here, as in Chicago; there is not even a system of departments. Each professor is master within the limits of his own chair, and the only common authority is the faculty, served by a committee on the curriculum. I have heard no suggestion of a reorganization, and I think we should all of us oppose any plan which should threaten to mar the present free play of individuality and independence amongst us. We are under the reign of "King Log" rather than "King Stork" here,[2] so far as our president is concerned. Dr. Patton is a man of marked individuality and personal force, but he does not command or interfere, and we are in no sense in leading-strings. I don't know of greater academic freedom anywhere.

Schools for the children!—question!—ah, there's the rub! The place is too small to have adequate schools for children,—at any rate for girls. Boys are fairly well provided for. My little ones are girls, and we are puzzled what to do with them for they have so far been taught at home. (There is a very good school, however,—including a kindergarten,—for very small girls.) We think we shall be able to manage for those a little more grown by some sort of combination amongst us to bring a competent college woman here for the purpose.

Society here is in no disagreeable sense exclusive. The intercourse within the college circles is free, natural, and delightful; and "new-comers" need not fear that they will be looked at askance, or received otherwise than cordially.

I think I can say without qualification that no religious tests are applied here. The president and trustees are very anxious that every man they choose should be earnestly religious, but there are no doctrinal standards amongst us, and I do not think that matter need embarrass this case at all. I will, of course, have a frank talk with the president about it before we reach the stage of official action.

And now, my dear Turner, I hope I have satisfactorily answered your questions. It has given me pleasure to attempt these answers because it gives me the deepest sort of pleasure to believe that there is a possibility of bringing you here. I sincerely believe that you would really profit by coming. I myself was bred in one region of our country, and have worked in another, and know from personal experience what a means of enlightenment that single circumstance has been. It, so to say, makes a man catholic in spite of himself, and every way quickens his historical imagination.

I am very glad to discuss this whole matter with the utmost fullness, and I sincerely hope that if there is any matter at which your judgment still sticks, you will ply me with more questions, and still further statements, pro and con. I am anxious to bring our correspondence, since it is confidential, to some definite issue of judgment before advising official action because I know that our trustees would not be willing to give a call before being informally assured of its acceptance; and you are the man I mean to ask them to call if you are willing. I will not use your expression of willingness, either, unless I can make sure of their taking my advice; so that your dignity in the case is secure in any event.

I verily believe that the spirit of American history is somehow very vitally present in Princeton, (see my Sesquicentennial address in the Dec. "Forum"!); and I also believe that no more favourable conditions for work exist in the atmosphere of any other place in the country. I often feel as if I, as a writer, should feel obliged to stay here, even if the college should treat me shabbily; and I feel that I am acting in wise friendship towards you, and not selfishly, in making this effort to bring you here.

Mrs. Wilson joins me in the warmest regards to you both, and I am, my dear Turner,

Your sincere friend,   Woodrow Wilson

EAWhwL, WWS (photostat in F. J. Turner Papers, MH).

¹ The Pyne Library, about which see EAW to WW, Aug. 13, 1896, n. 7, Vol. 9.

² A reference to the fable of the frogs who asked Jupiter for a king. When he sent them a log, they complained of its inaction. He then sent them a stork, which ate them all up.

To Albert Shaw

My dear Shaw,   Princeton, New Jersey.   16 November, 1896.

In spite of my threatened attack of writer's cramp, I am allowed to hammer a little at this machine; and I must use my liberty to thank you with all my heart for your generous letter of praise and friendship, just received.¹ Of course you shall have the photograph at once, under another cover.

I somehow seem to have my friends specially in mind when I try to write well; and that you think it well done is, I assure you, part of the reward I most covet.

Mrs. Wilson joins me in warmest regards to you both.

As ever,

Faithfully and cordially yours,   Woodrow Wilson.

TCL (in possession of Virginia Shaw English).

¹ It is missing.

A News Item

[Nov. 19, 1896]

PRELIMINARY HARVARD DEBATE.

The preliminary debate, to select the men who will represent Princeton in the joint debate with Harvard, was held in Murray Hall last night. Dean Murray presided and introduced the speakers, who debated on the same side that had been assigned to them originally in the contests in the Halls.¹ The men spoke in the following order: affirmative—Beecher '98, Sterling '97, Ramsay '97, Kirkwood '97, Yocum '98, McElroy '96; negative—Reeves '99.² The rebuttals were delivered in the same order and then the judges, who were Profs. Wilson, Fine, Perry and Daniels, retired, and returning in about a half hour announced that they had chosen as Princeton's representatives McElroy '96, Sterling '97, Yocum '98, Whig Hall, with Kirkwood '97, Clio Hall, as alternate.³

Printed in the *Daily Princetonian*, Nov. 19, 1896.

¹ For the question debated, see "A Bibliography on Cabinet Government," printed at Nov. 1, 1896, n. 1.

² Robert Livingston Beecher, Robert Fulton Sterling, William Boyd Ramsey, Robert Ogilvie Kirkwood, Howard Herr Yocum, Robert McNutt McElroy, and Nathaniel Smith Reeves.

3 The debate was held in Alexander Hall on December 18, 1896. Although, as the *Princeton Press* of December 19, 1896, put it, the Princeton debaters were superior "as speakers," the Harvard team, supporting the negative, was adjudged to have had the better argument.

From Leon Jourolmon

Dear Professor Wilson,   Knoxville, Tenn., Nov. 20, 1896.

The mere reception of your volume of essays[1] gave me great pleasure, and I anticipate much more from the reading. It recalled to memory your unfailing kindness in many delightful hours on board the Anchoria.[2] I hardly need assure you that I am very grateful for both book and remembrance.

Last night I read the first two essays with keen interest. You had told me the circumstances that caused the writing of "Mere Literature,"[3] and I therefore all the more closely watched the spirit that informs the essay. You have most distinctly the better of the argument,—as I imagine the argument on the other side. I never before got so clearly the idea of the triune nature of literature—fact (or thought), form and vital spark.

I was glad to find so much of yourself in the book. The reading of it was quite like hearing you talk. He who would find the personality of an author in historical work must search diligently, but in the essay the writer comes forward and shows himself in social and friendly way. And now for several evenings I shall have the pleasure of your company in these pages. If you could but step out and sit down and sip hot lemonade with me I should be only too happy; even as it is I feel that you have sent me part of your very self. One of these days, not far away, I hope some favoring bit of work or pleasure may bring your entire person to Knoxville.

With sincerest regards,

Yours ever,   Leon Jourolmon.

ALS (WP, DLC).
1 *Mere Literature and Other Essays.*
2 On which they had sailed from Glasgow to New York in the preceding August and September.
3 See the Editorial Note, " 'Mere Literature,' " Vol. 8.

From Walter Hines Page[1]

My dear Mr. Wilson,   [Cambridge, Mass.] November 21, 1896.

With the connivance of Mr. [H. E.] Scudder I take the liberty to remind you of two entries that we made on the engagement book of the Atlantic Monthly before you went abroad last summer. Although it takes two to make an engagement, and you, I believe, have never definitely given your assent, these things are so desirable and so excellent that we have been unable to look upon them in any other way than as engagements.

One request, you will recall, was that you would write an article after you came home about American residents abroad, the aim being to formulate the desirability of residence in the United States as compared with residence in Europe, but more especially to point out the obligations that American citizenship and its opportunities impose upon a citizen of the republic to live and work at home; all this tending toward the formulation of what constitutes the highest type of the American citizen.[2]

The other request, you will remember, was akin to this—that you would make a historical statement of the growth of American national feeling, showing its stages at the several periods of our history—aiming at a statement of what constitutes American nationality.[3]

We hope that you will be able to send us these things sometime during the winter when the pressure of your lecture engagements permits; and in order that you may be perfectly sure that we are not unmindful of you I add a third request.

We very much desire for the March Atlantic a review of President Cleveland's public career, and an estimate of his influence as a public character. We cannot turn to men who are active in political life for such an article, because we should receive from any such man either a mere catalogue of political events which he considers of importance, or a eulogy of Mr. Cleveland. Of course what we want is a piece of literature which shall interpret the effect upon our history and upon our national life of his career and of his personality. Scudder and I have talked over this subject very thoroughly, and we each, independently, reached the conclusion that in your hands the subject would receive much more satisfactory treatment than in the hands of any one else.[4]

Concerning the other essays which we hope to receive we do not venture to set any date, but we do hope that we may look for this paper on Cleveland in time for the March number, that is to say by the middle of January, and you must not say us nay.[5]

I do not think that the article will require much preparation in the way of research or of a review of our recent political history, because in the space of a single article you can do nothing more than sketch a large subject in outline and point out the greater events and larger tendencies.

I feel that I ought to add a word about the honorarium for

these papers. The frankest and fairest thing to say is to ask that you yourself set or suggest the price.

Very sincerely yours,   Walter H. Page

TLS (Houghton Mifflin Letterpress Books, MH).
    [1] At this time Assistant Editor of the *Atlantic Monthly*.
    [2] W. H. Page to WW, June 22, 1896, Vol. 9.
    [3] Page suggested this article either in conversation or in a letter which is missing. Wilson responded with "The Making of the Nation," printed at April 15, 1897.
    [4] Wilson responded to this invitation with "Mr. Cleveland as President," printed at Jan. 15, 1897.
    [5] Wilson's reply is missing, but see W. H. Page to WW, Dec. 3, 1896.

From Herbert Baxter Adams, with Enclosure

My dear Mr. Wilson: Baltimore. November 21, 1896.

I have just received from Dr. Fred. Bancroft[1] the enclosed extract regarding your latest book. You will perhaps be interested to read what Mr. Trescot has written. Our boys here are speaking with enthusiasm of your work and are hoping to hear you again in the department.   Very sincerely,   H. B. Adams

TLS (WP, DLC).
    [1] At this time Lecturer on the Political and Diplomatic History of the United States at Amherst College.

E N C L O S U R E

William Henry Trescot[1] to Frederic Bancroft

Pendleton, Anderson County,
Dear Mr. Bancroft: South Carolina. November 16, 1896.

I cannot thank you sufficiently for "Mere Literature" which you sent me and which I have read with a pleasure that I cannot well express. Of course I don't agree with everything he says but I cannot but feel indebted to the breadth and acuteness of the analysis and the elevation of tone in all his speculation. Ever since I read Wilson's "Congressional Government" I have wanted to know him and I came very near writing to him, but I doubt if he knows me by name, although I did hear that he grew up in Columbia, the capital of South Carolina, where I used to be a good deal some thirty years ago as a member of the Legislature, and his name is certainly not unfamiliar to me. . . .[2]

Wm. Henry Trescot.

TCL (WP, DLC).
    [1] Lawyer, diplomat, historian, and politician of South Carolina.
    [2] Elision in the original.

From Edmund Clarence Stedman[1]

My Dear Sir,   Bronxville, N. Y.   Nov. 22d, 1896.

The fact that *The Dial* has "got ahead" of me[2] shall not prevent me from telling you what satisfaction I experienced, though on a sick bed, when I read your Princeton oration. It is a too rare pleasure, nowadays, to come upon a piece of genuine, though contemporary, English prose. *The Dial*, I say, has forestalled me in expressing admiration of your closing passage—which seemed to me really Miltonic in nobility of cast and diction. My impulse was to tell you how fine I thought it—how truly in "the grand manner"—and even now, though so late, I make bold to do so. But, indeed, the whole oration has received the appreciation of all for whose judgment you have reason to care. I am, with respect,

Very truly yours,   Edmund C. Stedman

(Pray don't take the trouble to acknowledge my note)

ALS (WP, DLC) with WWhw notation on env.: "Ans."
[1] Poet, critic, and member of the New York Stock Exchange.
[2] He refers to an editorial, "The World's Memory," in the Chicago *Dial*, xxi (Nov. 1, 1896), 241-43, praising Wilson's "Princeton in the Nation's Service."

To Edmund Clarence Stedman

My dear Sir,   Princeton, 25 Nov., 1896

I cannot deny myself the pleasure of thanking you for your kind letter of the twenty-second. It was generous of you to think of writing. No one, I should fancy, can know better than you do how such words of appreciation, from one who has the right to assess values, heartens a writer and makes him fitter for his work. I thank you most sincerely.

No newspaper report had more than two-thirds of my address. It will appear for the first time in full in the December *Forum*, and I should rather have it judged as a whole than in its abbreviated form.

With warmest regards,

Most sincerely Yours,   Woodrow Wilson

ALS (WC, NjP).

From Frederick Jackson Turner

My dear Wilson: Madison Wisconsin November 27, 1896

I am very much indebted for your full replies to my enquiry, and should have replied before if I could have done so with advantage. But I have been working at the problem, which is not an easy one, and which means very much to me. I never regarded myself as particularly conservative, but I am beginning to doubt my opinion, as the difficulty of action in this case grows on me.

I notice by the press the announcement that Professor Sloane is called to Columbia,[1] I suppose to a chair of American history. Does this change—if it is to be a change—affect the matter in any way? It seems to render indefinite the question of the historical colleague, and while I am more than pleased with the Princeton system of independence, which is substantially our own, yet I am not, of course, indifferent to the personality of those who would work in history there, if I were to go.

I have just returned from Chicago where I consulted a specialist, who assures me that my catarrhal colds are likely to be greatly decreased, judging from the improvement he finds, and that climatic conditions need give me no concern hereafter, so this puts one question out of the way.

What you say regarding rent and provisions leads me to believe that, everything considered, there is no financial gain involved—at least not any very considerable advantage of that nature.

My library here is certainly a very important element in the problem, and I am increasingly reluctant to relinquish it without very clear reason. I know how difficult it is to do systematic investigation when the library is an hour or two away and involves a daily expense to reach it. And while it would be a pleasure to build up a library on my own ideals, yet you know that Americana, & public documents of the states, are not easily gotten, even with abundance of means. The relative inferiority of the Chicago libraries (in spite of their rich endowments) in American history has impressed this upon me.

So it comes to pretty nearly this: ought I to exchange my library advantage here, for the greater dignity of a professorship at Princeton, for the stimulus of new and undoubtedly more inspiring contact with the intellectual activity of the seaboard with its many centers of culture within short distances, and for companionship with yourself—for to me that is a very considerable factor. Over against these advantages lie also the removal from my people and my wife's people, now growing old,—the element of uncertainty in building up new work, and the separation from Haskins and my other friends in Madison. Here my work is shaping itself easily and naturally and I can look forward to increasing means, reputation and power in the University as it developes —not to consider the question of other calls.

There is the atmosphere of creative activity in the West, and now that it has laid the economic foundations, I look for the West to turn its youthful and vigorous enthusiasm and initiative into University lines. The men who rise with this uplift will have an influential and important place in American educational life. This may be dreamful; but it is a persistent thought with me, none the less. Wisconsin University is fitted by nature for a commanding place in this development of culture, and it is growing with the growth of the West; for American history it has remarkable advantages in our library.

For a year or more I have had reason to believe that it was the purpose of the authorities to raise my salary as soon as it seemed feasible. I ought not, therefore to reckon on my present income as the real factor; and I should do this University some injustice in deciding adversely to it before the real alternative could be placed before me.

I do not think you will misjudge my position. I need not say that I have no desire to trifle with this matter. It is simply not clear to me that I ought to make a definite and final pledge to go elsewhere under the conditions of salary and library mentioned, without knowing definitely what is the best thing Wisconsin can do by me.

If you reflect upon it, you will see that there is this Wisconsin side to the matter as well as the Princeton side, and you will recognize that my desire to do the fair thing all around is really the only course that you would wish a man to take. If, however, you think that it would be improper for Princeton to make a proposition that I could submit privately to the authorities here, I wish you would frankly let me know.

With frankness, also, I will tell you that I prefer not to give a final reply till hearing again from you in the matter, but that with the situation as it now appears to me, I am very doubtful of the advisability of agreeing to accept a call on the terms you suggest.

My wife, I suspect, would vote the other way, but she is in Chicago on a visit and is ruled out!

I may be wrong in this, but I shall look for your comments.

Mrs. Turner, if she were here, would join me in greetings to yourself and Mrs. Wilson.

I should like to get down to New York to the Association[2] and see you too; but I fear I can't do more than send a paper,[3] this time.

With regards   Yours Frederick J. Turner

ALS (WP, DLC).

[1] Sometime during the spring of 1896, President Seth Low of Columbia University nominated his old friend and fellow alumnus of Columbia College, William Milligan Sloane, Professor of History and Political Science at Princeton, to be the first incumbent of the Seth Low Professorship of History, established by the Columbia Board of Trustees in June 1895. President Patton and several of the Princeton trustees and faculty knew of the appointment as early as May 1896 but were sworn to secrecy by Sloane and later decided to keep the matter secret until after the Sesquicentennial Celebration. The Columbia trustees announced the appointment on November 16, 1896. The Low professorship was originally intended to be in American history, but the title was changed to conform to Sloane's interests in European history. See R. Gordon Hoxie *et al.*, *A History of the Faculty of Political Science, Columbia University* (New York, 1955), pp. 61, 226-27; F. L. Patton to James W. Alexander, Nov. 19, 1896, Patton Letterpress Books, University Archives, NjP; and the *New York Times*, Nov. 17, 1896.

[2] The annual meeting of the American Historical Association.

[3] Wilson, as it turned out, commented on Turner's paper, "The West as a Field for Historical Study," on December 31, 1896. See Wilson's remarks printed at that date.

To Frederick Jackson Turner

My dear Turner,   Princeton, N. J., Nov. 30, 1896.

I decline to believe that you are as unwilling as you seem to come here; not because I think your reasons poor, but because my desire to move you is so strong. I am the more prompt, therefore, in meeting every argument of yours that I can.

Let me begin again as it were at the beginning. I could not tell you before that Sloane was going away because he had bound me to secrecy in that matter until the Columbia people should themselves publish it. Now I can tell you that we shall need three men altogether: one to take European history with the upper classes and graduates, another to take American history in like manner, and a third to undertake the drill and stimulation of the lower classes in general history. Thats the whole programme.

About the men who shall fill the first and third of these chairs, I am both willing and anxious to hear your advice, and I think we could suit you in the matter of colleagues. I had thought of Haskins for the first chair I mentioned. I am, of course, perfectly satisfied about his scholarship and attainments; but I can't help remembering how shy he was, and I want to ask you one or two frank questions about him. Has he gained force and facility in lecturing, and can he command the attention of big classes without too much effort? Personal force and ease count for so much that I should hardly dare to think of a man who didn't have them. Please tell me while you are about it too what you would think of E. G. Bourne?[1] I hope Haskins will be at the American Historical Association; I should like to hear him read his paper, and get an idea of his manner.[2] Does anybody else, whose personality you know, occur to you?

Notwithstanding the fact[3] . . . made you, and such an addition to them while you are yet young as will add variety to your thought and point of view and a rich increase of intellectual experience.

As for money, to judge by my own experience it is easily made in the magazine and lecture region. I have not written when I felt disinclined, or spoken much oftener than I wanted to, and yet I have found no difficulty in adding $1500.00 to my yearly income when I chose. Moreover, as I said last time, it seems very likely that salaries of $4000.00 will be forth-coming here very soon.

Its under the head of libraries that I recognize your great advantage in our argument. I can only say that one or two of the rich men who are interested in building up our library are particularly bent upon getting rare Americana for us as rapidly as possible.

Long as it is, this letter is only preliminary to answering the important question of your letter, viz., whether it will not be possible to put an official assurance of your being called into your hands before asking you to decide the question of accepting. I don't know how that can be managed, and I am getting what I have written off my mind while the impression of your letter is still fresh. I will see what Dr. Patton says, and write you on that head as soon as possible.

Meanwhile think about what I have said, my dear Turner, as the earnest sentiments of a friend and get ready for your final decision. I have written bluntly as to one who knows me and will understand me; but a letter is a wofully poor thing, and I wish with all my heart that you *could* come to New York to read your paper, and have a talk with me and look at Princeton.

With warmest regards from us both,

Faithfully yours,   Woodrow Wilson

EAWhwL, WWS (photostat in F. J. Turner Papers, MH).
[1] Edward Gaylord Bourne, Professor of History at Yale University.
[2] Haskins did attend the meeting of the Association and read a paper, "The Life of Medieval Students as Illustrated by their Letters," later printed in the *American Historical Review*, III (Jan. 1898), 203-29. For Wilson's comment after hearing the paper, see WW to F. L. Patton, Jan. 4, 1897.
[3] A portion of the letter is missing at this point.

From John Huston Finley[1]

My dear Dr. Wilson: Galesburg, Illinois. Nov. 30, 1896.

It is difficult for me to address you without bringing in your Christian name. You should allow us to hyphenate it.

I have just sent a line of rather tardy congratulation to President Patten and I feel that I must send a postscript to you—for your part in the exercises of the festal season allowed me to say with a pardonable and particular pride to my friends here, "He was my teacher and friend."[2] I am not sure that I did not use the present tense in connection with the last, and if I did use it you allow it for the sake of the days long gone or for the friendship I cherish for him whom I still wish to claim as friend.

You must know too that you are one of our patron saints here. Your photograph hangs over the daily papers in the library—the most frequented spot[—]and I go in occasionally myself and worship a bit at the shrine. If one didn't have these "saints" about to help one what would one do?

I started out to give you my congratulations and to tell you how sorry I was and still am that I could not go to Princeton. I tried in a rather formal way to express the pleasure we should have in being present by proxy, and by vote of the Faculty I was the proxy (vicarius) or was to be, but at the last minute I was prevented from leaving. MacLaren[3] was the man who blocked the way. I succeeded in getting him to come here and was obliged to stay to prepare for his coming. I am the more sorry though MacLaren helps me to forget the sorrow because I shall never have again the pleasure of attending a sesqui-centennial, I fear.

Let me add my congratulations that you have won in foot ball.[4] I am afraid our house will fall. Mrs. Finley, who is by lineage of Harvard and in doctrine of Yale, holds for the crimson, or when that is down, the blue, while I am loyal to the orange and black. If you continue to take good students from us, however, I warn you that I shall have to withdraw my support.

We are having a good year and from all reports Princeton is making sesquipedalian progress.

Accept with my congratulations assurances of my most cordial regard.   Sincerely yours   John H. Finley

ALS (WP, DLC) with WWhw notation on env.: "Ans. 7 Jany, 1897."
  [1] At this time President of Knox College.
  [2] When Finley was a graduate student in history at the Johns Hopkins in 1888-89.
  [3] He was the Scottish Presbyterian minister and theologian, John Watson (1850-1907), who had become the literary rage in Great Britain and North America with his publication in 1894 and 1895 of two volumes of fictional sketches of Scottish rural life under the pen name of "Ian Maclaren." Watson

conducted the first of three highly successful lecture tours in the United States and Canada from October 12 to December 16, 1896.

[4] Princeton climaxed an undefeated football season by downing Harvard 12-0 on November 7 and Yale 24-6 on November 21, 1896.

William Milligan Sloane's Review of *George Washington*

[December 1896]

GEORGE WASHINGTON. By Woodrow Wilson. Illustrated by Howard Pyle. Harper & Brothers, 8 vo, $3.00.

BY WILLIAM M. SLOANE

It is said that the late Sir John Seeley, professor of history in the university of Cambridge, was greatly disturbed by the assumption of every intelligent man or woman that he or she had a right to an opinion in matters of historical science. This hallucination, the professor felt, was due to the established usage of employing plain, homely English words in the writing and in the discussion of history by its adepts, and he proposed, perhaps jocularly, that the men of his profession should invent a sesquipedalian terminology behind which the philosophic spirit of their learning should find a sacred asylum.

Professor Woodrow Wilson is of another mind. In the beautiful volume entitled "George Washington," he has made lavish use of his great resources for the benefit of every intelligent reader. The various chapters are each and all models of the historical essay, full of learning, yet with no suspicion of pedantry; rich in expressive style, yet carefully self-restrained in diction; adequate in presentation of the subject, yet free from rhetorical superfluity. The theme is one most difficult for any patriotic American, because the contemplation of that heroic age in our history, and of its shining example, arouses feelings which are not always compatible with sober discussion or unvarnished description. Professor Wilson has avoided the snare. He has a stately theme and he uses stately language, in places his style is magisterial, but from first to last his delineation of Washington in all the relations of life is marked by moderation and critical judgment.

The author is particularly fitted for his delicate task: he is a southern man with a northern training, and yet he is too young to have absorbed the bitterness of the civil war. He is therefore himself a catholic American, combining the sympathies of every section, representing the new generation which knows no sectionalism. These facts appear in his perfect appreciation of the same qualities as they stand forth in the life of his great subject.

With due regard for local flavor, for the virtues peculiar to a certain strain of blood, for environment and nurture, the writer nevertheless depicts for us in color, atmosphere, and proportion the man who was instinctively selected for leadership by the northern, middle, and southern colonies as combining in himself what was common to them all, as exhibiting in his person the vigor of a transition movement destined to become revolutionary, and as displaying the high qualities without which a successful conflict is not transformed into enduring victory.

This volume is not an exercise in the science of history, although it bears marks of independent investigation in certain directions, and is thoroughly philosophical in its arrangement. Nor is it chiefly an essay in historical ethics, although the lessons of the great theme are so presented that he who runs may read. It is rather a picture of Washington the man and of his times drawn in bold outline with the temper and skill of the artist, all the details being wrought into a harmonious unity which will compel the reader to take the book as a whole without emphasizing the details. Professor Wilson's theory of what a book should be, or at least what seems to be his theory, is more evident in this his latest work than in any previous one. It appears as if to him the product were vastly more important than the tools or the material, the result more precious than the process; his ideal is almost certainly to be a prose "maker" like the "makers" who use chisel, brush, or verse in the expression not of thoughts strung like pearls on a necklace, but of a single central conception brought into eminence by the matter and the work.

Of course in such an aim the essential thing is that elusive something which we call style. Every writer has mannerisms, the best transform what is peculiar into what is general, that is, into what we all believe ourselves vaguely to have thought, but which we admit that we never expressed even to ourselves exactly in this way. To this end the first essential is grasp or synthesis, a result which is always due to the finest analysis. In this book there will be found exactly this grasp; there are not half a dozen or more Washingtons,—Washington the surveyor, Washington the planter, Washington the general, Washington the statesman, Washington the Virginian, etc.,—there is a single Washington, displaying his permanent character in its adaptation to various pursuits, various duties, and various circumstances. This Washington is the man we have all desired to see, neither hero nor demigod, but a great, strong, struggling, modest American man, whose identity is never lost for an instant.

To depict this personage, Professor Wilson has developed his style into an admirable instrument. At times his periods have a roll which, though entirely his own, reminds the reader of Washington's great Irish contemporary, the true friend of America, the exponent in English speech of what was best in the conservatism of the age, as Washington was the exponent in English conduct of the same qualities. I mean, of course, Edmund Burke. For the most part, however, the charm of the author's writing lies in its directness and simplicity, monotony being avoided by an unexpected turn in some phrase or by the felicitous use of some word which, though expressive, must be considered etymologically before its true meaning appears. The meaning is thus brought home and fastened by an artifice which flatters the reader in its appeal to his erudition. If the writer had less store of words in his treasury this might be thought a trick or an affectation, but his vocabulary is uncommonly large, being especially rich in Anglo-Saxon terms. In the style of this volume there is likewise a certain old-time flavor of quaintness, not sufficient to cloy, but just enough to flavor. This too is an agreeable titillation to the literary palate, since it is in some sense reverential, a tribute from an essentially modern man to an age and place which were not merely picturesque, but which had in them such men and women with such breeding and principle as made possible the history in which they were one of the three great components.

If we were permitted to express a preference among the chapters of Professor Wilson's book, it would be for those which describe the *rôle* of Washington during the years of the Revolutionary war. The constitutional revolution antecedent to that epoch, although the determinative period of American history, left Washington characteristically unmoved. But the issue once defined, the consequences once confronted, there began under Washington's leadership a series of military movements which rank among the finest achievements of the human mind in the field of strategy. The discursiveness of history as generally and necessarily written makes it difficult to grasp these movements in their unity as the conclusive proof of Washington's superlative military genius. As Professor Wilson has gathered them together and displayed them they stand forth, as they should, the unsurpassed performance of a great mind face to face with physical force and reserve strength far superior to any at its command. The old, old lesson of organized moral power as the conqueror of numbers, resources, and size is told again with freshness and incisiveness. How apposite such teachings are at this juncture of our affairs the book-buyer needs not to be reminded.

But the close of the book is in its way quite as choice as any other part, displaying the author as the man of letters perhaps even better than do his military and political disquisitions. The thoroughly human elements of the great hero are less obstructed in their manifestation during the closing scenes of his life than in those where the man of action eclipses the man of sentiment, and these elements are portrayed in singular felicity by our author's sympathetic pen. We cannot fail to enjoy the picture of how the brains which planned the Jersey campaign grappled with an exhausted estate; of the general and statesman performing the commonplace duties of citizenship, or finding repose and refreshment in the tender intercourse of family life. The closing scenes of the story are told in fitting language, sympathetic, poetic, and adequate.

The volume owes much to the work of the artist. Mr. Pyle's pictures are in the truest sense illustrations of the text, not necessarily of the scenes depicted by the writer, but of the writer's thought and feeling. It is uncommon to find so strong a delineator of life willing to subordinate, or rather coördinate, his work to that of an author, and illustrated books by master hands are not always the joy to the purchaser which they are intended to be, for they sometimes divide the attention between two minds which are frequently inharmonious and sometimes at war. But Mr. Pyle is himself a charming writer, and the illustration of his own books has clearly given him a thorough understanding of the true relations beween pictures and text in a book which deals with a single important theme. The reader of this volume will find no friction between the conceptions of author and illustrator. Mr. Pyle is in his aims a kindred spirit with the true man of letters, his technique is clever, his fidelity to truth very high. It was a fine idea to bring the two men together in a performance of this character.

This book has a deep significance to the observer of his own times. Having seen the apotheosis of science in our age, we have also seen the revolt of the philosophic imagination against the trammels of systems which catalogue the facts of human evolution without regard to their proportion or relations. Further, we have noted the yearning for knowledge which shall be not merely scientific and philosophical, but artistic as well, and in the case of history artistic means literary. Professor Wilson has the sense of his age, he feels the demand for history written from the standpoint of the present time; with a firmly established reputation for research and analysis he has ventured to write a historical study which adds to both what we venture to designate as the quality of pertinence. This is not the same as either literary or ethical form, for while it includes both it does not emphasize them; to aim at either or at their combination constitutes an end in itself, to appeal by their means to a nascent sense in the world of readers is something different, it is further to develop that sense, to strengthen the already existing desire. There are many who will bid god-speed to Professor Wilson in his effort.

Printed in the New York *Book Buyer*, XIII (Dec. 1896), 724-29.

From the Minutes of the Princeton Faculty

5 5′ P.M., Wednesday, December 2nd, 1896.

. . . The President announced that the Dean and Professors Brackett, Fine, W. Wilson and Young had been appointed the Committee to prepare A Memorial to the Board of Trustees respecting the establishment of a Graduate College. . . .

Prof. Woodrow Wilson was added to the Committee on the Trask Lectures.[1] . . .

The Committee appointed for the purpose made the following report which was adopted and ordered to be transmitted to the Honorable, The Board of Trustees of Princeton University. . . .[2]

[1] Founded in 1891 with a gift of $10,000 from Spencer Trask, Class of 1866. The interest from the fund was used to sponsor lectures on subjects of special interest.
[2] The report, printed as the next document, was here spread upon the Minutes.

A Memorial to the Princeton Trustees

[Princeton, N.J., c. Dec. 2, 1896]

The Faculty of Princeton University hereby respectfully presents to the Honorable The Board of Trustees of Princeton University the following memorial respecting the establishment of a Graduate College.

Princeton has already committed itself to a development of its graduate work by assuming the University Title and by the appeals which have been made for the endowment of a Graduate College. In the judgement of the Faculty the Graduate College is not only the proper completion of our Academic System, but is necessary if Princeton is to maintain its place as one of the leading American Universities.

It is difficult to overestimate the value of such a college in training a body of the highest scholars. It will enable Princeton University from time to time to select for its Faculty well qualified men of its own teaching after such oversight and inspection as is hardly possible otherwise. It will enable Princeton to raise a body of well-trained men for other Universities and Colleges and the leading preparatory schools of the country, and thus vastly increase her influence. It will attract our best undergraduates to pursue higher studies here. The presence of a strong body of graduate students will also promote intellectual seriousness in the undergraduate body as no other influence could. In addition to its beneficial effects within the institution, it will do more than any other one thing to increase Princeton's reputation in the world of learning.

It is furthermore the judgement of the Faculty that the present time is not only most opportune for founding the Graduate College, but is critical. It is not to be expected that so many favorable influences will again conspire to this end for a long time to come. And it is equally clear that, unless prompt measures can be taken to found a Graduate College now, Princeton will be placed in a position of great discredit in comparison with other American Universities. We are beginning to experience already the loss of some of our own graduates, and graduates of other Colleges who desired to study in Princeton, to the non-professional graduate schools of Harvard, Cornell, Columbia, Johns Hopkins and Chicago. In the nature of the case this loss must increase unless arrested by the attractions of a strong Graduate College in Princeton; for the reason that there is an increasingly powerful tendency at the present time to develop graduate schools of pure studies in our greater Universities.

On the other hand, we are convinced that Princeton possesses certain important advantages over any other American institution for the development of a Graduate College representing the highest type of academic culture,—a type which is most attractive to the finest students and which we believe is not realized by any Graduate School yet founded in this country. This is because Princeton alone possesses in combination an ideal academic seclusion, an old and well developed undergraduate department,—the proper basis and feeder of the Graduate School,—and definite religious, patriotic, and intellectual traditions which command public confidence.

The Faculty realizes that the sums recently contributed to the endowment of the college are no more than sufficient for the proper equipment of the work already undertaken. But we feel that to confine them to that use exclusively would be to create an embarrassing presumption against a genuine University development, and thus discredit our public professions of purpose.

We therefore beg earnestly to suggest that, even at the cost of postponing for a time such a symmetrical strengthening of the undergraduate work as we all desire, some substantial portion of the new income be pledged toward the endowment of instruction in a Graduate College. We would, in pursuance of this idea, beg to suggest that this allotment of moneys be made contingent upon the addition by new subscriptions of gifts sufficient to warrant the definitive establishment of a Graduate College.

We are of the opinion that, were funds enough thus pledged now for the creation of two graduate professorships and several University fellowships, you would have given such an expression of your purpose in this matter as would inspire confidence in those to whom we hope to appeal for further gifts.

Such is our interest in this plan that we venture to urge that a conference regarding its details be granted our Committee by your Honorable Body.

James O. Murray
Charles A. Young
Cyrus F. Brackett
Woodrow Wilson[1]

HwS MS. (Trustees' Papers, University Archives, NjP).

[1] This memorial was presented to the Board of Trustees at their meeting on December 10, 1896. Following the reading of the memorial, the trustees conferred further on the subject with Professors Murray, Young, Brackett, and Andrew F. West. Why Wilson did not appear at the meeting with the other signers of the report is not clear. The addition of West to the faculty committee was a logical move since he was the Secretary of the Committee on the Sesquicentennial Endowment and a prime mover in the drive for a graduate school at Princeton. The trustees agreed on the need for a graduate college, or school, and elected a committee of five trustees (John J. McCook, Melancthon W. Jacobus, Moses Taylor Pyne, John Dixon, and President Patton) "to be in conference with the Faculty Committee on the Graduate College." Presumably, the faculty committee referred to was the one which had written the memorial, with the addition of West. Whether Wilson took any further part in the committee's work is not known.

At the meeting of the Board of Trustees on March 11, 1897, McCook reported for the trustees' committee that "The Committee on the Graduate College, in the absence of endowments to carry on the proposed work of the College, are able to report progress only and as a matter of form." The committee was to make similar statements at most of the meetings of the trustees during the next two years. The problem of money was the heart of the matter. West, in his final report as Secretary of the Committee on the Sesquicentennial Endowment, presented to the trustees on June 14, 1897, mentioned specifically that in recent months he had tried "every opening" to persuade one or more persons to provide an endowment of $1,000,000 for the Graduate College, but so far without success.

In its report presented on October 21, 1898, the trustees' committee as usual reported no progress but noted that "at a recent meeting of the Faculty Committee having this matter in charge, the conclusion was unanimously reached that the highest interests of the University demand that every effort should be made to secure the establishment of the Graduate College at the earliest practicable date, and they expressed the hope that its dedication might mark the beginning of the twentieth century's work at Princeton." The trustees' committee endorsed this stand, but with the usual stress on new endowment, by stating that "no effort should be spared to secure the funds to erect the necessary buildings and to adequately endow the Graduate College."

By December 8, 1898, the trustees' committee was again discouraged: "If it were not for the active interest of the Faculty in this matter and the discouragement to them likely to follow such action, your Committee would ask to be discharged." At the meeting of the trustees on March 9, 1899, the committee did in fact ask to be discharged, and the Board complied with their request, thus ending for a time the efforts to create a graduate school.

See, under the dates cited above, "Minutes of the Trustees of the College of New Jersey and Princeton University, 1894-98" and "Minutes of the Trustees of Princeton University, 1898-1901," bound minute books (University Archives, NjP).

From Walter Hines Page

Dear Mr. Wilson,   [Cambridge, Mass.] 3 Dec. 1896.

It is very gratifying to have your consent to prepare the two papers for the *Atlantic*—one on *Mr. Cleveland's Career* (Jan. 15) and the other on the *Development of American Nationality* later—when?[1]

The price that you name is reasonable and satisfactory.

Very sincerely yours,   Walter H. Page.

ALS (Houghton Mifflin Letterpress Books, MH).
[1] Wilson sent it in under the title of "The Making of the Nation" about April 15, 1897. It is printed at that date.

From Frederick Jackson Turner

Dear Wilson: Madison Wisconsin   3 December, 1896

I must say at once that I cordially appreciate your friendly letter and that I have no wish to conceal the fact that as a matter of inclination simply, I am strongly tempted to place the matter entirely in your hands at once. But it is an important step, and I would wish not to take it hastily, without fully considering the whole matter. Here I think I can see continued success; and I would change for some uncertainty at Princeton; and, as you say, the library matter is the real stumbling block; for, in history work this is the *sine qua non*. A man can use his philosophy in his own study, but he cannot go far in historical work that way. Tell me what you do yourself. How did you get up your Washington?—which I appreciate most highly! What did Johnston do for a library when working up his Lalor's Cyclopedia articles?[1] Do you have such collections as the colonial records, congressional annals, debates &c; and similar documents? I am less interested in the period of exploration etc. Do you find it possible to make frequent—(every day or so)—use of the New York or Phila. libraries, when you are investigating?

The outlined reorganization of the historical work at Princeton, certainly adds to the attractiveness of your suggestion. I do not know Mr. Sloane, while I do know Haskins thoroughly. I wouldn't trade him for any other Professor of European history in the country. You remember him when he was hardly more than a boy at Johns Hopkins. He has outgrown his nervousness and while he is not a "facile talker," he speaks freely, forcibly and lucidly, and holds the closest attention and respect of his classes. I regard him as an exceptionally good class lecturer. He has one elective class of 80 or 90 in Mediaeval History, to which he lectures three times a week with entire success. He has exceptional solidity of judgement and clearness of historical insight. In his seminary work he is all that you could ask for, and his year, spent chiefly in Paris, has given him a great incentive in his work. It may help you to an understanding of him to know that he is as enthusiastic over the *lecturing* of such great teachers as Lavisse,[2] in the École Normal[,] as he is over the criticism of men like Langlois.[3] He is one of the strongest reasoners and effective debaters in our faculty meetings. I am confident that he is as good or better lecturer than Bourne, and certainly as well trained a scholar. I think highly of Bourne also,—personally and as a scholar. Somewhere I have heard it said (to my surprise) that he was not as successful with undergraduates as might have been expected; but I cannot recall more than this vague impression, and even in this I may be under misapprehension. I should regard him as a good choice next to Haskins. What of Charles M. Andrews?[4]

But I cannot let you have Haskins, unless we both depart! Perhaps Princeton would object to a job lot of Wisconsin professors! but in fact Haskins belongs to the *comitatus* of Jameson and yourself and I grew up under the teaching of Allen and yourself, with [H. B.] Adams to keep me stirred up! So its a miscellaneous job lot after all.

Seriously, I should regard the knowledge that Haskins and I were to continue together as one of the most attractive elements in the proposal.

What you say of the unhistorical atmosphere of the West is undoubtedly true—at least its history tends strongly to run into present politics! I think the new environment is really a very important consideration, and I know I need it.

Regarding salaries, I should be glad to know a little more. Do the men who get $3400 there and have no other means live comfortably on it? Can they save anything? For a rental of $500 would we have modern improvements—water, gas or electricity, and sewage provision? How many rooms would such a place have? Are there such houses conveniently located? I notice that Mr. Cleveland is to "boom real estate" by removing to Princeton![5]

The finances of the matter I desire to know about, because I cannot of course expect such success as you in outside work, and I am tired of being worried and my freedom of work checked by the view of managing some project for keeping the domestic ship right side up. I am not anxious for riches, but I should be glad to feel that my modest household expenditures could be off my mind. That is why I am obliged to consider this aspect of the matter seriously.

I have imposed this long letter on you again, and without waiting for your promised later letter, so that I may be in a position to give you definite information for yourself whenever a final answer may be needed.

I see no way now to get to New York, but I may possibly manage it.   Cordially yours   Frederick J. Turner
ALS (WP, DLC).

[1] Alexander Johnston, the late Professor of Jurisprudence and Political Economy at Princeton, whom Wilson had succeeded. Johnston wrote most of the many articles relating to American history in John Joseph Lalor (ed.), *Cyclopaedia of Political Science, Political Economy, and of the Political History of the United States* (3 vols., Chicago, 1881-84).
[2] Ernest Lavisse (1842-1922), Professor of Modern History at the Sorbonne; author and editor of many historical works.
[3] Charles Victor Langlois (1863-1929), Professor of History at the Sorbonne; a distinguished medieval historian.
[4] At this time Associate Professor of History at Bryn Mawr College.
[5] Professor Andrew F. West had announced to the press on November 27, 1896, that President Cleveland had purchased a residence on Bayard Avenue and would make Princeton his permanent home soon after his retirement from the White House. *New York Times*, Nov. 28, 1896.

To Francis Landey Patton

                                                    Princeton,
My dear Dr. Patton,   Monday evening [Dec. 7, 1896].

Pardon me if I sit down the minute I get home to write you a note about the very matter I have just been discussing with you in your study. My own ⟨happiness⟩ and all my future here in the college seem to me so intimately dependent upon the ultimate decisiion [decision] in this matter, that I dare not leave anything undone which might serve to bring it to an issue which would assure me of the confidence and cordial trust of those who elect to places in the Faculty.

It occurs to me to ask that you permit me to appear before the Curriculum Committee of the Board to present the cases of

Haskins and Turner in the light in which it appears to me; that is, if you are willing to have their nomination actually advocated as you know I would advocate it; and if you are willing to have me come up[on] your invitation.

Hoping that you will deem this proporal [proposal] acceptable both to yourself and to the Committee,[1]

In haste,

Most cordially and frankly   [Woodrow Wilson]

WWTL (draft) (WP, DLC).
[1] For evidence of Wilson's appearance before the Committee, see the Minutes of the Curriculum Committee, printed at Dec. 9, 1896.

To Richard Watson Gilder

[Dear Mr. Gilder,]   Princeton Dec. 8, 1896.

You see I cannot even write with my own hand, being threatened with writer's cramp, and so am estopped from having literary plans for the present. I have promised to inform the readers of the Atlantic how Mr. Cleveland has succeeded in the interesting and difficult art of being President, about which I know so much; but I don't know how the job is to be managed, and I don't dare to have other plans beyond that just yet. . . .[1] Your suggestion about Li Hung Chang[2] is very timely, and I will put it to [Andrew F.] West in the way it deserves. The only objection I can think of is the pangs of chagrin it would cost us to tell His Excellency how small our salaries are and how much it costs us to live—how little a fellow can get for a literary essay!

[Sincerely yours,   Woodrow Wilson]

Extract printed in a publication of the Union Square Book Shop of New York, *The Book Hunter*, v (1930), 67.
[1] Elision in the text.
[2] Li Hung-chang (1823-1901), Chinese military leader and statesman for almost half a century, made an around-the-world tour in 1896 following his appearance as China's representative at the coronation of Czar Nicholas II in St. Petersburg. Li arrived in New York on August 28 and stayed there for a week. He then spent two days in Washington and departed from the United States by way of Niagara Falls, N.Y., on September 6. West may have met Li at one of the many social and diplomatic functions held in his honor. See Arthur W. Hummel (ed.), *Eminent Chinese of the Ch'ing Period (1644-1912)* (2 vols., Washington, 1943-44), I, 464-71; and the reports of Li's visit to the United States in the *New York Times*, Aug. 28-Sept. 15, 1896.

From Charles Dudley Warner[1]

My Dear Mr Wilson   Hartford Dec 8 1896

This will introduce to you Mr Joseph F. Swords, Chairman of the Committee on the Annual dinner of the Connecticut Sons of the American Revolution.

I bespeak for my friend a favorable hearing.

I knew when you finished that oration at Princeton that you had laid yourself open to a wide popularity and to requests of this kind from all parts of the country. You have to pay the penalty of success. I do trust that your sometime neighbors will get in this case the benefit of it. I do not know that you owe anything to Connecticut, but it is forward to claim help that will give the greatest distinction to its annual ceremony.[2]

Yours Sincerely   Chas. Dudley Warner

ALS (WP, DLC) with WWhw notation on env.: "Ans 7 Jan'y, '97."
[1] Editor-in-Chief of the *Hartford Courant;* Contributing Editor of *Harper's Magazine.*
[2] The Editors have not found any evidence that Wilson accepted this invitation.

From the Minutes of the Princeton Faculty

5 5' P.M., Wednesday, December 9, '96.

. . . Professors Brackett, Young and W. Wilson were elected a Committee by ballot to appear before and confer with the Board of Trustees if required[1]

[1] They did not confer with the trustees at their meeting on December 10, 1896.

From the Minutes of the Princeton Trustees' Curriculum Committee

The Committee on the Curriculum met at the call of the chairman in the Faculty Room on Wednesday, Nov. [Dec.] 9, 1896[,] 2:30 P.M.

Present: Dr. [E. R.] Craven
          Dr. Patton
          Dr. W. H. Green
          Geo. B. Stewart
          Col. [John J.] McCook. . . .

Prof. Wilson on invitation appeared before the com. and presented his views on the subject of the historical department.

It was unanimously carried that we report to the Board that we have had the filling of the vacancy caused by the resignation of Prof Sloane under consideration and that we hope to make definite recommendations at the March meeting respecting the department of history. . . .

Hw MS. (Trustees' Papers, University Archives, NjP).

From the Minutes of the Trustees of Princeton University

Princeton, N. J. December 10th, 1896.

. . . The Committee on the Curriculum respectfully reports to the Trustees of Princeton University as follows:

. . . 3. Resolved—That in consideration of the fact that this institution has recently assumed the title of Princeton University and entered upon a new era in its history, a special committee consisting of seven members of this Board, be appointed to inquire into the affairs of this University, to consider what changes if any are desirable in its policy, methods of administration, curriculum, or corps of instructors; and to make such recommendations to the Board of Trustees as they in their judgment may deem best.[1]

Committee appointed by the President:

Charles E. Green, Chairman,
E. R. Craven,
John A. Stewart,
M. Taylor Pyne,
James W. Alexander,
George B. Stewart,
John J. McCook.

"Minutes of the Trustees of the College of New Jersey and Princeton University, 1894-98," bound minute book (University Archives, NjP).

[1] For these recommendations, see the reports of the Special Committee on the Affairs of the University, printed at June 14, 1897, March 10, 1898, and June 13, 1898.

From Mosei Iakovlevich Ostrogorski[1]

Dear Mr. Wilson   Paris, 12 December 1896

I have returned only a few days ago to Paris and found to-day at the Société Historique the volume[2] you so kindly sent me. The feelings of pleasure and of gratitude it caused me would be quite justifiable by the mere publication of the volume. One is thankful when he sees magazine articles of a permanent value collected in book form. And opening yesterday the trunk of books I brought from the States, I put affectionately your "Old Master" on my shelves. The pleasure of being able to give him the next day a companion was the more intense that it is connected with our meeting which will remain one of the most pleasant reminiscences of my visit to America.[3] I could not resist the temptation of reading at once the essay on *the Truth of the matter.* I must abstain from giving any impression of the essay from fear of appearing, not of being, too complimentary. So I have to content myself with thanking you most cordially for your gracious souvenir.   Yours very sincerely   M. Ostrogorski

ALS (WP, DLC).
  [1] At this time living in Paris while doing the research for his famous work, *Democracy and the Organization of Political Parties* (2 vols., London and New York, 1902).
  [2] *Mere Literature and Other Essays.*
  [3] The circumstances of Ostrogorski's meeting with Wilson are unknown.

From Joseph Ruggles Wilson

My dearest Woodrow—   Richmond, Va., Dec. 15/96

Of course I knew you had not forgotten me nor had ceased to remember me affectionately: but I was pleased to receive your dictated letter of the 13th, not because of its reassurances, but because I love you with the devoted heart of a father and a friend, and am therefore always glad to get near to you even if it be only through the medium of written words that are not altogether perfunctory, or at all.

I have wondered at the Harpers' delay in issuing the 'Washington' book. A month earlier would certainly have been profitably better. Mr. W. Wirt Henry of this city has been asked to review it, but by what Magazine I do not know.[1] He will achieve a success in the way of exploiting his own superior knowledge. You know that he is the author of a Life of Patrick Henry,[2] his grandfather or great-grandfather: a big biography which is said to be well composed, and is much applauded by Virginians. He, by the way, told me that it was in the old episcopal church *here*, his revolutionary ancestor uttered the passionate words "give me liberty or give me death!" and not at Williamsburg.

I am very sorry that your arm still fails you. You do not say whether any *improvement* in its condition has been perceived: I was hoping that there would be something favorable to report. It is a pity that you continue to wrestle with more of the giant of work than your strength seems to justify. . . . Love to all.
                    Your affectionate   Father

ALS (WP, DLC).
  [1] By the *American Historical Review*. Henry's review is printed at April 1, 1897.
  [2] William Wirt Henry, *Patrick Henry: Life, Correspondence and Speeches* (3 vols., New York, 1891).

To Frederick Jackson Turner

My dear Turner,   Princeton, Dec. 15, 1896

A plague on boards of Trustees! Here I've been waiting for all this time for the Dec. meeting of our Trustees to get the plans concerning the history department made definite and final for next year, only to be disappointed at last, and left just where I was before. There is likely to be less money than usual for current expenses this year, it seems; some of the new monies are not to come in at once. The Trustees are afflicted with a sudden timidity about making definite plans for the near future, will *assure* me of nothing now, and—the next meeting of the board does not occur until March. I will say nothing about my chagrin. I will only beg you to be patient with these timorous gentlemen and to hold this matter still under advisement, if you possibly can, and indulgently will, until I can wring some definite action out of the board. Our president does not bother us by having a mistaken policy, he daunts us by having no will or policy at all.

I need not tell you how provoked I am to be obliged to leave this matter in so unsatisfactory a shape for you. There would be no impropriety, in my opinion, or breach of confidence either, in your saying to President Adams, if you cared to do so, that I had been sounding you in this business unofficially. You might thereby at least give your own people fair notice and ascertain informally how they would be disposed to act in case of a call; but of course this is a question for your own preference and judgment. I say what I have said only to make you perfectly free, and to relieve the situation of embarrassment as much as I can. I expect to see Haskins at the meeting of the [American] Historical Association, and shall seek a chance to sound him there. Might you not broach the subject to him now? I have made up my mind that he is the best man for us to get in European History.

And now let me answer some of the questions contained in your last letter as if nothing had happened in the meanwhile. In the matter of books I have done as follows in the past. Much of what I wanted, I found here; the trouble was the gaps and the incompletenesses in our collection. These I could note and make up for by a day or two's use now and again of the N.Y. libraries. Many of the libraries will send books to you for use. In getting up "Washington" I went down from Balt. and looked over some of his Mss. in the State Dept. There is really no trouble, our work being arranged as it is, (each man's class-work is bunched so as to come, all of it, upon two or three successive days only of the week;—for instance all of mine is on Monday and Tuesday) in going to N.Y. as often as may be necessary. We have very complete sets of the Govt. Records, Congressional Annuals, Debates, &c. I enclose you a list of the Colonial Records we now possess. I am ordering more at every opportunity, and the process will be speeded when the new money comes in. Alexander Johnston, by the way, did not write his Lalor articles here, but in a small Conn. town, where he was teaching before he came here, and where he had very poor library facilities indeed.[1] I heard the cheering news the other day, that one of our richest trustees had made up his mind that the library should not lack for Americana, even if we don't induce the New Jersey Historical Society to accept quarters in our new library building, as we are now trying to do.[2] There is really not much trouble about getting men interested in buying American material; European sources are the only real difficulty.

Regarding salary the men who get $3400.00 here and have no other means *do* manage to live very comfortably and to pay life insurance too. The projected salaries of $4000.00 ought to make such a prospect perfectly secure. It is not always easy to get a house conveniently located here because of the long drawn out shape of the town, but such a house as one would pay $500.00 [for] would of course have water, gas and sewage arrangements, and would have from eight to twelve rooms with bath-room, pantries, &c in addition. There are no signs yet that Mr. Cleveland's purchase will boom real estate amongst us very much. Mrs. Wilson is going to enclose an estimate of expenses based upon our own experience, and made upon a somewhat liberal scale.

After all March is not so very far off! Let me hear from you in the mean time if anything occurs to you; give my warmest regards to Mrs. Turner and to Haskins and believe me in warm friendship,

Most cordially yours,   Woodrow Wilson

P.S. Is Haskins married? I haven't heard of it if he is.

Monthly Account.

Food and lights	75.00
Servants	29.00
rent	42.00
coal	12.00
water	4.00
	$162.00

These items with the exception of the *first* are exactly what we pay ourselves. Our "food and lights" cost about $100.00 a month;

but our family, including the two servants, averages ten persons, two of them being very large and hearty college boys.[3] As a matter of fact when our family was the size of yours, I was able to keep that item down to $65.00.

Mr. Wilson says he forgot to mention that the salary now proposed for your chair is $3500.00 and he hopes to extract from them a definite promise to raise it to $4000.00 in—say—two years. May I add that you really could not *help* making at least $500.00 a year more,—people clamour so for lectures and "articles"! It would be a great mistake on your part to suppose that Mr. Wilson is their only victim. All who have any use whatever of tongue or pen are seized upon! Mr. Wilson makes $1500.00 every year; and last year when we were building, and he really tried himself, he made $4000.00 extra;—and almost killed himself doing it!

Please excuse this *very* informal introduction of myself! I have written you so many pages that I can scarcely believe you are not *my* friend too. With sincere regards to Mrs. Turner and yourself,   Yours very cordially   Ellen Wilson.

EAWhwL, WWS (photostat in F. J. Turner Papers, MH). Enc. missing.
   [1] Johnston was principal of the Latin School in Norwalk, Connecticut, before coming to Princeton.
   [2] The New Jersey Historical Society remained in Newark.
   [3] George Howe III, '97, Wilson's nephew, and Edward William Axson, '97, Ellen's brother.

From Annie Wilson Howe

My darling Brother,   N. Y. Dec. 15th 1896

Your sweet letter was a comfort to me in my anxiety and distress. I am sure I have warm sympathy from you and dear Ellie. I do not think I was ever placed in such a trying position. This is the seventh day, however, and the doctor says the disease generally runs its course, that is reaches its worst point by the seventh day. It is certainly diptheria, although a mild case.

Annie[1] is not quite so well this morning, the trouble having extended to the back of the nose. She is so good and so patient, and I have to distress her so often. The throat has to be sprayed *six* times a day, and it is so trying to her.

Wilson goes to work today.[2] It is just as well, for I cannot see him, except for a moment at a time, at the door of the room.

I write to George every day, and he will report to you. It may be better than for me to write to the house, although the doctor says there is no danger in sending a letter.

If anything goes wrong, I will certainly let you know at once. In haste and warmest love for you both,

Your devoted sister,   Annie.

ALS (WP, DLC).
[1] Her daughter.
[2] James Wilson Howe was not listed in the New York City directory for 1896, and the nature of his occupation is unknown.

From Francis Landey Patton

[Princeton, N. J.]

My dear Professor Wilson   December 18, 1896

I have received your letter of 15th Instant & beg to assure you that I shall have great pleasure in presenting to the Curriculum Committee your views in regard to the department of History.

Of course I can not predict what action will be taken by the Committee. They may conclude that the way is not clear for the establishment at present of a chair in American History; and of course there may be other names presented to the Committee for their consideration.

It is usual for us to consider very carefully the question of a vacancy in a department & to have a very free and full interchange of opinion before making a nomination to the Trustees.

I need not say that your opinion & your wishes will have very great weight with our Committee.

I am very sincerely yrs,   Francis L. Patton

ALS (Patton Letterpress Books, University Archives, NjP).

From Anna Underhill[1]

Dear Sir,   Sing Sing, N. Y. Dec. 19th '96.

At a meeting of the Regents' Centre—held after you left the room, Thursday evening—it was unanimously voted that we send you an additional expression of our pleasure in your lectures.[2] During the course, many such tributes as the following have been paid—"It raises my ideals." "It is a constant inspiration." "I am able to live a better and nobler life—in consequence of having heard these lectures."

Hoping you may some time come to Sing Sing again, on a similar errand,   Truly   Anna Underhill Secretary.

ALS (WP, DLC).

1 Secretary of the Regents' Centre in Sing Sing of the Extension Department of the University of the State of New York.

2 Myrtilla Avery to WW, June 27, 1896, cited as an Enclosure with EAW to WW, July 3, 1896, Vol. 9, indicates that Wilson was to give ten lectures at the Regents' Centre in Sing Sing. Aside from this intimation and the information in Miss Underhill's letter, nothing is known about Wilson's lectures there.

An After-Dinner Speech to the New England Society of Brooklyn[1]

[[Dec. 21, 1896]]

ADDRESS OF PROF. WOODROW WILSON, LL.D.

Mr. President,[2] *Ladies and Gentlemen:*—I am not of your blood; I am not a Virginia Cavalier, as Dr. Hill[3] has suggested. Sometimes I wish I were; I would have more fun. I come, however, of as good blood as yours; in some respects a better. Because the Scotch-Irish, though they are just as much in earnest as you are, have a little bit more gayety and more elasticity than you have. Moreover they are now forming a Scotch-Irish society, which will, as fast as human affairs will allow, do exactly what the New England Societies are doing, viz.: annex the universe. [Laughter.][4] We believe with a sincere belief, we believe as sincerely as you do the like, that we really made this country. Not only that, but we believe that we can now, in some sort of way, demonstrate the manufacture, because the country has obviously departed in many respects from the model which you claim to have set. Not only that, but it seems to me that you yourselves are becoming a little recreant to the traditions you yearly celebrate. It seems to me that you are very much in the position, with reference to your forefathers, that the little boy was with reference to his immediate father. The father was a very busy man; he was away to his work before the children were up in the morning and did not come home till after they had gone to bed at night. One day this little boy was greatly incensed, as he said, "to be whipped by that gentleman that stays here on Sundays." I do not observe that you think about your ancestors the rest of the week; I do not observe that they are very much

1 Wilson was speaking at the seventeenth annual dinner of the Society at the Pouch Mansion in Brooklyn on December 21, 1896, and was responding to the toast, "The Responsibility of Having Ancestors."

2 Stewart Lyndon Woodford, lawyer and former Member of Congress, soon to be appointed Minister to Spain by President McKinley.

3 David Jayne Hill, educator and future diplomat, who had recently resigned the presidency of the University of Rochester and was at this time studying the public law of Europe.

4 These brackets in the text.

present in your thoughts at any other time save on Sunday, and that then they are most irritating to you. I have known a great many men descended from New England ancestors and I do not feel half so hardly toward my ancestors as they do toward theirs. There is a distant respect about the relationship which is touching. There is a feeling that these men are well and safely at a distance and that they would be indulged under no other circumstances whatever; and that the beauty of it is to have descended from them and come so far away. Now, there are serious aspects to this subject. I believe that one of the responsibilities of having ancestors is the necessity of not being ashamed of them. I believe if you have had persons of this sort as your forefathers you must really try to represent them in some sort of way. And you must set yourselves off against the other elements of population in this country. You know that we have received very many elements which have nothing of the Puritan about them, which have nothing of New England about them; and that the chief characteristic of these people is that they have broken all their traditions. The reason that most foreigners come to this country is in order to break their traditions, to drop them. They come to this country because these traditions bind them to an order of society which they will no longer endure and they come to be quit of them. You yourselves will bear me witness that these men, some of them, stood us in good stead upon a very recent occasion: in last November. [Applause, hear, hear.] We should not at all minimize the vote of the foreign-born population as against the vote of some of the native-born population on the question of silver and gold. But you will observe that there are some things that it would be supposed would belong to any tradition. One would suppose it would belong to any tradition that it was better to earn a dollar that did not depreciate, and these men have simply shown that there are some common-sense elements which are international and not national.

One of the particulars in which we are drawn away from our traditions is in respect to the make-up and government of society, and it is in that respect we should retrace our steps and preserve our traditions; because we are suffering ourselves to drift away from the old standards, and we say, with a shrug of the shoulders, that we are not responsible for it; that we have not changed the age, though the age has changed us. We feel very much as the Scotchman did who entered the fish market. His dog, being inquisitive, investigated a basket of lobsters, and while nosing about incautiously one of the lobsters got hold of his tail, whereupon he went down the street with the lobster as a pendant.

Says the man, "Whustle to your dog, mon." "Nay, nay, mon," quoth the Scotchman, "You whustle for your lobster." We are very much in the same position with reference to the age; we say, whistle to the age; we cannot make it let go; we have got to run. We feel very much like the little boy in the asylum, standing by the window, forbidden to go out. He became contemplative, and said, "If God were dead and there were not any rain, what fun orphan boys would have." We feel very much that way about these New England traditions. If God were only dead; if it didn't rain; if the times were only good, what times we would have.

The present world is not recognizable when put side by side with the world into which the Puritan came. I am not here to urge a return to the Puritan life; but have you forgotten that the Puritans came into a new world? The conditions under which they came were unprecedent[ed] conditions to them. But did they forget the principles on which they acted because the conditions were unprecedented? Did they not discover new applications for old principles? Are we to be daunted, therefore, because the conditions are new? Will not old principles be adaptable to new conditions, and is it not our business to adapt them to new conditions? Have we lost the old principle and the old spirit? Are we a degenerate people? We certainly must admit ourselves to be so if we do not follow the old principles in the new world, for that is what the Puritans did.

Let me say a very practical word. What is the matter now? The matter is, conceal it as we may, gloss it over as we please, that the currency is in a sad state of unsuitability to the condition of the country. That is the fact of the matter; nobody can deny that; but what are we going to do? We are going to have a new tariff. I have nothing to say with regard to the policy of the tariff, one way or the other. We have had tariffs, have we not, every few years, ever since we were born; and has not the farmer become discontented under these conditions? It was the effort to remedy them that produced the silver movement. A new tariff may produce certain economic conditions; I do not care a peppercorn whether it does or not, but this is a thing which we have been tinkering and dickering with time out of mind, and in spite of the tinkering and dickering this situation has arisen. Are we going to cure it by more tinkering? We are not going to touch it in this way. Now, what are we going to do? It is neither here nor there whether I am a protectionist, or for a tariff for revenue, or whatever you cho[o]se to call me. The amount you collect in currency for imports is not going to make any difference. The right thing to do is to apply old principles to a new condition and get out of that new condition something that will effect a practical remedy. I do not pretend to be a doctor with a nostrum. I have no pill against an earthquake. I do not know how this thing is going to be done, but it is not going to be done by having stomachs easily turned by the truth; it is not going to be done by merely blinking the situation. If we blink the situation I hope we will have no more celebrations in which we talk about our Puritan ancestors, because they did not blink the situation, and it is easy to eat and be happy and proud. A large number of persons may have square meals by having a properly adjusted currency.

We are very much in the condition described by the reporter who was describing the murder of a certain gentleman. He said that the murderer entered the house, and gave a graphic description of the whole thing. He said that fortunately the gentleman had put his valuables in the safe deposit and lost *only his life*. We are in danger of being equally wise. We are in danger of managing our policy so that our property will be put in safe deposit and we will lose only our lives. We will make all the immediate conditions of the nation perfectly safe and lose only the life of the nation. This is not a joke, this is a very serious situation. I should feel ashamed to stand here and not say that this is a subject which deserves your serious consideration and ought to keep some of you awake to-night. This is not a simple gratulatory occasion, this is a place where public duty should be realized and public purposes formed, because public purpose is a thing for which our Puritan ancestors stood, yours and mine. If this race should ever lose that capacity, if it should ever lose the sense of dignity in this regard, we should lose the great traditions of which we pretend to be proud. [Applause.][5]

Printed in *Proceedings at the Seventeenth Annual Meeting and Seventeenth Annual Festival of the New England Society in the City of Brooklyn* (Brooklyn, 1897), 31-35.
[5] There is a one-page WWhw outline of this speech, dated "Dec. '96," in WP, DLC.

From Frederick Jackson Turner, with Enclosure

Dear Wilson: [Madison, Wis.] 27 December, 96.

I don't know how I came to leave the letter unposted so long. For the last two weeks I have been so absorbed in getting together the manuscripts from the Draper Collection for the Hist. MSS. Commission report at New York,[1] that I have hardly had time to think of anything else—so you will understand my absence of mind: my correspondence, association paper,[2] and even classes

have all been pushed to one side to get the MSS. off. Just turn
the Christmas greetings into New Year's wishes!

F. J. T.

ALI (WP, DLC).

  1 Turner was assembling and editing documents from the great Lyman C.
Draper Collection of manuscripts on western history at the State Historical Soci-
ety of Wisconsin to "elucidate the proposed French Expedition under George
Rogers Clark against Louisiana, in the years 1793-94." These were published as
a part of the "Report of the Historical Manuscripts Commission of the American
Historical Association" in the *Annual Report of the American Historical Associ-
ation for the Year 1896* (2 vols., Washington, 1897), I, 930-1107. See this same
Report, I, 478, for a brief description of Turner's project.

  2 "The West as a Field for Historical Study," read for Turner by Reuben Gold
Thwaites at the annual meeting of the American Historical Association in New
York on December 31, 1896. It is printed in *ibid*., pp. 281-87. For Wilson's com-
ments on Turner's paper, see "Remarks on an Historical Paper," printed at
Dec. 31, 1896.

E N C L O S U R E

My dear Wilson: Madison Wisconsin   18 December 1896

   In some respects it is just as well for me not to have to make a
decision now. Of course if your trustees act in March that would
be in time for notice to our own board which meets in April, in
case your suggestions were carried out.

   I will not deny the attractiveness of the proposition as you outline it, and even the library is in better shape, I judge, than I
imagined; but, as you say, there are odd gaps even in the list you
send me. I can't see how they should leave such broken sets. I
am glad you are to see Haskins in New York. He is not married,
but has rooms with us. His salary and rank are the same as mine.
I have confidentially told him that you had made enquiries of me
with regard to my willingness to consider a call to Princeton; and
I have talked with him on the basis of the Sloane vacancy. I merely sounded him and did not commit you. I judge he feels very
much as I do in the matter. His natural curiosity would be in
regard to library and well trained advanced students. You know
he had a call to Stanford and to Mass. Tech. a year or two ago.

   We shall see what Time brings forth and in the meantime, I
must thank you for the generous interest and kindness you have
shown in the matter. I wish to tell Mrs. Wilson also how much
Mrs Turner and I appreciate her information, and for myself I
must say that I am not only delighted but immensely relieved that she will admit me to the list of her friends after the
amount of writing that my enquiries have unwittingly imposed
upon her. My wife and I are agreed, Mrs Wilson, that you, like
Mr Gladstone, can make a budget interesting, and you have
helped us very much. If we ever do come to Princeton and Mrs

Turner fails to make her finances agree with yours I shall insist
that she get your recipe for the right management of the matter!

What a tremendous grist you have turned out this last year,
Wilson. I hope you have not really overworked; but I am appre-
hensive when I consider the amount of work it involves besides
your class duties. I don't see how you do it. Your Princeton oration
I have just gotten hold of.[1] It is a fine thing. Pres. Adams had
spoken of it before, but I had not been able to read it until this
week. It is stirring to read a university utterance like this with
real human ideals in it. If Princeton could revive her past, the
past of Madison and Witherspoon, and be equally effective in
furnishing us with leadership today, it would be a service of profound importance. I think that it is in the Universities that we
must look for this development, but the prospect in most of them
is not bright. I suspect that the men who catch your enthusiasm
are as likely to furnish the needed material as any others. The
writing on page 461 I like especially. It has a flavor of its own.

I am working hard over a lot of documents for the Historical
MSS. Commission—and haven't found time to do anything on my
Historical Association paper yet.

Mrs Turner joins with me in Christmas greetings and best
wishes for you and Mrs. Wilson.

Very cordially yours   Frederick J. Turner

ALS (WP, DLC).
   [1] "Princeton in the Nation's Service," New York *Forum*, XXII (Dec. 1896),
447-66.

From Ellen Axson Wilson

My own darling,   Princeton [Dec.] 30 1896

I must make haste and write you a little note to go by tonight's
mail, else it will be useless to write at all.[1] Florence[2] left this afternoon, at 3.35; so of course I was devoting myself to her this
morning;—feeling perhaps a little guilty at having left her so
much to her own devices since she has been here. I was even
obliged to leave her last night. Mrs. [Bliss] Perry came around at
five o'clock to beg me as a special favour to come and fill a gap;—
she had written to ask Miss Conover[3] and Mr. Dullas[4] instead of
us, and had heard nothing from Miss C.,—supposed she was out
of town. Now hear the sequel!—when I stepped into Guin's[5] cab
to go, behold *Miss Conover*! Was there *ever* such a predicament.
I opened the door and half sprang out, thinking I *must* make a
clean breast of it; but thought better of it. So we went up *together*!
I am sure Miss Conover thought me singularly distraught.

I had a lovely Xmas present today from Mrs. Norris,—a beautiful tall jar, or vase, with handles. It is an exquisite shape and in colour would seem to have been *made* for our parlour. It looks like a Rookwood.[6] I am simply delighted with it, chiefly of course because it is so exactly the *right* thing for the room,—besides being lovely in itself.

The receipt from the Insurance Co. duly arrived. I have a letter from Rose[7] which I am sure will please you and make you glad you sent the book. There is a nice letter from Mr. Turner—no other mail of special interest. Mr. Turner says he "sounded" Haskins but did not commit you. Also that Haskins is unmarried, but has there the same salary and rank as himself.

We are all well of course. I hope you are too, and are having a good time. I love you, dear heart, ah me, *how* I love! I am sure there is never a moment when you are absent that my thoughts are not hovering about you. Always and altogether

Your own Eileen.

ALS (WC, NjP).
  [1] Wilson was attending the annual meeting of the American Historical Association in New York.
  [2] Her first cousin, Florence Stevens Hoyt, then a student at Bryn Mawr College.
  [3] Juliana Conover, daughter of Helen Field and Francis Stevens Conover.
  [4] Joseph Heatly Dulles, Librarian of Princeton Theological Seminary since 1886.
  [5] William Guinn, who ran a hack service.
  [6] The Rookwood Pottery of Cincinnati, founded in 1880.
  [7] Rosalie Anderson Dubose to EAW, Dec. 27, 1896, ALS (WP, DLC).

From James Woodrow

My dear Ellen and Woodrow: Columbia, S. C., Dec. 31, 1896

I intended to write to you as soon as I reached home, but I found so much work awaiting me that it was utterly out of my power, and has been so until to-night.

I enjoyed my visit to your sweet home very much, and am grateful to you for all your kindness. My half-deafness, while it kept me from taking part in general conversation, did not keep me from pleasure in your home life, or even in more general society as much as you might have supposed.[1]

And what a delight it was to me to hear Woodrow's oration, and still more to see how justly it was appreciated, and has been since, far and wide. All the exercises were thoroughly enjoyable, but that far more than all.

I hope that both of you escaped suffering from reaction after the weeks of excitement[2] and that you and the little darlings are all perfectly well. Does Woodrow's health continue to improve?

I am glad to see you are going to have the Clevelands for not distant neighbors. I think Mrs. Cleveland must be a very sweet and sensible woman independently of all the present glare surrounding her. Then I am selfish enough to think that their coming may help to solve the question of a school for your girls, of which Ellen spoke so anxiously. The three little girls[3] would so far help in the forming of such a school as you want, and be even more important than "Grover's sending his boys to the University."

We are all well here, as are the absent members of our family.

Aunt Felie[4] joins me in much love to you both and the three girlies.   Your affectionate uncle,   James Woodrow.

Kind regards to the "boys."

ALS (WP, DLC).

[1] Dr. Woodrow attended the Sesquicentennial Celebration as a delegate of South Carolina College (now the University of South Carolina), of which he was president.

[2] Perhaps Dr. Woodrow was referring to the excitement of the presidential campaign of 1896, as well as that attending the Sesquicentennial.

[3] The Cleveland daughters were Ruth, five, Esther, three, and Marion, almost one and a half.

[4] His wife, Felexiana Shepherd Baker Woodrow.

A Report of a Session at the American Historical Association

[c. Dec. 31, 1896]

REPORT OF PROCEEDINGS OF TWELFTH ANNUAL MEETING OF THE AMERICAN HISTORICAL ASSOCIATION.

By Herbert B. Adams, Ph. D., LL. D., Secretary.

The twelfth annual meeting of this national society was held in New York, December 29-31, 1896, at Columbia University. It was generally agreed that this was one of the most successful conventions in the entire history of the Association. . . .

Considerable discussion was occasioned by Professor Turner's excellent paper on "The West as a Field for Historical study," which was read by his friend, Mr. R. G. Thwaites.[1] The contention was that Western history should be viewed in a large way as national and institutional history, and not merely as antiquarian or border history. The discussion was carried on by Professor McLaughlin,[2] of the University of Michigan, and Prof. Woodrow Wilson, of Princeton, both of whom made strong appeals for the independent treatment of Western history, instead of regarding it as an appanage of the East. . . .

Printed in *Annual Report of the American Historical Association for the Year 1896* (2 vols., Washington, 1897), 1, 13, 16-17.

1 In Hamilton Hall of Columbia University on December 31, 1896. See the reports in the *New York Times*, Jan. 1, 1897, and the *New York Herald*, Jan. 1, 1897.

2 Andrew Cunningham McLaughlin, Professor of American History at the University of Michigan.

Remarks on an Historical Paper

[[Dec. 31, 1896]]

REMARKS BY PROF. WOODROW WILSON

Mr. President, ladies and gentlemen of the Association: I want to begin by paying my personal tribute to Professor Turner. I believe he is one of those men who gain the affection of every student of history by being able to do what very few men manage to do, to combine the large view with the small one; to combine the general plan and conception with the minute examination of particulars; who is not afraid of the horrid industry of his task, and who can yet illuminate that industry by knowing the goal to which it is leading him, and the general plan by which it should be done. Such men ought to be not only appreciated, but they ought to be loved and supported. [Applause.][1] It is necessary to say this perhaps the more because a certain unpleasant impression might be created by such a paper as this. It is a dethronement of the Eastern historian. I think most of us would be inclined to reverse the expression which was used by Professor McLaughlin. He spoke of the materials being fresh and the students being young. We should speak of the materials being young and the students being fresh. [Laughter.] I say that is the natural inclination which we have, in our repulsion at being so prohibited from a field which we obviously do not understand. And yet I for my part have no feeling of being hurt, because at the same time we have to get used to the idea that we do not constitute the nation here on the Eastern Coast. It is an unpleasant idea, but we must prepare our stomachs for it, because it must be digested. I know we naturally have the feeling with regard to such matters that the country at large had when Andrew Jackson came to the Presidency. If you will let me tell you a rather rough story, of a rough region, it will illustrate, perhaps, what I am saying: An Eastern man, traveling in the West and putting up at one of those nondescript hostelries in that region, which had a barroom, and was used for a lodging house and for various other purposes, was shown to his room, which had a window opening on a balcony

1 All bracketed insertions in the original text.

where sat a number of men talking and smoking; and wishing to make his toilet in private and finding no shade to the window, he pinned up a waterproof cloak over the window. It was suddenly jerked down from the outside, and when he asked the intruding head what he meant by it, he said he just wanted to see what was so private in there. [Laughter.]

Now, I think we feel exactly that way about Andrew Jackson. The Westerners tore aside the veil of the old administrations in this country and said they wanted to know what was so very private about this Government. It had been run, they insisted, by a clique. It had been run by a dynasty. It had been run by people who pretended to own the Government. It had been run with the spirit of a corporation, with a provoking privacy, by those who felt that they had the prerogative to run it in the future as they had in the past. Andrew Jackson wanted to know what was going on. He dispelled the privacy of the Government, and the Government has been a public and a published Government ever since. Then came in the era of talk and gossip, and a Government which was characterized by shaking hands with the President until he was absolutely disarmed [laughter]—by using the Government as if it had been a part of the common property, and a very common sort of property indeed. Now, I welcome the more freely disclosures of the sort we have had in Professor Turner's paper this morning because it interests me particularly with regard to another region—I mean the South. Southerners are characterized by family pride, as everybody knows; and they have one characteristic which I am sorry to say is not common. They don't like to talk about themselves in public. In this autobiographic age that is a very singular characteristic; in this age when we all not only want to do things, but tell everybody how we do them, and tell everybody what we read in order to do them, and tell everybody what our fathers looked like and what our mothers' manners were. In this age of disclosures of private life such a characteristic is at least refreshing. Now, I can not claim that characteristic for myself, because I do not come by the strict Southern blood. I come of an enduring blood, the Scotch-Irish. Now the Scotch-Irishman has no objection to talking about himself. And if you will allow me to call your attention to it, a great deal of the history in regard to the South and the disclosures of the private affairs of the South is being done by the Scotch-Irish. The Scotch-Irish are following the admirable example set by New England. They are forming societies and proceeding to annex the universe. They are forming societies for the purpose of showing the United States that every element of any value or importance in this history of the country has been contributed by the Scotch-Irish; and I must say that I have the weakness to believe that a good deal of that is true. [Laughter.] And I believe this is another means of readjusting the perspective of American history.

Now, singularly enough, there are two sorts of irritation, or, rather, there are two bodies of irritation, that have prevented us from having the true history of this country written hitherto. The Northerner is irritated against the Southerner, and therefore he can not write the history of the Southern region; and until the Scotch-Irish popped up, there was nobody else to do it. Then the Eastern part is also irritated in regard to the Western. The Easterner regards it as a new eruption of the West into the East, and he is irritated by it; it disturbs the calm of his earlier studies. And it is eminently fortunate, it seems to me, that a man should arise like Professor Turner, who has self-possession, who is not bumptious, who has not any of the qualities we object to, and who yet knows the things which we want, unpalatable though they be, and who has the courage to put American history in its proper setting. Now, the Southern writers labor under a disadvantage. Have you never noticed how the Northern writer speaks about the South? He speaks about the South as he would speak of an inhospitable region which it was impossible for him to visit and see. I have noticed Northern historians almost always quote travelers in regard to the South, just as I would describe Kamchatka, a place to which I did not intend to go and did not hope to go. They quote by preference foreign travelers, those foreign travelers who have only been in a portion of the South and for a very brief period indeed. And they speak of the South as if it was not part of this country. They do not quote travelers in respect to the North. They know the North; they don't have to quote travelers. But the South is an inhospitable region with regard to which they believe travelers' tales, and they make up the picture of the South by matching this traveler's tale with that traveler's tale, and making a contradiction which I defy anybody to say is a valid picture of that region. It is a sort of phantasmagoria. I have lived in the South more than one-half of the length of years I have reached already, and I do not recognize it in these pictures. I am interested in them, because I recognize the atmosphere which I have breathed and yet never lived upon. I recognize ideas which I have heard currently attributed to people at the South, but which I myself have never entertained, and which my neighbors have never entertained, so far as I am aware. For one thing, the historian wishes the Southerner to be regretful in regard to his past. He wishes him to be apologetic in regard to his past. Now, no substantial history was ever of a sort to be regretted. Shall you regret your nature? Shall you regret your environment? Shall you regret your existence? Shall you apologize for not having done the impossible? Shall you change your spots? Shall you grow an inch in stature of your own choice? Shall you say, "I wish I had lived an unnatural life instead of a natural life?" Shall you say, "I wish I had imported ideas instead of inheriting ideas and developing ideas?" There is nothing to apologize for in the past of the South—absolutely nothing to apologize for. There is a great deal, however, cordially to accept in the present, and that is the consummation for which I pray and the consummation which has largely been brought about. The Southerner is proud of the past of his region, and he is cordially ready to accept the present and to help forward the tasks of the future. [Applause.]

Now, the man who is going to say all of this I fervently believe is a Scotch-Irishman, because, as I say, the Scotch-Irishman likes to hear himself talk. He has lived in this region and he is an animal who conforms his habits to his environment, and you will not find the Scotch-Irishman anywhere other than at home. If he can get good whisky and one or two of the other requisites of life, that is all he requires. The rest of the circumstances he can conform himself unto with great kindliness of spirit. And he has the appropriating spirit. The minute he lives in a region the region belongs to him. He does not belong to the region, but the region belongs to him, and he is responsible for its past as well as for its present and future. He has been adopted into the family; he has accepted the lineage; he has received the blood, and it is his purpose henceforth to apologize for nothing and to manage everything. Now, I say this conquering spirit is the spirit which ought to conquer its place in history. [Applause.]

Printed in *Annual Report of the American Historical Association for the Year 1896* (2 vols., Washington, 1897), I, 292-96.

A Diary for 1897

[Jan. 1-Dec. 31, 1897]

Inscribed (WWhw) on flyleaf: "Woodrow Wilson 12 Jan'y, 1897." Contents:

(a) WWhw entries for Jan. 1, 15, 16, 17, 20, and 21; July 24; Aug. 2, 3, 5, 6, 7, 12, 15, 20, 21, 23, 28, and 31; Dec. 27, 30, and 31, 1897, all printed at these dates.

(b) WWhw estimate of earnings from lectures and articles for the academic year 1897-98.

(c) Calendar for 1898 with some WWhw reminders of lecture dates.

Bound diary (WP, DLC).

From Wilson's Diary for 1897

Friday, January 1, 1897

Spoke at the Authors' Club,[1] about one o'clock in the morning, —invited there to see the new year in, along with the Historical Assn.

Heard anecdotes of Wm. Hamilton Gibson[2] wh. greatly engaged my fancy:

He sought once in the N. Y. libraries for a representation in colour of a certain very rare sort of butterfly wh. he wished to sketch for one of his illustrations; found it at last and sat down to make his picture. As he sketched one of the rare creatures fluttered into the very room where he sat, there in the midst of great New York, and settled just at his hand, and lingered there at rest, "as if," he said, "to have its picture taken." A marvel, surely!

He tried one day, sitting upon the piazza of a country house, to explain the markings upon the wings of a rare bird to a friend. Finding language a poor instrument, he walked to a cluster of bushes near by, thrust his hand within the leaves a minute, and came away holding one of the shy creatures nestling in his hand. He had that singular attraction for dumb creatures that love gives some pure men.

[1] The Editors have been unable to find any notes for or newspaper report of this speech.
[2] William Hamilton Gibson (1850-96), artist and magazine illustrator specializing in landscapes and nature subjects. He became well-known as a popularizer of nature study through a long series of illustrated articles in *Harper's*, *Scribner's*, and the *Century* magazines from the 1870's until his death.

An Autobiographical Sketch

[c. Jan. 1, 1897]

WOODROW WILSON, jurist, historian, man of letters, was born 28 December, 1856, in Staunton, Virginia. His mother, Jessie Woodrow, was born of Scots parents in Carlisle, England. His father, Joseph Ruggles Wilson, a noted divine of the southern Presbyterian Church, was born, of Scots-Irish parents, in Steubenville, Ohio. Woodrow Wilson was trained in private schools in Augusta, Georgia, and Columbia, South Carolina; and received his college and professional education at Princeton, where he graduated bachelor of arts in 1879, at the University of Virginia, where he got his schooling in the law, and at the Johns Hopkins University, where he began his special studies in the field of history and politics.

He practiced law in Atlanta, Georgia, 1882-1883; but, finding his taste for general study stronger than his taste for law practice, he turned, in 1883, to the work of his life by entering the Johns Hopkins University as a graduate student, and by undertaking, in 1885, the instruction in history and politics at Bryn Mawr College. From Bryn Mawr he went, in 1888, to Wesleyan University, Middletown, Connecticut; and in 1890 he accepted the chair of Jurisprudence at Princeton. Since 1887 he has been Lecturer in Administration at the Johns Hopkins University.

While a student at the Johns Hopkins Mr. Wilson published (1885) "Congressional Government, A Study in American Politics," which at once brought him applause and distinction on both sides of the Atlantic. He has since published "The State: Elements of Historical and Practical Politics," a text book (1889); "Division and Reunion, 1829-1889" (1893); "An Old Master and Other Political Essays" (1893); "Mere Literature," a volume of literary and historical papers, (1896); and "George Washington" (1896). While his position as a scholar and man of letters has become yearly more and more assured, he has also become widely known as a lecturer on literary and political subjects, and as a contributor to the leading magazines of the country.

WWT MS. (WP, DLC).

From Joseph Ruggles Wilson

My dearest Woodrow—   Richmond, Va January 3rd 1897

A prominent trustee of the "Washington and Lee" University called on me to-day to say that your name is prominently before members of the Board, as a suitable successor to Gen. Lee[1] whose resignation of the Presidency of this institution is to take effect on July 1st of the present year. The salary will be placed at almost any figure you might desire—say $4000 or $5000. In addition there is a President's house fine and roomy. It was built for Gen. R. E. Lee and is said to be all that can be desired in the way of a gentleman's residence. The faculty is a homogeneous body of disciplined scholars—12 or 14—which needs only an enthusiastic head to make it, throughout the several departments represented, a most efficient team of successful co-workers. The number of students is about 250. One of the most engaging peculiarities of this institution is that it is perfectly independent either of state aid or ecclesiastical control; and, with an endowment fund sufficient by its income to run the University were there no tuition fees to help it out—some $800,000 I believe. The President is not required to engage in class-room instruction; and is, if I understood aright, entitled to the services of a Secretary who is paid by the Board.

This, my precious son, seems like a very desirable, if not delightful opening—but whether you shall see it in the same rosy light as that which appeals to my vision, I of course cannot say. If you prefer, one or more members of the Board are prepared to call upon you in P.—on their own responsibility—for the purpose of laying the whole matter in its completed details before your attention.

Write me as soon as you conveniently may, in respect to this tentative offer. From your reply members of the Board will decide whether it shall be worth their while to see you in person.[2]

Much love to dear Ellie and to all, with New Year's greetings in addition,   I am as ever   Your devoted   Father

ALS, (WP, DLC).
[1] George Washington Custis Lee, President of Washington and Lee University, 1871-97.
[2] WW to EAW, February 16, 1897, suggests that Wilson returned a positive response to this overture; however, the absence in the Wilson Papers of any other letters relating to the Washington and Lee presidency indicates that the trustees did not engage in any negotiations with Wilson about the matter because they soon decided upon another man, William Lyne Wilson of West Virginia, at this time Postmaster General in Cleveland's Cabinet.

To Francis Landey Patton

My Dear Dr. Patton: [Princeton, N.J., c. Jan. 4, 1897]

I attended the three days' meeting of the American Historical Association last week,—wishing to see some men whom I had not seen, and make sure of my own judgment in the matter of the choice for ourselves. I have come away feeling, not only that we are shut in to the choice I have urged,—if we would have the best,—but that it is extremely fortunate we should be.

Professor Turner was not himself present at the meeting but he sent a paper on to be read, and the attention it attracted, the praise it drew forth (even from men like Justin Winsor,[1] ordinarily very churlish in praise) would, I think, have astounded you. He is obviously reckoned in that association the leading man in his field, a man who would lead in any field he chose. Professor Haskins was present and read a paper,[2]—the most delightful paper of the meeting, and made an impression of force and easy mastery such as I was not myself wholly prepared for.

I have no hesitation in saying that, if we can get these two men, the American Historical Association (with its historical scholars of the country) will say that we have not lost but gained by our changes.

We are, it seems to me, shut in to this reorganization of the History Department—even if that is the only considerable thing done with the new money by way of reorganization. We cannot get any man we should be willing to take to occupy an old-fashioned and really impossible chair such as Sloane so long endured. But we cannot afford to be behind colleges of the rank of Amherst in this capitally important department.

[Sincerely yours,   Woodrow Wilson]

Transcript of WWshL (draft) (WP, DLC).
  [1] Justin Winsor's remarks on Turner's paper are printed in the *Annual Report of the American Historical Association for the Year 1896* (2 vols., Washington, 1897), I, 287-88.
  [2] See WW to F. J. Turner, Nov. 30, 1896, n. 2.

To Walter Hines Page

My dear Mr. Page,   Princeton, N. J.   January 6th, 1897.

I have not forgotten that you want the article on President Cleveland by the 15th of January, and I am doing my best to make sure of its completion by that date. If I absolutely need a day or two of grace I will let you know promptly, so that there need be no uncertainty on your part.

With much regard

very sincerely Yours   Woodrow Wilson

TLS (Houghton Mifflin Letter Files, MH).

From Louis Clark Vanuxem[1]

My dear Tommie: Philadelphia   January 7th 1897

I have come across a great number of valuable letters to Benjamin Rush, which have never seen the light of publicity, written by John Adams and other prominent heroes of our revolution.

Col. Alexander Biddle, my neighbor, has them; they came to him by inheritance,[2] and his collection also includes a diary of Benjamin Rush in which our Ben gives his opinion of the characters of his fellow-signers of the Declaration of Independence.

Col. Biddle a couple of years ago, had fifty copies printed,[3] but after correspondeing with Adams' descendants, retained the fifty books in his possession, out of deference to the wishes of the Adams family.

Knowing that they would have an especial interest to you, I have obtained Col. Biddle's permission to send you copy of the aforesaid book, which he loaned me. Return it after digesting; and if your appetite is whetted to delve further into this Revolutiana, name a Saturday next month, when you will visit me, remaining my guest over the Lord's day, and I shall bring you and the owner of them together. It is needles[s] for me to say that such a visit would give me the greatest pleasure.[4]

May your best wishes for the New Year be realized, and happiness and prosperity attend you ever, says

Your friend,   L. C. Vanuxem

TLS (WP, DLC).

[1] Lawyer in Philadelphia and a member of the Princeton Class of 1879.

[2] Alexander Biddle (1819-99), a Philadelphia gentleman of leisure, who acquired his collection of Rush manuscripts through his marriage to Julia Williams Rush, granddaughter of Benjamin Rush.

[3] Alexander Biddle (compiler), *Old Family Letters: Copied from the Originals for Alexander Biddle*, Series A (Philadelphia, 1892).

[4] L. C. Vanuxem to WW, April 18, 1898, suggests that Wilson had not yet paid this visit to Vanuxem.

From Edward Dowden

Buona Vista, Killiney,

My dear Professor Wilson,   Co. Dublin, Jan. 7, 1897.

If "bis dat qui cito dat" be true I fear it argues that my belated thanks for your gift of "Mere Literature" are no more than half-thanks. But that can't be true. I feel grateful for the kind gift, & more for being in living contact through your book with the same mind (or character) that was present in your Princeton address. Your essays don't consist of clever things put together, but are the utterance of a person, with a way of thinking & feeling & speaking properly his own. I was naturally much interested in all you say of Burke,—I may add of Bagehot whose admirable articles in the *old National Review* I read very long ago. Your articles on American subjects make me feel that I have lost much in not knowing more of the great men & the history of the United States. "The supreme American," Lincoln, however, I knew in part, but, as far as it went, aright.

I have been busy—partly preparing my Princeton lectures for the press. They are on their way to Mr. Scribner.[1] I hope they are better than they seemed to me on the day I sent them off—with some sinking of the heart. I utilised for my lecture on Wordsworth matter properly belonging to an Introduction to a volume of Selections from Wordsworth which Ginn & Co. of Boston are slowly printing[2]—& I had to restore the stolen property, & insert what I did *not* read from my MS. in Alexander Hall.

Mrs. Dowden joins me in sending our kindest regards & good wishes for 1897 to Mrs. Wilson.

Again take my thanks & believe me

Very sincerely yours   Edward Dowden.

ALS (WP, DLC).

[1] Edward Dowden, *The French Revolution and English Literature; Lectures Delivered in Connection with the Sesquicentennial Celebration of Princeton University* (New York, 1897).

[2] Edward Dowden (ed.), *Poems by William Wordsworth* (Boston and London, 1897).

To John Franklin Jameson

My dear Jameson,   Princeton, New Jersey, 8 January, 1897.

I beg that you will not deem me selfish or churlish when I decline even this little scrap of work.[1] This disabling of my right hand (I am picking this labourously out with my left) has made an enormous difference in my life: for I cannot afford a secretary. I can manage to do the big pieces of work by which I earn my living; but the little jobs are just the very ones that are crowded absolutely out in the careful husbandry of minutes by which I manage to do the rest. I dare not promise to do them. And yet, spite of appearances to the contrary, I am

Your affectionate friend,   Woodrow Wilson

Warm regards from us both to you both.

WWTLS (J. F. Jameson Papers, DLC).

[1] This was probably a request for a short book review for the *American Historical Review*, of which Jameson was the managing editor.

The *New York Times*' Review of *Mere Literature*

[Jan. 9, 1897]

MERE LITERATURE AND OTHER ESSAYS. By Woodrow Wilson. Boston and New York: Houghton, Mifflin & Co. $1.50.

The title "Mere Literature" is an unfortunate one, as it fixes upon the whole collection of Woodrow Wilson's essays the name given to the poorest of these. It is a pity for a serious and gifted writer to juggle with words and array "scholar" and "scientist" against "artist" and "seer," as if to be a scholar fixed the limit of one's mind by rule and equation, and to be an artist precluded an accurate and careful method.

Probably Prof. Wilson's somewhat impatient rejection of "science" and "scholarship" is based on the feeling that Lowell expressed when he said that language should be a ladder to literature, and not literature a ladder to language, and that he would rather a young man were "intimate with the genius of the Greek dramatic poets than with the meters of their choruses," although he added, with his plain good sense: "I should be glad to have him on easy terms with both." But Lowell was never quite patient enough with his meters to be in the first degree a poet, and it is possible that in his histories Prof. Wilson gives almost too free a rein to his imagination. It is certainly a wild flight of fancy to assume that a thoroughgoing scholar dare not reflect, nor should we care too confidingly to accept this recipe for immortality.

"Let a man but have beauty in his heart, and, believing something with his might, put it forth arrayed as he sees it, the lights and shadows falling upon it on his page as they fall upon it in his heart, and he may die assured that that beauty will not pass away out of the world."

In fact, one feels painfully that in his essay on "Mere Literature," Prof. Wilson reveals the secret of his own weakness as a historian. "You must produce in color," he says, "with the touch of imagination which lifts what you write away from the dull levels of mere exposition. Black-and-white sketches may serve some purpose of the artist, but very little of actual nature is in mere black and white. Nothing is ever conceived completely when conceived so grayly, without suffusion of real light." What a confession for one who claims to be the champion of art! And it is a creed as dangerous for the young writer as it is for the young painter. There are many merits in the "dull level of mere exposition," and entirely to forswear the plain and patient statement of plain and simple fact is something like laying down a rule to eat nothing without sugar and cream—not even corned beef.

It is not until Prof. Wilson reaches Bagehot and Burke that he gives the reader anything like wholesome meat; and concerning Bagehot he is not enlightening, although there is some clever characterization—this, for example: "Bagehot is the embodiment of witty common sense; all the movements of his mind illustrate that vivacious sanity which he has himself called 'animated moderation.'"

Burke, however, is a genius after Prof. Wilson's own heart, and he renders him full justice. As a boy Burke turned his back on system and discipline, and read books too eagerly to read them very exactly. The course of events gave to this type of mind its opportunity. The American war for independence and the French Revolution were subjects demanding eloquence and a firm grasp of large principles—exact scholarship could very well be postponed. Under the influence of Burke's rich Irish sentiment and ringing phrases, Prof. Wilson loses the irritability of a special pleader, and shows himself at his genial best.

The essay entitled "The Course of American History" throws an interesting light upon Prof. Wilson's point of view as a historian. He has conceived the idea—not without reason—that our histories give only imperfectly the story of the South and West in tracing the outline of the Nation's development. It is not impossible that Prof. Wilson has some intention of himself becoming the historian who shall restore the just proportion, but there must first be a careful groundwork of accurate fact prepared by some poor grubber content—according to Prof. Wilson—to "prepare for oblivion" that the man of fancy may win immortality.

Printed in the *New York Times*, Jan. 9, 1897.

From Hans Carl Günther von Jagemann[1]

Dear Mr. Wilson: Cambridge Mass. January 14, 1897.

Mrs. von Jagemann and I finished last night reading your admirable biography of Washington to which we had treated ourselves at Christmas and I feel prompted to thank you sincerely for the great pleasure which it has given us. The world is always prone to look with a patronizing smile on a former generation for its worship of a hero, having forgotten the causes of such intense admiration. For this reason a new Life of such a man as Washington is needed from time to time to change the world's hazy ideas of his greatness into well-founded knowledge. I am sure that in your book "the impartial and eloquent historian" has succeeded in "exhibiting the life of George Washington . . . as a perfect model of all that is virtuous, noble, great and dignified in man."[2]

You probably receive a good many letters of this sort and you must not feel under obligation to answer this one. With the best wishes for your continued success and prosperity I remain

Yours very sincerely,   H. C. G. von Jagemann.

ALS (WP, DLC) with WWhw notation on env.: "Ans. 25 Jany, '97."
    1 At this time Assistant Professor of Germanic Philology at Harvard University.
    2 Von Jagemann was apparently quoting from an advertisement or review
which the Editors have been unable to find.

From Wilson's Diary for 1897

Friday, January 15, 1897

Finished and dispatched to the *Atlantic* article on *"Mr. Cleveland as President,"* begun Thursday last [January 7]. Much too hastily done to be either toned, judged, or written well: too distinctly hack work, and yet containing my deliberate and veritable judgment of the man, and so honest work.

Doctor sends Ellen to bed because of soreness in the vermiform appendix, first disclosed yesterday morning.

A Biographical Essay

[*Jan. 15, 1897*]

MR. CLEVELAND AS PRESIDENT.

It is much too early to attempt to assign to Mr. Cleveland his place in the history of our government and policy. That he has played a very great and individual part in our affairs no one can doubt. But we are still too near him to see his work in its just perspective; we cannot yet see or estimate him as an historical figure.

It is plain, however, that Mr. Cleveland has rendered the country great services, and that his singular independence and force of purpose have made the real character of the government of the United States more evident than it ever was before. He has been the sort of President the makers of the Constitution had vaguely in mind: more man than partisan; with an independent executive will of his own; hardly a colleague of the Houses so much as an individual servant of the country; exercising his powers like a chief magistrate rather than like a party leader. Washington showed a like individual force and separateness; but he had been the country's leader through all its Revolution, and was always a kind of hero, whom parties could not absorb. Jackson worked his own will as President, and seemed to change the very nature of the government while he reigned; but it was a new social force that spoke in him, and he re-created a great party. Lincoln made the presidency the government while the war lasted, and gave the nation a great ruler; but his purposes were those of a

disciplined and determined party, and his time was a time of
fearful crisis, when men studied power, not law. No one of these
men seems the normal President, or affords example of the usual
courses of administration. Mr. Cleveland has been President in
ordinary times, but after an extraordinary fashion; not because
he wished to form or revolutionize or save the government, but
because he came fresh to his tasks without the common party
training, a direct, fearless, somewhat unsophisticated man of
action. In him we got a President, as it were, by immediate choice
from out the body of the people, as the Constitution has all along
appeared to expect, and he has refreshed our notion of an American chief magistrate.

It is plain that Mr. Cleveland, like every other man, has drawn
his character and force in large part from his origin and breeding. It would be easy to describe him as a man of the people, and
he would, I suppose, be as proud as any other man of that
peculiar American title to nobility. But, after all, no man comes
from the people in general. We are each of us derived from some
small group of persons in particular; and unless we were too poor
to have any family life at all, it is the life and associations of the
family that have chiefly shaped us in our youth. Mr. Cleveland
had a very definite home training: wholesome, kindly, Christian.
He was bred in a home where character was disciplined and the
thoughts were formed, where books were read and the right rules
of life obeyed. He was early thrown, indeed, into the ordinary
and common school of life, had its rough work thrust upon him,
and learned, by his own part in it, the life of the people. But he
never got those first lessons, conned in plain village manses, out
of his blood. "If mother were alive I should feel so much safer,"
he wrote to his brother upon the night he was elected governor
of New York. Grover Cleveland certainly got good usury in his
steadfast youth out of the capital stock of energy and principle
he brought away, as his only portion, from his mother and father.

The qualities which have given him his place in his profession
and in the history of the country seem commonplace enough in
their customary manifestation: industry, thoroughness, upright-
ness, candor, courage. But it is worth while to remember that the
same force and adjustment that will run a toy machine, made
for a child's use, will also bring to bear the full might of a Corliss
engine, with strength enough to drive a city's industries. It is the
size and majesty of moral and intellectual qualities that make
them great; and the point the people have noted about Mr. Cleveland is that his powers, though of a kind they know and have
often had experience of, are made upon a great scale, and have

lifted him to the view of the world as a national force, a maker and unmaker of policies. Men have said that Mr. Cleveland was without genius or brilliancy, because the processes of his mind were calculable and certain, like a law of nature; that his utterances were not above the common, because they told only in the mass, and not sentence by sentence, were cast rather than tempered; that he was stubborn because he did not change, and self-opinionated because he did not falter. He has made no overtures to fortune; has obtained and holds a great place in our affairs by a sort of inevitable mastery, by a law which no politician has ever quite understood or at all relished, by virtue of a preference which the people themselves have expressed without analyzing. We have seen how there is genius in mere excellence of gift, and prevailing power merely in traits of chastened will.

When a city or a nation looks for a man to better its administration, it seeks character rather than gifts of origination, a clear purpose that can be depended upon to work its will without fear or favor. Mr. Cleveland never struck so straight towards the confidence of practical men as when he spoke of the tariff question as "a condition, not a theory." His mind works in the concrete; lies close always to the practical life of the world, which he understands by virtue of lifelong contact with it. He was no prophet of novelties, but a man of affairs; had no theories, but strove always to have knowledge of fact. There is as great a field for mind in thinking a situation through and through as in threading the intricacies of an abstract problem, and it has heartened men from the first to find that Mr. Cleveland could do thinking of that sort with a sure, unhurried, steadfast power, such as no less practical man could even have simulated. He was an experiment when he was chosen mayor of Buffalo, did not know his own powers, had given no one else their true measure; but he was thereafter a known and calculable force, and grew from station to station with an increase of vigor, and withal a consistency of growth, which showed his qualities such as waited only the invitation of fortune and opportunity. It may be that there are other men, of like parts and breeding, who could rise in like fashion to a great rôle, but it is certain that Mr. Cleveland has made a place of his own among the Presidents of the United States.

The ordinary rules of politics have been broken throughout his career. He came almost like a novice into the field of national politics, despite his previous experience as mayor and governor. He had always identified himself, indeed, with the Democratic party; but his neighbors in Buffalo had chosen him to better rather than to serve his party, when they elected him to local office. He had elevated the office of sheriff, when they called him to it, by executing it with conscientious energy and with an enlightened sense of public duty; and he had made it his business, when they chose him mayor of their city, to see municipal affairs put upon a footing of efficiency, such as might become a great corporation whose object was the welfare of its citizens, and no partisan interest whatever. It was inevitable that he should shock and alienate all mere partisans, alike by his temper and by his methods. He called himself a party man, and had no weak stomach for the processes of party management; but he had not sought office as a career, and he deemed his party better served by manliness and integrity than by chicanery. He was blunt, straightforward, plain-spoken, stalwart by nature, used to choosing and pushing his own way; and he had a sober audacity which made him no caucus man. His courses of action were incalculable to the mere politician, simply because they were not based upon calculation.

It commonly turns out that the fearlessness of such a man is safer than the caution of the professional party manager. A free and thoughtful people loves a bold man, who faces the fight without too much thought of himself or of his party's fortunes. Mr. Cleveland's success as mayor of Buffalo attracted the attention of the whole State,—was too pronounced and conspicuous to be overlooked. Party managers saw in him a man to win with, little as they understood the elements of his power. Even they stared, nevertheless, to see him elected governor of the State by the astounding majority of 192,854. He evidently had not studied the art of pleasing; he had been known as the "veto mayor" of Buffalo, and his vetoes as the "plain speech" vetoes. He had an odd way of treating questions of city government as if they were questions of individual official judgment, and not at all questions of party advantage. He brought his exact habits as a lawyer to bear upon his tasks as a public officer, and made a careful business of the affairs of city and State. There was nothing puritanical about him. He had a robust and practical spirit in all things. But he did not seem to regard politics as in any way a distinct science, set apart from the ordinary business of life. He treated the legislature of the State, when he became governor, as he had treated the city council of Buffalo, as if he were the president of a great industrial concern with incidental social functions, and they were its board of directors, often unwise, sometimes unscrupulous, in their action; as if it were his chief duty to stand between them and the stockholders, protecting the latter's interests at all hazards. He used his veto as freely when governor as he had used it when mayor. "Magnificent," cried the trained politicians about him, under their breath,—"magnificent, but it is not politics!"

And yet they found him thrust inevitably upon them as their candidate for President before his term as governor had drawn to its close. Evidence was accumulating that the country was ready to put an end to the long succession of Republican administrations which had held the federal executive departments for more than twenty years as a sort of party property; but it was also plain enough that the old, the real party leaders among the Democrats would by no means be acceptable substitutes. The Democratic party, moreover, had been too long in opposition to be ready to assume, as it stood, the responsibilities of government. It had no real union; it was little more than an assemblage of factions, a more or less coherent association of the various groups and interests opposed to the Republicans and bent upon breaking their supremacy. It did not itself know whether it was of one mind or not. For, though popular majorities had been running its way for ten years and more, and both Houses of Congress had once come into its hands, it had never had leave to undertake constructive legislation. The President's veto had stood always in its way, and its legislation had often been proposed for effect rather than with a view to actual execution. It was necessary it should go outside its own confused and disordered ranks if it would choose a successful presidential candidate, in order both to unite its own factions and to win the country's confidence: and so it chose Mr. Cleveland, and the country accepted him.

It was a novel experiment. The very considerations that made it wise to nominate Mr. Cleveland as President were likely to render it difficult to live under his presidency with an unbroken party discipline; and the circumstances of his election made it all the more probable that he would choose to be President of the country rather than leader of the Democrats. The Democrats, in fact, did not recognize him as their leader, but only as their candidate for the office of President. If he was leader at all in the ordinary sense,—if he spoke and acted for the views of any body of men,—he was the leader of those independent Republicans who had broken with their own party, and were looking for some one who should open a new era in party politics and give them efficient and public-spirited principles to believe in and vote for again. Men everywhere wished to see parties reform themselves, and old-line Democrats had more reason to expect to see their party fall apart into its constituent elements once more than to hope that Mr. Cleveland would unite and vivify it as an aggressive and triumphant organization. He had been made President, there was good reason to believe, rather because thoughtful men throughout the country wanted a pure and businesslike administration than because they wanted Democratic legislation or an upsetting of old policies; he had been chosen as a man, not as a partisan,—taken up by his own party as a likely winner rather than as an acceptable master.

Apparently there was no reason, however, to fear that Mr. Cleveland would arrogate to himself the prerogatives of political leadership, or assume the rôle of guide and mentor in matters of policy. At first he regarded the great office to which he had been chosen as essentially executive, except of course in the giving or withholding of his assent to bills passed by Congress. His veto he used with extraordinary freedom, particularly in the disapproval of private pension bills, vetoing no less than one hundred and forty-six measures during the sessions of the first Congress of his administration; and he filled his messages with very definite recommendations; but he thought it no part of his proper function to press his preferences in any other way upon the acceptance of Congress. In the public interest, he had addressed a letter to Mr. A. J. Warner, a member of Congress, and others, only eight days before his inauguration as President, in which he had declared in urgent terms his strong conviction that the purchase and coinage of silver should be stopped at once, to prevent radical and perhaps disastrous disturbances in the currency; and he joined with Mr. Manning, his Secretary of the Treasury, in speaking very plainly to the same effect when Congress met. But he deemed his duty done when he had thus used the only initiative given him by the Constitution, and expressly declined to use any other means of pressing his views upon his party. He meant to keep aloof, and be President with a certain separateness, as the Constitution seemed to suggest.

It cost him at least one sharp fight with the Senate to carry his purpose of executive independence into effect. Mr. Cleveland saw fit to remove certain federal officers from office before the expiration of their terms, and to appoint Democrats in their places, and the Senate demanded the papers which would explain the causes of the removals. The President declined to send them, holding that the Senate had no right to judge of anything but the fitness of the men named as successors to the officers removed. It was not certain that the moral advantage lay with the President. He had been put into the presidency chiefly because independent voters all over the country, and particularly in his own State, regarded him a tried champion of civil service reform; but his choice and method in appointments had by no means satisfied the reformers. They had stared to see him make Mr. Daniel Manning Secretary of the Treasury, not because Mr. Manning lacked ability, but because he was notoriously a politician of the very "practical" sort, and seemed to those who did not know him the very kind of manager Mr. Cleveland ought to have turned his back upon; and they did not like any more than the Senate did to see men deprived of their offices to make room for Democrats without good reason given, reason that had no taint of partisanship upon it. The truth was that the public service had been too long in the hands of the Republicans to be susceptible of being considered an unpartisan service as it stood. Mr. Cleveland said simply, to those who spoke to him in private about the matter, that he had not made any removal which he did not, after careful inquiry, believe to be for the good of the public service. This could not satisfy his critics. It meant that he must be permitted to use his judgment not only as a man, but also as a Democrat, in reconstructing a civil service which had been for a generation in the hands of the opposite political party. The laws could not be made mandatory upon him in this matter, under the Constitution, and he took leave to exercise his discretion here and there, as his judgment as a practical and strong-willed man suggested. That the operation of the laws passed for the reform of the civil service was strengthened in the main, and their administration thoroughly organized and very much bettered under him, no candid man could deny; and with that he asked the country to be content.

The whole question afforded an excellent opportunity for studying Mr. Cleveland's character. The key quality of that character is, perhaps, a sort of robust sagacity. He had never for a moment called himself anything but a party man. He had not sought personal detachment, and had all along known the weakness that would come with isolation and the absolute rejection of the regular means of party management; and he had dared to make his own choices in cases which seemed too subtle or exceptional for the law. It was unsafe ground often; blunders were made which appeared to defeat the purposes he had in view in making removals and appointments; it looked in the end as if it would have been wiser to make no exceptions at all to the ordinary rules of appointment: but the mistakes were those of a strong nature,—too strong to strip itself absolutely of such choice as might serve what was to him legitimate party strength. Who shall judge the acts in question who does not know the grounds upon which the President proceeded? Not all of government can be crowded into the rules of the law.

At any rate, criticism did not disturb Mr. Cleveland's serenity; and it pleased the fancy of men of all sorts to see the President bear himself so steadfastly and do his work so calmly in the midst of all the talk. Outsiders could not know whether the criticism cut or not; they only knew that the President did not falter or suffer his mind to be shaken. He had an enormous capacity for work, shirked no detail of his busy function, carried the government steadily upon his shoulders. There is no antidote for worry to be compared with hard labor at important tasks which keep the mind stretched to large views; and the President looked upon himself as the responsible executive of the nation, not as the arbiter of policies. There is something in such a character that men of quick and ardent thought cannot like or understand. They want all capable men to be thinking, like themselves, along lines of active advance; they are impatient of performance which is simply thorough without also being regenerative, and Mr. Cleveland has not commended himself to them. They themselves would probably not make good Presidents. A certain tough and stubborn fibre is necessary, which does not easily change, which is unelastically strong.

The attention of the country, however, was presently drawn off from Mr. Cleveland's pension vetoes and individual methods of appointment, from his attitude and temper as a power standing aloof from Congress, to note him a leader and master after all, as if in spite of himself. He was too good a Democrat and too strenuous a man of business to stand by and see the policy of the country hopelessly adrift without putting his own influence to the test to direct it. He could not keep to his rôle of simple executive. He saw his party cut into opposing factions upon the question of the tariff, upon the reform to which it had been pledged time out of mind. Mr. Carlisle, who wished to see the tariff brought to a revenue basis, was Speaker of the Democratic House, and Mr. Morrison was chairman of the Committee of Ways and Means; but Mr. Randall checkmated them at every turn, and nothing was done to redeem the party's promises. No man of strong convictions could stand there, where all the country watched him, waiting for him to speak, the only representative of the nation as a whole in all the government, and let a great opportunity and a great duty go by default. He had intended to make his a strictly business administration, to cleanse the public service and play his assigned part in legislation with a clear judgment to do right. But the President stands at the centre of legislation as well as of administration in executing his great office, and Mr. Cleveland grew to the measure of his place as its magnitude and responsibilities cleared to his view. The breath of affairs was at last in his lungs, and he gave his party a leader, of a sudden, in the plain-spoken, earnest, mandatory tariff message of December, 1887. It was such a stroke as no mere politician would have hazarded, and it sadly disconcerted the men who had supposed themselves the leaders of the Democrats. Mr. Cleveland had not consulted them about his manifesto. He had made the issue of the next presidential campaign for them before they were aware of it, and that campaign was immediately at hand. The Congress to which he sent his message showed already a sad cutting off in the ranks of the Democrats. In the first Congress of his administration his party had had a majority of close upon forty in the House, though the Senate was still against them. In the Congress of which he demanded tariff reform the Democratic majority in the House had dwindled to eleven, though the Senate was almost equally divided. It seemed as if he would commit his party to a dangerous and aggressive policy at the very moment when its power was on the decline, and risk everything with regard to the next choice of President. Some resented his action as a sudden usurpation; others doubted what they should think; a few took the changed aspect of politics with zest and relish. It was bravely done. The situation produced was even dramatic; and yet the calmest man anywhere touched by the business was Mr. Cleveland himself. It was no trick or impulse. It was the steadily delivered blow of a stalwart and thoughtful man, thoroughly sick of seeing a great party drift and dally while the nation's finances suffered waste and demoralization.

He had certainly settled the way the next campaign should go: that the country's reception of his message showed; and the politicians adjusted themselves as best they might to his policy of plain speech and no circumspection. The House passed a tariff measure, drafted by Mr. Mills, which was thrown aside in the Senate, but not rejected by the party. Mr. Cleveland was renominated for the presidency by acclamation, not because the politicians wanted him, but because their constituents did. The two parties went to the country, and Mr. Cleveland lost by the vote of his own State.

The odd thing about it was that defeat did not seem to lessen Mr. Cleveland's importance. Some persons did not like to see their ex-President return to the ordinary duties of legal practice, as he did in New York, apparently expecting a healthy, practical man to accept a merely ornamental part in society after once having been their chief magistrate. There was no denying the fact that he had wrought his own defeat and his party's by forcing a hot fight when matters were going peacefully enough. He himself kept as much as might be from unnecessary publicity. But the country could not cease to be interested in him, and he was the only man it would take seriously, even now, as the leader of the Democrats. Practical men could not for the life of them think of any more suitable candidate for the next campaign. Whether he had united or pleased his party or not, he had, in any case, given it a programme and made himself its chief representative. Through all the four years of Mr. Harrison's administration Mr. Cleveland was the most conspicuous man in the country out of office, and a sort of popular expectation followed him in all his movements.

The Republicans, moreover, delivered themselves into his hands. They took his defeat as a mandate from the people to make a tariff as little like that which Mr. Cleveland had desired as it might be possible to construct. The Committee of Ways and Means, of which Major McKinley was chairman, framed a measure unmistakably fit to meet the demand; and the congressional elections of 1890 went overwhelmingly against the Republicans. Apparently, the country had come at last to Mr. Cleveland's mind in respect of the tariff, and he became once more the logical as well as the popular candidate of the Democrats for the presidency. Once more he became President, and essayed the difficult rôle of leader of a composite party. He had created an additional difficulty, meanwhile, obeying an imperative conviction without regard to policy or opportune occasion. He had ventured a frank public letter in opposition to the free coinage of silver, notwithstanding the fact that he knew free coinage to be much more distinctively a Democratic than a Republican measure. The habit of independent initiative in respect of questions of legislative policy was growing upon him, as he felt his personal power grow and his familiarity with public questions; and he knew that he was striking straight home, this time, to the confidence, at any rate, of every enlightened man of business in the country. Such men he had known from his youth up, and could assess: his courage and self-confidence in such a case was stuff of his whole training and character, and he felt that he could afford to lose the presidency upon that issue.

Mr. Cleveland's second term has shown the full strength and the full risk of the qualities which, during his first administration, the country had seen displayed only in the disturbing tariff message of 1887, in his energetic treatment of the fisheries question, which the Senate did not like, and in certain appointments which the whole country had criticised. He gave warning at the outset of the individual rôle he meant to play in the selection of his Cabinet. He bestowed the secretaryship of state upon a man come but the other day out of the Republican ranks to support him; the secretaryship of war upon a man who had formerly been his private secretary; the post-office upon his one-time law partner; the department of the interior upon a Georgian whose name the country smiled to hear for the first time; the attorney-generalship upon a lawyer who was no politician; and the secretaryship of agriculture upon a quiet gentleman of his own picking out. Only the navy and the headship of the treasury went to men whom his party knew and followed in the House. His first Cabinet had contained men whom everybody knew as accredited leaders among the Democrats,—Mr. Bayard, Mr. Whitney, Mr. Lamar, Mr. Vilas; only the minority of his counselors had then been selected as if to please himself, rather than to draw a party following about him by recognizing the men who exercised authority among the Democrats. But his second Cabinet seemed chosen as if of deliberate and set purpose to make a personal and private choice, without regard to party support.

And yet there was less difference between the two Cabinets than appeared upon the surface. Though there had been some representative Democrats in the first Cabinet, they had not been men who controlled their party. Mr. Carlisle, of the second Cabinet, was undoubtedly more influential than any of them, and Mr. Herbert more truly a working, capital member of the party's force in the House. The truth was that Mr. Cleveland had, throughout his first administration, been all the while held at arm's length by his party,—an ally, perhaps, but not a partner in its undertakings,—had been compelled to keep the place of separateness and independence which had at first seemed to be his choice. In his second administration he apparently made no effort to force his way into its counsels, but accepted his place as the independent voters' President,—content if only he could have a personal following, carry out the real pledges of his party, and make his purpose felt as the nation's spokesman. Not that he broke with his party either in thought or in purpose; but he saw that it would not take counsel with him, and that, if he would fulfill his trust, he must force partisan leaders, for their own good, to feel his power from without. It might be they would draw about him more readily through mastery than through persuasion.

It was singular how politics began at once to centre in the President, waiting for his initiative, and how the air at Washington filled with murmurs against the domineering and usurping temper and practice of the Executive. Power had somehow gone the length of the avenue, and seemed lodged in one man. No one who knew Mr. Cleveland, or who judged him fairly, for a moment deemed him too covetous of authority, or in any degree disregardful of the restraints the Constitution has put upon the President. But the Democrats in the House were made conscious that the eye of the country had been withdrawn from them in matters of policy, and Washington seemed full of Mr. Cleveland, his Secretary of the Treasury and his Secretary of State. A position of personal isolation had been thrust upon him, but he used the power which had come to him to effect the purposes to which, as a Democrat, he felt himself pledged. If the party would not act with him, he must act for it. There was no touch of cant in him when he declared his allegiance to the Democratic party; there was only a danger that if the leaders of the party in Congress continued to follow him merely when they were obliged, he would himself presently be all the Democratic party that was left in the country.

On June 30, 1893, four months after his second inauguration, he took steps to force action upon the silver question. He called Congress to meet in extra session upon the 7th of August following, to deal with the finances of the country and prevent a panic; telling them plainly that the law which compelled the purchase and coinage of silver by the government ought to be repealed, and that this question must be settled even if the tariff had to wait. There was already serious disturbance in business circles, arising in large part from the condition of the currency, when, on the 26th of June, the British authorities in India closed the mints of that country to the free coinage of silver, and sent the price of the unstable metal down with a disastrous tumble in all the world's markets. It looked then as if there would certainly be a fatal panic, and Mr. Cleveland saw that Congress must meet and face the situation at once.

It was evident, even before Congress came together, that the battle was to be, not between Democrats and Republicans, but between the advocates and the opponents of the free coinage of silver, without regard to party. Conventions called by the silver men met in Denver and in Chicago before Congress as-

sembled, and denounced the proposal to repeal the silver purchase law as a scheme devised by American and English bankers,
with the assistance of Mr. Cleveland, to drive silver out of use
as money; and when Congress took the matter up, old party lines
seemed, for the moment at any rate, to have disappeared. It
was the "friends" of silver against its "enemies." The advocates
of Mr. Cleveland's policy of repeal won a decisive victory in the
House of Representatives, and won it at once, before August was
out; but in the Senate the fight dragged, with doubtful and wavering fortunes, until the very end of October,—would have ended
in some weak compromise had not the President stood resolute,—
and kept the country waiting so long for the issue that business
suffered almost as much as if repeal had been defeated.

It was the President's victory that the law was at last repealed,
and every one knew it. He had forced the consideration of the
question; he had told Senators plainly, almost passionately, when
they approached him, that he would accept no compromise,—
that he would veto anything less than absolute repeal, and let
them face the country as best they might afterwards. Until he
came on the stage both parties had dallied and coquetted with the
advocates of silver. Now he had brought both to a parting of the
ways. The silver men were forced to separate themselves and look
their situation in the face, choose which party they should plan
to bring under their will and policy, if they could, and no longer
camp in the tents of both. Such a stroke settled what the course
of congressional politics should be throughout the four years of
Mr. Cleveland's term, and made it certain that at the end of that
term he should either have won his party to himself or lost it
altogether. It was evident that any party that rejected the gold
standard for the currency must look upon him as its opponent.

He showed his fixed purpose in the matter once again by his
veto of the so-called Seigniorage Bill in March, 1894. The silver
men had already so far rallied as to induce substantial majorities
in both Houses to agree to the practically immediate coinage
of all the silver bullion owned by the treasury as a result of the
purchases of silver made under the law which had but just now
been repealed in the special session. It would not be wise to put
forth so great a body of silver, at such a time, to the fresh disturbance of the currency, said the President, and the bill was
negatived. The issue of more silver was defeated, and the silver
men quietly set about forming their party lines anew.

Meanwhile, issue was joined once more upon the question of
the tariff, not only as between Democrats and Republicans, but
also as between Democrat and Democrat, and new lines of di-

vergence were run through Mr. Cleveland's party. The Committee of Ways and Means, of which Mr. W. L. Wilson was chairman, had formulated a tariff bill during the special session, and
when Congress came together for its regular sittings they added
to their tariff scheme a bill providing for an income tax, to meet
the probable deficiency in the revenue likely to result from the
reduction of import duties which they had proposed. The two
measures were made one. There was keen opposition in the East
to the adoption of the income tax, and though the composite
bill went through the House by a majority of sixty-four, many
Democrats voted against it, and party lines were again broken.
In the Senate, the tariff bill was changed beyond recognition by
more than six hundred amendments. Many of the *ad valorem*
duties proposed by Mr. Wilson's committee were made specific;
the Senate would not consent to put iron and lead ores or coal
upon the free list with wool; above all, it insisted upon an increase rather than a reduction of the duty on sugar. In the Committee of Conference, irreconcilable differences of opinion
emerged between the two Houses; a letter from Mr. Cleveland
to Mr. Wilson, supporting the plans of the House and severely
criticising those of the Senate, only stiffened a little more the
temper of the Senate conferees; and the House at last yielded,
rather than have no change at all in the tariff.

Mr. Cleveland did not sign the bill, but suffered it to become
law without his signature. It was not such a law as he wanted,
he said, nor such a law as fulfilled the pledges of the party;
but the party had accepted it, and he would not cast himself
loose from it in this critical matter by the use of his veto. No
one believed that the Senators who had insisted upon the chief
matter of contention, the change in the sugar duties, had acted as
Democrats. It was the universal opinion that they had acted as
the representatives of a particular vested interest. But in the
nice balance of parties which existed in the Senate they were
in a position to dictate. The party leaders in the House thought it
better to pass some measure of tariff reform than to suffer a total
miscarriage; and Mr. Cleveland tacitly consented to their judgment.

The Supreme Court completed the discomfiture of the party
by declaring the income tax law unconstitutional. Without
that tax there was not revenue enough to meet the expenditures of the government, as presently became evident. Deficiency of revenue, coupled with the obligation of the government to redeem its notes in gold on demand, cut into the gold
reserve, and the money question grew acute again. To maintain

the gold reserve the administration was obliged again and again to resort to the issue of bonds. The President was in league, the silver men said, with the bankers and the men who controlled the gold of the world everywhere. Mr. Carlisle earnestly urged a radical reform of the currency system: the repeal of the law compelling a constant reissue of the government's legal tender notes, and such legislation as would make provision for a sufficiently elastic currency by means of liberal changes in the banking laws. But his plans were not acted upon; the revenue did not increase; the government was obliged to pay out gold, upon demand, from its reserve; and there was nothing for it but to obtain gold of the bankers, and of those who had hoarded it, by issuing new bonds and increasing the interest charges of the government. The silver men grew every day more hostile to the administration.

The administration bulked very large the while, not only in the business world, but also in the field of foreign affairs. A treaty providing for the annexation of Hawaii was pending in the Senate when Mr. Cleveland came into office in March, 1893; but Mr. Cleveland promptly withdrew it, and, in characteristic fashion, set about finding out for himself the real situation of affairs in the islands. The outcome showed his transparent honesty and rare courage very plainly, if not his skill in a delicate affair. He found that it was the countenance and apparent assistance of the agent of the United States in Hawaii that had facilitated the dethronement of the Queen and the setting up of a revolutionary government, and he took steps to undo so far as possible the mischievous work of interference. The apologies of the United States were made to the Queen, and the provisional government was informed that the government of the United States would expect it to withdraw and make way for the reëstablishment of the legitimate government of the islands. But the provisional government refused to withdraw, and the President was obliged to submit the whole matter to Congress, without whose sanction he did not feel justified in employing force or in taking any further step in the unhappy affair. It seemed a lame ending, and the papers found it easy to scoff, though hard to say what other honorable course could have been taken; and every man who was not a Jingo perceived that the President had not in fact lost credit. He had simply followed his conscience without regard to applause or failure, and given one more proof of his unsophisticated character.

At any rate, everybody forgot Hawaii upon the emergence of Venezuela. Diplomatic relations had been suspended between

Great Britain and Venezuela because of a dispute regarding the boundary line between Venezuela and British Guiana, and Mr. Cleveland's administration had intervened, and had insisted that the whole question be submitted to arbitration. The position it took was based explicitly upon the Monroe Doctrine, and the course it proposed was virtually a demand that the United States be accorded the right of intervention in all questions arising between South American states and European powers. Lord Salisbury declined to make any such concession to the United States, or to submit any more of the question between Great Britain and Venezuela to arbitration than he had already expressed his willingness to submit to adjudication in his correspondence with the Venezuelan government; and Mr. Cleveland sent to Congress his startling message of December 17, 1895.

Here again he showed himself a strong man, but no diplomatist. It was like a blunt, candid, fearless man to say that it was the duty of the United States to ascertain for herself the just rights of Venezuela, and resist any encroachment upon her southern neighbor by every means in her power, and to add that he fully realized the consequences that might follow such a declaration of purpose. But only our kinsmen oversea would have yielded anything or sought peace by concession, after such words had been spoken. England presently showed that she would not have taken such a defiance from William of Germany; but good feeling, good temper, good sense, soon brought the two governments to a better understanding. Our commission of inquiry acted with the utmost sobriety and tact; Mr. Olney pursued his correspondence with Lord Salisbury with a strength of good manners, good reasoning, and disinterested purpose that carried its own assurance of victory; we had in Mr. Bayard a representative in London of an old and excellent school of behavior; and the end was a diplomatic triumph for the United States which attracted the attention of the world. The successful settlement of the particular question in controversy was even followed by a treaty of general arbitration between England and the United States, such as multitudes of peace-loving men had prayed for, but few had dared to hope to see. What had at first seemed to threaten to mar Mr. Cleveland's fame once and for all turned out in the end its greatest title to honorable dignity. We are at last enabled to read the famous message aright. There spoke a man as desirous and capable of peace and moderation as any in the nation, but accustomed, when he spoke at all, to speak his whole mind without reserve, and willing to speak to Europe, if she must hear, as freely as he would speak to his own people. It was the perilous indiscretion of a frank nature incapable of disguises.

The Cuban question has shown us the same man. He has satisfied neither the Democrats nor the Republicans, because neither cared to observe the restraints of international law or set themselves any bounds of prudence; but he has made Spain feel the pressure of our opinion and of our material interest in the Cuban struggle none the less, and by his very self-restraint has brought the sad business sensibly nearer to its end.

In this, as in other things, he has been a man without a party. His friends have been the silent men who watch public affairs without caring too much about the fortunes of parties. He has carried civil service reform to its completion at last; but that did not give him a party. To extend the rules of the classified merit service to all branches of the public business was a work of non-partisanship, and no man need expect a party following because of that. Mr. Cleveland did not do this work hurriedly. At the close of his first administration the friends of reform stood disappointed and not a little disheartened. But he has done the work in his own way and thoroughly, and no man need doubt his record now. He can look back with deep satisfaction upon the fact that while he directed the affairs of the government vast tracts of the public lands were reclaimed for the use of the people; that he was enabled to put system and a little economy into the management of the Pension Bureau; that more than one of the executive departments has received a complete reorganization at his hands; that he gave the country the businesslike administration he promised. None of these things, however, secures any man the support of a party. Mr. Cleveland never seemed so utterly without a party as in the extraordinary campaign which has made Mr. McKinley his successor. But it is the country's debt to him now that he thus stood alone. He forced the fight which drove the silver men to their final struggle for a party. They chose the Democratic party, because it was strong in the West where the silver ore was mined, and in the South and in all the agricultural areas of the continent where those business interests are weak which most sensitively feel the movements of the money market. They drove thousands of men out of the Democratic party when they took it,—Mr. Cleveland, their chief enemy, with the rest. And the Republicans routed them upon the issue which Mr. Cleveland had made definite and final.

We need not pretend to know what history shall say of Mr. Cleveland; we need not pretend that we can draw any common judgment of the man from the confused cries that now ring everywhere from friend and foe. We know only that he has played a great part; that his greatness is authenticated by the passion of love and of hatred he has stirred up; that no such great personality has appeared in our politics since Lincoln; and that, whether greater or less, his personality is his own, unique in all the varied history of our government. He has made policies and altered parties after the fashion of an earlier age in our history, and the men who assess his fame in the future will be no partisans, but men who love candor, courage, honesty, strength, unshaken capacity, and high purpose such as his.[1]

Printed in the *Atlantic Monthly*, LXXIX (March 1897), 289-300.
[1] The only manuscript survival of this essay is a WWhw outline entitled "Notes: Grover Cleveland," in WP, DLC. It is interesting that, although he listed Coxey's Army and the Pullman strike in his outline, Wilson did not mention them in his essay.

From Wilson's Diary for 1897

Saturday, January 16, 1897

Finished reading letters of John Adams to Benj. Rush, now in possession of Col. Alex. Biddle, of Phila. Printed, not published, 1892, press of Lippincott,—loaned me, on loan fr. Col. B., by L. C. Vanuxem.[1] A few letters of Jefferson's included. Adam's amazingly frank, whimsical, indiscreet.

Ellen very comfortable,—soreness very slight,—but still kept in bed, for precaution's sake.

Went to New York to consult Mr. James W. Alexander,[2] at his request, about situation in history dept.,—came to a very cordial understanding.

[1] See L. C. Vanuxem to WW, Jan. 7, 1897, n. 3.
[2] James Waddel Alexander, Class of 1860 at Princeton, a member of the Princeton Board of Trustees, and an old friend and warm supporter of Wilson.

Sunday, January 17, 1897

Ellen still in bed,—soreness continuing to decrease. Did not go to church this A.M. partly because of disinclination to leave Ellen,—partly because of laziness.

If the diary of a man of letters sh. be made a place for the memoranda of his work it wd. doubtless be a truer record of his life than if its entries were matter of fact. An itinerary of his mind might even more truly reflect his fortunes and encounters than any chronicle of events he could make. If he were indeed a man of letters, and could take the colour of his life and reading into his thought:—if he could give his thought its perfect image in words. His record would be the test of his genuineness and his quality. If it were a commonplace book, that wd. settle him: if it were a living and effectual utterance of himself, it wd. validate him. It were in any case an unnecessary risk,—a hazardous exposure of his workshop and materials.

To John Huston Finley

My dear Mr. Finley,   Princeton, New Jersey, 18 January, 1897.

Alas! it is not so easy to arrange.[1] I spend all of February in Baltimore, lecturing every day at the Johns Hopkins, and Illinois is out of the question. After I get back to my tasks here I am tied till June, revising a text book I was once indiscreet enough to publish.

I am sincerely sorry. The programme you outline is extremely attractive; and I esteem it a great compliment that you should want me. At present I am doing what I must, not what I wish.

I write in haste, lest I should be obliged to disappoint your Chicago friends too.

With warmest regards and renewed thanks,

Faithfully Yours,   Woodrow Wilson

WWTLS (A. Krock Papers, NjP).
[1] Finley's letter, to which this was a reply, is missing.

From Wilson's Diary for 1897

Wednesday, January 20, 1897

Spent the day in Phila: *morning*, interview with Dr. Craven on the Historical Dept. (in wh. he was very non-committal, tho' showing liberal sympathies); *lunch* at Uncle Tom's;[1] *afternoon* with the masseur, having my arm massered.

[1] The Rev. Dr. Thomas Alexander Hoyt.

Thursday, January 21, 1897

Morning, interview with [Andrew F.] West, in wh. he showed the most stubborn prejudice about introducing a Unitarian into the Faculty.

Evening, dined at Dr. Murray's with Theodore Roosevelt, who lectured after dinner in Alexander Hall on "An Object Lesson in Municipal Reform,"—the application of the principles of civil service reform to the make-up and discipline of the N.Y. police force.[1]

1 Roosevelt's speech, the first Spencer Trask Lecture of the year, was reported at some length in the *Daily Princetonian*, Jan. 22, 1897.

To Ellen Axson Wilson

906 McCulloh Street,[1] Baltimore, Md.,

My own darling,   [Jan. 28, 1897]

I hate to write to you this way;[2] but no doubt it is most prudent for the present, and to-day, as it happens, I have not time to work out an epistle with my left hand.

I had my massage and electricity in Philadelphia, and a pleasant lunch at uncle Tom's, as I expected, and reached Baltimore, in a driving snow storm, at five minutes after seven last evening. It took me till bed time to get my dinner, empty my trunk and case, and get settled in my quarters. The room is as pleasant as I anticipated, and I am going to be as comfortable as possible.

I spent this morning "doing the polite" as usual, that is, calling on Mr. Gilman, Dr. Adams, and the other men in the Department, and seeing about the arrangements for my lectures. It is the same as last year, the lectures are to be semi-public. Fortunately, the subject[3] is not of quite so general an interest as last year's, and the attendance will probably not much of it be from outside.

I think I shall call on Mrs. Bird[4] to-day (to-night), if only for the pleasure of talking about you. I dare not think about you very much yet, because the flood of loneliness is just now very deep above me; but in company I can keep within bounds. I love you with all my heart, and am altogether

Your own   Woodrow

A heartful of love to dear sister,[5] and to each of the others that I love.

WWTLS (WP, DLC).
1 The address of Mary Jane Ashton's boardinghouse, where Wilson was again staying while in Baltimore to lecture—for the last time, as it turned out—on administration at the Johns Hopkins.
2 He was typing this letter.
3 The nature, scope, and method of administration. The notes that Wilson used in 1897 are printed, along with an Editorial Note, at Jan. 26, 1891, Vol. 7.
4 Sarah Baxter (Mrs. William Edgeworth) Bird, of 22 East Mt. Vernon Place.
5 Annie Wilson Howe.

From Ellen Axson Wilson

My own darling,   Princeton, Jan. 28/97

I intended to write this afternoon so that my letter might leave tonight, but sister Annie was writing here, and with the noisy children in the dining-room, and the upstairs rooms all too cold, there seemed no convenient time or place. But it is just as well to begin once for all writing at night, since it is by far the most satisfactory time & the only one when I can be regular.

There is of course no news to give you yet. There is a howling storm of snow, almost a blizzard, which has lasted now for twenty-four hours; it is much colder than it was yesterday, but we are doing very well; nothing has frozen! though the second story *is* uninhabitable. I am feeling almost entirely well,—am taking my medecine! I ordered a hack and sent Margaret to her lesson,—and found that Mrs. Hinton[1] was sick and it was postponed! I am thoroughly provoked at this repeated, though doubtless unintentional discourtesy, and if it were not for disappointing the child would never send her again.

I enclose your letters in another envelope;[2] one or two perfectly trifling ones I answered myself. I began one to Mr. Hotchkiss but decided his was too personal to be answered in the third person. How very singular is the one from the clipping bureau! I didn't know you had been secretly indulging your vanity by collecting "notices"!

Sister Annie sends her love. Little Annie is doing finely. I am glad they happened to be here when you left; but oh! how I miss you, my own darling! Nothing can serve to soften very much the pang when you are absent. I love you, dear, with all my heart.

                                        Your own   Eileen.

ALS (WC, NjP).
[1] Mary E. (Mrs. Charles Howard) Hinton, of 42 Mercer St., who seems to have given piano lessons.
[2] These letters are all missing.

The *Nation*'s Review of *George Washington*[1]

                                        [Jan. 28, 1897]
George Washington. By Woodrow Wilson. Harper & Bros. 1896.

. . . Prof. Woodrow Wilson's 'George Washington' first appeared in the pages of a magazine. . . . It is to be judged as a literary essay rather than as a study of character, and the skilful use of well-known incidents, described in flowing periods, makes it suited for the reader who is to be amused or easily instructed in the main features of Washington's life. As such it would suffer under a critical analysis, for the material is not infrequently of doubtful origin, and the statements of fact are sometimes not beyond question. Who, for example, ever knew that George Washington was the uncle of Lund Washington? No genealogy, however experimental, has ever said this, but Mr. Wilson states it as a fact. In these pages we meet with the commonly accepted view of Washington. He is the model son, the splendid soldier, and the transcendent statesman. The sense of proportion is not well maintained, and too little attention is paid to his second term as President. If it was intended to give an account of the social forces and conditions that made Washington, the book is inadequate; and it is also inadequate as a description of the man. We are left in doubt whether Mr. Wilson began to write a history or a biography; and as he appears to have had both undertakings in his mind, it would be unjust to dwell upon the shortcomings of either. He has produced a very readable sketch, but it is not what was to have been looked for from his pen.

Printed in the New York *Nation*, LXIV (Jan. 28, 1897), 72-73.
1 The author of this review was probably Worthington Chauncey Ford.

To Ellen Axson Wilson

My own darling,   Baltimore, Md., 29 January, 1897.

This letter of Mr. Stewart's,[1] which Hibben has just sent me, is as astonishing and as startling as a bolt out of a clear sky, isn't it? It adds one more sure sign of the practical impossibility of securing the election of Turner. I shall not give up the fight; but I fear I see how it will end. Of one thing I am convinced: I must on no account make it a matter personal to myself. The more I think over that the more convinced I am that to do that would be both unmanly and futile. Do not, therefore, as you love me, my darling, breathe anything about my resigning to anybody but your intimates to whom you have already revealed your thought and feeling in the matter; and bind them to strictest confidence. Such things *must* not get current, either directly or indirectly. We will fight the fight out on its merits; lose, no doubt; and take the consequences quietly and as Providence may show us the way. I know I need not pledge you to that policy. My own mind is made up. It adds to my peace of mind and to my self-respect and cheerfulness that it should be so.

I find that I forgot a few little things, my sweetheart. I think I ought to have my syphon[2] here to guard against the possible discomforts of away-from-home diet; I want two or three of your visiting cards, to send to the Executive Mansion; and I want the black portfolio in which I usually carry my lectures to class. It is, I think, in the third drawer of the left-hand tier in my desk. Please ask Ed. to pack the syphon in a small wooden box to guard against breakage.

I had a delightful call at Mrs. Bird's last night,—spent the whole evening there, working off my loneliness and my exasperation *in re* the Stewart letter. I came home to bed in a very wholesome frame of mind.[3]

I *must* add my little love message in my own hand,—to do anything else would be too much like *kissing* you by machinery. Ah, my darling, it sometimes seems to me as if my *life* consisted in my love for you. It steadies and heartens me and elevates me all the while,—makes me conscious of a quiet heart and an assured peace,—is a sort of still joy, offsetting everything that disquiets or would otherwise dismay. I am what I am *because* I am

Your own   Woodrow

Unbounded love to the chicks, dear sister, dear little Annie, and the boys.

WWT and WWhwLS (WP, DLC).
[1] The letter is missing, but its author was almost certainly the Rev. Dr. George Black Stewart, a member of the Princeton Board of Trustees and of the Curriculum Committee of that body. For further hints as to the letter's contents, see EAW to WW, Jan. 31, 1897, and WW to EAW, Feb. 16, 1897.
[2] The tube that Wilson used to siphon out his stomach.
[3] Beginning with the next paragraph, Wilson began writing with his *right* hand and completed the letter in this fashion. It was the first time, with one known exception—when he wrote his letter of October 27, 1896, to Edward Dowden—that he had used his right hand so much since his small stroke of May 1896.

From Ellen Axson Wilson

My own darling,   Princeton, Jan. 29, 1897.

I was bored to find when I came down this morning that my letter to you was still on the mantel,—overlooked by the boys; I am afraid before it reaches you you will begin to think me very neglectful. Your dear letter has arrived and was,—you know how welcome.

We are all doing nicely. It is a beautiful, bright day, still very cold, but pleasant because the wind has died down. The children, even little Annie, were able to be out and were very happy after their long confinement. What a quaint little thing Annie is! Just now Sister A. was telling about a child's chair in a toy-shop which had a very sweet music-box under it. Annie, she said, sat down in it and it immediately began to play. Then a crowd at once gathered about them, which embarrassed Annie extremely. Whereupon *she* explained to us, "You see, I didn't want to be an amusing man"!

Two of the thirty vol. set have arrived;[1] they seem to be very satisfactory. They begin with Abelard and end with Bagehot. There is no lack of *variety,*—Aeschylus, for example, and Miss Alcott in the same volume! The paper and print are fine and the binding neat. I have not read much in them, however, because Sister Annie has been reading "Northanger Abbey"[2] aloud; and in the intervals I have been absorbed in "Sentimental Tommy."[3] It is *delightful*! such a charming mixture of humour and pathos— and *absurdities,*—odd unexpected turns,—that I shall be heartily sorry to finish it.

I am *so* glad my darling is comfortable and seems so cheerful! With a heart full to overflowing with devoted love—I am, dearest,

Your little wife, Eileen.

ALS (WC, NjP).

¹ Charles Dudley Warner *et al.* (eds.), *Library of the World's Best Literature, Ancient and Modern* (30 vols., New York, 1896-97). A large advertisement for this work appearing in the *Daily Princetonian*, Jan. 25, 1897, included the following endorsement by Wilson and Dean Murray: "Princeton, N.J., Jan. 23rd, 1897. This work is thoroughly worth examining and thoroughly worth subscribing for. I am glad to commend it." There is a printed subscription agreement for the purchase of a set of the *Library of the World's Best Literature*, signed by Wilson and dated Jan. 23, 1897, in WP, DLC.

² By Jane Austen.

³ The novel by James M. Barrie, which had just been published.

To Ellen Axson Wilson

My own darling, Baltimore, Md., 30 January, 1897.

Your first letter reached me this (Saturday) morning. It does not seem to have reached Baltimore till four this morning, or to have left Princeton till three in the afternoon on Friday. But it is here at last, and my anxiety is relieved. Having left you sick, I was made very uneasy by not hearing anything.

I shall not write to-morrow. I shall be in Hampton,[1] you know; and it will probably not be possible for me to write. But that will make no interruption of the regularity of my letters, for you will receive this one on Monday. I leave for Hampton this evening on the Bay boat; reach Old Point at six to-morrow morning; and ride thence (about two miles) to Hampton, on an electric car. I shall come back on the night boat to-morrow.

I suppose you have not noticed that the *Nation* of this week again sneers at me, mildly, in a short notice of "George Washington"?[2]

I am very well, and am getting on quite as comfortably as any reasonable man could or should demand; but somehow the homesickness grows on me intolerably just now. This week-end is on some accounts the worst of all the stay here. The taste of home is so recent on my palate: the taste of Baltimore so raw and new! I am obliged diligently to think about nothing in particular: at any rate about nothing personal to myself.

I have seen cousin Mary.[3] She looks well, for her, though she is working as hard as ever.[4] She is nicely lodged,—very nicely indeed. I learned one shocking piece of news from her. Grace Worthington is divorced from her husband.[5] He applied for the divorce; she would not defend the case; and he has married another woman, a professional nurse who once nursed him in their own house here. There is some scandal at the bottom of it all; but I can only infer what is [it] may be: I could not ask,— nothing that touches her good name, I judge, of course (I suppose he charged her with desertion or something of that kind), but some scandalous act or intention of his. But this is all surmise, and worse than idle.

I went to the theatre last night to see a musical farce that was really diverting, and made me forget my loneliness for a little space.[6]

And now, my Eileen, how shall I find a word in which to relieve my yearning a little, by bringing me for a moment into your presence and making me conscious of you? No word of my own will do that. Some word of yours must do it. The most I can hope for is that some sentence wrung from my heart will seem so to live when you read it that you will know for the moment how passionately I love you,—how my heart lives with you all the while when I am away. I feel as if it would almost end me to wring such a sentence from my heart now, though! I can only cry out, I love you! and re-dedicate myself to you as

Your own   Woodrow

Unbounded love to all.

WWT and WWhwLS (WP, DLC).

[1] To speak at Hampton Institute. His address is printed at Jan. 31, 1897.
[2] It is printed at Jan. 28, 1897.
[3] Ellen's first cousin, Mary Eloise Hoyt.
[4] Teaching English literature at the Bryn Mawr School in Baltimore.
[5] Thomas Kimber Worthington, lawyer of Baltimore, a fellow-student of Wilson's at the Johns Hopkins.
[6] Either "Lost, Strayed or Stolen," by Woodson Morse and J. Cheever Goodwin, playing at Nixon and Zimmerman's Academy, or "Miss Philadelphia" (no author given), playing at Ford's Opera House.

An Address at Hampton Institute

[[Jan. 31, 1897]]

LIBERTY.

Address delivered on Founder's Day,[1]
by Prof. Woodrow Wilson.

It ought to hearten a man to come and stand in this place. It ought to hearten him to return to his native state to see such an institution as this. I cannot help feeling, as a Virginian, that Virginia is honored in having Hampton planted on her soil. I cannot help feeling that Virginia is honored in having the name of Armstrong enrolled upon her roster of brave and honorable men, for Virginia has given birth to many heroic souls, and while she did not produce Armstrong, he too has consecrated her soil.

It would be presumptuous in me, who did not know General Armstrong, to speak about him to you who did know him. I could only speak of him as the world at large can—as of one of whom I had heard great and noble things, as of the man whose name is known wherever devotion and the heroic performance of duty are held in grateful memory, but not as of one whom I had been privileged to know personally.

I think the best way to present General Armstrong to you to-day, will be by doing what I may suppose General Armstrong himself would have done—by speaking to you simply and frankly about things I know something of. General Armstrong knew a great deal about an astonishing number of things, of which he spoke out in characteristic fashion. He seldom spoke of anything he did not directly know: he spoke always of what he had seen, whether with the eyes of his body or the eyes of his spirit. It behooves any one, therefore, who would honor him in speaking in this place to this audience, to speak only of such things as he has seen or experienced for himself. Therefore, I am going to speak, not of a man but of a theme; a theme commonplace enough in a way, but a theme that is difficult and complex; a theme that it behooves every man to think about again and again. I am going to speak to you about Liberty; because liberty is a thing most dear to us, but a thing we are sadly ignorant how to use; a thing we talk much about but, it is to be feared, very imperfectly understand.

It is not permitted a layman to preach a sermon, but the Bible

[1] Commemorating the birthday, January 30, of Samuel Chapman Armstrong, who founded Hampton Institute in Hampton, Va., in 1868.

is full of texts that would fit this afternoon's subject.[2] You know that in one place we are told that Jesus said: "Ye shall know the truth, and the truth shall make you free," and that later, Paul, in his letter to the Galatians, said, "Stand fast, therefore, in the liberty wherewith Christ has made you free; and be ye not entangled again with the yoke of bondage." You will see at the outset that there is something of a practical contradiction in the meaning of these texts. We indeed know, in a measure, the blessedness of the freedom that comes from knowing "the truth" that Christ came into the world to show us; and yet we know also as Paul did, that "the liberty wherewith Christ has made us free" is expressed in a life of service[.] Our Christian liberty is expressed in a life of obedience to the Captain of our Salvation: and is obedience your ordinary conception of liberty? Does the man in the ranks think the order of his general a sign of his liberty? And yet does not his freedom in fact consist in the fact that he knows how to obey orders? That makes him part of the army. Do you yourselves think of a life of service as consistent with freedom? And yet service is efficiency, and efficiency is freedom.

We see a man working with a tool—a man without skill in its use. The tool slips and cuts his finger. Was he not enslaved to the tool by his own lack of knowledge, or skill in the mastery of the tool? Learn to use your tools well and you are free.

I am free, as men say, to go to the top of yonder tower and throw myself to the ground. But after I am down—what? Am I then free? Does not nature say to me in the hot language of the injury I have sustained, "You fool, not to know that to throw yourself down there would be destruction. Learn my laws and you shall be free; free from physical pain, free from damage, free to use as you will the forces of my power." It is my knowledge of the laws of health that keeps me from disease. It is my knowledge of the laws of society that makes me a free man in society;— those laws which say to a man "You are put upon your honor; obey and you are free, obey not and you must stand without, an outcast, or a prisoner.["]

We go out on the water in a boat. When she skims before the wind, we say "She sails free." When she is thrown up into the wind and we see her canvas quiver, we say "She is in irons." What do we mean? We mean that when the boat defies the wind, the wind takes her prisoner; when she goes with the wind, the wind sets her free. We mean that her freedom lies in her cooperation with the forces of nature, in her obedience.

---

2 Wilson was speaking on a Sunday.

We say a skein of thread is free when it is disentangled, and every thread is set in perfect order. We say we are free, when (and this is what makes the real difference between man and beast) the spirit is at the helm and we have the perfect use and control of all our faculties. If the steersman knows not the course, the vessel shall be thrown upon the shore, however anxious he may be to guide her safe to port. It is the spirit's knowledge as well as intention that sets a man free. It is free when it has found its adjustment to the forces about it.

Most men read books for this purpose. Judging from my own experience, I feel that it is not normal for the natural, carnal man to sit down and read a book; it is only an incentive for broader living that leads him to do it. I read books of adventure because I am exceedingly fond of active, out-of-door, life of which I cannot get all that I would get, and which I would rather have by proxy than not [at] all[.] I read to liberate myself from my limited surroundings. I read books of science, because I want my mind to be set free from misconceptions to which I have been in bondage. I enlarge my life by annexing the territory other men have discovered: patch out my thought by adding theirs: make myself free to wander at large and with knowledge in the world of men and nature. We study and read in foreign languages that we may become familiar with the thoughts and customs of other lands, and in some measure become citizens of the world.

You should follow Emerson's advice, to "Hitch your wagon to a star." But you say, what did he mean by that? He only meant, go the way all the forces of nature are going and you will feel the pull of the universe. You shall then be free indeed.

It is said of us Americans that we are immoderately vain of our continent, and we are laughed at for always boasting of its size; just as it is said of our English brother that

> "In spite of all temptations
> To belong to other nations,
> He remains an Englishman.
> And its greatly to his credit!"[3]

As if he had anything to do with his being an Englishman, or we could have made this continent small and snug instead of huge, if we had wished. But is there anything so ridiculous about it after all? It cannot but be said that it is a credit to have subdued so much of this continent to our own use; a puny race could not have done that. We matched ourselves with the size of the

[3] Adapted by Wilson from W. S. Gilbert's lyrics for *H.M.S. Pinafore*.

continent: we have used it and have not let anybody else use or share its immense domain. Power comes with real possession. A man possesses, not that which he stands upon, but that which he uses. A man may have a great deal of money and may surround himself with books, but if he has no education and cannot read the books they are none of his. I might line the walls of my room with books; but, if I do not use them, I might as well have walls of plaster. It would be cheaper; and, if I knew about plaster and did not know about books, it would be more fitting.

Such thoughts put us in the way of understanding the liberty of races and peoples. Many have speculated about liberty, few have understood or possessed it. What is the liberty of society? The subjection of men to the right laws of society, and their adjustment one to another in the life of communities.

The freedom of a machine comes from the perfect adjustment of all its parts. When it runs as if there was no restraint it does so because restraint is in fact perfected by adjustment. If it were not so, if each part was allowed to work independently of all the rest, would the machine be free? There would be no machine, it would fly to pieces and every part would suffer its separate destruction.

So the strength of society consists in the perfect and easy adjustment of each man to his fellows. The search after freedom, is a search after the best adjustment. I do not say adjustment simply, for some adjustments—ill adjustments,—cause friction, and men begin to find they are not free. There is now a constant friction between Labor and Capital for example, so that it is said that "Capital runs free and without friction, but Labor does not." This friction becomes so great now and again that we fear conflagration, if the sparks should fall anywhere into combustible matter.

We can hardly say that the laborer is in slavery, because there is a specific legal meaning attached to that word. Yet it is true that the laborer has not full liberty; we have not yet rightly adjusted him to the other parts of our social machinery, so that his associations with Capital may always be harmonious.

Look the world over, and you shall find find [sic] that everywhere men are striving for this particular thing—the adjustment of privilege and power; in order, that while every man shall have privilege and some men power, power shall not crowd or kill privilege.

We have what is called a constitutional government. There never has been a government of course, that did not have a constitution. Some constitutions have been written down, some have not been written, but every government that has ever existed has had a constitution—a way of doing things. By a "constitutional" government we do not mean simply a government with a constitution. What do we mean? We mean a government in which there is a constitution of liberty.

England has the oldest written constitution of liberty,—none other than the Charter itself. When, for example the great document says in the 29th Article, "No freeman shall be taken, or imprisoned, or disseised, or outlawed, or banished, or in any way distroyed; not [nor] will we pass upon him, nor will we set upon him, unless by the lawful judgment of his peers, or by the law of the land," it is giving a definition of liberty, a statement of the way Englishmen shall be treated,—a definition of their relations with the government. Did this curtail King John's lawful power? Not a bit. But it did change his attitude and method of rule. When England's barons met King John and parleyed and made terms with him at Runnymede they said in effect:—"Come not beyond this covenanted line, and we will kneel at your feet; overstep it and we meet you with swords." This is adjustment between power and privilege, and such should it be when power of necessity is lodged in a few persons.

No government can get along without a constitution of liberty, written or implied; and notice that a constitution of liberty is expressed in negative and not positive terms. We might think that Belgium's constitution differed from this, because Belgium does say "There shall be liberty of the press.["] Very well, what is meant by that? Is she going to admit absolute freedom of the press? No, society cannot permit that. You have got to have the liberty of the press defined. You have got to have definite laws of libel and sedition. English law says, not that you can say what [you] please, but that you can say or print anything that twelve of your fellow countrymen impanelled in a jury, shall say is not outrageous. If you want to pay your price, you can say anything you please, but you must pay for it. The average jury respects and serves public opinion.

Our Bill of Rights is our Constitution, and in the first clause of the 14th Amendment it says, that no man shall be deprived of "life, liberty; or property, without due process of law." Can I not be deprived of my life by my country? Yes: by any due process of law. If I do something for which the state has affixed the penalty of death, can it not demand that my life shall pay the forfeit? If the government is at war and needs every man in her service, cannot she draft me for her service; must I not go even if it be unto death? There is not a drop of blood in my body that is not at the disposal of the government, or the community in which I live:—but I must be treated as every other man is under the same circumstances. The picking out of a man because of personal dislike, or ill-will is despotism. Liberty consists in adjustments that are equal.

Cannot the government take my property? Do we not know that our property can be taxed out of our possession by our government if need be? We insist only that every man's property shall be treated just as every other man's property is. The law must be impersonal, impartial. It must say that *every* man who does such and such things must suffer the penalty. Our liberty consists, not in the fact that we are unmolested, but in the circumstance that we are not exasperated. If a man breaks a law of the government under which he lives, he is not exasperated if he is arrested and put in prison. It may disgrace him; it may break his heart; but he does not feel angry at the government. He knows that he has brought the shame on himself. But if we had such a state of things that we would never know for what reason we might be picked out and cast into prison, then the heart would rebel. We would say this was not a crime until I did it; we might die, but we would not feel that we were disgraced.

Think of the time of the French Revolution in France. The people who could best afford to pay the taxes were exempt by the laws of the land from paying them, but the poor people were taxed beyond all measure. One class was put as a weight upon another class that did not have the same chance of development or life. There was on [no] adjustment here; no equal place of equity for all who were governed.

Do not some of the characteristics of liberty begin to show themselves in such examples? In a community where all men are not equal under the law, there is no liberty. There must be a right adjustment of individuals to one another, of classes to one another, and of the government to all. But this adjustment is infinitely difficult to make, and must be made anew from age to age. No man ought to be impatient to see it speedily effected. It must come from day to day. Any man who expects to bring the millenium by a sudden and violent effort at reform, is fit for the lunatic asylum. No man in his senses believes that these things can be done in a night. It takes infinite patience to learn a trade, or to read a book; it takes an infinite deal of patience to solve a simple problem, and this is not a simple problem. It exercises the minds of all men, because it includes the welfare of all men.

I have no patience with those who are offering a panacea that shall do away with all the ills,—misfortunes, sickness, sin,—a pill to stop an earthquake,—but I am willing to do my share, however infinitesimal, in bringing about this perfect adjustment.

John Stuart Mill complains because the world is not more hospitable to new ideas: that men will not soon tolerate any thing that is brought forward in opposition to the common faith. . . .[4] He deplores this state of affairs, shall we deplore it?

I remember a legend about a man who dreamed that he went into a great hall in a cavern under the earth. On a dais at the head of the hall there lay a horn and a sword. Arranged around the room were knights in armor, standing beside their horses ready too for battle, but all cast into some mysterious sleep. Suddenly a voice said to him "Choose between the horn and the sword and wake these men." He raised the horn and blew a lusty blast upon it. Instantly the cavern, men, and horses vanished; and again he heard the voice cry, mockingly now:

> "Cursed be the fool that ever he was born,
> Who did not take the sword before he took the horn."

And so today, some men think they can rouse the world by blowing the horn rather than by using the sword. But you must first take your swords, and do your fighting, and that before you and not behind.

I do not want to see the world like Athens, running about after every new thing. The ship must have ballast as well as sails, or else suffer shipwreck. I do not want new ideas coming into the world that are not worth fighting for. I don't want to be led by a poltroon. Many a man is willing to speak about a new idea quietly in a parlor who would not fight for it in public. The man for us to follow is the man who is willing to fight for his ideas.

Is not this the lesson of the life of Armstrong? Did he expect every heart to beat in unison with his? Did he not meet contradiction, opposition, discouragement, in making visible to the world the idea that possessed him?

But are you sorry for Armstrong because he didn't have an easy time? Can any body here find it in his heart to pity him? Do you pity the forces of nature because of their hard work. Do you pity the sun because it cannot get out of its ecliptic? It must be burning work for the sun to keep on sending its rays down on our earth, but you wouldn't dream of pitying it. The man who wants things easy, and expects [to] have his ideals realized without a struggle, might as well have been left out of the world. The

[4] Elision in the text.

man I pity is the man who has no disposition to struggle. Without earnestness and mind to struggle we lose the prize, and what one man loses another man gains. Conquest is the crown of his liberty. The only nobility is the nobility of achievement. Never a man met with success without sweat of the brow or spirit. Never a man achieved anything without a perfect knowledge of what he wanted to achieve.

> "Slight those who say, amidst their sickly health,
> Thou livest by rule. What doth not so but man?
> Houses are built by rule and commonwealths.
> Entice the trusty sun if that you can,
> From his ecliptic line, beckon the sky.
> Who lives by rule, then, keep good company.—["]⁵

Printed in the *Southern Workman and Hampton School Record*, xxvii (March 1897), 51-53.
⁵ In George Herbert, "The Church-Porch," from *The Temple*.

From Ellen Axson Wilson

My own darling,   Princeton, Jan. 31, 1897.

I wonder where you are today!—if that telegram carried you to New York or not.¹ I rather hope it did not, so convinced do I feel that it will in the end be trouble, fatigue and money wasted. Then again I can't help hoping that you *did* go and may perhaps turn up here on the 9.30 to spend the night. But I ought not to think for a moment of that; doubtless you will need this evening for your consultations in New York—if you are there! Mr. Stewart's letter was certainly a revelation. It made me want to say so many things that I concluded it would be best to say nothing at first—I mean in my letters to you.

But the conclusion it forces upon us is so perfectly plain that it would be folly even to rage over it; why should we kick against the pricks,—expend nervous energy—life power—in an utterly hopeless struggle. If the *liberal* (!) trustees can show such appalling ignorance and prejudice as is exhibited in that letter,— especially the latter part of it—what *must* be the mental state of the McCooks,² &c.? It seems to me that the progressive party in the faculty has been as blindly ignorant concerning one set of facts as the trustees are concerning almost every other set when it even dreamed that Princeton under its present management could become a University. Mr. Hibben says, and I agree with him, that we must consider the Sesqui-centennial a great misfortune; we can't hope to be anything but a respectable, old-fashioned Presbyterian college; before we were that simply and without pretence; now we have merely made ourselves ridiculous before the whole academic world by making big promises that we have neither the will nor the power to carry out.

I quite agree with you as to the programme you have decided upon, and you may be sure I shall not breathe a word about the matter to anyone. Mrs. Perry you know is the only one to whom I was ever so imprudent as to speak of it in any way and she promised long ago never to breathe a word of it. The Hibben's are the *only* people who have the least idea that we feel it may end in our leaving; and of course they are safe.

We are all doing nicely except little Jessie whose turn has come to have the cold. She has fever today but I don't apprehend anything serious. She does not seem to be suffering. Old Dr. McIlvaine died yesterday;[3] I have heard no particulars. Mrs. Peabody, wife of the elocution teacher, is also dead.[4]

I am glad you had a pleasant evening with the Birds. Is she well and cheerful? Was it really her brother who died?[5] Give my love to her and to all friends,–of course to Minnie[6] especially.

I love you my darling, my own Woodrow, ah, how tenderly, how passionately[,] how entirely I love you! You are the very life of me, and I am in every thought

Your own   Eileen.

ALS (WC, NjP).

[1] The telegram is missing, but this and other letters reveal that it was from Cyrus H. McCormick and asked Wilson to attend a conference in New York on the matter of the history appointments at Princeton. As WW to EAW, Feb. 1, 1897, and EAW to WW, Feb. 1, 1897, make clear, McCormick's first telegram was superseded by a second, asking Wilson to come to Philadelphia for the conference.

[2] John James McCook, a New York lawyer and member of the Princeton Board of Trustees.

[3] The Rev. Dr. Joshua Hall McIlvaine, President of Evelyn College in Princeton, who died, actually, on January 29. Evelyn College, which had been in severe financial straits, failed to survive the blow of McIlvaine's death and closed its doors at the end of the academic year.

[4] Mrs. Stephen George Peabody, wife of the Associate Professor of Elocution at Princeton from 1866 to 1881, died on January 29.

[5] Mrs. Bird's brother, Dr. John Springs Baxter, had died in Macon, Ga., on October 12, 1896.

[6] Mary Eloise Hoyt.

Agnes Repplier's Review of *Mere Literature*

[February 1897]

MERE LITERATURE, AND OTHER ESSAYS. By Woodrow Wilson. Houghton, Mifflin & Co., 12mo., $1.50.

. . . Mr. Woodrow Wilson has been singularly happy in the naming of his book. He has taken Professor's Seeley's contemptuous phrase, "mere literature," with its complacent and most un-humorous air of depreciation, and, inscribing it reverently upon his title-page, has challenged all the supercilious scholarship of Christendom to find a nobler source of inspiration. It warms our hearts, and sends the blood dancing in our veins, to read this spirited defence of literature. Alas! that literature should ever need defence.—"There are still some who think that to know her is better than a liberal education." There are still some who believe that ideals and not facts rule the world. There are still some who would rather read and love the "Ode on a Grecian Urn" than study the principle of the common pump. The pump, it is true, has many clients; the urn has very few; yet these few must keep alive "the secret thinking of humanity," which, embalmed in imperishable art, survives from generation to generation, our heritage of beauty and of joy.

With the delicate insight of a student, Mr. Wilson combines that liberal tolerance dear to the wise old world which has learned in the course of many centuries that few things are so dangerous or so beneficial as they seem. He has a good word for Jeffrey, whom it is much easier to abuse. He understands the art, the alchemy he calls it, by which Horace Walpole transmuted things temporary and trivial into permanent literature. He probes, as far as critic may, the passionate, inexplicable impulse which sent the great reading public swaying with one strange rebound from the realistic fiction it professed to love to the romantic fiction it professed to scorn. He gives us a sympathetic study of Edmund Burke which will be read thankfully by those who are a little out of patience with the disparaging praise dribbled out to-day by English writers who really seem afraid to face Burke's honest greatness. Above all, he writes with clear-sighted enthusiasm concerning a man too little known by hurrying readers in this hurrying age, Mr. Walter Bagehot, who carried away with him when he died, sighs Mr. Birrell sadly, "more originality of thought than is now to be found in the four Estates of the Realm."

Nothing can be nicer or more pointed than some of Mr. Wilson's definitions. If we are prepared to edge away from an essay ominously entitled "A Literary Politician," he lures us on to its perusal by happily explaining in the very first paragraph that he does not mean by this phrase the literary man who affects politics, nor, sadder still, the politician who affects literature, "who seems to appreciate the solemn moral purpose of Wordsworth's 'Happy Warrior,' and yet is opposed to ballot reform." We know both those types well, and have no great liking for either; though perhaps the literary man who, like Macaulay, handles public af-

fairs for years with an unbroken and Arcadian confidence in the in-
fallibility of Whig principles is less harassing, on the whole, than
the politician who afflicts us with exhaustive treatises on Homer
or Milton, and whose review of a new novel is accepted as incon-
trovertible, because he *is* a politican and no critic. What Mr.
Wilson does mean is something very different from these nineteenth-century Crichtons who grow more oppressive every year,
and he offers his explanation with admirable lucidity and grace.

"Occasionally," he says, "a man is born into the world whose
mission is to clarify the thought of his generation and to vivify it;
to give it speed where it is slow, vision where it is blind, balance
where it is out of poise, saving humor where it is dry—and such
a man was Walter Bagehot. When he wrote of history, he made
it seem human and probable; when he wrote of political economy,
he made it seem credible, entertaining; when he wrote criticism,
he wrote sense. You have in him a man who can jest to your
instruction; who will beguile you into being informed beyond
your wont, and wise beyond your birthright." . . .

Printed in the New York *Book Buyer*, XIV (Feb. 1897), 60-61.

To Ellen Axson Wilson

My own darling,   Baltimore, Md., 1 February, 1897.
I got back this morning at eleven, having been obliged to return by way of Washington because the Bay boats do not run
Sunday nights, and having been very slow in getting to Washington (by boat) because of the heavy ice in the Potomac. I
find a telegram from McCormick[1] awaiting me, urging me to
meet him in Philadelphia tonight. Consequence: the omission
of my lecture this afternoon, the breaking of a dinner engagement at President Gilman's where I was to play the part of
principal guest, and a hurried note to the person I love best in all
the world and would rather see at this moment than get my
way in all particulars at Princeton. Wo[e] be to Cyrus if his
business does not justify all this disturbance of good manners,
business, and love-making!

I had a very interesting time at Hampton: and I hope my
audience also had while I was speaking. I do not know when an
audience has so moved me. I had at the outset a little trouble
to command my voice. There is something pathetic in the whole
thing that is strangely moving. But I must discourse upon that
at another time.

I love you and long for you, my Eileen, more than any words

can tell: more than anything can express but a life-long proof, by devotion, that I am   Your own   Woodrow

I am quite well, and not too tired. Unbounded love to all.

WWTLS (WP, DLC).
¹ It is missing.

From Ellen Axson Wilson

My own darling,   Princeton Feb. 1, 1897

I was most uncommonly stupid to forget so entirely your engagement at Hampton, and so fancy that you might go to New York! I didn't remember it 'till another fifty word telegram came from Mr. McCormick last night to me this time,[1] asking for further information as to your movements and explaining his own in detail. I sent an answer by Ed, who found the office closed last night and never thought of the matter again until lunch today (so intent was his mind upon your examination.) Of course it was too late then to send it at all, and I was extremely provoked; but I *hope* it made no real difference; for you would receive his second telegram early this morning, and answer at once. I wonder if you are in Philadelphia now; if you went after your lecture I fear you will be tired to death when all is over.

The children are much better today; both Jessie and Nellie had rather high fever last night, Jessie 102°, Nellie 103°, yet today they have none at all and seem almost perfectly well. The rest of us are all right.

The furniture has come from Krespach's[2] and it is *lovely*; Mr. K. says it is a $125.00 set! The velour is exactly the right colour and looks beautiful on it; the room is perfectly transformed and leaves nothing to be desired, I think. And the leather armchair is a great addition to the library.

But I have been interrupted & must now close in haste. With love inexpressible   Your little wife,   Eileen.

ALS (WC, NjP).
¹ This telegram is missing.
² John R. Krespach, general upholsterer, 38 University Place, Princeton.

To Ellen Axson Wilson

My own darling,   Baltimore, Md., 2 February, 1897.

Here I am again, back from Philadelphia; but the rush is not over. I must be at the Babcock's[1] for luncheon at one o'clock, and it is now nearly twelve. I am all ready, and can have a little chat with you; and you need not fear that the rush is too much for me. I hate it, but I feel first rate, even in this wretched dull weather.

The interview with Cyrus was about "the situation," of course, and brought forth very little but a very candid talk and a very cordial understanding between Cyrus and me. He is *in fact* liberal; but I am afraid he cannot effect much from the distance of Chicago. He has, besides, as you know, a strongly developed business cautiousness which is likely to make the affair go too slowly for success.

If [Of] course I cannot detail the conversation in a letter; and it really brought forth only one new thing. Cyrus told me that Dr. Patton had expressed himself as sincerely desirous to get both Haskins and Turner; and willing to stand for that course if it could be carried through. He believed, however, that it would not be possible to elect Turner at once. He proposes that we elect Haskins now to a chair of European History (giving Turner the proper intimations that a chair of American History will be created for him when the *funds* are available (not less than a year from now) and electing him when it could be managed more quietly and with less observation than now.[)] Or, rather, that is the policy Cyrus himself drew out of Dr. Patton's conversation, as perhaps a practicable programme. I do not think it is. I believe, as I told Cyrus, that it will lose us both men. But we shall pretty certainly lose them anyhow; and I would rather try this than nothing at all; and of course there is a possibility that it might succeed.

I am in a perfectly calm frame of mind about the whole matter now at last, and can look at it with perfect dispassionateness. The interview last night did not even fatigue me, and disturbed my spirits not for a single moment.

What an infinite comfort it is, my Eileen, to have your cordial support in my attitude in the matter! Bless your heart! It would be hard to say which heartens me most, your love, your loyalty, your prudence, your practical intelligence,—or which of the perfections I love you for. You seem to me to have everything I most love and admire! You have as complete a balance of faculties as Washington had, at the same time that you are so much more interesting than he was,—have such a lot of delightfully diverting feminine qualities, and such a deep colour taken from the best books. I can't love or admire you enough. And, ah, it is such a comfort to have settled this matter now in hand with such simplicity and dignity. I feel almost as independent of anything the Trustees may do as if they were running another institution!

Need I tell you again that I love you, and that I am altogether

Your own   Woodrow

I enclose check, endorsed. Please deposit it to the general account and use it. I will send you some more at the end of the week. Unbounded love to all. Make sister stay as long as possible.

WWTLS (WP, DLC).

[1] The Rev. Dr. and Mrs. Maltbie Davenport Babcock. He was pastor of the Brown Memorial Presbyterian Church in Baltimore.

From Ellen Axson Wilson

My own darling,   Princeton, N. J. Feb. 2/97

I am glad to hear that you enjoyed your Va. trip; and very sorry that you had to rush off to Phila. immediately after it. How extremely awkward about the Gilman engagement! How *did* you get out of it? I am *very* sorry for you—especially as I don't believe anything will come of the Phila. trip. And yet you were almost obliged to go; you must have the consolation of feeling when it is all over that you left nothing undone that you could do with propriety. I hope at least that you have not had to make your journey in such a tremendous snow-storm as we are having here.

We are at present curious to know how the weather will affect Miss Josephine Walton's[1] plans, she having invited two young ladies to spend the day with me tomorrow! It is decreed by the same power that Sister Annie shall go to the Junction to meet them on the ten o'clock train, that they shall dine as well as lunch with us, leaving on the eight o'clock train, and that the boys shall devote the day to their amusement. George has been rather bitter on the subject because of the examinations, but Ed is more philosophical;—which is fortunate, as the whole duty seems likely to devolve on him, George being quite sick tonight with a feverish cold. We have just put him to bed here. The children, I am glad to report, seem quite well today; I am doing finely.

I have one very sad item of news, Mrs. Hinton is de[s]perately ill with pneumonia. Mrs. Haggerty,[2] the nurse, told Mrs. Perry yesterday that there was *no* hope; but today I sent to enquire & Mr. Hinton told Ed that she seemed to him much better, though the doctor had expressed no opinion. Oh, how I hope he is right! What would become of that helpless crowd?

It is indeed shocking about the Worthingtons;—and so strange too that *he* should be able to get the divorce and put her in the wrong, for of course his immediate marriage proves him the offender. Apparently she has sacrificed herself utterly in order to avoid an open scandal and to preserve some appearance of a good name for her poor children. But how would such a course affect her claim to her children? Did you learn if she had them or not? Write me what you hear about it.

A telegram has just been handed in from those girls saying they will put off their trip on account of the storm.

Your syphon and portfolio went today. I enclose with your letters the cards. The little letter is to you from Ellie Erwin.[3]

Sister Annie and all send dearest love;—as for me I love you so much that I despair of sending it; no "common carrier" is equal to the burden; even this strong and mighty wind, just now storming the house, would I fancy faint beneath the weight before it reached Baltimore! But I send all I can, and will keep the rest for you until your return.   Your own   Eileen.

ALS (WC, NjP).

[1] Later letters furnish the only information that the Editors have about her—that she was a writer of sorts and a friend of James Wilson Howe in New York.

[2] Emma Haggerty, of 6 Charlton St.

[3] Ellen Woodrow Erwin, daughter of Elizabeth Adams Erwin of Morganton, N. C., girlhood friend of Ellen Axson Wilson. Her letter is missing.

To Ellen Axson Wilson

My own darling,   Baltimore, Md., 3 February, 1897.

It makes me very uneasy that you should say nothing explicit about the soreness from which you were suffering. Does it persist, grow less, grow more, vary,—*what* does it do? You say simply that you are 'all right'; but I know by sad experience what a multitude of small ailments such phrases can conceal. You know how desperately uneasy that soreness makes me; and, if you do not wish to torture me, you will say something explicit about it in every letter till it passes utterly away. You must not forget what a keen pang such little doubts can add to my loneliness.

I have to speak at a Harvard dinner here next week, dear.[1] Will you not look in one of the drawers of that spool case in my den (I think it is the bottom drawer of the right-hand tier) and send me all the after-dinner-speech notes there collected, especially the notes of a speech I made to the Harvard men in Philadelphia a few years ago?[2]

Will you not ask Ed. to pay the enclosed bill, getting the necessary amount in an international postal order, and sending the order, along with this bill, to Stauffer at the proper address?[3]

I suppose of course sister saw the letter from Dickinson[4] which you sent me the other day? It seems to make it extremely unlikely she can get the loan from them. If she does not care to arrange a personal loan in Columbia, I will arrange to get the money from some individual after I get back. Of course there is no hurry now. The present loan holds till May.

I got another letter from Wilder this morning, sent direct to my address here.[5] It seems that he wanted to see me with reference to a dinner which a lot of the Seventy-nine men want to give in my honour at the Princeton Inn![6] We are now trying to find a date; for of course I could not give them the February date (the nineteenth) which Billy suggested.[7]

I was not as much fatigued as I expected to be by my recent rushing around; but I stayed at home last night, and took things very quietly, talking with two friends here at the boarding house. I am very well indeed.

I go to Wilmington, Del., to speak to-morrow night, you know.[8]

Ah, my love, I feel somehow as if it would specially tear my heart to try to put my love for you into words to-day. That love seems to lie specially deep just now, far deeper than any words can go. I was reading some of Browning's love poems to his wife yesterday,—but even they seemed to lack the note I would have appropriated. I love you from the depths of my nature—whence no words can come!   Your own   Woodrow

Thank Ed. for the package, which came this morning. Unbounded love to all.

WWT and WWhwLS (WP, DLC).
   [1] Wilson's notes for this talk are printed at Feb. 10, 1897.
   [2] The date of Wilson's earlier talk to the Harvard alumni of Philadelphia is unknown; however, undated WWT and WWhw notes for the speech are in WP, DLC.
   [3] Theodor Stauffer, book dealer, 24 Universitätstrasse, Leipzig.
   [4] The letter is missing, but it was probably from Samuel Dickinson of J. Dickinson & Co., mortgage brokers of Richmond, Ind.
   [5] This letter from William Royal Wilder, secretary of the Class of 1879 and a New York lawyer, is missing.
   [6] A newspaper report of this affair is printed at March 18, 1897.
   [7] Wilson had promised to speak to the Princeton alumni in Baltimore on February 19.
   [8] See the two news reports printed at Feb. 5, 1897.

From Ellen Axson Wilson

My own darling,   Princeton Feb. 3, 1897

Those girls turned up after all today; it had stopped snowing this morning and twenty minutes before train time came a telegram from Wilson [Howe] saying they had started for Princeton. Sister Annie met them and took them sleigh-riding about the town. George was still in bed, but their arrival seemed to revive him; he is now up and out with the rest; the whole crowd including little Annie are now out sight-seeing. I hasten to take advantage of the quiet to scribble to you, for fear I shall not have the chance tonight; for Margaret now is quite sick with fever & cold and may need me all the evening. She seemed quite well when she went to bed but had a bad night, and her temperature has been 103° most of the day; she is in bed & has been sleeping a large part of the day. I have not yet sent for the doctor, hoping the regular treatment—the two pills,—may conquer it by tomorrow.

I am extremely glad, darling, that you still feel in such good form after all your running about,—and am equally glad that your spirits are good. It was certainly worth while to see McCormick. It must have been a comfort to find *one* trustee *actively* interested and alive to its importance. He showed a very praise-worthy determination to see you too!

But Margaret needs me & I must go. Your sweet words of praise make me feel very humble, my darling, but I comfort myself with thinking that at least you cannot overestimate my love and loyalty.   Your own   Eileen.

Don't put off or neglect the *massage.*

ALS (WC, NjP).

To Ellen Axson Wilson

My own darling,   Baltimore, Md., 4 February, 1897.

I go to Wilmington this afternoon at ten minutes after three, to lecture before the "New Century Club." I shall not get back, of course, until to-morrow morning, probably about half past ten.

I suppose you interpreted the receipt for fifty dollars sent me from Hampton, without much trouble?[1] Mr. Ogden,[2] the President of the Board of Trustees, tried to make me take fifty dollars for my address; but I knew that the School had to raise seventy-five thousand dollars every year to meet its necessary expenses, and I should have thought shame upon myself had I taken even my travelling expenses. I insisted that he turn the check intended to be mine over to the School treasury. I did not feel that it was in the least an act of generosity. The money would have burned a hole in my pocket. I am only explaining to you what may possibly have puzzled you a little bit.

Yes: Grace Worthington kept the children, and is living in Philadelphia. Had she taken the least step to defend the suit brought by Tom. for divorce, she could have defeated it outright. But she absolutely refused to take any steps at all, saying that if Tom. wanted to get rid of her she would do nothing to prevent him. I suppose it was tacitly (for all I know, expressly) agreed that she should keep the children. A fellow doing what Tom. was doing would not be anxious to be hampered by his rightful wife's children. But perhaps we should wait to know all before judging what seems so obvious a case even!

Nothing happens. I have nothing to do but think how lonely I am; and how little worth while what I am doing seems to be,— delivering lectures intended for a class of graduate students to a mixed audience, and unconsciously (not altogether unconsciously, either) spoiling, diluting, confusing the matter by popularizing it, and making little episodes of talk and anecdote as I go. Nothing could be (at any rate, I can hardly imagine anything calculated to be) more thoroughly unsatisfactory to the students and to me, or more confounding to outsiders! I sincerely hope this is the last year of it!

My one antidote against all ills and discouragements is my love for you. I should feel so absolutely *naught* without you,—so without weight or significance! I caught all the little moral force I have by a sort of contagion from you,—and all the atmosphere that makes my writing seem literary and gives it a momentary charm. Divorced from you, I should be nothing,—you would keep not only the children, but all my capital stock and character of every sort. I am not blue: this is one of my sane hours, when I can see without vanity or prepossession,—and can know what it means that I am   Your own   Woodrow

Unbounded love to all. When is Miss Walton to descend on you now? Is she coming to see the home life she is to describe in her biography of us?[3]

WWT and WWhwLS (WP, DLC).
[1] The receipt from Hampton Normal and Agricultural Institute, dated Feb. 1, 1897, is in WP, DLC.
[2] Robert Curtis Ogden, New York merchant, president of the Board of Trustees of Hampton Institute, 1894-1913.
[3] The Editors have been unable to find any published writings by Miss Walton.

From Ellen Axson Wilson

My own darling,   Princeton   Thursday [Feb. 4, 1897]

I *have* rather evaded the subject of that "soreness" because there was nothing in particular to say; until yesterday there was really no change since you went away. But it was better last night and tonight it really is scarcely to be found even by searching. I went out today for the first time in three weeks and it brightened me up immensely; it was a perfect day, mild and still and dazzlingly bright. I stopped in to see how Mrs. Brown[1] was,— you know she was quite ill when you left, but is about as usual now. I was just about to leave when Mr. de Vries[2] was announced, and she made me stay to be introduced. I only staid a few moments so could form no general impression, but he was very agreeable, extremely smiling and amiable but producing no impression of insincerity. They arrived yesterday. After some little conversation about their moving, reception, &c. Mrs. Brown began immediately upon her grievances anent his predecessor,[3] which frightened me promptly away, though I said I was,—and *was*—afraid to be out after the sun was low. Too bad that she should show such bad taste, and make things so awkward for him too!

Margaret is better today, though the fever is still not broken— temp. today was 101°. You will be glad to hear that Mrs. Hinton is thought to be decidedly better.

But I have spent the evening in a very long and tiresome because unsuccessful search for a receipt and have no time left for a real letter. It is the receipt for the taxes that were paid in Nov.,— I found the one for the *borough* taxes that I paid in July. What shall I do about it? Of course you can't tell me where it is,—indeed I have looked everywhere. The enclosed circular[4] explains the need of it. With dearest love,

Your devoted little wife,   Eileen.

ALS (WP, DLC).
[1] Susan Dod Brown, of 65 Stockton St.
[2] The Rev. John Hendrik De Vries, new minister at the Second Presbyterian Church.
[3] The Rev. Chalmers Martin, Instructor in Old Testament at Princeton Theological Seminary, Instructor in Hebrew at Princeton University, and Stated Supply at the Second Presbyterian Church, 1896-97.
[4] The enclosure is missing.

Two Newspaper Reports of an Address in Wilmington, Delaware

[Feb. 5, 1897]

PROF. WILSON ON "LIBERTY."

Entertaining Address Before the New-Century Club Last Evening.

The large audience that was privileged to listen to Professor Woodrow Wilson's lecture upon the theme of "Liberty" at the

New-Century Club last evening at eight o'clock, enjoyed a rare treat. The distinguished speaker was most charmingly introduced by Miss Mather,[1] president of the New-Century Club, and for an hour entertained his audience with an analysis of individual liberty.

"Liberty," said Professor Wilson, "calls up centuries of history. It is the keynote of politics, story, romance, adventure and heroism and even of infamy, for under misguided judgment men have shed blood and done deeds of violence in the name of liberty. The people who have deliberately desired liberty have enjoyed it the least and those who have enjoyed it most, as for instance the Anglo-Saxon race, have never sought for any abstract thing in any definite shape, and the ideas of liberty, of which we are proud to boast, we get not from the English, but from the French.

"The more we try to analyize [analyze] liberty the less we enjoy it; to seek an ideal state is to be constantly disappointed, and so, being a practical race, we should look at the subject in a practical way and try to realize a condition of things that is good to live by now and that will materialize before the millennium. Seek a practicable freedom, such as we believe we can attain to.

"One of the most potent elements in liberty consists of the institutions under which we live and not in the ways of doing things. To speak of families and pertinent institutions in order to illustrate the idea more fully, let us consider the institution of 5 o'clock tea, in which women habitually indulge, and the dress-coat with the two military buttons surviving their former significance; these were not evolved in a deliberate manner, but are simply habitual customs, whose origins no one has cared to fathom. The manners of society are the habitual ways prescribed to govern man's intercourse with his fellow-creatures. We speak of the ease of a man's manner, by which we do not in any sense mean the freedom of his manners, for the best-mannered man is the best-trained man, the one whose every move is adjusted to the rigorous demands of society. No one can imagine a perfectly natural man in society. A man uses a rifle skillfully, but is it the free hand or the one trained with the most sensitive schooling of the muscles that strikes the mark? Freedom does not mean isolation or a cutting loose from society when men become the slaves of their passions, but the freest man is he who is master of his passions. Perfect freedom is perfect self-mastery, a perfect adjusting of all the faculties and a co-operation with nature. If you have tried to drive two colts in double harness for the first time you have found that they do not co-operate to any extent and not until they are trained to yield to the restraint and help of the harness are they acceptable to their master; just so in society, its individual members must work with co-operation and not antagonism. Even though it is inconvenient crowding in society no one would wish to change places with Robinson Crusoe.

"Men speak of society as a necessary evil; that is because they have never given it one competent thought. It is rather a beneficent necessity. What differentiates man from the lower animals is the power of his spiritual development, and it is that that gives him a full and perfect manhood and makes him [in] the highest sense a man. In order that the spiritual nature of man may be developed, the eight-hour system is advocated for the working class so that those who do the manual labor of the world may not degenerate into mere beasts of burden, but may find some leisure for the development of their minds, and have their spiritual eyes opened. The love of books is not inherent except in rare cases, and the reason that most men read a book is because of the ambition to do everything anybody else does, and to have a share in all the affairs and interests which engross society in general. Book-worms rarely get anything out of books but dry facts in their head and the stiffness of the bindings in their lives.

"Society does much for us. It even authenticates our very existence by requiring a birth register to be kept. Society attends to the needs of sanitation and protects you from neglect on the part of your neighbor. It protects you in your rights to hold property and helps you make the possessions you acquire assured to you. Whether there is a natural right to hold property, an unrestricted individual right or not, if by the act of acquiring it, unlimited energy even though in a selfish purpose has been stimulated; let every man keep all he can get by his labor or his wits. Men acquire wealth for the power it brings: a million dollars in money is a million dollars' worth of power in the assemblage of their fellow-men.[2] Society assists even in the little affairs that take men's thoughts."

Printed in the Wilmington, Del., *Morning News*, Feb. 5, 1897.
[1] Mary H. Askew Mather, prominent in the social and civic affairs of Wilmington, and president of the New-Century Club from 1896 to 1898.
[2] Wilson would revive and expand this idea in "When a Man Comes to Himself," printed at Nov. 1, 1899, Vol. 11.

[Feb. 5, 1897]

NEW-CENTURY CLUB.

. . . In his lecture last evening on "Liberty," Mr. Woodrow Wilson proved by many witty illustrations and logical arguments that liberty can be enjoyed only by the apparent sacrifice of itself, or through obedience to law, human and divine. We cannot enjoy perfect freedom, only practical freedom. In society the man who has ease and freedom of manners is the well-bred man, the one who is thoroughly trained to obedience to society's laws. Heaven forbid that we should let a perfectly free, natural man loose in a dining-room. He who follows all his desires is not a free man, he is a slave to his passions, and is not free until he has become his own master.

Freedom comes not by isolation, but consists in co-operative adjustment. One must give up some of his liberty to be a member of society, but he cannot develop into what he would be except by what he gets from other men. Make a catalogue of what society does for you. It begins by registering your birth; otherwise you cannot even tell how old you are. It takes care of your health and your property. Do you claim that man has a natural right to property? Where would such right stop? He might have a natural right to a piece of property as long as he sat on it with a shot gun, or until two men with two shot guns claimed it. We want property we can go to sleep on; that we can go away from and come back and find still our own. A man who is worth a million cannot use it all unless he uses it for expense, regardless of pleasure, but he wants to be assured in its possession. He wants property because it means power; the most powerful man is the freest, the most helpless is a slave. We claim that our free government gives us liberty of speech; but have we absolute liberty of speech? Isn't there a law against libel? After all, we can only say the thing that 12 of our countrymen think we ought to be allowed to say.

Foreign critics laugh because we boast of the size of our continent, but our boast is of a conquered continent, reduced to our service because we know how to make nature co-operate with us. By putting our ear to the keyhole where she holds council we forced her to serve us by our obedience to her laws. If we had not made modern inventions how could we have used our continent? Even the eastern coast would have been too large to manage if steam and electricity had not lent us swift wings.

A constitutional government is one that, like nature, finds the line of least resistance for each individual, and allows the largest liberty consistent with good order. The Anglo-Saxon race has always stood for the present enjoyment of national and political liberty, but a Frenchman, Montesquieu, had to tell it what liberty meant. Yet his nation, that drank the deepest of the wine of liberty, went mad, because it had no thought of obedience, only of breaking its trammels.

Printed in the Wilmington, Del., *Every Evening*, Feb. 5, 1897.

To Ellen Axson Wilson

My own darling,   Baltimore, Md., 5 February, 1897.

I got back from Wilmington less than an hour ago. The lecture (on "Liberty," after all) was, it seemed, a decided hit; I stayed with delightful people; and had as pleasant a time as it is possible to have on a lecture trip. Of course the Wilmington people are more like southerners than like northerners, and one comes away from them feeling the warmth of their cordiality. This is the last trip away for me, so far as I can see, till I come to you on the twentieth, to speak at Lawrenceville on the twenty-second.[1] How jolly that the twenty-second should fall on a Monday! I need not start for Baltimore until Tuesday the twenty-third, and can be with you three nights!

It makes me desperately uneasy to think that you have to take care of the little patients in the next room through these chill nights in your present condition, my darling. Do you,—can you,—escape chill; and does it affect that soreness? I tremble to think what might happen should you yourself get a heavy cold, and give it a chance to descend to the sore part! You have told me not a word about your own condition yet that was explicit. Have you escaped heavy colds yourself? Do you take full precautions to protect yourself? You *must*, Eileen, obtain such help in the nursing as will shield yourself. If you wreck yourself my career is over, my heart broken. Do, please, tell me something,—everything!

I think the Walton-girl episode as deep a piece of cheek as ever I heard of. Has the woman lost her head and forgotten her breeding altogether? I hope you got at least a wee bit of amusement out of the performance!

I am very well, though tired. My lecture is the only engagement I have waiting me here to-day, and I shall take things quietly and get thoroughly rested. Nothing would rest me quite so much or so quickly as a moment with you! The principal source of my fatigue is anxiety about you and the chickens. To be away when you, as well as they, need to be taken care of, keeps my mind upon the rack, and tells on me keenly before the day is over. I love you, my sweetheart, my queen! I would give my life for you,—I *will* give my life for you, and always and in everything be   Your own   Woodrow

A heartful of love to all.

WWT and WWhwLS (WP, DLC).
    [1] Wilson gave his address, "Liberty," as a patriotic oration at the Lawrenceville School on February 22, 1897. *Lawrenceville School . . . Register 1896-1897* (Philadelphia, n.d.), p. 3. Neither the Trenton nor Princeton newspapers nor the school newspaper, *The Lawrence,* reported on this affair.

Four Letters from Ellen Axson Wilson

My own darling,   Princeton, Feb. 5 1897
    Yes, I understood perfectly about the receipt from Hampton. Of course you could not possibly have kept it. I had no idea any money was to be offered.

    Did you get Mr. Pyle's invitation before you left Baltimore. Which of these numerous invitations did you accept for the night? Did you remember that you had me excuse you to the first comers,—the Rodneys,—on the plea that you were obliged to return to Balt. that same night? Perhaps courtesy requires that you write a few words of explanation to them;—though of course I am in the dark as to the circumstances of the case.

    Margaret is a great deal better today,—the rest of us are well except that Sister Annie has a headache. It is another perfect day and I am about to go out again while the sun is high.

    I hope you are having good weather there, and that nothing else prevents your walking, so that you can have plenty of fresh air. I am disposed to think you *were* blue when this last letter was written, your assurances to the contrary notwithstanding. I am so sorry, my darling; and oh how I wish I were there! I hope that when you are feeling so especially *lonely* you will as often as possible escape from it by at least ceasing to be *alone*. Go to see some of those bright women or Mr. Babcock. The women especially by their appreciation of you ought to reassure you as to your "weight and significance." That reminds me that "The Bookbuyer" has a rather nice little review of your essays by Agnes Repplier.[1]

    I am distressed that the arrangement as to your lectures is so disagreeable to you. I would wager anything however that you are the only person who finds them unsatisfactory. I would talk it over with Gilman or Adams & either get your doubts as to their success removed or insist upon a change.

You say nothing about the massage, darling. I am *so* afraid you are neglecting it. *Please* have it done every other day at least; now while you are in Balt. is, you know, your *only* chance to have it done both systematically and scientifically. Miss Ward's bill was only $10.00.[2] But I am writing too long; I ought to be out if I am going.

I love you, darling, with absolute faith and devotion;—and my pride in you is as great as my love. Always and altogether.

Your own   Eileen.

[1] It is printed at Feb. 1, 1897.
[2] Jessie M. Ward, masseuse of Philadelphia. There is a receipted bill in WP, DLC, for $10.45 indicating that Ellen visited Miss Ward five times during December 1896 and January 1897.

My own darling,   Princeton, Feb. 7 [8], 1897

Though you *have* left only today[1] I know you will want me to write a few lines to tell you how the children are tonight. Jessie's temp. and Annie's were 101°, Margaret's 100°, and Nellie had no fever at all. Yet strange to say she seemed the most miserable of the four,—stomach ache and general prostration. The doctor had told me to give them cascara; and the dose made her frightfully ill,—poor little soul. She lost it, and it is quite out of the question to give her anything in its place, she is still so sick. The doctor said the trouble began with cold and that now they were just "run down." He ordered me to stop both sorts of pills and go back to the old powders. The children have seemed brighter all day but have been languid again this evening. I feel *quite* well.

I enclose in another envelope the proof of your Hampton speech.[2] I *hope* you won't let them persuade you to allow them to print any part of your regular lecture on "Liberty" in any form that would embarrass you in repeating it hereafter as a lecture! Can you not tell them you don't wish it printed *at all*?

Ah darling, how can I tell you how I enjoyed yesterday—and every moment of your stay? It is *impossible* to tell you,—therefore I am glad indeed that it is unnecessary; that you *know* what a comfort & delight your coming was, and how entirely I love you & am   Your own   Eileen.

[1] Wilson had come to Princeton, probably during the evening of Friday, February 5, and had stayed until Monday, February 8.
[2] Printed at Jan. 31, 1897.

My darling,   [Princeton, N.J.] Tuesday morning [Feb. 9, 1897]

The enclosed telegrams have just been received.[1] Sister Annie and I decided that you of course would not think of accepting as there was nothing whatever attractive in the prospect to pay for the trouble and interruption, and that I might safely decline for you. So I sent a telegram by the messenger boy to that effect. But just as I was signing my name to it, it occurred to me that there was a *bare* possibility that you might choose to accept for motives of policy connected with your fight for Turner;–that at any rate, I had best not decide the matter finally. I do hope you won't feel called upon to go though. This is the telegram I sent,– "Regret Prof. Wilson's absence from home now and until after fifteenth renders his acceptance impossible. Will forward telegram however."   In haste & love   Eileen.

ALS (WC, NjP).
    1 These telegrams are missing. One of them—the one to which Ellen soon refers—was undoubtedly an invitation to speak at the annual banquet of the Princeton Club of New York.

My own darling,   Princeton, Feb. 8 [9] 1897

I can only write a few hurried lines because I need to be up-stairs with Nellie. She has had a very sick day—great pain in her stomach & frequent vomiting. As our remedies failed and it seemed to increase I sent for the doctor tonight. He has just left; he says there is nothing to be anxious about; the cold has simply upset her stomach. I am to give her twenty drops of paregoric every half hour until she is relieved. The first dose seems to have already quieted her a little. I had already given it to her once today.

The other two seem quite bright even now after night-fall; they have very low fever 99½° and 100½°. I am perfectly well— no soreness at all. We had a very good night. But I must stop, dearest,—and not stay away from the nursery while poor little Nell is suffering. I love you with all my heart and soul and mind.

                    Your devoted little wife   Eileen.

ALS (WP, DLC).

To Ellen Axson Wilson

My own darling,   Baltimore, Md., 9 February, 1897.

Here I am again, settled down as if nothing had happened; and yet knowing, by the singing of my heart, that something has happened, and settling down in a humour that would have been impossible had I not renewed my strength by having been, only yesterday, in your arms. I am feeling very well; not a bit too tired; and renewed in spirits in a degree that cannot be measured!

There is no tonic for a weary (a heart weary) fellow like looking into the depths of your eyes when they are on fire with that wonderful love you have given him as a great gratuity.

Of course there is nothing to tell. I have no sick household, and no sore spot to report upon. I have only a routine of letter writing, the reading of examination papers, and the delivery of lectures. The only bit of news is distasteful: I have now to accept the invitation of the *Yale* Alumni to attend *their* banquet, to be given next Tuesday, the 16th.[1] By the way, Wilder now proposes March twelfth as the date of 'Seventy-nine's dinner to Tommy Wilson. I have accepted the date. I wish you would think of proper things for me to say on that embarrassing occasion, against my coming back.

Ah, my precious Eileen, how I love you: how infinitely happy your love makes me: how glad I am I went home and found out all over again the full delight of being

Your own   Woodrow

Love to all.

WWTLS (WP, DLC).
[1] Wilson's notes for this talk are printed at Feb. 16, 1897.

From the Minutes of the Princeton Faculty

5 5′ P.M., Wednesday, February 10th, 1897.
. . . Resolved, That the matter of the Eating Clubs be referred to the Committee on Discipline. . . .[1]

[1] For the committee's report, see the Princeton Faculty Minutes printed at March 24 and 31, 1897.

To Robert Means Davis[1]

My dear Professor Davis,   Baltimore, Md., 10 February, 1897.

You inadvertently addressed your letter of January first[2] to me at Princeton, *Pensylvania*: it consequently went a journey, and did not reach Princeton, New Jersey, till the other day, when I had come away to deliver my annual course of lectures here at the Johns Hopkins. I have it at last, however, and hasten to assure you that I have not been overlooking or neglecting it.

I wish very much that I could undertake the work you suggest. I have long had the matter in mind. I realize very keenly the unfairness to the South, the unveracity as history, of the existing text books, and I fear, as you do, the preparation and use of some partisan work on the other side. I have frequently been urged to write the book that is needed,[3] and such assurances as yours of your belief in my ability to write it hearten me more than I can say. But the truth of the matter is, that I am in the midst of other tasks which render the undertaking for the present impossible. I am in the midst of writing a history of the United States, indeed; but the history I am writing is upon the scale, and is being attempted in the method, of Green's "Short History of the English People."[4] It will cover much more than the political history of the country; its range covers all the colonial period; and I do not see how I can possibly finish it within less than six years.

By that time it may be too late to write the text book we want; but only by that time shall I be fully prepared to write it. My literary plans cover another big piece of work, in the study of politics,[5] for which the history I have referred to is, in a sense, a preliminary study; and it may be that the text book would in any case be crowded out. I feel that I have already turned aside too often to write occasional books. I do not want again to admit any serious interruption to my history; and I know that to stop now to write the book you suggest would involve very much more of an interruption than would be represented by the time it would take to write the smaller book.

I have troubled you with this full and confidential explanation and answer in order that you may see my deep interest in the subject of your letter and also the real reason why I do not feel that I can act upon a suggestion which I should, if free, be so glad to accept.

I have been much grieved to hear of Professor Le Conte's illness since his return home. I trust he is much better. We felt it a privilege to have him at Princeton.[6]

With much regard,

Most sincerely Yours,   Woodrow Wilson

WWTLS (R. M. Davis Papers, ScU).
[1] Professor of History and Political Economy at South Carolina College.
[2] It is missing.
[3] See, e.g., John Irenaeus McCain to WW, April 29, 1893, Vol. 8.
[4] See the Editorial Note, "Wilson's 'Short History of the United States,' " Vol. 8.
[5] His projected magnum opus, "The Philosophy of Politics," about which see the Editorial Note, "Wilson's First Treatise on Democratic Government," Vol. 5.
[6] The eminent geologist, Joseph LeConte, who had represented the University of California at the Sesquicentennial Celebration. LeConte had left South Carolina College to go to California in 1869.

To Mary Gresham Machen[1]

My dear Mrs. Machen,   Balto. 10 Feb'y, 1897

I am sincerely obliged to you for your kind invitation to dine with you on Saturday evening next, and accept with pleasure. I am the more complimented because of the anniversary character of the occasion. It is like being admitted in a very real sense to your family circle,—and I appreciate it accordingly.

With warmest regard,

Sincerely Yours,   Woodrow Wilson[2]

ALS (in possession of Arthur Webster Machen, Jr.)

[1] Mrs. Arthur Webster Machen, of 217 West Monument St. Wilson had been a frequent visitor in the Machen household since his graduate school days at the Hopkins.

[2] Wilson wrote this and the following letter with his right hand. They seem to have been the first letters that he wrote completely with his right hand following his small stroke in May 1896, except for his letter of October 27, 1896, to Edward Dowden.

To Ellen Axson Wilson

My own darling,   Balto., Md., 10 Feb'y, 1897

I must content my-self with a line or two with my pen to-day. Hammering out one or two long letters on the type-writer (e.g. to Prof. Davis of S. C.) has tired my left arm and made my left shoulder *hot*, in a way that warns me to beware and stop.

I am well,—have taken steps to have massage at once,—and am about to prepare for the Harvard men to-night. I have declined the N. Y. invitation.

Bless you for your prompt letter, darling, and for all your love! I am every moment more than ever

Your own   Woodrow

Love unmeasured, unstinted to all.

ALS (WP, DLC).

From Ellen Axson Wilson

My own darling,   Princeton, Feb. 10, 1897

I have just been doing what I suppose I should have done while you were here viz looking over the bills and check-book and seeing more particularly how we stand. You left $53.00 in bank, I deposited $89.00 making $142.00. I have paid Wanamakers, the servants, the German book-bill, the masseur and one or two little bills, and drawn a few dollars for the la[u]ndress &c., and now there is only $29.50 left in the bank, and the coal has not come yet! That and the water, $20.00, are the only bills left unpaid just now.

We had a very good night, and Nellie is much better today, not suffering at all,—since early morning,—though of course very weak and languid. Margaret seems rather the most miserable of the three today; she has a very bad looking tongue, and her ear is troubling her a little again. Jessie seems to feel quite well and so does little Annie. Sister Annie has caught a heavy cold now, but insists she must go tomorrow as she planned, having a good deal to do there before she starts south.

How disgusted you will be with the mail that I enclose:[1] a very typical day's collection—poor fellow!—a request for an article, a speech and a list of books!

You don't know how I hate to send you such letters as this, darling; nothing whatever in it that will not make you feel worse than before you read it! If I had the gift of ready speech I could partly atone for the necessary though dreary beginning by a pretty ending!—all made up of ingenious and original expressions of my love. But it is vain to attempt it,—that love,—yours for me and mine for you, is my comfort, my dependence, my supreme *joy* under all circumstances. But though it is *always* too deep for words, it is so most of all when care or anxiety renders it perhaps most dear to me. Always & altogether,

Your own   Eileen.

ALS (WC, NjP).
[1] The enclosures are missing.

Notes for Remarks at a Harvard Alumni Dinner[1]

Harvard Dinner,   Balto., 10 Feb'y, 1897.

It heartens a man to experience this fellowship of the great colleges of the country. *I* don't even object to the reading of *"the proceedings of the previous meeting."*

One spirit, tho a diversity of operations,—and I am, perhaps in a position to appreciate all: *Jane Collier.*

The old college *vs.* the new: *tradition: lambing in the Spring.* The Hopkins has the German tradition.

The private *vs.* the State Institution: common ideals *vs.* individual initiative. One wishes to partake of personal power. Don't feel thankful, however, that *"none of my colour dar."*

Princeton? Just now in transition, if not in parturition. *"Four children and—a sketch."*

WWhw MS. (WP, DLC).
[1] This dinner took place on February 10, 1897, at the Hotel Rennert in Baltimore. In its report of the affair, the Baltimore *Sun*, Feb. 11, 1897, noted about Wilson only that he replied to the toast, "Princeton."

To Ellen Axson Wilson

My own darling,   Baltimore, 11 February, 1897.

I feel rather "seedy" this morning: we did not get away from the Harvard dinner last night till after midnight, and the evening had not been lively at that. I am well, nevertheless, and feeling as well as any sensitive man would, no doubt, under the circumstances.

I actually began the massage treatment yesterday. A man, very skilful and very boastful, like all the rest, comes to my room to do the job, and does it in a very satisfactory manner,—at two dollars an hour. That seems to be the usual charge, and I could get it done at the hospital only as a patient there. It is jolly to have the thing done at home. The masseur is to come every other day.

I am *actually* at 906 now, and not on the other side of the street, at 909. A room (second storey front) was vacated on this side and I came over to escape the distressing cries of the poor ill woman next door to 909, who is so often delirious. I spoke of her, did I not, when I was at home? My present room, if less sunny, is just as big and pleasant, and expensive, as the one over the way.

Ah, sweetheart, how I adore you, and long for you: but it is now hardly more than *eight days* before I shall see you again, and be happy once more for a little! How I pity the dear little chickens in their troubles, and the dear anxious little mother who is my idol!   Your own   Woodrow.

Love to all.

WWTLS (WP, DLC).

From Ellen Axson Wilson

My own darling,   Princeton, Feb. 11 1897

The children all seem better this morning. They had a good night and are comparatively bright today. Margaret is the only one who had fever last night and hers was low. Their tongues are still very bad though, and of course until they clear we can't feel that the disordered condition is relieved.

Sister Annie is the ill one today; she has a very bad throat,—covered with white blotches. The doctor has ordered her quarantined until it is clear whether it is dipththeria or tonsilitis; she is sadly distressed, poor dear, at being here among the children. I havn't an idea it is dipththeria however; the doctor says it is much too late for her to have taken it from Annie; and she certainly has not been exposed to it here. Whatever it is, it is fortunate that she *is* here, for what would she have done with Annie in N. Y.[?] Little Annie is very reasonable so far; I don't know how she will behave at night when she finds she must sleep with me instead of her mother.

I am quite well,—feel no soreness. We are having beautiful weather—bright and not very cold. I hope it will help all our invalids; I had to go out this morning to get Sister A's medecines, —Annie[1] being 'out' you know,—and enjoyed my airing very much.

Miss [Henrietta] Ricketts having returned the Kiplings, I have just been glancing at the poem we were speaking of on Sunday. I am afraid it is very unregenerate to say so, but I have seldom read any "dream" of Heaven that seems to me so attractive. A place where "the Master of all good workmen shall set us to work anew"; where "we shall work for an age at a sitting and never be tired at all"; and better still—

"Where only the Master shall praise us, and only the Master
   shall blame;
Where no one shall work for money, and no one shall work
   for fame;
But each for the joy of the working, and each in his separate
   star,
Shall draw the Thing as he sees it for the God of Things as
   they are."[2]

But I am needed and must close abruptly. Good-bye, for today my love, my Woodrow! You must try & not worry about us. You know there is nothing serious the matter with anyone; I am feeling quite cheerful.   Your little wife   Eileen.

ALS (WC, NjP).
   [1] A servant.
   [2] "When Earth's Last Picture Is Painted."

To Ellen Axson Wilson

My Sweetheart and Queen,   Baltimore, Md., 12 February, 1897.

It is doleful news your letters bring, of illness for the precious little ones, and anxiety and labour for yourself; and I have a daily fight with sadness. But so sweet an image of yourself, the self-forgetful wife and mother, lurks in every word of what you write that I am made deeply happy after all! There are so many things about you to love that I am at a loss which to love first or most. I can therefore suit my mood in the matter. When I am sad,

I can make the sadness infinitely sweet by letting my thoughts dwell on all the touching loveliness of your devotion to me and the children; when I am gay, I think of how light-hearted and full of sunshine you are when you see the like mood in me, of what a deliciously winsome vein of fun and frolic runs through you, and with how engaging a face it shows itself in your bearing oftentimes; when I am grave and thoughtful, I feel so to the quick of your close companionship and quiet understanding in all affairs of the mind, and my thought is made easy by the inspiration; when I am in a mere lover's frame, I can recall scenes and embraces by the score which fairly make me thrill with pleasure. I can have any sort of wife I want, having you, who are so various, so full of sweetness, strength, and every womanly quality! Ah, Eileen, my matchless little wife, how shall I ever say how deeply, how delightfully, how passionately I am

Your own   Woodrow Wilson
(See the force of habit!)

WWTLS (WP, DLC).

Two Letters from Ellen Axson Wilson

My own darling,   Princeton Feb. 12 1897

I meant to write this afternoon in time for the five o'clock collection, but visitors prevented and now I am scribbling in great haste just before dinner in order that my letter may be mailed tonight, and reach you earlier than if I wrote this evening, for I know of course that you will be anxious about Sister Annie. She is decidedly better today in every respect, there is scarcely any white left on her throat; still the doctor "can't be sure" that it isn't dipththeria. He "took a culture" today and sent it off somewhere; we will hear the result tomorrow.

Jessie, Nellie, and Annie are improving rapidly; Margaret more slowly; the doctor says he is afraid it will be some time before she is quite herself again. Poor little girl, it makes my heart ache to look at [her], she is so unlike herself. I am quite well.

I am very glad you had so good an opportunity to change your room, though I am sorry too for your lost sunshine. I am *so* sorry to hear you were feeling badly when you wrote. What do you mean by "feeling as well as any sensitive man would under the circumstances." What circumstances? Did the speech go hard; didn't they seem to like it?

I am very, *very* glad the massage is begun at last.

With love beyond all words for my darling, believe me always & altogether,   Your own   Eileen.

Little Annie was as good as gold last night,—seemed to think it a great frolic to dress and undress with the other children and sleep so near them.

Poor little pet! She stood outside her mother's door today and asked if she "couldn't come in if she walked on tip-toes."

My own darling,   Princeton, Feb 13/97
I must scribble a line for the boys to mail to let you know that it is settled that Sister Annie has no dipththeria. The culture showed not a trace of it; moreover her throat is almost well. So things are looking much brighter with us today. The children, even Margaret, seem bright and playful. I am perfectly well. Moreover yesterday's storm is past and it is a glorious day. I have just been down town on business and have come in feeling much refreshed.

All send a heart full of love. Thank you, sweetheart[,] for that dear little letter you sent yesterday: How *lovely* you are to me in all you say and all you do! With a heart full to overflowing with love,   Your own   Eileen.

I enclose a letter from Stock[1] which seems much more cheerful than any other recent ones, does it not?

ALS (WC, NjP).
[1] It is missing.

To Ellen Axson Wilson

My own darling,   Baltimore, Md., 14 February, 1897.
I cannot love you enough for the qualities which have shone so finely in your recent letters: the self-possession, the courage, the quiet capacity, like a general's, to keep affairs in hand, whatever the crisis! To find such qualities going along with the sweet beauty of gentleness and trust and dependence upon the affection of others in you fills me with a joyful sort of admiration which is as intense as if it were new. Somehow your mastery in moments of crisis always comes upon me like a great surprise, often as I have seen it, confidently as I expect and count upon it. By what an extraordinary largess of fortune did you, who seem made by nature to excite all the ardors of romantic affection, a sort of poet's girl, get also an unlimited share of executive capacity, the right to rule the little world of your own life by the

sign of soft eyes which might seem meant only for love and dreams! Ah, how I have admired the tone and method of those wonderful letters, so hurried and yet so self-possessed: your ability to write of perplexities and yet not forget Kipling: to state facts that dismayed me, and yet without any of my dismay! With what would I not trust you,—*in* what would I not trust you! This is my valentine, my darling. Nothing has happened to me, except that I have been deeply anxious about you all, and have been overwhelmed with love for you. My very life seems summed up in that love; and now that the anxiety is relieved I can rejoice with a fuller heart than ever that I am, in all things,

Your own   Woodrow

WWTLS (WP, DLC).

From Ellen Axson Wilson

My own darling,   Princeton, Feb. 14 1897

I had hoped to find a long quiet time for writing to you today, but what with visitors and other things it has turned out otherwise. It is now after ten and I am just beginning;—and I am afraid the ending must follow in very short order for I am very sleepy and tired.

We are all better,—all who were not already quite well like myself. Sister Annie seems quite over her attack and expects to leave on Wednesday. The children all look "peaked" yet of course but are beginning to seem quite like themselves. The doctor does not let them go out yet which seems a great pity the weather being so extremely fine. I went out to church and heard a sermon from Mr. de Vries that I really think was as good as Dr. Purves'.[1]

By the way, while I think of it will you please send me at once some of your cards? And another thing;—hadn't you better write to Johnston,[2] tell him how unsatisfactory our heating system is in the upper story and ask him to send a man to meet you here on *Saturday*? If we wait until your return to stay it may be getting so warm that we can't furnish a complete demonstration of our case!

Ah what a comfort it is to think of 'Saturday,' and that it is actually *this* week! I am fairly living on the thought of it. I am already counting the hours that must pass before that happy one which finds me again in the arms of my darling, With all my heart   Your little wife   Eileen.

ALS (WC, NjP).
[1] Rev. Dr. George Tybout Purves, Professor of New Testament Literature and

Exegesis, Princeton Theological Seminary; Stated Supply, First Presbyterian Church of Princeton, 1895-99; Pastor, 1899-1900.

[2] Of Johnson and Company, manufacturers of steam and hot water heaters of 84 John St., New York, who had had the heating contract for the Wilson house.

To Ellen Axson Wilson

My owy [own] darling,   Baltimore, Md., 15 February, 1897.

Somehow I seem incapable of writing about anything but love to you these days! Ah, if I could only use my pen! I feel as if I might almost express my love, so much is the lover stirred in me! There is'nt any special reason: you are yourself the only exciting cause,—unless, indeed, what I was writing about yesterday has filled me with special thoughts of you: your courage and fine womanliness in the midst of the sickness and difficulty of the past week. It does not need that, or any other special act of circumstances, to make me realize my love for you. Whenever I think about you with the least degree of deliberation, a great enthusiasm floods my heart,—greater than any boy could feel for his sweetheart,—more romantic a thousandfold, more passionate, —compounded of every deep passion that can rule a man's spirit. There is the boy in it and the man too. It is sweeter to love one's wife than to love one's sweetheart: sweeter to love a wife of ten years than a wife of one: sweeter to spend a year with her now than a month at first,—ah, how much sweeter! What a strong savour of life and comfort and the real knowledge of love is in it now that was not in it then: and what would I give in exchange for you! There is no happiness imaginable without you, and next Saturday I shall know the full joy of being

                    Your own   Woodrow

Unbounded love to dear sister, and to all. Did you receive that check for fifty-three dollars?

WWTLS (WP, DLC).

From Ellen Axson Wilson

My own darling,   Princeton, Feb. 15, 1897

Your sweet letter—your valentine—is safely here and has made me very happy;—in spite of the fact that I am greatly puzzled to think how you could have found all those good things in those wretched little scrawls of mine! I am very much afraid, dearest, they would not have shown themselves so plainly if you had not "known just what you were looking for" and been very dertermined [determined] to find it! Yet I am so inconsistent as to deeply value every word you say in spite of these misgivings.

All goes well with us now. The children are steadily improving, and Sister Annie says she feels as well as ever. I am perfectly well.

So completely out of the woods are we that I [am] going to a reception tonight,—the one the Wikoffs give to the Smiths.[1] It is a great bore, especially as it is Sister Annie's last night, but you know we behaved so badly about their last "series," neither attending any nor sending cards, that I am afraid to stay away.

By the way, did you ever see any cards to the Frothingham receptions?[2] Was there any such thing in the wedding invitation? I remember that *it* was received. It seems they are giving two large ones at the Inn. I have never seen any invitation for us; of course if it did not come it is an oversight and I can only hope they won't notice that I neither come nor send cards. The second reception is on Wed.

Alice Owen, Bella's younger sister you know, died on Sat.;[3] it seems she has been ill for months,—an aenemic condition; just another form of consumption, they say. You know the father died of it.

Is'nt this a spicy letter and article a-pro-pos of you[r] oration?[4] It would be funny if it wern't so ominous. What absolute proof such things furnish of the truth of all you spoke,—of "the dangers under which we cower" &c. With love unbounded, inexpressible for my darling, I am as ever,   Your own   Eileen.

ALS (WC, NjP).

[1] The local newspaper was silent about this reception given by the family of James Holmes Wikoff, M.D., of 22 Nassau St.

[2] Arthur Lincoln Frothingham, Jr., Professor of Archaeology and the History of Art at Princeton University, was married to Helen Bulkley Post in Brooklyn on January 27, 1897. The *Princeton Press*, January 30, 1897, has an account of the wedding and dinner at the home of the bride's parents, but neither then nor later did it mention the two receptions referred to by Ellen.

[3] Alice Proctor Owen, daughter of Elizabeth Sheldon (Mrs. Henry James) Owen and sister of Isabel Sheldon Owen of 10 Mercer Street, died at Princeton on February 13 at the age of twenty-two.

[4] These enclosures are missing.

To Ellen Axson Wilson

My own darling,   Baltimore Md., 16 February, 1897.

I enclose the cards for which you asked. I do not remember whether cards for their receptions came with the Frothingham wedding invitation or not; but I feel quite sure I did not destroy the invitation. It ought still to be on my desk, in one of the little racks at the side,—probably the right hand side.

I received a letter this morning which enabled me to guage [gauge] my feeling with reference to the Turner matter. Hibben answered Mr. Stewart's former letter,[1] and now sends me the reply of Mr. S. to that. It expresses the belief that Turner would be unexceptionable from the academic point of view not only, but also in respect of his religious influence within the college; but it falls back upon the inexpediency of letting the orthodox Presbyterians who have given us money see us appoint a Unitarian. I find I take the folly with a sort of reminiscence of pain, and yet a real philosophy: much as it means with respect of all our future life.

I cannot write to Johnson in time to have him send a man to meet me on Saturday, my darling, because I do not know his address, and there are probably dozens of firms in New York who would be reached by a letter addressed "Johnson & Co."

I go to the Yale Alumni dinner to-night,[2] and have been napping most of the morning by way of preparation.

Of course you saw that W. L. Wilson had been elected at Lexington,[3] and would accept. I find myself a little disappointed. I should like to know now, to re-inforce my philosophy, just where we shall have to make our next home.

Do you wonder where I found the qualities set forth in my valentine in "those scrawls" of yours? (By the way, I wish you would not call letters that I love "scrawls." If you knew what sacred documents they were to your lover, you would not). I found them of course in their tone: in what they did not say; in their calmness, with no hint of panic or any haste but merely the haste of time; in their evidence of what was being done by the sweet mistress of the household; in all the method of the dear mind and the dear hand from which they came! Do you suppose I would have found them if they had been explicitly and deliberately expressed? Ah, sweet one, I know the motions of mastery in my darling, and my love for her is supreme. I am altogether   Your own   Woodrow

Love unmeasured to all.

WWTLS (WP, DLC).
 [1] See WW to EAW, Jan. 29, 1897, n. 1.
 [2] Wilson's notes for his talk at this affair are printed at Feb. 16, 1897.
 [3] William Lyne Wilson of West Virginia, who had just been elected President of Washington and Lee University.

From Ellen Axson Wilson, with Enclosure

My own darling,   Princeton, Feb. 16, 1897.

Dear Sister really got off today, and very lonely the house seems without her and dear little Annie. We have settled quite into our regular groove; the children had lessons this morning for the first time since their illness;—of course made rather easy. They were so pleased, however at the idea of having them that I concluded they must feel well enough.

I went to the Employment society;—where by the way we had a rather queer experience; Alice Owen's funeral was at 3.30 and not a soul came to get work until it was all over, so overpowering was their race instinct to stay where they could "see the procession." Some of the ladies, who had wanted to go to the funeral themselves, were quite bursting with indignation! After the meeting I went to see Mrs. de Vries[1] and liked her very much. By the way she had been told that I had "saved her" in the matter of the carpets and was quite grateful; and I was doubly glad that I interferred when I saw their parlour, the first glance at it revealing them to be persons of taste and refinement. The carpet they selected is a perfect beauty. She has great fun with some of her visitors who declare they think it "a perfect fright" and "can't imagine what the committee were thinking of not to get a 'real parlour carpet'; something *light*, with flowers on it instead of that dismal thing." It is in beautiful tones of brown.

I forward a letter from Jessie Brower; bring it back with you and we can answer it together while here. I should also like to see the second letter from Mr. Stewart. Mrs. Hibben was telling me about it.

At what hour will you reach here my darling? To think there are only three *whole* days left! Oh how wild I am for them to pass! I can scarcely sit still when I think of it. What a welcome you will find ready for you! (You wouldn't think it, but there is a little riddle-me-re in that last sentence. I wonder if you can guess it!) I love you my own Woodrow, ah how tenderly, how passionately I love you! In every heart-throb,

Your own   Eileen.

ALS (WC, NjP).

[1] At the manse of the Second Presbyterian Church at 16 Stockton St.

ENCLOSURE

From Jessie Bones Brower

My dear Cousin Woodrow: [Chicago, c. Feb. 14, 1897]

The time is approaching when we must make arrangements to board Le Foy in Princeton next fall,[1] and I write to you for advice. We would like to have him in a private family if possible, where he would be more or less under the eye of some responsible person.

Helen[2] tells me the Episcopal rector[3] takes boarders, and it seems to me that would be a good place. Can you advise me in this matter? Le Foy is a boy who is easily influenced, either for good or evil, by his associates. I may be doing him an injustice, but all the same, I would like to keep him from temptation as far as possible. He is a pleasant, amiable, obedient boy, but he has never been tried. And while we do not wish to keep him shut up, we would like the straight and narrow path made as easy to follow as possible.

I hope Ellie Lou and the youngsters are well. I should so much like to see you all again. Will you not be coming out West soon? The next visit you pay us must not be such a short one, my dear cousin. We have seen so many flattering things in the papers lately, about you and your last work. One of the Sunday Chicago papers had a first rate picture of you.

My dear cousin, when I look back to the days[4] when we played wild Indians, & frightened the little darkies so, & recall your favorite amusement of shaking me out of a tree, after throwing stones at me, you being a hunter & I a squirrel, I can scarcely believe we are the same couple. Those were dear old days, and you were my only brother.

I send you a picture of my Marion which has just been taken, & which is a most excellent likeness. My fourteen-year-old girl is 5-2 in—an inch taller than Helen.

What do you think of the International?[5] Is it improving? And have you read the little account of our trip to Florida?[6] I made all the pictures myself, & it is a *true, true* story. With much love to you all, I am

Your affectionate squirrel   Jessie B. Brower.

ALS (WP, DLC).
1 Her step-son, John LeFoy Brower, Princeton '01.
2 Jessie's sister, Helen Woodrow Bones.
3 The Rev. Dr. Alfred B. Baker, 22 Stockton St.
4 In Augusta, Ga.
5 A monthly magazine of travel and literature published in Chicago since

August 1896, of which her husband, Abraham Thew H. Brower, was the editor and manager.
6 Pathfinder, "A Trip to Florida," Chicago *International*, II (Jan. 1897), 87-94.

Notes for Remarks at a Yale Alumni Dinner[1]

Yale dinner   Balto. 16 Feb'y, '97

Name Freddie—5 years old—go to Hell!

Don't know you, but your manners are very familiar

Torch-light procession

Heaven lies about us in our infancy
In old age we lie about ourselves.

College dinners public dinners
    We are still a nation in the making: and shall be a nation by what we do and become, not by what we are and have.
    Progress not entrusted to select committees—but: the prevalent majority, as contradistinguished from the numerical majority.

The sword before the horn

Didn't know you was a candidate. We must be candidates for influence.

WWhw and WWsh MS. (WP, DLC).
    1 Held at the Hotel Stafford in Baltimore on February 16, 1897. In its report of the affair, the Baltimore *Sun*, Feb. 17, 1897, said about Wilson only that he made a brief address on Princeton.

To Ellen Axson Wilson

My dear darling,   Baltimore, Md., 17 February, 1897.

The Yale dinner is over and I am very sleepy, notwithstanding the hour-and-a-half nap I took yesterday by way of preparation. You will be pleased and surprised to learn that I made the best speech of the evening. The other fellows were so unconscionably new or awkward at the business that to beat them was easy and without credit.

The thing that sings in my head this morning, though, and makes me forget fatigue and everything that is not delightful, is the fact that you are only three days away from me. One more letter, and then I shall bring my own messages, and speak them with my arms about you, and your breath upon my lips! Ah, darling, it is a perilous business for a fellow to be as much in love as I am: it endangers his peace of mind. And yet it brings a sweet peace of its own, a great exultation, which I would not part with for all the world. It is a delicious uneasiness when you can know that the longing will be satisfied and more than satisfied at a sweet time not far off. I possess you, after all, even when you are not in my arms. I fancy often that you must feel my longing, for all the distance that lies between us!

I go to Dr. Griffin's[1] to dinner to-morrow evening, and to the Princeton dinner (with absolutely nothing to say) on Friday evening.[2] By the way, love, wont you look in my desk the minute you get this and send me the little blank book that is in the square pigeon hole with the brown stiff paper cards upon which I make the notes for my history? It is a little, square diary (with jokes in it!)[3] and beside it is a piece of paper (perhaps two pieces of paper) with similar records, which I also want. I have never a story in mind which I have not already told here.

Good-bye, my queen, but not for long. It will be day after to-morrow when you get this!   Your own   Woodrow

Unbounded love to all.

WWTLS (WP, DLC).
  [1] Edward Herrick Griffin, Professor of the History of Philosophy and Dean of the College Faculty at the Johns Hopkins.
  [2] The twelfth annual dinner of the Princeton Alumni Association of Maryland was held in the banquet room of Music Hall in Baltimore on February 19, 1897. President Patton made the principal address. Reporting on the affair, the Baltimore *Sun*, Feb. 20, 1897, said about Wilson only that he remarked that he was sorry that he was not older and could point to the two other speakers as his pupils.
  [3] The Editors have been unable to find this diary in the Wilson Papers.

From Ellen Axson Wilson

My own darling,   Princeton, Feb. 17, 1897

I have just had a little visit from Uncle Tom; he came on the one o'clock and left on the 8.30 tonight. I enjoyed it very much; though was sorry that it prevented my going to the installation services at the church tonight,[1] as I of course intended doing.

I did go to the Frothingham reception for a short time, while Uncle Tom went at the boy's invitation to their room. The reception was something new for Princeton and very fine; they had four or five fine musicians from New York down,—singers chiefly —and it was almost a continuous concert. There were a lot of people from the cities too among the guests,—all strangers to me of course except Mrs. Bayard Henry.[2]

I had a most surprising and amusing experience at this same reception: Mrs. Richardson[3] (of all people) taking me aside proceeds in the most earnest, serious and determined fashion to try to extort from me a promise "to do something to please her." And what do you suppose the "something" finally turned out to be? Why, that I should sit before the glass and paint my own portrait! And it must be "in the gown that you wore at the reception the other night," the white with the yellow lace. Her distress at the thought of my charms being lost to the world,—no permanent record left of them—was really touching! Now did you *ever* hear of anything funnier!

Your letter for tomorrow has turned up tonight and the little note-book you wanted has already gone. Am so glad the Yale speech was a success. I was *so delighted* with the Brooklyn one, the proof sheets of which I sent you.[4] Of course you know it is the first of your speeches of that sort I have ever seen,—except in the form of a few notes.

Good-night, my darling; we are all well and happy,—and I love you inexpressibly. Always and altogether,

Your own   Eileen.

ALS (WC, NjP).
  [1] The Rev. John Hendrik De Vries was installed as pastor of the Second Presbyterian Church on the evening of February 17, 1897. There is a lengthy report of the service in the *Princeton Press*, Feb. 20, 1897.
  [2] Jane Robeson (Mrs. Bayard) Henry of Philadelphia.
  [3] Grace Ely (Mrs. Ernest Cushing) Richardson, wife of the university librarian.
  [4] "The Responsibility of Having Ancestors," printed at Dec. 21, 1896.

To Ellen Axson Wilson

My own darling,   Baltimore, Md., 18 February, 1897.

I expect to reach home on the train which is due in Princeton at 1:54, which is, being interpreted, six minutes of two; so that it is at this present moment very little more (it is now exactly 11:42½) than forty-eight hours before my full happiness shall begin again. Your love makes me deeply happy even when I am away from you; but, ah, how much more that love means when I am with you and feel all the sweet power and unspeakable comfort of your presence!

Yes, I think I can guess the "riddle-me-re" of the dear letter I received last night. At least I know what it means in alternative. It means either that you will or that you will not be ready to show me *to the full* and at once how much you love me and how much you have missed me! Am I not a deep guesser, to be able thus to reduce it to one or the other of *two opposites*! I know this, at any rate: that no reception that you can give me can disappoint me, if only I see the right light in your eyes. If you love me, what do I care whether you indulge me or not? If you love me, I have my heart's desire. Ah, sweetheart, my precious Eileen, think of me constantly till I come; forget everything I have ever done or seemed amiss; remember only that I love you and have dedicated my life to you; make your heart warm for my coming, and you shall have such a welcome in store for me as will renew and thrill me in every fibre. Oh, how impatient I am to look in your eyes again, and say into your lips that I am

Your own   Woodrow

WWTLS (WP, DLC).

Two Letters from Ellen Axson Wilson

My own darling,   Princeton, Feb. 18 1897

I shall try and get my note off on the 2.30 today in order that it may certainly reach you before you leave. I have just finished the children's lessons;—and am sorry I had them at all, for they need sunshine more than lessons, poor little souls; and though the day began gloriously it has permitted "basest clouds" to "hide it[s] bravery."

By a distant association of ideas, that reminds me of poor Uncle Tom and his family. He really ran down for a few hours relief from the strain of all he has gone through in the last few weeks. Dr. Henry has fizzled out so completely that finally Uncle Tom had to go to New York, wind up their affairs, and take Allie[1] home to live.

Dr. Henry has made next to nothing in the last two years and of course they have got heavily in debt in spite of all Uncle Tom has done for them. Now he has had to give up his very office; being too much in arrears for the rent to hold it;—and besides he is drinking heavily. Was there ever a more unfortunate woman in the matter of marriage than poor "Sal"!

Ah, how everything that happens turns my heart with fresh wonder and joy to *you*, my darling, and to my marvellous good fortune in being loved by you. One would think I might have grown to take it as a matter of course by this time, as one sometimes does the sunshine,—though certainly that latter blessing is withdrawn often enough to keep us from growing too much dulled to its worth! You have never been ungenerous enough to take a similar precaution to ensure my "sense of your great merits." And yet the wonder of it all seems as fresh as on the first day; indeed, because I know you better now, it is much, much more wonderful to me,—as well as infinitely sweeter, now than then.

And now good-bye, darling,—good-bye for two days only,—delicious thought!

"Take all my loves, my love, yea, take them all;
What hast though [thou] then more than thou hadst before?"[2]

Your little wife   Eileen.

[1] Dr. Hoyt's daughter, Alice Louise Hoyt Truehart Henry, whose second marriage was going the way of her first. It is probably just as well that it is impossible to identify Dr. Henry in the New York city directory for 1897.
[2] From Shakespeare's Sonnet XL.

My own darling,   Princeton, Feb. 23/97

I have been this evening to the Miller Church[1] to hear a lecture,—a very interesting one!—by Mr. Perry on Thackery; and as that, coming after the Employment Society, has left me tired; and I am besides—most unaccountably!—overwhelmed by sleepiness, I will send only a *little* love-message tonight. Indeed it seems hardly endurable, after such full communion of soul, to go back the *same day* to the poor substitute of pen and ink. I write at all only because my darling must not be left tomorrow entirely without love token.

I do not think I have ever been so happy, dearest, as during these last three days; and I have never before been so happy, *with you away*, as I am now. The flood rose so high, you see, that it *cannot* subside all at once. I am still living on the delight of it all; I still feel you[r] presence almost as vividly as I did twenty-four hours ago. Ah my darling, how I love you, *love* you, *love* you! How absolutely I am yours! With what tender joy,— with what passionate delight does my heart echo my words when I call myself,   Your little wife,   Eileen.

ALS (WC, NjP).
[1] The University Place Cumberland Presbyterian Church, called the Miller Church because it had been founded by the late Rev. John Miller.

To Ellen Axson Wilson

My own darling,   Baltimore, Md., 24 February, 1897.

Here I am, settled to work again,—and realizing what a blessing it has been to me to be with you the past delightful days. I bring away from you such an impression of sweetness, tenderness, purity, love, and strength that it is a veritable benediction on me to have been with you and to bring your touch away with me! The intoxication of it all is in my blood almost as strongly to-day as it was yesterday,—and the happiness.

We are having exquisite weather, such as seems the suitable setting to my restored spirits. If I could know that that wretched soreness had not come back to you, and that the children were getting well by sure and perceptible stages, I could find it easy to be as bright and cheery as this perfect day,—into which I must go to shake off the dulling sensations of the twenty examination papers I have just finished reading.

Ah, my love, the last two or three days seem to me now like a delightful dream, in which I had seen all hopes of love and all my desires of happiness realized. They have made me more than ever,   Your own   Woodrow

I am quite well, and love the others as well as you!

WWTLS (WP, DLC).

From Ellen Axson Wilson

My own darling,   Princeton, Feb. 24, 1897

I am back from New York tonight rather tired but very well— *no* soreness. I didn't want to lose my chance at those dresses, so I telegraphed Sister that unless she telegraphed not, I would meet her today at Lord and Taylors.[1] The $23.00 dresses were very "natty" indeed, of rough "homespun"—as it is called,—just what I would like best for ordinary street wear, but more than *I* ought to pay for a dress for such purposes only; they were entirely unsuitable both in design and material for wear on "dress" occasions—receptions &c. So I ended by getting a perfectly elegant one for $34.00. That is about what my grey dress cost, but this is twice as fine. It is taylor-made & silk-lined throughout, and looks like a fifty dollar dress at least. It will do for either summer or winter, and would wear forever,—if it only wouldn't go out of style! It was economy to get it now; though of course I am "low in my mind" at having spent so much on dress. At any rate you will have the satisfaction of seeing me well dressed for once!

The children all seem better again; Margaret's cold, I hope is passing off. Little Annie and Sister both seemed well. They expect to start south next Tuesday.

Do excuse this superlatively bad scrawl, dear; something is wrong with either ink or pen.

I *love* you, *love* you, dear,—"with the smiles, tears, breath, of all my life, And if God choose I shall but love you better after death."[2]   Your own,   Eileen.

ALS (WC, NjP).
[1] The New York department store, then at 20th St. and Broadway.
[2] Elizabeth Barrett Browning, *Sonnets from the Portuguese*, XLIII.

To Ellen Axson Wilson

My own darling,   Baltimore, Md., 25 February, 1897.

You are the most charming person in the world. The more I think about you the more complete grows the spell you have wrought upon me! How sweet, how generous it was in you to write that little note that brought me such delight last night,— that little gem of a love letter that you wrote Tuesday evening, the very confession of sleepiness in which was a source of charm! Ah, Eileen, what has happened to us these sweet days gone by? I feel, as you do, an *abiding* sense of happiness, a comfort even in absence, such as I never felt before! Surely we drew closer together in that blessed love-making than we ever did before. I never before felt so to the quick the extraordinary fa[s]cination of your altogether lovely person and nature: I never brought so much of it away with me. The exaltation of it all remains with me as if it had entered into my very blood. I cannot think of anything else! I had a chance to talk about you last night, at Miss [Edith] Duer's dinner party, because some of the ladies there knew Stock, and it was such a delightful relief to have leave to talk about the only thing I really cared to speak of, the qualities of the dear little woman who has made me perfectly happy. You have enchanted me, dear; but it is not a spell that interferes with work: it only glorifies it and makes it seem more than ever worth while, if only in celebration of you! I would murmur back into your sweet lips your own words: "with what tender joy, with what passionate delight does my heart echo my words when I call myself"   Your own husband,   Woodrow

WWTLS (WP, DLC).

From Ellen Axson Wilson

My own darling,   Princeton, Feb. 25/97

What do you think I have been doing this afternoon? Writing out the Hoyt records, as far as they concern us, from the Hoyt book! Such tiresome work! Aunt Saidie[1] wanted the book returned, so I had to screw my courage to the sticking-point. But surely no one ever hated both the mental and manual exercise of writing with a more perfect hatred than I. I should have writer's cramp in a month if I made a business of it.

I send you in another envelope a very stupid lot of mail. Did you ever see anything so dreadful as the picture of you? The article on your Cleveland paper I enclose simply to point a moral

I want to draw.[2] I intended before this,—but it escaped my mind,—to try and extract from you a promise to take particular pains *not* to read any press comments on that subject. When papers can show such bitterness, as some of them have done, over your treatment of dead issues, or abstract questions, we can imagine how rabid they will become over a live subject like Cleveland. Of course neither of us were unmindful of that when you agreed to write it; it did not cause you to hesitate,—and I would not have had it to do so; because the writing of it was a good and worthy thing to do, and it would be utterly beneath you to swerve from your cause because of such clamours,—past, present or to come! But it is one thing to *act* in proud and brave disregard of such things and quite another to *feel* indifferent when the missiles are actually striking us in the face, one by one. I think it is only an act of self-preservation to turn one's back to them. They are not *worth* noticing,—there is nothing to be gained by it. As you know, I should like to extend this to the press notices of *all* your work, and persuade you to read absolutely *none* of them. It is part of a general policy of 'conservation of force' which I would have you adopt. To resist those little poisoned slings and arrows involves as much wear and tear of nerve and will as the doing of any other task that doesn't pay, and leaves just so much less life power for the things that do pay,—for the main issue. But I did not mean to harangue you at such length!

The children are doing well, and I am perfectly well. The boys are acting as ushers at the Evelyn [College] concert and dance tonight.

I love you, Woodrow dear, with my heart of hearts, and I am still oh! so happy in my love!

Your little wife,   Eileen.

ALS (WC, NjP).
1 Mrs. Thomas Alexander Hoyt. She had lent her David Webster Hoyt, *A Genealogical History of the . . . Hoyt Families* (Providence, 1871).
2 These clippings are missing.

To Ellen Axson Wilson

My own darling,   Baltimore, Md., 26 February, 1897.

I return Houghton and Mifflin's check, endorsed. Please have it deposited, and acknowledge the receipt of it, (to me).

I am so much obliged to you, my pet, for getting the proper sort of gown for yourself. You do not often spend enough on yourself; and I am really grateful. But, surely, that one gown will not be all you need.

What a comfort your sweet letters are, my Eileen: and how it goes to my head to realize that you are as much in love with me as I am with you! The only drawback about my recent supreme happiness with you is, that now I find other women almost entirely robbed of their charms. They are not like you (fortunately for my peace of mind!). They are interesting, and pleasantly feminine, but they are not fascinating in a sufficient degree to give a fellow pleasurable excitement in their presence. You have got my heart so in thrall that I cannot even play at feeling a romantic attachment for the most charming of them. Are you not ashamed to have spoiled my fun? I called on Mrs. [Edith Gittings] Reid last night. She is as interesting as ever: but not as delightful. My delight is all mortgaged and pre-empted! What shall I do? You don't want *all* of me, do you?

Ah, my Eileen, my little wife, it is sweet,—sweet beyond all words,—to make these confessions to you. Surely if ever woman took complete possession of her husband and lover, you have taken absolute possession of me. You are all the world to me, in very truth, and I am always and altogether,

Your own   Woodrow

WWTLS (WP, DLC).

From Ellen Axson Wilson

My own darling,   Princeton, Feb. 26, 1897.

I have been in something of a rush all day, and am still in fact. Until lunch was busy with the lessons of course. After lunch wrote a letter to Mrs. Williams,[1] dressed hastily and went down town with it so as to insure its getting off in time for tomorrow's mail steamer. (The clerk assured me that it would do so.) Then I called on Mrs. Phillips,[2] who receives on Fridays. She certainly is out of her element here,—a big, showy rather handsome young woman, half educated and, in a certain sense, half-civilized. But she isn't nearly so bad as "Mrs. Elton,"[3] for she seems thoroughly good-natured and well-meaning.

I spent the rest of the afternoon visiting,—saw Mrs. Hibben and her mother among others,—have just returned, and am hastily writing this before dinner, because after dinner I am going to the Trask lecture;—which in this case is no lecture at all but a rendition of "Midsummer Night's Dream";—a recitation with organ accompaniment.[4] Of course I am well or I wouldn't be flying around at this rate.

Dinner is over & I must close abruptly so as to see to the children before I go.

With all the love you want,

Your devoted little wife,   Eileen.

ALS (WP, DLC).

[1] Martha P. Williams, who was associated with a New York agency which recruited foreign teachers and governesses. The Wilsons were in process of hiring a German governess for their children, and Mrs. Williams was about to leave for Germany.

[2] Mabel K. Phillips, wife of Alexander Hamilton Phillips, Instructor in Mineralogy, of 41 Vandeventer Ave. The Phillipses had moved into Princeton from Stony Brook in 1896.

[3] Augusta Elton, vulgar and pretentious wife of the Rev. Philip Elton in Jane Austen's *Emma*.

[4] The Spencer Trask Lecture in Alexander Hall on February 26, 1897, was given by Charles F. Underhill, impersonator, who presented a dramatic reading of "A Midsummer Night's Dream," accompanied by selections from Mendelssohn's incidental music to the play performed by Hermann Rannefield, organist. For a news report, see the *Daily Princetonian*, Feb. 27, 1897.

Two Letters to Ellen Axson Wilson

My own darling,   Balto., Md., 27 Feb'y, 1897

I don't know whether what I write now will reach you before to-morrow's letter does or not, but I must send you a little "love token" anyhow,—and indulge myself with the pen,—so that the message may be more intimate. I have nothing to say, except that I am well and love you; but I could not tell more of my life, or of my health, than is told in so simple a declaration of love. My life is full and gracious, full of power and sweetness, full of a gladness that passes all expression and is itself strength and hope, *because* I love you, because you love me, because I am consecrated and accepted   Your own   Woodrow

ALS (WP, DLC).

My own darling,   Baltimore, Md., 28 February, 1897.

Few things are harder than to draw the line between self-defence and self-sufficiency in the matter of reading newspaper criticisms of what one has written or done; and I cannot yet quite make up my mind whether a resolution not to read what the papers say of my books and opinions would be wise or not. That it would be an admirable way of avoiding pain and the loss of nervous energy that goes along with pain cannot be doubted. It would, too, no doubt secure one's genuineness against damage. But genuineness is not incompatible with self-sufficiency and blindness to one's own faults; the man whose genuineness needs also shielding is apt to lack robustness and the steadfast bulk which tells in the world's competitions. I am not quite ready to go into that sort of moral infirmary. And yet I know that it would be folly to take press criticisms too seriously. One must have balance and judgment enough to distinguish the serious criticism from the superficial not only, but also to use his own critical knowledge of the qualities of his work to determine which of his critics it is worth his while to heed and take hints from. I ought to be old and self-possessed enough to do that, and not wince under petty wounds. After all, one does not write wholly for his own satisfaction; and my critics are not apt to succeed in driving me from my standards.

This is in the high philosophical style, I admit; and I very well know that it is much easier for me to formulate such rules than to follow them; but I can claim that my skin, and my self-possession, are much firmer than they used to be. That article about my estimate of Mr. Cleveland, for example, I read with a degree of philosophy but little removed from indifference. I can stand any amount of that sort of thing,—particularly when the critic is personally decent, as this fellow seems. At the same time, the mere fact that you are so sure of the wisdom of giving one's public critics no hearing at all makes me less sure than ever that I am right. I have learned that the presumption is violently in favour of your being right, whether in matters of taste or of practical judgment.

You are immensely entertaining in your little touches of characterization about Mrs. Phillips and all the other people you see, as well as in your brief sentences about what is doing at home. I would give my head if you were not the enemy of the pen you describe yourself to be:—and my head would be worth more as a gift. For the n'th time I declare, upon all the authority I may have as a critic, that you have a gift of expression more delightful than I can say. If you hate the pen, you have no right to take advantage of what others, less gifted than yourself, have generously written for your pleasure. They obtained this power at a great price,—of infinite endeavour,—you were born to the privilege of perfect speech. And to think that you should grudge your writing even to me,—and even when I am away and can't enjoy the fresh speech that is always on your lips! Heaven bring you to a better mind! I dare not say too much about it for fear of making what is so delightfully spontaneous self-conscious by never so little!

I love you, my sweet Eileen, more than words can say, and am in every way that you could wish

Your own   Woodrow

WWTLS (WP, DLC).

From Ellen Axson Wilson

My own darling,   Princeton, Feb. 28, 1897

I have just had a hearty laugh over a bit of conversation between the children—I think I must really report it. Margaret was helping Annie wash dishes, while Nellie looked on enviously. Says Nellie, "Annie is going to let me help her when you grow up." "No," says Margaret, "I will go on helping her anyhow"; "Well, I'll do it when you get married and go away." "But you'll get married and go away too." "No, I'll wait, I won't do it the same time you do!" Poor Nell! it is sad that she should be so early and so long the victim of hope deferred!

How I wish you could have been with me at the Kneisel concert last night! It was perfectly exquisite,—much the sweetest of all to my mind; there was so much soft, melting, angel music. I listened in a delicious dream, thinking of you unceasingly; and thought and sensation blended in such perfect harmony that,—altogether, I had a heavenly time![1]

And to think that I can already say, "he is coming *this* week!" How perfectly delightful! And curiously enough the idea has taken me this time something by surprise. I have been so intently *looking backward* all the week, delightedly living over and over again those three days, that I have postponed much later than usual resorting for my happiness to the joys of anticipation. Indeed I am not yet ready to turn my gaze altogether away from last week,—to *look forward only*. I see there is nothing for it but to be *double-faced*,—and doubly happy!

Yes, sir, I do want "all of you"—and I am quite unfeeling in the matter of "spoiling" your "fun." It is easy enough to define the "charm" which I have and other women lack, it is simply that I love you with all my heart, and they do not. Of course it is highly probable that they would love you if the way were clear. Still that is a matter for fancy and speculation; the *facts* remain as I have stated! That gives me a great,—perhaps an unfair advantage—over all the rest; but I shall be quite unscrupulous in making the most of it; since it is the only one I have.

We are all well; Margaret has suddenly begun to hear much better; almost as well as ever.

I love you, Woodrow, my darling, love you inexpressibly, and am in every heart-throb,   Your own   Eileen.

ALS (WP, DLC) with WWsh bibliographical reference on envelope.
  [1] The major works in the program of the Kneisel String Quartet in University Hall on February 27, 1897, were Dvořák's "American" Quartet in F Major, Opus 96, and Schumann's Piano Trio in F Major, Opus 80, with Mme. Mélaine de Wienzkowska as pianist. Ellen's comment about "angel music" probably refers to several shorter pieces on the program—a Bach "Air" (probably the famous "Air for the G-String"), a Haydn "Serenade," and a Boccherini "Minuet." See the *Daily Princetonian*, Feb. 27 and March 1, 1897, for the program and a review of the concert. About the Kneisel concert series in Princeton over the years, see EAW to WW, Feb. 4, 1895, n. 1, Vol. 9.

To Ellen Axson Wilson

My own darling,   Baltimore, Md., 1 March, 1897.

Monday morning is always a rather dismal time with me here, because neither your Saturday nor your Sunday letter gets away from Princeton till Monday morning, and I have to go forty-eight hours without news from my sweet one. This time, indeed, I have the delightful comfort of the thought that this is the last week of my exile. Everything becomes easier in the presence of that thought,—except that a great impatience comes upon me in a flood, and I suddenly forget how to wait!

I took dinner yesterday with Steiner, a Hopkins man who has succeeded his father as Librarian of the Pratt Library here;[1] and had a moderately stupid time. In the evening I took tea with Mr. and Mrs. Reid, and had an altogether delightful time. Remind me when I get home to tell you the stories I heard last night about their little boy.[2] I have three engagements for this week,—three dinner engagements. Tomorrow night I dine with Hiram Woods and "some fellows" whom he has invited to meet me; on Wednesday evening I dine with Mrs. Bird (our usual Sunday arrangements having failed); and on Thursday evening I dine with the Reids. They, by the way, are the most enthusiastic *competent* admirers of my Washington I have yet met. It is only *too* delightful to hear them praise it for the qualities I tried hardest to give it!

I keep very well indeed; and shall to-day finish these terrible examination papers, and feel like a free man once more. It's only painful to be well when you have to use your health in such labour. It would seem more suitable to sickness.

I love you, darling Eileen, more than I'd *dare* say if I could.
                    Your own   Woodrow

WWTLS (WP, DLC).
  [1] Bernard Christian Steiner succeeded his father, Lewis Henry Steiner, as

Librarian of the Enoch Pratt Free Library in Baltimore in 1892 at the age of
twenty-five and continued in the post until his death in 1926.
    2 Francis Fielding Reid, born in May 1891.

From Ellen Axson Wilson

My own darling,   Princeton, Mar. 1, 1897.

It is odd that I should have blundered in writing the date
tonight,[1] since the fact that it is "March 1st," Ed's birthday you
know, has been keeping me busy all day, and one would think
had been thoroughly impressed on my consciousness. The boys
are in the midst of their frolic now I suppose. We got them
packed off with their last goodies about half past seven.

I expected to come and write to you as soon as the children
were tucked in. But I was so tired that before I realized it I had
sunk into an arm-chair, with a new magazine, instead; I have
been there ever since; and it is now ten o'clock; and my eyes
simply decline to remain open.

I have just been reading among other things the "Review of
Reviews" on your Cleveland article;[2] and that reminds me to say
that I appreciate the force of all you say on the subject of your
critics; and that I did not mean to suggest that you read absolutely *no* criticism of your work. I would have you read those
that appear in the more thoughtful, serious, unprejudiced month-
lies and weeklies because they may be of possible service to you
in one or other of the ways you suggest, but I would absolutely
ignore the "common ruck" of "press notices." I have just read
"an auld true tale"—too long to tell,—will keep it till you come—
that illustrates beautifully the value of *such*.

With love beyond all measure,   Your own   Eileen.

ALS (WC, NjP).
    1 Ellen had first written "Feb." and then crossed it out.
    2 "Professor Woodrow Wilson's Estimate of Cleveland as President," New
York *Review of Reviews*, xv (March 1897), 327, a favorable notice.

To Edith Gittings Reid

My dear Mrs. Reid,   [Baltimore, c. March 2, 1897]

We agreed so thoroughly upon the doctrines contained in the
second and third of these essays[1] the other evening, as we talked,
in a conversation to me wholly delightful, of the danger literary
men run amidst the sophisticated set in our great cities, that I
venture to hope that you will read what I have here written, if
not for its own sake, at least as a generous mark of esteem for
                Your very warm friend,   Woodrow Wilson

ALS (WC, NjP).
1 "The Author Himself" and "On an Author's Choice of Company," in *Mere Literature and Other Essays.*

Francis Landey Patton to Cyrus Hall McCormick

My dear Mr McCormick: [Princeton, N. J.] March 2, 1897

I was very glad to get your letter of Feby 9 in regard to Professor Wilson & to have the assurance that you are able to give in respect to his attitude in regard to the department of History. I felt sure when I saw you that there must have been some mistake in supposing that Professor Wilson was offended: though I knew very well how much his heart was set upon having Professor Turner. I think however, that all things considered it is wise for us not to attempt just now to create a new chair of American History. With a deficit staring us in the face, it may be as well for the present to fill Professor Sloane's chair of general History: and I should be very glad to see Professor Haskins, whom Professor Wilson recommends, called to that Chair

Very sincerely yrs   Francis L. Patton

ALS (Patton Letterpress Books, University Archives, NjP).

To Ellen Axson Wilson

My own darling,   Baltimore, Md., 2 March, 1897.

Did you not send a cable message, as well as a letter, to Mrs. Williams about Fraülein Clara![1] If you did not, let me urge you still to do so. You cannot be in the least sure that the clerk at the Princeton post office knows the arrangements with regard to the German mails; and there is, in any case, a doubt about the letter reaching Leipzig before Mrs. Williams leaves.

How shall I thank you, my sweet Eileen, for that delicious love letter you wrote Sunday evening, and upon whose contents I have been drunk ever since last night? And how, my dear little mistress, are you going to maintain your thesis about your inability to speak your love, in the face of such epistles as this, which satisfy your lover as he did not suppose words,—even your words,—could *ever* satisfy him! This dear letter is as sweet, almost, as a kiss: contains sentences which, if they were to be murmured *with* a kiss, or spoken in my arms, would fill me with a delight more perfect than ever yet fell to me, even in your arms. Ah, my matchless little wife, surely you are consenting at last to study and practice *this* sweet art of love, too. I wonder if I am at last to have this crowning triumph: whether, having learned so much of the mystery and sweetness of love from me, you are not now about to add this completing touch of perfect speech, studying to *say* what is in your heart? And I wonder whether I could stand the joy of it, and the pride, too, of having won this final gift. Those were perfect days we spent together last week, my Eileen, but others are coming which will be sweeter still and more supremely delightful, if this is so! I wish I could give you a Kneisel concert every week to speed the process. I admit, my darling, that I cannot imagine anything more perfect than those intoxicating days, which will always be a sacred memory between us; but, after all, may they not have been but an earnest and foretaste of days to come when we shall have discovered the full speech of love. We have grown closer and closer together year by year, and shall we say that we have reached the limit! There is no limit between us!

See how you can excite me, my queen, by your perfect gift of speech, when you give it leave. Ah, how welcome you are to "all of me"! For what "fun" could I exchange this perfect happiness of having won all your heart and given you all of mine? Bless you, my sweetheart: I am yours wholly and with an absolute devotion, and there is no happiness to be compared with going back to you, to live as yours and yours alone! Only two more letters, and then I shall come myself, and the space will be closed up and forgotten between those heavenly days we now remember and the days of our reunion for the rest of the year!

Good bye, Eileen, my perfect darling. Think of me till I come and receive me as

Your own   Woodrow, your husband and your lover.

WWTLS (WP, DLC).
  [1] Clara Böhm of Leipzig, whom the Wilsons were considering as a governess for their children. Ellen had apparently asked Mrs. Williams to interview her for them.

From Ellen Axson Wilson

My own darling,   Princeton, Mar. 2, 1897

Before I forget it let me acknowledge the receipt and deposit of the $150.00 check.[1]

I have just come from an illustrated lecture by Mr. Libby[2] on Cuba,—at which I went fast asleep, leaning peacefully against the wall—(in the Miller Church.) Fortunately I was completely hidden from public view by a forest of tall hats and nodding plumes,—the appropriate insignia of our bourgeoisie on dress

parade. I went of course for the pictures, but found them,—
what I could see of them,—dull, and the lecture,—nothing.

I am getting quite gay—go out again tomorrow night, to dine
at the Perry's and meet the Smiths.[3] They had hoped you would
be here and are quite disappointed, but decided they wanted
me anyhow. But you are *really* gay! "Out every night!" How the
engagements always pile up in the last weeks of your stay there!
As for the Reids I am sure now that I should find her as charming
as you do, since she admires your work so much, and for the
right things.

Speaking of invitations,—of course you will decline for *me* the
invitation to the "tear" in New York![4]

The boys seem to have had a grand time last night,—kept it
up 'till nearly one o'clock. The fellows all declared it the best
spread they had ever seen, and gave me a vote of thanks and
"three times three."

Good-night, my darling, Only four nights alone now! Ah! how
glad I am!—and how I *love* you, *love* you, *love* you.

Your little wife,   Eileen.

ALS (WC, NjP).
  [1] Probably from the *Atlantic Monthly* for "Mr. Cleveland as President."
  [2] William Libbey, Professor of Physical Geography and Histology and Director of the E. M. Museum of Geology and Archaeology at Princeton.
  [3] The local newspapers do not tell us who these Smiths were.
  [4] The Editors have been unable to discover what the "tear" in New York was.

To Ellen Axson Wilson

My own darling,   Baltimore, Md., 3 March, 1897.

Will you not fulfil the following commissions for me? (1)
Please send Bob. Bridges one of those photographs I got not
long ago (of myse[l]f). (2) Please send a check for ten dollars
to the man whose note I return, making it payable to J. Max
Irwin, Superintendent.[1] (3) Please, ma'am, if you love me, accept
the invitation I return *for both of us*. I cannot decently decline
such an invitation, *but I will not go without you*. It fills me with
delight to think of your being so honoured *with* me, and I will not
bear the disappointment of going without you. Please write explaining that I am away, and saying that I have asked you to
accept for both of us. These last are *instructions*!

I feel rather "rocky" this morning, having been at dinner with
Hiram and the other men he had invited until after midnight
last night. Not that I feel ill in any sort or degree: I just do not
feel spry.

It's just as well. I have reached the stage (in view of the fact that this is the next to the last letter I shall write before going to you myself) when it has become again impossible to write love letters! The sweet ecstacy of having you in my arms and being with you as much as I please,—even to the preventing of everything you want to do,—is so near at hand that impatience grows upon me almost to the point of overmastering me. So completely am I, in every thought and movement of heart,

Your own   Woodrow

WWTLS (WP, DLC).
  1 Joseph Max Irwin, Stated Supply, 1895-98, of the University Place Cumberland Presbyterian Church. It is not known of what he was the superintendent.

From Ellen Axson Wilson

My own darling,   Princeton, Mar. 3, 1897
    Various things combined to prevent my writing earlier today as I expected; it is now half past ten; I have just come from the Perry's, slipped on a wrapper, and run down to write a few lines before I go to bed.
    I had an unusually pleasant evening; they were all people that I like well, the Smiths, the Hibben's and Mr. Fine. I went out with Mr. Hibben who was expressing profound regret that you had not been here during the past week,—and—shall I confess it? I *could not share his regret!*—not for the *reason he gave!* It seems the di[s]cipline committee have been in deep waters, and Mr. Hibben thought your brains had been much needed; but *I* was glad you escaped it all. I suppose you have heard echos of the trouble;—how the Sophomores kidnapped the light-weight wrestler, took him to New Brunswick and kept him there, so that they might *win* (!) the contest on Washington's birthday. They tried to secure all three of the champions but failed with the other two. The principal offenders have escaped, as usual; but two boys are sent away; one of them Gordon Johnston's brother.[1]
    Good-night, my dear one. To think that I have but one more letter to write:—and *then!*—ah then perfect happiness for

Your own   Eileen.

ALS (WC, NjP).
  1 Gordon Johnston, '96, and his brother, Robert Daniel Johnston, Jr., from Birmingham.

From Daniel Collamore Heath

My dear Professor Wilson: Boston March 3, 1897.

Yours of the 24th[1] received and I have read it with interest. I can easily understand that a man of your reputation cannot afford to have a book[2] which is not now correct sold unless it is sold under the date at which it was written. Why the date was not changed is more than I am able to tell you at this minute for the reason that my manufacturing clerk is not in and therefore I cannot ask him why the date was not changed. I supposed it had been changed. I assume, however, that he has printed none of the books since your request was made but has been simply binding up sheets that were printed before the request was made. He could have printed new title pages, even though it would have cost us something extra.

Now, as to resetting the book: I should like to refer that matter to my partners who will be in session in Boston from the 10th to the 20th of this month. I take it that you will be willing to await that length of time our final decision in the matter.

I enclose statement of sales for the six months ending December 31st[3] and I note that the sale of your book has during this period increased about 50 per cent. over last year's sales for the same period. It seems a pity to withdraw a book from the market that is increasing in sale.

By the way, since you think it would be the fairest arrangement for you to undertake half the expense of the revision, and since you will find it inconvenient to raise money to help on the book, would you be willing to allow us to put into the book on your account the royalties now due you, we to pay all the remaining expense. This would make you bear about ¼ part of the expense and we ¾?   Very truly yours,   D. C. Heath.

TL (WP, DLC).
  [1] It is missing.
  [2] *The State: Elements of Historical and Practical Politics.*
  [3] This royalty statement is missing.

To Ellen Axson Wilson

My own darling,   Baltimore, Md., 4 March, 1897.

My exile is nearly over, and a joy fills me which is surely the sweetest a man can feel. At dinner last night Mrs. Bird put her hand on the beautiful centre-piece and said, "This reminds me of Ellen: I used it first at that luncheon I gave her the last time she was here." I replied, "*Every*thing reminds *me* of her!" It was almost too true and intimate a thing to say aloud. My whole life reminds me of you: seems in some sort to proceed from you. Ah, how unspeakably I have been blessed: what a blessing and benediction it is upon our lives that such love should have come into them as that which holds us together. I know more fully and with a clearer consciousness every day of my life, it seems to me, that it has brought me the single thing which has put all my powers at their best. I needed just the love you have given me, and there is no one else in the world who could have given me this heart's desire, which I had not fully realized until it was satisfied. No one else ever gave a man just what you h[a]ve given me: that sweet love so subtly compounded of charm and tenderness, of engaging mental qualities and a distracting simplicity of womanly affection: so that there is no part of your mind or character which I do not love with the same touch of romance and ardour that a young man feels for his bride. All your qualities take me captive, and make me know myself free only when I am most completely

Your own   Woodrow

WWTLS (WP, DLC).

From Ellen Axson Wilson

My own darling,   Princeton, Mar 4, 1897.

Where do you think I have just been?—to the Trustee meeting! I feel like a magnate! To be sure I only stood outside the door, like the peri.[1] In your mail this morning came a note from Mr. Green[2] asking you to meet them there between 10 and 12; so I thought best to go and explain that you were absent. Is this *the* important meeting, or only some committee?[3]

I shall of course do as you insist and accept the N. Y. engagement. It might be very different, though, if you were here and I could "have it out with you"! Now if I only hadn't bought that dress I *couldn't* go; so I am being punished for my extravagance!

Did you see that Mr. Magie's father has been made Chief Justice of New Jersey?[4]

That is our only news except Cleveland gossip. She and the children have been here some time. She was at chapel Sunday. He I believe is to go South to shoot something,—or somebody,—before he comes here. By the way, you know the easy and cheerful manner in which you have always quieted the natural anxiety of our good friends as to what he should "do" here. (Poor souls! to be called upon to take charge of an ex-President *is* a heavy responsibility!) You always said he would "go fishing with Hough-ton Murray."[5] You will be interested to know that the same idea has occurred to another great man, viz. Houghton Murray him-self. He says he "expects to be Mr. Cleveland's most intimate friend."

You did not say whether you succeeded in getting a lecture appointment for last Saturday; so I don't know whether to expect you on the 2 o'clock or the late train Sat. But doubtless you will remember to tell me in tomorrow's letter.

And now goodbye, my darling, until I see you; the thought of all that implies fills me with a rapture that I cannot trust myself to speak of just now.　　　　　　　Your own　Eileen.

ALS (WC, NjP).

[1] According to Persian mythology an imaginary being, elf, or fairy, descended from fallen angels and forced to stand outside the door of heaven until penance is completed.

[2] Charles Ewing Green of Trenton.

[3] It was the Special Committee on the Affairs of the University, about the appointment of which see the extract from the Princeton Trustees' Minutes printed at Dec. 10, 1896. As the documents will soon reveal, Wilson appeared be-fore the Special Committee on March 10.

[4] William Francis Magie, Professor of Physics at Princeton, and his father, William Jay Magie, Chief Justice of the New Jersey Supreme Court, 1897-1900; Chancellor of New Jersey, 1900-1908; and trustee of Princeton from 1891 until his death in 1917.

[5] Haughton Murray, son of Dean Murray, who lived with his parents in the Dean's House at 73 Nassau St.

To Ellen Axson Wilson

My precious darling,　　　　Baltimore, Friday morning 5 Mar., '97

I delivered a Saturday lecture last week, and shall be free to take the best train of the day and reach Princeton at six minutes of two o'clock, God willing.

What my thoughts are I shall try to tell you when I have you in my arms,—but not till then. I seem to *know* and to *feel* nothing but that I am　　　　　　　Your own　Woodrow

ALS (WP, DLC).

From Charles Forster Smith[1]

My dear Sir:　　　　　　Madison, Wis.　March 10, 1897.

I have just read your great article on President Cleveland in the March *Atlantic*, and beg that you will allow me to thank you for it. Your treatment of the subject seems to me remarkably judicious and your manner of expression strikingly felicitous. Usually we have to wait long before one is found capable of writing so calmly, dispassionately, and judiciously about a great public character when every body is either praising or blaming. I am *satisfied* with your discussion of Mr. Cleveland's course. I never "went back on" Mr. Cleveland—pardon the phrase—but once, namely when he sent in the Venezuela message, and even then I tried to keep my mind open to the possibility of new light. And here again I am satisfied with your view. You have done a real service to political thought by this article, and those who are not partisans, but simply want good government, and are praying that leaders will from time to time appear about whom the real patriotism of the country can rally, will be especially grateful to you.

At this late day let me thank you also for the satisfaction your great sesquicentennial address gave me; and I might refer to still other public utterances of yours, were I not afraid of wearying you.

I recall with much pleasure an hour spent in showing you over the Vanderbilt grounds[2] (especially a remark you let fall then, that when you felt you needed a mental tonic you took up Elisha Mulford's *The Nation*), and with not less pleasure the evening spent at your house in July 1891, when I had the honor to renew my acquaintance with Mrs. Wilson, whom I had met at Mr. Ewing's in Nashville.[3] Begging that you will present my respects to her, I am,

Very truly yours,   Chas. Forster Smith.

ALS (WP, DLC).
[1] Professor of Greek and Classical Philology at the University of Wisconsin.
[2] In June 1886, when the Wilsons visited Robert and Harriet Hoyt Ewing in Nashville, and Smith was Professor of Greek at Vanderbilt University.
[3] Before Ellen's marriage.

From the Minutes of the Special Committee on the Affairs of the University

Trustees Room [Princeton, N. J.], Mch 10, 1897.
Present: Craven, Dixon, Stewart, & C. E. Green . . .
Prof Woodrow Wilson: discipline not effective
              3 Deans, graduate work shd be advanced. . . .

Hw minutes (Papers of the Special Committee on the Affairs of the University, University Archives, NjP).

Notes for Remarks at a Dinner[1]

12 March, 1897.

Can speak to any company except '79 and the N.Y. Alumni.
  With '79 I feel too much like a boy,—with the N.Y. alumni too much
  out of authority.
Present occasion not likely to set me at my ease
  My heart too much disturbed
  My head too much turned.
Certainly a red-letter day for me:
  Would rather be honoured by my class-mates than by any one else.
  They are not imposed upon,—unless by their affections
  They represent the training and the ideals wh. I feel to be most
  distinctively my own,—and Princeton's. As I said in my oration
  that there had been no such men since the Revolution, I thought
  of the back row[2] and my heart contradicted me.
  What heart and dignity in his work must it not give a man to be
  backed and cheered by such comrades.
I knew as I thought about the occasion what it must all mean:
  I have but carried out the ideals and purposes formed amongst
  you in the old days of our first fellowship here: you know that
  I am trying to be what I promised you,—what we promised each
  other.
I am a '79 man, and not one of those who write and lie in their graves
  "merely for pastime." Those who write not with bloody sweat will
  assuredly lie in their graves betimes.
Princeton has long had noble ideals—suitable to ennoble the nation;
  but it has not long sought the voice of literature to utter those
  ideals. It is that voice we would seek—if we do not find it, others
  may.
But enough: I have said my say. I won't carry you quite to "Pottsdam."
  I dared not learn a speech lest I sh. blurt the whole of a sudden,
  like the little boy: "My name's Johnny, I'm five yrs. old, go to Hell!"
Certainly these are novel enough proceedings, not open to the old
  negro's objection to the Episcopalian service. "Cy McCormick's."
I hope that they are not evidence that we are growing old and men-
  dacious about ourselves: "Heaven lies about us in our infancy[.]"
  In old age we lie about ourselves.
"Hope you will continue to approach me with your usual familiarity."

WWhw and WWsh MS. (WP, DLC).
  [1] A news report of this affair is printed at March 18, 1897.
  [2] Members of the Class of 1879 were seated on the back row in Alexander Hall
while Wilson delivered his Sesquicentennial oration.

From Daniel Collamore Heath

Dear Professor Wilson: Boston 15 March, 1897.

Yours of the 9th[1] received, and we have talked the matter over
fully and agree that we can afford to make an exception in your
case and pay for the new edition of your book ourselves, so please
go ahead on it as fast as you can.[2]

In re-setting the book we will make the page larger, but we shall probably have to use the same size type, which is easily read and will help us to keep the book within reasonable bounds.

I find that we have 338 copies of the book at the different offices and 346 in sheets. Now the question arises can you get the new edition ready in such season that we will not need to print any more of the old edition.

You may be sure that I could not have any feeling over any decision you might come to. I do not forget how fair you mean to be and have been in all matters, and that you treat this matter, as you have others, in a perfectly dispassionate and business-like way.   Yours very truly,   D. C. Heath.

TL (WP, DLC).
  [1] It is missing.
  [2] Wilson apparently began work soon afterward, for he wrote to Albert Bushnell Hart on May 18, 1897, that he was busy revising *The State* and had promised to complete the new version by the coming September. As subsequent documents will indicate, a variety of diversions prevented him from making such rapid progress. D. C. Heath's letter to Wilson of February 14, 1898, reveals that Wilson had just promised to send in copy for the revised edition on about May 1, 1898. Perhaps he finished before this date, for the preface to the new edition is dated March 31, 1897. In any event, his letters to his wife of June 18 and 19, 1898, show that he was then reading proof of the book. It appeared on about September 1, 1898.
  For the revision, Wilson rewrote and combined the first two chapters on the probable origin of government and its early development into one new first chapter entitled "The Earliest Forms of Government." He rewrote and divided old Chapter III on the governments of Greece and Rome into two separate chapters. In addition, he rewrote several sections in Chapter IV on Roman dominion and law and in Chapter V on Teutonic governments during the Middle Ages and the diffusion of Roman law in Europe, large portions of the chapters on France and Switzerland, and smaller portions of the chapters on Germany, Austria-Hungary, Great Britain, and the United States, in every case updating his text and incorporating the most recent scholarly findings. He went through the rest of the old text, updating and revising it where necessary, and tightening and improving its style. Finally, he updated his bibliographies by the addition of many new titles. Significantly, he made the fewest number of changes in the last four chapters on the nature and forms of government, the nature and development of law, the functions of government, and the objects of government. In fact, he made no important substantive changes in these chapters.
  One contemporary described the final product as follows: "The whole book has been carefully rewritten. The descriptive material is everywhere brought down to date, while nearly every page is improved by the introduction of some happy turn of expression or more telling illustration. Always an ardent believer in style as an indispensable adjunct to historical writing, the author in this latest work shows how much higher his own standard of literary execution has become since the book first saw the light in 1889." Unsigned review of *The State: Elements of Historical and Practical Politics*, revised edn. (Boston, 1898), in the *Annals of the American Academy of Political and Social Science*, XII (Nov. 1898), 417.
  The documentary materials in the Wilson Papers, Library of Congress, relating to Wilson's revision of *The State* are (1) Wilson's shorthand drafts of large portions of new Chapter III ("The Government of Rome") and the new sections for Chapter IV ("Roman Dominion and Roman Law"), Chapter V ("Teutonic Polity and Government during the Middle Ages"), Chapter VI ("The Government of France"), Chapter VII ("The Governments of Germany"), Chapter VIII ("The Governments of Switzerland"), Chapter IX ("The Dual Monarchies"), Chapter X ("The Government of Great Britain"), and Chapter XI ("The Government of

ministration of the federal Constitution, the guaranteeing of the cantonal constitutions, or the fulfilment of federal duties for their object"; and to effect revisions of the federal Constitution. *

This indefiniteness is due, in large part at least, to the fact that the federal Constitution has not yet been put upon a thoroughly logical basis. Though the drift of national sentiment has been strong enough to give the federal government great powers, it has not as yet been strong enough to give it complete powers within its own sphere. Cantonal jealousy has withheld logical roundness from the prerogatives of the central authorities: with the result of leaving their outlines a little vague.

514. Guarantee of the Cantonal Constitutions. — The Swiss federal Constitution is more definite in guaranteeing to the Cantons their constitutions than our federal Constitution is in guaranteeing to the States "a republican form of government." The guarantee is made to include the freedom of the people and their legal and constitutional rights; the exercise of those rights under representative democratic forms; and the revision of any cantonal constitution whenever an absolute majority of the citizens of the Canton desire a revision.

THE CANTONAL GOVERNMENTS.

515. The Cantonal Constitutions and the Federal Constitution. — So deeply is Swiss federal organization rooted in cantonal precedents, that an understanding of the government of the Confederation is best gained by studying first, the political institutions of the Cantons. At almost all points the federal government exhibits likeness to the governments of the Cantons, out of whose union it has grown. As our own federal Constitution may be said to generalize and apply colonial habit and experience, so the Swiss Constitution may be said to generalize and apply cantonal habit and experience: though both

A page of Wilson's autographed edition of "The State," showing a shorthand revision which he drafted for the 1898 edition

the United States"); (2) random WWhw and WWsh notes, outlines, and bibliographical references; and (3) numerous pages of the edition of 1889 with WWhw and WWsh additions and emendations.

A News Report

[March 18, 1897]

DINNER TO PROF. WILSON.

The Class of '79 Gives One in His Honor

All Princetonians share great pride in the various distinctions to which Prof. Woodrow Wilson has attained, and it was a happy idea on the part of the class of '79 to give a complimentary dinner in honor of their distinguished classmate. Owing to the recent publication and favorable reception of Prof. Wilson's book on "George Washington" it was originally planned, and very appropriately, to have the dinner on February 22nd. Owing to imperative previous engagements on Prof. Wilson's part, however, the date had to be changed, and the dinner was held last Friday night [March 12]. Every feature of it was carried out with the greatest success, several novelties being introduced which served to make the occassion a peculiarly pleasant one.

The table was set in the large dining room of the Inn and was tastefully decorated in orange and black. At one end of the table was a miniature cherry tree partially chopped down; in the center stood a large model of Nassau Hall, while at the other end was a representation of the historic cannon. At the foot of the table sat Mr. A. W. Halsey of New York who acted as toast-master, at the other end was William R. Wilder, Secretary of the class, and on his right sat Prof. Woodrow Wilson, the guest of the evening. On the menu card was an excellent engraving of Prof. Wilson, while on the back was a list of all his published works.[1] Another memento which each guest received was a little hatchet with the following inscription on the blade: "Dinner given Woodrow Wilson by the Class of '79, Princeton Inn, March 12, 1897." The toast-master, Mr. Halsey, made the principal address of the evening, and after speaking of the high appreciation in which Prof. Wilson is held by his class, presented him on behalf of the class with a bust of George Washington. It is a bronze bust executed by Houdon of Paris and when placed on a marble pedestal, stands seven feet high. Prof. Wilson responded in a few well chosen words, after which a number of impromptu speeches were made. Among those who spoke were James W. Alexander '60, Prof. W. F. Magie, Robert Bridges of New York, Charles Talcott of

Utica, W. B. Lee of New York, C. C. Cuyler of New York and
D. M. Barringer of Philadelphia. Mr. Wilder, the class secretary
read a number of letters from those unable to be present. . . .

Printed in the *Alumni Princetonian*, March 18, 1897.
    [1] A copy of the menu is in the Wilson Papers, Library of Congress, and is
autographed by all the '79 men present. They were (in the order in which they
signed) Woodrow Wilson, Charles A. Talcott, William F. Magie, Lawrence W.
Allibone, Cleveland H. Dodge, Harold Godwin, Peter A. V. van Doren, Mungo J.
Currie, Francis S. Phraner, Adrian Riker, George E. Shoemaker, Robert Bridges,
Chalmers Martin, Alexander J. Kerr, Abram W. Halsey, Frank H. Lord, William
T. Elsing, Fletcher Durell, Alfred J. P. McClure, Daniel M. Barringer, William
R. Wilder, John S. Baird, George L. Prentiss, Parker D. Handy, Charles O.
Brewster, Edward W. Sheldon, William B. Isham, Jr., Robert R. Henderson,
William B. Lee, John Farr, Robert H. McCarter, and Cornelius C. Cuyler.

To Robert Bridges

My dear Bobby,   Princeton, 18 March, 1897

It has taken me nearly a whole week to get over the emotional
effects of that extraordinary dinner,—so generously conceived, so
like the great class in the way it was done! I have never been quite
so overwhelmed as I was by the words of love and appreciation
spoken that night, or quite so eager to deserve the praise and
affection of the boys. I hope I shall never lose that eagerness; but
I am calm enough now to tell you what was in my heart as *you*
spoke. No man ever gave his friend greater joy, Bobby, than you
gave me. You said what I might have prayed my best friend
might be able to say; and it has heartened me beyond all expression. I do not know how to thank you, but I do know how to
appreciate your praise and your affection.
    As of old,   Your loving friend,   Woodrow Wilson

ALS (WC, NjP).

From Walter Hines Page

Dear Mr. Wilson,   [Cambridge, Mass.] March 20, 1897.

In some quiet half hour when you have nothing better to do,
will you not send me a little paper for "Men and Letters" in the
Atlantic? The short articles (from 1000 to 2000 words) that we
group under this general heading are really signed editorials on
literary subjects. Any subject, therefore, that has to do with
literature comes within the range of this little "Department"—
to give it a big name—for example:

How comes it that although there are multitudes of special
students of history in the United States who know more facts and
have a wider range of information than any great historical

writer in the world had down to twenty-five years ago, the amount of historical writing (properly so-called) is really very small, and most of it so dull as to be almost unreadable?

The forgotten necessity that a man who proposes to write anything worth while should steep himself in the great English literature in order to have the genius of the race as a basis of his style and a corrective of his thought. No foreign literature, not even the classics, will answer quite the same purpose. If a man do not have his own race behind him he will not write truly for his race: he cannot say a lasting word nor take hold on a permanent tendency.

These subjects happen to come into my mind at the moment. You may not care for either of them. I mention them only to show the kind of subjects that I hope to have taken up in "Men and Letters."[1]

I am hoping for your article on the Growth of American National Feeling for the July number (copy by the middle of May), although I remember that your promise to have it ready was conditional.[2]

In October the Atlantic Monthly will be forty years old, and we wish to celebrate that anniversary with a number that will be noteworthy. I am now making engagements for it with some of our best writers. We reckon on an article by you for that—may we not? You shall be in most excellent company and we need your help.[3]

All sorts of pleasant things come to us about your article on Cleveland.   Very sincerely yours,   Walter H. Page

TLS (Houghton Mifflin Letterpress Books, MH).

[1] Insofar as is known, Wilson never contributed to the "Men and Letters" column.

[2] This article, "The Making of the Nation," is printed at April 15, 1897.

[3] Wilson did not contribute to the October number.

From Octave Thanet[1]

Davenport, Iowa.
Dear Sir: March the twenty-second 1897.

Will you permit a fellow writer to express to you (not for herself alone but for everyone with whom she has talked on the subject) her admiration for your lucid, wise and strong article on President Cleveland. I am glad to see expressed the sentiments of seven out of ten business men who would like to be good citizens if they could hope that it would be of any use. And, to me who has studied Mr. Cleveland's career since his first election to the presidency, your analysis has been a great help.

Thank you: and thank you for your study of the *real* Washington. I feel you have deserved well of your country; and it is a comfort to me to say so.

Trusting that you will excuse a stranger for this frankness, I am, dear sir,   Very sincerely yours,   Octave Thanet.

ALS (WP, DLC).
[1] The pseudonym of Alice French (1850-1934), prolific author of novels, short stories, and works of non-fiction.

From the Minutes of the Princeton Faculty

5 5 P.M. Wednesday, March 24th, 1897.
. . . The report of the Committee in reference to Eating Clubs was considered and then recommitted to the Committee on Discipline.[1]

[1] For the report as approved, see the Princeton Faculty Minutes printed at March 31, 1897.

From Edward Ireland Renick

My dear Wilson: [Washington] Mar 25, 1897

Be sure to read Congressional Record March 24, 1897 page 212 beginning at the lower part of 1st column.[1]

Yours as ever with kind regards to Mrs Wilson,

E. I. Renick

I am alone at the Grafton [Hotel]—my wife being in Kentucky. Do come to see me when you are in Baltimore.

E. I. R.

ALS (WP, DLC).
[1] He referred to a portion of a speech on the Dingley tariff bill by Representative John Sharp Williams of Mississippi. Williams attacked the measure for reflecting "plutocratic influences" and not the will of the people. Williams also criticized the lack of leadership and legislative responsibility in a government which was not working as a harmonious whole and in which each branch tended to check the other with "nobody in particular responsible to the people for results."

From Charles Ewing Green

My dear Mr. Wilson,   Trenton 27, Mch. '97

Had your inquiry in regard to the chair of History[1] stood alone without reference to a possibility that the President might be withholding information from you for some reason unknown, I should have given you just what took place, which was entirely without discussion.

In view of the suggestion you have made, it seems to me that the information should come first and direct from the President; without the slightest criticism from me—I *have none, feel none*—because you have asked me in regard to the matter.

Possibly there may be a situation in which you think the President should send for you and tell you about the matter.

Can there be any possible reason why you should not say to Dr. Patton: You know my great interest in this subject, is there any reason why I should not know the action of the Board?

It would be impertinent in me to outline even anything further, to a gentleman of your tact and discrimination. I think my position is very clear, and correct. I shall always be glad to see and talk with you upon this or any other matter of university interest.

Very Sincerely Yrs   Charles E Green

ALS (WP, DLC) with WWsh notation on first page of letter: "Answered 28 March '97."
¹ Wilson's letter initiating this correspondence is missing, but for intimations of its contents see WW to F. L. Patton, March 28, 1897; WW to C. E. Green, March 28, 1897; F. L. Patton to WW, March 29, 1897; and, particularly, C. E. Green to WW, April 2, 1897.

To Francis Landey Patton

My dear Dr. Patton: [Princeton, N.J.] 28 March '97

I find myself forced to ask what action the Board of Trustees took with reference to the Department of History at its meeting nearly three weeks ago. You will remember the correspondence which you requested me to enter into with Professors Turner and Haskins and you will recall my having informed them that action was postponed in December to be taken in March. And you will perceive, therefore, how bound [I am] alike in mere friendship and courtesy to tell them at once of our full wish.

Let me add, that except for their sakes and for the sake of the duty I owe them, I would not inquire about this matter at all. Since, however, I feel myself forced to speak of it I must in all frankness add that I am deeply hurt by the way I have been treated in this affair. I have felt it something less than friendly, something less than courteous, that it should have seemed worth nobody's while all this time so much as to inform me whether the Board had acted at all or not. I have been treated like an employee rather than a colleague. But let me say again I should never have brought myself to speak of the matter of my own initiative had I not been under an obligation to others.

Very sincerely yours,   Woodrow Wilson

Transcript of WWshLS (draft) (WP, DLC).

To Charles Ewing Green

My dear Sir: [Princeton, N.J.] 28 March '97

Your letter of yesterday gave me a most painful surprise, and the feeling that it calls for an immediate reply.

You will remember that you took the initiative in consulting me about the reorganization of the History Department, and that when interviewed upon that subject I mentioned two men who seemed to me entirely qualified to undertake the history work of the University. I mean Professor Turner and Professor Haskins of Wisconsin University. You advised me to sound these gentlemen about their willingness to come to Princeton. I afterwards had several interviews with Dr. Patton upon the same matter— at his own invitation of course,—and got similar, very explicit advice from him. Both Professor Turner and Professor Haskins were intimately known to me, and I wrote to them with the utmost frankness, committing myself (though nobody else of course) quite unreservedly to the plan of calling them to Princeton. I had been led to expect action upon the matter at the December meeting of the Board of Trustees: when action was then postponed, I told Dr. Patton that I should write my friends of the postponement and tell them that the matter would be decided in March. I was bound alike in friendship and courtesy to let them know before March should run out what had been done. They had, of course, with a very proper pride, refused to be candidates for the appointment here; but they had known my action throughout, and it was my obvious duty to keep them informed of the action of the Board. For myself alone I should never have asked.

You, however, feel it your right to reprove me for my reference to the President. I wrote the letter I sent you in some haste and it was hardly out of my hands before I was aware that I had been guilty of a grave breach of taste; but I had hoped that under the circumstances you would have seen that it was justice to overlook it. Your letter was couched in the kindest terms, and I wish to say that I am in fact obliged to you for your words of appreciation. I wish also to add that, in performance of obvious duty it is my desire to apologize for my breach of college etiquette, which I perceive and sincerely regret. But I must in frankness admit myself deeply pained by the way in which you have replied to my proper inquiries about a business into which I was invited and did not thrust myself.

Very sincerely yours,   Woodrow Wilson

Transcript of WWshLS (draft) (WP, DLC).

Notes for a Religious Talk

                                                          28 Mar., '97.
                        Layman's Conference[1]
Collectivism of present age
  Effects upon our ideals and methods of social regeneration. We
    try to regenerate the poor and vicious by *social* motives:
    thr. their

          self-respect ⎫
          ambition   ⎬ of wh. they have none
          initiative   ⎭

  Booker Washington right,—we wrong.
"Expulsive power of a new affection."
  We never live nobly until we cease to live for ourselves. Only
    love transforms.
Christ the Saviour of the world.
  Individual salvation *is* national salvation.

WWhw MS. (WP, DLC).
  [1] This organization is described in n. 1 to the news item printed at April 6,
1894, Vol. 8. The meeting to which Wilson spoke on March 28, 1897, was, according to the announcement in the *Daily Princetonian*, March 27, 1897, a "union
meeting of the Mission Board and the Laymen's Conference" in Murray Hall on
the Princeton campus. No Princeton newspaper reported on Wilson's talk.

From Joseph Ruggles Wilson

My precious Son—   Richmond, Va. Mar. 28/97
    I write especially to say that I expect to start to-morrow on my
way to Durham, N. C.; but inasmuch as I am booked to stop
a couple of days in Wilmington N. C., I will probably not reach
my principal destination before Friday (April 2nd). Of course
you are interested in my simple movements and stay-ments. The
probability is that I shall trip it into Georgia during the interval
between leaving Durham and the meeting of General Assembly
at Charlotte, N. C. May 20th.[1]
    I hear occasionally from Josie and Kate,[2] never from Annie
(since her daughter was ill in New York), and from yourself
when you *can*. But old dads get—very naturally—to be postponed
for more immediate interests—and believe me, dearest son, that
I am content.
      Love to all   Your affectionate   Father

ALS (WP, DLC).
  [1] The General Assembly of the southern Presbyterian Church met in the First
Presbyterian Church of Charlotte, May 20-29, 1897.
  [2] That is, his younger son, Joseph R. Wilson, Jr., and Josie's wife, Kate.

From Francis Landey Patton

My dear Professor Wilson: Princeton, N. J. March 29th 1897

I have received your letter of March 28th & regret exceedingly that I have occasioned you any uneasiness through failure to communicate with you in regard to the action of the Board of Trustees respecting the Chair of History. I am greatly pained to know that you regard yourself as treated in a manner "something less than friendly, something less than courteous." I assure you that nothing could have been further from my mind than the thought of doing anything discourteous or of failing to do anything that my warm friendship for you would seem to call for.

I had expected to go and see you or to write: but I have been exceedingly busy since the meeting of the Board. I have had a number of engagements to meet that required time for preparation and that have taken me out of town from time to time. I did not suppose that the matter was so urgent and, therefore, preoccupied as I was, I very naturally allowed more time to pass before communicating with you than I had intended.

You may remember that the last conversation that you & I had upon the subject under consideration was in your own house during a visit which I paid you for that purpose. I wish that you had felt free to come & see me after the meeting of the Board of Trustees. I am always glad to see the Professors and whenever an appointment is under consideration the Professors interested are in the habit of coming to see me as frequently as the necessities of the case require: and it is always a great pleasure to me to discuss college problems with them.

In the conversation to which I have just referred I presented you at considerable length the way in which, after most careful reflection, the whole subject lay in my mind. I think therefore that you will not be surprised when I tell you what the action of the Board was.

At the meeting of the Curriculum Committee held the day before the meeting of the Trustees I stated again your views in regard to the Department of History and your estimate of the two gentlemen referred to in your letter. I then presented my own views substantially as I had submitted them to you: And said that in my judgment it was not expedient for the Trustees, in view of our present financial condition, to erect a new chair of American History, but that we should content ourselves for the present with filling the chair now vacant. I then said that I should be glad to see Mr Haskins elected to the chair of History, &

that I was entirely satisfied to act on your judgment without any further consideration of the subject.

The committee felt however that some member of the committee[,] preferably the President of the University[,] should see Mr Haskins before the chair was formally tendered to him & they decided that instead [of] making a nomination to the vacant professorship they would simply report progress and request the President of the University to make an oral statement. I made a very full statement of the case, giving my reason for not thinking it best to elect a Professor of American History at present and also for thinking that Professor Haskins is the best man to fill Professor Sloane's chair. But I said that the committee were of the opinion that I ought to see Mr Haskins before the Trustees go the length of inviting him to the Professorship. The Trustees were of the same opinion. Accordingly no action was taken looking to the establishment of a chair of American History: and an expression of opinion in regard to Mr Haskins, was all that transpired in regard to the filling of Prof Sloane's chair. It was understood however that at an early day I would seek an interview with Mr. Haskins, and if as the result [of] that interview the proposed relationship of Mr Haskins to our vacant chair should seem to promise to be mutually satisfactory I should have no hesitation in saying to him that he would be elected at the next meeting of the Board. In following this plan the Trustees are acting in accordance with their custom in such cases and I think are acting in great wisdom. I wish to say before I close that in all my references to this matter I have expressed my great obligation to you for the interest you have taken and the very kind assistance you have given me: & the reason I feel that your judgment should as far as possible be controlling. And I close as I began by repeating my expression of regret that anything so unfortunate should have occurred through any carelessness of mine that should cause you to feel that you had not been treated with proper consideration.

I am very sincerely yours   Francis L Patton

ALS (WP, DLC).

To Azel Washburn Hazen[1]

My dear Dr. Hazen,   Princeton, 29 March, 1897

I don't know how many long letters to you I have planned,—full of the many things I have thought,—*we* have thought,—of you and Mrs. Hazen, our dear friends, as our minds have turned again and again to Middletown and the two years, good to think of, which we spent there: and your letter[2] now more than two months old stirred me with an added impulse. But no letter was written,—simply because the flesh was weak! For almost a year now I have been suffering with neuritis in my right arm. For months I was forbidden to use the pen at all, and laboriously practiced the use of my left hand. I am a great deal better now; but it is still unwise to write more than a few lines,—and I must make them suffice. After all one can get as much affection into a line as in to a paragraph!

It has been a solace to us to feel that we were still members of your church, even if we could not see or hear you,—and the churches here have for long been in such a condition of would-be change that we have had no very ill conscience in the matter. But now we have settled conditions at last, and a clear duty in the matter:—we *must* ask for a letter to the Second Presbyterian Church of Princeton. Indeed we have waited already too long, reluctant to break the last actual tie to Middletown!

But I have written too much in writing this letter. Mrs. Wilson joins me in the most affectionate messages both to Mrs. Hazen and yourself, and I am, as ever

Your sincere friend,   Woodrow Wilson

ALS (in possession of Frances Hazen Bulkeley).
[1] Minister of the First Congregational Church in Middletown, Conn.
[2] It is missing.

To Frederick Jackson Turner

My dear Turner,   Princeton, New Jersey, 31 March, 1897.

I can grind out letters on this machine now with my left hand, and must write you at least a line or two (Mrs. Wilson being desperately busy with her "Spring sewing") to tell you of my disappointment.

I am probably at this writing the most chagrined and mortified fellow on this continent! The Trustees (or, perhaps, in fairness, I ought to say only the President and *some* of the Trustees, fully qualified to know and to plan for the rest) after having given me to understand that it would be possible, and that practically at once, to divide the work in history and erect a chair of American history, and having put me in the way of corresponding with you about the matter, have now discovered that the whole scheme must for the present be given up, for lack of funds, and nothing more attempted at present than the filling of the vacancy caused by Sloane's leaving! Of course they did not intend to treat me shabbily; and of course they have really found that the moneys they thought to have in hand next year will not be immediately available; but the blow is none the less distressing to me, and it is no doubt just as well that I have not just now a chance to go elsewhere! My disappointment is more keen than I can say, and my mortification that I should so elaborately have disturbed *you* about the matter.

I hope with all my heart that you will not have found a place to your permanent liking before these gentlemen really make up plans that will last; and that this does not mean that I am permanently cheated of a realization of my ardent desire to have you, my dear Turner, for a colleague. I naturally feel very pessimistic just at present; but I shall no doubt find it possible to hope again very soon. I have no real doubt, either, in the bottom of my heart, that Princeton is the most desirable place for national work in the country. May the present gloom pass very speedily!

I think it very likely that Dr. Patton will approach Haskins with a view to inducing him to accept the vacant chair of history; and that he will seek to make it to Haskins's taste by every possible modification of the work falling to it. May he succeed; and may that be our additional loadstone to draw you when the time at last comes!

But no more. I must write a line to Haskins; my left hand flags; and I am sick at heart.

Mrs. Wilson joins me in the warmest regards to you both, and I am, as ever,

Your affectionate friend,   Woodrow Wilson

N. B. The article in the April Atlantic[1] is really fine. I congratulate you!

WWTLS (F. J. Turner Papers, MH).
[1] F. J. Turner, "Dominant Forces in Western Life," *Atlantic Monthly,* LXXIX (April 1897), 433-43.

To Charles Homer Haskins

My dear Haskins,   Princeton, New Jersey, 31 March, 1897.

If there is a more deeply chagrined and mortified man in America to-night than I am, I am sorry for him! The Trustees have discovered at this eleventh hour that they will not have *money* enough at once to make the re-arrangements in history about which we talked at Christmas,—and all after letting me go forward with my part of the business all this while on the understanding that they would have, and that my wishes would be fully met in the matter! It is enough to make a man resign,—even to cast himself on the world!

Of course it is all done in innocence. They really were mistaken (quite inexcusably, I should suppose, if they can reckon in figures and *per cents*) about having money immediately available; but that hardly softens the blow for me, and I can hardly trust myself to write about it.

I think that it is Dr. Patton's intention to see you with reference to accepting the vacant chair of history as it stands,[1]—or, rather, no doubt, with all possible modifications to suit your tastes; and I hope with all my heart,—nay, I beg most earnestly,—that you will give the matter your most favourable consideration. Pray stretch a point to see the matter in a favourable light, as you love me, and as you value a thoroughly national place in which to work.

I am too much upset to write any more about the business just now; but hope to hear from you when it develops.

In the meantime, in suspended hope, with the most cordial regards, in which Mrs. Wilson very heartily joins, I am

Cordially and Faithfully Yours,   Woodrow Wilson

WWTLS (C. H. Haskins Papers, NjP).
[1] See F. L. Patton to WW, April 29, 1897, n. 2.

From the Minutes of the Princeton Faculty

5 5' P.M., Wednesday, March 31st, 1897.

The Faculty met, the Dean presiding in the absence of the President. . . .

The Committee on Discipline reported the following rules in reference to Eating Clubs which were adopted:

Whereas it is deemed by the Faculty that the privilege of undertaking the independent management of eating clubs or of leasing, owning or managing property for club purposes should be confined to the Junior and Senior Classes, the Faculty hereby adopt and declare the following

Rules for Freshman & Sophomore Eating Clubs:

No Club of Freshmen or Sophomores shall be permitted to lease, own, or manage any property for club purposes; neither shall any such clubs be permitted to organize any Eating Club except under the management of some responsible house-keeper authorized by the Treasurer to receive students as boarders; and no exception shall be made to this rule in any other way than by express vote of the Faculty, attested at the University Treasurer's Office in writing by the Clerk of the Faculty.

In no case shall a club of Sophomores be allowed to elect successors from the Freshman Class. . . .

The matter of the Lyman H. Atwater Prize in Political Science was referred to Professors Wilson and Daniels.[1]

The matter of the New York Herald Prize was referred to Professor Wilson. . . .[2]

[1] The Lyman H. Atwater Prize in Political Science, established by the Class of 1883 in memory of Professor Atwater and consisting of the interest on $1,000, was awarded annually to a senior for the best examination and essay on topics to be set by the professors of political and social science. The prize was offered in 1897 to the senior who passed the best examination on "The Referendum as Used in Switzerland" and wrote the best essay on "Theories of Representation." Henry Ford Stockwell of Hammonton, N.J., was the winner.

[2] The New York Herald Prize, consisting of the interest on $1,000 presented by James Gordon Bennett, was given to "the member of the Senior class or to the Special Student of satisfactory standing who shall have taken the prescribed course in Political Science and English Literature, and who shall have prepared the best essay in English prose upon some subject of contemporaneous interest in the domestic or foreign policy of the United States Government." *Catalogue of Princeton University . . . 1896-97* (Princeton, N.J., n.d.), p. 133. The winner in 1897 was Robert Comin of New Concord, Ohio. Princeton sources do not reveal the subject of his essay.

A Review of *George Washington*

[April 1897]

George Washington. By WOODROW WILSON. (New York: Harper and Brothers. 1897. Pp. ix, 333.)

. . . Professor Wilson, by a brilliant summing up of the claims of his hero, has justified the crowning of him as Prince of Men by that well-nigh universal acclaim which has pronounced him the "Best of Great Men, and the Greatest of Good Men." As a literary artist he has made with his pen as true a representation as did Houdon with his chisel.

The author commences with a fine chapter on the character, manners and customs of the Virginia society in which Washington was reared. As the immigrant ancestor of Washington was a royalist, and many royalists came to Virginia during the days of the Commonwealth, there was a temptation to enlist with those who maintain that Virginia got her character from her cavaliers. In doing so, however, our author has ventured on disputed ground. The late Hugh Blair Grigsby, than whom no one was more deeply versed in Virginia history, in his *Discourse on the Virginia Convention of 1776*, ably maintains that the character of Virginia society was first formed by the men of moderate means who came early to the colony, and that while many royalists came

during Cromwell's time, a number of these returned on the restoration of Charles II., and many adherents of the Commonwealth came in their stead; and he calls attention to the fact that
the valley of Virginia was entirely settled by Germans and Scotch-
Irish, while many Huguenots settled in eastern Virginia. The
truth probably lies between the different theories, and Virginia
character was simply pure Anglo-Saxon, with a slight admixture
of other European elements, developed in a mild climate, on a
generous soil, and under a system of agricultural labor which
made every landowner an English commoner, independent in
thought and action. This development the author points out.

In the chapter entitled "A Virginian Breeding" the author pictures the domestic circle and the early friendships which so po-
tently shaped the career of Washington. In doing so he gives due
credit to his mother and brother Lawrence. The mother, left a
widow before George was twelve years of age, he describes as
"a wise and provident mother, a woman of too firm a character
and too steadfast a courage to be dismayed by responsibility,"
and who "had shown a singular capacity for business." Of the
brother he says that, though but twenty-five when his father died
and left him the head of the family, he "proved himself such an
older brother as it could but better and elevate a boy to have."
We then have given us the traits of the boy that was father to
the man. "He was above all things else a capable, executive boy.
He loved mastery, and he relished acquiring the most effective
means of mastery in all practical affairs. His very exercise-books
used at school gave proof of it. They were filled, not only with the
rules, formulae, diagrams and exercises of surveying, which he
was taking special pains to learn, at the advice of friends, but
also with careful copies of legal and mercantile papers." The high
tone of the boy soon drew to him the best men in the community,
and among them Thomas, Lord Fairfax, a man of large landed
estate in Virginia upon which he had come to reside in 1746; a
man of taste and culture, who had written with Addison and
Steele for the *Spectator*. From him the boy learned "the scrupu-
lous deportment of a high-bred and honorable man of the world;
the use of books by those who preferred affairs; the way in which
strength may be rendered gracious and independence made generous." Left by his father in moderate circumstances, young
Washington realized the necessity of applying himself to business
at an early age, and so matured was he in the development of
business traits of a high order that at sixteen Lord Fairfax em-
ployed him to survey a large tract of land on the Shenandoah; a
dangerous enterprise, as it lay in a rough frontier region. The

task quickly and accurately performed brought him other business, which kept him busy for three years. He could hardly have had a better training for after life. It fitted him as an engineer when he afterwards entered military life. Upon the death of his brother Lawrence he found himself named as an executor of his will and the residuary legatee of his large estate on the death of his child. He had already been commissioned a major in the militia in the place of his brother. Thus at the age of twenty Washington was fully launched upon the stern business of life and placed under responsibilities difficult to be borne by matured men. How well he met those responsibilities our author shows, and in doing so traces the development of his noble character.

To the cares of business, thus early thrust upon him, were added within a year the responsibilities of public services of a grave character. In 1753 the French undertook to occupy the territory bordering on the Ohio, claimed by the English. Governor Dinwiddie was directed by the home government to warn them peaceably to depart, and if they did not heed the warning, to drive them off by force of arms. Young Major Washington was selected to serve the notice to quit, and he performed the task amidst great difficulties. His journey of 250 miles was through forests, often without even an Indian trail, amid snow and rain, over swollen rivers, and through the haunts of treacherous savages. Washington, with a guide and a small party, promptly appeared at a French outpost and received from the officer in command a flat refusal to the request to retire from the disputed territory. The next step to be taken was to drive off the intruders, and in the spring of 1754 we find Washington as lieutenant-colonel, with a small force, making his way over the Alleghanies for the purpose of executing this task. Camped at Great Meadows, just across the ridge of the mountains, while waiting for Col. Fry to join him, Washington with forty men came upon a party of thirty Frenchmen, May 28, 1754, and an engagement ensued in which the French were overcome, and Jumonville, their commander, was killed. This was the beginning of the war that was waged in Europe and America, and ended in 1763 by the surrender to the English of Canada and all the territory east of the Mississippi claimed by the French. Thus the skirmish at Great Meadows, in which Washington first snuffed the breath of battle and drew French blood, resulted in the final supremacy of the Anglo-Saxon race in North America. The man who thus commenced this momentous struggle was destined to wrest from England, within less than thirty years, her American colonies, including the very territory on which that struggle commenced.

But the flush of victory at Great Meadows soon turned to the pallor of defeat. The French at once sent against the rude fort a force double that of Washington. After exhausting his ammunition, the gallant colonel was forced to surrender on July 4, 1754, but on terms highly honorable, under which he withdrew his little force and returned to Virginia. Though the expedition had failed, because unsupported, Washington came back with increased reputation. The next year we find him with the unfortunate Braddock, rescuing his shattered army after its terrible reverse near Fort Duquesne. These early experiences taught Washington a lesson which was of infinite service in after life. He learned early how to bear defeat. In 1758 Col. Washington accompanied Gen. Forbes in another expedition against Fort Duquesne. Now they found the fort burned and deserted by the French, and Gen. Forbes hoisted the English flag and re-named the post Fort Pitt.

Washington returned to Mount Vernon, now his property, and in January, 1759, married Martha Custis, who added largely to his estate and immeasurably to his happiness. Soon we find him in the House of Burgesses, urging the claims of his soldiers to the pay withheld from them, and the watchful guardian of every interest of the military of the colony. Now he had time to indulge his passion for agriculture in the management of the large estates inherited from his brother and belonging to his wife. We find him fond of the manly recreations of the Virginians of his day, and in all respects a Virginia gentleman of the highest type. But the quiet of domestic life was soon to be replaced by political troubles of the gravest import. The determination of the English ministry to tax the colonies, manifested in the stamp duties imposed by Parliament, aroused America. The Virginia Burgesses rang the alarm-bell in the adoption, on May 30, 1765, of the resolutions offered by Patrick Henry, which looked toward resistance to the act. As is well known, this young man of twenty-nine, who had been a member of the House only a few days, carried his resolutions after a heated debate, in which all the older men who had been leaders in the body were arrayed against him. Our author leaves us in doubt as to Washington's vote on that fateful day, the beginning of the end of English rule of her American colonies. He was in his seat, as his diary shows, and that he voted with Henry may be fairly inferred from his letter to Francis Dandridge, September 20, 1765, in which he styles the act "unconstitutional," the ground taken by Mr. Henry.

With a rapid review of the continued troubles between Great Britain and her colonies, the author brings us to the Continental

Congress, the first clashing of arms, and the appointment of Washington to be commander-in-chief of the American army. He then brings out with remarkable distinctness his claims to true greatness, not only in his genius as a soldier but in his control of the political bodies and the leading men, whose aid was indispensable to the success of the Revolution. The story of the Revolutionary War, as told by Professor Wilson, reads like a grand epic poem with Washington as the hero. No one, indeed, can be familiar with the history of that memorable struggle without being impressed with the belief that but for Washington the cause of the colonies would have failed.

At its close, unlike Caesar, he met the suggestion of a crown with so much indignation that it was never renewed. Retiring to Mount Vernon, with the fond hope of spending his remaining days in quiet domestic life, he found himself too famous to be allowed the rest he coveted. Very soon, too, the weakness of the Confederation became painfully evident, and those who had won free institutions became alarmed about their preservation amid state jealousies and anarchical tendencies. Washington now bent his energies towards the realization of a federal government which would be strong enough to ensure the general welfare, while leaving to the states the management of their local affairs. Such a government he had recommended in 1783 in a letter to the governors of the states on the disbanding of the army.

The work of the National Convention accomplished in framing the Federal Constitution, Washington set himself earnestly to work to have it adopted. Beyond question, the statement of Count Moustier, the French minister to the United States, was true. He wrote in 1789, "The opinion of General Washington was of such weight that it alone contributed more than any other measure to cause the present Constitution to be adopted." Professor Wilson, in describing the struggle for adoption, does not do justice to the Virginians who opposed the unamended Constitution. He says, "It disturbed him (Washington) keenly to find George Mason opposing the Constitution—the dear friend from whom he had always accepted counsel hitherto in public affairs—and Richard Henry Lee and Patrick Henry, too, in their passionate attachment to what they deemed the just sovereignty of Virginia." These three statesmen did not oppose the Constitution as a plan of government. They saw plainly, however, that the guards against encroachment by the great powers brought into existence upon the rights of the people and of the states were not sufficient; and they proposed amendments, which they wished engrafted before adoption, to strengthen those guards. The amendments they suggested were urged by the Virginia Convention and the most important were adopted very soon by the states. These constitute the first ten amendments, and nine of them are for the protection of the individual citizen, eight being taken from the Virginia Bill of Rights. The tenth alone refers to the states and reserves to them, or to the people, the powers not delegated to the United States, or prohibited to the states. The wisdom of these amendments has been amply vindicated in the history of the national government, and has been acknowledged by courts and jurists. It is high time that historians should give due honor to those far-seeing statesmen who insisted on their adoption.

The account of Washington's administration is mainly taken up by Professor Wilson with relating his wise sending-off of the new government, and his firm resistance to the tendency of the country to take active sides in the passionate struggle in Europe, caused by the French Revolution. No one now doubts the great wisdom of his administration. The last scenes in the life of the hero and statesman are well told.

On the whole, it may be said that Professor Wilson has given us no new facts, but he has taken the well-known events of Washington's life and, with a pen of genius, has thrown around them a fresh charm. The volume is beautifully printed and illustrated, and will add permanently to the author's well-established reputation. . . .

WM. WIRT HENRY.

Printed in the *American Historical Review*, II (April 1897), 539-45.

The *Atlantic Monthly*'s Review of *George Washington*

[April 1897]

. . . It is a long stride from a thing to a man, and as the real history of the United States is epitomized in the careers and characters of a few men, though illustrated by multitudes, the prowess of a historian may be pretty fairly measured by his capacity to deal with these men. Indeed, in the case of Washington it may almost be said that the only possible treatment is that which takes him as a symbol rather than as a man, and Mr. Woodrow Wilson in his George Washington (Harpers) gives a fresh argument in support of those who persistently maintain that the first citizen of the American people was a statue, and not a man. In vain, they say, do you tell us stories of his profanity and collect the instances of his laughter; you cannot make us really believe he was alive. He was a great figure, we grant, but the

evidences of his humanity are feeble. Mr. Wilson reinforces this
position by a new method. He gives over the attempt at vivifying
Washington; he scarcely attempts even a lifelike portrait-statue,
but expends his energy upon what may be termed the bas-relief
treatment of a great man. He does not avail himself of some of
the minor facts hoarded for the proper building-up of a human
character, nor does he give a very close or detailed itinerary of
Washington's course as that great figure moves through history.
Rather, he takes his subject in the large way as a person moulded
by nature out of great historic material, and shows him chiefly in
his relation to the place from which he sprang, the time in which
he lived, and the men amongst whom he moved.

Mr. Wilson's studies in government and history have given
him an admirable equipment for this task. They have accustomed him to seeing life in its broad masses and movements, so
that when he comes to particular narrative he gives the person
the benefit of the class. Nothing could be better than his characterization of the Virginian life out of which Washington came.
Without confusing the reader with too many details, he sets
forth the old contrast between New England and Virginia in a
luminous fashion, and enables readers of history to perceive
clearly the sources of power which made Virginia the mother of
Presidents. Facts with regard to Washington may be had with
little difficulty from various biographies, but we know of no
other writer who has come so near to accounting for him as it
is reasonable to expect; and if, in addition, he could have sent
this creation along its way with the vigor of a dramatic narrator,
he would unquestionably have achieved a great work of bio-
graphic art. As it is, he has given an agreeable and illuminating
philosophy of Washington which ought to be of great service
to some writer who is a story-teller as well. . . .

Printed in the *Atlantic Monthly*, LXXIX (April 1897), 567-68.

From Azel Washburn Hazen

My dear Dr Wilson—   Middletown, Conn. 1 April [1897]

Please accept my grateful thanks for your very kind note. The
letters will be sent by our Clerk at once.[1] You do not speak of
one for Edward Axson. If that is desired, of course it will be
cheerfully granted.[2]

Now, my dear friend, I cannot let you sever this formal tie
which has for nine years bound you to our Church, without telling you once more of my esteem and my love for Mrs Wilson

and yourself. You were *ideal* parishioners while here and your expressions ever since have been most friendly.

I can never forget your reverent, worshipful bearing in our services, nor your *patient* attention to my too barren words, while your many utterances of regard for myself will long be cherished as a comfort and an inspiration. Receive again my warmest gratitude for all.

I am exceedingly sorry to learn of your physical ailment, and beg to express my tender sympathy.

Mrs. Hazen joins me in love to you all

Believe me always   Faithfully yours,   A. W. Hazen

A new boy came to the Armstrong home[3] yesterday afternoon.

ALS (WP, DLC).
   [1] The letters were sent immediately, and the Wilsons were received into the membership of the Second Presbyterian Church of Princeton by its Session on May 5, 1897.
   [2] Edward Axson did not join the Second Church in Princeton with the Wilsons, and does not seem ever to have become a member of it.
   [3] The home of Andrew Campbell Armstrong, Professor of Philosophy at Wesleyan University, and his wife, Mabel Chester Murray Armstrong. The new boy was Sinclair Wallace Armstrong.

A News Report of a Religious Talk

[April 2, 1897]

MURRAY HALL

Prof. Woodrow Wilson Speaks on Christian Example.

Professor Woodrow Wilson addressed the students [of the Philadelphian Society] last night in Murray Hall. His text was from the fifth chapter of Matthew, and the subject was the necessity of a Christian life which sheds abroad light and directs others to Christ. Certain lights are psychologically connected with certain emotions; so certain influences are connected with certain characters. A concealed light always goes with a furtive purpose and no man can go among men without having some rays of his character shed light on their lives. What a man does, expresses what he is, and it is a sad thing when a life is not emphatic enough to show its aim. The way to convert men is to live before them[,] not to rebuke them and the glory for an influential life is to be given to God. When a man lives for a cause he does not desire honor for himself, but the success of the principles he advocates. Unchristian men keep watch over their lives when in the presence of those who carry about with them a pure atmosphere; and a Godly life is the most efficient means of saving men from immorality and unbelief.[1]

Printed in the *Daily Princetonian*, April 2, 1897.
[1] There is a brief WWhw outline of this talk, dated April 1, 1897, in WP, DLC.

From Charles Ewing Green

My dear Prof. Wilson,   Trenton, 2d April, 1897.

I hoped to have found time when I was in Princeton on Wednesday last, to have a talk with you, but was fully occupied till the hour of leaving.

I must be very frank in saying that your letter of 28 March was as painful a surprise to me, as mine could have been to you; and perhaps your first letter as much as the second.

My letter to you was perfectly frank, perfectly kind, with nothing to be deciphered or inferred between the lines, and with absolute freedom from all spirit of criticism. I had no thought or desire to "reprove," or even to intimate any "breach of taste." Any injustice to you was farthest from my thought, and if you think any was done you, though I do not see it, I wish very cordially to apologize for it; and to say on the other hand, though your courtesy has dictated an apology to me, I do not see that I am entitled to it, or that you owed it in any sense. Now: you are quite right in saying that I first talked with you about the reorganization of the History Department. I believe you did mention two gentlemen, and I have no doubt, though I do not recall it—(that is unnecessary, for I have absolute confidence in your statement)—that I advised you "to sound those gentlemen about their willingness to come to Princeton." That was in October, five months ago. In all that time you never said to me what you had done, or once referred to the matter in any way. (There was no necessity that you should, and I am not taking any exception to this). I understood however that there had been correspondence and interviews upon the subject, with the President, and perhaps with a trustee. Suddenly, you write me asking for information about the matter, and in the same letter say that the President has said nothing to you about the action of the Trustees in the matter, and *intimate a fear* that there was some reason for this. My reply was to the effect, if I recollect aright, I would write you as you desire, but for that *intimation*; in view of *that*, it seemed to me that you should see the President and talk with him. Was not that right? Was there injustice to you in this?

Ever sincerely & faithfully yours   Charles E. Green

ALS (WP, DLC).

From Frederick Jackson Turner

Dear Wilson: Madison, 3 April 1897

Don't be disturbed over the outcome of our migration correspondence. While I gave the serious consideration to your letters that they were entitled to, I never pressed your enquiries beyond the cautious statement that you gave them, and so I have not built improperly on this foundation. Not having before me at any time the Wisconsin alternative to your proposition, I did not even come to full face with the question of the change. As between the prospect you offered, and my present position, your suggestion was attractive, and the prospect of having you for a colleague might have broken my roots here in any case; but it would have been a choice difficult to make, for my library and our lakes are pretty strong grappling hooks here. Perhaps it was after all a ladylike act in the fates to settle it for me! and I value the incident as a proof of your regard.

I shall not willingly let Haskins go,—as I told you before. Of course I like him so much that I could not wish him to suffer disadvantages by remaining with us; but if you secure him it will be President Adams' fault, not mine. The truth is, that barring salaries and the distance from the fellow workmen of our craft, Madison has some exceptional advantages for historical work, and I confess I do not know many places where I could be as well content,—so long as no upturning of our University traditions is effected. So I am not likely to make any pilgrimage that I can foresee.

Mrs. Turner, I know, would have found a delightful friend in Mrs. Wilson—at least they both have certain common traits, I imagine, for my Penelope is also just now engaged in administering nursery and sewing girl. We both hope to welcome you and your wife here some time, and show you some of the reasons why we could find it difficult even to look forward to answering the query you proposed.

I am glad you did not disapprove of the *Atlantic* article. I am arriving at the conviction that the magazine is not my proper platform.

With cordial regard   Yours   Frederick J. Turner

ALS (WP, DLC).

To Charles Ewing Green

My dear Mr. Green: [Princeton, N. J.] 3 Apr. '97

Allow me to thank you for your letter of yesterday. I am sincerely obliged to you for the plans which it contains. I followed the advice of your first letter at once: wrote to the President of the University, and received from him a very full explanation of what the Trustees had done.

I am not a little chagrined to learn from your letter that you were not informed of the several stages of the consultations concerning the calling of Professors Turner and Haskins to the History Department. I had frequent interviews with the President about the matter, in more than one of which he spoke of consulting with you. I was also heard, at my own request, before the Curriculum Committee. I had no idea that the matter stopped with those gentlemen. If I had known that you were not informed of every step taken, I should have made it my business to inform you and consult with you. I can now only regret my own ignorance.

Very sincerely yours,   Woodrow Wilson

Transcript of WWshLS (draft) (WP, DLC).

To Richard Watson Gilder

My dear Mr. Gilder,   Princeton, 5 April, 1897

I am so very sorry to have missed you this morning! I was at the College lecturing and attending committee meetings all the forenoon, and got your message *just* too late to catch you before your train time. I was very much chagrined. Would that you could have stayed longer.

I have had the ill luck, by all sorts of accidents, not to meet Mr. Cleveland yet. I hope I shall early have an opportunity.

Faithfully yours,   Woodrow Wilson

ALS (R. W. Gilder Papers, NN).

Notes on de Tocqueville's *Recollections*[1]

Mem., April 11, 1897.

Alexis de Tocqueville

Seer, but no guide.[2]

It is harder to accept Tocqueville as a political guide after reading his Recollections than it was before

or—

These recollections concern the stirring years—and are written by one who was an active public man in these days of revolution,—and yet they move with the quiet style of one who looks calmly on from a distance and feels no compulsion either to guide or not. Here is food for reflection!

Not necessary to be the second in order to be the first? France abounds with examples.

And yet Tocqueville not quite a Frenchman,—with the Norman transfusion that made him so admirable a man.

Extraction, breeding, life, and time.

The air of France in his day bred theories,—and yet he was calm and aloof.

It stung to action, and yet he cd. in no time of crisis be more than an observer (The extraordinary scenes he sat thr. in the Ass.—What he said and did)

Are seer and guide to be separated? Can the calm record of things observed guide or stimulate others, if made by a mind so unmoved, a will so child-like? Is there no vitiating weakness wh. permeates the whole[?]. Is it good *philosophy* wh. is so conceived?

WWhw MS. (WP, DLC).
¹ Comte de Tocqueville (ed.), *The Recollections of Alexis de Tocqueville*, trans. by Alexander Texeira de Mattos (New York, 1896).
² At this point Wilson indicated that the following two sentences were alternative openings for this memorandum.

From Joseph Ruggles Wilson

Carrolina Hotel
My precious son—   Durham, N. C., April 12/97.

I am sorry that you ever thought at all of that interest on the $800.00¹—and I am sorely tempted to tell a falsehood and say that a portion was paid before. You on[c]e mentioned the matter in connection with something that may have suggested it, but, as it [you] ought to have done of course, you forgot to write a check at that time and would have done better to have forgotten the thing altogether.

I have now preached two Sundays here,² but the work is up a very steep hill. What I wrote to you about the people last week,³ I am constrained now to reiterate. They seem utterly soulless[.] My room in the hotel (which by the way I am not sure the church will pay for, although I am not to be paid for my services in any other way) is quite good, with bathroom and accompaniments—and were the solitude not so intense I might not complain.

I am very sorry that both Ellie and yourself are under the physician's care. Indeed, since George's[4] death I am for myself afraid to trust a doctor; but possibly you have one in whom confidence may be justly placed.

Yes—I read, and with pleasure, the article in the Atlantic with reference to Mr. Cleveland. I have no doubt he has read and prizes it, especially as now-a-days he is not receiving from many folk his due commendation. I am glad that you will have opportunities for personal friendship with him—almost—if not quite—the only man who can be styled a statesman left to the country. McKinley is small, the Senate is a fraud, and the House is—indiscribable.

Love to dear Ellie and the boys—to the girls, too, if they can be brought to recollect the grandfather who truly loves them.

Your loving Father   Joseph R Wilson

ALS (WP, DLC).
  [1] A mysterious reference.
  [2] Dr. Wilson was guest preacher at the Durham Presbyterian Church, of which the Rev. Dr. Lennox Birkhead Turnbull was the pastor.
  [3] This letter is missing.
  [4] George Howe, Jr., M.D., his late son-in-law.

A News Report

[April 15, 1897]

THE DEBATERS AGAINST YALE.

The Debate was Intensely Interesting
and the Decision Close.

The Inter-Hall Preliminary Yale Debate was held in Murray Hall at 7.30 last evening, upon the question, *Resolved*: That the power of the Speaker of the House of Representatives is detrimental to public interests.

The competitors spoke in the following order: *Affirmative*: H. H. Yocum, J. Jones, Ivy Lee, A. C. Fulton. *Negative*: R. F. Sterling, N. S. Reeves, R. O. Kirkwood, R. L. Beecher, A. H. Throckmorton. The speeches were eight and five minutes in length respectively. At the close of the debate the judges[1] announced that the following men had been chosen to debate against Yale: R. F. Sterling, N. S. Reeves, H. H. Yocum; alternate, Ivy Lee.[2]

The speakers all showed careful preparation and a thorough knowledge of the subject, and, taken as a whole, the debate gave evidence of a clearer insight into the question and a more direct and forcible method of dealing with the points at issue than has been shown in any previous contests of this kind in Princeton. In announcing their decision the judges said that they had selected Princeton's representatives only after long deliberation and a close discussion of the merits of the contestants.

Printed in the *Daily Princetonian*, April 15, 1897.
 1 Wilson, Bliss Perry, W. F. Magie, and W. B. Scott.
 2 The debate was held in New Haven on May 7. The Princeton team defended the negative and won a unanimous decision.

An Historical Essay[1]

[*c. April 15, 1897*]
THE MAKING OF THE NATION.

The making of our own nation seems to have taken place under our very eyes, so recent and so familiar is the story. The great process was worked out in the plain and open day of the modern world, statesmen and historians standing by to superintend, criticise, make record of what was done. The stirring narrative runs quickly into the day in which we live; we can say that our grandfathers builded the government which now holds so large a place in the world; the story seems of yesterday, and yet seems entire, as if the making of the republic had hastened to complete itself within a single hundred years. We are elated to see so great a thing done upon so great a scale, and to feel ourselves in so intimate a way actors in the moving scene.

Yet we should deceive ourselves were we to suppose the work done, the nation made. We have been told by a certain group of our historians that a nation was made when the federal Constitution was adopted; that the strong sentences of the law sufficed to transform us from a league of States into a people single and inseparable. Some tell us, however, that it was not till the war of 1812 that we grew fully conscious of a single purpose and destiny, and began to form policies as if for a nation. Others see the process complete only when the civil war struck slavery away, and gave North and South a common way of life that should make common ideals and common endeavors at last possible. Then, when all have had their say, there comes a great movement like the one which we call Populism, to remind us how the country still lies apart in sections: some at one stage

 1 There is a brief WWhw outline of this essay dated April 11, 1897, in WP, DLC, hence the date ascribed to it. No manuscript copy seems to have survived. [Eds.' note]

of development, some at another; some with one hope and purpose for America, some with another. And we ask ourselves, Is the history of our making as a nation indeed over, or do we still wait upon the forces that shall at last unite us? Are we even now, in fact, a nation?

Clearly, it is not a question of sentiment, but a question of fact. If it be true that the country, taken as a whole, is at one and the same time in several stages of development,—not a great commercial and manufacturing nation, with here and there its broad pastures and the quiet farms from which it draws its food; not a vast agricultural community, with here and there its ports of shipment and its necessary marts of exchange; nor yet a country of mines, merely, pouring their products forth into the markets of the world, to take thence whatever it may need for its comfort and convenience in living,—we still wait for its economic and spiritual union. It is many things at once. Sections big enough for kingdoms live by agriculture, and farm the wide stretches of a new land by the aid of money borrowed from other sections which seem almost like another nation, with their teeming cities, dark with the smoke of factories, quick with the movements of trade, as sensitive to the variations of exchange on London as to the variations in the crops raised by their distant fellow countrymen on the plains within the continent. Upon other great spaces of the vast continent, communities, millions strong, live the distinctive life of the miner, have all their fortune bound up and centred in a single group of industries, feel in their utmost concentration the power of economic forces elsewhere dispersed, and chafe under the unequal yoke that unites them with communities so unlike themselves as those which lend and trade and manufacture, and those which follow the plough and reap the grain that is to feed the world.

Such contrasts are nothing new in our history, and our system of government is admirably adapted to relieve the strain and soften the antagonism they might entail. All our national history through our country has lain apart in sections, each marking a stage of settlement, a stage of wealth, a stage of development, as population has advanced, as if by successive journeyings and encampments, from east to west; and always new regions have been suffered to become new States, form their own life under their own law, plan their own economy, adjust their own domestic relations, and legalize their own methods of business. States have, indeed, often been whimsically enough formed. We have left the matter of boundaries to surveyors rather than to statesmen, and have by no means managed to construct economic units in the making of States. We have joined mining communities with agricultural, the mountain with the plain, the ranch with the farm, and have left the making of uniform rules to the sagacity and practical habit of neighbors ill at ease with one another. But on the whole, the scheme, though a bit haphazard, has worked itself out with singularly little friction and no disaster, and the strains of the great structure we have erected have been greatly eased and dissipated.

Elastic as the system is, however, it stiffens at every point of national policy. The federal government can make but one rule, and that a rule for the whole country, in each act of its legislation. Its very constitution withholds it from discrimination as between State and State, section and section; and yet its chief powers touch just those subjects of economic interest in which the several sections of the country feel themselves most unlike. Currency questions do not affect them equally or in the same way. Some need an elastic currency to serve their uses; others can fill their coffers more readily with a currency that is inelastic. Some can build up manufactures under a tariff law; others cannot, and must submit to pay more without earning more. Some have one interest in a principle of interstate commerce; others, another. It would be difficult to find even a question of foreign policy which would touch all parts of the country alike. A foreign fleet would mean much more to the merchants of Boston and New York than to the merchants of Illinois and the farmers of the Dakotas.

The conviction is becoming painfully distinct among us, moreover, that these contrasts of condition and differences of interest between the several sections of the country are now more marked and emphasized than they ever were before. The country has been transformed within a generation, not by any creations in a new kind, but by stupendous changes in degree. Every interest has increased its scale and its individual significance. The "East" is transformed by the vast accumulations of wealth made since the civil war,—transformed from a simple to a complex civilization, more like the Old World than like the New. The "West" has so magnified its characteristics by sheer growth, every economic interest which its life represents has become so gigantic in its proportions, that it seems to Eastern men, and to its own people also, more than ever a region apart. It is true that the "West" is not, as a matter of fact, a region at all, but, in Professor Turner's admirable phrase, a stage of development, nowhere set apart and isolated, but spread abroad through all the far interior of the continent. But it is now a stage of development with a difference, as Professor Turner has shown,[2] which makes it practically a new thing in our history. The "West" was once a series of States and settlements beyond which lay free lands not yet occupied, into which the restless and all who could not thrive by mere steady industry, all who had come too late and all who had stayed too long, could pass on, and, it might be, better their fortunes. Now it lies without outlet. The free lands are gone. New communities must make their life sufficient without this easy escape,—must study economy, find their fortunes in what lies at hand, intensify effort, increase capital, build up a future out of details. It is as if they were caught in a fixed order of life and forced into a new competition, and both their self-consciousness and their keenness to observe every point of self-interest are enlarged beyond former example.

That there are currents of national life, both strong and definite, running in full tide through all the continent from sea to sea, no observant person can fail to perceive,—currents which have long been gathering force, and which cannot now be withstood. There need be no fear in any sane man's mind that we shall ever again see our national government threatened with overthrow by any power which our own growth has bred. The temporary danger is that, not being of a common mind, because not living under common conditions, the several sections of the country, which a various economic development has for the time being set apart and contrasted, may struggle for supremacy in the control of the government and that we may learn by some sad experience that there is not even yet any common standard, either of opinion or of policy, underlying our national life. The country is of one mind in its allegiance to the government and in its attachment to the national idea; but it is not yet of one mind in respect of that fundamental question, What policies will best serve us in giving strength and development to our life? Not the least noteworthy of the incidents that preceded and fore-tokened the civil war was, if I may so call it, the sectionalization of the national idea. Southern merchants bestirred themselves to get conventions together for the discussion, not of the issues of polities, but of the economic interests of the country. Their thought and hope were of the nation. They spoke no word of antagonism against any section or interest. Yet it was plain in every resolution they uttered that for them the nation was one thing and centred in the South, while for the rest of the country the nation was another thing and lay in the North and North-

[2] American Historical Review, vol. i. p. 71. [WW's note]

west. They were arguing the needs of the nation from the needs of their own section. The same thing had happened in the days of the embargo and the war of 1812. The Hartford Convention thought of New England when it spoke of the country. So must it ever be when section differs from section in the very basis and method of its life. The nation is to-day one thing in Kansas, and quite another in Massachusetts.

There is no longer any danger of a civil war. There was war between the South and the rest of the nation because their differences were removable in no other way. There was no prospect that slavery, the root of those differences, would ever disappear in the mere process of growth. It was to be apprehended, on the contrary, that the very processes of growth would inevitably lead to the extension of slavery and the perpetuation of radical social and economic contrasts and antagonisms between State and State, between region and region. An heroic remedy was the only remedy. Slavery being removed, the South is now joined with the "West," joined with it in a stage of development, as a region chiefly agricultural, without diversified industries, without a multifarious trade, without those subtle extended nerves which come with all-round economic development, and which make men keenly sensible of the interests that link the world together, as it were into a single community. But these are lines of difference which will be effaced by mere growth, which time will calmly ignore. They make no boundaries for armies to cross. Tide-water Virginia was thus separated once from her own population within the Alleghany valleys,—held two jealous sections within her own limits. Massachusetts once knew the sharp divergences of interest and design which separated the coast settlements upon the Bay from the restless pioneers who had taken up the free lands of her own western counties. North Carolina was once a comfortable and indifferent "East" to the uneasy "West" that was to become Tennessee. Virginia once seemed old and effete to Kentucky. The "great West" once lay upon the Ohio, but has since disappeared there, overlaid by the changes which have carried the conditions of the "East" to the Great Lakes and beyond. There has never yet been a time in our history when we were without an "East" and a "West," but the novel day when we shall be without them is now in sight. As the country grows it will inevitably grow homogeneous. Population will not henceforth spread, but compact; for there is no new land between the seas where the "West" can find another lodgment. The conditions which prevail in the ever widening "East" will sooner or later cover the continent, and we shall at last be one people.

The process will not be a short one. It will doubtless run through many generations and involve many a critical question of statesmanship. But it cannot be stayed, and its working out will bring the nation to its final character and rôle in the world.

In the meantime, shall we not constantly recall our reassuring past, reminding one another again and again, as our memories fail us, of the significant incidents of the long journey we have already come, in order that we may be cheered and guided upon the road we have yet to choose and follow? It is only by thus attempting, and attempting again and again, some sufficient analysis of our past experiences that we can form any adequate image of our life as a nation, or acquire any intelligent purpose to guide us amidst the rushing movement of affairs. It is no doubt in part by reviewing our lives that we shape and determine them. The future will not, indeed, be like the past; of that we may rest assured. It cannot be like it in detail; it cannot even resemble it in the large. It is one thing to fill a fertile continent with a vigorous people and take first possession of its treasures; it is quite another to complete the work of occupation and civilization in detail. Big plans, thought out only in the rough, will suffice for the one, but not for the other. A provident leadership, a patient tolerance of temporary but unavoidable evils, a just temper of compromise and accommodation, a hopeful industry in the face of small returns, mutual understandings, and a cordial spirit of coöperation are needed for the slow intensive task, which were not demanded amidst the free advances of an unhampered people from settlement to settlement. And yet the past has made the present, and will make the future. It has made us a nation, despite a variety of life that threatened to keep us at odds amongst ourselves. It has shown us the processes by which differences have been obliterated and antagonisms softened. It has taught us how to become strong, and will teach us, if we heed its moral, how to become wise, also, and single-minded.

The colonies which formed the Union were brought together, let us first remind ourselves, not merely because they were neighbors and kinsmen, but because they were forced to see that they had common interests which they could serve in no other way. "There is nothing which binds one country or one State to another but interest," said Washington. "Without this cement the Western inhabitants can have no predilection for us." Without that cement the colonies could have had no predilection for one another. But it is one thing to have common interests, and quite another to perceive them and act upon them. The colonies were first thrust together by the pressure of external danger. They needed one another, as well as aid from oversea, as any fool could perceive, if they were going to keep their frontiers against the Indians, and their outlets upon the Western waters from the French. The French and Indian war over, that pressure was relieved, and they might have fallen apart again, indifferent to any common aim, unconscious of any common interest, had not the government that was their common master set itself to make them wince under common wrongs. Then it was that they saw how like they were in polity and life and interest in the great field of politics, studied their common liberty, and became aware of their common ambitions. It was then that they became aware, too, that their common ambitions could be realized only by union; not single-handed, but united against a common enemy. Had they been let alone, it would have taken many a long generation of slowly increased acquaintance with one another to apprise them of their kinship in life and interests and institutions; but England drove them into immediate sympathy and combination, unwittingly founding a nation by suggestion.

The war for freedom over, the new-fledged States entered at once upon a very practical course of education which thrust its lessons upon them without regard to taste or predilection. The Articles of Confederation had been formulated and proposed to the States for their acceptance in 1777, as a legalization of the arrangements that had grown up under the informal guidance of the Continental Congress, in order that law might confirm and strengthen practice, and because an actual continental war commanded a continental organization. But the war was virtually over by the time all the reluctant States had accepted the Articles; and the new government had hardly been put into formal operation before it became evident that only the war had made such an arrangement workable. Not compacts, but the compulsions of a common danger, had drawn the States into an irregular coöperation, and it was even harder to obtain obedience to the definite Articles than it had been to get the requisitions of the unchartered Congress heeded while the war lasted. Peace had rendered the makeshift common government uninteresting, and had given each State leave to withdraw from common undertakings, and to think once more, as of old, only of itself. Their own affairs again isolated and restored to their former separate importance, the States could no longer spare their chief men for what was considered the minor work of the general Congress. The best men had been gradually withdrawn from Congress before the war ended, and now there seemed less reason than ever why they should be sent to talk at Philadelphia, when they were needed for the actual work of administration at home. Politics fell back into their old localization, and every public man found his chief tasks at home. There were still, as a matter of fact, common needs and dangers scarcely less imperative and menacing than those which had drawn the colonies together against the mother country; but they were needs and perils of peace, and ordinary men did not see them; only the most thoughtful and observant were conscious of them: extraordinary events were required to lift them to the general view.

Happily, there were thoughtful and observant men who were already the chief figures of the country,—men whose leadership the people had long since come to look for and accept,—and it was through them that the States were brought to a new common consciousness, and at last to a real union. It was not possible for the several States to live self-sufficient and apart, as they had done when they were colonies. They had then had a common government, little as they liked to submit to it, and their foreign affairs had been taken care of. They were now to learn how ill they could dispense with a common providence. Instead of France, they now had England for neighbor in Canada and on the Western waters, where they had themselves but the other day fought so hard to set her power up. She was their rival and enemy, too, on the seas; refused to come to any treaty terms with them in regard to commerce; and laughed to see them unable to concert any policy against her because they had no common political authority among themselves. She had promised, in the treaty of peace, to withdraw her garrisons from the Western posts which lay within the territory belonging to the Confederation; but Congress had promised that British creditors should be paid what was due them, only to find that the States would make no laws to fulfill the promise, and were determined to leave their federal representatives without power to make them; and England kept her troops where they were. Spain had taken France's place upon the further bank of the Mississippi and at the great river's mouth. Grave questions of foreign policy pressed on every side, as of old, and no State could settle them unaided and for herself alone.

Here was a group of commonwealths which would have lived separately and for themselves, and could not; which had thought to make shift with merely a "league of friendship" between them and a Congress for consultation, and found that it was impossible. There were common debts to pay, but there was no common system of taxation by which to meet them, nor any authority to devise and enforce such a system. There were common enemies and rivals to deal with, but no one was authorized to carry out a common policy against them. There was a common domain to settle and administer, but no one knew how a Congress without the power to command was to manage so great a property. The Ordinance of 1787 was indeed bravely framed, after a method of real statesmanship; but there was no warrant for it to be found in the Articles, and no one could say how Congress would execute a law it had had no authority to enact. It was not merely the hopeless confusion and sinister signs of anarchy which abounded in their own affairs—a rebellion of debtors in Massachusetts, tariff wars among the States that lay upon New York Bay and on the Sound, North Carolina's doubtful supremacy among her settlers in the Tennessee country, Virginia's questionable authority in Kentucky—that brought the States at last to attempt a better union and set up a real government for the whole country. It was the inevitable continental outlook of affairs as well; if nothing more, the sheer necessity to grow and touch their neighbors at close quarters.

Washington had been among the first to see the necessity of living, not by a local, but by a continental policy. Of course he had a direct pecuniary interest in the development of the Western lands,—had himself preëmpted many a broad acre lying upon the far Ohio, as well as upon the nearer western slopes of the mountains,—and it is open to any one who likes the sinister suggestion to say that his ardor for the occupancy of the Western country was that of the land speculator, not that of the statesman. Everybody knows that it was a conference between delegates from Maryland and Virginia about Washington's favorite scheme of joining the upper waters of the Potomac with the upper waters of the streams which made their way to the Mississippi—a conference held at his suggestion and at his house—that led to the convening of that larger conference at Annapolis, which called for the appointment of the body that met at Philadelphia and framed the Constitution under which he was to become the first President of the United States. It is open to any one who chooses to recall how keen old Governor Dinwiddie had been, when he came to Virginia, to watch those same Western waters in the interest of the first Ohio Company, in which he had bought stock; how promptly he called the attention of the ministers in England to the aggressions of the French in that quarter, sent Washington out as his agent to warn the intruders off, and pushed the business from stage to stage, till the French and Indian war was ablaze, and nations were in deadly conflict on both sides of the sea. It ought to be nothing new and nothing

strange to those who have read the history of the English race
the world over to learn that conquests have a thousand times
sprung out of the initiative of men who have first followed private
interest into new lands like speculators, and then planned their
occupation and government like statesmen. Dinwiddie was no
statesman, but Washington was; and the circumstance which
it is worth while to note about him is, not that he went pros-
pecting upon the Ohio when the French war was over, but
that he saw more than fertile lands there,—saw the "seat of a
rising empire," and, first among the men of his day, perceived by
what means its settlers could be bound to the older communities
in the East alike in interest and in polity. Here were the first
"West" and the first "East," and Washington's thought mediating
between them.

The formation of the Union brought a real government into
existence, and that government set about its work with an energy,
a dignity, a thoroughness of plan, which made the whole country aware of it from the outset, and aware, consequently, of the
national scheme of political life it had been devised to promote.
Hamilton saw to it that the new government should have a definite party and body of interests at its back. It had been fostered
in the making by the commercial classes at the ports and along
the routes of commerce, and opposed in the rural districts which
lay away from the centres of population. Those who knew the
forces that played from State to State, and made America a partner in the life of the world, had earnestly wanted a government
that should preside and choose in the making of the nation; but
those who saw only the daily round of the countryside had been
indifferent or hostile, consulting their pride and their prejudices.
Hamilton sought a policy which should serve the men who had
set the government up, and found it in the funding of the debt,
both national and domestic, the assumption of the Revolutionary
obligations of the States, and the establishment of a national
bank. This was what the friends of the new plan had wanted, the
rehabilitation of credit, and the government set out with a programme meant to commend it to men with money and vested
interests.

It was just such a government that the men of an opposite
interest and temperament had dreaded, and Washington was not
out of office before the issue began to be clearly drawn between
those who wanted a strong government, with a great establishment, a system of finance which should dominate the markets,
an authority in the field of law which should restrain the States
and make the Union, through its courts, the sole and final judge

of its own powers, and those who dreaded nothing else so much, wished a government which should hold the country together with as little thought as possible of its own aggrandizement, went all the way with Jefferson in his jealousy of the commercial interest, accepted his ideal of a dispersed power put into commission among the States,—even among the local units within the States,—and looked to see liberty discredited amidst a display of federal power. When the first party had had their day in the setting up of the government and the inauguration of a policy which should make it authoritative, the party of Jefferson came in to purify it. They began by attacking the federal courts, which had angered every man of their faith by a steady maintenance and elaboration of the federal power; they ended by using that power just as their opponents had used it. In the first place, it was necessary to buy Louisiana, and with it the control of the Mississippi, notwithstanding Mr. Jefferson's solemn conviction that such an act was utterly without constitutional warrant; in the second place, they had to enforce an arbitrary embargo in order to try their hand at reprisal upon foreign rivals in trade; in the end, they had to recharter the national bank, create a national debt and a sinking fund, impose an excise upon whiskey, lay direct taxes, devise a protective tariff, use coercion upon those who would not aid them in a great war,—play the rôle of masters and tax-gatherers as the Federalists had played it,—on a greater scale, even, and with equal gusto. Everybody knows the familiar story: it has new significance from day to day only as it illustrates the invariable process of nation-making which has gone on from generation to generation, from the first until now.

Opposition to the exercise and expansion of the federal power only made it the more inevitable by making it the more deliberate. The passionate protests, the plain speech, the sinister forecasts, of such men as John Randolph aided the process by making it self-conscious. What Randolph meant as an accusation, those who chose the policy of the government presently accepted as a prophecy. It was true, as he said, that a nation was in the making, and a government under which the privileges of the States would count for less than the compulsions of the common interest. Few had seen it so at first; the men who were old when the government was born refused to see it so to the last; but the young men and those who came fresh upon the stage from decade to decade presently found the scarecrow look like a thing they might love. Their ideal took form with the reiterated suggestion; they began to hope for what they had been bidden to dread. No party could long use the federal authority without coming to feel it national,—without forming some ideal of the common interest, and of the use of power by which it should be fostered.

When they adopted the tariff of 1816, the Jeffersonians themselves formulated a policy which should endow the federal government with a greater economic power than even Hamilton had planned when he sought to win the support of the merchants and the lenders of money; and when they bought something like a third of the continent beyond the Mississippi, they made it certain the nation should grow upon a continental scale which no provincial notions about state powers and a common government kept within strait bounds could possibly survive. Here were the two forces which were to dominate us till the present day, and make the present issues of our politics: an open "West" into which a frontier population was to be thrust from generation to generation, and a protective tariff which should build up special interests the while in the "East," and make the contrast ever sharper and sharper between section and section. What the "West" is doing now is simply to note more deliberately than ever before, and with a keener distaste, this striking contrast between her own development and that of the "East." That was a true instinct of statesmanship which led Henry Clay to couple a policy of internal improvements with a policy of protection. Internal improvements meant in that day great roads leading into the West, and every means taken to open the country to use and settlement. While a protective tariff was building up special industries in the East, public works should make an outlet into new lands for all who were not getting the benefit of the system. The plan worked admirably for many a day, and was justly called "American," so well did it match the circumstances of a set of communities, half old, half new: the old waiting to be developed, the new setting the easy scale of living. The other side of the policy was left for us. There is no longer any outlet for those who are not the beneficiaries of the protective system, and nothing but the contrasts it has created remains to mark its triumphs. Internal improvements no longer relieve the strain; they have become merely a means of largess.

The history of the United States has been one continuous story of rapid, stupendous growth, and all its great questions have been questions of growth. It was proposed in the Constitutional Convention of 1787 that a limit should be set to the number of new members to be admitted to the House of Representatives from States formed beyond the Alleghanies; and the suggestion was conceived with a true instinct of prophecy. The old States were not only to be shaken out of their self-centred life, but were even to see their very government changed over their heads by the rise of States in the Western country. John Randolph voted against the admission of Ohio into the Union, because he held that no new partner should be admitted to the federal arrangement except by unanimous consent. It was the very next year that Louisiana was purchased, and a million square miles were added to the territory out of which new States were to be made. Had the original States been able to live to themselves, keeping their own people, elaborating their own life, without a common property to manage, unvexed by a vacant continent, national questions might have been kept within modest limits. They might even have made shift to digest Tennessee, Kentucky, Mississippi, Alabama, and the great commonwealths carved out of the Northwest Territory, for which the Congress of the Confederation had already made provision. But the Louisiana purchase opened the continent to the planting of States, and took the processes of nationalization out of the hands of the original "partners." Questions of politics were henceforth to be questions of growth.

For a while the question of slavery dominated all the rest. The Northwest Territory was closed to slavery by the Ordinance of 1787. Tennessee, Kentucky, Mississippi, Alabama, took slavery almost without question from the States from which they were sprung. But Missouri gave the whole country view of the matter which must be settled in the making of every State founded beyond the Mississippi. The slavery struggle, which seems to us who are near it to occupy so great a space in the field of our affairs, was, of course, a struggle for and against the extension of slavery, not for or against its existence in the States where it had taken root from of old,—a question of growth, not of law. It will some day be seen to have been, for all it was so stupendous, a mere episode of development. Its result was to remove a ground of economic and social difference as between section and section which threatened to become permanent, standing forever in the way of a homogeneous national life. The passionate struggle to prevent its extension inevitably led to its total abolition; and the way was cleared for the South, as well as the "West," to become like its neighbor sections in every element of its life.

It had also a further, almost incalculable effect in its stimulation of a national sentiment. It created throughout the North and Northwest a passion of devotion to the Union which really gave the Union a new character. The nation was fused into a single body in the fervent heat of the time. At the beginning of the war the South had seemed like a section pitted against a section; at its close it seemed a territory conquered by a neighbor nation. That nation is now, take it roughly, that "East" which we contrast with the "West" of our day. The economic conditions once centred at New York, Boston, Philadelphia, Baltimore, Pittsburg, and the other commercial and industrial cities of the coast States are now to be found, hardly less clearly marked, in Chicago, in Minneapolis, in Detroit, through all the great States that lie upon the Lakes, in all the old "Northwest." The South has fallen into a new economic classification. In respect of its stage of development it belongs with the "West," though in sentiment, in traditional ways of life, in many a point of practice and detail, it keeps its old individuality, and though it has in its peculiar labor problem a hindrance to progress at once unique and ominous.

It is to this point we have come in the making of the nation. The old sort of growth is at an end,—the growth by mere expansion. We have now to look more closely to internal conditions, and study the means by which a various people is to be bound together in a single interest. Many differences will pass away of themselves. "East" and "West" will come together by a slow approach, as capital accumulates where now it is only borrowed, as industrial development makes its way westward in a new variety, as life gets its final elaboration and detail throughout all the great spaces of the continent, until all the scattered parts of the nation are drawn into real community of interest. Even the race problem of the South will no doubt work itself out in the slowness of time, as blacks and whites pass from generation to generation, gaining with each remove from the memories of the war a surer self-possession, an easier view of the division of labor and of social function to be arranged between them. Time is the only legislator in such a matter. But not everything can be left to drift and slow accommodation. The nation which has grown to the proportions almost of the continent within the century lies under our eyes, unfinished, unharmonized, waiting still to have its parts adjusted, lacking its last lesson in the ways of peace and concert. It required statesmanship of no mean sort to bring us to our present growth and lusty strength. It will require leadership of a much higher order to teach us the triumphs of coöperation, the self-possession and calm choices of maturity.

Much may be brought about by a mere knowledge of the situation. It is not simply the existence of facts that governs us, but consciousness and comprehension of the facts. The whole process of statesmanship consists in bringing facts to light, and shaping law to suit, or, if need be, mould them. It is part of our present danger that men of the "East" listen only to their own public

men, men of the "West" only to theirs. We speak of the "West"
as out of sympathy with the "East": it would be instructive once
and again to reverse the terms, and admit that the "East" neither
understands nor sympathizes with the "West,"—and thorough
nationalization depends upon mutual understandings and sympathies. There is an unpleasant significance in the fact that the
"East" has made no serious attempt to understand the desire for
the free coinage of silver in the "West" and the South. If it were
once really probed and comprehended, we should know that it is
necessary to reform our currency at once, and we should know
in what way it is necessary to reform it; we should know that a
new protective tariff only marks with a new emphasis the contrast in economic interest between the "East" and the "West,"
and that nothing but currency reform can touch the cause of the
present discontents.

Ignorance and indifference as between section and section no
man need wonder at who knows the habitual courses of history;
and no one who comprehends the essential soundness of our
people's life can mistrust the future of the nation. He may confidently expect a safe nationalization of interest and policy in
the end, whatever folly of experiment and fitful change he may
fear in the meanwhile. He can only wonder that we should continue to leave ourselves so utterly without adequate means of
formulating a national policy. Certainly Providence has presided
over our affairs with a strange indulgence, if it is true that Providence helps only those who first seek to help themselves. The
making of a nation has never been a thing deliberately planned
and consummated by the counsel and authority of leaders, but
the daily conduct and policy of a nation which has won its place
must be so planned. So far we have had the hopefulness, the
readiness, and the hardihood of youth in these matters, and have
never become fully conscious of the position into which our peculiar frame of government has brought us. We have waited a
whole century to observe that we have made no provision for
authoritative national leadership in matters of policy. The President does not always speak with authority, because he is not
always a man picked out and tested by any processes in which
the people have been participants, and has often nothing but his
office to render him influential. Even when the country does
know and trust him, he can carry his views no further than to
recommend them to the attention of Congress in a written message which the Houses would deem themselves subservient to
give too much heed to. Within the Houses there is no man, except
the Vice-President, to whose choice the whole country gives heed;

and he is chosen, not to be a Senator, but only to wait upon the disability of the President, and preside meanwhile over a body of which he is not a member. The House of Representatives has in these latter days made its Speaker its political leader as well as its parliamentary moderator; but the country is, of course, never consulted about that beforehand, and his leadership is not the open leadership of discussion, but the undebatable leadership of the parliamentary autocrat.

This singular leaderless structure of our government never stood fully revealed until the present generation, and even now awaits general recognition. Peculiar circumstances and the practical political habit and sagacity of our people for long concealed it. The framers of the Constitution no doubt expected the President and his advisers to exercise a real leadership in affairs, and for more than a generation after the setting up of the government their expectation was fulfilled. Washington was accepted as leader no less by Congress than by the people. Hamilton, from the Treasury, really gave the government both its policy and its administrative structure. If John Adams had less authority than Washington, it was because the party he represented was losing its hold upon the country. Jefferson was the most consummate party chief, the most unchecked master of legislative policy, we have had in America, and his dynasty was continued in Madison and Monroe. But Madison's terms saw Clay and Calhoun come to the front in the House, and many another man of the new generation, ready to guide and coach the President rather than to be absolutely controlled by him. Monroe was not of the calibre of his predecessors, and no party could rally about so stiff a man, so cool a partisan, as John Quincy Adams. And so the old political function of the presidency came to an end, and it was left for Jackson to give it a new one,—instead of a leadership of counsel, a leadership and discipline by rewards and punishments. Then the slavery issue began to dominate politics, and a long season of concentrated passion brought individual men of force into power in Congress,—natural leaders of men like Clay, trained and eloquent advocates like Webster, keen debaters with a logic whose thrusts were as sharp as those of cold steel like Calhoun. The war made the Executive of necessity the nation's leader again, with the great Lincoln at its head, who seemed to embody, with a touch of genius, the very character of the race itself. Then reconstructions came,—under whose leadership who could say?— and we were left to wonder what, henceforth, in the days of ordinary peace and industry, we were to make of a government which could in humdrum times yield us no leadership at all. The

tasks which confront us now are not like those which centred
in the war, in which passion made men run together to a common work. Heaven forbid that we should admit any element
of passion into the delicate matters in which national policy must
mediate between the differing economic interests of sections
which a wise moderation will assuredly unite in the ways of harmony and peace! We shall need, not the mere compromises of
Clay, but a constructive leadership of which Clay hardly showed
himself capable.

There are few things more disconcerting to the thought, in any
effort to forecast the future of our affairs, than the fact that we
must continue to take our executive policy from presidents given
us by nominating conventions, and our legislation from conference committees of the House and Senate. Evidently it is a purely
providential form of government. We should never have had
Lincoln for President had not the Republican convention of 1860
sat in Chicago, and felt the weight of the galleries in its work,—
and one does not like to think what might have happened had
Mr. Seward been nominated. We might have had Mr. Bryan for
President, because of the impression which may be made upon
an excited assembly by a good voice and a few ringing sentences
flung forth just after a cold man who gave unpalatable counsel
has sat down. The country knew absolutely nothing about Mr.
Bryan before his nomination, and it would not have known anything about him afterward had he not chosen to make speeches.
It was not Mr. McKinley, but Mr. Reed, who was the real leader
of the Republican party. It has become a commonplace amongst
us that conventions prefer dark horses,—prefer those who are not
tested leaders with well-known records to those who are. It has
become a commonplace amongst all nations which have tried
popular institutions that the actions of such bodies as our nominating conventions are subject to the play of passion and of
chance. They meet to do a single thing,—for the platform is really
left to a committee,—and upon that one thing all intrigue centres.
Who that has witnessed them will ever forget the intense night
scenes, the feverish recesses, of our nominating conventions,
when there is a running to and fro of agents from delegation to
delegation, and every candidate has his busy headquarters,—can
ever forget the shouting and almost frenzied masses on the floor
of the hall when the convention is in session, swept this way and
that by every wind of sudden feeling, impatient of debate, incapable of deliberation? When a convention's brief work is over,
its own members can scarcely remember the plan and order of it.
They go home unmarked, and sink into the general body of those

who have nothing to do with the conduct of government. They cannot be held responsible if their candidate fails in his attempt to carry on the Executive.

It has not often happened that candidates for the presidency have been chosen from outside the ranks of those who have seen service in national politics. Congress is apt to be peculiarly sensitive to the exercise of executive authority by men who have not at some time been members of the one House or the other, and so learned to sympathize with members' views as to the relations that ought to exist between the President and the federal legislature. No doubt a good deal of the dislike which the Houses early conceived for Mr. Cleveland was due to the feeling that he was an "outsider," a man without congressional sympathies and points of view,—a sort of irregular and amateur at the delicate game of national politics as played at Washington; most of the men whom he chose as advisers were of the same kind, without Washington credentials. Mr. McKinley, though of the congressional circle himself, has repeated the experiment in respect of his cabinet in the appointment of such men as Mr. Gage and Mr. Bliss and Mr. Gary. Members resent such appointments; they seem to drive the two branches of the government further apart than ever, and yet they grow more common from administration to administration.

These appointments make coöperation between Congress and the Executive more difficult, not because the men thus appointed lack respect for the Houses or seek to gain any advantage over them, but because they do not know how to deal with them,— through what persons and by what courtesies of approach. To the uninitiated Congress is simply a mass of individuals. It has no responsible leaders known to the system of government, and the leaders recognized by its rules are one set of individuals for one sort of legislation, another for another. The Secretaries cannot address or approach either House as a whole; in dealing with committees they are dealing only with groups of individuals; neither party has its leader,—there are only influential men here and there who know how to manage its caucuses and take advantage of parliamentary openings on the floor. There is a master in the House, as every member very well knows, and even the easy-going public are beginning to observe. The Speaker appoints the committees; the committees practically frame all legislation; the Speaker, accordingly, gives or withholds legislative power and opportunity, and members are granted influence or deprived of it much as he pleases. He of course administers the rules, and the rules are framed to prevent debate and individual initiative.

He can refuse recognition for the introduction of measures he disapproves of as party chief; he may make way for those he desires to see passed. He is chairman of the Committee on Rules, by which the House submits to be governed (for fear of help-lessness and chaos) in the arrangement of its business and the apportionment of its time. In brief, he is not only its moderator, but its master. New members protest and write to the news-papers; but old members submit,—and indeed the Speaker's power is inevitable. You must have leaders in a numerous body,—leaders with authority; and you cannot give authority in the House ex-cept through the rules. The man who administers the rules must be master, and you must put this mastery into the hands of your best party leader. The legislature being separated from the ex-ecutive branch of the government, the only rewards and punish-ments by which you can secure party discipline are those within the gift of the rules,—the committee appointments and prefer-ences: you cannot administer these by election; party govern-ment would break down in the midst of personal exchanges of electoral favors. Here again you must trust the Speaker to or-ganize and choose, and your only party leader is your moderator. He does not lead by debate; he explains, he proposes nothing to the country; you learn his will in his rulings.

It is with such machinery that we are to face the future, find a wise and moderate policy, bring the nation to a common, a cordial understanding, a real unity of life. The President can lead only as he can command the ear of both Congress and the coun-try,—only as any other individual might who could secure a like general hearing and acquiescence. Policy must come always from the deliberations of the House committees, the debates, both secret and open, of the Senate, the compromises of committee conference between the Houses; no one man, no group of men, leading; no man, no group of men, responsible for the outcome. Unquestionably we believe in a guardian destiny! No other race could have accomplished so much with such a system; no other race would have dared risk such an experiment. We shall work out a remedy, for work it out we must. We must find or make, somewhere in our system, a group of men to lead us, who repre-sent the nation in the origin and responsibility of their power; who shall draw the Executive, which makes choice of foreign policy and upon whose ability and good faith the honorable exe-cution of the laws depends, into cordial coöperation with the legislature, which, under whatever form of government, must sanction law and policy. Only under a national leadership, by a national selection of leaders, and by a method of constructive choice rather than of compromise and barter, can a various nation be peacefully led. Once more is our problem of nation-making the problem of a form of government. Shall we show the sagacity, the open-mindedness, the moderation, in our task of modification, that were shown under Washington and Madison and Sherman and Franklin and Wilson, in the task of construction?

Printed in the *Atlantic Monthly*, LXXX (July 1897), 1-14.

From James Waddel Alexander

My dear Professor Wilson,   N. Y. April 21, 1897.

I remember that one of your classmates, at the '79 dinner given to you, while pronouncing a panegyric on your "Washington," was asked if he had read it, whereupon he promptly and all to [too] candidly answered "No!"

I am better prepared to express an opinion on it. I only got the book a day or two ago, although I have been clamoring for it a long time; and I have just laid it down, five minutes ago, finished, and wished there was more.

I cant help saying to you that it is a splendid success. You know this already, and have heard it from a hundred mouths; but I may nevertheless have the personal satisfaction of contributing my modest bay to the garland you wear. I feel as if I know the immortal George better than I did, and take a more hopeful view of our country's affairs than I did last week, after being refreshed in my mind by your account of what Washington had to face in the early days of the republic and the way he faced it.

I am proud, too, that the author of this book is a Princeton man, and that Princeton is enjoying the influence of his culture and character; and this pride is not tempered by the knowledge I have that this "Washington" is only a sort of sport compared with your more serious work.

Wishing you a continuing career of increasing usefulness and renown,   I am faithfully yours,   James W Alexander

ALS (WP, DLC) with WWhw notation on env.: "Ans. 26 April, '97."

An Announcement

[April 24, 1897]

University Place Cumberland Presbyterian Church, J. Max Irwin, pastor. Mr. S. M. Jordan[1] will preach to-morrow morning at 11. Prof. Woodrow Wilson will speak at the evening service at 7.45.

Printed in the *Daily Princetonian*, April 24, 1897.
1 Samuel Martin Jordan, then a student at Princeton Theological Seminary. He later served as a missionary to Persia for many years.

Notes for a Religious Talk

(Miller church, 25 April, 1897.)

Ps. XIX., 7 & part of 8: "The law of the Lord is perfect, converting (restoring, healing) the soul: the testimony of the Lord is sure, making wise the simple. The statutes of the Lord are right, rejoicing the heart." Human desires and ambitions

Strength,—wisdom,—happiness. (The three things of men most desirable)

General and growing dissatisfaction with the wisdom that is not *spiritual*.

Of what other testimony (truth) can it be said that it maketh wise the *Simple*? Not of any *intellectual* truth. Hence the efficacy of very simple preachers.

What other *right* rejoices the heart?

What other *law* makes the *soul* whole & sound?

Why? Why should there be this efficacy? *Because* we are made in the image of God, and it is thus that our true energy is released, our true adjustment restored.

WWhw and WWsh notes (WP, DLC).

To Albert Bushnell Hart

My dear Professor Hart,   Princeton, New Jersey, 26 April, 1897.

I asked Mr. Richardson, our Librarian, to reply to your question about the New Jersey Archives;[1] and he told me the other day he had done so,—I hope satisfactorily.

With regard to the revision of the bibliographies in the *Epochs*,[2] I can see no sufficient objection to inserting references to the "Guide"[3] with regard to the minor literature of the subject; but I think that all the chief works ought to be directly referred to in the lists.

I saw Haskins for a little while on his way back from the Committee meeting in Cambridge,[4] and we talked over its job a little. I shall be interested to see just how far it departs from our programme made at Madison.[5]

With much regard,

Most sincerely Yours,   Woodrow Wilson

TCL (RSB Coll., DLC).

¹ *Documents Relating to the Colonial, Revolutionary and Post-Revolutionary History of New Jersey* (47 vols., Newark and Trenton, 1880-1949). This series is commonly referred to as the "New Jersey Archives" because this title is stamped on the spine of the original bindings. Nineteen volumes had appeared by 1897.

² Wilson's *Division and Reunion* was a volume in this series edited by Hart.

³ Edward Channing and Albert Bushnell Hart, *Guide to the Study of American History* (Boston and London, 1896).

⁴ The meeting in Cambridge, Mass., which took place during the week of April 12-18, 1897, was one of five meetings held by a committee of seven historians appointed by the American Historical Association in December 1896 to "consider the subject of history in the secondary schools and to draw up a scheme of college-entrance requirements in history." The members of the committee, besides Hart and Haskins, were Andrew C. McLaughlin (the chairman), Herbert Baxter Adams, George L. Fox, Lucy M. Salmon, and Henry Morse Stephens. The final report of the committee was printed under the title, "The Study of History in Schools," in the *Annual Report of the American Historical Association for the Year 1898* (Washington, 1899), pp. 427-564, and was also issued in 1899 as a separate volume.

⁵ See the Editorial Note, "The Madison Conference on History, Civil Government, and Political Economy," Vol. 8, and the minutes of the conference printed at Dec. 28, 1892, *ibid.* The American Historical Association's committee studied the somewhat narrower subject of history in secondary schools over a much longer time span than the Madison committee and arrived at basically similar recommendations, although there were many differences in detail and emphasis.

Two Letters from Theodore Roosevelt

My dear Mr. Wilson: [Washington] April 27, 1897.

It is always a pleasure to hear from you,¹ but I am happy to say that as regards the subject of this letter I have already been doing all I can for Mr. Renick.² The Chief Clerk has rarely, indeed of late years never, been retained as such, but he has always been given another place, and I have been doing everything I could to get Mr. Renick the other place. My efforts failed in other departments, and now I am trying to get him a position under Secretary Long.

This is one of the matters in which I have been especially interested, and you may be sure that, so far as my efforts avail anything, they will be put forth heart and soul in Mr. Renick's behalf.   Faithfully yours,   Theodore Roosevelt

¹ Wilson's letter to Roosevelt is missing.
² He had been dismissed as Chief Clerk of the State Department upon the return of the Republicans to power under McKinley.

My dear Mr. Wilson: [Washington] April 29, 1897.

I write you at once to tell you bad tidings about our friend Renick, and I request you to keep this letter entirely confidential. I called on Secretary Long as soon as he got back here from New York and put the case on behalf of Renick as strongly as I knew how. However, he was very decided in refusing to entertain the suggestion that Renick should be given the position of appointment clerk, or even a smaller position in the Brooklyn Navy Yard. I am, of course, merely a subordinate and can only acquiesce, and I hardly know what else to do. I wonder, however, if Secretary Long would not pay some heed to a letter from a man of your standing? He is a man of cultivation himself and of entire kindness of heart, and desires to do justice. Of course he knows I am what would be called a professional civil service reformer, and I am all the time asking favors in the way of retention of democrats in all branches of the service, so that they get to regard a request from me as something to be expected and discounted. Now, if you write him at once a statement of the case, not using too strong language in condemning the State Department, but expressing your regret that the invariable custom of giving a turned-out chief clerk something has not been followed, and saying how civil service reformers and gold democrats generally would appreciate an act on behalf of Renick, I think it barely possible that some good would result. Of course I don't want to appear as your adviser in the matter, and this must be kept purely confidential.[1]

Very sincerely yours,   Theodore Roosevelt

TLS (Letterpress Books, T. Roosevelt Papers, DLC).

[1] It is not known whether Wilson wrote this letter to Secretary of the Navy John Davis Long. It has not been found.

From Francis Landey Patton

Princeton, New Jersey.

My dear Professor Wilson: April 29, 1897

I have received your letter enclosing Professor Haskins's to you.[1]

In my conversation with Prof Haskins[2] I put the whole matter before him; & I have written him embodying the same ideas.[3] The department of Political Science, I have said, will be eliminated from the chair. The salary [–] $3,000–will at no distant day be raised to the maximum of $3,400. The department of History will be developed as speedily as we can wisely do it; & meanwhile, with Mr Coney[4] teaching all the required Sophomore work & also offering lectures in Modern History to Juniors & Seniors, Mr Haskins on a schedule say of eight hours–(he has 12 hours now)–could arrange his lectures so as to employ his time very largely upon his own special fields of inquiry.

I feel about it in this way:

Mr Haskins is a young man, unmarried, & is offered $3,000 in a leading chair of one of the foremost universities in America. In my judgment he would be wise to come on the salary offered. If Princeton is the place of vantage which I trust he thinks it is, then the additional $400 ought not to be made the condition of his coming: especially as he has been told that the increase of salary will come in a short time.

I did not say to Professor Haskins but I had in mind the fact that there are several of our Junior Professors who ought to be raised to $3400 before a man as young as Prof Haskins is given $3400[.] I refer to such a man as Prof Fine.

At the same time, I can anticipate your rejoinder, that if Prof Haskins is presumably the man to fill the vacant chair we ought not to hesitate long in regard to the difference between $3000 & $3400. At the present state of the negotiations I think the committee[5] is in favor of the proposition as I made it & I hope very sincerely that Professor Haskins will see it as I do. I have assured him of the most cordial desire on my part to have him and & [*sic*] of a very cordial election if he indicates his willingness to come. I cannot help feeling that he will see in a call to Princeton an opportunity to do his life work under very exceptional conditions.

          I am very sincerely yours   Francis L Patton

ALS (WP, DLC).

  [1] Both letters are missing.

  [2] Haskins visited Princeton and conferred with Patton on April 19 and 20, 1897.

  [3] F. L. Patton to C. H. Haskins, April 29, 1897, ALS (C. H. Haskins Papers, NjP).

  [4] John Haughton Coney, Instructor in History.

  [5] That is, the Curriculum Committee of the Board of Trustees.

To Charles Homer Haskins

My dear Haskins,   Princeton, New Jersey, 11 May, 1897.

I have not returned sooner to the charge because I preferred to let the President do the talking. We are both most sincerely anxious to have you come, and do not think that you would ever regret it. I hope that Dr. Patton has put his case persuasively; and I do not know what I could say that I have not already said. You will not be pressed for time. Our Trustees can do nothing until June anyway, and I hope you will by that time have thought about Princeton long enough to make up your mind to come.

In short, my dear fellow, I want you very much, and I believe that you would be happy and prosperous here.

My love to Turner.

          Faithfully Yours,   Woodrow Wilson

WWTLS (C. H. Haskins Papers, NjP).

To Albert Bushnell Hart

My dear Professor Hart, Princeton, New Jersey, 18 May, 1897.

I am afraid I have shown myself very stupid about your letter *in re* the revision of the book lists in the "Epochs."[1] You did not say so explicitly, but I suppose I ought to have understood that the Messrs. Longmans want *me* to revise those in number three.[2] I did not so understand you at first; and that is my excuse for not having made a definite reply at once.

It will involve a good deal of gratuitous labour;[3] but I am willing, for the sake of the little book, to attempt the revision as soon as possible. I do not see, however, how that can be before the Autumn.[4] I am busy now upon a revision of "The State" which has long been necessary, and which I have promised to complete by September. I do not see how I can possibly stop for anything else.

With much regard,
In haste, Sincerely Yours, Woodrow Wilson

TCL (RSB Coll., DLC).
[1] Hart's letter is missing.
[2] That is, his own *Division and Reunion*.
[3] Because he had received a flat payment of $500 for his manuscript.
[4] Actually, Wilson was not able to complete his revision of the bibliographies until about April 14, 1898. The so-called eleventh edition of *Division and Reunion*, which embodied his revisions, came out later in 1898.

From Maltbie Davenport Babcock

My dear Friend: Baltimore. May 18, 1897.

We come home with our garments smelling of the myrrh, aloes and cassia of Princeton. We do not know when we have had such a happy Sunday as the one we spent in your home and the University.

The tree in your side yard I should say was the June Berry (or Shad Bush, or Service Tree). It is the only tree that I can find that answers at all to the description. When some Princeton botanist settles this, let me know whether I am right or wrong.

I enclose a copy of the lines on the Dogwood Mrs. Wilson asked for. I have ordered "The Sowers"[1] to be sent you. It is a book that will pass some vacation hours pleasantly.

Very truly yours, M. D. Babcock

TLS (WP, DLC) with WWhw notation on env.: "Poem—Dogwood." Enc.: TC of poem, "To the Dogwood," presumably by M. D. Babcock.
[1] Henry Seton Merriman [Hugh Stowell Scott], *The Sowers* (New York, 1895).

From the Minutes of the Princeton Faculty

5 5′ P.M., Wednesday, May 19th, 1897.

. . . The Committee on Discipline presented the following Resolution which was adopted and ordered to be communicated to the Treasurer of the College;

Resolved, That no housekeeper taking Sophomores or Freshmen as Table Boarders shall be permitted to supply such boarders with the use of Pool Tables. . . .

A News Item

[May 22, 1897]

At a congregational meeting of the Second Presbyterian Church, held on Wednesday [May 19] evening, Professor Woodrow Wilson, Mr. L. W. Freund and Mr. Matthew Bergen were chosen ruling elders and Messrs James E. Burke and W. Percy Gibby deacons.

Printed in the *Princeton Press*, May 22, 1897.

A News Report

[May 22, 1897]

THE LIT. BANQUET.

The '98 Board Dines the Retiring Editors.

The annual banquet given by the newly elected editors to the retiring members of the *Nassau Literary Magazine* Board was held at the Inn last evening. The room was decorated with the University colors, and potted plants and dog-wood were tastefully arranged in various parts of the room, the general appearance of things being quite attractive.

Covers were laid for about thirty, the company present consisting of the members of the English department of the faculty, representatives from *The Daily Princetonian* and the *Tiger*,[1] several invited guests, and a few undergraduates.

Prof. Bliss Perry was the toastmaster, and he called for the following toasts:

"The Faculty," Prof. Woodrow Wilson.

"The Alumni," Mr. Robert Bridges, '79.

"The '98 Board," R. D. Dripps.

"The '97 Board," A. W. Leonard.

Informal addresses were also made by James Barnes '91, Jesse Lynch Williams '92, Laurence Hutton of *Harper's Magazine*, and a representative of the *Yale Literary Magazine*.

Printed in the *Daily Princetonian*, May 22, 1897.
[1] An undergraduate magazine of wit and humor "in prose, picture, and poesy," founded in 1882.

To Edith Gittings Reid

My dear Mrs. Reid,   Princeton, New Jersey, 30 May, 1897

If you have read my little volume of essays, remember the impression of defects made upon you at the time of reading, and can forget that it was written by a friend, will you not help me by telling me where you found my writing or my thought lacking in form, in force, or in truth?

I know it is presumption in me to ask this; but I earnestly hope that you will pardon the liberty I am taking, simply because you know,—as I am sure you do,—to what straits a man is put to get frank criticism such as will really help him to be somebody in the world. It is not my profession to write essays; but essays test a writer's quality, perhaps, as no other form of prose writing can,—show his touch, his notion of form, his ideal of phrase, his range of ideas, his mental and artistic make-up; and it is for that reason that I crave your judgment upon these.

If you do not feel perfectly ready to write as I ask,—if you don't remember what impressions the essays made upon you, or haven't the time or the inclination,—pray prove that you think me genuine by saying that you will not or cannot. You may be sure that I shall only be a little more distinctly ashamed of my presumption in asking you to be my literary adviser.

Please give my warmest regards to Mrs. Gittings[1] and Mr. Reid, my love to Francis, whom I have never seen, and my deferential compliments to the Paradise Club;[2] and believe me, with many misgivings,

Most sincerely Yours,   Woodrow Wilson

ALS (WC, NjP).
[1] Mary E. (Mrs. James) Gittings, Mrs. Reid's mother, who lived with her.
[2] This seems to have been the subject of a private joke between Mrs. Reid and Wilson. There is no record of a Paradise Club in Baltimore at this time.

To Albert Shaw

My dear Shaw,   Princeton, New Jersey. 31 May, 1897.

Do you remember my speaking to you once about a young nephew of mine for whom I was anxious to find an entrance into magazine work? He is now about to graduate here; and much as it goes against the grain for me to be an applicant for a place of any kind, either for myself or for another, I feel that it is my duty to help him in every way I can, and that, seeing what a really lovely and capable fellow he is, it ought not to be hard for me to put him forward.

His name is George Howe. He had his schooling in part at Lawrenceville, our admirable training place near at hand here, and his college course with us. He has been under my eye, in my house, all the four years he has been an undergraduate, and I know him thoroughly. He has grown steadily in studious power from year to year, now stands among the best men of his class—among the very best in all literary study, and seems to me of a most satisfactory type. He has an odd mixture of hard sense, such as seems to make him very fit for business, and sensibility of the finer effects of style and literary force. I have from the first thought that he had the sort of calmness and matter-of-fact tone of judgment that fitted him for the business side of literary work, such as editors have to deal with; and I can on that account write such a letter as this with an unusual degree of confidence.

Will you not have some chance this summer to try him in your office, while Lanier[1] is away?—without pay, even, and as an experiment, for him an experience. He is a docile fellow, and would be easy to teach, as well as very quick, I think, to take teaching; and I feel a sort of confidence that you could readily make him an exceedingly useful helper. You will not often find such a combination of literary taste and training and balanced common sense—an utter absence of all nonsense.

And now, my dear fellow, pardon me for the liberty I have taken. I love this boy and admire him. I could not do less than this for him; and I have the hope that I shall in the end be serving you also, if you can give him something to do that will test his qualities.[2]

Mrs. Wilson joins me in warm regard to you both, and I am, as ever,   Your sincere friend,   Woodrow Wilson

TCL (in possession of Virginia Shaw English).

[1] Charles Day Lanier, at this time Assistant Editor of the New York *Review of Reviews*. Wilson had no doubt taught Lanier when he was a graduate student at the Johns Hopkins, 1888-89.

[2] As future correspondence will reveal, George Howe III did not go to work for Shaw, but obtained a position as a tutor in August 1897.

A Commencement Address[1]

[[June 2, 1897]]

ON BEING HUMAN.

"The rarest sort of a book," says Mr. Bagehot slyly, is "a book to read"; and "the knack in style is to write like a human being." It is painfully evident, upon experiment, that not many of the books which come teeming from our presses every year are meant to be read. They are meant, it may be, to be pondered; it is hoped, no doubt, they may instruct, or inform, or startle, or arouse, or reform, or provoke, or amuse us; but we read, if we have the true reader's zest and palate, not to grow more knowing, but to be less pent up and bound within a little circle,—as those who take their pleasure, and not as those who laboriously seek instruction,—as a means of seeing and enjoying the world of men and affairs. We wish companionship and renewal of spirit, enrichment of thought and the full adventure of the mind; and we desire fair company, and a large world in which to find them.

No one who loves the masters who may be communed with and read but must see, therefore, and resent the error of making the text of any one of them a source to draw grammar from, forcing the parts of speech to stand out stark and cold from the warm text; or a store of samples whence to draw rhetorical instances, setting up figures of speech singly and without support of any neighbor phrase, to be stared at curiously and with intent to copy or dissect! Here is grammar done without deliberation: the phrases carry their meaning simply and by a sort of limpid reflection; the thought is a living thing, not an image ingeniously contrived and wrought. Pray leave the text whole: it has no meaning piece-meal; at any rate, not that best, wholesome meaning, as of a frank and genial friend who talks, not for himself or for his phrase, but for you. It is questionable morals to dismember a living frame to seek for its obscure fountains of life!

When you say that a book was meant to be read, you mean, for one thing, of course, that it was not meant to be studied. You do not study a good story, or a haunting poem, or a battle song, or a love ballad, or any moving narrative, whether it be out of history or out of fiction,—nor any argument, even, that moves vital

---

[1] Delivered, according to a brief news item in the *Boston Evening Transcript*, June 3, 1897, at Miss Hersey's School on Chestnut Street in Boston on June 2. The school had been founded in the late 1880's by Heloise Edwina Hersey, an educator and writer of some note. No manuscript of this address survives, undoubtedly because Wilson sent his only copy to the *Atlantic Monthly* as soon as he returned from Boston, and the office of that magazine did not return the copy to him. This and following notes by the Editors.

in the field of action. You do not have to study these things; they reveal themselves, you do not stay to see how. They remain with you, and will not be forgotten or laid by. They cling like a personal experience, and become the mind's intimates. You devour a book meant to be read, not because you would fill yourself or have an anxious care to be nourished, but because it contains such stuff as it makes the mind hungry to look upon. Neither do you read it to kill time, but to lengthen time, rather, adding to it its natural usury by living the more abundantly while it lasts, joining another's life and thought to your own.

There are a few children in every generation, as Mr. Bagehot reminds us, who think the natural thing to do with *any* book is to read it. "There is an argument from design in the subject," as he says; "if the book was not meant for that purpose, for what purpose was it meant?" These are the young eyes to which books yield up a great treasure, almost in spite of themselves, as if they had been penetrated by some swift, enlarging power of vision which only the young know. It is these youngsters to whom books give up the long ages of history, "the wonderful series going back to the times of old patriarchs with their flocks and herds,"—I am quoting Mr. Bagehot again,—"the keen-eyed Greek, the stately Roman, the watching Jew, the uncouth Goth, the horrid Hun, the settled picture of the unchanging East, the restless shifting of the rapid West, the rise of the cold and classical civilization, its fall, the rough impetuous Middle Ages, the vague warm picture of ourselves and home. When did we learn these? Not yesterday nor to-day, but long ago, in the first dawn of reason, in the original flow of fancy." Books will not yield to us so richly when we are older. The argument from design fails. We return to the staid authors we read long ago, and do not find in them the vital, speaking images that used to lie there upon the page. Our own fancy is gone, and the author never had any. We are driven in upon the books *meant* to be read.

These are books written by human beings, indeed, but with no general quality belonging to the kind,—with a special tone and temper, rather, a spirit out of the common, touched with a light that shines clear out of some great source of light which not every man can uncover. We call this spirit human because it moves us, quickens a like life in ourselves, makes us glow with a sort of ardor of self-discovery. It touches the springs of fancy or of action within us, and makes our own life seem more quick and vital. We do not call every book that moves us human. Some seem written with knowledge of the black art, set our base passions aflame, disclose motives at which we shudder,—the more because we feel their reality and power; and we know that this is of the devil, and not the fruitage of any quality that distinguishes us as men. We are distinguished as men by the qualities that mark us different from the beasts. When we call a thing human we have a spiritual ideal in mind. It may not be an ideal of that which is perfect, but it moves at least upon an upland level where the air is sweet; it holds an image of man erect and constant, going abroad with undaunted steps, looking with frank and open gaze upon all the fortunes of his day, feeling ever and again

> "the joy
> Of elevated thoughts; a sense sublime
> Of something far more deeply interfused,
> Whose dwelling is the light of setting suns,
> And the round ocean and the living air,
> And the blue sky, and in the mind of man:
> A motion and a spirit, that impels
> All thinking things."[2]

Say what we may of the errors and the degrading sins of our kind, we do not willingly make what is worst in us the distinguishing trait of what is human. When we declare, with Bagehot, that the author whom we love writes like a human being, we are not sneering at him; we do not say it with a leer. It is in token of admiration, rather. He makes us *like* our humankind. There is a noble passion in what he says; a wholesome humor that echoes genial comradeships; a certain reasonableness and moderation in what is thought and said; an air of the open day, in which things are seen whole and in their right colors, rather than of the close study or the academic classroom. We do not want our poetry from grammarians, nor our tales from philologists, nor our history from theorists. Their human nature is subtly transmuted into something less broad and catholic and of the general world. Neither do we want our political economy from tradesmen nor our statesmanship from mere politicians, but from those who see more and care for more than these men see or care for.

Once,—it is a thought which troubles us,—once it was a simple enough matter to be a human being, but now it is deeply difficult; because life was once simple, but is now complex, confused, multifarious. Haste, anxiety, preoccupation, the need to specialize and make machines of ourselves, have transformed the once simple world, and we are apprised that it will not be without effort that we shall keep the broad human traits which have so far made the earth habitable. We have seen our modern life ac-

2 From Wordsworth's "Lines Composed a Few Miles Above Tintern Abbey."

cumulate, hot and restless, in great cities,—and we cannot say that the change is not natural: we see in it, on the contrary, the fulfillment of an inevitable law of change, which is no doubt a law of growth, and not of decay. And yet we look upon the portentous thing with a great distaste, and doubt with what altered passions we shall come out of it. The huge, rushing, aggregate life of a great city,—the crushing crowds in the streets, where friends seldom meet and there are few greetings; the thunderous noise of trade and industry that speaks of nothing but gain and competition, and a consuming fever that checks the natural courses of the kindly blood; no leisure anywhere, no quiet, no restful ease, no wise repose,—all this shocks us. It is inhumane. It does not seem human. How much more likely does it appear that we shall find men sane and human about a country fireside, upon the streets of quiet villages, where all are neighbors, where groups of friends gather easily, and a constant sympathy makes the very air seem native! Why should not the city seem infinitely *more* human than the hamlet? Why should not human traits the more abound where human beings teem millions strong?

Because the city curtails man of his wholeness, specializes him, quickens some powers, stunts others, gives him a sharp edge and a temper like that of steel, makes him unfit for nothing so much as to sit still. Men have indeed written like human beings in the midst of great cities, but not often when they have shared the city's characteristic life, its struggle for place and for gain. There are not many places that belong to a city's life to which you can "invite your soul." Its haste, its preoccupations, its anxieties, its rushing noise as of men driven, its ringing cries, distract you. It offers no quiet for reflection; it permits no retirement to any who share its life. It is a place of little tasks, of narrowed functions, of aggregate and not of individual strength. The great machine dominates its little parts, and its Society is as much of a machine as its business.

"This tract which the river of Time
Now flows through with us, is the plain.
Gone is the calm of its earlier shore.
Border'd by cities, and hoarse
With a thousand cries is its stream.
And we on its breast, our minds
Are confused as the cries which we hear,
Changing and shot as the sights which we see.

"And we say that repose has fled
Forever the course of the river of Time,
That cities will crowd to its edge
In a blacker, incessanter line;
That the din will be more on its banks,
Denser the trade on its stream,
Flatter the plain where it flows,
Fiercer the sun overhead,
That never will those on its breast
See an ennobling sight,
Drink of the feeling of quiet again.

"But what was before us we know not,
And we know not what shall succeed.

"Haply, the river of Time—
As it grows, as the towns on its marge
Fling their wavering lights
On a wider, statelier stream—
May acquire, if not the calm
Of its early mountainous shore,
Yet a solemn peace of its own.

"And the width of the waters, the hush
Of the grey expanse where he floats,
Freshening its current and spotted with foam
As it draws to the Ocean, may strike
Peace to the soul of the man on its breast—
As the pale waste widens around him,
As the banks fade dimmer away,
As the stars come out, and the night-wind
Brings up the stream
Murmurs and scents of the infinite sea."[3]

We cannot easily see the large measure and abiding purpose of the novel age in which we stand young and confused. The view that shall clear our minds and quicken us to act as those who know their task and its distant consummation will come with better knowledge and completer self-possession. It shall not be a night-wind, but an air that shall blow out of the widening east and with the coming of the light, that shall bring us, with the morning, "murmurs and scents of the infinite sea." Who can doubt that man has grown more and more human with each step of that slow process which has brought him knowledge, self-restraint, the arts of intercourse, and the revelations of real joy?

[3] Matthew Arnold, "The Future."

Man has more and more lived with his fellow men, and it is society that has humanized him,—the development of society into
an infinitely various school of discipline and ordered skill. He has
been made more human by schooling, by growing more self-
possessed,—less violent, less tumultuous; holding himself in hand,
and moving always with a certain poise of spirit; not forever
clapping his hand to the hilt of his sword, but preferring, rather,
to play with a subtler skill upon the springs of action. This is our
conception of the truly human man: a man in whom there is a
just balance of faculties, a catholic sympathy,—no brawler, no
fanatic, no Pharisee; not too credulous in hope, not too desperate
in purpose; warm, but not hasty; ardent and full of definite
power, but not running about to be pleased and deceived by every
new thing.

It is a genial image, of men we love,—an image of men warm
and true of heart, direct and unhesitating in courage, generous,
magnanimous, faithful, steadfast, capable of a deep devotion
and self-forgetfulness. But the age changes, and with it must
change our ideals of human quality. Not that we would give up
what we have loved: we would add what a new life demands.
In a new age men must acquire a new capacity, must be men
upon a new scale and with added qualities. We shall need a new
Renaissance, ushered in by a new "humanistic" movement, in
which we shall add to our present minute, introspective study of
ourselves, our jails, our slums, our nerve-centres, our shifts to
live, almost as morbid as mediæval religion, a rediscovery of the
round world and of man's place in it, now that its face has
changed. We study the world, but not yet with intent to school
our hearts and tastes, broaden our natures, and know our fellow
men as comrades rather than as phenomena; with purpose,
rather, to build up bodies of critical doctrine and provide ourselves with theses. That, surely, is not the truly humanizing way
in which to take the air of the world. Man is much more than a
"rational being," and lives more by sympathies and impressions
than by conclusions. It darkens his eyes and dries up the wells
of his humanity to be forever in search of doctrine. We need
wholesome, experiencing natures, I dare affirm, much more than
we need sound reasoning.

Take life in the large view, and we are most reasonable when
we seek that which is most wholesome and tonic for our natures
as a whole; and we know, when we put aside pedantry, that the
great middle object in life,—the object that lies between religion
on the one hand, and food and clothing on the other, establishing
our average levels of achievement,—the excellent golden mean, is,

not to be learned, but to be human beings in all the wide and genial meaning of the term. Does the age hinder? Do its mazy interests distract us when we would plan our discipline, determine our duty, clarify our ideals? It is the more necessary that we should ask ourselves what it is that is demanded of us, if we would fit our qualities to meet the new tests. Let us remind ourselves that to be human is, for one thing, to speak and act with a certain note of genuineness, a quality mixed of spontaneity and intelligence. This is necessary for wholesome life in any age, but particularly amidst confused affairs and shifting standards. Genuinenesss is not mere simplicity, for that may lack vitality, and genuineness does not. We expect what we call genuine to have pith and strength of fibre. Genuineness is a quality which we sometimes mean to include when we speak of individuality. Individuality is lost the moment you submit to passing modes or fashions, the creations of an artificial society; and so is genuineness. No man is genuine who is forever trying to pattern his life after the lives of other people,—unless indeed he be a genuine dolt. But individuality is by no means the same as genuineness; for individuality may be associated with the most extreme and even ridiculous eccentricity, while genuineness we conceive to be always wholesome, balanced, and touched with dignity. It is a quality that goes with good sense and self-respect. It is a sort of robust moral sanity, mixed of elements both moral and intellectual. It is found in natures too strong to be mere trimmers and conformers, too well poised and thoughtful to fling off into intemperate protest and revolt. Laughter is genuine which has in it neither the shrill, hysterical note of mere excitement nor the hard metallic twang of the cynic's sneer,—which rings in the honest voice of gracious good humor, which is innocent and unsatirical. Speech is genuine which is without silliness, affectation, or pretense. That character is genuine which seems built by nature rather than by convention, which is stuff of independence and of good courage. Nothing spurious, bastard, begotten out of true wedlock of the mind; nothing adulterated and seeming to be what it is not; nothing unreal, can ever get place among the nobility of things genuine, natural, of pure stock and unmistakable lineage. It is a prerogative of every truly human being to come out from the low estate of those who are merely gregarious and of the herd, and show his innate powers cultivated and yet unspoiled,—sound, unmixed, free from imitation; showing that individualization without extravagance which is genuineness.

But how? By what means is this self-liberation to be effected,—this emancipation from affectation and the bondage of being like other people? Is it open to us to choose to be genuine? I see noth-ing insuperable in the way, except for those who are hopelessly lacking in a sense of humor. It depends upon the range and scale of your observation whether you can strike the balance of genuineness or not. If you live in a small and petty world, you will be subject to its standards; but if you live in a large world, you will see that standards are innumerable,—some old, some new, some made by the noble-minded and made to last, some made by the weak-minded and destined to perish, some lasting from age to age, some only from day to day,—and that a choice must be made amongst them. It is then that your sense of humor will assist you. You are, you will perceive, upon a long journey, and it will seem to you ridiculous to change your life and dis-cipline your instincts to conform to the usages of a single inn by the way. You will distinguish the essentials from the accidents, and deem the accidents something meant for your amusement. The strongest natures do not need to wait for these slow lessons of observation, to be got by conning life: their sheer vigor makes it impossible for them to conform to fashion or care for times and seasons. But the rest of us must cultivate knowledge of the world in the large, get our offing, reach a comparative point of view, before we can become with steady confidence our own masters and pilots. The art of being human begins with the prac-tice of being genuine, and following standards of conduct which the world has tested. If your life is not various and you cannot know the best people, who set the standards of sincerity, your reading at least can be various, and you may look at your little circle through the best books, under the guidance of writers who have known life and loved the truth.

And then genuineness will bring serenity,—which I take to be another mark of the right development of the true human being, certainly in an age passionate and confused as this in which we live. Of course serenity does not always go with genuineness. We must say of Dr. Johnson that he was genuine, and yet we know that the stormy tyrant of the Turk's Head Tavern was not serene. Carlyle was genuine (though that is not quite the *first* adjective we should choose to describe him), but of serenity he allowed cooks and cocks and every modern and every ancient sham to deprive him. Serenity is a product, no doubt, of two very different things, namely, vision and digestion. Not the eye only, but the courses of the blood must be clear, if we would find serenity. Our word "serene" contains a picture. Its image is of the calm evening, when the stars are out and the still night comes on; when the dew is on the grass and the wind does not stir; when the day's work is over, and the evening meal, and thought falls clear in the quiet hour. It is the hour of reflection,— and it is human to reflect. Who shall contrive to be human without this evening hour, which drives turmoil out, and gives the soul its seasons of self-recollection? Serenity is not a thing to beget inaction. It only checks excitement and uncalculating haste. It does not exclude ardor or the heat of battle: it keeps ardor from extravagance, prevents the battle from becoming a mere aimless mêlée. The great captains of the world have been men who were calm in the moment of crisis; who were calm, too, in the long planning which preceded crisis; who went into battle with a serenity infinitely ominous for those whom they attacked. We instinctively associate serenity with the highest types of power among men, seeing in it the poise of knowledge and calm vision, that supreme heat and mastery which is without splutter or noise of any kind. The art of power in this sort is no doubt learned in hours of reflection, by those who are not born with it. What rebuke of aimless excitement there is to be got out of a little reflection, when we have been inveighing against the corruption and decadence of our own days, if only we have provided ourselves with a little knowledge of the past wherewith to balance our thought! As bad times as these, or any we shall see, have been reformed, but not by protests. They have been made glorious instead of shameful by the men who kept their heads and struck with sure self-possession in the fight. No age will take hysterical reform. The world is very human, not a bit given to adopting virtues for the sake of those who merely bemoan its vices, and we are most effective when we are most calmly in possession of our senses.

So far is serenity from being a thing of slackness or inaction that it seems bred, rather, by an equable energy, a satisfying activity. It may be found in the midst of that alert interest in affairs which is, it may be, the distinguishing trait of developed manhood. You distinguish man from the brute by his intelligent curiosity, his play of mind beyond the narrow field of instinct, his perception of cause and effect in matters to him indifferent, his appreciation of motive and calculation of results. He is interested in the world about him, and even in the great universe of which it forms a part, not merely as a thing he would use, satisfy his wants and grow great by, but as a field to stretch his mind in, for love of journeyings and excursions in the large realm of thought. Your full-bred human being loves a run afield with his understanding. With what images does he not surround himself and store his mind! With what fondness does he con travelers' tales and credit poets' fancies! With what patience does he follow science and pore upon old records, and with what eagerness does he ask the news of the day! No great part of what he learns immediately touches his own life or the course of his own affairs: he is not pursuing a business, but satisfying as he can an insatiable mind. No doubt the highest form of this noble curiosity is that which leads us, without self-interest, to look abroad upon all the field of man's life at home and in society, seeking more excellent forms of government, more righteous ways of labor, more elevating forms of art, and which makes the greater among us statesmen, reformers, philanthropists, artists, critics, men of letters. It is certainly human to mind your neighbor's business as well as your own. Gossips are only sociologists upon a mean and petty scale. The art of being human lifts to a better level than that of gossip; it leaves mere chatter behind, as too reminiscent of a lower stage of existence, and is compassed by those whose outlook is wide enough to serve for guidance and a choosing of ways.

Luckily we are not the first human beings. We have come into a great heritage of interesting things, collected and piled all about us by the curiosity of past generations. And so our interest is selective. Our education consists in learning intelligent choice. Our energies do not clash or compete: each is free to take his own path to knowledge. Each has that choice, which is man's alone, of the life he shall live, and finds out first or last that the art of living is not only to be genuine and one's own master, but also to learn mastery in perception and preference. Your true woodsman needs not to follow the dusty highway through the forest nor search for any path, but goes straight from glade to glade as if upon an open way, having some privy understanding with the taller trees, some compass in his senses. So there is a subtle craft in finding ways for the mind, too. Keep but your eyes alert and your ears quick, as you move among men and among books, and you shall find yourself possessed at last of a new sense, the sense of the pathfinder. Have you never marked the eyes of a man who has seen the world he has lived in: the eyes of the sea-captain, who has watched his life through the changes of the heavens; the eyes of the huntsman, nature's gossip and familiar; the eyes of the man of affairs, accustomed to command in moments of exigency? You are at once aware that they are eyes which can see. There is something in them that you do not find in other eyes, and you have read the life of the man when you have divined what it is. Let the thing serve as a figure. So ought alert interest in the world of men and thought to serve each one of us that we shall have the quick perceiving vision, taking meanings at a glance, reading suggestions as if they were expositions. You shall not otherwise get full value of your humanity. What good shall it do you else that the long generations of men which have gone before you have filled the world with great store of everything that may make you wise and your life various? Will you not take usury of the past, if it may be had for the taking? Here is the world humanity has made: will you take full citizenship in it, or will you live in it as dull, as slow to receive, as unenfranchised, as the idlers for whom civilization has no uses, or the deadened toilers, men or beasts, whose labor shuts the door on choice?

That man seems to me a little less than human who lives as if our life in the world were but just begun, thinking only of the things of sense, recking nothing of the infinite thronging and assemblage of affairs the great stage over, or of the old wisdom that has ruled the world. That is, if he have the choice. Great masses of our fellow men are shut out from choosing, by reason of absorbing toil, and it is part of the enlightenment of our age that our understandings are being opened to the workingman's need of a little leisure wherein to look about him and clear his vision of the dust of the workshop. We know that there is a drudgery which is inhuman, let it but encompass the whole life, with only heavy sleep between task and task. We know that those who are so bound can have no freedom to be men, that their very spirits are in bondage. It is part of our philanthropy— it should be part of our statesmanship—to ease the burden as we can, and enfranchise those who spend and are spent for the sustenance of the race. But what shall we say of those who are free and yet choose littleness and bondage, or of those who, though they might see the whole face of society, nevertheless choose to spend all a life's space poring upon some single vice or blemish? I would not for the world discredit any sort of philanthropy except the small and churlish sort which seeks to reform by nagging,—the sort which exaggerates petty vices into great ones, and runs atilt against windmills, while everywhere colossal shams and abuses go unexposed, unrebuked. Is it because we are better at being common scolds than at being wise advisers that we prefer little reforms to big ones? Are we to allow the poor personal habits of other people to absorb and quite use up all our fine indignation? It will be a bad day for society when sentimentalists are encouraged to suggest all the measures that shall be taken for the betterment of the race. I, for one, sometimes sigh for a generation of "leading people" and of good people who shall see things steadily and see them whole; who shall show a handsome justness and a large sanity of view, an opportune tolerance for the details that happen to be awry, in order that they may spend their energy, not without self-possession, in some generous mission which shall make right principles shine upon the people's life. They would bring with them an age of large moralities, a spacious time, a day of vision.

Knowledge has come into the world in vain if it is not to emancipate those who may have it from narrowness, censoriousness, fussiness, an intemperate zeal for petty things. It would be a most pleasant, a truly humane world, would we but open our ears with a more generous welcome to the clear voices that ring in those writings upon life and affairs which mankind has chosen to keep. Not many splenetic books, not many intemperate, not many bigoted, have kept men's confidence; and the mind that is impatient, or intolerant, or hoodwinked, or shut in to a petty view, shall have no part in carrying men forward to a true humanity, shall never stand as examples of the true humankind. What is truly human has always upon it the broad light of what is genial, fit to support life, cordial, and of a catholic spirit of helpfulness. Your true human being has eyes and keeps his balance in the world; deems nothing uninteresting that comes from life; clarifies his vision and gives health to his eyes by using them upon things near and things far. The brute beast has but a single neighborhood, a single, narrow round of existence; the gain of being human accrues in the choice of change and variety and of experience far and wide, with all the world for stage,—a stage set and appointed by this very art of choice,—all future generations for witnesses and audience. When you talk with a man who has in his nature and acquirements that freedom from constraint which goes with the full franchise of humanity, he turns easily from topic to topic; does not fall silent or dull when you leave some single field of thought such as unwise men make a prison of. The men who will not be broken from a little set of subjects, who talk earnestly, hotly, with a sort of fierceness, of certain special schemes of conduct, and look coldly upon everything else, render you infinitely uneasy, as if there were in them a force abnormal and which rocked toward an upset of the mind; but from the man whose interest swings from thought to thought with the zest and poise and pleasure of the old traveler, eager for what is new, glad to look again upon what is old, you come away with faculties warmed and heartened,—with the feeling of having been comrade for a little with a genuine human being. It is

a large world and a round world, and men grow human by seeing all its play of force and folly.

Let no one suppose that efficiency is lost by such breadth and
catholicity of view. We deceive ourselves with instances, look at
sharp crises in the world's affairs, and imagine that intense and
narrow men have made history for us. Poise, balance, a nice
and equable exercise of force, are not, it is true, the things the
world ordinarily seeks for or most applauds in its heroes. It is
apt to esteem that man most human who has his qualities in a
certain exaggeration, whose courage is passionate, whose generosity is without deliberation, whose just action is without pre-
meditation, whose spirit runs towards its favorite objects with an
infectious and reckless ardor, whose wisdom is no child of slow
prudence. We love Achilles more than Diomedes, and Ulysses
not at all. But these are standards left over from a ruder state
of society: we should have passed by this time the Homeric stage
of mind,—should have heroes suited to our age. Nay, we have
erected different standards, and do make a different choice,
when we see in any man fulfillment of our real ideals. Let a
modern instance serve as test. Could any man hesitate to say
that Abraham Lincoln was more human than William Lloyd Gar-
rison? Does not every one know that it was the practical Free-
Soilers who made emancipation possible, and not the hot, im-
practicable Abolitionists; that the country was infinitely more
moved by Lincoln's temperate sagacity than by any man's enthusiasm, instinctively trusted the man who saw the whole
situation and kept his balance, instinctively held off from those
who refused to see more than one thing? We know how serviceable the intense and headlong agitator was in bringing to their
feet men fit for action; but we feel uneasy while he lives, and
vouchsafe him our full sympathy only when he is dead. We know
that the genial forces of nature which work daily, equably, and
without violence are infinitely more serviceable, infinitely more
admirable, than the rude violence of the storm, however necessary or excellent the purification it may have wrought. Should
we seek to name the most human man among those who led the
nation to its struggle with slavery, and yet was no statesman, we
should of course name Lowell. We know that his humor went
further than any man's passion towards setting tolerant men
a-tingle with the new impulses of the day. We naturally hold back
from those who are intemperate and can never stop to smile,
and are deeply reassured to see a twinkle in a reformer's eye.
We are glad to see earnest men laugh. It breaks the strain. If it be

wholesome laughter, it dispels all suspicion of spite, and is like the gleam of light upon running water, lifting sullen shadows, suggesting clear depths.

Surely it is this soundness of nature, this broad and genial quality, this full-blooded, full-orbed sanity of spirit, which gives the men we love that wide-eyed sympathy which gives hope and power to humanity, which gives range to every good quality and is so excellent a credential of genuine manhood. Let your life and your thought be narrow, and your sympathy will shrink to a like scale. It is a quality which follows the seeing mind afield, which waits on experience. It is not a mere sentiment. It goes not with pity so much as with a penetrative understanding of other men's lives and hopes and temptations. Ignorance of these things makes it worthless. Its best tutors are observation and experience, and these serve only those who keep clear eyes and a wide field of vision.

It is exercise and discipline upon such a scale, too, which strengthen, which for ordinary men come near to creating, that capacity to reason upon affairs and to plan for action which we always reckon upon finding in every man who has studied to perfect his native force. This new day in which we live cries a challenge to us. Steam and electricity have reduced nations to neighborhoods; have made travel pastime, and news a thing for everybody. Cheap printing has made knowledge a vulgar commodity. Our eyes look, almost without choice, upon the very world itself, and the word "human" is filled with a new meaning. Our ideals broaden to suit the wide day in which we live. We crave, not cloistered virtue,—it is impossible any longer to keep to the cloister,—but a robust spirit that shall take the air in the great world, know men in all their kinds, choose its way amidst the bustle with all self-possession, with wise genuineness, in calmness, and yet with the quick eye of interest and the quick pulse of power. It is again a day for Shakespeare's spirit,—a day more various, more ardent, more provoking to valor and every large design even than "the spacious times of great Elizabeth," when all the world seemed new; and if we cannot find another bard, come out of a new Warwickshire, to hold once more the mirror up to nature, it will not be because the stage is not set for him. The time is such an one as he might rejoice to look upon; and if we would serve it as it should be served, we should seek to be human after his wide-eyed sort. The serenity of power; the naturalness that is nature's poise and mark of genuineness; the unsleeping interest in all affairs, all fancies, all things believed or done; the catholic understanding, tolerance, enjoyment, of all classes and conditions of men; the conceiving imagination, the planning purpose, the creating thought, the wholesome, laughing humor, the quiet insight, the universal coinage of the brain,—are not these the marvelous gifts and qualities we mark in Shakespeare when we call him the greatest among men? And shall not these rounded and perfect powers serve us as our ideal of what it is to be a finished human being?

We live for our own age,—an age like Shakespeare's, when an old world is passing away, a new world coming in,—an age of new speculation and every new adventure of the mind; a full stage, an intricate plot, a universal play of passion, an outcome no man can foresee. It is to this world, this sweep of action, that our understandings must be stretched and fitted; it is in this age we must show our human quality. We must measure ourselves by the task, accept the pace set for us, make shift to know what we are about. How free and liberal should be the scale of our sympathy, how catholic our understanding of the world in which we live, how poised and masterful our action in the midst of so great affairs! We should school our ears to know the voices that are genuine, our thought to take the truth when it is spoken, our spirits to feel the zest of the day. It is within our choice to be with mean company or with great, to consort with the wise or with the foolish, now that the great world has spoken to us in the literature of all tongues and voices. The best selected human nature will tell in the making of the future, and the art of being human is the art of freedom and of force.

Printed in the *Atlantic Monthly*, LXXX (Sept. 1897), 320-29.

From Edith Gittings Reid

My dear Mr. Wilson   [Baltimore] June 2nd [1897]
I have just read your letter, and though I must be off in five minutes to go to the country for a few days, I want to tell you what great pleasure your letter gave me. The Essays are very distinct in my memory and in a few days I will write you just the impression they made upon me at the first, and second readings.
                    Very faithfully your friend   Edith G. Reid

ALS (WP, DLC).

Ellen Axson Wilson to John Bates Clark[1]

My dear Dr. Clark,   Princeton, June 3, 1897.

I am about to do a very odd thing;—I am going to write you a confidential letter; not only without Mr. Wilson's knowledge, but with the full assurance that if he *did* know he would veto it flatly! Naturally I am feeling dismayed at such an unprecedented procedure,—and yet I *will* "do the deed["]!

As I suppose you know, Mr. Wilson gives a course of twenty-five lectures at the Johns Hopkins every winter; having when he first came to Princeton arranged for a yearly furlough of five weeks. But, being singularly dependent upon his home life, this long absence is a great and increasing trial to him,—so much so, that last winter he declared, to my great relief, that he would not renew the engagement. Now, however, when it becomes necessary to decide the matter, he thinks that he must renew it,—that we cannot afford to give it up. And the worst of it is that I am afraid he is right.

Of course a man,—or woman,—of the world would think us a pair of silly children to make a tragedy of a five weeks separation. But his temperament;—his way of putting *his whole self* into every lecture, and every written page, really makes it rather important for his physical and mental well-being that I should be constantly at hand, to "rest" him, as he says.

I have often thought longingly how pleasant it would be if these lectures were given in New York instead of distant Baltimore;—and now I have had a very bold thought! It has occurred to me that "something might come of it" if one of his friends would just say to Mr. Low:[2] "By the way, Wilson of Princeton, who really is an uncommonly good lecturer, has a yearly furlough of five weeks in which he gives a course at the J. H. U. Wouldn't it be a good scheme if we tried to capture him ourselves for those five weeks?" Would you "mind" saying that to Mr. Low,—"only that and nothing more"?

By his practice of making his courses alternating,—open to juniors and seniors,—the lectures would really number fifty and cover more ground than a full college lecture course of one hour a week for the year. It is almost like adding another professor to the faculty for $1,000, or less, instead of $5,000 or $7,000. The Hopkins has shown her cleverness in securing a number of such courses. It is a cheap method of borrowing brains and reputations from other institutions!

The course he gives there is for graduates on "Administration." Personally, (of course I have no idea what he would think of it,)

I should like him to give at Columbia some such course as his Princeton one on "Public Law"; because it is really to some extent a course on good citizenship, and I have seen what a stimulating and bracing effect it has had on many of our fellows. They are all most enthusiastic over it. In that subject, more directly perhaps than in some others, his strong, high character "tells"; no less than his capacity for clear thinking and forcible, vivid expression. I should like to see him a "power for good" in that great city,—provided he did not have to *live* in it!

But I must "stop this";—and I am sorely tempted to let it end its career in the waste basket, so much do I fear you will think me foolish or presumptuous. But no, I will not turn coward!

Mr. Wilson is in Boston, where he has gone to deliver an address; and cannot therefore,—were I willing to give him the opportunity!—join me in warmest regards to all. Believe me, dear Mr. Clark,   Yours most cordially,   Ellen A. Wilson.

ALS (WP, DLC).
   [1] An old friend of Wilson, at this time Professor of Political Economy at Columbia University.
   [2] Seth Low, President of Columbia University.

From Francis Landey Patton

My dear Professor Wilson: [Princeton, N. J.] June 5, 1897
   I received a letter from Professor Haskins last evening in which, I regret to say[,] he informs me that after giving the whole question the fullest consideration he has decided to remain in Madison.
   I am   Very sincerely   Francis L. Patton

ALS (Patton Letterpress Books, University Archives, NjP).

To Charles Homer Haskins

My dear Haskins,   Princeton, New Jersey, 7 June, 1897.
   I shall not try to express my disappointment at your decision to decline the call to Princeton. It is very keen, I assure you. At the same time, I fully appreciate the reasons you give, and have no sort of fault to find with the conclusion. I think you underestimate the development here. The very atmosphere counts for a chair or two in each branch, and I think the future very secure. But no man not of the place can understand what I mean by this, and I cannot wonder that you kept to your anchorage.
   I find that the President has no other candidate in mind, so that our plans are *nil* for the moment.

Give my love to Turner, and keep for yourself the most cordial good wishes both of Mrs. Wilson and myself.

Faithfully Yours,   Woodrow Wilson

WWTLS (C. H. Haskins Papers, NjP).

From Albert Bushnell Hart

My dear Wilson: Cambridge, Mass. June 7, 1897.

Your stay here gave great pleasure to your friends, old and new. We all hope that you will repeat it, with Mrs. Wilson, who will find the wives of the fraternity in no way inferior to the men whom you say you liked.

Tonight I am laboring over the *Epochs*. You wrote the *Suggestions for Readers and Teachers*, did you not? I think that may now be extended and enlarged, to make room for the new literature. I have just been doing the same thing for the other volumes. Could you cast the result into three groups: (1) to cost about $10.00; (2) to cost about $20.00; (3) to include the other two groups, and all to cost say $150.00. Could you also add a short section on *Sources*.[1]

I hope your conscience will allow you to leave out Andrews' *History*—a thing so unworthy might justly be ignored. Perhaps you will feel that you must refer to the *Quarter Century*[2]

I assume that you prefer to do this part of the job yourself. I think you are entitled to charge Longmans $50.00 for the necessary revision of Suggestions and bibliographies. Of course the page numbering (except in the Roman figures) cannot be altered; but they will cut and fit, and if necessary insert pages, to accomodate your changes.

Sincerely yours,   Albert Bushnell Hart

You ought to write a special preface for the "Ninth edition"

ALS (WP, DLC).

[1] Wilson prepared new "Suggestions for Readers and Teachers" and a section on sources, as well as a new preface, dated April 14, 1898, for what was called the eleventh edition of *Division and Reunion*, published in 1898.

[2] Elisha Benjamin Andrews, *History of the United States* (2 vols., New York, 1894) and *The History of the Last Quarter-Century in the United States, 1870-1895* (2 vols., New York, 1896).

Ellen Axson Wilson to John Bates Clark

My dear Prof. Clark,   Princeton, June 8, 1897.

I cannot tell you how deeply I appreciate the kind and reassuring manner in which you have received and answered my letter.

With all my heart I thank you; your goodness helps to restore my self-respect, somewhat shaken by my own extraordinary conduct!

Your plan[1] is certainly an excellent one, and I shall be exceedingly obliged to you for suggesting it to Mr. Plimpton,[2] as you propose. And after doing that, let me beg you to take no further trouble in the matter,—not even the trouble of *thinking* about it. It would deeply distress me to feel that I had betrayed you into anything resembling a "campaign" in Mr. Wilson's interest. My only thought has been to have a good friend like yourself insinuate into the proper brain the idea that it might be practicable and desirable to secure him! Then if nothing came of it, well and good. I do not expect anything to come of it, for a reason that escaped me when I wrote before. Some time after, it occurred to me that if a course were in question belonging, not to Mr. Sloane's department,[3] but to Mr. Burgesses,[4] President Low would naturally consult Mr. Burgess and defer to his wishes; and he and Mr. Wilson do not exactly constitute a mutual admiration society![5] So please realize fully that I shall not be in the least surprised or mortified if I never hear of it again, and let me beg you, in any event, to feel no uneasiness about it.

With renewed thanks for your great kindness, which I shall never cease to remember with gratitude, believe me, dear Mr. Clark,   Yours most cordially,   Ellen A. Wilson.

ALS (WP, DLC).

[1] The nature of Clark's plan is not disclosed in the extant documents.

[2] George Arthur Plimpton, partner in the Boston publishing firm of Ginn and Company, book collector, long-time trustee and treasurer of Barnard College, treasurer of the Academy of Political Science, and financial backer of the *Political Science Quarterly* in its early years.

[3] That is, the Department of History at Columbia University.

[4] The Department of Political Science at Columbia.

[5] In part because of Wilson's highly critical review of Burgess's *Political Science and Comparative Constitutional Law* (2 vols., Boston, 1891), printed at May 1, 1891, Vol. 7.

To Francis Landey Patton

My dear Dr. Patton,   Princeton, New Jersey, 8 June, 1897.

In one of our conversations on the reorganization of the Historical Department, I said that, if the Trustees would create and fill two history chairs, one in European and the other in American history, and appoint an assistant in history as at present, I would take the instruction in political science. Of course I know that I am not bound by that promise, because the condition precedent has not been complied with; but I am bound to help the University out as best I can, and I wish, moreover, to control the instruction in political science. I have, therefore, the following requests to make, for submission to the Curriculum Committee and the Board of Trustees:

1. That (with Mr. McCormick's consent) the title of my chair be made *The McCormick Professorship of Jurisprudence and Politics*.[1] I am very anxious to lift the word Politics out of its low meaning to the Aristotelian use, as several of the best universities in the country have already done. Johns Hopkins, for example.

2. That, instead of the course in International Law, I be authorized to give a course in the *Elements of Politics*: the genesis and action of the body politic; the nature and forms of government; the character and lodgment of Sovereignty.

3. That, instead of the course in Public Law, in which I have treated of the legal side of institutions, I be authorized to give a course in *Constitutional Government*, a study of the political side of those institutions in which our own life is founded.

4. That I be authorized to merge my present course in the history of Law into my present course in *English Common Law*, and give lectures on the genesis, growth, character, and general principles of English Common Law, running through *both terms of the year*.

My courses in Jurisprudence would then be, one in General Jurisprudence, one in American Constitutional Law and one in English Common Law; and my courses in Political Science would be those on Elements of Politics and on Constitutional Government.[2]

Confidently hoping that these new arrangements will be approved,   Very sincerely Yours,   Woodrow Wilson

WWTLS (Trustees' Papers, University Archives, NjP).

[1] The Estate of Cyrus McCormick had given $100,000 in 1896 to endow the McCormick Professorship of Jurisprudence. "Minutes of the Trustees of the College of New Jersey and Princeton University, 1894-98," p. 418. No record of Wilson's election to the professorship can be found, most probably because the McCormick family had simply endowed Wilson's existing chair, and no formal election occurred.

[2] As will soon become apparent from subsequent documents, the Board of Trustees approved Wilson's requests. His new course program, which he continued to offer through the academic year 1901-1902, is outlined and described more fully in "Wilson's New Course Program in Political Science and Jurisprudence," printed at Dec. 1, 1897. Wilson's notes for his first new course, Elements of Politics, are printed at March 5, 1898; the notes for his second new course, Constitutional Government, are printed at Sept. 19, 1898, Vol. 11.

Notes for a Talk

11 June, 1897

Cottage Club[1]

A place of comradeship, a centre of sentiment. Let the sentiment *remember*. "This isn't a horse; it's a hobby."

II.

Impression made by college, not one of progress, but of repitition— always young;—and yet there are the professors! "Heaven lies about us in our infancy," &c.

III.

Even professors forget as they hasten from one new generation to another. *Beg* your pardon. Quite forgot the 4th,—an excellent woman!

IV.

The power of democracy is in individual groupings—and a club can both make and carry ideals and traditions. I *believe* in the "proceedings of the previous meeting."

WWhw MS. (WP, DLC).
¹ An undergraduate eating club at Princeton.

From Edith Gittings Reid

Charmian P.O.   Franklin Co. Pa.
My dear Mr. Wilson   June 14th 1897

Alas! this must be a laudatory instead of a critical letter, and I feel very sure that you will be sorry. I recall the very words I used after first reading your volume of Essays. They were: "Mr Wilson always throws courage and generosity even into his finest literary phrases. After reading anything he writes I feel as I felt when a child and 'Ivanhoe struck the shield of Brian de Bois Guilbert until it rang again!' "

My dear friend, you must be content to have me, should you need one, your advocate—not your judge. It is the very fact that I never assume the critical attitude with you that your presence is always a pleasure and rest.

I know very well how difficult it is to have a true opinion, one, as you say, that "will really help you to be somebody in the world[.]" You *are* a great deal to-day, and, I believe, more absolutely, that when the end comes you will be with the very great— in an incomparably higher atmosphere than the clever, literary coster-mongers of the day.

This much I can do for you—when I hear anyone speak of your writings (anyone worth considering) I will listen attentively and, if anything is said that might be helpful, I will send it to you with perfect frankness.

And now I have a favor to ask of you. Won't you persuade your wife to come with you and pay me a visit? We have bought a cottage up here in the mountains, the air is good, and the country attractive. I want to know your wife, and it would be, *will be*, so delightful to have you both with me.

Harry sailed for England Saturday and I want to fill the sum-

mer with pleasant things to keep down a certain inevitable loneliness. There is a little study that shall be entirely yours, and I
will see that you have better pens, ink, and paper than I am now
using.

Let me know when to expect you. The journey is short—only
two hours from Baltimore; but I will send you a time table this
afternoon. With kind regards to Mrs. Wilson, I am your very faithful friend   Edith G. Reid

ALS (WP, DLC) with WWhw notation on env.: "Ans. 21 [18] June /97."

From the Minutes of the Trustees of Princeton University

Princeton, N. J., June 14th, 1897.
. . . The Committee on The Curriculum reported. The Report
was accepted, approved, its recommendations adopted, and is as
follows:

Report of the Committee on The Curriculum.

. . . II. That the request of Prof. Woodrow Wilson be granted
and the suggestions adopted, as set forth in the following communication from him: . . .[1]

◊

The Committee on the Affairs of the University made the following Report of progress, and was continued. The Report was
approved, and its suggestions were adopted.

Report of Committee on University Affairs.

To the Board of Trustees of Princeton University:
A special Committee was appointed at the December (last)
meeting of the Trustees to make investigation of the several
Departments of the University, with the view of reporting to the
Board such suggestions as might be of general advantage to the
Institution; and more especially to report a plan of re-organiza-
tion of the School of Science, if that should seem desirable. . . .

The Committee regret that their labors are not yet completed,
and that they can report only in part, and as to that part in a
way not altogether satisfactory to them; as to the matters covered,
however, the voice of the Committee is unanimous.

It would have been gratifying, had the way seemed clear, to
report such changes in the School of Science as would have relieved, measurably at least, the imperfect co-ordination existing
there. This, however, the Committee hopes to remedy without
undue delay.

The time that has elapsed since the appointment of the Committee may seem ample to have accomplished all that was desired. It should be borne in mind, that the Committee is composed in the main of very busy men whose time is fully occupied with their ordinary engagements, and who have many additional demands upon it.

Frequent meetings of men living remote from each other are practically impossible; nor can busy men take consecutive days from their regular occupations.

The Committee, however, has been far from idle. It has held meetings on seven days, and been in session altogether more than twenty five hours. The President; the Dean; Professors Young, West, Woodrow Wilson, Scott, and Perry, of the Academic Faculty; and Professors Brackett, McMillan, Cornwall, Magie, Rockwood, Harris, and F. N. Wil[l]son of the School of Science Faculty, have appeared before the Committee at its request, and been examined some eighteen or twenty hours in free and searching inquiry on discipline, curriculum, and administration. They were requested to give their views fully and with perfect freedom on these several matters. On some questions there was practical unanimity of view; on others, perhaps not less important, there was wide variance.

While there was decided adverse criticism, there was no manifestation of an offensive or even unkind spirit.

Statements, free and strong when made to the individual trustee, lost all color, and became mild and gentle hedgings, harmless shafts at most, when the ear of the Committee was opened to them.

The opinion had undoubtedly obtained that the President was not as much in evidence in the class rooms as he should be. This, perhaps, is true, and there was not wanting the inferential suggestion that he could not therefore be advised as to workings of the departments, and what was being done in them. It was very clear to the Committee, however, that the President had fully acquainted himself with what was being done, and how it was done, even to minute detail; and with the needs of the various departments. Not only so, he knew what was being done in other universities, and with what means. It was also apparent to the Committee that he had a full and comprehensive grasp of the situation here, and, broad, intelligent, and forceful views of the lines on which the logical development of Princeton University should proceed.

It would be well, however, that discipline be administered with firmer hand; that studies should be better co-ordinated; and methods of administration be somewhat changed in order to greater efficiency.

In the matter of administration, the general opinion prevailed that the system of Deans should be adopted.

On this head, it is enough to say, that even if the Committee were practically a unit in its favor—which they are not,—there seem to be serious difficulties in the way of appointing any of the professors now in the service of the University as Deans of the Academic and Scientific Faculties; and even if men of high and unquestionable qualifications for these offices were known to your Committee and could be procured, there are absolutely no funds available to pay their salaries.

The Committee, however, is seriously considering this question, and it may be that upon further light and reflection the Committee will recommend the appointment of Deans.

It should further be said in regard to the matter of administration, it is true that there has been much criticism. The Committee has not failed to consider this, and it is quite evident to them and it so reports with great pleasure that if there has been just ground for such criticism heretofore, the President is now taking this matter in firmer hand and, as it seems to the Committee, on wise lines. It must not be inferred, however, that the Committee has ceased its labors or made its final report on this matter of administration.

The Committee is fully alive to the gravity of the situation, and of the urgent importance of taking some measures of relief as early as practicable, and to this end they are ready to consider these matters further during the summer recess.

They beg leave therefore to suggest that, if it commends itself to the Trustees, the Committee be empowered to take such action, the Committees on Finance and Curriculum concurring, in any of the matters before them, including changes in Faculties and retirement of its members, as may seem to them clearly demanded by the best interests of the University; and further that the President be added to the Committee.

The Committee are clearly of the opinion that one of the most pressing needs of the institution at this time is a University Secretary.[2] His office should, in a measure, correspond to the confidential clerk of a great business House. The University has become a great business concern. It cannot longer proceed with the old fashioned methods unchanged. Such an officer should aid in the organization of the President's and Dean's offices. He should be thoroughly acquainted with the general workings of the institution, conduct the general correspondence and be prepared to give such information as is authorized to be made public, or that patrons or intending patrons may desire and are entitled to have. He should be an alumnus; of business capacity and habit, of established loyalty to trust, prompt, courteous, and of good address, and should have a general acquaintance with the alumni. He should of course be entirely acceptable to the President.

In the judgment of the Committee, the President can render no greater service to the University or to himself, nor one that would commend itself more heartily to its best friends everywhere, than the preparation and delivery in the University Chapel, commencing at the earliest practicable date, if possible during the next academic year, of at least ten sermons on great themes, uplifting to the student body, and prepared with a view to publication for upholding and increasing the historic, philosophic, and religious repute of the University.

Dr. Patton's great power is in the pulpit, and here he can do more to mould and guide in high and right thinking than in any other way.

The pulpit of Princeton University should be of commanding dignity and influence and should be jealously guarded. The President should name or approve and personally invite every preacher that occupies it.

The President should preach in the Chapel at least once a month, and on the same Sabbath of the month, as far as possible. The students would not only be benefitted by the service, but, it is believed, they would be highly gratified by it.

It is further earnestly hoped that the President may see his way clear to preside at all Sabbath morning services in the Chapel, whoever may be the preacher of the day. His presence would greatly enhance the dignity of the service.

There are occasions of course when the President must be absent; there are calls which properly command his services. Of these he must be the judge. But these should be mainly when his response thereto promises advantage to the University, and which he cannot wisely decline.

It is further hoped that all the President's great powers shall be concentrated here; that all his time shall be given to the University.

In these suggestions there is no intended criticism whatever upon any action of the President in the past, but only a very earnest expression of opinion of what seems to the Committee most desirable in the interests of the University.

Respectfully submitted by order of the Committee,

(Signed) Charles E. Green, Chairman.

Princeton, June 14th, 1897. . . .

1 At this point, all but the first paragraph of Wilson's letter to F. L. Patton of June 8, 1897, was spread on the minutes.
2 Despite the pressing need, a Secretary was not appointed until 1901, when Charles Williston McAlpin assumed that post.

From Francis Landey Patton

My dear Professor Wilson: [Princeton, N.J.] June 16, 1897

Your letter of today was received.[1] I read it to the Board. Your motive in not desiring to receive the degree in the absence of Dr. van Dyke was thoroughly appreciated and you will have the opportunity of receiving the degree in the autumn with Dr. van Dyke, if he should conclude to accept it then and you should then not be unwilling to accept it.[2] I hope that you will feel free to accept it at that time. I need not assure you of the cordiality with which it was voted to you by the Trustees. I am

Very sincerely yours,   [Francis L. Patton]

TLS (Patton Letterpress Books, University Archives, NjP).
1 It is missing.
2 Wilson and Henry van Dyke were nominated for honorary L.H.D. degrees at the meeting of the Princeton Board of Trustees on June 14, 1897. Later in the meeting, the Committee on Honorary Degrees reported on the nominations; its report was accepted and placed *in retentis*. The degrees were to be conferred in the autumn of 1897, but the conferral never took place, whether because of Wilson's and van Dyke's refusal to accept the degrees is not known.

To Charles Ewing Green

My dear Sir,   Princeton, N. J., 17 June, 1897.

I append, as requested, answers to the several questions, concerning my own work and the work of the University, received from you this afternoon.[1] The answers bear the same numbers as the respective questions to which they are replies.

1. The topics taught in my department next year will be and the year 1898-'99: General Jurisprudence; The Elements of Politics; Constitutional Government; The Constitutional Law of the United States; and The Development of English Common Law. I have no assistants.

2. I give instruction four hours a week, entirely by lectures.

3. Pollock's *First Book of Jurisprudence*; Wilson's *The State*; Boutmy's *Essays in Constitutional Law*; Boutmy's *English Constitution*; Dicey's *Law of the Constitution*; Cooley's *American Constitutional Law*.[2]

4. The only written exercises I give are the final examinations in each course, and an occasional written recitation.

5. Besides class room instruction, I direct the reading and thesis writing of one or two graduate students.

6. I have no laboratory work.

7. The studies in my department are not properly co-ordinated with those in History because there is no proper History Department, and cannot be until a considerable differentiation is possible in the instruction in history.

8. With regard to required studies, I do not favour an increase of their number. I could wish, however, that a place might be found for Political Economy in the Sophomore, instead of in the Junior, year.

I think that electives should be added in the Junior year only in accordance with a carefully devised plan of co-ordination. Electives might well be added very freely to the list of Senior studies.

9. My pupils are not prepared sufficiently to understand the historical groundwork of their studies, because of the very scant allowance of training in history,—perhaps beca[u]se of mistaken methods,—in Sophomore year, and because of lack of differentiation, thoroughness, and scope in historical instruction in Junior year.

10. My department can amount to very little so long as there is no distinct chair of Political Science, and no provision for assistants.

11. During the academic year 1896-'97 I have published two books: "Mere Literature and Other Essays," Boston, Houghton, Mifflin, & Co., November, 1896; and "George Washington," New York, Harper & Brothers, December, 1896.

Articles: several in *Harper's Magazine* on the life of Washington, afterwards collected in the volume mentioned above, and one entitled "Mr. Cleveland as President," published in the *Atlantic Monthly* for March, 1897.

Very Respectfully Yours,   Woodrow Wilson

WWTLS (Papers of the Special Committee on the Affairs of the University, University Archives, NjP).

1 Wilson is responding to a letter from the Special Committee on the Affairs of the University to the professors of Princeton University, dated June 10, 1897, and quoted in full in the report of the Special Committee on the Affairs of the University printed at June 13, 1898.

2 Full bibliographical information about these works (except for Wilson's *The State*), which Wilson was using as textbooks, is given in "Wilson's New Course Program in Political Science and Jurisprudence," printed at Dec. 1, 1897, ns. 1, 3, 4, 5, and 6.

To Edith Gittings Reid

My dear Mrs. Reid,   Princeton, 18 June, 1897

I cannot easily express the pleasure your letter gave me. It did not bring me what I sincerely wanted, a revelation of my faults in writing; but its generous applause and cordial friendship made me forget what I had wanted in my deep satisfaction in what I had received.

I must straightway prove my right to call myself a critic by pointing out to you two cardinal defects in what I write. There is, first, a serious structural defect, noticeable most of all in the literary essays, but to be found also elsewhere,—for example, in the "Washington," particularly in the earlier parts. The transitions are managed *too* smoothly: the several stages of the argument are not distinct enough: you bring away no definite outline, but only a recollection of certain passages and a general impression of the whole meaning. The treatment plays in circles; it does not move with directness along a clear course.

There is, besides, a fault of style: and here, again, the literary essays are the best field of observation. The phrasing is too elaborate: has not the easy pace of simplicity. The sentences are too obviously wrought out with a nice workmanship. They do not sound as if they had come spontaneously, but as if they have been waited for,—perhaps waited for anxiously. The fact is not so. They come fast and hot enough usually, and seem natural moulds for my thought. But I am speaking of the impression they make when read;—the impression they make upon *me* after they are cold,—when read in the proof, for example. I write in sentences rather than in words: they are formed *whole* in my mind before they begin to be put upon the paper, usually,—and no doubt that is the reason they seem *cast*, rather than naturally poured forth, and have lines of artificiality in their make-up.

I might carry the criticism into other points,—but these will, I trust, sufficiently illustrate my critical capacity! I feel bound, once and again, to study my work objectively.

You must have been conscious of these defects, architectonic and of detail, but were too generous to speak of them. Then, too, it is my serious business to study my own art,—particularly as I have a big piece of work in hand in which such faults are apt to be telling—a history of the country from the settlement till 1889, written with an attempt to let the story tell itself, as nearly as possible without commentary by the historian, and keep the atmosphere and illusion of each age as it passes. Alas, that I should have set up an impossible ideal in "The Truth of the Matter"![1]

In a way your generous appreciation stimulates me as much as your critical analysis of what I have *not* done might have instructed me. Knowing you, I know how much it means that you should take, not the critical, but the sympathetic attitude when I write or talk for you. It must mean that you find me at any rate genuine; and it heartens me as it should that you so believe in me. A man who wishes to make himself *by utterance* a force in the world must,—with as little love as possible,—aply [apply] critical tests to himself; and the best critical tests, surely, are the standards of those he can trust to see and utter the truth about the art he practices.

It is not likely I shall be in Baltimore another winter. The Hopkins' losses[2] have made it necessary to cut off all lectures not essential to instruction, and, though they were willing, I believe, to renew their engagement with me, I did not see my way clear to allow it. By admitting a general, mixed audience to my lectures, they had made it impossible to preserve their original character as class lectures; and by allowing them to *count* as class lectures they made it impossible for me to make them really popular.[3] They were unable to enter into any new arrangement,— and I find myself *reduced* to letter writing to preserve my hold on the dear friendships I have made in a place that had come to seem to me almost like a second home. This is one reason I am sending you a long epistle,—like a man afraid to be cut off. This deepens, too, more than I can say, my regret,—*our* regret,—that we cannot accept your kind invitation to make you a visit. I know of nothing that would be more delightful, more refreshing after a year of grinding,—and I know, as she does, that Mrs. Wilson would enjoy it as much as I would. But we have company with us now, and are likely to have until I am released from imperative tasks here late in July,—invited kinsfolk, coming and going; and when July is nearly out we shall be due, bag, baggage, and children, at a distant boarding place in Va.,[4] where we have quarters engaged. I wish I could think of some way of turning aside; but an army must go straight to its destination and its commanders cannot leave their posts! It goes hard to say this; but I see no choice.

Please send my warmest regards to your husband, and believe me, in all gratitude, my dear friend,

Faithfully Yours, Woodrow Wilson

ALS (WC, NjP).

[1] An essay in *Mere Literature and Other Essays*, printed in this series as "On the Writing of History" at June 17, 1895, Vol. 9.

[2] This was the latest in the recurring financial crises at The Johns Hopkins University caused by the fact that the bulk of Johns Hopkins's original bequest to found the university had been stock of the Baltimore and Ohio Railroad Company, which the founder in his will had urged the trustees not to sell. The Baltimore and Ohio was forced into receivership in February 1896, and all dividends were suspended. Not until after 1898 did the Hopkins trustees begin gradually to dispose of their large holdings of Baltimore and Ohio stock in order to diversify their investments. See John C. French, *A History of the University Founded by Johns Hopkins* (Baltimore, 1946), pp. 94-100.

3 For a fuller explanation of Wilson's reasons for discontinuing his lectures at the Johns Hopkins, see WW to Edith G. Reid, Oct. 3, 1897.

4 Col. Robert M. Stribling's "Mountain View," at Markham, Fauquier County, Va., near Front Royal.

Two Letters to Albert Shaw

My dear Shaw,   Princeton, New Jersey, 21 June, 1897.

I am going to send my nephew, George Howe, about whom I wrote you, to see you, with a note of introduction, not in the least, as I am sure you will believe, to hasten your conclusion, but to give you some personal impression of the boy to go on.

I had an interview with Mrs. Abbe[1] the other day about an address she wants me to give in November; and she said you were intending to write to me about it. If you could give me some very definite pointers about what, exactly, would be expected of me, it would help me greatly in making up my mind whether or not the thing was feasible for me. The work is certainly worth all encouragement; but ought not some New York man to attempt this November function?[2]

How sad and shocking Finley's sudden death![3] It has saddened me not a little.

With warm regards,
As ever,   Faithfully your friend,   Woodrow Wilson.

1 Catharine Amory Palmer (Mrs. Robert) Abbe, President of the City History Club of New York and wife of a distinguished surgeon.

2 Actually, Wilson gave the lecture—entitled "Patriotism Begins at Home"— before the City History Club in New York on Dec. 10, 1897. See the news report printed at Dec. 11, 1897.

3 Robert Johnston Finley, Wilson's former student and brother of John Huston Finley, died of a heart attack at his home in New York on June 8, 1897. At the time of his death, he was manager of the McClure Newspaper Syndicate.

My dear Shaw,   Princeton 21 June, 1897.

This is to introduce my nephew, George Howe, about whom I wrote you. You shall not have to know him long to discover a sterling and most capable fellow.

                    Yours as ever,   Woodrow Wilson.

TCL (in possession of Virginia Shaw English).

To Albert Bushnell Hart

My dear Hart,   Princeton, New Jersey, 21 June, 1897.

I thank you for your letter of June seventh. Commencement tasks and distractions have prevented my answering it sooner.

I think I can do the revision of prefaces, bibliographies, etc. for my Epoch some time this Summer; but just what time I cannot say. It shall be as soon as possible. I think, with you, that it might be well to have a little special Preface for the new edition; and you may be sure that E. Benj. Andrews' vulgar volumes will not appear in any of my lists. I will observe the limitations about the pagination; but there may be one or two passages in the text of the volume which I shall wish to change.

I trust that Mrs. Hart continues to improve, and that you have pleasant plans for the Summer.

With warm regard,

Faithfully Yours,   Woodrow Wilson

TCL (RSB Coll., DLC).

Two Letters to Elijah Richardson Craven

My dear Dr. Craven,   New York, 1 July 1897

I have just had an interview with Prof. Morse.[1] As you may have seen by the papers, he has been induced to withdraw his resignation at Amherst,[2] and this makes the matter much less plain sailing for us. I shall have to see you again before the [Curriculum] Committee comes together, and shall come down to Phila. to-morrow,—Friday. I shall hope to be at your office by 11:20 or 11:30.

In haste, with warm regard,

Sincerely Yours,   Woodrow Wilson

[1] Anson Daniel Morse, Professor of History at Amherst College.
[2] Morse sent a letter of resignation to the President of Amherst College, Merrill Edwards Gates, and the Amherst Board of Trustees at some time during the latter half of June 1897. The exact circumstances surrounding this event are unclear from contemporary newspaper accounts, but it is evident that Morse was in conflict with Gates over the staffing and control of the Department of History. One account had it, for example, that an assistant had been appointed to the department without Morse's knowledge. Morse's resignation created a furor among alumni returning for reunions at the end of June. The quarrel was resolved in some manner, at least temporarily, and President Gates was able to announce on Commencement Day, June 30, that Morse had withdrawn his resignation. The foregoing incident was part of a growing revolt among faculty, students, and alumni against the arrogantly incompetent Gates administration, which would culminate in his forced resignation on June 9, 1898. See the *New York Tribune*, June 23 and 28 and July 1, 1897; the *New York Times*, July 1, 1897; and Claude M. Fuess, *Amherst: The Story of a New England College* (Boston, 1935), pp. 249-57.

My dear Dr. Craven,   Princeton, 10 July, 1897

This afternoon's mail at last brings me a letter from Professor Morse.[1] As I feared and expected, he feels it his duty to remain at Amherst, at any rate until the present crisis is past, and the

Trustees, at the November meeting, either have or have not acted, —have met the situation squarely or not met it at all.

I am deeply disappointed. This seemed an opportunity to make the best of a very unfortunate situation in our history department next year; but it has slipped away.

You spoke of wishing to have a consultation with the Curriculum Committee in any event. If I can be of any service to you, I hope you will feel free to call upon me. My own interests are deeply concerned. I shall be in Princeton for the next ten days or two weeks.

With warm regard,

Most sincerely Yours,   Woodrow Wilson

ALS (Trustees' Papers, University Archives, NjP).
¹ It is missing.

Two Letters from Elijah Richardson Craven

My dear Prof. Wilson—   [Philadelphia] July 12th, 1897.

I regret to learn that Professor Morse will not be available for us. Under the circumstances, more especially since the President is absent from the country, I do not think it will be necessary to call a meeting of the Committee on the Curriculum.

Very sincerely yours,   E. R. Craven   per C. E. C.

ALS (E. R. Craven Letterpress Books, University Archives, NjP).

My dear Professor Wilson: [Philadelphia] July 19th, 1897

It gives me pleasure to inform you that at the June meeting of the Board of Trustees of Princeton University, your requests concerning the title of your Chair and the changes in your courses of lectures, were acceded to.

I remain,   Yours, most truly,   E. R. Craven

TLS (E. R. Craven Letterpress Books, University Archives, NjP).

From Julia Gardiner Gayley¹

Dear Sir,   Putney, Vt. July 20, 1897.

Understanding from some members of the Committee on University Extension work in Pittsburgh, Pa., that there is a possibility of your lecturing for them in October,² I write to ask if you could at that time, give a talk (morning or afternoon) before the ladies of the department of Social Economics of the Twentieth Century Club of Pittsburgh.

This is a women's club of a membership of three hundred.

Up to this time we have been rather a frivolous club in that we have listened to many wise and charming things but have not studied or worked much.

But we have resolved to change that, and have projected a plan of work along several lines of study for next winter, the enclosed being one of them. Some of us feel rather anxious about the success of the venture or appeal.

I say this somewhat in apology for the outline I send which will seem to you very shallow and sketchy and which was indeed framed somewhat on the principle of a sugar coated pill, in the hope that thereby it might commend itself to more than two or three.

Having myself been deeply a debtor to your books I feel sure that if our winter's work could be started with a talk by yourself, much interest would be stirred.

Doubtless it would be an easy matter for you[,] out of the fulness of your knowledge, to talk to us on the first or second subjects of my outline[3]—somewhat as to a class of beginners and with due regard to our limitations.

Will you kindly write me to the above address what such a talk would cost us in case you come to Pittsburgh for the U.E. people,[4]—and if you do not come to them what it would be to us alone.

I should like also to know whether you are lecturing this summer before any summer school.

Hoping to hear favorably from you[5] I am

Very sincerely yours   Julia G. Gayley

ALS (WP, DLC) with WWhw notation on env.: "Pittsburg (?) Ans. 27 July, 1897." Enc.: printed outline of topics to be studied by the Twentieth Century Club of Pittsburgh.

[1] Mrs. James Gayley of Pittsburgh, wife of the managing director of the Carnegie Steel Co. and chairman of the Department of Social Economics of the Twentieth Century Club, a woman's organization.

[2] Wilson gave "Democracy" before the University Extension Society in Pittsburgh on Oct. 28, 1897. See the news report printed at Oct. 29, 1897.

[3] The first two subjects on the outline are "The Beginnings of Government" and "Forms of Government."

[4] Wilson's fee was $50, as an undated entry in the diary described at Jan. 1, 1897, reveals.

[5] Wilson's reply is missing, but he did speak before the Department of Social Economics of the Twentieth Century Club on "Forms of Government" on October 29, 1897. His notes for this lecture are printed at that date.

From Joseph R. Wilson, Jr.

My dearest Brother: Clarksville, Tennessee, July 23, 1897

I would have written to you before this, but I have only recently recovered from what came near being a serious spell of sickness which originated in a "misery in my midst" ending in some fever and the necessity to remain at home for several days. The physician warned me of the danger of typhoid fever if I was not careful, so I *was* careful, you may be sure. I have been at work for several days but am still compelled to be careful and various and sundry rumblings and other signs of another possible eruption in the troubled regions warn me that any but the simplest food and the best care in other ways may result unpleasantly. I hope to be entirely well before long. My new "boss"[1] was kind enough to allow my salary to go on during my sickness, an unusual thing in a newspaper office, so I did not suffer financially except in the way of a moderate sized doctor's bill.

Under the new management *The Times* is taking rapid strides forward much to the discomfort of a spleenful contemporary who delights in the revengeful "slinging of mud" at our offending persons. This simply affords us a source of amusement, however, and does no one any harm unless it be the mud slinger himself. Business is good, pay regular, and, the entire establishment on a better basis.

It is hard to realize that I have passed the 30 year mark, but such is the case. The anniversary of my birth was last Tuesday and I was pleased to receive an excellent large photograph of my better half and sweet daughter,[2] nicely framed for my office. It makes me feel rather sad to think that life has commenced to pass away so rapidly and so little yet done.

Kate and Alice are in moderately good health and we are enjoying the happiness of our sweet home, made doubly dear by the little one, now over two years old, who is the joy of our hearts.[3] She is exceedingly cute, can say almost anything she pleases and is a very companionable little girl. I wish you could all come to see us in our home. Would this be possible? Cheap rates to the Centennial at Nashville[4] are now to be had from everywhere, you know, and that city is only sixty miles from us. The Centennial, too, is well worth seeing. I was there on Wilmington, N.C. day and renewed many pleasant friendships of days gone by. Geo. Chadburn, Jr., for instance, was there, and many others that I had almost forgotten. Kate was with me and I was proud to introduce her to the friends of my boyhood days. Think of this trip, dear brother, and you all come if you can. If this would be too expensive, and I fear it would, could you and sister Ellie arrange to come?

I have not heard from dear father very recently and we are anxiously awaiting for news of his promised visit to us. Do you know how he is? We are so anxious to have him with us.

Write to us soon, please. Kate joins me in unbounded love to sister Ellie, yourself and the little folks.

Your devoted brother   Joseph.

ALS (WP, DLC) with WWhw notation on env.: "*Ans.* 30 July/97."
  1 James G. Rice, proprietor of the Clarksville, Tenn., *Evening Times.*
  2 Kate and Alice Wilson.
  3 That is, Alice, born May 7, 1895.
  4 The Tennessee Centennial Exposition, held a year late at Nashville from May 1 through October 30, 1897. Modeled upon the World's Columbian Exposition of 1893 in Chicago, the Tennessee Exposition was housed in a "White City" of wood and stucco buildings, including a replica of the Parthenon (later replaced by a permanent concrete reproduction). The exposition attracted over 1,200,000 visitors, including President McKinley, during its six-month duration. Louise Littleton Davis, "The Parthenon and the Tennessee Centennial: The Greek Temple that Sparked a Birthday Party," *Tennessee Historical Quarterly*, XXVI (Winter 1967), 335-53.

From Lyon Gardiner Tyler

Dear Dr. Wilson,   Williamsburg, Va., July 23 1897

Your letter is everything I could wish,[1] and I am sure you show the true historic spirit in manifesting the disposition that you do, to revise and correct. I am aware that the history of the country has been written mainly from the Massachusetts standpoint, and that a writer feeling indifferent in the matter would be certainly imposed upon by the thousand and one books, with which they have occupied the avenues of history. I found out long since that it was improper to accept any statement made by a Northern historian regarding Southern men or Southern motives, without material modification. Not because the Northerner intentionally erred but because the glasses he looked through were altogether different. Even where Northerners and Southerners joined together for a common purpose, the reasons for the union were apt to be contradictory. Thus if the majority of National Republicans in Massatts. were Whigs in 1834, all the Whigs were Democrats in Georgia where there *never* had been a National Republican party. They were *Whigs* because to them the Democratic party was not Democratic *enough*. They regarded Jackson as the embodiment of nationalism.

I am with kind regards   Lyon G. Tyler

ALS (WP, DLC).
  1 Wilson's letter to which this was a reply is missing. However, Tyler had

written to Wilson earlier (L. G. Tyler to WW, April 19, 1897, ALS [WP, DLC]), objecting to Wilson's accusation of bad faith against President John Tyler, in *Division and Reunion*, pp. 138-39, for vetoing the Fiscal Corporation bill on September 9, 1842, after that measure had been approved in Cabinet meeting. In a lengthy discussion with many references, Tyler claimed that the bill had been discussed in Cabinet in principle only, that the measure itself had been prepared later, and that when it came to the President's desk it did not contain the provision he had insisted upon for the consent of the states to the establishment of branch banks within their jurisdictions. Wilson modified his text in the so-called eleventh edition of 1898 to meet Lyon Gardiner Tyler's criticisms.

From Wilson's Diary for 1897

Saturday, July 24, 1897

Arrived with Ellen and the children at Col. Robt. M. Stribling's, Markham, Fauquier C., Va.

From Walter Hines Page

My dear Mr. Wilson: Cambridge, Mass[tts] 25 July 1897.

Alas! alas! alas! you can't afford, of course, to interrupt your larger plan even for a History of the Civil War—unless, indeed, the History of the Civil War be the bigger plan of the two; whereof I cannot judge.[1] But this leaves the History of the Civil War stranded—*the* history, I say, for I know the two or three that are dragging their slow selves along, convoluted ponder[o]sities, perfunctory traditionalities, the labor of your "professional" historian, d—n him! for if he be not the worst enemy of the simple direct human joy of mankind in reading what mankind aforetime have done, I am doing him wrong. But I have suffered much from the wretch who smothers the story even of a good fight, in learning, and I like to hit his dull head every time I see it.

If you have said the final word about your doing it, can't you help me find a man who can do it? You have been about several of the great factories where they turn out historians, Adams's factory at Baltimore, the Smiths'[2] at Columbia, Hart's here. Hasn't it happened that some fellow who has the story-telling faculty has ever gone through these mills? The mill is necessary: if they could only get the right grist! When I ask Adams and Hart and the rest, they proceed to tell me of men who *know* history, whereas I want men who can also write it.

Now, as to the other—the History of the People: I once asked you prematurely, about the publication of it; and you said, very wisely, that you wished to do this task without even any thought of a publisher[,] much less any obligation, definite or implied;

and that you would let me know when you were ready to talk about publishing. That reply was wise and kind, and I shall bide my time in silence, wishing you to know in the meantime that I am a great deal more eager to read it than I am to publish it, and that if I can ever render a publisher's service my chief pleasure will be that I serve you and it.

But there comes up one other aspect of the subject mention of which also may be premature: when you get to turning-off the story, the Atlantic Monthly then as now will gape voraciously for good matter. Without showing your hand—saying nothing about the history—you may feel inclined to let me publish chapters of it from time to time. Certain parts of it at least will be capital magazine-matter, and I am sure that (as an incident of some importance) that [sic] I can do fairly by you in the matter of payment.

Do not take the trouble to write me anything about this now: I am not trying to extract any promise from you. I wish you to know, however, that I see the value of this to the magazine and also to you and to the country; and, when the time comes for you to consider it, I wish you to remember that I have said this much to you on this 25th day of July 1897.

In the meantime and all the time, pray remember that I shall be grateful for whatever incidental pieces—essays, addresses, whatnot—you have ready for publication. I have indeed always in my desk a dozen subjects that I wish you'd take up. In fact you will never know what forbearance I exercise towards you in not keeping up a constant fire of this kind of grape and canister.

Very sincerely yours,   Walter H. Page.

ALS (WP, DLC).
1 Wilson's letter, to which this was a reply, is missing.

2 The only Smiths on the Columbia faculty at this time were Munroe Smith, Professor of Roman Law and Comparative Jurisprudence, and Richmond Mayo-Smith, Professor of Political Economy and Social Science.

From Wilson's Diary for 1897

Monday, August 2, 1897

Went from Markham to Hot Springs, to attend Va. State Bar Ass'n.[1] Spent 4 hours at Manassas *en route*, reading Dowden's *Shakspere*,[2] and visiting Prince William Co. court, wh. I found in session.

Found Prof. Echols of the Univ.[3] on the train, with his second wife, a bride,—a most interesting looking woman.[4]

1 Wilson's address to the Association on August 5, 1897, is printed at that date.

² Dowden wrote widely on Shakespeare and edited his works, but Wilson is undoubtedly referring to his highly regarded *Shakspere, A Critical Study of His Mind and Art* (London, 1875; many later edns.).

³ William Holding Echols, Jr., Professor of Mathematics at the University of Virginia.

⁴ Elizabeth Harrison Echols, whom Echols had married in June 1897.

Tuesday, August 3, 1897

Met many old friends and acquaintances, among the rest, Patterson (Archie) and Eugene Massie of Richmond, Judge J. K. M. Norton (Keith) of Alexandria, Richard Byrd of Winchester, Julian Cocke (and his wife, née Leila Smith) of Roanoke, Profs. Peters and Lile of the University.[1]

[1] The full names of these "old friends and acquaintances," all of whom Wilson had known while a law student at the University of Virginia, were Archibald Williams Patterson, Eugene Carter Massie, James Keith Marshall Norton, Richard Evelyn Byrd, Lucian Howard Cocke, Leila Smith Cocke (daughter of Professor Francis H. Smith of Charlottesville), William Elisha Peters, Professor of Latin, and William Minor Lile, Professor of Law.

To Ellen Axson Wilson

Hot Springs, Bath Co., Va.

My own darling,   Tuesday, 3 August, 1897

Of course there is no time, amidst these busy and talkative men and women, to write letters fit to read; but there is time to love,—and great provocation. I never feel quite so lonely as when amongst a multitude of new acquaintances,—and of old acquaintances whose lives have not touched my own since boyhood. I feel, if anything, more strange with the latter than with the others. The change in them daunts me and holds me off from being their chum again. But that will wear off, no doubt, before the Association adjourns

Mr. Henry's paper,[1] read this morning, was very interesting indeed, and very well done. There was nothing new in it; but a thing well done is almost as good as a thing newly done

Everybody is very kind and cordial and complimentary. It is likely I shall have a conference or two this afternoon, with individuals, about the presidency of the University;[2] but, for myself, it has already ceased to be a personal question.[3] The plan proposed is, to elect for a term of four years,—and that is deeply and absurdly foolish. It does not appear that anything but the question, president or no president, will be considered by the Committee of alumni here. I enclose copies of the full majority and minority reports to the Board of Visitors.[4] I shall advise against a presidency such as is proposed. The majority report seems to me extremely weak,—the minority report extremely sentimental, though better done than the other.

Everybody asks and wishes for you. I am well, and love and miss you oh, so deeply, so ardently, my incomparable darling. God bless you and keep you.   Your own   Woodrow

ALS (WP, DLC).
¹ The address delivered by William Wirt Henry of Richmond as president of the Virginia State Bar Association. It is printed in the *Report of the Ninth Annual Meeting of the Virginia State Bar Association* (Richmond, 1897), pp. 239-69.
² The university had been governed since its foundation by a Board of Visitors, together with, later, a Chairman of the Faculty, elected annually. Rapid increase in the external business and educational relations of the university during the latter half of the nineteenth century prompted many discussions about and suggestions for a modernization of the administrative hierarchy, but a concerted move in that direction did not materialize until 1896. On June 16 of that year, the Board of Visitors appointed a committee to report on the advisability of the election of an executive officer who would give his full time to the university's affairs. The reports of this committee were being considered by the alumni as well as the faculty at this time. Philip A. Bruce, *History of the University of Virginia, 1819-1919* (5 vols., New York, 1920-22), v, 1-36.
³ This is the first documentary evidence that Wilson had been considered by his friends at the university and among the alumni as a possible candidate, and that someone had spoken to him about the matter. For additional evidence, see Wilson's diary entry printed at Aug. 20, 1897.
⁴ The enclosures are missing. The majority report, stating that "competition is no less keen in the educational world than in that of business," urged that the university be conducted according to the best standards of business management and under an executive "unhampered in the discharge of his administrative duties by the duties of a professor." It further recommended that the new head or president be appointed for a term of four years at a salary of $5,000.
The minority report argued that the appointment of a president would violate the spirit in which Jefferson had founded the university; that it would be difficult if not impossible to find a man who combined all the necessary qualities for the position of president; that the university could not afford the salary and expenses of a president; and that the election of such an executive would place the professors in a subordinate position and hamper their traditional independence. P. A. Bruce, *History of the University of Virginia*, v, 20-23.

From Ellen Axson Wilson, with Enclosure

My own darling,   Markham [Va.], Aug. 3 1897

I suppose that if I write this afternoon you will not get the letter until Thursday morning; so perhaps I had best not postpone longer, though you would, I dare say, prefer to wait for later news. Who knows however but the spirit may move me to write again tomorrow!

Nellie and Jessie were both quite sick all day yesterday. They were evidently feverish and I began to think of sending for the doctor; in fact I should have been obliged to do so for the sake of getting the proper medecine if Mrs. Taylor¹ had not kindly given me her bottle of chalk mixture,—her own doctor's prescription. They are both *much* better today;—no touch of fever. Jessie seems really well. I have been reading "The Fairie Queene" to them and they seem quite absorbed in it; I have read six cantos. Apparently they are more entertained than I am! Much of it I find decidedly tedious.

Margaret has just returned from the picnic,—the others of course were not well enough to go. She says they had "a lovely time." She dieted *herself* strictly all day yesterday, she was so afraid of being kept from the picnic.

I was interrupted here by a call from an old lady who stayed until night! so my letter could not be finished in time for last night's mail. Jessie is quite well this morning but Nellie is not quite *so* well. I gave her only toast and a little rice a[nd] chicken yesterday, but that seems to have been too much for her delicate stomach; so I have her on milk and lime-water today. I would send for the doctor, only I hear of his giving such large doses of calomel on all occasions that I am really afraid of him.

I enclose a note from your cousin which needs an immediate answer. Mr. Hunt[2] sends a postal to say that he has secured a watchman for August for a reasonable price, and that all is well at our house so far. From Houghton and Mifflin comes a check for $57.98 for your two books.[3] The University Extension sends you your dates for Wilmington, Oct. 21, Nov. 4, Nov. 18.[4]

I have a letter from Sister Annie[5] saying that George has a place and was to begin *Aug.* 2. He is taken "on trial,"[6]—but I can't make out *where*! He [She] says George called on Mr. Bridges "who sent him to Mr. Seymour,[7] who sent him to Mr. Wright the editor."[8]

Sister seems disgusted with her flat and says she and the boys have decided that if, as the agent thinks likely, they can sublet it, and if Stock and Madge wish to board with them, they will take a house in Brooklyn in Oct. She says they can live much more cheaply in Brooklyn. Wouldn't that plan be *delightful* for Madge?[9]

I am writing very hastily to get this off to the mail, so I can't tell you how much I love you, for that would take a great deal of time you know! But I love you just as much as you care to have me, darling, and I think of you and long for you *every moment*. I hope you are well & having a delightful time. Always & altogether　　　　　　　　　　Your own　Eileen.

ALS (WC, NjP).

　¹ Presumably another boarder at "Mountain View."

　² Professor Theodore Whitefield Hunt, who lived next door to the Wilsons at 48 Library Place.

　³ Houghton Mifflin's royalty statement, dated July 31, 1897, is in WP, DLC.

　⁴ These lectures were to be on Burke, de Tocqueville, and Bagehot; see the newspaper reports printed at Oct. 22 and Nov. 5 and 19, 1897.

　⁵ It is missing.

6 See WW to R. Bridges, Aug. 30, 1897, for an explanation of George Howe's "trial."

7 James S. Seymour, associated with the *New York Evening Post.*

8 Henry John Wright, editor of the New York *Globe and Commercial Advertiser.*

9 Her sister, Margaret Axson, who planned to live with Stockton Axson in Brooklyn while attending Adelphi Academy. Axson taught English in Adelphi's college division. Mrs. Howe did sublet her flat and rented a house at 474 Waverly Avenue in Brooklyn, where Stockton and Margaret took rooms.

E N C L O S U R E

From James Wilson Woodrow

Colorado Springs, Colorado,
Dear Cousin Woodrow   July 29th, 1897

I am on my way to Chillicothe where I expect to be married to Miss Nancy M. Waddle,[1] during the first week in August.

The wedding will be a very quiet one—without formal invitation. I can understand how it may be inconvenient to you to be present, yet it would be such an intense delight to us that we wish to most urgently request your presence if it can possibly be granted.

With warmest love to yourself and family—

Your cousin   J. Wilson Woodrow

ALS (WP, DLC).

1 Nancy Mann Waddel of Chillicothe, Ohio, assistant editor of the Chillicothe *Daily News,* 1896-97. She later moved to New York and wrote short stories, verse, and novels, most of them under the name of Mrs. Wilson Woodrow.

To Ellen Axson Wilson

My own darling,   Hot Springs, Bath Co., Va. 4 August, 1897

The weather here has grown intolerably hot. I sincerely hope Markham is cooler.

Nothing further has come to the surface about the presidency of the University. The men who wanted to talk with me have several times said that they wanted a little conference, but have not yet had it,—though opportunities have not lacked. It is evident that the whole thing is an effort on the part of the Board of Visitors, of which Col. McCabe[1] was until the other day a member, to create an office for McC. I am not inclined to go near the business in any way.

Nothing happens here except pleasant talk,—and *very* pleasant talk it is; a more intelligent and individual body of men I never met, and I should greatly like to make my home amongst them.

You will be relieved to hear that I am reasonably well prepared for the banquet to-morrow evening: I have eight very manageable stories noted down. Mr. Henry, the President of the Association, has notified me that he will toast me personally,—and, since the theme thus assigned me is *myself*, I can say what I please,—wander whithersoever my stories lead me!

The number of old University and family acquaintances increases from day to day, and I am beginning to feel quite like "home folks" here.

I am well, and, barring the heat, comfortable. I love you with an increasing and deepening affection, and am in all that is best in me altogether　　　　　　Your own　Woodrow

ALS (WP, DLC).
1 William Gordon McCabe (1841-1920), founder and headmaster (1865-1901) of the University School at Petersburg and Richmond, member of the Board of Visitors of the University of Virginia, 1888-92, vice rector, 1892-96.

Notes for a Reply to a Toast

[Aug. 4, 1897]

Heaven lies about us in our infancy
1 *Myself*, a fascinating theme,—but the French saying. (Definition of a bore).
2 *Might*, if I had but the gift, make even that theme palateable. "Sugar coat your head and go as a pill."
3 Has, at any rate, the virtue of novelty. Cannot object that it is merely "the proceedings of the previous meeting."
4 "This is no place to get religion."
5 Accustomed to trying situations, have spoken and acted in all kinds: "a faithful and loving wife of the seven following persons."
6 And I speak as a native,—not afraid of the *sting* of the retort, "Every man for his own country."
7 As for the morning's address, "This isn't a horse,—it's a hobby."
8 If I would insist on anything it would be a disposition of mind open to moderate change, and wise improvement. *Doctrine of election*,—must be *candidates* for efficiency.
9 Must not forget the originative ardour of our first generations of statesmen—"A very estimable woman she was, too."
10 "Whustle to the lobster."

WWhw and WWsh MS. (WP, DLC).

A Newspaper Report of an Address

[*Aug. 5, 1897*]

THEIR CLOSING DAY.

The Virginia Bar Association at Hot Springs.

THE GREAT FEATURE

The Address of Professor Woodrow Wilson, of Princeton University—His Subject a Leaderless Government—A Fine Effort.

Hot Springs, Va., August 5.—(Special.)—The attendance at the third day's session of the State Bar Association was larger than that of the two previous days, and all present unite in saying no meeting in the past has been so generally satisfactory.

Of course, the feature of the day was the address by Professor Woodrow Wilson, of Princeton University, on "A Leaderless Government." Dr. Wilson is a Virginian, a graduate of the University of Virginia, and consequently the social atmosphere was thoroughly congenial. He has a most attractive personality, and his polished and ornate address was delivered in a clear, well-modulated voice, each word being well enusciated [enunciated] and emphasized. His paper showed long and close study and a logical and trained mind. After a graceful introduction he showed that it was literally true that our government was without a leader. . . .[1]

Professor Wilson was frequently interrupted with applause.

The banquet to-night was a decided success. The menu was most tempting, the chef was on his mettle, the speeches were sparkling and bright, the wines of good vintage, and the cigars choice. The dining-room was brilliantly fringed with a selection of beautiful women, and good fellowship reigned supreme.

Among the toasts and responses were:

"Our Guests," Dr. Woodrow Wilson, of Princeton University.

"The Judiciary," James Keith [Marshall Norton], of Supreme Court of Appeals of Virginia.

"Medicine," Dr. D. A. Costa [Jacob Mendez Da Costa], of Philadelphia.

"The Ladies," Professor William G. Peters, of University of Virginia.

Printed in the *Richmond Dispatch*, Aug. 6, 1897.

[1] Here follow long extracts from Wilson's address, "Leaderless Government," printed below as the next document.

An Address

[[Aug. 5, 1897]]

LEADERLESS GOVERNMENT

Gentlemen of the Virginia State Bar Association:

Before I enter upon the discussion of my theme, permit me to express my keen gratification at finding myself in this congenial company. I am a lawyer and a Virginian. I feel here the sort of exhilaration that must always come to a man who returns from a distance to breathe his native air again and mix once more with those to whom he feels bound by a sort of intellectual consanguinity. I am proud of Virginia's traditions, as you are. I feel, as you do, that she gave the country its first life, long kept a sort of presidency in its affairs, and has always been one of the strategic centres of its society and its politics. I feel as if her great University, where, like so many of you, I was trained in the law, were still in no small part my academic home; and I know that here, among men of my own race and breeding, I can speak my mind frankly upon any theme, as the best men have always spoken in Virginia ever since Sir George Yeardly summoned that first assembly in the little church at Jamestown in the far year 1619.

It heartens a man not a little to know that he may speak his real thought and be understood, if he but speak it in the right temper. It is my purpose to-day to speak of public affairs; and we have a longer tradition than that of Virginia, even, to give us warrant for free speech in that field. We have the immemorial practice of the English race itself, to which we belong. Nowhere else has the pure strain of the nation which planted the colonies and made the independent government under which we live been kept so without taint or mixture as it has been in Virginia, and hitherto in all the South. One feels here that the origin and breeding, the impulse and the memory of the men he deals with are unmistakable; that he reckons with an ascertained force and a certain habit—a force and a habit that have not changed since the great days of the Revolution, when Virginia led the country in the making of the Constitution; and that he ought to be able to count now, among the offspring of that achieving generation, upon the same fearless examination of policies and institutions that enabled Washington and Mason and Henry and Madison to win triumphs in their heroic day.

This is not a day of revolution; but it is a day of change, and of such change as may breed revolution, should we fail to guide and moderate it. Institutions, if they live, must grow, and suffer the alterations of growth—must rise to new uses; must lose some parts and take others on. They cannot stand still; they cannot even stiffen to a single shape and use. The nation must at every turn make its choice, not only as to legislative policy, but also as to the uses to which it shall put its fundamental law and its very principles of government.

If ever a nation was transformed, this nation has been, under the eyes of a single generation—and processes that run so fast are perilous. The choices made in the midst of them are not deliberate, but hasty and almost at hazard; the necessary adjustments of life and institutions are made, not by plan, but upon the suggestion of the instant. It is matter, surely, of common prudence that we should pause and look the time through when we can, with a purpose to gain distinct knowledge of what is going forward, discover its force and direction, and make ourselves ready to assume control of it for the future, seeing that the pace is now set, the running determined. It is time we should speak frankly with each other about the present and about the future.

I mean to go, if I can, to-day, to the centre of some of the chief topics of government. We chose the forms of political life under which we live, and it is our duty to scrutinize them from season to season, if we would keep them incorrupt and suitable to our use. We talk of statesmanship and of policy sometimes as if they arose out of institutions; but we know that they do not. They are the children of individual initiative and of individual strength of character. The framers of our Constitution in this country made a great deal of institutions; but, after all, institutions only create the condition under which action must be planned: they do not breed action. No government will run itself. The excellence of any form of government depends upon the provision it has made for the action of those who conduct it and choose its policies. It gets its character from what they find it possible to do. The men who chose our present forms of government made much of law and of method because they were engaged in a work of actual creation. They were constructing a polity which was novel and without model, and they knew that definiteness of plan was, for the time being, everything. They were forging, and fitting and bolting the structural iron of the whole fabric of which they were the originating architects. But we are now choosing policies, not forms of government. The nation is made—its mode of action is determined; what we now want to know is: What is it going to do with its life, its material resources and its spiritual strength? How is it to gain and keep a common purpose in the midst of complex affairs; how is its government to afford it wisdom in action?

This is the question I have chosen to discuss. Put in its most direct form it is this: How is the nation to get definite leadership and form steady and effective parties? Take what government you will, this question includes all others, if you inquire concerning efficiency. Among a free people there can be no other method of government than such as permits an undictated choice of leaders and a strong, unhampered making up of bodies of active men to give them effective support. When party government fails, all definiteness goes out of politics. Who is to be held responsible for policy? By what legerdemain are you to get anything done? Shall you convince one man at a time the nation through, assume that your neighbor counts for as much in affairs as any one else, hazard the fortunes of the nation upon a chance concurrence of opinion? Policy,—where there is no absolute and arbitrary ruler to do the choosing for a whole people—means massed opinion, and the forming of the mass is the whole art and mastery of politics. How is the massing done among us? Who chooses our leaders, and by what process? What guides our parties and what do we know them to stand for? These are questions of fact, to be answered first without attention to the criticisms our answers may suggest with regard to some of the radical features of our constitutional arrangements. Let those criticisms follow after, if they must. We cannot afford to blink either the facts or their necessary revelation.

I have told you my own conclusion with regard to our present constitutional usage in the title I have chosen for this address. By the words "Leaderless Government" I mean to describe the government of the United States. I do not utter the words with the least touch of censoriousness or cynicism or even discouragement. In using them I am simply speaking a careful and, if I may say so, a dispassionate judgment. I do not believe it a necessary feature of our government that we should be without leaders; neither do I believe that we shall continue to be without them; but as a matter of fact we are without them, and we ought to ask ourselves, Why? I mean, of course, that we are without official leaders—without leaders who can be held immediately responsible for the action and policy of the government, alike upon its legislative and upon its administrative side. Leaders of some sort we, of course, always have; but they come and go like phantoms, put forward as if by accident, withdrawn, not by our choice, but as if upon some secret turn of fortune which we neither anticipate nor as a nation control—some local quarrel, some obscure movement of politics within a single district, some manipulation of a primary or some miscarriage in a convention. They are not of the nation, but come and go as if unbidden by any general voice. The government does not put them forward, but groups of men formed we hardly know where, planning we hardly know what; the government suffers no change when they disappear—that is the private affair of some single constituency and of the men who have supplanted them.

Look at the familiar system for a little with this matter in view, and you shall see that, as we now use it, it seems devised as if to prevent official and responsible leadership. The President cannot lead. We call his office great, say that the Queen of England has no power to be compared with his, and make choice of nominees for the presidency as if our votes decided a constructive policy for the four years to come; but we know that in fact he has as little power to originate as the Queen has. He may, no doubt, stand in the way of measures with a veto very hard to overleap; and we think oftentimes with deep comfort of the laws he can kill when we are afraid of the majority in Congress. Congressional majorities are doubtless swayed, too, by what they know the President will do with the bills they send him. But they are swayed sometimes one way and sometimes the other, according to the temper of the times and state of parties. They as often make his assured veto a pretext for recklessness as a reason for self-restraint. They take a sort of irresponsible and defiant pleasure in "giving him the dare": in proposing things they know many people want and putting upon him the lonely responsibility of saying that they shall not have them. And if he stand for long in the way of any serious party purpose, they heat opinion against him and make his position more and more unpleasant, until he either yields or is finally discredited. It is a game in which he has no means of attack and few effective weapons of defence.

Of course he can send a message to Congress whenever he likes—the Constitution bids him to do so "from time to time," in order to "give the Congress information of the state of the Union, and recommend to their consideration such measures as he shall deem necessary and expedient"; and we know that, if he be a man of real power and statesmanlike initiative, he may often hit the wish and purpose of the nation so in the quick in what he urges upon Congress that the Houses will heed him promptly and seriously enough. But there is a stubborn and very natural pride in the Houses with respect to this matter. They, not he, are the nation's representatives in the making of law; and they would deem themselves subservient were they too often to permit him leadership in legislative policy. It is easy to stir their resentment by too much suggestion; and it is best that a message should be general, not special—best that it should cover a good many topics and not confine itself too narrowly to one, if a President would keep in credit with those who shape matters within the House and Senate. In all ordinary times the President recognizes this and preserves a sort of modesty, a tone as if of a chronicler merely, and setter forth of things administrative, when he addresses Congress. He makes it his study to use only a private influence and never to seem a maker of resolutions. And even when the occasion is extraordinary and his own mind definitely made up, he argues and urges—he cannot command. In short, in making suggestions to Congress the President of the United States has only this advantage over any other influential person in the nation who might choose to send to Congress a letter of information and advice. It is the duty of Congress to read what he says; all the larger newspapers will print it; most of them will have editorial comments upon it; and some will have letters from their Washington correspondents devoted to guessing what effect, if any, it will have upon legislation. The President can make his message a means of concentrating public opinion upon particular topics of his own choosing, and so force those topics upon the attention of the House. But that is all; and under ordinary circumstances it is not much.

It was not so in the early years of the government. Roughly speaking, Presidents were leaders until Andrew Jackson went home to the "Hermitage." Sometimes they have been leaders since; but in the old days it was a matter of course that they should be. Since Jackson's masterful figure passed off the stage, the ordinary courses of politics have been drawing us away from the state of things which once made the country, and politicians themselves, instinctively turn to the President for guidance, as if he were a sort of prime minister as well as the official head of the permanent administration. Washington led, of course, and fashioned the government itself—for reasons no man any longer needs to have stated to him; and his first cabinet, as everybody knows, was made up of the party masters of the day—men whom all knew to be chief political figures, for the moment not only, but also for the years to come. John Adams, the second President, was almost as great a figure in all civil affairs as Washington himself. Jefferson was a born leader of men, who not only led his party, but first created it and then taught it the methods of power. Madison felt, in no small measure, that compulsion by which later Presidents by the half dozen have been led and mastered, the compulsion of Congressional initiative—resident in that day of change in the persons of Henry Clay and John C. Calhoun, under whom, themselves youngsters in the arena, a young party was coming to self-consciousness and authority. But Madison was of a stature and eminence in affairs which even the high and taking qualities of these men could not dwarf. Monroe saw times of quiet peace, when parties seemed for a little to have fallen asleep. John Quincy Adams but kept the seat warm for Jackson—and not very warm at that; and with Jackson came in a new democracy, which was to change the whole face of affairs.

Merely to name these men is to call the roll of the leaders of two generations. It was taken for granted at the first that the real leaders of the nation would be put into the presidential chair. For a little while Vice-Presidents succeeded Presidents, as if of course; and then for a season Presidents were allowed to name their own successors in their appointment to the office of Secretary of State—or, rather, were expected to fill that great office with men whom their party accepted as second only to the Presidents themselves in weight and influence, their natural successors. The management of these things was left in that day to well known groups of men which all the country knew to constitute, each for its own party, a sort of unofficial ministry. Nominations were arranged in Congressional caucus, by men in whose hands rested not only the conduct of these matters, but the whole shaping of party policies as well; and they naturally chose according to some recognized plan, compatible with the immediate objects of their organization, putting those in authority who were their actual leaders, and to whom they looked for guidance whether in office or out.

It was no doubt inevitable that this system of Congressional nomination should come to an end. The nation began before very long to look upon it as a system which bred intrigue and threatened to put affairs of the first importance into the hands of cliques and "rings." But in rejecting that system to pass to the use of nominating conventions we certainly rendered it impossible—or, at any rate, in the highest degree unlikely—that our Presidents should ever be leaders again. Do what you will in such a matter, you do not very much lessen the overwhelming weight of Congress. You still leave the real energy of the government with the men who make the laws, pay the bills, and create the conditions under which Presidents must act. Roger Sherman declared very bluntly, in the Constitutional Convention of 1787, that "he considered the executive magistracy as nothing more than an institution for carrying the will of the Legislature into effect"; and, although we may not be willing to go the length of saying quite so much as that, we see even more clearly now than Roger Sherman did at the beginning that, in the last resort, it lies with Congress, and not with the executive, to choose what the government shall be and do. And we know that it is a serious matter that the intimate relations which once existed between Congress and the President should have been so completely broken.

The men who are sent to our nominating conventions are men, for the most part, little known—and in other matters little regarded; men who have nothing to do with legislation, and who are without any responsible part whatever in the choice of policies for the nation. An incalculable number of local influences, utterly obscure to the country at large, and unconnected, as we know, with any general party purpose or policy of which the country can know anything, determine the instructions with which delegates are sent. They run together to press the claims of a score of candidates, selected, not by the general voice of any party, but upon grounds of preference which only their special friends and partisans can explain. Generally it turns out that the candidates whom all the country knows have been too much talked about beforehand, too definitely preferred or rejected in the preliminary contests in which the delegates were chosen. Some "dark horse"; some man hitherto little thought of; some one whom his friends have astutely known how to push in the secret conferences of separate delegations; some man whose personal tact or force has caught of a sudden the enthusiasm of the convention itself and of the crowds in its galleries; some man unheralded and untried, it may be, catches the drift of the vote and is nominated. A good man he may be, and a fair President—Providence has been kind to us much beyond the encouragement we have given it; but he is not always a man whom we know, and he is seldom a man accepted in Washington as of course a leader and maker of affairs.

Singular things happen in the process. A new figure emerges, sometimes, behind the accepted candidate, the figures of his backer and manager. Nobody has known him, until now, outside his State. Men hear his name with curiosity. But, if his candidate be elected, they hear it for a little while with awe—and behold, a new Colossus in the midst of our shifting politics! Seasoned Congressmen smile in their beards, no doubt, to see the new man come radiant to Washington, beaming authority on every side; but they court him for a brief space, as one who has the ear of the President in the making of appointments; and then, when the appointments are made and the President has found his

Woodrow Wilson, Princeton Sesquicentennial Orator

1.

Princeton in the Nation's Service

We pause to look back upon our past today, not as an old man grown reminiscent, but as a prudent man still in his youth and ~~hardy~~ lusty prime and at the threshold of new tasks, who would remind himself of his origin and lineage, recall the pledges of his youth, assess as at a turning in his life the duties of his station.

We look back only a little way to our birth; but the brief space is quick with movement and incident enough to crowd a great tract of time. Turn back only one hundred and fifty years, and you are deep within quiet colony times, before the French and Indian war or thought of separation from England. But a great war is at hand. Forces ~~hitherto~~ long pent up and local presently spread themselves at large upon the continent, and the whole scene is altered. The brief plot runs with a strange force and haste:— First a quiet group of peaceful colonies, ~~not a little~~ very placid and commonplace and dull, to all seeming, in their patient working out of a slow development; Then, of a sudden, a hot fire of revolution, a quick release of power, as if of forces long pent up, but set free at last in the generous heat of the new day; the mighty processes of a great migration, the vast spaces of a waiting continent filled almost suddenly with hosts bred to the spirit of conquest, a constant making and renewing of governments, a stupendous growth, a perilous expansion. Such days of youth and nation-making must surely count double the slower days of maturity and calculated change, as the Spring counts double the ~~dull~~ sober fruitage of the Summer.

Princeton was founded upon the very eve of the ~~revolutionary~~ stirring changes which put the Revolutionary ~~them~~ drama on the stage,—not to breed politicians, but to give young men such training as, it might be hoped, would fit them handsomely for the pulpit and for the ~~high~~ grave duties of citizens and neighbours. A small group of Presbyterian ministers ~~took~~ had the initiative in its foundation. They ~~could~~ acted without ecclesiastical ~~thought~~ authority, as if under obligation to society ~~as well as~~ rather than to the church. They had no more vision of what was to come upon the country than their fellow colonists had; they knew only that the pulpits of the southern colonies lacked properly equipped men ~~to the~~ and all the youth middle and in those parts ready means of access to the higher sort of schooling. They thought the discipline at Yale a little less than liberal and the training offered as a substitute in some quarters a good deal less than thorough. They wanted "a seminary of true religion

The first page of Wilson's manuscript of
"Princeton in the Nation's Service"

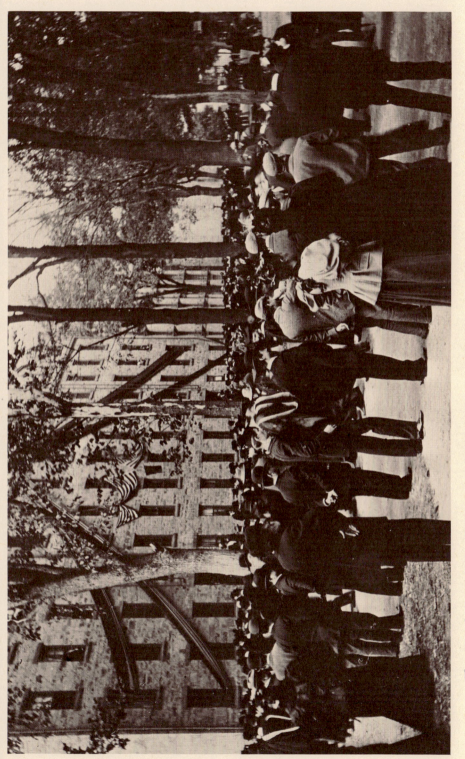

The crowd viewing the Sesquicentennial academic procession as it passed in front of West College

Andrew Fleming West, Professor of Latin

Henry Burchard Fine,
Dod Professor of Mathematics

George McLean Harper,
Professor of Romance Languages

Pyne Library, erected in 1896-97

Edward William Axson,
Class of 1897,
brother of Ellen Axson Wilson

George Howe III,
Class of 1897,
nephew of Woodrow Wilson

The earliest known photograph of Joseph Ruggles Wilson,
taken in 1866, recently discovered

place, they draw aside to see whether this crack coach will slip into oblivion or not. And so each man has his entry and his exit.

And even if things go differently, even when the man whom the convention nominates is some one of whose career and influence we know or can assess, how often does it happen that he is such a man as will be accepted as a real leader at Washington—where alone he can lead? Nobody supposes, I take it, that Mr. McKinley was ever the real leader of the Republican party. He did not even play a really constructive part in the framing of the celebrated tariff law which we call by his name; but the country thought that he did and rejected what they deemed his handiwork in the most emphatic manner, by name and title. Whatever personal admiration Mr. McKinley may have excited by reason of the sincerity, simplicity, and directness of his character, he was clearly dwarfed in all matters of party choice by Mr. Reed and Mr. Lodge, and the real leaders of the Republican ranks. It was much the same as if Mr. Depew had been taken in his stead, a prominent person, but no master of policy—except that Congressmen particularly resent the selection of an outsider. Mr. McKinley had at least been bred to politics in the atmosphere of Washington, and might be expected to know something of the temper and tact of dealings between the President and the Houses. Plainly the nominating convention has separated legislature and executive much more sharply than the makers of the Constitution intended; has brought utterly incalculable forces into play for the choice of our Presidents; and has cut us off once and for all from the old traditions of party leadership. We must take our Presidents somewhat at haphazard and by a special, clumsy machinery out of the general body of the nation; and the Houses must provide themselves with purposes and leaders of their own.

And yet the Houses show a notable lack of efficient organization; for I take it for granted that when one is speaking of a representative legislature he must mean by "an efficient organization," an organization which provides for deliberate, and deliberative, action, and which enables the nation to affix responsibility for what is done and what is not done. The Senate is deliberate enough; but it is hardly deliberative after its ancient and better manner; and who shall say who is responsible for what it does and for what it does not do? The House of Representatives is neither deliberate nor deliberative. We have not forgotten that one of the most energetic of its recent Speakers thanked God, in his frankness, that the House was not a deliberative body. It has not time for the leadership of argument; it has not time, therefore, to disclose the individual weight of its members. Debate takes time. It also lets the nation hear the prevailing voices and the reasons for action. For debate and leadership in that sort the House must have a party organization and discipline such as it has never had.

The Speaker of the House is its master—how absolutely members of the House have known these two generations and more; but the general public have only recently begun to find out. It has time out of mind been the custom amongst us to elevate the leader of the dominant party in the popular House to its Speakership—ever since Colonial times, when the Speaker of the Assembly was our spokesman against the domineering Governor and Council whom the Crown had appointed. We have long been familiar with the idea that, for some reason which we have not very carefully looked into, the presiding officer of our representative chamber is not a mere moderator, but also a guiding spirit in legislation: and so we have not very carefully noted the several steps by which he has come to be a sort of dictator. In the first place, the House sifts and handles all its business by means of standing committees. Thousands of bill[s] are presented for consideration every session; it would be impossible to consider them all, or even to vote upon them all, were the House to give itself up exclusively to voting. They naturally fall into classes, according to their subjects, and for each class there is a standing committee to which they are referred. But it is a critical matter for a bill that it should pass into the hands of a committee along with hundreds of other bills, relating to the same or like matter. It may be it will not come back alive. The committee is very likely to pocket most of the proposals sent it, and to modify the rest, and the net result is that all legislation in effect originates with the committees, or, at any rate, comes before the House unmistakably marked by their handling.

And the Speaker appoints the committees. Of course he has not a perfectly free hand in the matter. Length and priority of service entitle certain members to certain chief posts of honor on the committee lists; and the Speaker, besides regarding their claims, must take counsel in some decent degree with the other leaders of his party before he finally makes up his mind whom he shall put upon the committees; but he none the less determines their make-up, and their make-up determines legislation. That is the Speaker's power of creation; and that is the reason the session disappoints the country and discredits the party if the Speaker be not a consummate party leader.

But that is only a part of the Speaker's power. He also retains control of the business of the House from day to day in a very autocratic manner. The rules of the House themselves in part determine what the course of business shall be. They give precedence to the reports of the committees which have charge of bills touching the raising and the spending of revenue; and they determine in what order and at what times the other committees shall be allowed to report. When important matters pile up and it becomes necessary to fix a special order by which questions of the first consequence shall gain precedence and the docket be relieved of its congestion, the Committee on Rules is authorized to bring in a temporary programme for the purpose. But the Speaker appoints the Committee on Rules and is himself its chairman. He steers as well as presides.

The rules are adopted afresh at the opening of every new Congress, with such modifications as the committee may have to suggest—and that committee is always the first to be appointed. Its regulations, alike in ordinary and in extraordinary cases, aim always at this single and consistent object—to keep business in the hands of the committee and rigidly exclude personal initiative on the part of individual members. It requires unanimous consent for a member to get any matter before the House independently of the committees: and you cannot even ask for unanimous consent unless you can obtain recognition and get the floor. The Speaker's eye is his own. He can see whom he pleases: and he must know your object before he will recognize you. If he do not know it, he will not see you. He will never see you even when he does know it, if he knows it to be something that will upset or interfere with party plans or the settled programme of the session—if only by taking up time. You may remonstrate with him and pray to him in private as you will, he will not let you cross the purposes he has in view as the leader of his party. Or, if, by reason of your importunity, he should at last seem to yield, and agree to accord you recognition and a chance to make your motion, you may be sure he will take very good care to get some member's promise that he will promptly object, and you will fail of unanimous consent and be silenced after all.

Here, then, is your silent master of men and of policies in the House, the Speaker, who appoints the committtees which originate legislation, determines the order of business at every critical point through the Committee on Rules, and sees whom he will amongst those who would put themselves forward in the business of the House. I have not described him to condemn him. I do not see how else business could go forward in an assembly which would otherwise be a mere mass meeting. But I do wish to make it evident that this is an extraordinary picture, and that it sets our national legislature apart as unique among the representative assemblies of the world—unique in having its leader silent and in the form of his office a mere moderator, and in having its course of action determined by management and not by debate.

And what of leadership in the Senate? When you have described the House of Representatives you have described but half of Congress, and that, Senators would say, the lower half. The Senate unquestionably, whatever we may say of the House of Representatives, stands unique among legislative bodies in the modern time. Whether we relish its uniqueness in the present generation quite as much as it was relished among our fathers is an open question, but its individuality is indubitable. This singular body has assumed of late what I may, perhaps, be allowed to call a sort of Romo-Polish character. Like the Roman Senate, it has magnified its administrative powers and its right of negative in the great fields of finance and foreign affairs, as well as in all ordinary legislation; and, following Polish precedents, it has seemed to arrogate to its members the right of individual veto. Each senator, like each prince of ancient Poland, insists, it would seem, upon consulting his own interests and preferences before he will allow measures to reach their final consideration and passage. In the field of administration, it seems plain, the Senate expects the executive very generally to submit to its oversight and suggestion, as Roman magistrates submitted to the Senate of their singular republic.

I am anxious not to distort the true proportions of the picture, even in pleasantry; and, if to put the matter as I have just put it savours too much of exaggerating temporary tendencies into established practices, let us rest content with saying merely that this noted assembly has at almost every critical juncture of our recent political history had an influence in affairs greater, much greater, than that of the House of Representatives; and that the methods by which this great council is led are likely to be of the utmost consequence to the nation at every turn in its fortunes. Who leads the Senate? Can any one say? It, too, has its standing committees, to which all of its business is in the first place sent, as to the committees of the House; but it accords them no such mastery as is accorded the committees of the House. Debate and amendment make free with committee reports, as with any other matter, and upon the open floor of the Senate no man is master. The Vice-President is an outsider, not the leader of his party— even if his party have the majority in the Senate—and generally not a very influential outsider—timid about asserting even the natural powers of a parliamentary moderator. Among the Senators themselves there is an equality as absolute as the equality of the sovereign states which they represent. It is give and take amongst them. Personal conferences are the only means for the adjustment of views and the compounding of differences. One senator [Senator] is as formidable as a dozen in the obstruction of business. The Senate as a whole is jealous of its dignity and of its prerogatives; and its members severally stand out distinct units in every matter of controversy. Who shall say who leads and who obeys amongst them?

And so we have the composite thing which we call the Government of the United States. Its several parts are seve[r]ally chosen; it is no unified and corporate whole. Its President is chosen, not by proof of leadership among the men whose confidence he must have if he is to play an effective part in the making of affairs, but by management—the management of obscure men—and through the uncertain chances of an ephemeral convention which has no other part in politics. Its popular chamber shapes its affairs, not by conference with those who must execute the laws and show them feasible, nor yet by any clarifying process of debate, but chiefly by means of the silent management of its moderator, whose office is fixed for a two years' term, and who represents, not the country, but a single constituency. Its Senate is a band of individuals, amongst whom it is impossible to maintain leadership, and to whom it is difficult to extend the discipline of party organization. This is not a government of systematic checks and balances,—a *system* of checks and balances would enable you to distinguish causes and calculate effects. It is a government without definite order, showing a confused interplay of forces, in which no man stands at the helm to steer, whose course is beaten out by the shifting winds of personal influence and popular opinion.

On the whole, however, it has not worked ill, you will say; and what was good enough for our fathers is good enough for us. I heartily assent to the one proposition, but not to the other. A colonial government was once good enough for our fathers, if you will but go back so far; but it was not good enough for their sons, and our government as we use it is not as good as when they used it. Our fathers were choosing men, and so must we be. They chose governments to suit their circumstances, not to suit their ancestors; and we must follow the like good rule—praying that we may choose wisely as they did. The colonial governments were not failures so long as they were good enough to last; and certainly the government of the United States has been no failure, but a success so conspicuous, for the most part, that the nations of the world have stood at gaze to see so great a thing done in the West, upon the new continent whither they supposed none but radicals had gone. You shall not find me uttering aught in dispraise of the great work of that memorable body of statesmen who met in Philadelphia in that year 1787, which they have made illustrious. They have won an imperishable name in the history of politics, and no man can take it away from them, were we churl enough to wish to do so. Neither shall you find me an advocate of radical changes. The men who made our government showed themselves statesmen in nothing so much as in this, that they adapted what they had to a new age; and we shall not be wise if we outrun their great example. But let us know the facts; and, if need be, fit our institutions to suit them. There is cowardice, sometimes, in mere self-satisfaction.

The Government of the United States as we use it, besides, is not the Government of the United States as they used it. Why is it that this leaderless character of our government did not disclose itself to an earlier generation as it has disclosed itself to us? The government has the same formal structure now that it always has had: why has its weakness been so long concealed? Why can it not serve the new time as well as it served the old? Because the new time is not like the old—for us or any other nation; the changes which we have witnessed have transformed us. The tasks set the government now differ both in magnitude and in kind from those set it in days gone by. It is no old man's fancy that the old days were different from those we now see. For one thing—and this can be no news to any man—an industrial revolution separates us from the times that went by no longer ago than when the war between the States came on; and that industrial revolution—like the war itself—has not affected all parts of the country alike—has left us more various and more unequal, part by part, than ever before. We speak nowadays of a new sectionalism, and I, for one, deprecate the phrase. I rejoice to believe that there are no longer any permanent sectional lines in this country. But there is an unprecedented diversification of interests—and for the time, no doubt, differences of interest mark also differences of region and of development. And these differences of condition and of economic growth as between region and region, though temporary, are more sharply marked than they ever were before. Moreover, there is a confused variety: region differs from region in an almost incalculable number of significant details. And there is added to this everywhere a swift process of change, a shifting of elements, a perplexing vicissitude in affairs. Here and there communities have a fixed life, and are still and quiet as of old, but these lie apart from the great forces that are making the nation, and the law is change.

These things do not need demonstration; they hardly need illustration. No man is so ill-informed as not to know that the conditions which existed before the war were simple and uniform the country through, as compared with those which have sprung up since the war. And where conditions are comparatively simple and uniform, constructive leadership is little needed. Men readily see things alike and easily come to a common opinion upon the larger sort of questions: or, at any rate, to *two* general opinions, widespread and definite enough to form parties on. For well-nigh a generation after the war, moreover, the problems which the government of the Union had to settle were very definite problems indeed, which no man could mistake, and upon which opinion could readily be concentrated. I think the country sadly needed responsible and conscientious leadership during the period of Reconstruction, and it has suffered many things because it did not get it—things of which we still keenly feel the consequences. But the tasks, at least, were definite and unmistakable, and parties formed themselves upon sharp-cut issues.

Since then, how has the scene changed! It is not now fundamental matters of structure and franchise upon which we have to centre our choice; but those general questions of policy upon which every nation has to exercise its discretion: foreign policy, our duty to our neighbors, customs tariffs, coinage, currency, immigration, the law of corporations and of trusts, the regulation of railway traffic and of the great industries which supply the necessaries of life and the staffs [stuffs] of manufacture. These are questions of economic policy chiefly; and how shall we settle questions of economic policy except upon grounds of interest? Who is to reconcile our interests and extract what is national and liberal out of what is sectional and selfish? These are not questions upon which it is easy to concentrate general opinion. It is infinitely difficult to effect a general enlightenment of the public mind in regard to their real merits and significance for the nation as a whole. Their settlement in any one way affects the several parts of the country unequally. They cannot be settled justly by a mere compounding of differences, a mere unguided interplay of rival individual forces, without leadership and the courage of definite party action. Such questions are as complex and as difficult of adequate comprehension as the now infinitely varied life of the nation itself; and we run incalculable risks in leaving their settlement to the action of a House of Representatives whose leaders are silent and do not tell us upon what principle they act, or upon what motive; to a Senate whose undisciplined members insist upon making each an individual contribution to the result; and to a President chosen by processes which have little or nothing to do with party organization or with the solution of questions of State. We can seldom in this way see a single year ahead of us.

I, for my part, when I vote at a critical election, should like to be able to vote for a definite line of policy with regard to the great questions of the day—not for platforms, which, Heaven knows, mean little enough—but for *men* known and tried in the public service; with records open to be scrutinized with reference to these very matters; and pledged to do this or that particular thing, to take definite course of action. As it is, I vote for nobody I can depend upon to do anything—no, not if I were to vote for myself. It may be that, if I vote with the successful party, my representative in the House is a perfectly honest, well meaning, and moreover, able man; but how do I know upon which committee Mr. Speaker will put him? How do I know where his influence will come in, in the silent play of influences (it may be perfectly legitimate influences) that runs through the committee rooms in so heady a stream? How do I know what the Speaker and those with whom he takes counsel will let the House do? I do not vote for the Senators of my State: I do not always know just why those who do choose them make the particular selection they hit upon. When I vote for Presidential electors, I know only what the candidate's friends say that he will do. He accepts a platform made for him by a convention which he did not lead and which does not have to carry out its own programme; and I know that he may have no constructive power at all when he gets to Washington. No man can vote with real hope or confidence, or with intelligent interest even, under such a system.

What would I have? I feel the embarrassment of the question. If I answer it, I make the unpleasant impression of posing as a statesman, and tempt those who wish to keep every man in his place to remind me that I am only a college professor, whom it would better become to stick to his legitimate business of describing things as they are, leaving it to men of affairs to determine what they ought to be. I have been trying to describe things as they are, and that has brought me, whether I would or no, straight upon this question of the future. I am not addressing a college class, but men of affairs, who want their doctrine in the concrete and with no shirking of hard questions. Moreover, the things I have been describing are the proper objects of my study. In lecturing upon Politics I try, indeed, not to lecture as a politician; but I try also not to lecture as a fossil. I must study affairs of the day as well as things dead and buried and all but forgot. I remember, too, that this is not a convention, but a body of students. You will want from me, not a programme of reform, but a suggestion for thought.

My studies have taught me this one thing with a definiteness which cannot be mistaken: Successful governments have never been conducted safely in the midst of complex and critical affairs except when guided by those who were responsible for carrying out and bringing to an issue the measures they proposed; and the separation of the right to plan from the duty to execute has always led to blundering and inefficiency; and modern representative bodies cannot of themselves combine the two. The Roman Senate, the only efficient administrative assembly that I know of in the history of the world, was a permanent body, made up for the most part of men who had served their terms as executive officials through a long succession of offices. It undertook actually to direct the affairs of the state, as our Houses do; but its members had had varied executive experience, and—what was of still more significance—its mistakes came back upon itself. The shame of failure fell upon it, and not upon those who were merely its agents. Moreover, it was a thoroughly *national* power: it stood for no constituencies; in its days of success it represented, not a divided, but a thoroughly homogeneous state. If you would have the present error of our system in a word, it is this, that Congress is the motive power in the government and yet has in it nowhere any representative of the nation as a whole. Our Executive, on the other hand, is national; at any rate may be made so, and yet has no longer any place of guidance in our system. It represents no constituency, but the whole people; and yet, though it alone is national, it has no originative voice in domestic national policy.

The sum of the matter is, that we have carried the application of the notion that the powers of government must be separated to a dangerous and unheard of length by thus holding our only national representative, the Executive, at arm's length from Congress, whose very commission it seems to be to represent, not the people, but the communities into which the people are divided. We should have Presidents and Cabinets of a different calibre were we to make it their bounden duty to act as a committee for the whole nation to choose and formulate matters for the consideration of Congress in the name of a party and an Administration; and then, if Congress consented to the measures, what they are already—a committee to execute them—make them work and approve themselves practicable and wise. And that is exactly what we ought to do. We should have not a little light thrown daily, and often when it was least expected, upon the conduct of the Departments, if the heads of the Departments had daily to face the representatives of the people, to propose, defend, explain administrative policy, upon the floor of the Houses, where such a plan would put them: and heads of departments would be happy under such a system only when they were very straightforward and honest and able men. I am not suggesting that initiative in legislation be by any means confined to the Administration—that would be radical, indeed—but only that they be given a free, though responsible, share in it—and that, I conceive, would bring the government back very nearly to the conception and practice of Washington. It would be a return to our first models of statesmanship and political custom.

I ask you to put this question to yourselves: Should we not draw the Executive and Legislature closer together? Should we not, on the one hand, give the individual leaders of opinion in Congress a better chance to have an intimate part in determining who should be President, and the President, on the other hand, a better chance to approve himself a statesman, and his advisers capable men of affairs, in the guidance of Congress? This will be done when the Executive is given an authoritative initiative in the Houses. I see no other way to create national figures in the field in which domestic policy is chosen, or to bring forward tested persons to vote for. I do not suggest methods—this is not the place or the occasion; I suggest an idea—a way out of chaos: the nationalization of the motive power of the government, to offset the economic sectionalization of the country; I suggest the addition to Congress, which represents us severally, of a power, constituted how you will, which shall represent us collectively in the proposing of laws; which shall have the right as of course to press national motives and courses of action to a vote in the Congress. This will not subordinate Congress; it may accept the proposals of the Administration or not, as it pleases (it once took a scolding from Washington himself for not accepting them); but the country will at least have a mouthpiece and not all of policy will lurk with committees and in executive sessions of the Senate.

Printed in Virginia State Bar Association, *Annual Address Delivered by Hon. Woodrow Wilson, at the Ninth Annual Meeting, Held at the Hot Springs of Virginia, August 3, 4 and 5, 1897* (Richmond, 1897).

From Wilson's Diary for 1897

Thursday, August 5, 1897

Delivered address before the Ass'n. on "Leaderless Government," and in the evening, at banquet, responded to the toast, "Our Honored Guest, Dr. Woodrow Wilson. In giving him to Princeton the South has discharged her many obligations to that great institution."

To Ellen Axson Wilson

My own darling,   Hot Springs, Bath Co., Va. 5 August, 1897

I have been persuaded to stay until Saturday morning. It was put so that I could hardly with courtesy decline,—tho. my longing inclination is for to-morrow.

I think I may say that the address was really a *great* success. Everybody seems enthusiastic,—even allowing for southern warmth of expression.

I am well and love you with all my heart, passionately, romantically, altogether.

Your letter came this morning.

Your own   Woodrow

ALS (WP, DLC). Enc.: unidentified newspaper clipping with cut of Wilson and announcement of his address to the Virginia Bar Association.

From Wilson's Diary for 1897

Friday, August 6, 1897

Went driving to Warm Springs, with Mrs. Camm, Mrs. Axtell, Miss Lulie Lyons, Archie Patterson, and Mr. Jackson Guy.[1] Delighted to find the old place unchanged. The very bath houses over the beautiful bathing pools looked every stick the same. Brought back so vividly my boyhood trip there with dear mother, Aunt Marion, and the rest,—the climb to the 'Flagpole,' &c.[2] The *smell* of the baths recalled so much!

[1] Lulie Lyons was from Richmond, as were Archibald Williams Patterson and Jackson Guy, both of whom were lawyers. Mrs. Camm and Mrs. Axtell cannot be identified.

[2] Wilson visited Warm Springs in Bath County, Va., during the late summer of 1880, when he was staying at Fort Lewis, also in Bath County, with his mother and his aunt, Marion Woodrow Bones.

Saturday, August 7, 1897

Returned to Markham.

Thursday, August 12, 1897

Provisionally chose the following topics for Brooklyn Institute lectures:

1. Origins of Our City Governments.—2. Principles of Organization.—3. The City Executive.—4. The City Council.—5. Reform. Sent to Prof. Hooper, subject to change.[1]

[1] The correspondence is missing, but Wilson had promised Franklin William Hooper, Director of the Brooklyn Institute of Arts and Sciences, that he would give a lecture course at the Institute on municipal government on April 30 and May 7, 14, 21, and 28, 1898. See "Appointments for the year," in the diary described at Dec. 9, 1897. As it turned out, the lectures were postponed, and Wilson delivered them in November and December of 1898. See the notes for these lectures printed at Nov. 18, 1898, Vol. 11, and the news reports printed at Nov. 19 and Dec. 17, 1898, *ibid.*

From Jabez Lamar Monroe Curry

"Hardy Cottage,"

My dear Sir—   Bar Harbor, Me 12 Aug. 97

I have just read in *Dispatch* a part of your very able & philosophical address before the Va. Bar Association.[1] I hope it will be published in more permanent and bindable form. If so, tell me how I can procure a copy. In the Con. Convention was a very astute and wise Wilson[2] and now we have two more, although not "chips of the old block." Your address and Pres. Wilson's (W. L.) before the Law Assoc. at Albany[3] should be published together in cheap form and placed in the hands of every Congressman (doubtful, whether he desires of enlightenment), Cabinet officer, governor and leading (are any of them "leaders" now?) editor.

I wish the Visitors of the Univ. had had the wisdom and firmness to elect you as President.

Yours very truly   J. L. M. Curry.

PS. If you have never seen my little book on The Southern States,[4] I should like to send you a copy.

ALS (WP, DLC) with WWhw notation on env.: "Ans. 15 Aug/'97."

[1] This report is printed in part at Aug. 5, 1897.

[2] James Wilson of Pennsylvania, who played an important part in the Constitutional Convention of 1787.

[3] William Lyne Wilson delivered an address, "Some Points in the Working of our Constitutional System," before the annual meeting of the New York State Bar Association in Albany on January 19, 1897. See *Proceedings of the New York State Bar Association: Twentieth Annual Meeting* (Albany, N.Y., 1897), pp. 22-41.

4 *The Southern States of the American Union Considered in their Relations to the Constitution of the United States and to the Resulting Union* (New York, 1894). There is a copy of this book in the Wilson Library, DLC.

From Wilson's Diary for 1897

Sunday, August 15, 1897

Col. Stribling repeated to me what he had said more than once before, that the northern troops in the war were *mostly* foreigners, at any rate in all but the final stages of the war,—at any rate the troops encountered by the Army of Northern Virginia. 'He never saw a batch of prisoners that was not made up chiefly of foreigners,—often of men who could not speak or understand English.' He also told me that some of McClelan's [McClellan's] cavalry at the beginning of the War were *strapped to their horses* because of their inexperience in riding. Lee's armies were, $\therefore$, much superior in *personnel*,—immensely superior in the cavalry arm of the services. It will be interesting to verify these impressions.

From Francis Landey Patton

My dear Professor Wilson: Princeton, N. J.   August 16 1897

I have been ill nearly all the time since my return from Bermuda or I should have replied to your letter[1] before this. I have just put Mrs Patton on the train for Boston & am in Princeton preparatory to a start for Toronto tonight.

I have not seen Mr Armstrong & do not know whether he will accept the chair that has been offered him.[2]

As soon as I can I will try & write more definitely though I think I may say that there is nothing definite to say beyond this:

1. Armstrong is called to a chair in the department of History.

2. Professor Sloane's chair is distinctly understood to be vacant[.] You may be sure that in reorganizing the department of History I shall do everything that lies in my power for the good of the department: but of course I cannot say in advance just how the work of the department will be distributed: nor would I like to undertake the distribution without the advice & approval of the Curriculum Committee of the Trustees.

I do not understand however that Mr. Armstrong is to teach Sophomore history during the present winter. That will remain for the present in the hands of Mr Coney.

I shall hope to see Mr Armstrong soon & I will write again. Meanwhile with best wishes & kindest regards to Mrs Wilson

                    I am very sincerely   Francis L Patton

ALS (WP, DLC).
   1 It is missing.
   2 Andrew Campbell Armstrong, Jr., Professor of Philosophy at Wesleyan University, who, as F. L. Patton to WW, Sept. 21, 1897, reveals, declined the invitation.

From Wilson's Diary of 1897

                                    Friday, August 20, 1897

Went, with Ellen, to Charlottesville, to see Montecello and the University. Saw Montecello for the first time. The rebuilding at the Univ. was still in progress,[1] and it was very hard to form a just idea of the new buildings at the foot of the Lawn.

In the evening saw Heath Dabney, at his house on 'Preston Heights.' He introduced the mooted subject of a President for the Univ.—said that, so far as he could see, *my* name was the only one now prominently put forward in connexion with the office. The Faculty very heartily and unanimously oppose the creation of the office; but Heath thinks it will be created nevertheless, and said that he thought the friction of the change would be reduced to a minimum if I would take the office. If they *must* have a President (I don't wonder they don't want one), they would, he felt sure, rather have me than any other man in the country,—would welcome me most heartily, and coöperate with me with entire and unaffected cordiality. All this makes the matter very serious subject for thought, should the office in fact be offered me.

   1 A fire had swept the campus of the University of Virginia on October 27, 1895, destroying the Annex building and the Rotunda. Restoration was still under way when Wilson visited Charlottesville, the new buildings not being dedicated until June 1898.

                                    Saturday, August 21, 1897
Returned to Markham,—afternoon.

To Frank William Taussig[1]

                          Markham, Fauquier Co., Virginia,
My dear Professor Taussig,   22 August, 1897.
I am sorry to say that I cannot sign the little paper you sent me.[2] I have no sympathy whatever with President Andrews' views on the silver question, as I am sure you have not; but I think

the Brown Corporation made a collossal blunder in forcing his resignation upon a matter of opinion. It seems a very ominous blow at freedom of opinion. At the same time I do not see that the error would be corrected by his reinstatement. To invite him now to resume the presidency will be interpreted to mean that the Corporation has yielded to criticism, and not to mean that it has seen its error. It will be no retrieval of the mistake; and will create a very false relation between Dr. Andrews and those whom he serves. I do not think that we ought to ask Brown so to embarrass herself; but I most profoundly hope this may be a lesson, a warning to Boards of Trustees. In short, I feel as you do about the whole matter; but I think this particular mistake remediless.

With warm regard,

Most sincerely Yours,   Woodrow Wilson

WWTLS (J. F. Jameson Papers, DLC).

[1] Professor of Political Economy at Harvard University.

[2] Taussig had sent Wilson a brief petition to the Brown Corporation requesting the reinstatement as President of Brown University of Elisha Benjamin Andrews, who had resigned after a contretemps over bimetallism.

Andrews had long held opinions decidedly favorable to international bimetallism. Although he had never aired these views in public, in at least two letters to alumni during the early summer of 1896, he had expressed his belief that the United States might on its own initiative safely adopt a double monetary standard, and that other nations would then follow suit. These letters, widely printed and quoted without Andrews' consent, aroused considerable apprehension among conservative friends of the university at the very time that opinions were being overheated by the so-called battle of the standards between McKinley and Bryan. Andrews was in Europe on a year's leave of absence and took no part in the presidential campaign. However, by the time of his return several members of the Brown Corporation had become convinced that his views were impairing the ability of the university to attract gifts and legacies. Accordingly, the Corporation, at its meeting on June 16, 1897, appointed a committee to confer with President Andrews. In a subsequent written statement, the committee requested of the President "a forbearance, out of regard for the interests of the University, to promulgate" his views on bimetallism. In his reply on July 17, Andrews submitted his resignation, adding that he could not meet the request without "surrendering . . . that reasonable liberty of utterance . . . in the absence of which the most ample endowment for an educational institution would have but little worth."

The controversy, which had already gained wide attention, now became a *cause célèbre*. A number of letters and petitions were addressed to the Brown Corporation. Some, like Taussig's "little paper," sought the reinstatement of Andrews; others demanded an apology by the Corporation for its infringement of the freedom of expression. At its meeting on September 1, 1897, the Corporation assured Andrews that it had intended no "official rebuke" or restraint on his freedom of opinion and asked him to withdraw his resignation. Expressing satisfaction with this statement, Andrews returned to his post. He left Brown a year later to become superintendent of schools in Chicago, and in 1900 he became Chancellor of the University of Nebraska, where, presumably, his bimetallic views were more acceptable. Walter Cochrane Bronson, *The History of Brown University, 1794-1914* (Providence, R. I., 1914), pp. 461-67, and Elizabeth Donnan, "A Nineteenth-Century Academic Cause Célèbre," *New England Quarterly*, xxv (March 1952), 23-46.

From Wilson's Diary for 1897

Monday, August 23, 1897

Stories: Little boy (missionary's son?) said babies were some-times born twins so that cannibals could eat *philopoena*. (Miss Lucy Smith)[1]

Irishman, after hearing silver debate: "16 to 1! Next thing you know you'll have *nothing to ate* (8)" (Miss Mary Smith).

[1] Lucy Marshall Smith and her sister, Mary Randolph Smith, shortly to be mentioned in this entry, were the daughters of the Rev. Dr. Henry Martyn and Lucy Marshall Coleman Smith. Dr. Smith, a native of Carlisle, Pa., and a graduate of Jefferson College and the Columbia Theological Seminary, was pastor of the Third Presbyterian Church of New Orleans, 1857-88; editor of the New Orleans *Southwestern Presbyterian*, 1869-91; and Moderator of the General Assembly of the southern Presbyterian Church, 1873. He was also an old friend and associate of Joseph Ruggles Wilson.

The Smith sisters were soon to become intimate friends of the Woodrow Wilsons. Lucy Marshall Smith was born on her maternal grandfather's plantation in Madison Parish, La., in 1862, while her father was serving as a chaplain in the Confederate Army. Mary Randolph Smith was born in New Orleans in 1866. They grew up in the manse of the Third Presbyterian Church on Chartres Street in New Orleans and, upon the retirement of their father in 1888, moved to a home at 1468 Clay Avenue. Dr. and Mrs. Smith both died in 1894, and their daughters lived in the house on Clay Avenue until their deaths. They were active in the social, religious, and charitable life of their city. Mary Randolph Smith died on Nov. 14, 1941, Lucy Marshall Smith on Feb. 16, 1951.

From Edith Gittings Reid

Blue Ridge Summit Pa.

My dear Mr. Wilson   August 24th [1897]

I was so disappointed in receiving your letter and Mrs. Wilson's[1] telling me that you could not come that I evinced anything but a Christian spirit. Miss Bessie King and Dr. Adams,[2] walking under the trees, filled me with scorn instead of my usual kindly interest: They were prodding for stones and talking an ethe-realized moonshine which they called religion—and imagined themselves in love. Love and Dr. Adams! Then before I had time to do very much harm Edge Bird[3] came and his vocabulary reduced me to a docile state of imbecility from which I am only just recovering—and give my first rational moment to you.

I write you of all this ill nature, caused merely by not having the friends I wanted, as I should like Mrs. Wilson to know the worst about me—and then, when we meet, and she likes me, we will be the best of friends—so this egotistical preamble is more for her than for you.

I wanted very much to re-read your Essays in the light of your own criticism but have not had the opportunity. I don't think you

a fair critic of yourself. Your style is strong, and rings true always. I remember no "effort" in it whatever. It is the organ not
the flute[.] You are not toying with words. I remember your
thought not your language—and it came to me in strong outlines
rather than in finished etching. Take, for instance, Henry van
Dyke whose writings I read with much personal interest—I remember his style but alas! for the thought. You are eager to give
all of yourself, anxious to convince, you think your audience
worthy—and you will succeed as no other historian will succeed
of whom I know! And, indeed, I know most of them a little—
well enough to have caught their flavor. Take Dr. Adams[—]he
will never be an historian—everything is fretted from the mind[,]
nothing springs from the heart. Never the strong rider going
through life guiding his steed to be sure, but with a light hand,
a firm seat, his eye and soul lying open to every light and shadow
that falls[,] every breath that stirs—his soul to the soul of the
unknown—not he! He would prefer to take his excursions on a
trolly car and get his information from a conductor.

There is, it seems to me, a spirit in every day, an atmosphere,
that unless you feel you and the day are strangers. There are no
two alike, each brings its peculiar message to you and you your
response. And if this is true of the days, what must it be of the
ages.

The inspired historian—who sees down the ages and brings
their warning and message to us, with its prophecy, has more
truly than any other heard the voice from the grave, caught his
glimpse of Eternity. I can hear you laugh—and hear you say:
"Won't you allow one an inconsequent moment? a joke or two by
the wayside?"

I want to see you so much. If it is at all possible for you to run
up for a few days even—won't you come? We expect to be here
until the last of October and you and Mrs. Wilson could not name
a day that would not be the one I would choose. I am sure if you
send me a telegram saying "Expect me to-morrow" I should
say: "I call that Providential!" So come if you can—and believe me
most faithfully your friend   Edith G. Reid

One thing I want to ask you. In the lives of individuals it is the
apparent trifles that have counted—is it true of Nations? For instance: I remember when a very little child my Aunt gave me
some bon bons; the box was pink, tied with white ribbon, and the
bon bons were prodigal in colors and shapes. I rushed down and
embraced her, and thanked her with an abandon of delight,

That evening my eldest brother came up with a book for me from my Aunt and said in his scornful way, "Aunt C. was so over-powered by your gush, she thought you must be hinting for something else. So she sent you this book." I secretly put that book in the fire. I cried myself to sleep, and unconsciousness of self died in me that night and even to this day I never thank anyone without a sudden pang. But what a letter I am writing! And I don't feel the least inclined to stop. Ah! but that day years ago taught me self control—& I will. Give my best regards to Mrs. Wilson, and tell her that I have not said a word about next winter because I still hope to see you both soon.

ALS (WP, DLC) with WWhw notation on env.: "Ans. Oct. 3/97."
  1 Mrs. Wilson's letter is missing.
  2 Their mutual friend, Herbert Baxter Adams.
  3 Mrs. Bird's grandson, Edgeworth Bird.

To Edwin Robert Anderson Seligman[1]

Markham, Fauquier Co., Virginia.
My dear Professor Seligman, 26 August, 1897.

I should have been very glad to subscribe to the petition you sent me,[2] had it reached me in time. Professor Taussig sent me the briefer paper, requesting the Brown Corporation to reinstate Mr. Andrews; and I wrote to him that I could not sign it. I believe that the Corporation have made an irreparable mistake, and that to ask them to retain Mr. Andrews is to ask them to do something that would be considered the fruit, not of repentance, but merely of timidity. I can subscribe to every word of the paper you send me; but I confess I do not see what the Corporation can now do that will be understood "to uphold and affirm, without possibility of misunderstanding, the principle of academic freedom." They must seek another opportunity if they would be thought to be sincere. The whole thing is most lamentable.

With much regard,

Very sincerely Yours, Woodrow Wilson
P.S. I send the paper, anyway. It may be in time.[3] W. W.

WWTLS with WWhw PS (J. F. Jameson Papers, DLC).
  1 Professor of Political Economy and Finance at Columbia University.
  2 Seligman's letter in which the petition was enclosed is missing.
  3 Since the Brown Corporation did not meet until September 1, the petition may have reached it in time to have some influence.

From Wilson's Diary for 1897

Saturday, August 28, 1897

Jessie's birth-day (10 yrs. old).

In the evening the children acted a little play written by Jessie herself, and acted it most charmingly, in pretty costumes devised by the ladies,—Miss Lucy Marshall Smith (New Orleans) stage manager.

Miss Lucy spoke of Collins's as the best *History of Kentucky*[1] and of Martin's as the best *History of Louisiana*;[2] and said that Mr. B. R. Forman, of New Orleans knew most of the events of the "14th of September" (1872?)—the Kellogg crisis in the politics of the State.[3]

[1] Lewis Collins, *Collins' Historical Sketches of Kentucky . . .* , revised and enlarged by Richard H. Collins (2 vols., Covington, Ky., 1882).

[2] François Xavier Martin, *The History of Louisiana* (New Orleans, 1882).

[3] The "Kellogg crisis" of 1874 was only one of a series of crises that erupted during the postwar struggle for power between the conservative Democratic party and the Republican or "Radical" party in Louisiana. William Pitt Kellogg, entering politics after his appointment by Lincoln as Collector of the Port of New Orleans, had served as United States senator until his election as Governor in 1873. His administration was beset by turbulence and bitter opposition, climaxed by an organized riot begun on September 14, 1874, during which Kellogg was driven from the State House and took refuge in the customhouse. The federal government supported Kellogg, and a presidential proclamation restored him to power.

From George Howe III

Dear Uncle Woodrow,   Brooklyn, Aug 29/97

Ed[1] has by this time told you all about my plans and there is little more for me to add except to thank you for all the trouble you have taken in helping me to secure a position, and also to ask if my plan meets with your approval. I went in to see Mr. Bridges one morning to find out if he had heard of any place that I might apply for. He said that just two minutes before he had given my address to Jesse [Lynch] Williams who had two jobs to offer me. He introduced me to Williams who gave me the choice of going to Europe with Mr. Alexander's son[2] or of doing some work (travelling, we supposed) in connection with a book entitled "Universities and Their Sons."[3] I was at first in favor of the latter but we found out that it didn't amount to much. I went down to see Mr. Alexander and had a long talk which proved afterwards to be satisfactory to both of us. His main anxiety was for the character of the boy he wished to engage—he wished to have one who is certainly a gentleman, inasmuch as he will be one of his family for a year to come. My references to you and Mr. Bridges satisfied him on that point. He then made some inquiries about me among "my friends," he said, and told me that all he had heard was extremely complimentary. I should like to know who those friends are. So he engaged me from the 8th September till next June or perhaps September, suggesting $50 per month and all expenses as the terms. Until October 13th I am to be at Seabright. On the 13th we sail for England, I believe, then go to Paris. Most of the winter we shall be in the south of France whence it is possible that we shall go to Rome and Naples. It depends upon the boy whether we shall return in June or Sept. I consider myself very fortunate and don't know how I can thank you enough for your trouble. I hope it meets with your entire approval. Ed can tell you anything else that you may wish to ask. I expected to tell you all about myself yesterday but you did not turn up. Our house here is fine. Come up and see it. I wish I could live in it for a while.

All send lots of love   George Howe

You will probably be happy to learn that the people are named *Alexander* so that you may still call me Aleck.

ALS (WP, DLC) with WWhw notation on env.: "Ans. 2 Sept., 1897."
  [1] Edward William Axson.
  [2] Frederick Beasley Alexander, son of James Waddel Alexander.
  [3] Joshua Lawrence Chamberlain *et al.* (eds.), *Universities and Their Sons* (5 vols., Boston, 1898-1900).

To Robert Bridges

                                         Markham, Fauquier Co., Virginia,
My dear Bobby,   30 August, 1897.

There was a singular miscarriage in the matter of securing a place on the *Commercial Advertiser* for my nephew, George Howe.[1] Your friend turned him over to some one else in the office of the *Advertiser* who told him to report for trial under the impression that he had had experience as a reporter. Of course it at once came out that he had had no experience of any kind, but was just out of college, and the trial ended before it began. It was an entirely different sort of work I was hoping they would find for him, upon the re-organization of the staff of the paper, as you know. If you can, and have the opportunity, I would be very grateful if you would call your friend's attention to the mistake, and see if the thing can be approached again de novo.

We have been here in this quiet mountain place for five weeks, having a perfect rest from the world; but we return to Princeton on Friday.

With constant affection,

As ever,   Faithfully Yours,   Woodrow Wilson

WWTLS (WC, NjP).
¹ See EAW to WW, Aug. 3, 1897, ns. 7 and 8.

From Wilson's Diary for 1897

Tuesday, August 31, 1897

Reading Savigny's "System des heutigen Römischen Rechts," at the following passage (I., p. 30), "Individuals constitute the State, not as such and according to their number *per capita*, but only in their constitutional articulation," had this note suggested to me:

Caption for section of P.o.P.¹ and for lectures on Sovereignty:²
The Consent of the People (its nature, forms, significance, &c.)

Legislation *may* mean,—often *should* mean,—*modification*,— such modification as would quite certainly be defeated upon *Referendum*, and would yet, as every statesman might see, benefit the whole people. Hence the necessity for *leadership* and for originative authority in every Legislature.

¹ His projected *magnum opus*, "The Philosophy of Politics."
² This does not occur as a "caption" in his notes for the lectures on sovereignty in his new course on the Elements of Politics. These notes are printed at March 5, 1898.

To Robert Bridges

My dear Bobby,   Markham, Virginia, 2 September, 1897.

Hurrah for Howe's luck, and thank you from the bottom of my heart for your watchful kindness in looking up a job for the boy! It takes a weight off my mind. I agree with you that such an engagement, though it leads directly to nothing, will bring just the additional training and experience the lad needs at this stage of his life, and I approve of it thoroughly.

I am delighted that you are at last free for a vacation. The more pity you cannot have a jolly long one such as I have had, and am just finishing. We go home to-morrow, and an immense pile of work awaits me. But I shall attack it with zest and finish it, I have little doubt, without distress. The only distress I suffer will come from the conditions under which the college is administered!

With lasting affection,

Faithfully Yours,   Woodrow Wilson
WWTLS (WC, NjP).

To Lucy Marshall Smith

My dear friend,   Princeton, 15 Sept., 1897

Mrs. Wilson had written you a letter, in reply to your last, but will not send it now from motives of prudence.

Just after you left Markham, our little Nellie developed a little fever and a very pronounced irruption all over her body and limbs. The doctor was called in and thought it merely the result of indigestion. Nellie proceeded promptly to get well, besides. When we got home we called our physician here, showed him such traces as remained of the irruption, and got the same verdict,—indigestion. During the last few days, however, Nellie's skin has been peeling off in minute flakes, and *now* the doctor says she must have had an extremely mild attack of *scarletina*. This peeling stage is the stage at which the disease is most apt to be communicated,—and so the poor little chick has been quarentined, and Mrs. Wilson with her. Ellen therefore thinks she had better not send her letter, and asks me to write in her stead.

It may be that she will be quarentined for ten days,—and that would bring us to the period of your coming. Scarlet fever, it seems, is wholly a child's disease, and grown persons are not susceptible to the infection; but if you would be made uneasy by the fact of its having been in the house, she hopes you will not feel obliged to come. At the same time it would almost break her heart to miss your visit. We are all looking forward to it with the keenest pleasure; and Ellen hopes that, if you are *not* rendered uneasy about coming by the situation, you will not postpone your visit another day beyond the time mentioned in your last letter. Her brother has promised to come down for Saturday and Sunday, the 25th and 26th, for the express purpose of meeting you; Nellie is perfectly well now, and by that time may be expected to have stopped shedding, and,—in short, Ellen's heart is set! You don't know how you have both taken hold on our hearts! Ellen begs (particularly since New Orleans doesn't now seem a good place to go to for some months to come)[1] that you will not promise your Kentucky kinsfolk to come to them at the very first of October, but that you will generously give us the full time at first agreed upon, at least, and I cry a loud *Amen*.

With every good wish and hope

Yours with affectionate regard,   Woodrow Wilson

ALS (photostat in RSB Coll., DLC).

[1] In September 1897 public notice was given of the presence of yellow fever in New Orleans, evoking memories of the severe epidemic of 1878, when over

four thousand residents had died. Fear swept through the city. The mayor arranged to set up a temporary yellow fever hospital in a school, but a mob,
afraid that the presence of the hospital would endanger them, set fire to it and
then engaged in a battle with the firemen. Order was restored, and the outbreak
in New Orleans proved to be less serious than previous epidemics—1,900 cases
and 300 deaths. However, it received wide notice since it spread up the Mississippi Valley at least as far as Memphis. Hodding Carter (ed.), *The Past as Pre-
lude: New Orleans 1718-1968* (New Orleans, 1968), p. 113.

From Francis Landey Patton

My dear Prof Wilson: [Princeton, N. J.] Sept 21/97

My illness has prevented me from carrying out my promise
to write you respecting the result of my interview with Prof.
Armstrong.

Of course you already know that after carefully considering
the whole question he has decided to remain at Wesleyan.

The work in the Department of History will go go [*sic*] on this
year as last, Mr. Coney conducting the Sophomore required class
& offering electives to Juniors & Seniors.

I had arranged this with him before I left Princeton in June

                    Sincerely   Francis L. Patton

ALS (WP, DLC).

From the Minutes of the Princeton Faculty

                    5 5′ P.M., Friday, Septem. 24th [1897]

... The Dean called the attention of the Faculty to the action
of the Com. on Discipline in reference to Sophomore Eating Clubs.
The action of the Com. was approved, and upon the recommendation of the Com. the the [*sic*] Inca, Vampa & Sioux Clubs, having
complied with all the requirements of the Faculty and having
promised to abstain from hazing, were duly authorized. . . .

To Robert Randolph Henderson

My dear Bob.,   Princeton, 29 Sept., 1897

I have not overlooked or forgotten your letter,[1]—you may be
sure of that; but it came at a time when it was impossible for
me to give it the sort of consideration it demanded. It came just
as we got back from our summer outing in Va., and we had just
discovered that one of the children *had had* scarlet fever a few
days before, which the country doctor in Va. had failed to recog-

nize, and that she was in the after stage, of peeling &c., when it is most contagious!! Quarantine was established, we were advised to write as few letters as possible; and our lives, so to say, stood still. Now at last, I am deeply thankful to say, we are out of the woods. The other children have not contracted the disease; the quarantine is over; we have been fumigated; and I return to my correspondence.

And what am I to say? It tears my heartstrings to say No to what *you* ask, my dear fellow; and yet I do not see what else I *can* say. Next summer is, indeed, a long way off; but not so far as not to be covered by my present engagements. Summer, you know, though nominally our "vacation," is really the time when we college fellows have to do most of our consecutive writing. I have a book promised for the end of '98: and next summer must take the bulk of the work on it.

You have no idea how much an address costs me, if it is for an Association[2] one wishes to talk his best to. I have absolutely nothing in hand that would be suitable,—even tolerably suitable, and it is really out of the question for me to consent to write one.

You must forgive me, my dear boy. The hard thing about saying No in this case is, that I must say it to you. I have said it to half a dozen other people without compunction. I would do anything for you but slight work already undertaken. The only engagements I have made to speak during the next twelve-month involve no *new* work at all,—and that is the only sort I *dare* make.

Mrs. Wilson unites with me in warmest regards to Mrs. Henderson as well as to yourself; and I am, in spite of present appearances,

Your affectionate friend,   Woodrow Wilson

ALS (WC, NjP).
  [1] It is missing.
  [2] Its name is unknown to the Editors.

EDITORIAL NOTE

WILSON'S HISTORY OF THE UNITED STATES FOR SCHOOLS

The book promised for the end of 1898 to which Wilson referred in the letter to Robert Randolph Henderson, just printed, was to be a brief history of the United States for schools. His object in writing such a work was, as he wrote to Charles Scribner, that it might "win a place in southern schools which have become discontented with what they regard as 'northern' views of the war and are much too apt to swing to the opposite extreme and use partisan 'southern' accounts." He had become interested in such a book as early as 1893 and eventually accepted the undertaking virtually as an obligation, for, as he also wrote to Scribner, so many "men of influence" in the

South had urged the task upon him that it "came to look like a sort of public duty."[1] When he began the actual work, he realized an additional benefit. He could, as he explained to Edith Gittings Reid, use it as a "preliminary sketch and study in proportions for the larger canvas upon which I am at work."[2] He was referring, of course, to his "Short History of the United States," which he had begun in 1893 and which is described in an Editorial Note in Volume 8.

At some time during the fall or early winter of 1897-98, Wilson successfully broached the idea of the school history to Harper and Brothers, for there is in the Wilson Papers a signed contract dated January 31, 1898, for a volume to be entitled "A History of the United States for Schools." Even before signing this contract, Wilson had set about compiling bibliographical references and notes for his school history. There is a substantial body of these materials in the Wilson papers, most being memoranda and outlines of incidents, topics, and chapter sections. Among these materials are two drafts of a chapter outline indicating that he contemplated a volume of nine or ten chapters and 500 pages. In what appears to be the second draft, he listed the following chapters: "Before the English Came," "The Swarming of the English," "The Discipline of Common Undertakings," "The Approach of Revolution," "The War for Independence," "Founding a Federal Government," "The Making of a Nation," "The Parting of the Ways," and "Armed Division." In the other draft he had included a tenth chapter, "Reunion."

Wilson began writing his first chapter, "Before the English Came," on March 19, 1898, and completed it on April 8, 1898, as his dating on the handwritten draft reveals. Wilson also prepared a typescript of the chapter; it is printed at April 8, 1898. There are in addition shorthand, handwritten, and typed fragments extant of some sections of Chapter II, "The Swarming of the English." These sections indicate that he had probably finished that part of the second chapter covering Virginia, New Netherlands, Plymouth, Massachusetts Bay, Maryland, the expansion of New England, and the English Civil War by the end of the summer of 1898. But work proceeded slowly, for although Wilson had before him drafts of the early parts of "A Short History," he was in fact creating a new and briefer text, and he obviously encountered more difficulty in writing a simplified version in broad strokes than he had in composing in more detail the original chapters of the longer work. For example, the handwritten drafts include more emendations and alterations than usually appear in Wilson's manuscripts.

Given this method of composition, his progress was slow for an additional reason: he quickly outran the "Short History" manuscript, for it included only a complete first chapter and six of ten projected sections of his second chapter which would have carried his narrative through the Glorious Revolution. Therefore, before he could proceed with the school history, he had to digest new materials and prepare new notes and outlines. By the early spring of 1899 he had undoubtedly completed the remainder of Chapter II covering the Restoration, the Carolinas, and Pennsylvania. There are brief shorthand notes for these sections in the Wilson Papers. There is no question

[1] WW to C. Scribner, Feb. 28, 1899, Vol. 11.
[2] WW to E. G. Reid, Oct. 3, 1897.

but that shortly afterward he finished the third and fourth chapters as well, for also in the Wilson Papers is a shorthand draft, dated April 15, 1899, of Chapter III, now called "Common Undertakings," together with a shorthand draft of "The Approach of Revolution," later changed to "The Parting of the Ways." The school history, however, never moved beyond this point; in fact certain events soon destined it to become abortive.

Harper and Brothers, encountering severe financial difficulties, sold its educational publications and contracts to the American Book Company, a large publisher of school texts, in the autumn of 1899. Hearing of the sale, and fearing that his contract might be included, Wilson wrote at once to Harper's, insisting that the contract be returned to him. He could not, he said, "consent to the transfer of the contract to any firm with which I did not myself wish to write a book."[3] But the transfer had already been made. In a sharply worded letter to the American Book Company, Wilson insisted that he had intended his book to be "primarily literary and not a text," and that he did not wish to consider writing his school history for a publishing house "exclusively or principally engaged in the publication of school books." He urgently requested that he be released from any obligation under the contract with Harper's.[4] The American Book Company was unwilling to let Wilson go, even though it was clear at this time that he was in no mood to complete the book. Finally, Henry Hobart Vail, Editor-in-Chief of the firm, in an interview with Wilson on January 20, 1900, achieved the best possible understanding in the circumstances. The contract was to stand, Wilson and Vail agreed, on the possibility that Wilson might some day change his mind and complete the book. Meanwhile the company would not press him for the manuscript, nor would it interfere with his plans to write a history of the United States "on other lines."[5] And so the school history came to an end, "cut off," as Wilson later wrote, "almost at its birth."[6]

[3] WW to H. D. Newson, Dec. 1, 1899, Vol. 11.
[4] WW to the American Book Company, Dec. 11, 1899, *ibid.*
[5] See the memorandum of an interview, printed at Jan. 20, 1900, *ibid.*
[6] WW to E. G. Reid, Jan. 27, 1901, Vol. 12.

An Outline of an Address

29 Sept. '97[1]

(*Not delivered*)[2]   Princeton, 30 Sept. 1897
Patriotic Citizenship

1. We are too apt, perhaps, to associate patriotism with periods of storm and stress and crisis, like that of the Revolution,—when there is scope for heroic action.
2. *In peace*, what is Patriotism? It is the same as it is in times of war,—only harder to see in the *items of conduct*, in terms of action. It is always
3. *Identification with the Community*. And Patriotism in such communities as these of ours is *No mere sentiment*. It must be sentiment founded on *knowledge*.

4 Did you never reflect *what sort of order this is*, under wh. we live? An order based upon *a common understanding, a common intelligence, a common morality*. We are *self*-governed,—or else self-*disordered*.

5 And the *Liberty* for wh. Mercer died,—what is it? The right to do what we individually please to do? No, but *the right to do what we ought under such a polity*.

5½ It was *for that right the Revolution was fought*,—to compel the ministers *and the king* in England to do what they *ought* under such a polity. Washington and Mercer were of the same breed with Hampden, and Chatham, and Burke.

6 And what *does* the polity demand? We have it all in Tennyson:
  (1) We must remain "*a nation yet*, the rulers and the ruled"— "a body of people organized for law."
  (2) "Some sense of *duty*."
  (3) "Something of a *faith*."
  (4) "Some *reverence for the laws* ourselves have made."
  (5) "Some *patient force*—to change them when we will."
  (6) "Some *civic manhood* firm against the crowd."[3]

Following this model and ideal, we shall know the true meaning and might of citizenship and feel at its flood the full sentiment of patriotism.

WWhw MS. (WP, DLC).
  [1] Wilson's composition date.
  [2] Mercer Engine Company No. 3 of Princeton, a volunteer fire-fighting organization, observed its semicentennial by commemorating the death of General Hugh Mercer at the Battle of Princeton. Exercises in Alexander Hall on Thursday evening, September 30, 1897, were followed by the unveiling of a tablet at the battlefield on October 1. Wilson was to have been the third speaker on Thursday evening. However, the second speaker, Judge Beverley Randolph Wellford, Jr., of Richmond, Va., discoursed at such length that Wilson's speech had to be canceled, causing the *Princeton Press*, Oct. 9, 1897, to lament, "It is a common matter of regret that on account of the lateness of the hour on Thursday evening Professor Wilson's address on 'Patriotic Citizenship' was omitted." There is a copy of the program of the two-day affair in the Wilson Papers, Library of Congress, entitled *Program Semi-Centennial Celebration of Mercer Engine Company No. 3 Princeton, New Jersey September 30 and October 1 1897* (n.p., n.d.).
  [3] Tennyson's "The Princess, Conclusion."

To Edith Gittings Reid

My dear Mrs. Reid,   Princeton, New Jersey, 3 October, 1897

I fear that you have wondered with something like indignation why I have not answered your letter written in August. Five weeks have gone by since it found me, in Virginia, and I have not answered it though it contained another cordial invitation to visit you at Charmian! The reason is all too sufficient. When your letter reached me we were just on the point of starting homeward with a sick child,—Nellie, our youngest. The country doctor said that it was merely her digestion that was disordered; but she had been more or less out of sorts for some weeks and it was evident that we ought to go directly home with her. When we reached home it was discovered that she had had a mild attack of scarlet fever,—which is more infectious in its later stages than in its earlier! She was quarentined, with her mother, at once. The administration of the household fell to me; and, inasmuch as she had been shut into one room later than she should have been, our physician advised me not to write letters to any one who had children. I did not go much to public places, and I did not shake hands with my friends when I chanced to meet them. That's the whole story. The other children, I am deeply thankful to say, have not contracted the disease; the quarentine is raised; and we are free again, in mind as well as in body. I write as soon as possible.

It made our hearts warm that you should urge us so cordially to come to see you. It would have made us feel richer and younger, could we have gone. Mrs. Wilson already feels you her personal friend, having taken her knowledge of you from me; and I feel my life fuller by reason of your friendship, so generously and cordially given; but it is my ardent desire that you and Mrs. Wilson should know each other without intermediary. You must both lose by imperfect transmission of your qualities. It must be managed some day, some way. Not next winter, alas! I fear; for, what with my own increasing engagements and the Hopkins straits for money, my lectures there have gone by the board. Dr. Adams proposed ten instead of twenty-five; I did not think that worth while, either for the students or myself; and they could not afford more. It seems like the breaking of a tie that I had come to regard almost as permanent.

It makes me the more glad that you do not mind writing letters, and that your letters contain so much of yourself. I feel it a special privilege to have such authentic news of what you think about the matters that lie so near the heart of my own occupations and ambitions,—and that you "don't feel the least inclined to stop" when you are writing. Perhaps, if you will think of it seriously, you are encouraging a vice in me by talking to me of the matters about which I ask your critical judgments! I sometimes fear that it is a mistake to think too much about the way in which the things I seek to do ought to be done. I hate to hear *other* fellows talk solemnly about 'their art'; and I often feel foolish when I realize how very seriously I am taking myself. And yet, if I know my own heart, it is not myself, but my work that I study and would perfect! Take the matter I have in hand: it is impossible, if I would do it worthily, not to study it critically as a question of art. I am about to begin a school history of the United States, partly as a preliminary sketch and study in proportions for the larger canvas upon which I am at work; partly in order that the southern schools may at least be offered a history written in the national spirit and yet thoroughly just, with the justice of sympathy, to the South's principles and point of view. And yet it would be folly to add to the almost numberless manuals of this kind another manual. It must be a work of art or nothing,—and I must study the art. I must cultivate a new style for the new venture: a quick and perfectly pellucid narrative, as clear as the air and coloured with nothing but the sun, stopped in its current here and there, and yet almost imperceptibly, for the setting in of small pictures of men and manners, coloured variously, as life is. I have never yet done anything of the kind and I do not know that I can do it. Neither the style of the essays, nor the style of the Washington will do,—and I have no other, except that of "Division and Reunion," which is equally unsuitable.

And thoughts of these things bring me back to your letter, with its delightful suggestion that ages, like days, have their own spirit and atmosphere, each bringing a peculiar message and demanding a peculiar response. Unquestionably it is so, and what the writing of history demands is that the historian give himself wholly and with entire resignation of his own crotchets, to the sympathetic rendering of these, being as careful to *belong* for a little to the age of which he writes as to know what its events were. Oh to be a seer and to have an imagination that would enable one to be of all ages a contemporary!

But tell me how a school history ought to be written,—and read with leniency my essay,[1] sent under another cover.

Mrs. Wilson joins me in warmest greetings and shares my sense of privation in not having seen you.

Faithfully Your Friend,   Woodrow Wilson

ALS (WC, NjP).
[1] Wilson probably sent a reprint of his "The Course of American History" (printed at May 16, 1895, Vol. 9), which the New Jersey Historical Society had just published in its *Semi-Centennial of the New Jersey Historical Society, at Newark, New Jersey, May 16, 1895* (Newark, 1897).

An Announcement

[Oct. 8, 1897]

MASS-MEETING.

There will be a mass meeting this evening, in Murray Hall, at 7 p.m. The meeting will be held to arouse interest in the Halls. There will be two speakers, one from each Hall. Whig Hall will be represented by Prof. Woodrow Wilson, and Clio Hall by W. B. Hornblower '71, of New York.

Printed in the *Daily Princetonian*, Oct. 8, 1897.

From Isaac Minis Hays[1]

American Philosophical Society, Independence Square,

Sir: Philadelphia, October 15th 1897

I have the honour of informing you, that you have been this day elected a Member of the American Philosophical Society, held at Philadelphia, for promoting useful knowledge.

I am, Sir,

Your obedient Servant,   I. Minis Hays, Secretary.

Printed LS (WP, DLC).

[1] Philadelphia physician, editor of medical journals, student of the life and writings of Benjamin Franklin, and one of the secretaries of the American Philosophical Society.

From Daniel Collamore Heath

Dear Mr. Wilson: Boston, Oct. 16, 1897.

I quote the following in a letter just received from our London agents, with respect to "The State."

"Please let me know your stock of this book. We have 60 or 70 which may not be sufficient for this year's needs. You say that you have a revised edition of the book in hand. Is this to be published soon? Please say when. It would be a very great pity for you to let the book run out of print even for a short time as if we were unable to supply Cambridge needs another book would probably be substituted in place of 'The State' and we might never be able to get the latter reinstated. We look upon this matter as of much importance."

We find that we have but 50 copies on hand here. We have written our Chicago and New York offices to learn how many copies they have and how many they will likely need during the rest of the school year, and we now write to you for any suggestion you can give us as to reprinting of the old edition and also to inquire when you think the new edition will be ready.

Very truly yours,   D. C. Heath

TL (WP, DLC).

From Longmans, Green and Company

Dear Sir: New York, Oct. 16, 1897.

We are obliged by your favor of the 13th of October, and regret that we are not to have the pleasure of seeing you here. We quite understand however the difficulty of making time in these days.

Your understanding of our desire as to the revision of "Division and Reunion" is quite correct, and we hope you will be able to do it in such good season, that we shall be able to make the necessary changes before the Autumn demand begins next year. Will you allow us to suggest that to do this comfortably we ought to have the matter all in hand by July.

Of course we hope that it will be found unnecessary to do a great deal of rewriting: but we must leave this in your hands.

Very truly yours,   Longmans, Green & Co.

TLS (WP, DLC).

To Isaac Minis Hays

My dear Sir,   Princeton, New Jersey, 20 October, 1897

Allow me to acknowledge with deep appreciation the receipt of your official announcement of my election to membership in the American Philosophical Society. I am sincerely gratified and accept the election with the liveliest pleasure.

Very truly Yours,   Woodrow Wilson

ALS (Archives, PPAmP).

From the Minutes of the Princeton Faculty

5 5′ P.M., Wednesday, October 20th, 1897

. . . Upon recommendation of the Com. on Discipline, It was Resolved That Mr. —— be suspended from [blank] until Thanksgiving for being present when hazing occurred in his room on the evening of Saturday, Oct. 9th. He is a member of the Academic Sophomore Class (1900)

Upon recommendation of the Com. on Discipline the following action was taken:—Whereas The Faculty has been informed that Students have been using the golf links on Sundays, Resolved, That the authorities of the golf links be requested to enforce their rule against Sunday playing. . . .

Two Newspaper Reports of a Lecture on Edmund Burke in Wilmington, Delaware

[Oct. 22, 1897]

PROF. WILSON'S TALK

The first lecture in the interesting series[1] that has been arranged for the coming winter by the New-Century Club for its members and the general public was delivered last night before an appreciative audience by Woodrow Wilson, Ph.D., LL.D., Professor of Jurisprudence, Princeton University, upon the subject: "Burke, the Interpreter of English Liberty."

Professor Wilson was introduced by Miss Mather,[2] president of the New-Century Club, and he said in part:[3]

"It is extremely difficult to bring the man from his writings. Thoughts are intangible and unless we hear them spoken and get the flavor of the man, we cannot estimate their force. We have some intimation of the force of great actors, such as Garrick or Siddons, because we know how audiences have been thrilled, and yet there is nothing so evanescent as the fame of an actor who, in every instance, merely repeats another's words. There must be an atmosphere belonging to both writer and actor that shall animate the writings of the one and the acting of the other, or they will not live. Many men whose writings we do not consider good reading, had in their day a following because of the atmosphere they carried around with them.

"Emerson, whose writings so largely influence the young of the present generation, does not sati[s]fy mature minds who want sequence of thought. His deductions follow no logical sequence, and as you read them you feel as if you were riding over a corduroy road, not level, not speedy, but a fairly good road. We cannot appreciate the forensic flights of Rufus Choate, because we realize as we read that what was vital is missing, namely the time and the circumstances, neither of which we can reproduce. Good speeches are said never to read well, but he who thinks thus has not in mind those of Webster, Erskine or Burke. As we read the writing of Burke we feel that some of the atmosphere has been carried over from the life of the man into them and that he is the only man who ever lived, who could have written such sentences.

"As is generally the case, there is more of Burke in his writings than in his life, for men put the best of themselves, their lives and thoughts into the books they design to live. Good talkers are not always good writers; the latter must send a vitality through pen and ink which shall test the ability to think. Open Edmund

Burke's writings anywhere and you will be caught by the current force and carried from page to page, every line said to a purpose. . . ."

Printed in the Wilmington, Del., *Morning News*, Oct. 22, 1897; some editorial headings omitted.
   [1] Reports of Wilson's other two lectures—on de Tocqueville and Bagehot—are printed at Nov. 5 and 19, 1897.
   [2] Miss Mather is identified in the first of the newspaper reports printed at Feb. 5, 1897, n. 1.
   [3] For this lecture, Wilson used the notes on Burke described in the Editorial Note, "Wilson's Lectures on Great Leaders of Political Thought," Vol. 9.

[Oct. 22, 1897]

NEW-CENTURY CLUB.

. . . Before a goodly audience in the auditorium of the New Century Club last evening, Woodrow Wilson, Ph.D., LL.D., professor of jurisprudence in Princeton University, began a course of three lectures on Great Leaders of Political Thought. His subject for the evening was "Burke, the Interpreter of English Liberty," a subject which he treated most interestingly and instructively. His consideration of Burke's principles with respect to party were especially interesting in the light of present day politics.

Prof. Wilson came upon the stage accompanied by Miss Mary A. J. Mather, president of the New Century Club, and Mrs. Charles S. Howland, chairman of the educational committee of the club. Miss Mather, in a felicitous speech, spoke of the pleasure which had been derived from hearing Prof. Wilson in a previous series of lectures, and referred to him as a real voice. The speaker of the evening was warmly applauded as he arose at Miss Mather's gracious introduction.

In prefacing his consideration of Edmund Burke, Prof. Wilson explained the difficulty of getting the character of a man of letters, for character is always an intangible thing. According to Walter Bagehot, some men carry an atmosphere about them. Such men as Emerson and Choate made a great impression upon their generation, but it is difficult for later generations to see the cause of their influence. Gladstone made good speeches, but they are not good reading. Burke did have an atmosphere in his writings. When you read the sentences of Burke you feel that only one man could have written them. In his writings you find the man that wrote them. He did the thing not for the sake of doing it, but for the sake of what it was to accomplish.

Edmund Burke, by dying, removed some of the obstructions from his work: he had an Irish brogue: he was angular and he was melodramatic in manner. Taking these things away there was left an atmosphere that was engaging, the force that was to last. He was born of Irish parents in Dublin, but we never think of him as an Irishman. Goldsmith and he came to England about the same time, and they were alike in some respects, but one always thinks of Goldsmith as an Irishman. Burke had a way of borrowing money from friends and forgetting to repay it, and the friends also forgot to ask him for it. His brother Richard and his cousin William engaged in some unsavory transactions, but he had no hand in them; it was inconceivable that he should have soiled his hands by it; he was the most incorruptible man of his age. However, the Burkes made the money and the Burke[s] spent it, but never knew where it came from. He thought it good luck to have so much money and did not ask its source. When the scheme failed and the men were brought to ruin, Burke went manfully to work and supported them by literary hack work. He read law and thought it an interesting science to know but not to practice. His father, who was an attorney in Dublin, cut off his supplies, and then, irresponsible Irishman that he was, he got married. He started the Annual Register, a sort of "Review of Reviews," and wrote nearly the whole of it. He wrote an account of the settlements in America. He was one of the group that met at the "Turk's Head," which included Sir Joshua Reynolds, Garrick, Goldsmith and Dr. Johnson. In 1765 he formed the friendship with the Marquis of Rockingham, through whom he obtained a seat in Parliament, and made the most extraordinary speeches of the day. We must realize the times in which he lived to realize the effect he produced. The members soon found themselves listening to words concerning the general empire and that made for liberty. When they got used to it they stopped listening, for they began to notice his brogue. Some of the speeches which we read with amazement were delivered to empty benches. They were in reality addressed to future generations.

Burke was practical as to parties. His view was that you cannot act except in parties, and if you act on your own judgment you would be a minority of one, and so you must have concert of action. "When men are not acquainted with each others principles," said Burke, "nor experienced in each others talents, nor at all practiced in their mutual habitudes or dispositions by joint efforts of business; no personal confidence, no friendship, no common interest subsisting among them; it is evidently impossible that they can act a public part with uniformity, perseverance or efficacy." That is why, continued Prof. Wilson, that committees of 100[1] seldom amount to anything for they have not acted together before and by the time they understand each others idiosyncracies the campaign is over and the other side has won. Burke also said that when bad men combine, good men must associate. It is not enough that a man means well and always votes according to his conscience, but duty demands that what is right should not only be made known, but made prevalent. Continuing Prof. Wilson said that this does not mean that you must blindly serve old parties, but good men must associate in sufficient numbers to defeat the bad.

He stood with ardor for freedom and men said he belied himself in his attitude toward the French Revolution, but they saw the evils of the monarchy and not what the principles of the people were leading France to stagger through. The revolutionists said, "We can cut down the structure of government and rear you another," but he said, "Change is not reform; the thing you touch is alive and you cannot make another full grown in a night; it will not have the gristle to last nor the muscle to endure; a government is made of the tested experience of a race." He feared the entrance of French radical philosophy with [into] England and fought it with all his might.

He championed the cause of America. He drew attention to the lineage of the people of America and said, "You can no more impose on them than you can impose on yourselves." He declared that the people must be taken as they are. This was his doctrine of expediency, the doctrine of doing the wisest thing under the circumstances. Wisdom in practical things is expediency. It is the expedient thing which is the wise thing when you are dealing with masses of men. As Burke said: "I do not know how to draw up an indictment against a whole people." To achieve reform you must get the opinion of the most instructed people. Burke understood India and America. He did not live in England; he lived where his mind was.

Burke took in all the details and thus his generalizations are so strong. He took questions of the moment to the light and held them up to be seen where great principles of conduct might shine upon them from out the general experience of the race. And the voices of the finer passages in Burke are like the voices of prophecy as well as the voices of history.

The next lecture will be given on November 4th on De Tocqueville.

Printed in the Wilmington, Del., *Every Evening*, Oct. 22, 1897.
1 That is, reform groups.

A Looseleaf Notebook

[Oct. 24, 1897-Nov. 2, 1898]

First page begins (WWhw): *"For Donovan lectures:* (Balto. 1898."
Contents:

(a) WWhw list of Donovan lectures at the Johns Hopkins. (About the Donovan lectures, see WW to D. C. Gilman, Nov. 14, 1897, n. 2.)

(b) *"The Fashion of the Age* (in Literature)," WWhw notes for a lecture, printed below at Oct. 24, 1897.

(c) *"Forms of Government,"* WWhw notes for a lecture, printed at Oct. 29, 1897.

(d) WWhw memorandum for an essay on "The Sentiment of History" and list of subjects for essays, printed at Oct. 29, 1897.

(e) WWhw list of names of residents of Richmond, Va.

(WP, DLC).

Notes for a Talk[1]

(24 Oct., '97)[2]
(Sewickley, Pa., 27 Oct., '97)
The Fashion of the Age (in Literature)

All the world has become readers and the court of taste is not the same it once was: but the old court is still open, and still preserves its old precedents and standards of judgment,—and this is the court that grants franchises for the future.

There are several "reading publics": the cultivated, the uncultivated, the chaste, the unchaste, the modest, the prurient. You may appeal to wh. you will and win success,—i.e. sales and vogue—and you may make your calculations as to which of these will outlive the others.

The fashion of the age is no doubt represented by the novel and the essay that attempts the solution of moral problems: but for the majority the old answers are still conclusive, and the next age will have different problems.

Note the revival of the essay,—and that the moralist cannot get accepted as an essayist. An essay is none when it becomes an argumentative brief. Let the age have out its arguments; but the essayist must comment with no partisanship except that wh. makes him a genial partisan of his own opinions! He is a living soul *looking on*, uttering his reflections upon things new and old.

This revival may mean that the age is getting its offing, its quiet air, again, and beginning to observe itself without distorting emotion. Beginning, too, to become once more tolerant of individualities,—admitting men individually, as well as in parties, to its favour. And then? Perhaps the masculine and permanent works of personal conviction,—not fashionable accents but the voices of men. Once let them know that they will be heard, and they will speak out.

WWhw and WWsh notes in looseleaf notebook described at Oct. 24, 1897.
1 To the Woman's Club of Sewickley, Pa. See the news report printed at Oct. 28, 1897.
2 Wilson's composition date.

Three News Reports of a Visit to Sewickley and Pittsburgh

[Oct. 27, 1897]

PROF. WOODROW WILSON.

Arrangements for His Entertainment While in the City.

Dr. Woodrow Wilson, professor of jurisprudence in Princeton university, was a passenger on the Southwestern express this morning. He will be in Pittsburg three days. He was met at the depot by Edward A. Woods,[1] who escorted him to his home in Sewickley. This afternoon the professor will be the guest of the Women's Club of the Sewickley valley and will address them in the Edgeworth clubhouse. This evening Mr. and Mrs. Woods[2] will tender a reception to him at their Sewickley home.

To-morrow morning Mr. Wilson will come back to Pittsburg. In the evening he will lecture in the Carnegie Music hall on "Democracy," his well-known talk on popular government. This lecture is under the auspices of the Pittsburg center of the University Extension society and is given for the purpose of opening the courses of study provided by the society. The University club will have the professor for its guest Friday evening [October 29], when a smoker will be given in his honor.

Printed in the *Pittsburg Press*, Oct. 27, 1897.
   [1] Edward Augustus Woods, insurance executive and broker, whose office was in Pittsburgh.
   [2] Gertrude Macrum Woods.

[Oct. 28, 1897]

MR. WILSON LECTURES.

The Woman's club of Sewickley tendered a reception yesterday afternoon to Dr. Woodrow Wilson, professor of jurisprudence in Princeton university. It was one of the club's "artist days" when a special meeting is held to do honor to a distinguished visitor. Mrs. Edward A. Woods presided. Prof. Wilson delighted the ladies assembled with an address on the "Fashions of the Age," in which he referred to the style of literature of the present time. He said that the object of much of the literature of the day is to deal with some moral problem and explained the evident reason for some prominent works. He elaborated the subject in a clever and pleasing manner that called forth frequent applause from the fair hearers. . . .

This evening Prof. Wilson will open the annual course of lectures for the University Extension society. He will speak on "Democracy" in Pittsburgh Carnegie Music Hall. . . .

Printed in the *Pittsburgh Commercial Gazette*, Oct. 28, 1897.

[Oct. 29, 1897]

WILSON TALKS ON GOVERNMENT.

Princeton's Professor of Jurisprudence Lectures at Carnegie Music Hall.

The first of the season's lectures in the University Extension course was given last evening in the Pittsburg Carnegie Music hall by Woodrow Wilson, professor of Jurisprudence in Princeton university. A large audience was present to greet the distinguished guest. . . .

In introducing Prof. Wilson Mr. Briggs[1] said the society felt it could do no better than to begin its season with a lecture on popular government, and it was a pleasure to introduce one of its most prominent exponents. Among other things Dr. Wilson said. . . .[2]

Printed in the *Pittsburg Post*, Oct. 29, 1897; some editorial headings omitted.
[1] C. C. Briggs, president of the Pittsburgh Center of the University Extension Society.
[2] Here follow extracts from "Democracy," printed at Dec. 5, 1891, Vol. 7.

Notes for an Address[1]

Pittsburgh, Oct. 29/97

Forms of Government.

"Of forms of gov't. let fools contest;
Whate'er is best administered is best."—*Pope*

While this is not true, the importance of *forms* of gov't. may be much exaggerated.

The qu., what is the best form of government? must be answered by the other, For whom? For here you must bring in Montesquieu's philosophy of "the spirit of the laws," and consider many circumstances.

Monarchy, ancient and modern, simple and absolute—such as a mayor might exercise,—and complex, systematic, of necessity limited.

Aristocracy, ancient and modern,—the *privileges* of a class: the political service and ascendency of a class.

Democracy, the ancient 'demos' contrasted with the modern people. The people infinitely various. And there is the *proletariat*, besides,—cleft in two: labourers, unemployed.

None of these was ever simple in form for long,—and none had any place until a modern time for the conception of *constitutionalism*.

What is a constitution, and when and how did the idea arise of a separate and distinct body of constitutional law,—a power outside the gov't.?

England's a test case: What can Parliament change?

The State *vs.* the Government,—a notion modern in its origin and application.

Written constitutions make the existence of the State more definite and explicit, but not more real.

A constitutional State:
   (a) A law-making body representative of the State, not of the gov't., —set to control the gov't.
   (b) An administration subject to the laws.
   (c) A judiciary secured vs. improper influences.
   (d) A more or less formal and complete formulation of the rights of individuals as *vs.* the gov't.

Monarchy, aristocracy, or democracy may be "constitutional"; but constitutionality depends upon
   1) Temper and habit of people, and, ∴ , of officials
   2) Practical means of control and methods of administration. (Pope again)

Montesquieu's notion as to the corruption of gov'ts by the decay of their characteristic principles, fits into

Aristotle's opinion: "It is clear that the best political association is the one wh. is controlled by the middle class, and that the only states capable of good administration are those in wh. the middle class is numerically large enough at least to hold the balance of power,"—because a middle class is more apt to conserve a principle of action than is either an aristocracy or a proletariat.

The *real problem of Politics* (said Aristotle) is, How, out of heterogeneous elements, to make the best combinations for moral progress.

WWhw notes in looseleaf notebook described at Oct. 24, 1897.
   ¹ Before the Department of Social Economics of the Twentieth Century Club of Pittsburgh, a woman's organization, in the morning of Oct. 29, 1897.

Memoranda

[c. Oct. 29, 1897]
For an Essay on *The Sentiment of History.*

This is *not* the sentiment of the historian himself, or of the historian's own age, towards what he is recording, but the sentiment wh. went with the acts and events themselves in their own age.

These sentiments the historian ought to reproduce, after as lively a sort as possible. The sentiment of the present-day reader will take care of itself, and will save the historian the necessity of comment.

◊

Subjects for Essays:
What it Heartens a Man to Know.
In Case of Doubt.
When Duty is Plain.
The Zest of Action.

Men of Action and Men of Books.
The Unhappy Immunity of Fools.
A Man of the World[,] What in the best sense?
Concerning Honour.
Concerning Vanity.
Leisure.
Pleasure.

◊

When *Mr. A. L. Lowell's book* on English party organization and dis-
cipline comes out,[1] and [an] article to be written on
The Boss and the Machine.
The Leader and the Party.

WWhw and WWsh memoranda in looseleaf notebook described at Oct. 24, 1897.
  [1] Abbott Lawrence Lowell, "The Influence of Party upon Legislation in England and America," *Annual Report of the American Historical Association for
the Year 1901* (2 vols., Washington, 1902), I, 319-542.

Francis Landey Patton to John Aikman Stewart

My dear Mr. Stewart: [Princeton, N.J.] November 3 1897

You may remember that the Trustees at their late meeting referred the matter regarding the Princeton Inn to a committee
of five to be appointed by the President & of which he was to be
the chairman.[1]

That committee consists of the following gentlemen besides
myself: Rev Dr. [John] Dixon, Mr. Charles E. Green, Mr. J. Bayard
Henry and the Hon W. J. Magie.

Mr. Green & I agreed in consultation that though we greatly
desired your counsel you would prefer not to be asked to take a
place on the committee.

I have called a meeting of the com. for Saturday Nov. 6th in
the Trustees' room at 2 o'clock P.M. . . .

I am greatly disturbed by this matter & reflection does not
serve to show me an easy way out of our difficulty. Today I called
the Faculty discipline com. together & asked from each one an
expression of opinion.

Various shades of opinion were represented as you can imagine
when I tell you that those present were the Dean & Professors
Cornwall, Packard, Woodrow Wilson, Winans, McCloskie, Duffield, Hibben and Young. But there was an unanimous expression
of opinion that no change in our existing law is needed, & that
it would be impossible to carry into execution a law prohibiting
students going into drinking places. I am more sorry than I can
say that so many of our Presbyterian Synods have condemned us
without a hearing & have done us damage so unjustly

I am very sincerely yours   Francis L. Patton

ALS (Patton Letterpress Books, University Archives, NjP).
  [1] Earlier in 1897 a group of Princeton professors and townspeople, including Charles Woodruff Shields and Grover Cleveland, signed a petition for the grant of a license to the Princeton Inn to serve beer and wine at meals and in the grill room. The signers hoped to lessen the temptation of local saloons for Princeton students. The petition soon set off a violent controversy within the Presbyterian Church. The Reform Committee reported, "with humiliation and astonishment," to the Synod of New York on October 21 that a bar had been set up in Princeton with the connivance of Princeton professors. "How long," the committee asked, "may we hope to keep the pulpit, and even the ministry from the calamity of the cup?" Patton and the Princeton trustees and professors stood their ground, and Professor Shields resigned from the Presbytery of New Brunswick after that body had voted to discipline such of its members as had signed the petition. He joined the Episcopal Church and was ordained priest in 1899. Thomas J. Wertenbaker, *Princeton, 1746-1896* (Princeton, N.J., 1946), pp. 374-75.

From G. P. Putnam's Sons

Dear Sir: New York Nov. 4th, 1897

Replying to your favour of 3rd inst. we shall be more than pleased to supply you a set of the Writings of Jefferson,[1] the terms of payment being entirely to suit your own convenience. We shall prefer, if you say so, to deliver at once all the volumes that are published, and you may pay as you suggest, at the rate of $5.00 per month, or at any intervals that you see fit.

We are always glad to meet the convenience of professional men in the matter of settlement of account.

Very respectfully,   G. P. Putnam's Sons. [per] K. W.

TL (WP, DLC).
  [1] Paul Leicester Ford (ed.), *The Writings of Thomas Jefferson* (10 vols., New York, 1892-99). There is a copy of this work in the Wilson Library, DLC.

From Joseph Ruggles Wilson

My precious Son—   Columbia, S. C. Nov. 5/97

I expect to leave for Clarksville, Tenn., on Monday the 8th—stopping a few days in Augusta and in Nashville.

I have been asked to supply my old Wilmington pulpit[1] during the months of February March and April—and have, more or less wisely, consented conditionally.

I have been in a very good boarding house here for nigh a month now, and rather than move again I would remain if duty did not seem to call me to Tennessee; and Josie and Kate really seem to *want* me with them; at any rate I am glad to believe that this is the case: old men as well as young like to be welcome.

With much love to Ellie and the children,

I am your   devoted Father

ALS (WP, DLC) with WWhw notation on env.: "Ans."
  [1] Of the First Presbyterian Church.

A Newspaper Report of a Lecture on Alexis de
Tocqueville in Wilmington, Delaware

[Nov. 5, 1897]

NEW-CENTURY CLUB.

. . . A large audience listened last evening to the address by
Prof. Woodrow Wilson on "Tocqueville, the Student of Democracy." He said:[1] "Alexis Clerel de Tocqueville was a leader of
political thought, but not in the same sense as Burke, who was a
leader of the policy of his nation and who would have felt that
he had failed in his mission if that policy had not been translated
into active politics. Though de Tocqueville was a man of action,
he was not meant to be; he was a member of the Assembly under
one of the short-lived governments of France, but he stood among
affairs as a looker-on. We feel as if he were an American, his
reputation at least belongs to us, since it was built on the book
he wrote of us, and which first made us conscious of ourselves,
and known as we would be to the world.

["]Yet we do not know him; he seems to us a name that has
not body, nor character. If through and through a man's writings
are pure, the man must be pure, and this man was nobler than
the things he wrote. It has been said that he was a sad writer,
but though lacking in the sharp wit of Montesquieu, he was not
of those upon the surface of whose writing no smile appears. He
was contemplative, pure and serene.

["]He came of Norman blood—not a Frenchman, if you will,
but a Northman—the things that make us steady in government
we get from the Normans. The old castle, blown through and
through by air from the North Sea, overlooked the narrow seas
to England. He lived like an English gentleman; he turned the
grounds about Tocqueville into an English park. He brought a
wife out of England and she gave him sympathy in the quiet
soothing way that a wife must give to make it possible for a man
to do what he did. He imbibed the English notion that a man must
take part in public affairs or not do his duty, yet he was not fitted
for public affairs and shrank from the public eye; it was deeply
to his credit that he tried. A public man must do as Lord Salisbury
does, never read the newspapers and not know what is said of
him, or read them and suffer, or read them and not care. De
Tocqueville had too thin a skin, he could not stand the rough
conduct of public life: a man must rough hew a course; he cannot be logical, for affairs are not logical; if he does not get co-
operation, he cannot get leadership.

["]De Tocqueville was an aristocrat; his family suffered in the Revolution, one on the guillotine; his parents were in prison under Robespierre. Tocqueville felt he must serve the country that had given his family only pain and despair; he had the nobility of a man who receives wrong and repays it with service. He witnessed the revolution of 1848, but felt there was nothing genuine in it. He said, 'We Frenchmen are apt to be so theatrical; the people are engaged in trying to re-enact the French Revolution, but I was unable to persuade myself that I or any one was in danger and I returned to the Assembly as to a play; when the armed mob entered the hall the president seemed reduced to fluidity as he slid off the bench.'

["]In 1832 De Tocqueville was appointed with Beaumont to inspect our penitentiary system, which was then regarded as a model for the world, and was adopted in France from their report, but the greatest result of the visit was the work on 'Democracy in America.' It gained for De Tocqueville admission among the 'Forty Immortels.'

["]He happened here in the reign of Andrew Jackson and supposed things were in their normal condition. He did not know that when Jackson stamped his foot and said 'By the Eternal!' he meant his foot to stay down. But though Tocqueville saw the nation in abnormal times he yet understood its essential principles. He did not write his book for us; he wrote it to steady his own countrymen, to make them understand the essentials of democratic government; to show them that if they would have our principles, they must have our character, our conditions, our political intelligence. He knew that France was capable of all that can be accomplished by a single effort, but unable to abide—was swayed by sensation—that general reasoning about mankind would not fit the French.

["]He found there was little independence of opinion in America. He came from a country where all thought differently, and felt it could not succeed as a republic because not enough thought alike. He was surprised to find so much distinguished ability among our people, so little in our rulers. A democracy may render corruption more dangerous than an aristocracy; it is worse to witness immorality that leads to greatness. If we see above us men who inherited wealth and power, whose station we cannot reach, we are not tempted, but if a man understands he can achieve greatness by corruption, how surely is he drawn.["] Mr. Wilson added: "We should be awake every moment to the dangers of corruption; a democracy cannot be led by corrupt men and not suffer. No man dare sleep in vigilance in a democratic country.

["]De Tocqueville had the sagacity to see that our government is one of States, that Congress is only the part that shows. He said 'town meetings are to liberty what primary schools are to science.' They are the places where we learn our mistakes and first lay our minds alongside our fellow citizens' minds. The ability to conduct a meeting by parliamentary procedure seems born in our blood. Tocqueville saw that this knowledge makes a self-governing race. On the adoption of the Constitution in 1789 he said: 'It is a novelty to find a nation that turns a scrutinizing eye upon itself until it finds a remedy and then adopts it without shedding a drop of blood or wringing a tear.'

["]His observations all touch beneath the surface; he was even able to see beneath Andrew Jackson. He saw that the fundamental belief of the race was homogeneous. William of Germany elevates his eagles as the host is elevated. We put the flag on our schoolhouses as an object of worship. If we worship symbols of nationality and forget the living God, if we substitute worship of ourselves, we have lost what the flag stands for."

Printed in the Wilmington, Del., *Every Evening*, Nov. 5, 1897.
1 For this lecture, Wilson used the notes on de Tocqueville described in the Editorial Note, "Wilson's Lectures on Great Leaders of Political Thought," Vol. 9.

To John Percy Nields[1]

My dear Sir,   [Princeton, N. J., c. Nov. 8, 1897]

I have read the papers which you put into my hands last week[2] with astonishment, and, I must add, with not a little amusement. It seems to me a notable case of "much ado about nothing."

I do not remember in what terms I told the anecdote about Judge Story, for I was speaking extemporaneously,[3] but I certainly did not mean to attribute to him any habits that would discredit his memory. I said nothing that might not have been said of half the public men of his generation,—that he drank freely,—and am sure his own generation would not have blamed him for doing what everybody else did. I should be the last man to say anything to discredit Judge Story.

For the sake of historical accuracy I am glad to have been corrected (though I told the anecdote as I had heard it in Washington). As Senator Gray told it, it transfers the point to Judge Marshall, an immeasurably greater man; and I am sure Judge Marshall's friends, knowing the habits of his generation, will not regard his reputation as in the least degree jeopardized by the story.   Very truly yours   [Woodrow Wilson]

Transcript of WWshL (draft) (WP, DLC).
    [1] Lawyer of Wilmington; Harvard '89; Harvard Law School, 1889-90 and 1891-92.
    [2] When Wilson lectured on de Tocqueville before the New-Century Club in Wilmington on November 4.
    [3] When he lectured on Burke before the New-Century Club on October 21.

To James Barr Ames[1]

My dear Sir: [Princeton, N.J.] (8 Nov. 1897)

Mr. John P. Nields of Wilmington has put into my hands a correspondence[2] which fills me with astonishment. He has taken very seriously indeed an anecdote which I told, by the way, in a public lecture. I was speaking extemporaneously; yet must have been more than usually careless in the way I expressed myself if I said anything that could justly offend any friend of Justice Story's. I told nothing that I thought to his discredit, except a freedom in drinking which was common to practically the whole generation of the public men to which he belonged, and I simply told the story as I had heard it in Washington. If it was untrue, I shall of course drop it at once. I am sorry to have given anyone pain by telling it; and nothing could be farther from my thoughts than any detraction of Judge Story.

Very truly yours   [Woodrow Wilson]

Transcript of WWshL (draft) (WP, DLC).
    [1] Dean of the Harvard Law School.
    [2] Including, presumably, correspondence between Nields and Ames about Justice Story.

Notes for a Talk

12 Nov., 1897.

Whig Hall[1]

The life of the University becoming infinitely *diversified—these Halls* must be *the literary centre* of its life.
None but literary men can make a literary centre, either in a Hall or in a class-room. Suppose the professor is the *only* literary man in the room!
How become literary men? By literary associations,—by reading,—reading for companionship. This not to be done in Hall, but out of Hall, by individual reading and by Reading Clubs.
The inducement? (1) The sheer, incomparable pleasure of it.
            (2) The nation's enrichment and advancement, both in action and in expression. The nations that have transmitted their force, the literary nations, which have put their ideals into speech.

WWhw MS. (WP, DLC).

¹ At a business meeting on November 3, 1897, the members of the American Whig Society resolved to hold a special meeting of the Society on November 12 at which new members would be received and several "graduates of Hall" would speak. The meeting of November 12 was addressed by nine speakers, including Robert Bridges and Wilson. "Minutes of the American Whig Society," bound minute book (University Archives, NjP), Nov. 3 and 12, 1897.

To Daniel Coit Gilman

My dear Mr. Gilman,   Princeton, 14 Nov., 1897

I was just about to write to you when your letter of the eleventh reached me,¹ and made necessary a reconsideration of the matter I was about to speak of.

I had carefully thought over my resources for doing what you suggested to me in our chapel on the 22nd of last month, and had come to the conclusion that I could offer you three lectures,— on Burke, Bagehot, and Maine—which I could make very suitable for a Donovan course,² dwelling on these men rather as men of letters than as writers upon politics merely. And I had concluded that I might offer to add Mill to the list, should you prefer four lectures to three. I should have to work these lectures up for the occasion, particularly in the case of Maine and Mill; but I should be quite willing to do that, since you wished it, and since the terms you named would make it worth my while.

I am sorry to say I cannot fall in with the plan Dr. Adams has worked out. I have no course of six lectures that would be at all suitable for the purpose, and it would be quite out of the question for me to prepare such a course in addition to the other work that is pressing upon me. Until you urged the matter upon me last month, I had determined to keep February clear for some literary work I am engaged upon, and it is still my preference to do so. I feel the more constrained, therefore, to say that it will not be possible for me to fall in with this later plan.

Please present my warmest regards to Mrs. Gilman and your daughters, and believe me

Most cordially and faithfully Yours,   Woodrow Wilson

I return the *prospectus* under another cover.

ALS (D. C. Gilman Papers, MdBJ).
¹ It is missing.
² Caroline Donovan had given $100,000 to the Johns Hopkins in 1889 to endow a chair of English literature, but the first incumbent was not chosen until 1905. Meanwhile the income from the fund was used in part from time to time to sponsor short series of lectures on literary subjects.

A Newspaper Report of a Lecture on Walter Bagehot
in Wilmington, Delaware

[Nov. 19, 1897]

NEW-CENTURY CLUB.

. . . Mr. Woodrow Wilson concluded his course of lectures last evening.[1] He said, "One often asks one's self 'why should a man go up and down the world of books and only read of affairs when he might take part and live in the midst of them?' College men must be book men, but they pray not to be book worms—to explore books as if they were the chief end of man, when the chief end ought to be the affairs of the world. But it is worth making a business of books because the past is contained in them. We cannot know the present if we do not know the standards by which men have been guided in the past. A man can see with his own eyes what goes on around him, but cannot get the proper perspective to enable him to understand it without the aid of books in making connections with the great moving powers in history. We can only meet the dead in books; why should we let them pass out of our lives when we can keep their fine flavor. A man writes that what is good in him may live. Emerson says 'We have in books what men have chosen as best to be perpetuated.' Some books might have been written by a dictionary. No man ever liked an abstract thought because it was abstract: he wants a pulse in it.

["]We find a distinctive personal flavor in Charles Lamb, but nowhere can be found so distinctive a personal flavor as in Walter Bagehot. It is a pleasure to introduce anyone to him. We plume ourselves on recognizing English genius before it is recognized at home. When a quick intelligence appears we claim that it is talking to us. Yet we have not discovered Bagehot, although he is well known in England. He did not write for our magazines, nor for those we read. He wrote for a heavy Unitarian journal[2] that must have been given an electric shock by finding such bright wit between its dull pages. The only collected edition of his works is printed by an Accident Insurance company of Hartford.[3] One ought to be obliged to them since one can buy for $5 what would otherwise cost $48. You meet an individual in Bagehot worth going out of the way to find. Some have thought his life could not have been interesting because it was so successful, and it is true some successful people are not interesting. If the critical situations that make life vivid are not outside of you they may be inside.

["]He was born in Somersetshire in 1826. His father was vice-president of a banking company. He married the niece of its founder and stepped into a solid business. Such banking companies in England are the solidest in the world. They stand up alongside of the Bank of England. But his greatest inheritance was his wife [mother] with her quick wit and such a tongue to hand down to her son. She could not go into a company without changing the character of it. She seemed to make it vital and alive. She always said what she thought. This woman, the mother of so remarkable a son, gave him all her brilliant qualities to which was added a little more steadiness from his father. An extremely dull person said of Mrs. Bagehot that she was 'queer,' but after all, craziness is a relative matter. Such craziness as hers is a condition of the minority; the majority of people are dull. She only gave too much rein to her mind. Clever talkers are usually poor writers: they need an audience; some human face to address. Mrs. Bagehot's son had staying qualities; he could keep his thoughts organized: he could deploy bodies of thought and see with a general's eye what the outcome would be. The power to marshal thoughts is power to write. An author must not have separated valuable thoughts, but united ones. This power his father added to what Walter got from his mother, that was why her bright wit was translated on to the page. He meant to be a lawyer, but it was too slow. He married a daughter of John Wilson, who established the London Economist, and succeeded him as editor. He possessed an immense capacity for affairs. Chancellor after chancellor resorted to him to get in touch with the business of the economic world. He was consulted on the great affairs of the nation's politics. He also wrote literary essays. The business and money side of politics is most interesting to an Englishman. It makes a business man uneasy to know that his banker writes essays. Why should he go into literary affairs when he can study the affairs of the market. He wrote about ancient society, but what have we to do with men starting a nation? Had we not better stick to a nation that has come, in business[,] than learn how it got here? But unless we know the past we cannot understand the present. We can get a better knowledge of human nature by reading Shakespeare than by studying business men of to-day. There is a permanence in human nature; men think it would be different to-morrow by reason of some reform they wish to effect, but the change would be all over by to-morrow night. Bagehot found life bigger than the accounts of his bank.

["]He was a good while making up his mind to be married (not after he met Miss Wilson, though). His mother urged him to marry, but he said, "No, a man's mother is his misfortune, but his wife is his fault." When asked what party he belonged to he said he didn't know, he was "between sizes in politics." A large number of men in this country have found themselves between sizes in politics, too. They do not want to be classed under a party name they have always disliked, even if they have found it best to vote with it.

["]Walter Bagehot would study each man he met and prod him on to reveal himself. He used to walk alone, talking to himself. What he thought it worth while to say to himself must have been worth hearing. If asked his opinion on a doubtful question he would say: "My mind is to let on that subject." He quaintly sat apart and listened while the world deployed before him. His essay on "Physics and Politics" is an incomparable guide to point out interesting things. I've often found ideas in what people have written that they have gotten unconsciously from Bagehot. I find I use his thoughts myself. He stripped the English Constitution of its literary theory. Ours needs a like operation. The hardest thing we have to do is to forget the Federalists. We forget that constitutions are living things, vehicles of a life that changes from time to time. Bagehot enables us to understand what the English Constitution is. People thought the government consisted of the Queen and Houses of Parliament. They should substitute the Ministry for the Queen. If a minister is not supported by the House of Commons he must resign. The Queen may be called the sovereign of England, but not its government. Her use in a dignified capacity is incalculable, but only to hold the imagination and veneration of the people, but she has three rights: To be consulted, to encourage and to warn. Having no others she uses these with great effect. She says: 'The responsibility of this measure is upon you: it is my duty not to oppose it, but I warn you that I do not approve.' She is always in office whether a Ministry goes in or out. She will say 'I believe you were in the Ministry in—.' (perhaps mentioning a date before he was born). 'You can try it, but I think it will not succeed.' That is calculated to take the nerve out of a man.

["]Ours has been called an astronomical government, lasting by months and years. In the middle of a term an administration may offend very badly, and if the people remember to the end they can turn it out. The theory is that we are governed by the President, whom we elect, but the truth is that the Speaker rules. The President cannot do what he said he would do unless the Speaker consents to let it be done. The House has tied its hands with rules and has to abide by them. We need men like Bagehot, who thought for himself, who will not hesitate to ask: 'Shall I get my opinion out of the New York "Nation," or make my own, or from an "outlook,"[4] or have an outlook of my own.' "   A. S.

Printed in the Wilmington, Del., *Every Evening*, Nov. 19, 1897.
[1] For this lecture, Wilson used the notes on Bagehot described in the Editorial Note, "Wilson's Lectures on Great Leaders of Political Thought," Vol. 9.
[2] Bagehot did publish some of his early essays in the Unitarian journals, the London *Prospective Review* and the London *Inquirer*, but most of his later work appeared in periodicals such as the London *Economist*, which had no Unitarian connections.
[3] Forrest Morgan (ed.), *The Works of Walter Bagehot with Memoirs by R. H. Hutton* (5 vols., Hartford: Travelers Insurance Company, 1889).
[4] That is, the New York *Outlook*.

To Daniel Coit Gilman

My dear Mr. Gilman,   Princeton, 23rd., Nov., 1897

Your letter of this morning[1] is thoroughly kind and thoroughly like you in its cordiality, but I am sorry to say you did not understand my last note. No doubt I expressed myself obscurely; for I *thought* I was declining!

The fact is, that I have no lecture on Burke or on Bagehot that I would deliver at the Hopkins,—but only University Extension lectures intended for a very different sort of audience; and on Maine I have no lecture at all of any kind. When I saw you in October I understood you to say that, by putting me on the Donovan foundation, you could offer me one hundred dollars a lecture for a course of from two to four (the sum I nowadays get for lectures); and I concluded that I could afford,—at any rate, that I *would* afford,—to prepare lectures on Burke and Bagehot and Maine on those terms. For less I do not think I ought to interrupt the literary work I shall, by February, be deeply absorbed in.

This does not sound as I would like it to sound. It sounds as if the only question with me were a question of money. But I say it without misgivings to you because I know that you know me and will not misunderstand. I am perfectly well aware, and can say without the least affectation, that the lectures would not be worth a hundred dollars apiece to the Hopkins, and that, under the circumstances it would be unwise to pay so much when quite as good lecturers can be had for less. I would not have mentioned the sum had I not understood you to offer it. I now see that I was mistaken as to what you said, or else that it has turned out to be impossible for you to act upon that first suggestion (it was of course in no case a definite or formal offer); and I shall not only not be hurt but my judgment shall wholly approve, if you kindly say nothing more about the matter.

Whether I speak for you or not, I am a loyal Hopkins man, wishing more for her than for myself,—and, in all affection,

Faithfully Yours, Woodrow Wilson

ALS (D. C. Gilman Papers, MdBJ).
¹ It is missing.

From Daniel Coit Gilman

[Dear Professor Wilson:]   [Baltimore] Nov. 28 [1897]

Our D[onovan]. fund can afford to give you $100.00 per lect. for 2 or 3 freshly written lectures on Burke[,] Bagehot & Maine & this I offer you provided we can agree on dates. My other suggestions were based on Dr. A[dams]'s impressions that you had at command some 'ready made['] lectures[.]

Vy scy yrs.   [D. C. Gilman]

Hw draft written on WW to D. C. Gilman, Nov. 23, 1897.

To Daniel Coit Gilman

My dear Mr. Gilman,   Princeton, 29 Nov., 1897

You are very generous, and I appreciate it most heartily. You may count on me for lectures on Burke, Bagehot, and Maine; and you may choose any week for them in February that you prefer,—my only request in the matter being that you put them as *late* as possible, to give me time for preparation,—for the lectures must be as good as I can make them.

I heartily congratulate Baltimore on your appointment on the Commission to draft a charter for the city.¹ I trust you have colleagues who stand somewhere near you in fitting gifts for the work!

With warmest regards,

In haste,   Faithfully Yours,   Woodrow Wilson

ALS (D. C. Gilman Papers, MdBJ).
¹ The commission appointed by the Mayor of Baltimore in November 1897 to draft a new charter for the city included, besides Gilman, such important political and reform leaders as William Pinkney Whyte, Ferdinand C. Latrobe, George Gaither, and Lewis Putzel. Gilman's main contribution to the new charter was to consist of provisions for the reform of the city school system. The charter, enacted by the Maryland legislature in March 1898, greatly improved the efficiency of the government of Baltimore. See James B. Crooks, *Politics & Progress: The Rise of Urban Progressivism in Baltimore, 1895 to 1911* (Baton Rouge, La., 1968), pp. 93-97; and Clayton Colman Hall (ed.), *Baltimore: Its History and Its People* (3 vols., New York, 1912), I, 304-307.

Wilson's New Course Program in Political Science and Jurisprudence

[c. Dec. 1, 1897]

DEPARTMENT OF PHILOSOPHY. . . .

IV. Jurisprudence and Politics.

Professor Wilson.

1 I. Outlines of Jurisprudence: an exposition of Jurisprudence as an organic whole, exhibiting the nature of its subject-matter, its relationship to cognate branches of study, the inter-relationship of its several parts to each other, and their proper function and aim. Lectures and collateral reading. Junior and Senior Elective; first term [2], alternating with course 1 II. Given 1897-98. Professor Wilson. *Pollock*: A First Book of Jurisprudence.[1]

2 I. The elements of Politics: the genesis and action of the body politic; the nature and forms of government; the character and lodgment of sovereignty. Lectures and collateral reading. Junior and Senior Elective; second term [2], alternating with course 2 II. Given 1897-98. Professor Wilson. *J. R. Seeley*: Introduction to Political Science.[2]

1 II. Constitutional Government: its nature, genesis, and operation. Lectures and collateral reading. Junior and Senior Elective; first term [2], alternating with course 1 I. Given 1898-99. Professor Wilson. *E. Boutmy*: Studies in Constitutional Law;[3] and *W. Wilson*: The State.

2 1 [II]. American Constitutional Law. Lectures and collateral reading. Junior and Senior Elective; second term [2], alternating with course 2 I. Given 1898-99. Professor Wilson. *Cooley*: American Constitutional Law;[4] and *A. V. Dicey*: The Law of the Constitution.[5]

3, 4. English Common Law: its genesis, growth, character, and general principles; with a general introduction on European legal history. Lectures and collateral reading. Senior Elective; both terms [2]. Open only to those Seniors who take or have taken course 1 I. [*E. Boutmy*, English Constitution.][6]

Printed in *Catalogue of Princeton University* . . . 1897-98 (Princeton, N.J., n.d.), pp. 38-43; brackets are in the original and denote the number of lectures each week.

[1] Frederick Pollock, *A First Book of Jurisprudence for Students of the Common Law* (London and New York, 1896).

[2] John Robert Seeley, *Introduction to Political Science, Two Series of Lectures* (London and New York, 1896).

[3] Émile Gaston Boutmy, *Studies in Constitutional Law: France—England—United States* (London, 1891).

[4] Thomas McIntyre Cooley, *The General Principles of Constitutional Law in the United States of America*, 2nd edn. (Boston, 1891).

5 Albert Venn Dicey, *Introduction to the Study of the Law of the Constitution*, 5th edn. (London and New York, 1897).

6 Émile Gaston Boutmy, *The English Constitution* (London and New York, 1891).

To the Rector and Board of Visitors
of the University of Virginia

Gentlemen,   Princeton, New Jersey, 5 December, 1897

Having learned that your honourable body is likely to take early action in the matter of filling the vacancy caused by the death of Professor Holmes,[1] I take the liberty to write you in the hope that you may see fit to consider the claims of my friend Professor Richard Heath Dabney to promotion to the full chair of Historical and Political Science.

I have long known Professor Dabney and have long been familiar with his written work,—particularly with his "Causes of the French Revolution"; and I feel for him not only the strong affection springing from an almost life-long friendship, but also the admiration of a fellow-student, who knows the first class quality of his work. I cannot speak of Professor Dabney as a teacher, because I have never had the good fortune to be associated with him in academic work; but I know how well he is spoken of,— and I have no doubt his pupils can give the most unequivocal testimony to his strength in the class-room.

I have the deepest affection for the University of Virginia, as all her sons must have; and I should rejoice to see her advance and reward the sons who have been faithful in her service as they deserve. I know with what zeal and devotion,—I think I know with what scholarship, Professor Dabney has served her,—and I should rejoice to see him rewarded with what I feel sure he has earned.[2]

I am, Gentlemen, with great sincerity and with great respect,

Very truly Yours,   Woodrow Wilson

ALS (R. H. Dabney Papers, ViU).

[1] George Frederick Holmes, Professor of History, Literature, and Political Economy at the University of Virginia, died on November 4, 1897.

[2] Dabney was elected to the Chair of History and Political Economy at the meeting of the Board of Visitors on December 10, 1897.

A News Report

[Dec. 6, 1897]

PRINCETON CLUB OF TRENTON DINE.

The first annual dinner of the Princeton Club of Trenton, was held Thursday evening [December 2]. The dinner was served in the banquet room of the Trenton House, which was handsomely decorated with orange and black streamers. Many prominent alumni were present.

Dr. Charles E. Green, of Trenton, presided, and before the company was seated, "Old Nassau" was sung. Colonel Morris R. Hamilton '39, was cheered as the oldest living graduate.

After dinner, Dr. Green introduced President Patton, of the University, as the first speaker of the evening. Judge Edward G. Bradford, of Yale, was the next speaker, and he was followed by Hon. J. L. Cadwalader, of New York. Then followed speeches by Rev. Wilton Merle Smith, Professor Woodrow Wilson and Professor Andrew F. West.

Printed in the *Daily Princetonian*, Dec. 6, 1897.

To Albert Shaw

My dear Shaw,   Princeton, New Jersey. 6 December, 1897.

No: I had not heard from Mr. Mabie.[1] I am sincerely obliged for the invitation.[2] I esteem it a high compliment and should heartily like to be present. But I have promised to dine that very night with the Quill Club,[3] and the laws of nature prevent my being with the Aldine under the circumstances. It would give me great pleasure to be present and to take part in honouring Dr. Hale, and I wish it were possible; but, under the circumstances, I must send only my hearty regrets, and my warm thanks to you and your committee.[4]

With warm regards,
     As ever
          Cordially and faithfully Yours,   Woodrow Wilson

TCL (in possession of Virginia Shaw English).
   [1] Hamilton Wright Mabie, Associate Editor of the New York *Outlook*.
   [2] From the Aldine Club, 75 Fifth Avenue, New York City, incorporated in 1889 as a club of men, each of whom was "a publisher, author, artist or printer, or who is engaged in the publishing business, or in literature, painting, sculpture, engraving, architecture or music, or who is known to be in sympathy with the objects of the club." Both Shaw and Mabie were members at this time. The Aldine Club merged with the Up Town Association in 1898 to form a luncheon club known as the Aldine Association. See *Club Men of New York, 1898-99* (New York, 1898), p. 5, and *Club Men of New York, 1901-2* (New York, 1901), p. 7.
   [3] On December 14, 1897. See the news report printed at Dec. 15, 1897.
   [4] The Aldine Club held a dinner in honor of Edward Everett Hale on December 14, 1897. The toastmaster was Richard Watson Gilder, and the speakers included Hale himself, William Dean Howells, and Paul Leicester Ford. The report in the *New York Times*, December 15, 1897, noted that "letters of regret" were read from Edmund C. Stedman, Carl Schurz, Seth Low, George F. Hoar, Woodrow Wilson, Daniel C. Gilman, and Francis L. Patton.

From the Minutes of the Princeton Faculty

5 5′ P.M. Wednesday, December 8, 1897

. . . Upon recommendation of the Com. on Discipline it was Resolved That no person hereafter be permitted by the Faculty to lease or occupy a house for the purpose of keeping therein an Eating Club composed either altogether or chiefly of members of the Sophomore Class. . . .

A Diary for 1898

[Dec. 9, 1897-Dec. 28, 1898]

Inscribed (WWhw) on flyleaf: "Woodrow Wilson, 9 December, 1897." Contents:

(a) Entry for Jan. 1, 1898, printed at that date.
(b) "Appointments for the year."
(c) "Estimate of Extra Earnings, 1898."
(d) Calendar for 1898 with reminders of lecture dates.

Bound diary (WP, DLC).

Notes for a Lecture on Patriotism[1]

New York, 10 Dec., 1897.

For City History Club.

PATRIOTISM BEGINS at HOME

There are some words which attract or repel as if they were living things. The word *Liberty* is one of these, and the word *Patriotism* is one.

"The last refuge of scoundrels"? Who shall assess the motive of those who live?

Conceived aright, Patriotism is *not a sentiment,* though it breeds a sentiment. It is an *energy of character* which manifests itself and seeks its object *beyond the circle of self-interest.* It is a sort of thoughtful energy which looks abroad for its satisfaction. We deem it a form of cant to profess it and yet after all seek personal ends. Illustration: *the flag*

Patriotism was *once a simpler thing* with us than it is now: for once the objects of this self-forgetful energy were simple. It requires more and more vision to conceive society as it grows more and more vast, more and more complex and various,—as the very community in which you live semms [seems] by degress [degrees] to grow as complex and various as the nation itself. You cannot see and know your leaders as villagers do; and patriotism has become *harder to see and express in items of conduct.*

Days such as *our "Fathers"* saw were of necessity days of achievement,—days when the very country itself was a-making, and when Nature herself, and every foe to the daring venture, *compelled energy that was more than private* and individual and selfish.

Note the *use of the frontier* to us, and of her colonies to England,—
to satisfy the feet of the young men. The flame of energy spreads
eagerly from outpost to outpost, like a prairie fire.

And so we get our test and standard, and learn how far the *Jingos* are
right,—why sober and enlightened men are drawn on to cheer them:
—shows us where the real source of life lies for the nation, in the
tasks that are comprehended and lend themselves to the rougher
sorts of strength. *Provided we have none but rough and unthought-
ful strength to use!*

Our Tasks, from being obvious and suitable for rough strength, *have
now become delicate*, requiring nicety of thought and a purged
temper, a just self-restraint. We shall get the thoughtful energy we
need only by understanding the task: by deliberately knowing it
and seeing it in its items.

This is the way *all minds take fire*,—upon all subjects,—*by contact* with them.

What, in this case, *will the vision of knowledge* bring us, here, in this
great community, which has not yet awakened to a common consciousness, a common purpose, or even a common thought regarding its tasks or its destiny?

Did you never reflect *what sort of an order this is* under which we live?
An order based upon a common understanding, a common intelligence, a common morality. We are self-governed or else self-dis-
ordered.

Tocqueville saw even in his simpler day that institutions complex and delicate as ours required an extraordinary *"variety of information and excellence of discretion"* on the part of the people,—
that it presupposed information and capacity of quite unp[r]ece-
dented compass and flexibility.

Moreover, *the test of this policy is Patience*: patience that knows and
steadily pursues what it desires,—*that* distinctly *plans what to wait
for*. A patient perseverence in details.

Can you deliberately breed a motive? Certainly: by deliberately *breeding an interest*,—if in yourself, why then a selfish motive,—if in
your community, why then a patriotic motive.

Understand the conditions, then. *You cannot touch the life of the
nation directly*. We must touch and move it indirectly, by thought
and motive where we are. Hence local study and intensive effort.

This community will never awake to its own betterment and salvation
through any abstract motive of duty, but only through a concrete
image of its own life and interests:—through a sort of ardent and
enduring self-consciousness.

Take examples: take *Boston, Glasgow*. You shall find a pride in
the past, a consciousness of eclat, a desire for self-development.

Hope for these things comes to us through the *revival of historical interest* in our day,—with its vivid imaginative reconstitution of the
past.

Hope comes *also* with *the necessity to stay where we are* and spend
our lives in a single community, alongside old neighbours,—a necessity which has come with the filling in of the free lands of the West.

You cannot build a national system of thought or motive unless you
first get your local foothold. Let us address our spirits to the task:
and first of all *let us see and love our nearest duty*.[2]

WWT MS. (WP, DLC).
1 See the following document for a news report of this lecture.
2 There is a WWhw outline of these notes in WP, DLC.

A News Report of a Lecture

[Dec. 11, 1897]

WHAT PATRIOTISM MEANS

Under the auspices of the City History Club, Prof. Woodrow Wilson of Princeton University delivered a lecture on "Patriotism Begins at Home" at Sherry's, Thirty-seventh Street and Fifth Avenue, last evening.

The club, which was founded in 1895, with Mrs. Robert Abbe as President, has for its object the formation of popular classes for the study of the history of the City of New York, in the hope of awakening such an interest in its traditions, and in the possibilities of the future as shall tend to civic betterment. The lecture last night was intended as a contribution along this line, and it brought together a brilliant and fashionable company.

Prof. Wilson was introduced by James W. Alexander. Patriotism, he said, was not a sentiment; it bred sentiment. It was, rather, a sort of energy of character which expressed itself outside the narrow circle of selfish interests. It was not blind loyalty to the flag, for on that flag was written more than loyalty; there was written resolution. The springs of patriotism were in character—instructed, chastened, purified, unselfish character. As the community became more complex, patriotism became more difficult. In the early days of this country it consisted chiefly in securing a foothold. Now tasks of nicety were substituted for feats of strength.

The speaker contrasted the patriotism of the soldier, which, he said, was largely a sentiment, with the patriotism of the citizen. It was easy to recruit armies with a sentiment, he declared, and, speaking as a Southern man, he added:

"One-third of the armies of the Confederacy could not have given a reasonable explanation of what they were fighting for. They knew somebody had insulted somebody they cared for, and that was enough.

"The true patriot," said the professor, "must have the critical frame of mind. He must be willing to part company with his best friend, if necessary. Patriotism is a thing to con and study. If you are not studious you cannot be usefully patriotic. You must study your fellow-men honestly and laboriously, yet we see men fling themselves out of politics because the toilets of the men they meet in a party caucus displease them.

"You must remember that the trained minds of a democratic community do not set the running for that community. A company like this, for instance, of trained minds and interchangeable ideas, is in no sense representative of the community, because the masses of men act from preconceived notions and are predisposed to reject new ideas.

"To be patriotic, you must understand the common people, but the common people are no one thing. There is no common pattern or mold for men of the unthinking classes. You need infinite agility of mind to conceive your fellow-citizens in terms of fact. Yet how are you to help them if you do not so know them? The polity we live under is based on a common understanding. Yet I doubt if you have a common understanding with your fellow-citizens. You confess that you have not when you express surprise at the result of an election in your own city."

Answering the question, "Why does patriotism begin at home?" Prof. Wilson said: "Because a man cannot understand a whole unless he understands the part. You cannot be patriotic at long range. Unless you set the air about you aglow with the heat and virtue of your action, you cannot expect to have it reach the outer world. Another reason is that no man can understand all the parts of this great Nation, whereas he can measurably know his own people and his own neighbors, their antecedents, and their history.

"The first thing to do, if you are going to be patriotic, is to get a firm foothold where you are. If in the midst of your own community you take pains to understand and advance its interests, you are fulfilling the duties of a patriot.

"Now, ladies and gentlemen," said Prof. Wilson, in conclusion, "I have been saying one thing throughout this whole lecture, and that is, you must love because you understand, and seek to help because you have studied, your own people."[1]

Printed in the *New York Times*, Dec. 11, 1897; some editorial headings omitted.
[1] For one listener's recollection of comments on this lecture, see B. N. Harrison to WW, Feb. 3, 1900, printed as an Enclosure with WW to EAW, Feb. 5, 1900, Vol. 11.

From the Minutes of the Princeton Faculty

8 P.M., Monday, December 13th, 1897.

A special Meeting of the Faculty was held at the call of the President.

The Dean reported that much damage had been done to the Gymnasium by the Senior Class at their Class Meeting on the night of Friday, 9th inst. . . .

The Treasurer of the College was present and presented an estimate of the sum necessary to repair the damages to the Gymnasium and also read the written promise to secure the University against loss which had been given by Messrs. Loofbourrow & Dripps,[1] respectively President and Secretary of the Class.

After full discussion and careful consideration it was Resolved that the Treasurer be requested to present the bill for damages done to the Gymnasium by the Class of 1898 at their recent meeting to Messrs. Loofbourrow and Dripps, and to inform them that payment must be made by January 15th, 1898. . . .

Resolved That a Committee be appointed to consider the question of the manner of conducting the Senior Class Elections hereafter.

The Dean and Professors Wilson, West, Winans, Fine and Cornwall were appointed the Committee.[2]

The question as to whether any additional penalty shall be imposed upon the Senior Class for their recent misconduct at their Class Meeting in the Gymnasium be referred to the same Committee.

[1] Milton Floyd Loofbourrow and Robert Dunning Dripps.
[2] For the committee's report, see the Princeton Faculty Minutes printed at Dec. 22, 1897.

Notes for an Address on Patriotism[1]

14 December, 1897

"*Quill Club*," N.Y.

"PATRIOTISM IN TIME OF PEACE,"
Or, "The Duty of LIVING for One's Country."[2]

I take it as *a subtle compliment* that you should have taken it for granted that I would maintain this thesis against the Jingoistic sentiment of the day.

But let us do the Jingos justice: they speak that *spirit of the frontier* that has so far had the chief part in the making of the country. *Our protest* means this, we must have *an equal mastery in the tasks of peace,—the spiritual aggrandizement of the country.*

Consider the nature of the polity,—the self-poised polity,—under which we live,—*the nature of Liberty* in a country with institutions such as ours. = "*Americanism?*"

What sort of men ought we to be under such a polity? Observe that *it is preëminently an intellectual and a debating polity.*

We should *understand and be ready to demonstrate. We should,
therefore, be*
    Studious of the life of the *nation,*—and *community.*
        "   "   " conditions of practical success in politics.
    Fearless in criticism,—fearful of radical change.
    Partisans of the right.
    Unclouded by books,—unduped by men.
    Lovers and followers of good men.

WWhw MS. (WP, DLC).
  ¹ See the following document for a news report of this lecture.
  ² A printed title, which Wilson pasted on his notes.

A News Report of an Address

[Dec. 15, 1897]

PATRIOTISM IN PEACE.

There was a large attendance at the sixty-third regular meeting
and dinner of the Quill Club of New York at the Windsor Hotel
last evening. J. Cleveland Cady presided. The topic was "Patriotism in Time of Peace; or, the Duty of Living for One's Country,"
and the speaker was Prof. Woodrow Wilson of Princeton University.

Prof. Wilson said he spoke of patriotism with diffidence. It is
better for a man to pray that he may act with patriotism when
the occasion arises than to say that he will. Prof. Wilson said he
spoke from the standpoint of an anti-jingo, though he was ready
to admit that the jingo might have his uses; to shake us out of
a too comfortable lethargy.

"Material aggrandizement," he said, "is not worth having unless
we have the proper spiritual accomplishments. How are we to
get the proper spirit? By knowing more of each other. There is a
lamentable mutual ignorance between the various sections of the
country. They have not yet a common interest. Our policy rests
upon a common knowledge, a mutual understanding; it presup-
poses a comradeship of thought. You must be comrades in this
country with men wholly unlike yourselves. If you cannot do that
you must give the task up.

"Who shall show us the silent, invisible hosts that gather
within the country to threaten it, the enemies that are worthy of
our metal? The most of our fellow-citizens do not stand on an
elevation whence they can see. I am afraid of no one so much
as the good man who is wrong. Multitudes will follow him to the
death, even though he lead the country to destruction. I would
prefer that all wrong men were knaves. Let no man suppose that
peoples live by logic, by ratiocination, for they do not. We must

study the self-poised policy. Self-possession is the highest mark of political capacity.

"Unless the thoughts of this Nation run a common course, the affairs of this Nation cannot run a common course. It is a good thing for the academic man to go abroad and mix with the men who do not believe a word he says. The college classroom is no place to get the final word on any subject. It is a fighting thing to belong to a democracy. What is liberty—political liberty? It is the right to do what anybody else in the community can do, without having any arbitrary distinctions. It is the assurance that a man will be treated exactly as everybody else is treated. It is being on parole.

"There is that word 'American' that we have thrust down our throats, though no one has yet told us what it is. Some say it is un-American to criticize one's country. That nation is safe that will see its own faults and has the courage and patience to correct them. Not all at once, not by revolution, but one at a time."

Prof. Wilson concluded by advising his hearers to be unclouded by books and not duped by men, and to be lovers and followers of good men—good men and true. . . .

Printed in the *New York Times*, Dec. 15, 1897; one editorial heading omitted.

To Richard Watson Gilder

Princeton, New Jersey,
My dear Mr. Gilder,   22 December, 1897.

Pardon my delay in replying to your question of the seventeenth. A rush of imperative engagements has made it impossible for me to attend properly to my correspondence, and it has fallen sadly into arrears.

I am afraid that the Franklin is as impossible as the Cromwell. I declined the latter, not because it was not deeply interesting and attractive, but simply for lack of time. It would be, for me, more interesting to write about Cromwell than to write about Franklin; but I cannot write about anybody in the way you suggest at present. That is the whole matter.

As for the "Home Patriotism,"[1] that is gone beyond recall (peace to its memory!). I have no one to dictate to, no experience in dictating, and no knack at recollecting what I said on any special occasion, which itself suggested what I said. To send you an essay on the subject would be to write an entirely different thing; and the lectures on Burke and the rest for the Johns Hopkins must take precedence of everything else now. I am not in any sense a ready writer. Things come by great deliberation to me.

You must not think, therefore, that I do not attach enough importance to what you suggest. I am pleased away down to the bottom that you should want these things; but I know by what economy and by what concentration of effort I must rule myself, and try to resist all temptation.

With warmest regard and appreciation,

Faithfully Yours,   Woodrow Wilson

WWTLS (WC, NjP).

[1] He refers to his address, "Patriotism Begins at Home."

From the Minutes of the Princeton Faculty

12 33′ P.M., Wednesday, Dec. 22, 1897.

The Faculty met, the Dean presiding in the absence of the President.

The Committee on Discipline made a report and upon its recommendation it was

Resolved That the Father of Mr. —— (So. C.) be informed that for participation in hazing and neglect of study he cannot be allowed to return to the University after the vacation and that he must be withdrawn from the University.

On recommendation of the Committee on Discipline it was Resolved That —— (Sci. Sp.) and —— (J. C. Sc. Sci.) for connection with disorderly conduct in forcing entrance into the room of a fellow-student be suspended from the University until January 15th, 1898.

Also Resolved That Mr. —— (S. C., Sc. Sci.) for participation in the maltreatment of a fellow student be suspended from the University until March 1st, 1898.

Also Resolved That the Father of Mr. —— (J. C. Sc. Sci.) be informed that his son must be withdrawn from the University for forcing entrance into the room of a fellow-student and maltreating him.

The Committee on Senior Elections reported the following Resolutions which were adopted: viz.,

Senior Class Elections.

Resolved, That hereafter no meeting of the Senior Class for the transaction of business connected with the Election of Class Officers be allowed to take place in the evening.

Resolved, That the actual Election of Class Officers in Class Meeting be forbidden, and that the Class be requested to adopt some method of balloting which will avoid the necessity of Class Meetings for that purpose.

Resolved, That the Committee be authorized to hold a conference with the present Junior Class with regard to the adoption of a convenient system of election. . . .

From Wilson's Diary for 1897

Monday, December 27, 1897
Started for St. Louis, leaving Princeton 9:38 A.M., Phila., 12.20.

An Outline of an Address[1]

St. Louis 29 Dec. '97
The College Man and Society.

College = a place from which to look around.
   "   "   "   "   "   " forward
  " " where to take stock of what has been done, and *forecast* what may be done.

Not, primarily, a place of immediate preparation for the practical tasks of business.

A place, rather, for *detached* thought. Thought nowadays suffers from a too narrow attachment to particular interests.

The college man ought to be the purveyor of thoughts to the community

Not thoughts of Utopia,—but

Thoughts of life and achievement,—whether in the sphere of matter or in the sphere of spirit.

And so furnish *yeast* for Society

That's the argument: Keep Society full of *wholesome* yeast.

A university not the cloistered place it once was,—but a place of quick and eager ferment,—only *free* and apart,—not in the midst of 'interests.'

Chapman's notion (January *Atlantic*, 1898) of a new *Middle Age*,[2]— and the function of the college in it? Cannot be the same function that the *old* Schoolmen performed.

The college keeps even practical ideals in heart nowadays,— e.g., foot-ball: the ideal of self-mastery and battle,—for those who are battle-stuff.

The college should be the source of *reasoned conviction* for a doubting age.

(*a*) Colleges of belief,—albeit not sectarian,
(*β*)   "   " doubt.

Which can serve the age best in its present temper.
Which will quicken a strong generation?
Which will give America intellectual primacy?

"Smoker" at St. Louis University Club

WWhw MS. (WP, DLC).
    [1] Two news reports of this affair are printed at Dec. 30, 1897.
    [2] Henry G. Chapman, "Belated Feudalism in America. II," *Atlantic Monthly*, LXXXI (Jan. 1898), 41-50.

From Wilson's Diary for 1897

Thursday, December 30, 1897

Lunched again at Noonday Club, with pretty much the same company as yesterday,—with the notable addition of Mr. Henry Hitchcock.[1]

Drove after luncheon with Mr. [blank]

Dined with the Princeton Club of St. Louis.

    [1] Distinguished St. Louis lawyer, defender of the Union during the Civil War, organizer and first dean of the Washington University Law School, author, and President of the American Bar Association, 1889-90.

Four News Reports of a Visit to St. Louis

[Dec. 30, 1897]

PROF. WILSON THE GUEST OF HONOR AT A LUNCHEON.

A very enjoyable luncheon was given yesterday at the Noonday Club rooms, at which James L. Blair was the host and Prof. Woodrow Wilson, who occupies the chair of jurisprudence at Princeton College, was the guest of honor. There were also present John D. Davis, Henry T. Kent, Col. James O. Broadhead, James A. Seddon, Capt. Henry King, Fielding Oliver, Thomas S. McPheeters and Edward Cunningham, junior.

The luncheon began at 1 o'clock, and was served in a private dining room. The table was tastefully decorated with cut flowers. When the coffee and cigars had been served the company sat for some time exchanging stories, which were more frequently of college life than of later experience. The luncheon was ended at 3 o'clock, and the guests dispersed.

Prof. Wilson arrived in St. Louis Tuesday [December 28], and came to attend the banquet to be given by the Princeton Alumni Association. He is stopping with John D. Davis.[1] Prof. Wilson is comparatively a young man, but has attained quite a reputation as an authority upon constitutional law. He has written a number of books, among which is a life of Washington. The men who were entertained at luncheon with him yesterday were not all Princeton men, but were all college men.

Printed in the *St. Louis Globe-Democrat*, Dec. 30, 1897; one editorial heading omitted.
    [1] John David Davis, Princeton, 1872, a lawyer of St. Louis.

[Dec. 30, 1897]

PROF. WILSON'S VISIT.

Reception at the University Club—
To-Night's Princeton Club Dinner.

Prof. Woodrow Wilson of Princeton University is receiving the cordial hospitalities of the Princeton men and their friends. His first day in St. Louis closed with a reception at the University Club last night. The reception was attended by many of the members. Prof. Wilson gave an informal talk on the general subject of the part the colleges and the collegions should fill in society. He urged an active, efficient interest in public affairs. He said that educated men were needed to give intelligent direction to the forces of society and to reformatory movements. They should keep in touch with public sentiment and public needs and should contribute to the work of molding the changing forms of laws.

Prof. Wilson made a strong plea for freedom of opinion and speech in the universities and for the teaching of truth regardless of consequences. He criticised the timidity of men with regard to their convictions and to the defense of truth. He believed that the way to combat error was not by persecution or the arbitrary exercise of power, but by meeting it with truth.

Incidentally he defended athletics in colleges as a means of developing manly qualities. He wanted to see the fighting spirit kept alive, not to engage in senseless and wrongful wars, but to combat injustice and to fight when there was something worth while to fight for.

To-night Prof. Wilson will be given a dinner by the Princeton Club of St. Louis at the St. Louis Club. The list of Princeton graduates who have signified their intention to be present indicates that it will be the largest reunion that has ever been held by the Princeton Club. Besides the alumni, the dinner will be attended by twenty-five undergraduates of St. Louis, who will contribute the latest Princeton songs and yells to the after-dinner jollities.

Printed in the *St. Louis Post-Dispatch*, Dec. 30, 1897.

[Dec. 30, 1897]

PROF. WILSON'S RECEPTION AT THE UNIVERSITY CLUB ...

Prof. Woodward Wilson, noted professor of jurisprudence in Princeton University and lecturer on political economy in Johns Hopkins, is in St. Louis, the guest of the Princeton alumni. He arrived yesterday morning[1] and was entertained at luncheon at the Noonday Club by James L. Blair. Among those who met him here were Captain King, Chancellor Chapman [Chaplin], Major Cunningham, Henry T. Kent, Colonel James O. Broadhead and T. S. McPheeters.

He was tendered a reception last night at the University Club, and after an hour of conversation he was introduced by B. B. Graham, the president of the club. His address was a short one, in which he spoke of the college man and society. He took the stand that the college man should not be isolated.

The college of to-day is not the cloistered place that it once was; it is a place in which to look forward and around and the graduate should be a purveyor of thought in the community. The college is a place to furnish yeast for society, and society should be kept full of yeast, so the college should be a place of quick and eager ferment.

He expressed himself as in favor of athletics. He did not believe that a college man should be enabled to enter the world and battle for his livelihood as well, if not better, than the man without the advantages of an education, and he should not be looked upon as a man incapable of fighting his way with the rest because of his collegiate education.

The address was frequently interrupted with applause. . . .

During his brief sojourn in St. Louis Prof. Wilson has become favorably impressed with the city's far-famed reputation for hospitality. Clubs have invited him to be present at feasts prepared in his honor; lawyers have sought to do the social graces in welcome of the distinguished guest. It could be said with truth that nearly every minute of the day is taken up with some social function. Friends of old college days insist upon making it pleasant for him, and the noted visitor finds in such hearty reception a memory of his hospitable native State, Virginia.

While the honored guest of the city and the Princeton Club, he is the especial guest of John D. Davis of Vandeventer place. He and Mr. Davis are friends of long standing. Both affectionately refer to Princeton as Alma Mater. Yesterday Mr. Davis and James L. Blair, president of the Princeton Club, showed Prof. Wilson the city. Prof. Wilson's visit to the city was occasioned by a pressing invitation to be present at the banquet of that organization.

"I had heard of St. Louis hospitality," remarked the professor yesterday, "and the warmth and grace of the welcome that greeted me explained why the city's reputation in that respect was not only national but international.

"We have 25 students from St. Louis this year, and the institution is growing in favor with the people of this community every year. Meeting so many old college friends is a refreshment akin to the pleasure of a general alumni meeting of tried and true friends.["]

Prof. Wilson is in the prime of life, having celebrated his forty-first birthday Tuesday. He looks younger. No one would take him for 35. As an essayist, a writer upon legal, historical and political subjects he has a reputation as wide as the country. In the domain of treatises upon jurisprudence he ranks among the most eminent of the continent. His "Life of Washington" attracted much attention and favorable comment from the critics. He has prepared a text book, "The State," which is used at Harvard and Yale. Besides contributing thoughtful and interesting articles to the magazines, he lectures at the Johns Hopkins University and the New York Law School.

Prof. Wilson was graduated from Princeton. He belongs to the class of '79. He studied law at the University of Virginia and took a post graduate course at the Johns Hopkins University, and for awhile practiced law at Atlanta, Ga. He soon gave up the practice of the profession and accepted a chair at the Wesslian [Wesleyan] College in Connecticut. From there he was called to the chair of jurisprudence at Princeton.

Printed in the *St. Louis Republic*, Dec. 30, 1897.
1 Actually, on the morning of December 28.

[Dec. 31, 1897]

PRINCETON CLUB'S TWENTY-THIRD
ANNUAL DINNER.

Prof. Woodrow Wilson the Guest of Honor
at the St. Louis Club.

The twenty-third annual dinner of the Princeton Club of St. Louis was held last night in the palatial dining-room of the St. Louis Club. The dinner was given in honor of Prof. Woodrow Wilson, Ph.D., LL.D., who is at present visiting in St. Louis as the guest of the Princeton alumni. Nearly half a hundred members of the alumni were seated around the festal board in addition to seventeen undergraduates of that noted institution. An excellent menu was served.

The banquet was attended exclusively by Princeton men, and the central figure of the evening was, of course, Prof. Wilson. He is a man who would command attention in any place. His features are strong and at the same time classic and his mode of delivery is clear, deliberate and distinct. He also possesses the remarkable faculty of knowing when he has said just enough to suit the occasion, a faculty so painfully lacking in so many after-dinner speakers of the present day. Prof. Wilson's address last night consumed less than a half an hour's time, but in that period he had treated of his subject in a thorough manner. . . .

Prof. Wilson said that when he read on the menu card that the banquet was complimentary to him, he felt that he had attained a certain giddy eminence. It reminded him, he said, of the young man who had succeeded in becoming elected to the Legislature from an obscure county and immediately became a candidate for the speakership of that body. Some of his fellow-members concluded that it would be a good joke to put him in the Speaker's chair, and afterwards take him away from there. A committee, appointed for the purpose, escorted the young member to the chair, whereupon the latter thanked them for the honor and expressed a hope that they would continue to approach with their usual familiarity.

He was pleased with the reception that had been accorded him. He compared his position to that of a young man who visited Princeton in 1877, and was royally treated one night. So much so, in fact, that when he stepped off the ferry in New York on his return he remarked he was glad "that it was cold or he wouldn't keep." But he felt at home, as he was in the presence of Princeton men, and could speak his own mind. The poet had said that "heaven lies about us in our infancy," and a wag added that he [we] could lie about ourselves in our old age. So, he said, we can freely talk among ourselves.

Princeton was not a young college. When a college reaches a certain age, it can congratulate itself on having attained a certain standard. It was not young and did not have a job lot of professors, like the university at Chicago. There was a certain impulse about an old college for which nothing can be substituted. One of the oldest functions of a college was to act as an organ of memory for the community. The organ of recollection was the organ of identity, and the organ of identity was the organ of power. So you feel that the power of an old institution like this was immense. It dealt in an impalpable stock, which made a nation rich from generation to generation.

The speaker compared private institutions, such as Princeton is, to State institutions. The State institution depended upon the inexhaustible supply of taxation, but the private institution was different. Consequently, the State institutions produced the average voter, but those from the private institutions were the more cultured, something that is absolutely necessary in a certain portion, at least. A private institution consequently was infinitely to be preferred. Princeton had distinctive ideals. Her beautiful type of architecture, he said, was one of them. True, science of law and literature could be found at Princeton. The science of the age was cosmopolitan, has no home, no parallels of latitude. If you want a national university, you should build it out of nationality. Science has no nationality. If a university was to breathe a national spirit, it must breathe a spirit of history and literature.

At the conclusion of Prof. Wilson's address a number of Princeton songs were sung by the guests.

Printed in the *St. Louis Republic*, Dec. 31, 1897; some editorial headings omitted.

From Wilson's Diary for 1897

Friday, December 31, 1897

Started for home at 8 o'clock.

From Wilson's Diary for 1898

January 1, 1898

Reached home from St. Louis, middle of the afternoon. Found Madge,[1] Mary and Florence Hoyt.

[1] His sister-in-law, Margaret Axson.

To Charles Greene Rockwood, Jr.

My dear Sir,   Princeton, 6 Jan'y 1898

Allow me to thank you for your note of today informing me of my election as a resident member of the Nassau Club.

I accept the election with pleasure and appreciation.

Very truly Yours,   Woodrow Wilson

ALS (Nassau Club, Princeton, N.J.).

From Charles Dudley Warner

My dear Mr Wilson   New York, January 6th, 1898

Perhaps you are familiar with the edition of the *American Men of Letters* which I am editing, and which is published by

Messrs Houghton, Mifflin and Company. It has been somewhat difficult for me to find writers, in this series, who have the requisite knowledge of the times and of the authors included in the series, and at the same time the literary touch necessary for these brief biographies. They are really long biographical essays, in which the man's life is sufficiently told, and his works dwelt upon, together with a certain estimate conveyed in this process of the man's rank and value as a man of letters.

The compensation in this series has so far been the ordinary ten per cent., and of course that pay is not magnificent, but the series has a constant sale for libraries and otherwise, and no doubt this sale will have a long life. Going into this series is not taking the risk of an isolated book.

I wish very much to have your help in this, and to offer you the life of Francis Parkman. I do this with a great deal of confidence, because I have such a high idea of your sense of historic perspective, and knowledge of the field which Parkman covers. In my judgment he is quite at the head of American historians, both in his style and the grasp of his subject; and I could not offer you, it seems to me, a more attractive subject than Parkman.

If you are willing to consider this, I should like to hear from you at your earliest convenience.

Yours sincerely   Chas. Dudley Warner

TLS (WP, DLC).

To John Forrest Dillon[1]

My dear Sir,   Princeton, New Jersey, 10 January, 1898.

I take real pleasure in commending to you my young friend Mr. Alfred Hayes, Jr.[2] Mr. Hayes studied general Jurisprudence under me for two years, and I can say without hesitation that I never had a more satisfactory pupil. His work was more than intelligent; it was spirited and thoughtful, besides being thorough. I feel sure that he would prove a most valuable associate in any office; and I hope that it will be possible for you to find a place for him in your business. He needs but a little addition of practice to theory to make him a thorough-going lawyer. He may confidently be counted on to keep his study of the law abreast of his practice in it, and more.

With much regard,
Very sincerely yours,   Woodrow Wilson

TCL (RSB Coll., DLC).
[1] New York corporation lawyer and legal scholar.
[2] Princeton, 1895; LL.B., Columbia, 1898. Hayes apparently did not obtain a position in Dillon's office.

To Charles Dudley Warner

My dear Mr. Warner,

Princeton, New Jersey
12 January, 1898

You have offered me an extremely attractive piece of work in asking me to write a life of Parkman for the American Men of Letters series, and you have in the mere offer paid me a compliment which I deeply appreciate. I think as you do of Parkman's work and rank among historians, and it would be a veritable privilege to speak at length of so beautiful and devoted a life. It has been very hard for me to make up my mind that I could not do it.

But a very little reflection has shown me that I *must* decline. I have work in hand to which I am every way pledged and which must take, at the least, four or five years in the doing,—besides a textbook promised which must serve as a sort of preliminary sketch and study in proportions. Practically all of my work so far,—with the exception of the little volume I published first of all,—has been in the nature of by-products. I believe I have something better in me, and that it is high time I got it out. I owe it to myself to decline even what I should so much like to do.

With warmest regards and heartiest thanks,

Most sincerely Yours,   Woodrow Wilson

TCL (RSB Coll., DLC).

Notes for an Address in New York on Patriotism[1]

16 Jan'y, 1898.

Religion and *Patriotism*: Patriotism the Duty of Religious Men.

Make a duty of a Sentiment?

This, a sentiment based on principle, a principle of *service*. A sentiment of *devotion*

Devotion has definite duties, based upon the *nature of its object*.

The object of patriotic devotion is the community, the country, the nation.

Is all so-called patriotism suitable to the country as it is,—so situated, so governed?

Serve the country as you would serve your *friend*.

The object of national, even more than of individual, life, is character. The nation has *only this world*.

National character a means to individual character, as to individual fortunes

A religious man turns from his duty when he turns from public duty and endeavour. He is neglecting the means of moralization.

Means going into politics? Politics does not mean *office*,–and even office does not mean cynicism for the Christian. Only that dirt stains that sticks.

Means also going in for all the endeavours of communal life. It means *translating principle into social action*.

WWhw MS. (WP, DLC).
1 See the following document for a news report of this address.

A Newspaper Report of an Address

[Jan. 17, 1898]

SERVICE FOR STUDENTS.

A special service for students and college men was held last night, with the co-operation of the Students' Club, in Calvary Episcopal Church, at Fourth-ave. and Twenty-first-st. It was largely attended, the body of the church being filled by men. Addresses were made by President Franklin Carter of Williams College, who spoke on "Patriotism and the Republic"; by Professor Woodrow Wilson, of Princeton University, who spoke on "Patriotism the Duty of Religious Men," and by Bishop Potter,[1] whose theme was "Religious Men the Best Patriots." President Charles Cuthbert Hall of Union Theological Seminary read the lesson. . . .

Professor Wilson said in part: "Patriotism, as the duty of a religious man, is not a sentiment, but a devotion of his time and service to the object of his love—his country. It is not an expression of words, but an act. Don't be afraid to go into politics, which does not necessarily mean into office. You may go into politics and you may stay in without receiving the least suspicion of stain; and if office comes to you honorably you may occupy it also without stain. For, observe that a man is not stained by handling the vilest thing in the world: the skin only may be stained, and from that the apparent stain may be purged. Don't be afraid to handle dirt, if only you can work it to your good purpose. Socialize your religious motives in working for your country; then patriotism will not have to be hastened by speeches.

"I have confidence, for my own part, in the future of our country. I do not believe our Republic will be lacking in the proper amount of stuff in the time of trial; it is the light-headed who do the greatest amount of talking, and, paradoxical as it may sound, we may best open our ear to the man who is not talking. . . ."

Printed in the *New-York Tribune*, Jan. 17, 1898; one editorial heading omitted.
1 Henry Codman Potter, Bishop of the Protestant Episcopal Diocese of New York.

Two Reports of an Address at Oberlin, Ohio

[Jan. 18, 1898]

"DEMOCRACY."

Professor Woodrow Wilson, of Princeton, Lectures in the U. L. A. Course.

The third U. L. A.[1] lecture of the year was given at the First Church last Friday evening [January 14] by Prof. Woodrow Wilson, of Princeton University. His subject was "Democracy." It was not a "popular" lecture in the sense in which the term is ordinarily used. It was scholarly and eloquent; in it was gathered the ripe fruitage of Prof. Wilson's years of research in the science of politics. It was an intellectual treat for those who have made the science a subject of careful thought or special study; and for all who heard it with attention—and those who did not, heard it to little purpose—it was replete with interest. The fault of the lecture, if it may be called a fault, was that the matter of it was too vast to be gathered into the mind of a person of ordinary mental capacity, in one brief evening. Its content would furnish the backbone for many heavy books on political philosophy; and, possibly, there were others besides the NEWS man who found themselves at the close of the lecture with pronounced symptoms of mental dyspepsia. . . .[2]

Printed in the *Oberlin News*, Jan. 18, 1898.
[1] The Undergraduate Lecture Association.
[2] Here follows a long summary of "Democracy," printed at Dec. 5, 1891, Vol. 7.

[Jan. 19, 1898]

WOODROW WILSON ON "DEMOCRACY."

Oberlin audiences are accustomed to meet distinguished men. But it is seldom that they listen to one more eminent in his chosen field than Professor Woodrow Wilson. As a master of history and political science much was anticipated from him in his lecture on "Democracy." Much was realized.

His impressive manner, his pleasing voice and the conviction that he had something to impart caused the closest attention on the part of his hearers. Indeed, close attention was necessary for a satisfactory comprehension of the argument. For, although the diction was clear and forceful, the progress slow and the exemplification abundant, the lecture was so abstract in its character and withal so suggestive that it required a continual application of the mind.

For students of political science it had great interest. As a popular lecture it was somewhat heavy, even for an Oberlin audience. It would be more satisfactory to read it, with opportunity for reflection, than it was to hear it from a lecture platform. But while it might not be called an entertaining lecture, it was certainly scholarly. It awakened the mind to new conceptions of the actual structure and workings of our government, and brought its citizens to a greater realizing sense of their duty and opportunity. . . .[1]

Printed in the *Oberlin Review*, xxv (Jan. 19, 1898), 247-48.
  [1] Here follows a brief summary of "Democracy."

To George Chase[1]

                                              Princeton, New Jersey,
My dear Professor Chase,   20th. January, 1898.

Allow me to thank you for the cheque for three hundred dollars, and to hand you, herewith, the receipt.

I think I ought, in acknowledging the completion of this business transaction, to say that I fear this must be my last year of lectures with you. I am well aware that I am laying myself open to the response of the nursery song: "Nobody asked you to, Sir, she said"; but there has been so far a sort of tacit continuance of the arrangement from year to year, and I think I ought to let you know at once what to expect.

The simple fact is, of course, that the arrangement long since ceased to be pecuniarily advantageous to me. For a year or two past I have continued it, however, out of a genuine interest in the school. That interest is not abated a jot; but my engagements have greatly multiplied, and I feel as if I could no longer spare the time and the energy.

I need not say how I regret to break a connection which has been in every way so agreeable to me. I am sure you will appreciate my action at its true meaning.

With warmest regard and appreciation, and with the best possible wishes for the continued prosperity of the School, which so richly deserves it,

                    Very sincerely Yours,   Woodrow Wilson

WWTLS (RSB Coll., DLC).
  [1] Dean of the New York Law School, where Wilson had delivered an annual series of lectures on constitutional law since 1892. See the Editorial Note, "Wilson's Lectures at the New York Law School," Vol. 7.

A News Report

[Jan. 21, 1898]

PROF. WILSON'S LECTURE.

The Second of a Series Given in the
University Place Church.

The second of a course of three lectures for the benefit of the
University Place [Cumberland Presbyterian] Church, was delivered last evening, by Professor Woodrow Wilson, in the University Place Church; his subject being "Leaders of Men."[1]

Professor Wilson said, in part, that those only are leaders of
men who lead in action and forcible expression of thought, rather
than literary men who convey their thoughts through books.

The man who acts stands nearer to the hearts of the people
than the man of silent thought, and the arguments of an orator
to urge on the mass to action must be broad and easily comprehended.

He spoke of the impossibility of a statesman to write fiction
or a literary man to be a public orator. Disraeli could not be a
novelist any more than Browning a statesman.

Men cannot be led by being told what they do not know, but
the mass likes to be led by firm, resolute arguments, and an
orator to lead must be pleasing to the eye and the ear, with a
musical voice and a sturdy appearance.

Style has much to do with popular speaking and an orator
must be sympathetic with his audience.

Prof. Wilson referred to a number of the world's most influential leaders, giving the characteristics of each.

Printed in the *Daily Princetonian*, Jan. 21, 1898.
  [1] Printed at June 17, 1890, Vol. 6.

To George Chase

Princeton, New Jersey,

My dear Professor Chase,   25 January, 1898.

Allow me to thank you for your very cordial letter,[1] every word
of which I deeply appreciate. It gives me very keen pleasure to
know how you have felt about my work at the School, and I
have gained *that* satisfaction from the otherwise painful necessity of withdrawing, at any rate.

Of course, as you suppose, I feel obliged to stop because there
are more and more demands upon my time from year to year,
and I would fain make such additions to a college salary as are

necessary in some way that will take less time and (to be plain) bring more money. I did not suggest an increase in the compensation simply because I did not suppose that so short a course of lectures would be worth to the School what the time taken in their delivery would be worth to me. So far as one can make definite calculations in such matters, they ought to bring me, not three, but six hundred dollars; and that sum I did not,—I *do* not,—feel like asking. I thought it best for the School that I should simply, and with the best possible will towards it, withdraw.[2]

I knew, too, that you would take it in all kindness, as you have taken it; and that I should have the satisfaction of having lost an engagement that has interested me very much indeed, without losing a friend or even my cordial relations with the School itself. I thought, however, that this additional explanation would make the matter even more satisfactory to you, by stating my grounds of withdrawal even more explicitly and frankly than before.

With the warmest regard,

Faithfully Yours,   Woodrow Wilson

WWTLS (RSB Coll., DLC).
  [1] It is missing.
  [2] Chase's reply is missing, but he did not attempt to meet Wilson's terms.

To Harry Fielding Reid

My dear Mr. Reid,   Princeton, 25 January, '98

That was a most generous note of yours, of the thirteenth.[1] I hardly know what to say in reply. I expected to see Mr. [Maltbie D.] Babcock here last week, but was disappointed,—and so could not straighten matters out.[2]

I shall certainly expect to come to you on the evening of February twenty-first,—to stay, if you can put up with me so long, till I deliver my last lecture, on the twenty-fifth, and I shall be perfectly happy if I can induce Mrs. Wilson to join me there. She has never left the children for so long.

I shall be in Washington from next Monday until the twenty-first of February, when I come to Baltimore. I have some writing to do which can best be done here.

You must have thought me rude not to mention in my last the little volume of Watson's poems[3] you said Mrs. Reid was to send Mrs. Wilson. The fact is, it did not come. I was waiting till Mrs. Wilson should have a chance to see it and make her own acknowledgments. Since it has not made its appearance at all, I fear it has miscarried.[4]

Sincerely hoping that Mrs. Reid is entirely well again, and with warmest regards (from us both) to you both,

Most cordially Yours,   Woodrow Wilson

ALS (WC, NjP).
  [1] It is missing.
  [2] Dr. Babcock had invited Wilson to stay at his home while he gave his Donovan lectures at the Johns Hopkins in February.
  [3] *The Collected Poems of William Watson* (New York and London, 1899).
  [4] E. G. Reid to EAW, Feb. 4, 1898, explains the delay in sending the book.

Two Letters to Ellen Axson Wilson

The St. James, Washington, D. C.

My own darling,   1 February 1898

Here I am, well and all right,—but when I shall get settled it would be hard to say. It is so *desperately* cold just now that it is positively painful to go about and look up a boarding place. I have seen Meriwether,[1]—with inconclusive results,—but I shall not look up Renick, I think, till to-morrow morning. Meanwhile, I shall try to keep warm, and shall at any rate keep my *heart* warm by thinking of you. Ah, my darling, each separation from you is harder than the last,—and this time there is anxiety added to the pain of separation! May God keep my darling! Please write me *just* how you feel, and what Dr. Van Valzah[2] says. I love you more than I ever did before and am altogether,

Your own   Woodrow

  [1] Colyer Meriwether, Secretary and Treasurer of the Southern History Association, of which Wilson was a Vice President from 1896 to 1907. Wilson was undoubtedly speaking to Meriwether on behalf of Renick, who wished to publish an article on Christopher Gadsden in the *Publications of the Southern History Association*. Renick's article appeared in that journal, Volume II, July 1898, pp. 242-55, under the title of "Christopher Gadsden."
  [2] William W. Van Valzah, M.D., 10 East 43rd St., New York.

The Grafton, Washington, D. C.

My own darling,   2 February, 1898

I've been all day looking for a place to *stay*, and write, therefore, rather too late, I am afraid, to send this letter promptly off for to-morrow's delivery.

I am settled,—or rather settling—here at the *Grafton*,—where the Renick's *were*. They moved away to-day, to go to housekeeping again. I am sorry, of course; and yet I am not *wholly* sorry, I am a little ashamed to say, not to be thrown *too* much with *Mrs. R.* I find her rather trying,—and yet could not have R. himself without her.

It is quite high here—$15.00 a week—but I found that I would have to pay almost as much at a really comfortable boarding-house,—with various risks, besides,—and not be my own master, either, in various ways. Here I am independent, very comfortable, and properly regardful of my standing in the world. I can admit my whereabouts to the swells, who are, I am afraid, sure to find me out. Is that an improper motive to admit? Like other people who live beyond their means for appearance sake, I shall try to economise in other matters!

I am writing in the writing room in the midst of a lot of talkative men, and I hardly know what I am writing about. But I know how glad I am to get settled,—and I know how much I love you. My room is warm (even in this weather) and has plenty of good light, and I shall be very cosy in it indeed.

Ah, how homesick I am! How I long to go back and give the whole thing up! I feel so anxious to know how my darling is! I hope she went to New York to-day and has come back knowing what to do with herself.

Good night, pet. I love you passionately and altogether. I am quite well.   Your own   Woodrow

ALS (WP, DLC).

From Ellen Axson Wilson

My own darling,   Princeton Feb. 2, 1898.

Your note came duly to hand and glad I am that you can report yourself well and safely arrived, in spite of the frightful weather. It is fortunate you are not bound in the *other* direction; Mr. Perry, for instance, is snow-bound in New England, whither he went to lecture.

Of course in such weather I did not try to go to New York today, but will do so tomorrow if it does not rain or snow. It was quite bright this afternoon, though intensely cold, and I went out to test my strength and judge if it will hold out for New York tomorrow. It will undoubtedly for I went up to the Perry's and Westcotts, and the walk did me nothing but good. I am feeling *very* well tonight. Have just finished my German and seen Fraülein[1] and the children go off to bed; am writing at the library table. There is a beautiful fire burning, and the room is as warm and cheerful as possible, but oh, so lonely! Last night it was really *desperately* lonely; but tonight—perhaps because of having been out in the fresh air,—my courage is a little higher. But how does *anyone* bear to *live* alone! Did you see these lines in the "Century"?

"High thoughts and noble in all lands
Help me; my soul is fed by such.
But ah, the touch of lips and hands—
        The human touch!
Warm, vital, close, life's symbols dear,—
These need I most, and now, and here."[2]
I love you, dear, with all my heart and am altogether

                              Your own   Eileen.

ALS (WC, NjP).
    [1] Clara Böhm, the Wilsons' German governess.
    [2] Richard Burton, "The Human Touch," *Century Magazine*, LV (Feb. 1898),
521.

To Ellen Axson Wilson

My own darling,   Washington, D. C.   3 February 1898

This is my "black day,"—when I have been away from home over forty-eight hours and have had no letter from home. It is inevitable, no doubt, and must always be so; but such things are not governed by reason, and I must always be blue just at this stage. Philosophy is out of the question. I can only love you with a sort of deep pain of longing, and live as best I may till a letter come. I trust everything is all right and that my darling is well, but I cannot know it yet.

I began work at last this morning, on the Bagehot, and the first three or four pages have gone very well; but it is too soon to tell how smoothly the machinery will run when I enter the more serious matter of criticism.

I love you darling—ah, *how* I love you and yearn for you. Love to all, and kindest regards to Fraülein.

Will you not ask Ed. to make an *express* package out of the following things and send them to me.

(1) 100 sheets of the square paper in the front of the third drawer in my desk in the tier nearest the window. There is a big square envelope in the window seat in the corner nearest the drawer which will hold them *unfolded*.

(2) 25 copies of my Va. Bar address[1] (on top of my safe)

(3) The clothes from the last wash

(4) The strychnine tablets that came from the drug store the day I left home.

(5) My Roget's *Thesaurus* from my desk (on the right of the pigeon-holes.)

(6) (*Please get these yourself*) My after-dinner speech notes

in the right hand top drawer of the little chest of drawers in the *den*, in an envelope just about the size of this sheet.

And your humble petitioner will ever be

Your own   Woodrow

ALS (WP, DLC).
[1] "Leaderless Government," printed at Aug. 5, 1897.

From Ellen Axson Wilson

My own darling,   Princeton, Feb. 3, 1898.

Here I am safely back from New York, and very thankful to be here,—out of the terrible cold. The doctor found nothing seriously wrong with me; stomach and liver misbehaving a little, the former in the same way that yours did, he said, liquids remaining in it. I was also found to be "nervous." I am to take calomel and salts for four nights & mornings, and report again if I am not all right. I am not at all the worse for the day, though tired, of course. I spent much of it after leaving the doctor's, at the water-colour exhibition, and enjoyed myself.

Found your letter from the Grafton awaiting me. Am very glad, dear, that you have established yourself at a pleasant place; where your outing won't be spoiled for you by sordid surroundings.

I also found two or three letters that needed a prompt answer. I hastily did them up and had Ed mail them.[1] These banquet invitations have been the only requests for speeches so far.

But I shan't write a "letter" tonight, only the necessary "report." All quite well. With love beyond all words,

Your devoted little wife   Eileen.

ALS (WP, DLC).
[1] They are missing.

To Ellen Axson Wilson

My own darling,   Washington, D. C.   4 February, 1898

The embargo is raised: a letter has come, and my spirits have gone up to above normal! It's always a nice test of endurance, those first three days,—I should not care to risk more. And is my darling free from nausia,—is she really well? I wish she were more detailed and specific about the subject that makes more difference to me than any other in the world,—*herself*, and all that concerns her personally!

I begin to fear that it is imprudent for me to be staying here in Washington. I have sat and watched the Houses a good deal in the afternoons, and the old longing for public life comes upon me in a flood as I watch. Perhaps I should be safer somewhere else, where I should be kept from a too keen and constant discontent with my calling,—perhaps, too, this feeling will wear off when I have seen enough!

There is absolutely no news. I do nothing and see nobody. I am well,—and infinitely unhappy to be separated from you, my love and my life. Your own Woodrow

ALS (WP, DLC).

From Ellen Axson Wilson

My own darling, [Princeton, N.J.] Friday [Feb. 4, 1898].

Did you *ever* see anything so comically absentminded as the way I have begun this letter!—putting the address where the date ought to [be]! There is no help for it now, so I proceed!

I have had rather a busy day; was trying to finish a dress for Nellie in the morning after lessons. Just after lunch I hurried to Mrs. Phillips,[1] being anxious to see her and tell her about the Hibben lot[2] before they had decided on something else. From there I went to the German class at the Duffields.[3] And this evening I became so interested in my German book that I read on 'till after nine. I find I am rather tired, and my hand especially so nervously jerky, that it is really a pain to write. Otherwise I am quite well, except that my appetite is not so good as usual. Jessie and the other children are quite well again. It has been a splendid day, though cold, and they have all been up to see Beth Hibben.[4] All our good towns-folks have betaken themselves with one accord to sleighs, and were chasing each other like mad up and down Nassau St. I was glad to see the children come home safely through the hurly-burly.

I will send the various things you want tomorrow morning,—will get the notes and send with this. The pills have already gone. They with your neatly packed lunch lay on the library table when you left, and I neglected to give them to you! I was *so* sorry! Am sorry my letter was delayed too. It is because I write at night but must of course wait till morning to mail.

With love beyond all words, believe me, darling, as ever, Your own Eileen.

No mail of consequence today. I find the "notes" so numerous that I will send them, as you doubtless intended me to, in the express package

ALS (WC, NjP).

¹ Identified in EAW to WW, Feb. 26, 1897, n. 2.

² Ellen was trying to interest Mrs. Phillips in the lot on Washington Street which the Wilsons had sold to John Grier Hibben in 1895. See J. W. Fielder, Jr., to WW, March 18, 1895, n. 1, Vol. 9. The Phillipses bought or built a home on Hodge Avenue.

³ Probably the home of Professor John Thomas Duffield at 23 University Place.

⁴ Elizabeth Grier Hibben.

Edith Gittings Reid to Ellen Axson Wilson

My dear Mrs. Wilson   [Baltimore] Feb. 4th 1898

You really *must* come on the 21st. I have been fairly beset with ladies indignantly trying to seize Mr. Wilson—it is not safe and utterly ruinous to his humility. If you are here it may force some reticence upon these benighted females. I am not strong—and grey hairs in a woman are not what they are cracked up to be as regards influence. So do come. The little copy of Watson I ordered for you, my bookseller tells me is in process of going through a new edition. So it may be some time before you have it, but I want you to like the poem "Wordsworth's Grave"

Hoping and believing that I am to see you very soon

I am very sincerely   Edith G. Reid

ALS (WP, DLC).

From Ellen Axson Wilson

My own darling,   Princeton, Feb. 5 1898

I had intended to write a long letter to you tonight, but I was stupid enough to become a little sick at the tea-table; and I have been loafing all the evening waiting for the spell to pass, so that I could sit up comfortably and write after all. I am better, but it is bed-time; and I am quite ready for it. I have no pain, only nausea; I seem to be seized with a sick loathing at the sight of food; between meals I am usually perfectly well. I think it must be partly due to the medecines;—calomel every night, salts every morning. Don't concern yourself, dear, it will doubtless pass very soon, and is a very small matter at its worst;—this evening, for instance, when it has not prevented my browsing with much entertainment through a vol. of the "Library of the World's best Literature."

We have had a beautiful day, and the night with its full moon is glorious. *Isn't* it good to have the bitter cold end. Even old Mrs. Brown¹ was able to get out today. It was communion Sunday, you know. Mr. Devries gave us an especially good sermon.

All your things were forwarded you yesterday morning, and I hope will reach you safely by tomorrow at latest.

And now goodnight, darling. We are all well—with the slight reservation mentioned,—and love you *dearly*. It is *such* a pleasure to think of you there, enjoying yourself thoroughly I hope, quite free to do your own work in your own time and way, and amid interesting and agreeable surroundings. If you could only burn those wretched examination papers, I should be *quite* happy about you!

Please excuse this hideous scrawl. Somehow I can't control my hand at all.

Believe me, darling, in every heart-throb,

Your devoted little wife,   Eileen.

ALS (WP, DLC).
[1] Susan Dod Brown of 65 Stockton St.

Two Letters to Ellen Axson Wilson

My own darling,   Washington, D. C. 6 February, 1898

I am staying away from church this morning, largely because of the disinclination I have to appear at a place of worship as (apparently, at any rate) one of the innumerable crowd of curious strangers that throngs this unnatural place. I say 'unnatural' because Washington is nothing *but* the seat of the national government,—and of an idle society of rich people. It would be a great deal more wholesome, both for the country and for the government, if the seat of the latter were one of the great cities, with an independent life of its own,—out of which the representatives of non-commercial communities might take the instruction they so sadly lack, and can't get in Washington.

I have not made any calls yet, but am afraid I must begin early this week. There are a number of people here upon whom I really *ought* to call, despite my shyness and disinclination in the matter,—some whom I do not know. Whether I can accommodate my pride to seeking the acquaintance of the latter or not I don't know; but I really ought to stretch a point in the matter, I suppose, to break in some degree my quite anomalous personal isolation. I do not know enough interesting people. My acquaintanceships are altogether too haphazard. I ought, for example, to call on the Speaker of the House,[1] and upon Henry Adams, the historian, and upon 'Tom' Page, the husband,[2]—and upon various notables like unto these,—but *will* I? I fear not. I am too proud to *seek* acquaintance even with men who, I feel sure, would like to know me. My vanity takes the form of pride,—and you are deeply deceived when you call me 'modest.' I may be too critical to esteem my own work very highly, but I am not above thinking most extravagantly of my personal dignity! It's all one, in the long run.

Speaking of visits, darling, don't you think that, now that I know that I am not expected at the Babcock's and that no complications can arise to embarrass us, I can write to the Reid's that *you* will join me at their house on the evening of the twenty-first? Of course if anything *special* should happen to keep you at home, you could withdraw, even at the last moment; but there is no *general* reason why you should not go, and I have set my heart on having you with me those four days, the 22th–25th. Write me Yes, darling, so that I may send definite assurances to the Reids. It is hardly courteous to leave the matter uncertain.

I have written something over a third of my lecture on Bagehot, and hope to finish it by Friday next, so as to begin on Maine, the hardest of the three, on Saturday. That will leave me only eight working days for the Maine,—no more than I shall have spent on Bagehot,—not so many as I gave to Burke,—and that makes me feel rather nervous; but I shall no doubt manage the spurt, since it is necessary! In case of disaster, I can command a couple of mornings in Baltimore for the completion or last touching of No. III. I fancy that the Reid's big library (a jolly fine room,—spacious and impressive, like Sir Henry [Maine] himself) would be a very fit place for that particular bit of composition! And *ten* days' imprisonment ought to be sufficient discipline for the preparation of *any* lecture. If the thing is going to net me $250.00, that will be $25.00 a day,—very fair pay!

The poem you quote from the *Century is* singularly sweet and appropriate *now*, my pet. And that illustrates one law of poetic conception, I suppose. I read that poem before I left home, and saw nothing in it,—thought it rather weak. *Now* it seems infinitely sweet and true,—and stirs my longing for you as if it were very vital indeed. The verses I enclose[3] I have also appropriated to my own case, and they have comforted me not a little. Even *looking forward* to you is a source of deep, deep joy to me, Eileen. I do not think my life could ever seem wholly lonely and forlorn so long as I felt your *spiritual* presence in it, and could expect some day to hold you in my arms again. I do not find these little letters of yours very satisfactory in the matter of your *health*, my pet. They lack reassuring details. I can't be put at ease by being told that, though your appetite is not good, you are "otherwise quite well." I know with how many different intonations and with how many correspondingly different shades of meaning you can utter those (conventional) words. They need your voice, and above all your *eyes*, to interpret them. I know how I left you,—I have yet to learn how I should find you, were I to return *now*. You must learn the art of detail, dearest!

I am *perfectly* well in all respects. My spirits are not quite normal yet. I am still under the weight of the first loneliness,—I am still sadly homesick. But you love me,—that I know,—and I love you as only he can who knows you and adores you as

Your own   Woodrow

¹ Thomas Brackett Reed.
² Thomas Nelson Page, who after his second marriage, to Florence Lathrop Field of Chicago on June 6, 1893, had given up the practice of law to take up residence in Washington. The Pages' home became a center of social activity.
³ This enclosure is missing.

My own darling,   Washington, D. C.   7th February, 1898

The express package came this morning. The box of pills never turned up, either at the St. James or here. It's no matter. I got others here, of course. The express package was all right, and I am very much obliged, both to you and to Ed., darling. I rather expected some handkerchiefs to be with the clean underclothes. Did Maggie¹ have none? I'm quite short in the number I have with me.

I advanced Bagehot to page seventeen this morning, with the aid of several long quotations, and so am well past the halfway (I stop at p. 28 or 29) point, and may finish him on Thursday and have another day for Maine. It's a great bore to be *obliged* to write so much *per diem*, but the pressure will soon be off,—*and I shall see you*. How sweet it is to think of seeing you *week after next* in Baltimore, and of having you off on a jolly little holiday and spree with me! Of course you will remember to bring *all* your large wardrobe of evening clothes. We shall probably have at least a couple of dinners given us. I am head over ears in love with you, and am altogether   Your own   Woodrow

ALS (WP, DLC).
¹ Maggie Foley, a servant.

From Ellen Axson Wilson

My darling,   [Princeton, N.J.] Tuesday [Feb. 8, 1898]

I did not write as usual last night, but by doing it so soon after breakfast I hope to make the usual mail. I am *very* much better, feel *quite* well this morning, actually had an appetite for lunch yesterday, and had only a *slight* touch of nausau at night.

I had an anxious time with Nellie, who just at dinner-time struck herself a violent blow in the eye with the sharp corner of the nursery desk lid, which was open for writing upon. It was impossible to be sure last night that the ball was not hurt, for of course it was much inflammed with crying &c. But both the iris and the pupil look perfectly clear this morning, and I think there is no reason to apprehend further trouble. I cannot feel too thankful that it is so; a fraction of an inch more would perhaps have put it out. The main wound was a sharp little cut on the extreme upper edge of the lower lid, which bled a good deal. She was also bruised a little above the eye on the brow. It looks very well this morning; scarcely swollen at all.

This sort of thing makes my courage rather fail me about leaving them to go to Balt. I had a letter from Mrs. Reid yesterday insisting that I come;—havn't answered it yet.

The carpenter is here and has just begun with the book-case.

In *greatest* haste, and with a heart full of over-flowing with love,   Your devoted little wife,   Eileen.

Ed sent your examination papers and I think he sent the pills in the same package. They went to the St. James.

ALS (WC, NjP).

To Ellen Axson Wilson

My own darling,   Washington, D. C. 8th February, 1898

I can't help being deeply distressed, and anxious too, that your nausea should continue and you should be so nervous,—as shown by your inability to command your hand in writing! I sent a telegram this afternoon, in my impatience to get *late* news of your condition, and am writing now in hopes that a reply will come before I finish my letter (it is now about half-past five).

My work gets on very equably and well. I reached page twenty-two of the Bagehot this morning (about two p.p. ahead of my schedule); but, if you don't get better, I don't see how I can go on here. I shall feel that I must go to you before very long. I can't think of anything else.

As for what we a little feared, in spite of all likelihood, that ought to be settled this week. It is four weeks to-day (this afternoon) since your last courses began. They ought to come again within a day or two, if they are coming. But why should I talk of *this*, it is surely quite out of the question!

I went to the new Library of Congress[1] this afternoon (to be doing something). I had not been before,—for of course I shall not reach the work I thought of doing there.[2] The decoration seemed to be altogether too *loud*,—too much in the red-and-gilt taste of the modern city hotels and theatres. Of course much of the mural painting is very fine and very beautiful,—but much of it is also very commonplace, and some of it is a mere display of very fleshly young women in very seductive attitudes.[3] I cannot pretend that I, personally, object to this, but it seems undignified and very far short of great imaginative art such as one would like to see represent our national achievement. I spent only about three quarters of an hour in the building, however, and ought not to judge it upon so brief an examination.

You may be sure that looking at works of art proved a poor device for getting you out of my mind (such was my purpose, madam!), and I think it will not be easy for me to excape [escape] a certain pensive association with the place when I shall go there hereafter,—though if it should turn out that you are going to get well right away (which God grant!), that very thing may make me feel glad there next time! Ah, my darling, with how intense and passionate a love I love my little wife,—how almost tragically is it true that I am   Your own   Woodrow

ALS (WP, DLC).

[1] Work had begun on the new Library of Congress in 1887. Opened in November 1897, it was hailed as a masterpiece of Italian Renaissance architecture. For the first time in the construction of a public monument, the government had called exclusively on American artists to execute the decoration. About forty of them contributed murals and sculpture, mosaics and workings in bronze. The Library's most imposing features were the highly ornate entrance hall and grand staircase—"a vision in polished stone"—and the gallery under the great dome of the main reading room, containing bronze statues by MacMonnies, French, Bartlett, and Saint-Gaudens, among others.

[2] Probably research for his school history of the United States.

[3] Most of the murals were executed on canvas in the various artists' studios and then affixed to the walls of the Library. They are allegorical or historical in theme—ranging from Edwin H. Blashfield's series on "The Progress of Civilization" and "Human Understanding" in the dome of the great rotunda to "The Evolution of the Book" by John W. Alexander, "The Government of the Republic" by Elihu Vedder, and "The Muses" by Edward Simmons. It may well have been this last series, or George W. Maynard's paintings—floating figures in the Pompeian style—to which Wilson refers.

From Ellen Axson Wilson

My own darling,   Princeton, Feb 8 1898

I came home at dinner-time to find your telegram awaiting me,[1] much to my distress, for it shows that you have taken the record of my small ailments much too seriously. Such things make me greatly doubt the wisdom of the "compact," upon which you insist so strenuously, that I should tell you "the whole truth, the exact truth," as to my feelings. That would be all right if the corresponding effect on you could be counted on to be equally *exact* in preserving the due and scientific relation between cause and effect. But my darling's anxious temperament makes these little things affect him to an exaggerated degree, and the *truth* itself would "*ultimately* prevail" more entirely, if I were allowed to say nothing about them. However that may be, it *is* the exact truth that I feel *quite* well, and have eaten my *dinner*,—not merely milk—for the first time. I was at the Employment Society too, but most of the women having gone to a big funeral, I did very little except loaf; so am not at all tired. Stopped to see Mrs. Brown on my way home and found her well and bright.

Your bookcase is up and looks *fine*,—*much* better than I expected. I am delighted with it. It is a great improvement, merely as regards the appearance of the room, on the organ. It only cost $1.75 to put it up. Shall I have Briner[2] do the finishing, or try and get the man who did the house?[3] I learn from the carpenter that the latter's name is "Will Davis" and that he lives in Trenton. And here is another little matter perplexing me;—the enclosed card came tonight.[4] Are we under any social obligation to pay the extra $2.00?

I hope, dear, you *will* see some of the men you speak of; if for nothing else because it will be of service to you in your work, to know such people as the Speaker of the House, and get informal inside views of "present history." I sympathize with you so entirely in the feeling you confess in these matters. It is so exactly *my* disposition too, that it is difficult for me to press such a point! But I can see that we are not "wise in our generation." Perhaps it might be better for you if I were to some mild degree a woman of the world, with "social ambitions" (!) That reminds me that I wrote to Mrs. Reid today accepting her invitation, though with some misgivings both of heart and conscience. I am delighted that you are getting on so well with your work. I think you are doing famously. How delightful that I am to *hear* them as well as read them! That is beyond comparison the greatest inducement for the Balt. visit.

Thank you, dearest, for the sweet lines you enclose. They went straight to my heart, which echoes them every one. It is literally true that for years your return from Balt. has been, subconsciously perhaps, identical in my mind with "the breaking up of winter,"—the coming of spring. It has really come to seem as if there were some necessary scientific connection between the two! Only one month more of winter then, and I must try to learn for my "waiting" "a great patience." Believe me Woodrow, darling, in every heart-throb,   Your own   Eileen.

ALS (WC, NjP).
  [1] It is missing.
  [2] George W. Briner, painter, 18 Edgehill St.
  [3] That is, the painter who did the finishing work on their house.
  [4] It is missing.

To Ellen Axson Wilson

My own darling,   Washington, D. C. 9 February, 1898.

I know that you will pardon an occasional typewritten letter. After several hours of writing, my arm sometimes feels more than a little queer, and I think I had better indulge it in a change of exercise.

Your last letter, and the telegram[1] of yesterday, have re-assured me a great deal, and I am much better in my mind to-day. God send the good news may continue! I wrote very easily and rapidly on the Bagehot this morning,—too easily by half, I am afraid; and shall very readily bring it to a conclusion to-morrow morning, if nothing happens to interrupt me. It has gone very smoothly from start to finish, and for that reason I suspect it. But I cannot tell what to think of it until you hear it.

And you *must* hear it, sweet. Don't let one little accident prevent your coming to Baltimore, or rob you of your self-possession. Poor little Nen! It was indeed a narrow escape, and makes me shiver and give fervent thanks to God for the providential escape! And how are *you* feeling *now*, sweetheart? Do you continue better? Do you seem to be getting really well? *Please* tell me *in detail*!

When Dr. Wikoff sends the papers Mrs. Garrett mentioned in her letter, will you not send them on to me, my pet? I should try to act in the matter.[2]

Poor Stockton, he has gotten himself, and perhaps me too, in to a hole. I have written him that, if it is necessary to do so to redeem him, I will speak for Mrs. Mason, but that he must get me off if he possibly can.[3]

There is no news. The Princeton dinner here comes off to-night,[4] and I am to have the usual sort of a time, but I shall bear it with what fortitude I may.

I have made no calls yet, except on Renick.

With a heart full to overflowing with love,—a love that possesses my whole life and force,   Your own   Woodrow

WWTLS (WP, DLC).
  [1] The telegram is missing.

² Mrs. Thomas Harrison Garrett of Baltimore, who had lived at 3 Stockton Street while her three sons attended Princeton. The youngest, Robert, was graduated in 1897. Mrs. Garrett's letter and the papers are missing, and the matter about which Wilson felt constrained to act remains unknown to the Editors.

³ Stockton Axson's letter and Wilson's reply are missing, and this affair remains mysterious. However, there is no known record of Wilson speaking for a Mrs. Mason.

⁴ See the news report printed at Feb. 10, 1898.

Two Letters from Ellen Axson Wilson

My own darling,   Princeton, Feb. 9/1898

I am delighted to hear of better spirits, and such good progress in your work. All goes well here too. I am feeling perfectly well again,—appetite as good as ever too.

Speaking of the Balt. trip.—I think I had better arrange to get there on the evening of the 22nd, for of course I must remain until Sat morning in order to hear your three lectures, and that would make the trip too long for me to get the advantage of a return ticket;—longer too than I care to be away from the children. Unless there is something very fine to be expected in the way of a speech on the 22nd, I shan't be sorry to miss it. Write me about trains, &c., picking out for me one that will not interfere with anyone's plans.

I have been busy today making a new brown silk waist "for Balt." Went out this morning though just before lunch. 'Twould have been a sin against nature to have stayed in! Was there ever such weather here before so early! *wonderful!* the very "promise of May[.]" It sent a wave of delicious excitement and expectation thrilling through me, with actually a catch of the breath, as I walked. "A feeling as when eager crowds await before a palace gate, some wondrous pageant."

I love you, *love* you, with all my heart and soul, and am always and altogether,   Your own,   Eileen.

My own darling,   Princeton, Feb. 9, 1898.

I have just received at the door the note from Dr. Shields enclosed in the other envelope.¹ I told the messenger to tell him you were out of town. The old doctor is so formal that you had better drop him an answer yourself.

I feel perfectly well today again, have been out a good deal, and enjoyed intensely "the feeling of spring" in the air,—the first day of *promise*! It made me almost fancy that you must be on your way home, and not, alas, with three-fourths of the time still to go. But I have vowed to myself not to indulge in any complainings, or self-pity!

I saw Mr. [W. M.] Daniels on the street, looking,—and, he says, *feeling*,—very well. Am glad he had such a short siege. The only other Princeton news is the death of Dr Schank's wife,[2] which took place this morning.

What will you do about the Clarksville invitation? I *hope* it is at an impossible time; I don't at all like the tone in which they *summon* you![3]

And by the way what *did* you reply to that Miss Lyon's invitation?[4] How *could* she have so little delicacy and sense of propriety as to invite you? And to do it so many months before too, so as to make sure of getting ahead of everyone!

But I must stop at once as there are several matters of business that must be seen to tonight. You would have laughed to see me trying to make out a check for 80 cts! I failed utterly,—spoiled the check,—didn't know how to do it for less than a dollar! Had to make Ed hunt up the man & pay him the cash!

With love beyond all words.

Your devoted little wife,   Eileen.

ALS (WC, NjP).
  1 It is missing.
  2 Maria Robbins Schanck, wife of J. Stillwell Schanck, Professor of Chemistry and Hygiene, Emeritus.
  3 Wilson had promised to speak at Vanderbilt University in Nashville and at Lincoln's birthplace in Hodgenville, Kentucky, in June 1898. The "summons" that annoyed Ellen is missing, but it was undoubtedly a peremptory invitation from Joseph R. Wilson, Jr., to his brother to spend the interval between the addresses with him and his family in Clarksville, Tenn. This Wilson did.
  4 Wilson was scheduled to deliver five lectures on constitutional government at Richmond College (now the University of Richmond) in late October and early November 1898. See the news reports of these lectures at Oct. 28 and 29 and Nov. 1, 2, 4, and 17, 1898, Vol. 11. "Miss Lyon" was Lulie Lyons of Richmond, whom Wilson mentioned in his diary entry of Aug. 6, 1897. Her invitation is missing.

Notes for Remarks at an Alumni Dinner[1]

"Hotel Wellington," 9 February, 1898.

Washington Dinner (Alumni)

Shall *never love another college*!
Yet here is a certain comfortable home feeling: not always the *"proceedings of the previous meeting."*
A sense of comradeship, too: I may not know you personally, but *"your manners are very familiar."*
Subject: The University a place of disinterested guidance, detached from interests. Too big a theme? *"Mark off a figure* no bigger than I am on him, and if I don't hit it, it wont count.["]

Attentions lately paid us by *our friends*: I prefer to sleep with our enemies. "You coward!"

Certain irresponsible journals remind me of the Irishmans eight Day clock. *"How long will they run if you wind them?"*

But enough. *"I hope that you will continue to approach me with your usual familiarity."*

WWT MS. (WP, DLC).

1 See the news report which follows for an account of this affair.

A News Report of an Alumni Dinner in Washington

[Feb. 10, 1898]

NASSAU'S SONS FEAST

Banquet of Princeton Alumni Association.

With words of affection for their alma mater, songs of college days reciting the valorous deeds of the sons of Old Nassau, and with a feast of many delicacies, the twenty-seventh annual dinner of the Princeton Alumni Association of the District of Columbia was celebrated last night at the Wellington Hotel. Around the banquet board were seated the representatives of graduating classes of half a century—men who have become widely known and prominent in their chosen professions—and the younger alumni who have left the university in the last few years. The gathering was a representative one. The banqueters came early in the evening and made merry until a late hour, the dinner being one of the most enjoyable since the organization of the association.

The banquet hall was decorated with palms and potted plants, the walls being hung with orange and black bunting and banners. The tiger colors prevailed in the decorations, the effect being most pleasing. The tables were arranged in T shape, the invited guests being seated at the head table to the right and left of Hon. Joseph K. McCammon, President of the Alumni Association, who presided and acted as toastmaster. A strip of orange and black ribbon ran lengthwise of the long board. Roses and carnations formed the floral decorations of the table. . . .

There were no formal toasts or set speeches, but many of the more prominent guests present were called upon for remarks, and in each instance responded in a most happy vein. When the coffee and cigars had been served President McCammon rapped for order, and stated that President Patton, of Princeton, had been unable to attend the dinner on account of an engagement to speak in Baltimore. He said it was with great pleasure, however, that he introduced Prof. Woodrow Wilson, one of the most distinguished members of the Princeton faculty. Three lusty cheers were given as Prof. Wilson arose. His speech was very witty, abounding in good humor and touching upon topics of especial interest and importance to Princeton men just now. Prof. Wilson was frequently interrupted by loud applause. . . .

Printed in the *Washington Post*, Feb. 10, 1898; some editorial headings omitted.

Two Letters to Ellen Axson Wilson

My own darling,   Washington, D. C.   10th February, 1898

That was a very, very sweet letter you wrote Tuesday night, after sending me the telegram,—so full of womanly sense and tenderness. Of course you are right, my darling. I am unreasonably anxious, and I will try to do better,—to be more self-possessed and sensible. My only excuse is, that it is no ordinary case. I *would* not be so anxious about anybody or anything *but you*. You evidently can't imagine what a part you play in my mind: it is as if the body were anxious about the heart. My life centres in you, and nothing can touch me so to the quick as what affects you,—particularly what affects your health or spirits. You need not doubt the wisdom of our compact. If it were not for that, I should be always torturing myself with fears and doubts far worse than those I suffer under the treaty. But I *have* been foolish, and I will try to behave more reasonably.

The Princeton dinner came off, but was rather tame. Some of the speeches were good, but mine was not. However, they did not seem to know that it was poor, and I slept well, despite a good deal of mild chagrin.

I am so glad, my darling,—so delighted and grateful, that you have accepted Mrs. Reid's invitation. How I shall look forward to those happy days! How sweet of my love to do this for my sake! God bless you, sweetheart! You certainly know how to love! And I am sure you will like the Reids.

Hurrah for the bookcase. I am so relieved that you really like it. I saw from the first that you were a little doubtful how it was going to look, and I am proportionately relieved that you should actually admire it. I would *try* to find the Trenton painter, I think; but, if he cannot be promptly found by letter, no doubt Briner can strike the shade of the rest of the woodwork in the room very well. I am anxious to have the case dry and ready for use when I get back. I suppose the shelves should be oiled.

Bagehot was finished before noon to-day. He's a little too long for his hour, I am afraid; but I do not know how to shorten him. To-morrow, *Sir Henry Sumner Maine*!

Ah, darling, I slept with your sweet letter under my pillow, and feel bouyant to-day. I am heart and life

Your own Woodrow

I am perfectly well

My own darling, Washington, D. C. 11th February, 1898

I sit down to my letter a little earlier than usual to-day because it is so mild and Spring-like out of doors that I have determined to go out to Mt. Vernon about two o'clock and spend the afternoon. I might get back too late to write in time for my regular mail.

Yes, I think we are socially bound to send the enclosed card. I wrote to Dr. Shields at once.

I have spent the early part of the morning in "reading up" Sir Henry Maine's life. It is going to be hard, I foresee, to give life and reality to my discussion of him. He does not lend himself to quotation very readily, and the men who have written about him have written like clams; but probably, by unstinted use of the "big bow wow" manner which both he and his friends employ, I may manage to take up a great deal of space in saying very little. It's a decided change after Bagehot! It will affect my style, see if it don't!

I love you darling,—and somehow it increases my love for you to read other men's lives. I seem the more vividly to appreciate the inspiration of my own! Your own Woodrow

ALS (WP, DLC).

From Ellen Axson Wilson

My own darling, Princeton, Feb. 11 1898

Your sweet letter written yesterday has been read over I don't know how many times today, and I can't say with how much pleasure. Not only the sweet words, but the cheerful spirits it revealed gave me deep satisfaction. *How* happy you make me, darling!—in how many ways!

I am very glad the article is finished,—and the dinner too. Am sorry for the "chagrin"; but am quite sure that if the speech *was* a failure,—in *your* opinion,—the fact remained a secret from your hearers!

I enclose a letter from Brooklyn[1] which I hope will come as a relief to you. It seems to me it will make things much easier for you to give them in the fall, now that the New York Law School is out of the way; especially as they were new lectures; and you have new lectures to prepare for the college too. And as the money was to go on the [house] debt, the postponement will make only the little difference of interest there.

We are all very well; only I am "unwell," and a little tired, having had a busy day, partly because Lizzie[2] is sick, and the German class was to be here this afternoon. Fraülein and Ed have gone to an organ recital given by the college organist. I have been putting the children to bed in her place;—stayed up and had a "cosy time" with them. It is now after nine; and I, somehow, am overcome by *sleep*,—so must close.

Ah, Woodrow, darling, how I *love* you, and how I long for you! Somehow I feel tonight an inexpressible yearning, tenderness towards you! With love unspeakable,

Your little wife   Eileen.

There was so little mail today that I enclose it with this.[3]

ALS (WC, NjP).
  [1] This letter is missing, but it was from Franklin William Hooper, Director of the Brooklyn Institute of Arts and Sciences, asking Wilson to postpone his lectures there from April to the autumn of 1898. See Wilson's diary, Aug. 12, 1897, n. 1.
  [2] Another servant, whose last name is unknown.
  [3] The enclosures are missing.

To Ellen Axson Wilson

My own darling,   Washington, D. C.   12th February, 1898

I shan't insist on your coming to Baltimore on the 21st.,—I *can* wait until the 22nd, if I *must*, but I doubt one of the reasons. I don't think the tickets are limited to five days, are they? Did you inquire at the R. R. office?

While I think of it, I had better mention the one or two things I wish you would bring to Baltimore with you. If you have room in your trunk, I wish you would bring,—oh no! I forgot you would not come on the 21st.,—I was going to say my academic costume—cap and all—for use on the morning of the 22nd.[1] It's not important enough to make it worth while to *send* them. The other thing I had thought of may occur to you independently: will you not bring the little bundle of *rubbers* in the bottom drawer of the washstand?

You ask me what I said in answer to Miss Lyons' note. What *could* I say? I never was more bored in my life, but I could not refuse point-blank. I tried to temporize. I told her it was not to be one 'address' (as she seemed to think) but five lectures, running through almost a whole week; that I was a nervous 'literary fellow' who would be a very uncomfortable sort of guest, and that they[2] had better let me stay at an hotel. If she takes the hint, all right,—if not, what can I do but accept—and I have little hope that she will, and I feel as if I were in a very deep hole.

Of course I shall have to let those Brooklyn lectures go over till the Autumn,—though I confess I should rather have gotten them out of the way this Spring.

Maine was set up on the stocks yesterday (I am now writing on Sunday), and a little more than a day's stint put on it. I begin to hope that I shall have something to say, after all, but I may have to spread it a little thin. I can at any rate enlarge upon some of my favourite ideas about style. Both Maine's own ideas about writing and his practice offer excellent texts for comment. His practice is admirable, but his maxims are ridiculous. Not every artist can expound the methods of his art, or analyze the effects he produces. *I* can tell how the thing is done, alas! very well,— but I am in the greater dispair at not being able to *do* it. It's odd that I write better when I am explaining the theory than when I am trying to practice it. I sometimes suspect that I am a better critic than artist! The worst of my present job is, that Maine does not excite any such enthusiasm as Burke or Bagehot excites. If he had any personal charm, his friends, in writing about him, have given us no taste of it. It is going to be hard work, and work of the imagination, to reconstruct the image of the *man,*— and yet you cannot in this case understand the writer without a clear conception of the man. Whether I can trust my imagination to re-make a man I never saw and have the most inadequate report of remains to be seen. That is to-morrow's (Monday's) task.

I made my first formal call last night,—on Mrs. Col. Winthrop,[3] who once wrote about Bagehot in a Roman Catholic magazine,[4] quoting largely from me, and sent me the article, with a letter.[5] Her husband called on me on Friday. They proved to be exceedingly interesting and really attractive people. She is touched a little more than my taste relishes with the qualities of the fashionable society of which she forms a part; but she is no ordinary woman of fashion, is admirably well read and appreciative of good things, and lives in an atmosphere of right ideas. The Colonel said, amongst other naïve things, that he supposed all 'educated people' were free traders! All *properly* educated people *are*. They are people worth knowing, and I am booked, of course, to dine with them,—the day not yet appointed.

I began this letter on Saturday, darling, and am finishing it on Sunday,—I know no letter can get to you till Monday, anyway. I am in excellent health and spirits,—and my thoughts are all day long deeply engaged with you,—even while I write at my lectures. I find myself wondering what you would think of this, that, or the other judgment or expression; as my writing goes forward from sentence to sentence, it seems somehow to address itself to you and to be toned for your ear. When I read the lectures in Baltimore I know it will seem to me that *you* are my only auditor, —the only one to catch *all* the thought, its flavour and slight aroma as well as its substance and obvious form. You have crept into my life and into my *consciousness* as a sort of additional mind and personality,—to soften, to beautify, to enlarge and vivify all that I see,—and I seem to take from you some subtle feminine quality of refinement and pure joy of appreciation which my natural powers would lack. It must be for some such reason that I feel *complete* when you are close within my arms and our very breath seems *one*,—and that, away from you, I feel as if living on imagination and in an atmosphere in which there does not seem to be air enough to *fill* my lungs.

I am in every breath and power   Your own   Woodrow

ALS (WP, DLC).
  1 Wilson sat on the stage during the Founder's Day exercises at the Johns Hopkins.
  2 Miss Lyons and her mother.
  3 Alice Worthington Winthrop, wife of Col. William Woolsey Winthrop.
  4 Her article was undoubtedly "Walter Bagehot and His Attitude Towards the Church," by "An American Contributor," in the London *Month, a Catholic Magazine and Review*, LXXXVI (Jan.-April, 1896), 556-61.
  5 Her letter is missing.

From Ellen Axson Wilson

My own darling,   Princeton, Feb 13, 1898

I have read some German, and also had a call from Mr. Wykoff[1] and am as a consequence somewhat belated in beginning to write.

I am sorry Sir Henry Maine promises to be a hard task. I have always understood that his personality was rather shadowy. Is it because he is more scholar than man, or because he simply objected to having his private life and character exploited, and found friends to respect his views? It *is* unsatisfactory, after all, not not [sic] to be told what sort of *men*, one's favourite writers are;—and if they are the right sort of men why should they object to our knowing, why shouldn't their friends wish us to know it? *I* would like for all the world to know what a splendid, lovely fellow *you* are! That biographical question, with which you left "the club"[2] struggling, has several sides to it;—and I am on *all* of them! We have another question for tomorrow, on which also we are probably not destined to say "the last word"! viz: "Is literary taste declining?" What is your opinion on that subject? We are to meet after the Kneisel Concert tomorrow, it having proved impossible to find another free day in the week. I have so many little things on hand for this week that I am already feeling rather hurried in prospect. Must make candy for the church in the morning, for it seems they have decided to begin an "Exchange" in a small way, sell candy and take orders for cakes. Wednesday I must try to see the doctor as he wanted me to come again soon.

And what do you do with yourself, dearest, when you arn't writing essays. You tell me nothing of that. Do you still spend your afternoons in Congress? I hope you have made a beginning with those *calls*! Are there any good plays for you to go to at night? Or are you struggling with those hateful exam papers by way of amusement. By the way, you never said whether they reached you; the pills *were* with them.

We are all *perfectly* well; I have been a little *blue* for my darling all today. The sweet sunshine has done something for me; I have followed it around the house, so as to be exactly *in* it all the time, but it doesn't atone for the lost warmth and comfort of your dear presence. Oh love, my love, I *want* you; ah how intensely I want you! how entirely I love you! You are the very life of me.   Your own   Eileen.

ALS (WC, NjP).
    [1] Walter Augustus Wyckoff, Lecturer in Sociology.
    [2] The Present Day Club of Princeton, a women's club organized in 1898 and incorporated in 1900.

To Ellen Axson Wilson

My own darling,   Washington, D. C.   14 February, 1898

I brought that tiny volume containing Arnold's essay on "Sweetness and Light"[1] away with me when I left home, to read on the train,—and here it lies on my little table and looks at me with a sort of wistful meaning,—not because I have not read it,—for I have read it,—but because a certain sweet lady who loved me, and who has brought sweetness and light into my life, once wanted to read to me out of it a passage which interpreted her loving judgment of me, and I was absent-minded and rude, not knowing what she intended, and wounded her, turning her unselfish pleasure into pain and bitterness! I shall not soon forget the pang I suffered when I discovered what I had done,—and this little book reminds me of it I don't know how many times a day. It is good for me. I have much to learn from the recollection,— not love—I *could* not *love* you more—but considerate tenderness and a more self-forgetful love. Somehow, it is not a bitter memory, for all it brings a keen pang of veritable remorse at every recurrence: a sort of chastened joy at what you meant to do remains as the chief emotion of it all. I don't think you knew what a shock it sent to my heart to find that I had actually put you off with a sort of impatience when you were trying, with an exquisite tact, to show me by a new way what sort of an image your heart held of me! It is one of the little things that will *tell* in my life like a sort of crisis and revelation. It connected itself in my thought at once with the time when you found that the date of my birth corresponded with the date put above the quotation in your Jean Ingelow Birthday Book which you had picked out as describing me![2] I had robbed myself of what I would go through fire to get,—the coming back into your eyes of that unspeakably sweet, brooding, dreamlike look of love that was in your eyes then, in the sweet dawn of our happiness:—this time there were *tears* instead, and *I* had brought them there! Ah, my Eileen, my little wife,—this is my Valentine, my love token—this confession of that intense moment of suffering, in which I saw you in all your loveliness and knew my heart about you!

Your own   Woodrow

ALS (WP, DLC).
[1] The title of the first chapter of Matthew Arnold's *Culture and Anarchy* (London, 1869). "Sweetness and Light" was reprinted as a separate essay several times in the 1890's.
[2] See WW to ELA, Dec. 8, 1883, Vol. 2.

From Ellen Axson Wilson

My own darling,   Princeton Feb 14/98

It is ten minutes of ten and I must write a mere line just to say we are all perfectly well. I have been in a rush all day and am very ready for bed;—first lessons, then a business call from Mrs. Devries & Mrs. Duffield, then candy-making, then one or two notes and a *rush* down town to get some *valentines* for the children before the three o'clock concert. After the concert the club, then dinner, and at half past seven a meeting at the Devries from which I have just returned. The meeting of course was with regard to the "Exchange" work which the church women have decided to begin.

How I wish you could have heard the concert! It was one of the best of all! *exquisite*![1]

With *devoted* love,   Your own   Eileen.

ALS (WC, NjP).
[1] The program by the Kneisel String Quartet included Beethoven's Quartet No. 9 in C Major, Opus 59, No. 3; Schubert's "Theme and Variations," from the Quartet No. 14 in D Minor ("Death and the Maiden"); and Schumann's Quintet for piano and strings in E Flat Major, Opus 44, with Adele Lewing at the piano. *Daily Princetonian*, Feb. 11, 1898.

From Daniel Collamore Heath

Dear Professor Wilson: Boston 14 February, 1898

Yours of the 12th received. If the revised copy of the State gets to us by the 1st of May it will be in season for our purposes I think.

I have been serious about the civil government though I may not have written always in a serious vein. You will remember that some years ago you thought you would make such a book,[1] and if I remember rightly you wrote us an announcement of it. You may have forgotten the matter, and I therefore send with this a page torn from an old catalog to show you just what I mean.[2] You will see, therefore, that I had some strong reasons for being serious and hoping you would make the book. Still, I do not want to press the matter unduly. I believe you would make a far better book than has yet been made or is likely to be made, and I naturally want you to do it, and to do it for the best publishers. I do not blame the other publishers for setting you at work[3] and keeping you at work so you wont have time for the other fellow, and I do not balme [blame] you for doing the thing that you can best do *con amore* and that will bring you the largest return, so we will consider the whole thing off if you say so.

                    Yours very truly,   D. C. Heath.

TL (WP, DLC).
[1] See the Editorial Notes, "Wilson's Plan for a Textbook in Civil Government," Vol. 5, and "Wilson's Elementary Textbook in American Government," Vol. 6.
[2] The enclosure is missing, and a copy cannot be found because the files of D. C. Heath and Company are not extant for this period.
[3] On Wilson's school history of the United States.

To Ellen Axson Wilson

My own darling,   Washington, D. C. 15 February, 1898

So you want to know what I do with my afternoons and evenings, do you? It isn't very interesting. I have read a few examinations,—not many yet, I am sorry to say; I have spent two or three evenings at Renick's, one calling, two or three seeing indifferent plays, one at the alumni dinner and the rest reading in my room, generally an old biography I have picked up here. After luncheon my routine is to write a letter or two, go to the Houses or take a long stroll in this beautiful place, drop in at Lowdermilk's (the huge and fatally seductive old-book store here), look in at Renick's office[1] and discuss some law question, and then come to my room in time to write my letter to you before dinner. Yesterday afternoon I went to a reception (a small one) at Miss Lichfield's (I don't know who Miss Lichfield is—I know only that she is very nice), to which my friend Mrs. Winthrop (who receives with Miss L.) had bidden me,—I went *after* my Valentine was written, at six o'clock.

I quoted two whole pages from Maine this morning, and was set much 'forarder' by the act. I have reached page 15 and shall finish on Friday, if nothing happens. I am trying to weave the matter, life with works, *a la* Winchester,[2] and am having reasonable success (I *believe*—I have not *read* any of it yet); but I am writing *currente calamo* and I am afraid that the style, though it may sound very well, will not stand the eye of the critical reader quite so well. I went to the Library of Congress this afternoon and read the notice of Maine which appeared in the London *Times* just after his death in 1888,—evidently written by a close and intimate friend,—and got some hints out of it which will be of service: but my portrait must be largely imaginary after all,—in the legitimate sense of the word.

But I must not write more,—my arm is very tired from the morning's exertion. I am well and in excellent spirits,—and in everything   Your own   Woodrow

ALS (WP, DLC).
[1] Renick had become associated with the Washington office of Coudert Brothers, a New York law firm, after his dismissal from the State Department in 1897.
[2] His old friend, Caleb Thomas Winchester of Wesleyan University.

From Ellen Axson Wilson

My own darling,   Princeton   Feb 15 1898

I have just come from the Employment Society and must scribble a little note before dinner, for alas! after dinner I *must* dress and go to a Wikoff reception! They are giving one of their "series," and this is the only possible evening for me; and having, as you may remember, behaved atrociously the last time,—neither attending any, nor sending cards, it is a matter of life and death to get there now.[1] Our doctor has us too much in his power to be insulted with impunity!

I found at the Society that Mrs. Hibben goes into the doctor too tomorrow, so I feel more cheerful than usual at the prospect. We can gossip together ad libitum. She was so naive and funny yesterday at the Club,—spent all her time telling us what Mr. Dulles and *Prof Thomson*[2] thought on the subjects. Her sense of humour, usually in such excellent working order, must have been gone to the shop for repairs. She also wanted Mrs. [E. C.] Richardson to repeat what Mr. R. had said to them,—as if *Mrs. R.'s* opinion was not very much more to the point. If she shows always such a flattering respect for masculine intelligence *as such* no wonder they find her charming; that added to all her intrinsic fascinations must make her utterly irresistible—bless her heart! I *hope* this doesn't sound as if I have been making fun of her.

What a sweet, *sweet* letter you have sent me, my darling, for a Valentine, so sweet that it made me cry for very love and longing. Ah, if you were only here, and I were *close* in your arms and could close your mouth with kisses when you begin to talk so. For sweet as it all is, you know, dear, that part of it you ought not to think or feel; you are magnifying the merest accident into an offense on your part. As far as there was any fault, it was *altogether mine* for being so full of my thought that I could not wait to choose my occasion better. Dearest love, don't let yourself feel any "pang" because of it.

I love you Woodrow, darling, *inexpressibly*

Your little wife,   Eileen.

Ed has come in. I asked him at lunch to enquire at the station about the return tickets. You are right, they are good for ten days. Ed misinformed me before. So unless you have already written to the Reids that I will go on the 22nd, I think I *had* better reach there on evening of the 21st. I am *so* afraid that by arriving on such a busy full day as the 22nd, I will put someone to inconvenience. I *would* almost certainly embarrass you in *your* plans!

ALS (WP, DLC).
 [1] See EAW to WW, Feb. 15, 1897, n. 1.
 [2] Joseph Heatly Dulles, Librarian of Princeton Theological Seminary, and Henry Dallas Thompson, Professor of Mathematics at Princeton University.

To Ellen Axson Wilson

My own darling,   Washington, D. C.   16 February, 1898.

I wrote five more pages on Maine this morning, and must let my pen hand off this afternoon from more exertion. I know you wont mind. I am a little belated, besides, because I read several pages of the afternoon paper to find out what I could in addition to the morning's news about the blowing up of the Maine at Havana. Itnt is [Isn't it] dreadful,—and mysterious? How can one help suspecting foul play under all the circumstances? And yet very likely it was a most inoportune accident. Let us hope that sufficient evidence remains to make it certain what happened.

I went to the theatre last night, for I felt rather more than usually tired by yesterday morning's work. The play[1] was foolish and not good enough to rest me. To-day I feel in excellent condition, and I shall spend the evening answering the batch of letters Ed. forwarded this morning, and reading examination papers.

I do not know whether I hope that you are in New York to-day or not, anxious as I am to have you see the doctor promptly and get taken care of by him. It has turned so bitterly cold that I rather dread the idea of having you exposed to the winds in New York. They get a terrible sweep here too.

Just think, my love, it is less than a week before we shall be in one another's arms, God willing! It is just six days, to be exact. It quickens my pulse to think of it, and seems to make everything so much easier.

I shall probably make several calls now. I have been postponing them in order to escape invitations to dinner; and fortunately there are not many to make.

I love you with all my heart and am altogether
                              Your own   Woodrow

P.S. Somehow I cannot form love phrases on the machine, and I have a feeling that you would not care to have me form them!

WWTLS (WP, DLC).
    [1] There were four plays and musicals running in Washington on February 15, 1898, and Wilson's comment might have applied to any one of them. See the reviews in the *Washington Post*, Feb. 15, 1898.

From Ellen Axson Wilson

                                        [Princeton, N. J.]
My own darling,   Wednesday night [Feb. 16, 1898]

I am at home again, safe and well, and not much tired after my day in New York. I write in extreme haste, thinking you might like a *prompt* note better than a longer letter,—so Ed is to mail this for me now.

Mrs. Hibben and I had a pleasant day,—spent much of it together. The doctor found me better, though he was not quite satisfied.

I got me a nice *little* trunk for this,—and other *little* journeys; a thing we have often needed, but the need for *such* things must grow *very* acute before one actually buys! I also bought a fire screen for the library fire; which will save us many anxious moments.

Isn't the Maine disaster perfectly awful! What *will* happen next! It must be intensely exciting in Washington just now.

All perfectly well. With love unspeakable

Your little wife,   Eileen.

ALS (WC, NjP).

From Daniel Collamore Heath

Dear Mr. Wilson: Boston 17 February, 1898

Yours of the 16fh [16th][1] is received and I hasten to assure you that I do very well remember that I wrote you asking whether the announcement of the book had better be left standing in the catalog or not, and I also remember that you replied that you saw no prospect of being albe [able] to write the book; but I hoped the prospect was better now. There was something in your last letter that led me to think you might have forgotten the old announcement, and I called your attention to it not to have you feel that you must be held by it, but rather that you might refresh your memory as to the character of the book I wanted.

I readily understand the situation and shall of course let the matter drop, and yet we want a good book on civil government and we do not know who else can make one that will suit us. Who is the next best fellow for such a book in your judgment?

I am gratified at the willingness on your part to do something for us some day in case you find the leisure.

Yours respectfully,   D C Heath

TLS (WP, DLC).
[1] It is missing.

To Ellen Axson Wilson

My own darling,   Washington, D. C.   17th February, 1898

I suppose, from what you said in your Tuesday letter about going with Mrs. Hibben, that you *did* go to New York yesterday. I shall be impatient to learn, to-night, how my pet fared in the cold, and what the doctor said about her health.

I went to the House of Representatives this afternoon and called on the Speaker. He had said to Renick that that would be the best place to find him, for he is much out of the chair during the seasons of routine debate and division. He proved not only agreeable but even attractive, keeping the floor indeed in conversation, like most public men accustomed to command attention, but frank, sensible, and interesting. I could not have *much* talk with him, for he was soon called away, but I enjoyed the ten minutes or so I *did* have very much indeed,—and think that I got his point of view about his office and its tendencies.[1] He told me he had read "Congressional Government" and had been astonished to find how admirably one outside affairs had been able to group the features of our "government by helter-skelter."

Since I began writing your sweet little note written after your return from N. Y. *has* come. Thank you, you sweet thing, for writing so promptly, to relieve my anxiety. I am so glad the doctor thinks you better, does he promise to get you *well* at once? Write me by what train you will reach Baltimore on Monday, sweetheart. Do you think you will have room in the *little* trunk for my academic toggery, cap included? By the way, the address on the 22nd is to be delivered by Charles Kendall Adams, President of the University of Wisconsin,—*not* a very enlivening prospect, I am sorry to say.[2]

My Maine will be completed, I confidently expect, to-morrow morning. I hope *it* wont blow up! When it is finished I shall relax my mind by reading examination papers! This is a pleasure trip only in a very modified degree.

My pleasure, my delight will come next week,—will be complete to overflowing the minute I see you. My heart waits for you with a yearning I cannot quiet except by that sweet hope.

                                        Your own   Woodrow

ALS (WP, DLC).

[1] For Wilson's later comment on his conversation with Speaker Reed, see the extract from the diary of Beatrice Webb printed at April 25, 1898.

[2] At the Founder's Day Celebration of the Johns Hopkins on February 22, Adams gave an address supporting the university's application for state aid. See the Baltimore *Sun*, Feb. 23, 1898.

From Ellen Axson Wilson

My own darling,   Princeton Feb. 17 1898.

I am delighted at the progress you are making with the Maine! You will soon have it off your hands entirely and then I hope the rest of your stay in Washington will be one of more pleasure.

By the way, I was shocked to learn from one of your letters,— was it Kennard's[—]of Mr. Faison's death![1] When and how was it? and what has become of his children? I cut out and enclose the article to which Mr. *Patterson* alludes in his letter today.[2] What a dreadful thing!—I can't remember "Mr. Patterson." Is he a special friend of yours? He evidently thinks you are engaged to stay with him in the fall; and that will get you out of a "hole," for it *must* antedate Miss Lyon's, since it was accepted so long ago that you had forgotten it! Of course it would *never* do to go to Miss Lyon's; it would be even better to be rude to her! though that will not be necessary.[3] She at least has sense enough to see that you can't go without me.

What will you say to Mr. Patterson in answer to his friend?[4] I suppose if you give them any encouragement they will consider you bound to accept in case their plans succeed![5]

Is it too late to change *my* plans again? I don't want to reach there on Tuesday because I will be sure to inconvenience everybody, and Monday is *so* soon,—will keep me so long from the children. It would really be best for me to leave here *Wednesday* on the 9.38, if it goes through; that would get me there about lunch time, would it not? Unless I get a letter or telegram from you vetoing that plan, I will so decide it.

I suppose you hear of nothing but the "Maine." Its happening then and there is certainly a most extraordinary coincidence. Yet surely it is nothing more. That it was an accident, due to some unknown chemical cause, seems much easier to believe than anything else,—when one considers the variety & enormous quantity of explosives aboard. Don't you think the people on the whole are behaving well?—showing sense and self-posession? I can't express my contempt for people who talk as some of the senators have done,—*trying* to cause a still worse explosion!—the very ones who *should* set the example of self-control to the nation!

We are all well; and *I love you* Woodrow, darling, more than I can say, or you can realize.   Your little wife,   Eileen.

ALS (WC, NjP).
[1] This letter, apparently from John Hanson Kennard, Jr., of New Orleans, telling about the recent death of Walter Emerson Faison, an old friend of Renick and Wilson, is missing.

2 This letter from Archibald Williams Patterson of Richmond, Wilson's friend from University of Virginia Law School days, is missing.

3 Wilson did stay with the Pattersons when he gave his lectures at Richmond College.

4 Patterson's friend was George Washington Miles of Radford, Va., a member of the Board of Visitors of the University of Virginia.

5 Miles had asked Patterson whether Wilson would accept the Chairmanship of the Faculty at the University of Virginia. For an intimation of Wilson's reply to Patterson, see G. W. Miles to WW, March 21, 1898.

To Ellen Axson Wilson

My own darling,   Washington, D. C.   18th February, 1898

This is actually the last letter I shall write to you before *seeing* you! A letter written you to-morrow or Sunday would not get to you till Monday,—and on Monday I shall *see* you. How my heart beats to think of it! The very novelty and loneliness of my situation here have made me miss you more acutely than ever, if possible. I have been amused and comfortable here, and am sure that I have by coming here done my faculties the right sort of service, given them the most refreshing and stimulating sort of variety,—but variety is not what my *heart* wants. It wants only and always *you*, and it is beyond measure delightful that you are actually to be part of my outing. And to think that you will hear my Bagehot and Maine both for the first time when you hear them *read* in public gives quite a novel and exciting touch of variety to the prospect of lecturing. It's great fun to think of it! The Maine was finished this morning, as per programme, just after eleven o'clock, having been written in six mornings, at the rate of a little more than four pages,—at the rate of nearly five pages,—*per diem*. Isn't that an ominous facility? Haven't you forebodings about the quality of a paper written so easily,—considering the fact that I never wrote about Sir Henry before? It must be in this talkative Washington air. I have not read the thing myself yet, and know very little more about its literary quality than you do. It is probably in the "same old style." But I am to see you so soon that I am not worrying about that, or about anything else just now. With your eyes beaming love and sympathy at me as I read, I can make *any*thing go off well enough in the reading. But I *ought* always to write with you in the house. No matter where I write, it is true, you are always present, in my consciousness even, to set a standard of taste for the sentences and the judgments they carry. But when you are actually at hand, and all is to be read to you at once, the whole power you exercise is so vivid! Ah, my darling, you are coming, and I am happy,—being altogether   Your own   Woodrow

ALS (WP, DLC).

From Ellen Axson Wilson

My own darling,   [Princeton, N. J.] Friday [Feb. 18, 1898]

I have quite inexcusably neglected a promise to Ed,[1] made some days ago, viz to secure from you a "character" to add to his collection for Chicago.[2] It—the collection—is almost complete now, and should be sent off; so I write a hasty note to catch the early morning mail, to ask you to send it as soon as possible.

The Trenton man was too busy to do your book-case, so Mr. Briner has just been here and will put on the first coat tomorrow. Please write me at once whether you are willing to have him finish it in my absence or would rather have him wait until week after next.

We are all quite well. Please, dear, don't let either [of] the Balt. "Christians" doctors impose on you and squeeze a speech out of you![3] Dr. Mitchell ought really to be ashamed to put it as he does, when he *knows* how you have suffered from over-work! I am rather indignant with him. I am very busy, but I think of you *all the time*, my *darling*, my Woodrow.

Your little wife   Eileen.

ALS (WP, DLC).

[1] Her brother, Edward Axson, who at this time was a graduate student in chemistry at Princeton.

[2] Perhaps he was about to apply for a fellowship at the University of Chicago. In any event, he went to the Massachusetts Institute of Technology in the autumn of 1898 to study chemical engineering.

[3] Dr. Charles Wellman Mitchell and Dr. Hiram Woods, Jr., Wilson's classmates at Princeton, had asked Wilson to speak to their respective church groups while he was in Baltimore for the Donovan lectures. Their letters are missing. Wilson seems to have declined.

A News Item

[Feb. 19, 1898]

The choice of electives for the second term in the upper classes has been announced. In the Senior Class Politics under Professor Wilson leads with 91 students. Bible is second with 89, American Literature third with 61, and History of Philosophy fourth with 57. In the Junior Class Politics has 100, English Literature 92, Bible 58, History of Philosophy 54 and French 46.

Printed in the *Princeton Press*, Feb. 19, 1898.

To Ellen Axson Wilson

My own darling,   Washington, 20 Feb'y, 1898

This is indeed a bitter, a cruel disappointment, that you are not coming till Wednesday, and I could wish it had not been kept till the last moment; but no doubt it is wise, and I acquiesce as best I may. I have telegraphed the Reids when to expect me on Monday, and that they are not to look for you till Wednesday. The 9:38 train is quite slow, and does not reach Baltimore in time for luncheon. It arrives at 2:00 P.M. The 10:42 is much better, and reaches Baltimore only 22 minutes later,—at 2:22. Unless you telegraph to 608 Cathedral St., Baltimore, to the contrary, I shall expect you on the latter train. Either train brings you through without change. Very likely the Reids will insist upon waiting luncheon for you,—but that cannot be helped; if you mean to get to Baltimore before night, those are the only trains to choose from. I shall tell the Reid's that you will bring lunch with you on the train. Of course you will,—you could not eat the sandwiches or the fried oysters you get on the way. By the way, I have a suggestion to make. Ask Ed. to telegraph us a few words (Care Prof. H. F. Reid, 608 Cathedral St.) every day,—in the morning, say,—as to how they all are and fare. That will serve to keep your mind easy,—as easy, at any rate, as possible.

I am very well, but bored by social duties. I dined last night with Mrs. Winthrop. She is always interesting and attractive, but her guests, with the exception of a very bright Irishman,[1] were decidedly unexciting. The chief woman guest did, indeed, excite me disagreeably by showing herself an anti-liquor and anti-tobacco fiend, with more ardour than sense,—and I came very near being curt and rude with her. I shan't always, I foresee, treat fools with courtesy,—even women fools,—and I told *this* one very plainly what my *opinions* were. To-night I go again to Mrs. Winthrop's—to *tea* (it being Sunday), to meet Professor Langley of the Smithsonian.[2] I wonder that she entertains on Sunday, for she is a devout Roman Catholic. Now that the social function is upon me, I shall be glad to get away.

I love you, darling. You must not think, from the rather businesslike and low-spirited tone of this letter, that I am *vexed* at my disappointment. I have only lost my spirits for a little, and shall be all right again presently. My heart was keyed up to a great and joyful expectation, and has run down rather painfully—that is all. I shall wind it up again to its normal tension,—for I shall see you on Wednesday, and I am always, with all my heart

Your own   Woodrow

ALS (WP, DLC).

¹ Maurice Francis Egan, at this time Professor of English Language and Literature, Catholic University of America. See M. F. Egan to WW, Oct. 20, 1902, Vol. 14, recalling the meeting.

² Samuel Pierpont Langley, noted astronomer and pioneer in aviation, at this time Secretary of the Smithsonian Institution.

From Ellen Axson Wilson

My own darling,   Princeton, Feb. 20, 1898.

I have been, in spite of all I could do, *blue* all today at the thought that I *might* have seen you tomorrow, but will not. I am sure I decided for the best;—but I wish I could, without giving trouble, have made it *Tuesday* at two. Oh how my heart *aches* to see you!

I was *so* afraid you would misunderstand, or rather take it too seriously and think me really sick, that I did not give the real reason for my change of plan, thinking I would explain fully when I saw you; but perhaps it is better to confess the truth at once. Dr. Van Valzeh himself was dubious about a whole week of social engagements for me,—having found my liver and nerves somewhat awry, but I felt so well that night that I didn't regard his warning. When however, to my surprise and disgust, I awaked the next morning with a violent sick head-ache I was so discouraged that I decided I had better curtail the trip;—though the headache was *all* gone when I wrote. But you know, dear, nothing fatigues your little country-bred wife,—not any amount of *work*— so much as society functions; and it would not contribute to your pleasure, your friend's, or my own, for me to be there half sick. I am now *quite sure* however that the *calomel*, which he gives me every other night, is the chief cause of the head-aches. I felt *perfectly* well last week after I had finished taking them. They will of course do good in the long run, but their *immediate* effect is to sicken. I shall have to take another tonight I suppose, but after that I shall certainly stop until my return from Baltimore, and so I shall expect to reach you in excellent condition. I have no head-ache today, but just now by way of variety, I am indulging in a little vertigo, which explains this more than usually erratic hand-writing.

Thinking you *might* send word that Mrs. Read had been notified, and it was too late to change my plans[,] I got *quite* ready to go tomorrow, so I shall *rest* thoroughly tomorrow and Tuesday. I will take the "10:42 A.M." train on Wednesday, reaching Balt at 2.25. Ed says that train gets there only 20 minutes later than the 9.37, so I had as well take the later. *Beg* Mrs. Reid to have *nothing* for me to eat but a *glass* of *milk* and a *wafer*,—it is really all I *ought* to eat.

Madge[1] turned up yesterday unexpectedly to us all. They[2] have holiday Monday & Tuesday on account of Washington's birthday. She say[s] Stock *may* come over tomorrow. Of course he *won't*.

Do you know that,—you having the address book with you,—I have not the slightest idea what Mr. Reid's initials or address are? Just suppose this shouldn't reach you! I had a letter from her; but like a perfect goose I tore it up after I answered it. I write in haste, so that Ed may mail this tonight.

Please, my own darling, don't be worried, and fancy I am sick. I *assure* you I am *not*.

I love you unspeakably, dear, and oh how happy beyond all words I will be when I am at last in your arms once more. I long to be there so much indeed that I don't dare trust myself to write about it tonight. I am afraid as it is I will have to end this evening with a little cry all by myself in the dark, so much do I want you! My *darling*, my Woodrow, my *husband*!

Your little wife,   Eileen

ALS (WP, DLC).
  [1] Margaret Axson, her younger sister.
  [2] At Adelphi Academy and College.

To Ellen Axson Wilson

My own darling,   Washington, D. C.   21 February, 1898

I write in the midst of packing and of the hurry of last things to do this morning, not knowing whether I shall have time to write after reaching Baltimore this afternoon. I leave at 3:15 and expect to reach Baltimore at 4:20.

I am very well and in my usual spirits again.

I supped last evening with Mrs. Winthrop, and met Senator Lindsay,[1] Professor Langley, and a Miss Aldis,—a most interesting company. After they were gone (at 10:30) I stayed and read my Bagehot lecture to Col. and Mrs. Winthrop and Miss Winthrop, the Colonel's maiden sister,—finishing about 11:45 with the Colonel nodding, but the others alert!

I love you, my precious Eileen, with all my heart, and long for you so intensely that I am thankful there isn't time to write about or dwell on it. I am in all eagerness and unspeakable love

Your own   Woodrow

P.S. I forgot your question. Briner ought not to be trusted to strike the shade without you.

ALS (WP, DLC).
¹ William Lindsay of Kentucky.

From Ellen Axson Wilson

[Princeton, N. J.]

My own darling,   Monday morning [Feb. 21, 1898]

Your letter just read. It is nearly 10 o'clock and I scribble a line to be sent to the *right* address. Madge will take it to the office. I hope it will make the 10.42. I wrote last night, but had forgotten the address, and found the address book gone. Sent my letter "Care Prof. Harry Reid Mount Vernon Place," so perhaps you won't get it. In it I said that I would take the 10.42 on *Wednesday.* And also explained as I should have done frankly at first, that I was postponing the start because I was not quite strong enough for a whole week of social functions. Ah, if I were only to visit *you* quietly in Washington how happy I should be! for then I should be in your arms tonight! But then I should miss the lectures, and that would break my heart. I [am] feeling better this morning and expect to reach you in excellent condition.   Your devoted little wife,   Eileen

Your lectures *are* late in the afternoon, are they not? If, by any chance, I am mistaken there, and will miss one by not getting there till Wed. at 2.22 you will telegraph, will you not? so that I may go on *Tuesday* afternoon? It would be an overwhelming disappointment to miss one of the lectures.

ALS (WC, NjP).

Notes for Remarks on Washington's Birthday¹

J. H. U. [Feb. 22] '98

Washington not a Saint,—not patronizing
    Heaven lies about us in our infancy
Mark off a space on him.
W. no prig (Sugar coat your head)
    Home sense and sense of simplicity at Mt. Vernon
    Breed of Lee and Jackson.
    Sense of neighbourhood—sense of home-bred honour.
Doctrine of *service*—serve with your*self,*—the *best* that is *in you.*
    Guard only vs. "*indecent* exposure of private opinions"
There is no cloying of sweetness here,—and we cannot be cloyed with *strength.*
    Good word, better word, bad word.

Pottsdam.

Lift the suspicion of lack of practical pol. sagacity from colleges by enlightened, tolerant service.

WWhw MS. (WP, DLC).

[1] For the occasion of this speech, see the news report which follows.

A News Report of Founder's Day Exercises at the Johns Hopkins

[Feb. 23, 1898]

HOPKINS UNIVERSITY

The principal feature yesterday of the Commemoration Day exercises celebrating the twenty-second anniversary of the Johns Hopkins University was the announcement by President Daniel C. Gilman that the university trustees had decided to ask for State aid. . . .

A Prize Awarded.

Prof. Herbert B. Adams announced that the John Marshall prize, one of the highest honors in the gift of the university, had this year been awarded to Dr. Charles D. Hazen, Dartmouth, '89, Johns Hopkins University, Ph.D., '93, now professor of history in Smith College, for his scholarly treatise upon "Contemporaneous American Opinion of the French Revolution."

The prize is a relief portrait in bronze of Chief Justice Marshall and was established by a New England lady. It has been awarded in successive years to the most distinguished alumnus of the Johns Hopkins University, the first recipient being Professor Woodrow Wilson,[1] now of Princeton University, who yesterday occupied a seat upon the stage. . . .

Alumni Reunions.

At night the general Hopkins Alumni Association had the eleventh annual banquet at the Hotel Rennert. It was the largest reunion of the sort for several years, the presence of alumni of the eighties being particularly noticeable. One hundred and thirty-five sat down to the tables.

The orators of the night were President Gilman, Mr. Charles J. Bonaparte, Major Richard M. Venable and Prof. Woodrow Wilson, who spoke upon "Our Patron Saint." The university banjo club rendered selections, Dr. Thomas S. Baker sang, and Messrs. Harwood and Clunet gave topical songs. . . .

Printed in the Baltimore *Sun*, Feb. 23, 1898; some editorial headings omitted.

[1] About this award, see EAW to WW, June 17, 1892, n. 6, Vol. 8.

An Announcement of Wilson's Donovan Lectures

[Feb. 23, 1898]

PROF. WOODROW WILSON'S LECTURES.

Prof. Woodrow Wilson, of Princeton University, will begin his annual course of lectures at the Johns Hopkins University today. Professor Wilson is a Ph.D. of the university, and has become widely known in the past few years by his historical writings. His subject this year, "Three Prominent [Literary] Statesmen," is of more general interest than his former lectures, and the lectures are open to the public.

Today Dr. Wilson will speak upon Edmund Burke, tomorrow upon Walter Bagehot and on Friday his subject will be Sir Henry Sumner Maine.

Printed in the Baltimore *Sun*, Feb. 23, 1898.

Two Public Lectures at the Johns Hopkins

[Feb. 23, 1898][1]

Edmund Burke: A Lecture.

Much has been said and written about Edmund Burke, and the whole world knows his fame; but it is not necessary to repeat it all to see him alive again. It is not necessary to tell the entire story of his life to make it clear what measure of man he was or of what force and consequence in his day. It is possible to view him from a single point of observation and in a single situation and yet see him complete and whole, in his habit as he lived.

There is often to be found in the life of a great man some point of eminence at which his powers culminate and his character stands best revealed, their characteristic excellence brought to light and illustrated with a sort of dramatic force. Generally it is a moment of success that so reveals them at their best, when their will has had its way and their genius its triumph. But Edmund Burke seems to me to give the most striking proofs of his character and genius in the evil days in which his life ended,— not when he was a leader in the Commons, but when he was a stricken old man at Beaconsfield. That Burke was a great states-

[1] All three of Wilson's Donovan lectures are printed at their delivery date, and all notes are by the Editors. The definite composition date of this Burke manuscript is unknown; however, Wilson certainly composed it between November 29, 1897, when he agreed to give the Donovan lectures, and February 1, 1898, when he left for Washington to write the lectures on Bagehot and Maine. In all probability Wilson wrote the Burke lecture during the Christmas holidays of 1897-98. There are some WWhw notes taken for the Burke lecture in WP, DLC.

man no thinking man can read his pamphlets and speeches and deny; but a man can be a great statesman and yet not be a great man. Burke makes as deep an impression upon our hearts as upon our minds. We are taken captive, not so much by his reasoning as by the generous warmth that steals out of it into our hearts. There is a tonic breath of character and of generous purpose in what he writes,—the fine sentiment of a pure man; and we are made to know that he who wrote thus was great not so much by reason of what he said or did as by reason of what he was. What a man was you may often discover in his days of bitterness and pain better than in his seasons of cheer and hope; for if the noble qualities triumph then, showing themselves still sound and sweet; if his courage sink not; if he show himself still capable of self-forgetfulness; if he still stir with a passion for the service of causes and policies which are beyond himself, his stricken age is greater than his full-pulsed middle age. This is the test that Burke endures,—the test of fire. It has not often been judged so; but let any man of insight take that extraordinary *Letter to a Noble Lord*, which was written in 1796, and which is Burke's *apologia pro vita sua*, consider the circumstances under which it was written, its tone, its truth, its self-revelations, and the manner of man that is revealed, and say whether this be not the real Burke, undaunted, unstained, unchanged in purpose and in principle.

Some of Burke's biographers have turned their faces away from these last scenes and last writings of his life with a sort of sad reverence, as if loath to blame and yet unable to approve. They have bidden us draw the veil over these days of disturbed judgment and unbalanced passion and think only of the great days when he was master of himself, the foremost political thinker in all Europe. His vision had until now been so clear, his judgment so sane and sure footed, his knowledge of the facts with which he dealt so comprehensive and unerring; and it is simple pity, they say[,] that he should have gone mad about the French Revolution. For that is the fact they are at a loss to account for, and despair of justifying. Burke threw all his magnificent resources against the French Revolution, and with a sort of fury assisted to carry England into the war wh. monarchical Europe was waging to suppress it. And yet that Revolution was France's salvation: without it she could not have been set in the way of a free life and a reformed and purified gov't. Frightful as were its excesses, they were but the violent purgings of a wholesome and cleansing disease, and Burke with his knowledge of France and of affairs ought to have seen it. Burke, they will tell you, knew France better than any other Englishman living, except Arthur Young. He was not arguing for or against France, you suggest, but only crying out vs. the introduction of the French revolutionary ideas into England, whither the disease might be carried by contagion and where it would feed upon a healthy, not upon a distempered society, working death, it might be, instead of purification. There was no such danger, they reply, and Burke of all men should have known that there was none. They will cite you that famous passage in which, in the days of his calm vision, Burke had described the placid content of England and had laughed at those who supposed that the noise of a few politicians could disturb it. "Because half a dozen grasshoppers under a fern make the field ring with their importunate chink,"— he had laughed,—["]while thousands of great cattle beneath the shadow of the British oak chew the cud and are silent, pray do not imagine that those who make the noise are the only inhabitants of the field, that of course they are many in number, or that, after all, they are other than the little, shrivelled, meagre, hopping, though loud and troublesome, insects of the hour." Had he now himself at last been betrayed into mistaking the insects of the field for the great cattle of the British herd, and did he fear a stampede because these chirped with excited clamour?

The question is radical. Settle it, and you have analysed Edmund Burke. You are easily able to prove that, at any rate in the late year 1791, the year after he wrote his great pamphlet against the Revolution,—his "Reflections on the Revolution in France,"— he was as clear sighted as ever, and as poised in judgment. A correspondent in France—a member of the Nat. Ass.—had asked him to suggest a course of action for those who were seeking to guide affairs in the unhappy kingdom; but he had declined and had given these luminous and statesmanlike reasons for declining. "Permit me to say," he wrote, "that if I were as confident as I ought to be diffident in my own loose general ideas, I never should venture to broach them, if but at twenty leagues' distance from the centre of your affairs. I must see with my own eyes; I must in a manner touch with my own hands, not only the fixed, but momentary circumstances, before I could venture to suggest any political project whatsoever. I must know the power and disposition to accept, to execute, to persevere. I must see all the aids and all the obstacles. I must see the means of correcting the plan, where correctives would be wanted. I must see the things: I must see the men. Without a concurrence and adaptation of these to the design, the very best speculative projects might become not only useless but mischievous. Plans must be made for men. People at a distance must judge ill of men. They do not always answer to their reputation when you approach them. Nay the perspective varies, and shows them quite other than you thought them. At a distance, if we judge uncertainly of men, we must judge worse of *opportunities* which continually vary their shapes and colours, and pass away like clouds." Here, certainly, was a lucid interval, if the man was mad! It is a matter of common knowledge, too, that in the very midst of his excitement about French affairs he was able to give counsel with all his old-time wisdom and self-possession about the deeply disturbed affairs of Ireland,—counsel that rang true to the sane and tolerant standards he had stood by while there was revolutionary war in America. He wrote, too, the while, calm "Thoughts and Details on Scarcity," from every line of which spoke the hopeful and informed economist. His thought held steadily on its way, without excitement or serious error. His training held good as in every previous effort of his mind. "I had earned my pension before I set my foot in St. Stephen's chapel," he said with quiet pride. "The first session I sat in Parliament, I found it necessary to analyze the whole commercial, financial, constitutional, and foreign interests of Great Britain and its empire." He keeps to the last the assured and confident step of the veteran. I take leave to say again that the real Burke may be found and admired in the *Letter to a Noble Lord*, written in the midst of the French frenzy, no less than in the noble utterances in which he defended his opposition to the American war.

The *Letter* was written in defence of the pension which had been granted him in 1794, and contained his own estimate of his public services. If a man can be petty, expect him to be so when he defends a bounty bestowed upon himself; if ever an old man may be petulant, it is when the rewards of his old age are sneered at and condemned. Burke is neither. There was everything to sting him in the circumstances of the attack. He had accepted a pension from the government of William Pitt, his arch opponent in politics till their common fear of the French Revolution drew them together and brought about an artificial coalition in affairs. It was possible for malicious men to make him out an apostate Whig and twit him cruelly with being a beneficiary of the court, though all his life he had championed a proud independence and talked against the extravagance of private grants. Pitt had not brought the grant of his pension before Parliament, but had arranged it by gift from the Crown, and Burke had the mortification of feeling that Pitt had taken this course because he feared the opposition the grant would excite in Parliament. Outside Parliament it raised a storm of animadversion and abuse as it was, and its discussion was not wholly avoided in the Houses. The Duke of Bedford and the Earl of Lauderdale attacked the pension in the Lords, as part of their general indictment of the ministry; and it was to their attack that Burke replied. "Loose libels ought to be passed by in silence and contempt," he says, with his accustomed gravity. "By me they have been so always. I knew, that, as long as I remained in public, I should live down the calumnies of malice and the judgments of ignorance. If I happened to be now and then in the wrong, (as who is not?) like all other men, I must bear the consequence of my faults and my mistakes. The libels of the present day are just of the same stuff as the libels of the past. But they derive an importance from the rank of the persons they come from, and the gravity of the place where they were uttered. In some way or other I ought to take some notice of them. To assert myself thus traduced is not vanity or arrogance. It is a demand of justice; it is a demonstration of gratitude." (V., 177)[2]

The year 1794, the year in which the pension was granted, had been the darkest year of all Burke's strenuous career. The active work of his life was ended. The long trial of Hastings had that very year at last been concluded and with it the last, as it was also the most arduous, public business he was to engage in. He had recognized this as the end of active duty, had withdrawn from the House of Commons, and had but just turned to Beaconsfield for the solace of a quiet old age, when a cruel blow fell upon him which poisoned the sources of happiness and snatched hope away. He had loved Richard Burke, his son and only child, with all the passion of his ardent nature; and the year had opened bright with the hope that Richard was to succeed him as member for Malton in the Commons; but death had come of a sudden and taken his son away. "The storm has gone over me," he cried; "and I lie like one of those old oaks which the late hurricane has scattered about me. I am stripped of all my honours, I am torn up by the roots, and lie prostrate on the earth. . . . I live in an inverted order. They who ought to have succeeded me have gone before me. They who should have been to me as posterity are in the place of ancestors."

There was nothing to break the force of the blow. Only absorbing labour can lighten such a man of grief like this. Quiet Beaconsfield, lying remote from the busy world, out upon the gentle plains of Buckinghamshire, was no place in which to seek for-

---

2 Wilson is referring to *The Works of the Right Honorable Edmund Burke,* 5th edn. (12 vols., Boston, 1877).

getfulness. Here was leisure for every memory; here were days
open to be possessed by any thoughts that might come; here was
no business, but only a desolated home, with an old man for
tenant. The very sympathy of his tender wife, bereaved like himself, was but a part of the same grief. Even the relish of old
friendships was not vouchsafed him. His friends of the old days
that had seen his life run strong, with the full sunlight on it,—the
friends whose comradeship and sympathy and counsel had given
to his days of labour their keenest zest and confidence, no longer
sought him out, or could bring him any succour. They had not
cast him off; he had withdrawn himself from them, because they
would not think as he did of the Revolution over sea, in France.
He had feared and hated it from the first: they had been tolerant
towards it. He had turned from them. Most of them had followed
him at last, indeed,—the great Duke of Portland, Lord Fitzwilliam,
Windham, and Grenville, and a great company of the rank and
file of the old Whigs, till men laughed and said there were not
enough members left to the minority that clung to Fox to fill a
hackney coach,—for the atrocities of the revolutionists in France
had wrought a deep change in England; but Burke must have felt
it, though no humiliation or dishonour, yet a thing unpalateable
and in need of explanation that he should be the pensioner of a
Tory government with which his old-time associates were acting
only because political necessity and the critical stress of affairs
for the time compelled them. He could have no such *satisfaction*
in old associations under the new order of affairs as he had had
under the old. We may blame him for his break with Fox, and
say that it was unnecessary and wanton; but we are not assessing
praise or blame, we are seeking to understand a character, and
shall know it better when we realize how exquisite the pain of
that separation was for it, and yet how inevitable. We must seek
to know what the struggle of that day of crisis meant for Burke,
and meant, Burke being the judge, for mankind itself. It was,
after all, no ignoble fault that Burke had committed,—if fault
it was.

Upon a first reading of Burke's utterances against the Revolution in France, no doubt, every man of the modern time must
feel them to be intemperate. "Astronomers have supposed," he
says in that famous letter, "that, if a certain comet, whose path
intersected the ecliptic, had met the earth in some (I forget what)
sign, it wd. have whirled us along with it, in its eccentric course,
into God knows what regions of heat and cold. Had the portentous comet of the Rights of Man (wh. 'from its horrid hair
shakes pestilence and war,' and 'with fear of change perplexes

monarchs') had that comet crossed upon us in that internal state of England, nothing human could have prevented our being irresistibly hurried out of the highway of heaven into all the vices, crimes, horrors, and miseries of the French Revolution." (V., 181) *"To innovate is not to reform.* The French Revolutionists complained of everything; they refused to reform anything; and they left nothing, no, nothing at all, *unchanged.* The consequences are *before* us,—not in remote history, not in future prognostication: they are about us; they are upon us. They shake the public security; they menace private enjoyment. They dwarf the growth of the young; they break the quiet of the old. If we travel, they stop our way. They infest us in town; they pursue us to the country. Our business is interrupted, our repose is troubled, our pleasures are saddened, our very studies are poisoned and perverted, and knowledge is rendered worse than ignorance, by the enormous evils of this dreadful innovation." (V., 187)

Here, if you look nowhere else, is a sufficient explanation of the critical matter of his life's history: there need be no mystery about Burke's attitude towards the French Revolution after reading this luminous *Letter,*—and there need no longer be any pitiful apology for it, either. He had not mistaken the noisy insects of the hour for the great cattle of the British pasture. Some of the first minds of the kingdom, whether for philosophy or for statesmanship, had hailed the doctrines of the French revolutionists as the true gospel of liberty; men of both parties in the State, and not a few of those who were most studious in affairs, looked to see the world liberalized by the gracious power of the Rights of Man. No doubt it was clear enough in the end that the mass of the steady English people were safe against the infection, and that Burke's fears were exaggerated: the "thousands of great cattle beneath the shadow of the British oak" continued to chew the cud and look forth upon their quiet fields with an undisturbed philosophy. But who could certainly foresee that they would thus keep the subtle breath of war and panic out of their nostrils? Who can say how much of their quiet they took from the voice of their herdsmen, crying out the familiar words of gov't. and control? This was no common or vulgar danger that Burke set himself first to expose and then to neutralize. It was no mere French spirit of disorder that he feared would cross the Channel, but a spirit of change that was without nationality or country,—an abstract thing of dogma and belief like the spirit of the Reformation, which had ignored all boundaries of states and moved the world as if it had been but a single community.

"The present Revolution in France," he said, "seems to me to bear little resemblance or analogy to any of those which have been brought about in Europe, upon principles merely political. *It is a Revolution of doctrine and theoretic dogma.* It has a much greater resemblance to those changes which have been made upon religious grounds, in which a spirit of proselytism makes an essential part. The last revolution of doctrine and theory wh. has happened in Europe is the Reformation. It is not for my purpose to take any notice here of the merits of that revolution, but to state one only of its effects. That effect was, *to introduce other interests into all countries than those which arose from their locality and natural circumstances.* The principle of the Reformation was such as, by its essence, could not be local or confined to the country in which it had its origin. For instance, the doctrine of 'Justification by Faith or by Works,' which was the original basis of the Reformation, could not have one of its alternatives true as to Germany and false as to every other country. Neither are questions of theoretic truth and falsehood governed by circumstances any more than by places. On that occasion, therefore, the spirit of proselytism expanded itself with great elasticity upon all sides: and great divisions were everywhere the result." (IV., 318, 319). Similarly, Burke saw, the new gospel of the Rights of Man might be counted on, if unchecked, to divide the nations of the world. "The political dogma," he said, "which, upon the new French system, is to unite the factions of different nations, is this: 'That the majority, told by the head, of the taxable people in every country, is the perpetual, natural, unceasing, indefeasible sovereign; that this majority is perfectly master of the form as well as the administration of the State, and that the magistrates, under whatever names they are called, are only functionaries to obey the orders which that majority may make; that this is the only natural government; that all others are tyranny and usurpation.' " (IV, 322). He did not pretend to prescribe for France; but he saw her leaders engaged in a mad work of destruction; he knew that such doctrines logically and inevitably breed a corresponding practice; he believed that such a way of reform as it had produced in France would mar not only the institutions but also the whole moral and political habit of the English people; and he meant to keep out the infection if he could. He meant to keep England, if he might, from "the dreadful contagion" of revolutionary principles,—"to preserve, pure and untainted, the ancient, inbred integrity, piety, good nature, and good humour of the people of England,"—so he put it,—"from the dreadful pestilence which, beginning in France, threatens to lay waste the whole moral and in a great degree the whole physical world, having done both in the focus of its most intense malignity." (V., 204-205)

There is here the whole philosophy of his course with regard to the Revolution in France. If his excitement rose beyond measure in the struggle, who shall say that it was an unnatural excitement, or an unhallowed? If you would see him at his best, Miss Burney said, you must not mention politics. "His irritability is so terrible on that theme," she declared, "that it gives immediately to his face the expression of a man who is going to defend himself from murderers." We should not expect a man to be easy and affable when he deems himself in a death grapple with the enemies of his country. If the French revolutionary doctrines *had* taken root in England,—what then? They did not? Who shall say how much this vehement Irishman did to keep them out?

At any rate, it turned out that he was speaking the real mind of England about the Revolution. When once they saw the monstrous projeny it brought forth in action, Englishmen flocked, rank and file, to the defense of authority and orderly government, and Burke found himself for the nonce a European power. Statesmen of every opinion sought his advice. He had once sent his son to Coblenz to act as his representative in helping the exiled noblemen of France to form practicable plans of action. Richard Burke had neither the talents nor the nobleness of disposition with which his father credited him. The great hearted man gave his love as his nature bade him; chose his intimates by rules of affection and duty, rather than by rules of interest; and had fewer connections to commend him to the great than any other public man of his generation; and yet ruled by the sheer force of genius amongst those who sought counsel. "Burke has now got such a train after him," writes Gilbert Elliott in 1793, "as would sink anybody but himself. His son, who is quite *nauseated* by all mankind; his brother, who is liked better than his son, but is rather oppressive with animal spirits and brogue; and his cousin, William Burke, who is just returned unexpectedly from India, as much ruined as when he went years ago, and who is a fresh charge on any prospects of power Burke may ever have. Mrs. Burke has in her train Miss French, the most perfect *She Paddy* that ever was caught. Notwithstanding these disadvantages Burke is in himself a sort of power in the state."—It is noteworthy that this critical contemporary should have seen it.—"It is not too much to say that he is a sort of power in Europe, though totally without any of those means or the smallest share in them which give or maintain power in other men." (*Ency Brit.* IV., 549)

Sir James Mackintosh, who had written an earnest defence of the Revolution in answer to Burke's first and great pamphlet vs. it, himself surrendered at discretion when he saw what things the years brought forth in France, confessed that he had been 'the dupe of his enthusiasm'; and sought Burke out in his retirement at Beaconsfield to seek his friendship and render him homage in his closing days. There he saw Burke roll on the carpet, a gleeful participant in the sports of children, and heard such talk as no man else could utter,—so full of life and power was it, so amazingly various, so free and unpremeditated in its copiousness and beauty. This was not the morbid and unbalanced man some have thought they saw, who now look back to the French Revolution as, after all, a wholesome, though terrible, catastrophe, and feel themselves repelled by Burke's savage onslaught upon it.

These were the days in which Burke wrote his defence of his pension, and surely that masterly *Letter* is a wonderfully perfect mirror in which to see the man and the meaning of his life. We are first of all struck by the splendid pride of this once obscure attorney's son, with his queer following of discredited Irishmen,—his own tongue, as we know, touched with the brogue of that volatile race which Englishmen half despised, half feared, and wholly distrusted. It was a sad indiscretion on the part of the Duke of Bedford, it turned out, to have ventured to attack this apparently broken old man. "Why will his Grace, by attacking me," cries this formidable Celt, "force me reluctantly to compare my little merit with that wh. obtained from the Crown those prodigies of profuse donation by which he tramples on the mediocrity of humble and labourious individuals? I would willingly leave him to the Herald's College." (V., 200) "The merit of the grantee he derives from was that of being a prompt and greedy instrument of a *levelling* tyrant, who oppressed all descriptions of his people, but who fell with particular fury on everything that was *great and noble*. Mine has been in endeavouring to screen every man, in every class, from oppression, and particularly in defending the high and eminent, who, in the bad times of confiscating princes, confiscating chief governors, or confiscating demagogues, are the most exposed to jealousy, avarice, and envy." (V., 202) Had the Duke forgot that the first peer of his name was a Mr. Russell, "raised by being a minion of Henry the Eighth," (V., 201)—or was he too young to know, that he should attack the pension of this man, who had, by his steadfast defense of the existing order, "strained every nerve to keep the Duke of Bedford in that situation" of power and of property which alone gave him privilege and precedence? "Let him employ all the energy of his youth," exclaimed the indignant old statesman, "and all the resources of his wealth to crush rebellious principles which have no foundation in morals, and rebellious movements that have no provocation in tyranny. Then will be forgot the rebellions which, by a doubtful priority in crime, his ancestor had provoked and extinguished." (V., 206) "My merits, whatever they are, are original and personal." (V., 200) "I was not, like his Grace of Bedford, swaddled and rocked and dandled into a legislator: *'Nitor in adversum'* is the motto for a man like me. I possessed not one of the qualities, nor cultivated one of the arts, that recommend men to the favour and protection of the great. . . . At every step of my progress in life (for in every step was I traversed and opposed,) and at every turnpike I met, I was obliged to show my passport, and again and again to prove my sole title to the honour of being useful to my country, by a proof that I was not wholly unacquainted with its laws and the whole system of its interests both abroad and at home." As we read, how much greater does the recent house of Burke seem in the person of this single man, than all the generations of the ancient house of Bedford, and how noble, without patent from the Crown.

In this great *Letter* are set forth, too, Burke's own estimate of the services he had rendered. "If I were to call for a reward, (which I have never done,) it should be for those in which for fourteen years without intermission I showed the most industry and had the least success: I mean in the affairs of India. They are those on which I value myself the most: most for the importance, most for the labour, most for the judgment, most for constancy and perseverance in the pursuit." (V., 192) There is here no egotism. It is a great mind's satisfaction in great tasks, to which it justly feels itself equal. More than that, it is a great mind's satisfaction in great ideals. This *Letter* is, indeed, from first to last, a defence of his own life and motives, and, knowing it to be this, you can but wonder at its noble dignity, its largeness of spirit, its essential importance, as if it were a state paper. And yet, if you will analyze it, if you will look again at the quality that has struck you, you will find that you do not think of Burke's life as you read. First you think of the indiscretion the young Duke of Bedford has committed in attacking this veteran master of argument and retort. His young bones hardly so much a[s] crack in the jaws of the lion, so soft are they,—so swift and utter is there annihilation. There is a sense of overwhelming if not of pitiless power to be got from those terrible sentences in which fame of the house of Bedford is to be seen engulphed and ruined. But there ensues upon this another impression. You feel that there is no personal passion,—no anger,—no spirit of retaliation or revenge. You have risen, imperceptibly, into a region of high principle. You begin to realize that the Duke of Bedford has not offended Burke (that is a mere detail) so much as he has outraged great principles of moral order and political wisdom. Burke is taking you straight to the uplands of the region of thought in which he finds himself,—not so much by deliberation, it would seem, as by instinct,—and is placing you at the point he knows and loves so well: the point from which you can see all the ancient kingdoms of government, their old landmarks and strong defences.

He must always have a concrete object for his thought. It is the folly of Bedford that has brought him out of Beaconsfield into the familiar forum of public controversy again. This peer of the realm has shown himself ready to consort with those who justify the revolutionists over sea,—and has found fellows in the Lords to cheer him while he questioned the very principles of ancient privilege upon which that House and the peerage itself were founded! Burke runs upon the challenge to the defense of the realm and its immemorial Constitution. It is there he feels his passions deeply engaged. He writes a manual of statesmanship for the rebuke of a heady young Duke and the behoof of all England. A single, very celebrated, passage from the *Letter* will illustrate the whole purpose and habit of this great mind. "As long," he says, with deep and solemn passion, "as long as the well-compacted structure of our Church and State, the sanctuary, the holy of holies of that ancient law, defended by reverence, defended by power, a fortress at once and a temple, shall stand inviolate on the brow of the British Lion,—as long as the British monarchy, not more limited than fenced by the orders of the State, shall, like the proud Keep of Windsor, rising in the majesty of proportion, and girt with the double belt of its kindred and coëval towers, as long as this awful structure shall oversee and guard the subjected land,—so long the mounds and dikes of the low, fat Bedford level will have nothing to fear from all the pickaxes of all the levellers of France. As long as our sovereign lord the King, and his faithful subjects, the lords and commons of this realm,—the triple cord which no man can break,—the solemn, sworn, constitutional frank-pledge of this nation,—the firm guaranties of each other's being and each other's rights,—the joint and several securities, each in its place and order, for every kind and every quality of property and dignity,—as long as these endure, so long the Duke of Bedford is safe, and we are all safe together,—the high from the blights of envy and the spoliations of

rapacity, the low from the iron hand of oppression and the inso-
lent spurn of contempt." (V., 210) Here is to be had a key to the
whole *Letter*,—a key to Burke's thought when he spoke of government,—a key to his method, and to his style throughout all his
writings.

He did not erect "the proud Keep of Windsor" there, in that
famous passage, merely as a majestic ornament of style, nor in
any way as an object of pleasure. It in fact stands not very far
away from the "low, fat Bedford level.["] There is but Buckinghamshire and a slender arm of Hertford between; and Burke
means you to see it as an actual bulwark of the land. But as his
own eye turns southward to the majestic pile his thought is
quickened, as always, by the simile of power. It seems to him a
type and image of the law,—upon its walls "the awful hoar of innumerable ages,"—within it the title deeds of a nation grown old
in privilege and in ordered liberty. It is this that exhilerates the
mind in Burke,—this *reality* of great thought. You stand ever with
your feet upon the earth, you are always in the midst of affairs,
men and concrete powers round about you, and yet your vision is
not of them, it is of the great verities in the midst of which they
move. You are strengthened by a sense of the nearness, the im-
manence of great principles of action. They are seen to dwell at
the very heart of affairs, and to form as it were an intrinsic part
of circumstance. They are abroad and operative in the world.
Burke's thought has, therefore, a certain *visible* quality. It does
not seem wholly bred of the mind. It has always about it the
scenery and atmosphere of action. That you should be moved by
such thinking is of course inevitable: it comes from a mind itself
stirred and quick with practical effort. Never, while it keeps to its
normal processes, is that mind betrayed into preferring the
speech it uses to the meaning it would convey,—and that meaning carries the superb ornaments with which it is so often
adorned with a quite inevitable appropriateness. If images abound,
it is because the mind that here speaks conceives the world always thus in concrete and almost tangible shapes. It is because
its eye is ever upon the object of its thought. It is not reflecting;
it is observing: it *sees* the field of action. Men and nations are
not still before it, but move always with the large variety and
dramatic force of life itself. Its retina is crowded with images
and deeply touched with colour, like a little world.

It is this vivid realization of the world of fact and of spirit
as it is that makes Burke's thought seem so conservative, and
makes us wonder whether, after all, we should call him a liberal
or not. There is no element of speculation in it. It keeps always

to the slow pace of inevitable change and invents nothing, content to point out the accepted ways and use the old light of day to walk by. Nevertheless there is one infallible test by which you know Burke's thought to have the power of life in it,—and, if the power of life, the power of growth. You are exhilarated by it. It does not hold your powers back; it quickens them mightily. There are visions of the future in it, as well as of the past,—and the future is bright with a reasonable hope of healing change. But he loved above all things, and very wisely loved, a sober, provident, and ordered progress in affairs;—the balanced force of government seemed to him more likely to work out results that would last and could be lived by than the wilful and too hasty ardour of enthusiasm. "I have ever abhorred," he said in that memorable *Letter*,—"I have ever abhorred, since the first dawn of my understanding to this its obscure twilight, all the operations of opinion, fancy, inclination, and will, in the affairs of government, where only a sovereign reason, paramount to all forms of legislation and administration, should dictate. Government is made for the very purpose of opposing that reason to will and to caprice, in the reformers or in the reformed, in the governors or in the governed, in kings, in senates, or in people." (V., 189) This is our own doctrine. It is with a hope to have such moderation and restraint in affairs that we have made our written constitutions,—that they may govern the course of law and of policy. "It was my aim," said Burke, "to give to the people the substance of what I knew they desired, and what I thought was right, whether they desired it or not," (V., 186) and this must ever be the best maxim of statesmanship amongst a free people.

It was this very genius for slow action and confident self-mastery that Tocqueville found and praised as the first and greatest of all political qualities in the conduct of our own affairs. He had seen France stagger from revolution to revolution like a tipsy lad, high-spirited, generous, full of an engaging dash and hope, but incapable of self-government or of sober effort, sustained and manful, and he knew how to appreciate the maturer powers of a self-governing race. "The temperament of our nation," he said, speaking of his own France, "is so peculiar that the general study of mankind fails to embrace it. France is ever taking by surprise even those who have made her the special object of their researches; a nation more apt than any other to comprehend a great design and to embrace it, capable of all that can be achieved by a single effort of whatever magnitude, but unable to abide long at this high level, because she is ever swayed by sensations and not by principles, and that her instincts are better than her morality; a people civilized among all civilized nations of the earth, yet, in some respects, still more akin to the savage state than any of them, for the characteristic of savages is, to decide on the sudden impulse of the moment, unconscious of the past and careless of the future."[3] Tocqueville knew, as Burke did, with his vivid insight, that it is a long drill in the moderate processes of an ordered liberty that makes a people conscious of the past and careful of the future; and it was under the influence of this thought that, with a half envious admiration, he paid us that incomparable compliment, whose perfect phrases linger in the memory like the tones of verse. "It is a novelty in the history of society,"—he is speaking of the self-possession and capable deliberateness of those critical days during which we exchanged the flimsy Confederation for our present firm and consistent frame of government: "It is a novelty in the history of society to see a great people turn a calm and scrutinizing eye upon itself, when apprised by the legislature that the wheels of government are stopped; to see it carefully examine the extent of the evil, and patiently wait for two years until a remedy was discovered, which it voluntarily adopted without having wrung a tear or a drop of blood from mankind." (I., 109)[4]

It was this superlative gift of sobriety and good-temper in affairs that Burke feared to see England lose should she too weakly indulge herself in any feeling of partiality for the feverish reforms of France. Those who blame him dispraise the very qualities that made him great. Burke had the supreme literary gift of vision: he saw things steadily and saw them whole, and other men were daunted and in doubt about his trustworthiness because they could not see so much;—but he had not the literary mind in affairs, and protested it should not be used in matters of government. "I have lived long and variously in the world," said he. "Without any considerable pretensions to literature myself, I have aspired to the love of letters. . . . I can form a tolerable estimate of what is likely to happen from a character chiefly dependent for fame and fortune on knowledge and talent. . . . Naturally men so formed and finished are the first gifts of Providence to the world. But when they have once thrown off the fear of God . . . and the fear of man, . . . nothing can be conceived more hard than the heart of a thorough-bred metaphysician. . . . It is like that of the Principle of Evil himself, incorporeal, pure, un-

---

[3] Quoted in the translator's introduction to Alexis de Tocqueville, *Democracy in America*, translated by Henry Reeve, new edn. (2 vols., London, 1875), I, xix-xx. This is the edition in the Wilson Library, Library of Congress, and the passage quoted is marked in pencil.

[4] *ibid.*, I, 109.

mixed, dephlegmated, defecated evil. . . . Their imagination is
not fatigued with the contemplation of human suffering through
the wild waste of centuries added to centuries of misery and
desolation. Their humanity is at their horizon,—and, like the horizon, it always flies before them. . . . These philosophers consider
men in their experiments no more than they do mice in an air-
pump or in a recipient of mephitic gas." (V., 215-218) Only
philosophers, and philosophical historians—philosophical after
the fact,—blame Burke for his hot antipathy for the French Revolution. It is all very well for the literary mind to brood in air, high
above the levels whereon men breathe the atmosphere of their
own time and neighbourhood, and from this aerial point of vantage look down with unruffled composure, cool tolerance, and a
final reckoning of loss and gain upon the troubled affairs of generations gone, looking before and after, and saying all was well,
like a minor Providence. But statesmen cannot afford thus to
withdraw from affairs. Opportunities change from moment to
moment, like the colour and shape of summer clouds, as Burke
said. After you have seen and done your duty, then philosophers
may talk of it and assess it as they will. Burke was right and was
himself when he sought to keep the French infection out of
England.[5]

◊

WWhw MS. (WP, DLC).
  [5] This lecture was published, *mutatis mutandis*, as "Edmund Burke and the
French Revolution," *Century Magazine*, LXII (Sept. 1901), 784-92.

[Feb. 24, 1898]

Walter Bagehot.—A Lecture.

We are often very glib and confident in our generalizations
about the characteristics of the English race,—not noting, perhaps not caring to note, when the mood for generalization is
upon us, how many individuals of that race escape our classification and show what qualities they please. Under which characteristic of that sturdy and for the most part matter-of-fact
people do we place its extraordinary fecun[d]ity in every kind of
individual genius? Is Shakespeare a typical product, or is he
not,—or has the race changed since the open and sunny times of
great Elizabeth? Is Milton more natural and native in his kind?
It is not a gay nation, nor yet is it saturnine, nor always sober.
If it sometimes laugh, it is always in earnest. But it has produced
some,—nay very many,—excellent wits. No doubt this might be
made a mystery, if we chose. The great majority of Englishmen,

it is safe to say, look upon a jest with uneasiness and feel towards a jester a deep distrust. They do not wish the things they think about whipped into a syllabub, and they prefer to take counsel with grave and serious men,—as if life were all counsel and all counsel matter of logic and calculation, with never a laugh in it anywhere. You remember Sydney Smith's jest to his brother. "We have reversed the law of Nature," he said; "you have risen by your gravity, and I have sunk by my levity." It deeply shocked Englishmen to find a clergyman given to jesting. And then there was Charles Lamb. How uncomfortable he made most sober men. How many good men thought him light-headed, besotted, a sort of whimsical, irreverent, unbalanced child,—and what pleasure he took in making them think so! He is delivered of their company now. He is read and loved only by the juster, clearer spirits, bred by nature to be like those who welcomed and relished his comradeship while he lived. This is a large and goodly company, and is likely always to be, God be praised,—but it is not a representative company of Englishmen, any more than his immediate comrades were in his own generation. You must not demand of the ordinary man,—even of the ordinary reading man,—that he know his Lamb,—and nobody is in the least likely to think of Lamb as of a typical English mind. You do not feel about him as you would feel about a French wit,—ah, what a race for the fine turn of the phrase and for the poignant thrusts of a nice wit! And so Congreve and Sheridan seem to belong, of right, across the Channel, and you look to see English comedy, in all ordinary seasons, produce its laugh by comic incident rather than by subtle jest or apt rejoinder.

The subject is a most alluring one, and yet very dangerous. Every prudent writer must avoid it. It defies analysis. No one can explain why the English race has brought forth so much genius of the lighter as well as of the graver sort,—and enough readers to keep a wit in countenance. One must simply say that the fact is so, and discreetly pass on. The only excuse I can give for having ventured upon so elusive a topic is, that Walter Bagehot was a wit, one of the most original and audacious wits that the English race has produced, and because, being a wit, he seems himself to have perceived the incongruity of his being an Englishman. "I need not say," he wrote in his youth,—"I need not say that in real sound stupidity the English people are unrivaled: you'll hear more wit and better wit in an Irish street row than would keep Westminster Hall in humour for five weeks." Bagehot had no literary lineage behind him, nor anything very unusual in his bringing forth that would lead the historian of letters to expect him to be what he so delightfully turned out to be. Upon a plain street in the quiet little town of Langport in the midst of Somersetshire there stands a plain but broad and home-like house, with its threshold upon the very footway of the street; and here, in an upper room Walter Bagehot was born, on the third of February, 1826. The house is the residence of the man-ager of the Somersetshire bank whose offices are but a few rods away upon the same street, where it turns about towards Glaston-bury and Wells. This was the business to which Bagehot was born. His father, Thomas Watson Bagehot, was Vice-President of the private banking company which Mr. Samuel Stuckey had established there in Langport in the last century, and which had so prospered that its branches were after a while to be found in every considerable place in the County,—wh. was, indeed, des-tined to become in our own day the largest private bank of issue in England. The Stuckeys are still the magnates of the little town, the owners of ample green acres that stretch away northward and broaden from the hill which the parish church crowns and adorns. Thomas Bagehot married a niece of Samuel Stuckey. But not before she had seen a good deal of the large world outside the sequestered town in which her great son was to be born. She had first married a Mr. Estlin of Bristol,—and her life and companionships in Bristol, that old city which had so teemed through more than one great age with commerce of the mind, as well as with trade in the stuffs of the Indies and the ends of the world, had enriched her lively mind not a little in the days when she was most susceptible. She was older than Mr. Bagehot by a goodly number of years,—perhaps it would be ungallant to say how many,—but she was not the kind to grow old or stagnate, even if she had lived all her life in that quiet house in Langport; and her son Walter Bagehot took a good measure of genius by inheritance from her.

Somersetshire is a sunny county, and lies at the heart of that brightest part of England which is thrust with its rising coasts southward towards the heart of the Atlantic; but many dull wits are born thereabouts. For all there is so much poetry in the soft air, with its sun-lit mists and its fine, mysterious distances, look-ing towards the sea, it has not bred many poets. Its levels of in-telligence have, in all ordinary times, been nearly as flat and featureless as its own fat interior meadows, wh. used now and again to hold a flood of waters like the sea, with only here and there an island hill like that of Avalon, where monks built their abbey of Glastonbury. It is pleasant to see Langport perched upon one of these infrequent hills, a landmark for the traveller, and to think that it was from this haven Walter Bagehot set out to make his bold voyage into the world of thought,—that "high-spirited, buoyant, subtle, speculative nature, in which the imaginative qualities were even more remarkable than the judgment," —as one of his comrades and fellow voyagers has said,[1]—a man of a "gay and dashing humour which was the life of every conversation in which he joined"; and of a "visionary nature to which the commonest things often seemed the most marvelous, and the marvelous things the most intrinsically probable." This was the man who was to set the facts of English politics in their true light,—and not the facts of English politics only, but also many of the facts of the world's political development as well; for it is in the vision of such men that facts appear as what they are,—are seen to consist not simply of what is *in* them, but also, and even more, of what is *behind* them and about them, their setting and atmosphere,—and are seen not to be intelligible without these. No doubt it was a signal advantage to have a very brilliant woman for his mother, as Bagehot had, and a woman who had come to the maturity of her charming gifts; and to have had so sterling a man as Thomas Bagehot for his father,—a man of cultivated power and of great good sense and balance of judgment. But brilliant women are not always generous in giving wit to their sons, and the best of men have begot fools. Neither Somersetshire air nor any certain custom of mental inheritance can explain Walter Bagehot. We must simply accept him as part of the largess of Providence to a race singularly enriched with genius.

Nor is the breeding of the boy much to our purpose. He was not made by his breeding. His mind chose its own training,— as such a mind always does,—and made its own world of thought in the days of his formal schooling in Bristol and at University College, London, whither he went because his father would not have him stomach the religious tests imposed at Oxford and Cambridge. Schools and colleges are admirable for drill and discipline of the mind and give many an ordinary man his indispensable equipment for success; but that is not their use for the exceptional mind of genius. Such a mind does not accept their drill. It takes only their atmosphere, needs only the companionship they afford, uses them with a sort of sovereign selection of what it desires. Bagehot has given us his own vivid statement of the habit of such minds, in an article on "Oxford Reform" which he published in the *Prospective Review* for August, 1852. "In

[1] Richard Holt Hutton in Forrest Morgan (ed.), *The Works of Walter Bagehot with Memoirs by R. H. Hutton* (5 vols., Hartford, Conn., 1889), I, xxv.

youth," he says, "the real plastic energy is not in tutors or lectures or in books 'got up,' but in Wordsworth and Shelley; in the books that all read because all like; in what all talk of because all are interested; in the argumentative walk or disputatious lounge; in the impact of young thought upon young thought, of fresh thought on fresh thought, of hot thought on hot thought, in mirth and refutation, in ridicule and laughter: for these are the free play of the natural mind, and these cannot be got without a college." "*These* cannot be got without a college"! Here is food for reflection for those who look to be made men of thought by diligence in attending lectures and thoroughness in 'getting up' examinations! No doubt Bagehot was writing thus out of his own experience, as Mr. Hutton says. Such minds make their own laws and ways of life, and the rest of us, being duller, must take care not to use prescriptions which do not suit our case. Mr. R. H. Hutton, who was Bagehot's college mate and life-long friend, tells us that "youth, buoyancy, vivacity, velocity of thought were of the essence of the impression which he made. Such arrogance as he seemed to have in early life was the arrogance as much of enjoyment as of detachment of mind; the *insouciance* of the old Cavalier as much at least as the calm of a mind not accessible to the contagion of social feelings. He always talked, in youth, of his spirits as inconveniently high: and once wrote to me that he did not think they were quite as 'boisterous' as they had been, and that his fellow-creatures were not sorry for the abatement; nevertheless, he added, 'I am quite fat, gross, and ruddy.' He was indeed excessively fond of hunting, vaulting, and almost all muscular effort; so that his life would be wholly misconceived by any one who . . . should picture his mind as a vigilantly observant, far-away intelligence,—such as Hawthorne's for example. He liked to be in the thick of the *mêlée* when talk grew warm, though he was never so absorbed in it as not to keep his mind cool." (I., xxxii, xxxiii.)[2] He liked to talk indeed even when there was no one to talk to but himself; for there are elderly men still to be found at the bank in Langport who remember the overflowing vivacity of the bank's one-time director, and recall how he could often be overheard talking to himself in his characteristic eager fashion as he paced all alone up and down the directors' room, in the intervals of business. He was a sore puzzle to the sober citizens of his native town, who did not know any means of calculating what this tall, athletic, stirring gentleman

---

[2] Wilson is again referring to the first volume of the *Works*. In Wilson's subsequent references to this edition, the appropriate volume number will be added where helpful *in situ*.

would be at next, or what he would say in his whimsical humour. He was asked once (and only once) to read a lecture to the literary society of Langport. His subject was Reading, and he advised his amazed hearers, amongst other things, to read *all* of the *Times* newspaper every day, the advertisements included. They did not see the jest, and deemed the advice quite as incomprehensible as the man himself! He was as careless and as whimsical, it would seem, as Lamb himself with regard to the impression he made on most sorts and conditions of men.

London, it turned out, and not Somersetshire, was to be Bagehot's chief place of residence. Somersetshire was always his home, but London was his place of work. As usual, the provinces were to enrich the capital. Though he first studied law for a little, Bagehot eventually turned to the practical business affairs which have for so many generations seemed the chief and most absorbing interest of all Englishmen. It was, of course, the intellectual side of business that really engaged him, however. He was something more than a Somersetshire banker. He became editor of the London *Economist*, and brought questions of finance to the light in editorials which clarified knowledge and steadied prediction in such fashion as made him the admiration of the Street. The City had never before seen its business set forth with such lucidity and mastery. London had taught Bagehot a great deal in the days when he was an undergraduate in University College and he had roamed its streets, haunted by all the memories of deeds and of letters of which the place was so full. Now he learned by a new sort of companionship, a companionship with the men who were the living forces of the time in business and in politics. It is not easy to overestimate the influence of a great capital upon affairs, or the influence of affairs upon a great capital. London, like Paris, is so much more than a political capital. No public man can live at the heart of that great, abounding life; or mix even for a little in that society, where men of every sort of thought, and power, and experience, and habit of reason throng and speak their minds, without in some way receiving a subtile and profound instruction in affairs. And the men of the city are themselves instructed by their acquaintances at short range with the processes and the forces which control in the policy and business of the state. Such a capital as London is a great intellectual clearing house, and men get out of it, as it were, the net balances of the nation's needs and thoughts. Bagehot both gave and took a great deal in such a place. His mind was singularly fitted to understand London, and every complex group of men or interests. He had the social imagination that Burke had, and Carlyle,—that

every successful student of affairs must have, if he would scratch
but a little beneath the surface, or lift the mystery from any
transaction whatever. For minds with this gift of sight there is a
quick way opened to the heart of things. Their acquaintance
with any individual man is but a detail in their acquaintance with
men; and it is noteworthy that, though they gain in mastery, they
do not gain in insight by their contact with men and with the
actual business of the world. Burke saw as clearly and with as
certain a penetration when he was in his twenties as when he had
lived his life out. The years enriched his knowledge with details,
and every added experience brought him some concrete matter
to ground his thought upon; but the mastery of these things was
in him from the first.

Bagehot showed the same precocious power, and saw as clearly
at twenty-five as at fifty, though he did not see as much or hold
his judgment at so nice a balance. You have evidence of this in
the seven remarkable letters on the third Napoleon's *coup d'état*
which he wrote from Paris while he was yet a law student. They
are evidently the letters of a young man. Their style goes at a
spanking, reckless gait that no older mind would have dared
attempt or could have kept its breath at. Their satirical humour
has a quick sting in it; their judgments are offhand and unconscionably confident; their crying heresies in matters of politics
are calculated to shock English nerves very painfully. They are
aggressive and a bit arrogant. But their extravagance is superficial. At heart they are sound, and even wise. The man's vision
for affairs has come to him already. He sees that Frenchmen are
not Englishmen, and are not to be judged, or very much aided
either, by English standards. You shall not elsewhere learn so
well what it was that happened in France in the early fifties, or
why it happened and could hardly have been staved off or
avoided. "You have asked me to tell you what I think of French
affairs," he writes. "I shall be pleased to do so; but I ought perhaps to begin by cautioning you against believing, or too much
heeding, what I say." It is so he begins, with a shrewd suspicion,
no doubt, that the warning is unnecessary. For he was writing
to the editor of *The Inquirer*, a journal but just established for
the enlightenment of Unitarian dissenters,—a peo[ple] Bagehot
had reason to know, and could not hope to win either to the
manner or to the matter of his thought. They would think the
one flippant and the other radically misleading and erroneous.
But it was the better sport to write for their amazement. He
undertook nothing less bold than a justification of what Louis
Napoleon had done in flat derogation of the constitutional liber-

ties of France. He set himself to show an English audience, who he knew would decline to believe it, how desperate a crisis had been averted, how effectual the strong remedy had been, and how expedient at least a temporary dictatorship. "Whatever other deficiencies Louis Napoleon may have," he said, "he has one excellent advantage over other French statesmen,—he has never been a professor, nor a journalist, nor a promising barrister, nor by taste a littérateur. He has not confused himself with history; he does not think in leading articles, in long speeches, or in agreeable essays." ([II] 377) "He has very good heels to his boots, and the French just want treading down, and nothing else,—calm, cruel, business-like oppression, to take the dogmatic conceit out of their heads. The spirit of generalization which, John Mill tells us, honourably distinguishes the French mind, has come to this, that every Parisian wants his head *tapped* in order to get the formulae and nonsense out of it. . . . So I am for any carnivorous government." ([I, xlvii])[3] Conscious of his audacity and of what will be said of such sentiments among the grave readers of *The Inquirer*, he hastens in his second letter to make his real position clear. "For the sake of the women who may be led astray," he laughs, affecting to quote St. Athanasius, "I will this very instant explain my sentiments." ([II] 378)

He is sober enough when it comes to serious explanation of the difficult matter. Laughing satire and boyish jibe are put aside, and a thoughtful philosophy of politics,—Burke's as well as his own,—comes at once to the surface, in sentences admirably calm and wise. In justifying Napoleon, he says plainly and at the outset, he is speaking only of France and of the critical circumstances of the year 1852. "The first duty of society," he declares, "is the preservation of society. By the sound work of old-fashioned generations, by the singular painstaking of the slumberers in churchyards, by dull care, by stupid industry, a certain social fabric somehow exists; people contrive to go out to their work, and to find work to employ them actually until the evening; body and soul are kept together,—and this is what mankind have to show for their six thousand years of toil and trouble." ([II] 379) You cannot better the living by political change, he maintains, unless you can contrive to hold change to a slow and sober pace, quiet, almost insensible, like that of the evolutions of growth. If you cannot do that, perhaps it is better to hold steadily to the old present ways of life, under a strong, unshaken, unquestioned government, capable of guidance and command. "Burke first taught the world at large," he reminds us, "that politics are made

3 Wilson left this space blank.

of time and place; that institutions are shifting things, to be tried by and adjusted to the shifting conditions of a mutable world; that in fact politics are but a piece of business, to be determined in every case by the exact exigencies of that case,—in plain English, by sense and circumstances. This was a great step in political philosophy, though it *now* seems the events of 1848 have taught thinking persons (I fancy) further: they have enabled us to say that of all these circumstances so affecting political problems, by far and out of all question the most important is national character." ([II] 394)

"I need not prove to you that the French *have* a national character," he goes on, "nor need I try your patience with a likeness of it: I have only to examine whether it be a fit basis for national freedom. I fear you will laugh when I tell you what I conceive to be about the most essential mental quality for a free people whose liberty is to be progressive, permanent, and on a large scale; it is much *stupidity*. I see you are surprised; you are going to say to me, as Socrates did to Polus, 'My young friend, of *course* you are right; but will you explain what you mean? as yet you are not intelligible.'" [II, 397] His explanation is easily made, and with convincing force. He means that only a race of steady, patient, unimaginative habits of thought can abide steadfast in the conservation and businesslike conduct of government, and he sees the French to be what Tocqueville had called them,—a nation apt to conceive a great design, but unable to persist in its pursuit, impatient after a single effort, "swayed by sensations and not by principles," her "instincts better than her morality." "As a people of 'large roundabout common-sense' will as a rule somehow get on in life," says Bagehot, "no matter what their circumstances or their fortune, so a nation which applies good judgment, forbearance, a rational and compromising habit, to the management of free institutions will certainly succeed; while the more eminently gifted national character will but be a source and germ of endless and disastrous failure if, with whatever other eminent qualities, it be deficient in these plain, solid, and essential requisites." It is no doubt whimsical to call "large roundabout common-sense," ([II] 395) good judgement, and rational forbearance "stupidity," but he means, of course, that those who possess these solid practical gifts lack that quick inventive originality and versatility in resource which we are apt to think the characteristics of the creative mind. "The essence of the French character," he explains, "is a certain mobility: that is, a certain [']excessive sensibility to *present* impressions,' which is sometimes 'levity,' for it issues in a postponement of seemingly fixed principles to a momentary temptation or a transient whim; sometimes 'impatience,' as leading to an exaggerated sense of existing evils; often 'excitement,' a total absorption in existing emotion; oftener 'inconsistency,' the sacrifice of old habits to present emergencies," ([II] 401-2)—and these are qualities which, however engaging upon occasion, he is certainly right in regarding as a very serious if not fatal empediment to success in self-government. "A real Frenchman," he exclaims, "can't be stupid: *esprit* is his essence, wit is to him as water, *bon-mots* as bonbons." ([II] 399) And yet 'stupidity,' as he prefers to call it, is, he rightly thinks, "nature's favourite resource for preserving steadiness of conduct and consistency of opinion: it enforces concentration; people who learn slowly, learn only what they must." ([II] 399)

This, which reads like the moral of an old man, is what Bagehot saw at twenty-six; and he was able, though a youth and in the midst of misleading Paris, to write quick sentences of political analysis which were fit to serve both as history and as prophecy. "If you have to deal with a mobile, a clever, a versatile, an intellectual, a dogmatic nation," he says, "inevitably and by necessary consequence you will have conflicting systems; every man speaking his own words, and always giving his own suffrage to what seems good in his own eyes; many holding to-day what they will regret to-morrow; a crowd of crotchety theories and a heavy percentage of philosophical nonsense; a great opportunity for subtle stratagem and intriguing selfishness; a miserable division among the friends of tranquility, and a great power thrown into the hands of those who, though often with the very best intentions, are practically and in matter of fact opposed both to society and civilization. And moreover, beside minor inconveniences and lesser hardships, you will indisputably have periodically—say three or four times in fifty years—a great crisis: the public mind much excited; the people in the streets swaying to and fro with the breath of every breeze; the discontented *ouvriers* meeting in a hundred knots, discussing their real sufferings and their imagined grievances with lean features and angry gesticulations; the parliament all the while in permanence very ably and eloquently expounding the whole subject, one man proposing this scheme and another that; the Opposition expecting to oust the ministers and ride in on the popular commotion, the ministers fearing to take the odium of severe or adequate repressive measures, lest they should lose their salary, their place, and their majority; finally a great crash, a disgusted people overwhelmed by revolutionary violence or seeking a precarious, a pernicious, but after all a precious protection from the bayonets of military despotism." ([II] 416-417) Could you wish a better analysis of the affairs of that clever, volatile people, and can you ascribe it wholly to his youth that Bagehot should in 1852 have deliberately concluded that "the first condition of good government" in France was "a really strong, a reputedly strong, a continually strong executive power"? ([II] 412)

Henry Crabb Robinson, that amiable man of letters and staunch partisan of constitutional liberty, could never recall a name,—especially in his old age, you remember,—and in conversation with Mr. R. H. Hutton he used to refer to Bagehot by description as "that friend of yours—you know whom I mean, you rascal!—who wrote those abominable, those most disgraceful letters on the Coup d'État—I did not forgive him for years after!" (I., xlvi) We must, of course, admit, with Mr. Hutton, that the letters were "airy, and even flippant, on a very grave subject"; but their airiness and flippancy were not of the substance: they were but a trick of youth, the playful exuberance of a lusty strength,—the colt was 'feeling his oats.' What the critic must note is, that there is here already the vivid and effectual style that runs like a light thr. everything that Bagehot ever wrote. Mr. Hutton tells us that Bagehot used to declare that his early style affected him 'like the joggling of a cart without springs over a very rough road'; (I., 1) and no doubt the writing of his maturer years does often go at a more even and placid pace. But you shall not find in him anywhere the measured phrases of the formal, periodic writer, or any studied grace or cadence. The style has always, like the thought, a quick stroke, an intermittent sparkle, a jet-like play, as if it were a bit of sustained talk, and recorded, not so much a course of reasoning, as the successive, spontaneous impressions of a mind alert and quick of foot. It is singular to find him preferring the dull, English way of writing editorials to the sprightly pointed paragraphs of the French journals, as he does in the extraordinary sixth Letter on the *Coup d'État*, in which he hits off the characteristics of the French press with a point and truth I do not know where to match elsewhere. We are apt, upon a superficial impression, to regard him as himself touched with a certain French quality and to think of his own writing as we hear him exclaim, of the French journalists, "How well these fellows write! . . . How clear, how acute how clever, how perspicuous!" ([II] 423) But he tells us with what relief and satisfaction, after running with these voluble and witty fellows, he opened the quiet columns of an English paper. "As long walking in picture galleries makes you appreciate a mere wall," he says, "so I felt that I understood for the first time that really dullness had its interest." "There was no toil, no sharp theory, no pointed expression, no fatiguing brilliancy." ([II] 423-424) He quotes an English judge as having said, "I like to hear a Frenchman talk: he strikes a light, but what light he will strike it is impossible to predict; I think he doesn't know himself," and he frankly expresses his own distaste for such irresponsible brightness. "Suppose, if you only can," he cries, "a House of Commons all Disrealis. It would be what M. Proudhon said of some French Assemblies, 'a box of matches.'" ([II] 404-405) You cannot be with the man long without seeing that, for all he is so witty and as quick as a Frenchman at making a point, there is really no Gallic blood in the matter. His processes of thought are as careful and as conservative as his style is rapid and his wit reckless.

In 1852 the very year in which the Letters on the *Coup d'État* were written, the period of Bagehot's preparation in the law was completed and he was in due course called to the bar. But he decided not to enter upon the practice. He had read law with a zest for its systematic ways and its sharp and definite analytical processes, and with an unusual appreciation, no doubt, of the light of businesslike interpretation which it applies to the various undertakings and relationships of society; but he dreaded the hot wigs, the unventilated courts, and the night drudgery which the active practitioner would have to endure, and betook himself instead to the less confining occupations of business. His father was interested in large commercial undertakings and was a ship owner as well as a banker, and his son found, in association with him, an active life, full of travel and important errands here and there upon which he could spend his energies with not a little satisfaction. We are not apt to think of commerce and banking as furnishing matter to satisfy such a mind as Bagehot's,— but business is just as dull, and just as interesting, as you make it. Bagehot always maintained that "business is much more amusing than pleasure,"—and of course it is if you have mind enough to appreciate it upon all its sides and in all its bearings upon the life of society. Give such a mind as Bagehot's such necessary stuff of life to work upon as is to be found in the commerce of a great nation, and it will at once invest it with the dignity and the charm of a great theme of speculation and study. Bagehot's contact with business made him a great economist,—an economist sure of his premises and big-minded and scrupulously careful and guarded in respect of his conclusions. Mr. Hutton tells us that Bagehot "was always absent-minded about *minutiae*" and himself admitted that he never could 'add up.' He was obliged to leave details to his assistants and subordinates. But such has often been the singular failing of men who could nevertheless reason upon details in the mass with an unexampled certainty and power. Bagehot turned always, it would seem, as if by instinct, to the larger aspects of every matter he was called upon to handle, and had, no doubt, that sort of imagination for enterprise which has been characteristic of great business men (as of great soldiers and statesmen) in all generations. Such men can put together colossal fortunes but Bagehot's career did not lead him that way. The literary instinct was more deep-seated and radical in him than the money-making, and he found his right place as a man of business when he became editor of the London *Economist*. He did not long keep to Langport. His marriage, in 1858, brought him to the characteristic part of his career. His mother had urged him some time before to marry, but he had put her off with his characteristic banter. "A man's mother is his misfortune," he had said, "but his wife is his fault." Whether delay brought wisdom or not (when a man of genius gets a wife to his mind it is apt to be mere largess of Providence!), certain it is that his marriage endowed him with happiness for the rest of his life and introduced him to a new and more fruitful use of his gifts. He married the eldest daughter of the Right Hon. James Wilson, who had founded the *Economist*, and whose death, two years later, in India, in the service of the government, left Bagehot, at thirty-four, to conduct alone the great weekly which his genius was to lift to a yet higher place of influence.

Mr. Hutton believes that it was Bagehot's connexion with the inner world of politics in London to which his marriage gave him entrance that enabled him to write his great works of political interpretation,—for he was undoubtedly the first man to strip the English constitution of its "literary theory" and show it to the world as men of affairs knew it and used it. Mr. Hutton was Mr. Bagehot's life-long intimate, and one hesitates to question his judgment in such a manner, but it may at least be said that it can be established only by doubtful inference, even tho. uttered by a companion and friend. It is not necessary for such a mind as Bagehot's to have direct experience of affairs or personal intercourse with the men who conduct them in order to comprehend either the make-up of politics or the intimate forces of action. A hint is enough. Insight and imagination do the rest. The gift of imaginative insight in respect of affairs carries always with it a subtle, unconscious power of construction which suffers not so much as the temptation to invent, and which is equally free from taint of abstract or fanciful inference. Somehow,—no man can say by what curious secret process or exquisite delicacy and certainty of intimation,—it reconstructs life after the irregular patterns affected by nature herself, and will build you the reality out of mere inference. Bagehot may have been quickened and assured by an intimate and first-hand knowledge of men and methods, but it seems like mistaking the character of his genius to say that he could not have done without this actual sight of concrete cases and personal instances of motive and action. The rest of his work justifies the belief that he could have seen without handling.

The power and the character of his imagination are proved by the extraordinary range it took. Most of the extraordinary literary studies in which he has given us so memorable a taste of his quality as a critic and all-round man of letters were written before his marriage, between his twenty-sixth and his thirty-second years,—the most extraordinary of them all, perhaps,—the essay on "Shakespeare—the Man,"—in 1853, when he was but twenty-seven; and there is everywhere to be found in these studies a man whose insight into life was easy and universal,—and yet the centre of life for him was Langport in far Somersetshire. His fame as a political thinker was made later when he was more mature and his imagination had been trained to its function by his travels in the high company of the men of genius of whom he had written. "Variety was his taste, and versatility his power," as he said of Brougham,—and the variety of his taste and the versatility of his power showed in what he wrote of economy and of institutions no less than in what he wrote of individual men and books. In his "English Constitution," which he published in 1867, he gave an account of the actual workings of parliamentary government, so lucid, so witty, so complete, and for all so concise and without delay about details (which seemed in its clear air to reveal themselves without comment) that it made itself instantly and once for all a part of every man's thinking in that matter. Everybody saw what he intended them to see, that the English government is a government shaped and conducted by a committee of the House of Commons, *called* "her Majesty's ministers"; that the throne serves only to steady the administration of the government, to hold the veneration and imagination of the people; and that the House of Lords is only, at most, a revising and delaying chamber. The book is now a classic. Two years later (1869) he turned to a broader field of thought in his "Physics and Politics," in wh. he sought to apply the principles of heredity and natural selection to the development of society, showing how political organization was first hardened by custom; then altered and even revolutionized by changes of environment and by the struggle for existence between banded groups of men; and finally given its nice adaptations to a growing civilization by the subtle, transmuting processes of an age of discussion. There are passages in this little volume which stimulate the thought more than whole treatises written by those who have no imagination whereby to revive the image of older ages of the world. Here, for example, is his striking comment upon the nations which, like the Chinese and the Persian, have stood still the long centuries through, caught and held fast, as he puts it, beneath a cake of antique custom: "No one will ever comprehend the arrested civilizations," he says, "unless he sees the strict dilemma of early society. Either men had no law at all, and lived in confused tribes hardly hanging together, or they had to obtain a fixed law by processes of incredible difficulty; those who surmounted that difficulty soon destroyed all those that lay in their way who did not—and then they themselves were caught in their own yoke. The customary discipline, which could only be imposed on any early men by terrible sanctions, continued with these sanctions, and killed out of the whole society the propensities to variation which are the principle of progress. Experience shows how incredibly difficult it is to get men really to encourage the principle of originality." There is here the same thesis his Letters on the *Coup d'État* had advanced, with a sort of boyish audacity seventeen years before. This is the philosophy of *dullness*. No nation, while it is forming, hardening its sinews, acquiring its habits of order, can afford to encourage originality. It must insist upon a rigid discipline and subordination. And even after it has formed its habit of order, it cannot afford to have too much originality or to relax its fibre by too rapid change,—cannot afford to be as volatile as the French. Progress is devoutly to be wished, and discussion is its instrument,— the opening of the mind; those nations are the great nations of the modern world which have dominated the European stage, where there is movement and the plot advances from ordered change to change. But conservation and order must even yet be preferred to change, and the nations which do not think too fast are the nations which advance most rapidly. Bagehot speaks somewhere of "the settled calm by which the world is best administered."

Bagehot's thought is not often constructive. Its business generally is analysis, interpretation. But here, in "Physics and Politics," it is distinctly creative and architectonic. It is always his habit to go at once to the concrete reality of a subject, lingering

scarcely a moment upon its conventionalities: he sees always
with his own eyes, never with another's; and even analysis takes
from him a certain creative touch. The object of his thought is
so vividly displayed that you seem to see all of it, instead of only
some of it. But here, in speaking of ages past and gone, his object is reconstruction, and that direct touch of his imagination
makes what he says seem like the report of an eye witness. You
know after reading this book, what an investigator the trained
understanding is,—a sort of original authority in itself. Nor is
his humour gone or exiled from these solemn regions of thought.
There is an intermittent touch of it even in what he says of the
political force of religion. "Those kinds of morals and that kind
of religion which tend to make the firmest and most effectual
character," he explains, "are sure to prevail" in every struggle
for existence between organized groups or nations of men, "all
else being the same; and creeds or systems that conduce to a
soft limp mind tend to perish, except some hard extrinsic force
keep them alive. Thus Epicureanism never prospered at Rome,
but Stoicism did; the stiff, serious character of the great prevailing nation was attracted by what seemed a confirming creed, and
deterred by what looked like a relaxing creed. The inspiriting
doctrines fell upon the ardent character, and so confirmed its
energy. Strong beliefs win strong men, and then make them
stronger. Such is no doubt one cause why Monotheism tends to
prevail over Polytheism; it produces a higher, steadier character,
calmed and concentrated by a great single object; it is not confused by competing rites, or distracted by miscellaneous deities."
"Mr. Carlyle has taught the present generation many lessons, and
one of these is that 'God-fearing' armies are the best armies.
Before his time people laughed at Cromwell's saying, 'Trust in
God, and keep your powder dry.' But we now know that the trust
was of as much use as the powder, if not more. That high concentration of steady feeling makes men dare everything and do
anything." (76)[4] Is it a misuse of the word to say that a quiet,
serious sort of humour lurks amidst these sentences and once
and again peeps out at you, with solemn eyes? And there are
bold, unconventional sallies of wit in the man as there were
in the boy. Take, for example, what he said of one of the qualities
which seemed to him very noticeable in that extraordinary and
very uncomfortable man, Lord Brougham. "There is a last quality," he says, "which is difficult to describe in the language of
books, but which Lord Brougham excels in, and which has per-

---

[4] As Wilson indicates, he is now quoting from *Physics and Politics*. The copy
in his library bears the imprint, "New York, 1884."

haps been of more value to him than all his other qualities put together. In the speech of ordinary men it is called 'devil'; persons instructed in the German language call it 'the dæmonic element.' . . . It is most easily explained by physiognomy. There is a glare in some men's eyes which seems to say, 'Beware, I am dangerous; *noli me tangere.*' Lord Brougham's face has this. A mischievous excitability is the most obvious expression of it. If he were a horse, nobody would buy him; with that eye no one could answer for his temper." (393)[5] With what apparent irreverence, too, he opens his chapter on the Monarchy in his "English Constitution." "The use of the Queen in a dignified capacity," he begins, "is incalculable. . . . Most people when they read that the Queen walked on the slopes at Windsor—that the Prince of Wales went to the Derby—have imagined that too much thought and prominence were given to little things. But they have been in error; and it is nice to trace how the actions of a retired widow and an unemployed youth become of such importance." (101)[6] And yet he is not laughing. "The best reason why Monarchy is a strong government" he goes on, very seriously, "is, that it is an intelligible government. The mass of mankind understand it, and they hardly anywhere in the world understand any other." (Id.) His thought turns back to the *coup d'état* which he had seen in France. "The issue was put to the French people," he says; "they were asked, 'Will you be governed by Louis Napoleon, or will you be governed by an assembly?' The French people said, 'We will be governed by the one man we can imagine, and not by the many people we cannot imagine.'" (102)[7] The man is a conservative, but his wit is a radical.

His "Lombard Street" is the most outwardly serious of his greater writings. It is his picture of the money market, whose public operations and hidden influences he exhibits with his accustomed, apparently inevitable, lucidity. He explains, as perhaps only he could, the parts played in the market by the Chancellors of the Exchequer, whose counsellor he often was, by the Bank of England, and by the joint-stock banks, such as his own in Somersetshire; the influences, open and covert, that make for crisis or stability,—the whole machinery and the whole psychology of the subtle game and business of finance. There is everywhere the same close intimacy between the fact and the thought. What he writes seems always a light playing in affairs, illuminating

[5] *The English Constitution and Other Political Essays.* The copy in Wilson's library bears the imprint, "New York, 1882."
[6] *ibid.*
[7] *ibid.*

their substance, revealing their fibre. "As an instrument for arriving at truth," one of Bagehot's intimate friends once said, "I never knew anything like a talk with Bagehot." It got at once to the heart of a subject. He instantly appreciated the whole force and significance "of everything you yourself said; making talk with him, as Roscoe once remarked, 'like riding a horse with a perfect mouth.' But most unique of all was his power of keeping up animation without combat. I never knew a power of discussion, of cooperative investigation, of truth, to approach to it. It was all stimulous, and yet no contest." (lxi)[8] The spontaneity with which he wrote put the same quality into his writings; they have the freshness, the vivacity, the penetration of eager talk, and abound in those flashes of insight and discovery which make the talk of some gifted men seem like a series of inspirations. He does not always complete his subjects, either, in writing, and their partial incompleteness makes them read the more as if they were a body of pointed remarks and not a set treatise or essay.

No doubt the best samples of his style are to be found in his literary and biographical essays, where his adept words serve him so discerningly in the disclosure of very subtle things: the elements of genius, the motives and constituents of intellectual power, the diverse forces of individual man. But you will find the same qualities and felicities in his way of dealing with the grosser and more obvious matters of politics. Here, as everywhere, to quote his own language about Laurence Sterne, his style "bears the indefinable traces which an exact study of words will always leave upon the use of words"; (II, 157)[9] here, too, there is the same illuminative play of sure insight and broad sagacity. You may illustrate his method by taking passages almost at random. "The brief description of the characteristic merit of the English Constitution is," he says, "that its dignified parts are very complicated and somewhat imposing, very old and rather venerable; while its efficient part, at least when in great and critical action, is decidedly simple and rather modern. We have made, or rather stumbled on, a constitution which—though full of every species of incidental defect, though of the worst *workmanship* in all out-of-the-way matters of any constitution in the world—yet has two capital merits: it has a simple efficient part which, on occasion, and when wanted, *can* work more simply and easily, and better, than any instrument of government that has yet been tried; and it contains likewise historical, complex,

[8] *Works*, I.
[9] *Works*.

august, theatrical parts, which it has inherited from a long past—
which *take* the multitude—which guide by an insensible but an
omnipotent influence the associations of its subjects. Its essence
is strong with the strength of modern simplicity; its exterior is
august with the Gothic grandeur of a more imposing age." (78)[10]
He is interested to bring out the contrast between English political arrangements and our own. "When the American nation
has chosen its President," he explains, "its virtue goes out of it,
and out of the Transmissive College through wh. it chooses. But
because the House of Commons has the power of dismissal in
addition to the power of election, its relations to the Premier are
incessant. They guide him, and he leads them. He is to them what
they are to the nation. He only goes where he believes they will
go after him. But he has to take the lead; he must choose his
direction, and begin the journey. Nor must he flinch. A good
horse likes to feel the rider's bit; and a great deliberative assembly
likes to feel that it is under worthy guidance. . . . The great leaders of Parliament have varied much, but they have all had a certain firmness. A great assembly is as soon spoiled by over-indul-
gence as a little child. The whole life of English politics is the
action and reaction between the Ministry and the Parliament.
The appointees strive to guide, and the appointors surge under
the guidance." (199-200)[11] "The English constitution, in a word,
is framed on the principle of choosing a single sovereign authority, and making it good; the American, upon the principle of
having many sovereign authorities, and hoping that their multitude may atone for their inferiority. The Americans now extol
their institutions, and so defraud themselves of their due praise.
But if they had not a genius for politics; if they had not a moderation in action singularly curious where superficial speech is so
violent; if they had not a regard for law, such as no great people
have yet evinced, and infinitely surpassing ours, the multiplic-
ity of authorities in the American Constitution would long ago
have brought it to a bad end. Sensible shareholders, I have heard
a shrewd attorney say, can work *any* deed of settlement; and
so the men of Massachusetts could, I believe, work *any* constitution. But political philosophy must analyse political history; it
must distinguish what is due to the excellence of the people and
what to the excellence of the law; it must carefully calculate the
exact effect of each part of the constitution, though thus it may
destroy many an idol of the multitude, and detect the secret of
utility where but few imagined it to lie." (296-297)[12]

[10] *The English Constitution and Other Political Essays.*
[11] *ibid.*   [12] *ibid.*

These are eminently businesslike sentences. They are not consciously concerned with style; they do not seem to stop for the turning of a phrase; their only purpose seems to be plain elucidation, such as will bring the matter within the comprehension of everybody. And yet there is a stirring quality in them which operates upon the mind like wit. They are tonic and full of stimulous. No man could have spoken them without a lively eye. I suppose the 'secret of their utility' to be a very interesting one indeed,—and nothing less than the secret of all Bagehot's power. Young writers should seek it out and ponder it studiously. It is this: he is never writing 'in the air.' He is always looking point-blank and with steady eyes upon a definite object; he takes pains to see it, alive and natural; he uses a phrase, as the masters of painting use a colour,—not because of its own beauty,—he is not thinking of that,—but because it matches life and is the veritable image of the thing. Moreover, he is not writing merely to succeed at that: he is writing, not to describe, but to make alive. And so the secret comes to light. Style is an instrument, and is made imperishable only by embodiment in some great use. It is not of itself stuff to last, neither can it have real beauty except when working the substantial effects of thought or vision. Its highest triumph is, to hit the meaning; and the pleasure you get from it is not unlike that which you get from the perfect action of skill. The *object* is so well and so easily attained! A man's vocabulary and outfit of phrase should be his thought's perfect habit and manner of pose. Bagehot *saw* the world of his day, saw the world of days antique, and showed us what he saw in phrases which interpret like the tones of a perfect voice, in words which serve us like eyes.[13]

10 February, 1898[14]

WWhw and WWT MSS. (WP, DLC).
[13] This lecture was published, *mutatis mutandis*, as "A Wit and a Seer," *Atlantic Monthly*, LXXXII (Oct. 1898), 527-40.
[14] Wilson's composition date.

From Fabian Franklin[1]

Dear Mr. Wilson,   Baltimore Feb 24, 1898
I had hoped to come to your lecture on Bagehot this afternoon, and to have an opportunity at the close of it to tell you how much I enjoyed and admired the lecture on Burke which we had the privilege of hearing yesterday. I thoroughly sympathized with the view you took; the way in which you brought it out was masterly.

It is not often that one has an opportunity of hearing a great subject treated with such a combination of strength, impressiveness and warm and sincere feeling; and I could not let the occasion go by without an expression of my gratitude.

Yours sincerely,   Fabian Franklin

ALS (WP, DLC) with WWhw notation on env.: "From Dr. Fabian Franklin—in re Burke."

1 At this time editor of the *Baltimore News*.

A Public Lecture at the Johns Hopkins

[Feb. 25, 1898]

A Lawyer with a Style[1]

Sir Henry Maine was a lawyer with a style, and belongs, by method and genius, among men of letters. The literary world looks askance upon a lawyer, and is slow to believe that the grim and formal matter of his studies can by any [alchemy] of style be transmuted into literature. Calf-skin seems to them the unlikeliest binding in the world to contain anything engaging to read. Lawyers, in their turn, are apt to associate the word 'literature' almost exclusively with works of the imagination, and to think 'style' a thing wholly misleading and unscientific. They demand plain business of their writers and suspect a book that is pleasing of charlatanry. And yet a really great law writer will often make his way easily and at once into the ranks of men of letters. Blackstone's *Commentaries* have been superceded and re-superceded, again and again, by all sorts of changes and restatements of the law of England, but they have lived serenely on through their century and more of assured vitality, and must still be read by every student of the law, in America no less than in England, because of their scope, their virility, their luminous method, their easy combination of system with lucidity,—their distinction of style, their quality as of the patriciate of letters. It does not seem to make any difference whether they are correct or not,—and we return to them, after reading Bentham and Austin, their arch critics,—a little shame-facedly, it may be,—to find our zest and relish for them not a whit abated. It is noteworthy that, though the profession has so thumbed and subsisted upon them, they were not written for the profession, but for the young gentlemen of England, whom the learned Vinerian professor wished to instruct in the institutions of their country. They are stripped as

1 There are WWhw and WWsh notes for this lecture in WP, DLC.

much as might be of technical phrase and detail, and are meant to stand in the general company of books, the servants and instructors of all comers. They are meant for the world and seem instinctively to make themselves acceptable to it.

Sir Henry Maine, whether he was conscious of it or not, wins his way to a like standing among men of letters by a like disposition and object. His books were, without exception, I believe, made up out of lectures delivered either to young law students, not yet masters of the technicalities of the law, or to lay audiences to which professional erudition would have been unintelligible. He never seemed to stand inside the law while he wrote, but outside,—not explaining its interior mysteries, but setting its history round about it, showing whence it came, whence it took its notions, its forms, its stringent sanctions,—what its youth had been, and its growth, and why its maturity showed it come to so hard a fibre of formal doctrine. He viewed it always as something that the general life of man had brought forth, as a natural product of society; and his thought went round about society to compass its explanation. He moves, therefore, in a large region, where it is refreshing to be of his company, where wide prospects open with every comment, and you seem as he talks to be upon a tour of the world.

Of course this does not explain the style of the man, but that is in any case a mystery. His method of thinking carries with it that style,—thinking in that way, he *must* write in that way. You shall not find a near-sighted man looking out for landscapes, nor a man without gift of speech sallying forth to explore the thoughts which he cannot express. I am not going to attempt the heart of the mystery: I do not know whether men can think without words or not. I only know that flight is a question of wings, and that you do not find mind, without strong pinions poised very high in the spaces of the air.

I do not think that Sir Henry Maine himself understood this matter—it was not necessary that he should. In an address which he delivered to the native students at Calcutta, he warned them, very sensibly, to beware, if they wished to write effective English, of too deliberately striving to write well. "What you should regard," he says, "is, not the language, but the thought, and if the thought be clearly and vividly conceived, the proper diction, if the writer be an educated man, will be sure to follow. You have only to look," he goes on, "to the greatest masters of English style to satisfy yourselves of the truth of what I have said,"— and yet his example is not very convincing. "Look at any one page of Shakespeare," he says. "After you have penetrated beneath the poetry and beneath the wit, you will find that the page is perfectly loaded with thought." ⟨(Life, 5)⟩[2]

"After you have penetrated beneath the poetry and beneath the wit"!—this is a dark saying, who shall receive it! After you have penetrated beneath the exquisite form of the features, have ceased to observe the curve of the cheek and the sweet bloom upon it, and the seductive light in the eye, no doubt you shall find flesh and blood,—but there is everywhere flesh and blood to be found without line or colour to give it distinction. Weight of thought, no doubt, but books by the thousand have been foundered and sunk by mere weight of matter. Sir Henry Maine himself shall not survive by reason of the abundance and validity of his thought, but by reason of his form and art. "Maine can no more become obsolete through the industry and ingenuity of modern scholars," Sir Frederick Pollock declared, "than Montesquieu could be made obsolete by the legislation of Napoleon. Facts will be corrected, the order and proportion of ideas will vary, new difficulties will call for new ways of solution, useful knowledge will serve its turn and be forgotten; but in all true genius, perhaps, there is a touch of Art; Maine's genius was not only touched with Art, but eminently artistic; and Art is immortal." ⟨(Life, 48)⟩ Aye, *art* is immortal,—not thought alone and of itself, but thought perfectly conceived, formed, and vivified. Maine disliked what is called 'fine' writing, as every man of taste must; and he was no coiner of striking phrases. The only sentence he ever wrote which his friends claim to have seen going abroad upon its own merits as a Saying is this: "Except the blind forces of Nature, nothing moves in this world which is not Greek in its origin," ⟨(Life, 30, 48)⟩—which is neither true nor epigrammatic. Epigrams were not in his way. If the cat's question to the ugly duckling in the fairy tale had been put to him, and he had been asked "Can you emit sparks?" he would have been obliged to admit, with the duckling, that he could not;—but, like the ugly duckling, he turned out to be a swan, sovereign in grace, if not in dexterity. His style does not play in points of light, but acts far and wide and with a fine suffusion, like the sun in the open.

You will best understand the power and the art of the man if you study his life and work, what he did and the manner in which he did it. Not that you will know any better, after the story is told than before, how to analyze his power or explain his art; but you will know very clearly just what he was and stood for,—of just

2 Mountstuart E. Grant Duff and Whitley Stokes, *Sir Henry Maine: A Brief Memoir of His Life . . . with Some of His Indian Speeches and Minutes* (London, 1892).

what he was a master and how his mastery displayed itself. What a master in any art did is always inseparable in the last analysis from what he was. The life of a writer has in it very little that can be told, and delicate health had held Sir Henry Maine always to a very quiet level. He had no adventures as a boy,—except that his mother and aunt came near killing him with an overdose of opium; and his youth was without any irregularity except over-study,—which for a normal youth would be very irregular. His father was a Dr. James Maine, of whom we are told nothing except that he was born at Kelso, near the Scottish border, and that he lived for short time after his son Henry's birth on the island of Jersey. The boy's full name was Henry James Sumner Maine, his godfather being the excellent Dr. Sumner, Bishop of Chester, and afterwards Archbishop of Canterbury. He was born near Leighton, August 15, 1822. His mother was Eliza Fell, who came of a family of good position living in the neighbourhood of Reading. She is said to have been a clever and accomplished woman, and it turned out that she was to be her gifted son's sole guardian. Family difficulties separated her from her husband and she removed while the lad was in his second year to a residence at Henley-on-Thames. There Henry Maine got his first schooling; thence he went, when he was but seven, to Christ's Hospital, where Dr. Sumner had been able to place him; and from Christ's Hospital he went, as Exhibitioner, to Pembroke College, Cambridge, in 1840, at the age of eighteen,—a slender, clear-voiced, alert lad, as fragile almost as a tender girl, but full of a masculine energy which showed in his lively eye, at once bright and deep, perceiving and thoughtful, and in his speech, which was very definite and sure of its mark,—a lad whom one could have wished to see much in the sun, to put colour in his cheeks, but who could not often be drawn away from his books and showed pale, like the student. He went in for all the prizes, and got most of them: was elected Foundation Scholar of his College; won medals for English verse, Latin hexameters, Latin odes, Greek and Latin epigrams; became Craven University Scholar and Senior Classic; and finally won the Chancellor's Senior Classical Medal, putting himself through the unpalateable discipline of taking the honours in mathematics necessary to qualify him for winning it. Pembroke had no vacant Fellowship to offer him, but he was made Tutor at Trinity Hall immediately upon his graduation, in 1844, and three years later, when he was but twenty-five was appointed Regius Professor of Civil Law.

"I was curious," said a gentleman who had had the good luck to be coached by Maine at Trinity Hall, "I was curious to see how this tutor of mine, so young as he was, about two years my junior, would get on at first. . . . The result removed all doubts and surpassed my most sanguine expectations. I could feel that I was being admirably jockeyed. He had the greatest dexterity in impressing his knowledge upon others, made explanations that came to the point at once and could not be misunderstood, corrected mistakes in a way one was not apt to forget, supplied you with endless variety of happy expressions for composition and dodges in translation—in short," was just the man to make the pace for a pupil who wanted to study. "Dodges in translation"! ⟨(Life, 9)⟩—are we to understand that this young gentleman of twenty-two had already learned how to march straight across a subject, how to avoid details, and yet imply them within a general proportion? Here is certainly the Henry Maine we have read, with his explanations that come "to the point at once and cannot be misunderstood," and his skill at inclusive statement. He was "backward to speak before his elders," the same witness tells us, and "had the rare merit of being a talker or a listener, as circumstances demanded, but, when he did speak," put in "keen and rapid remarks that told like knock-down blows." ⟨(Life, 10)⟩ This will not do for a description of Maine's written style. That is not keen and rapid, and there is nothing like the accent of a blow about it. It is deliberate, rather, and calm, and makes serene show of strength. But men who write thus, with a sort of restrained and chastened force, often speak in forms more direct and eager. It may well be, besides, that mere illumination has the effect of point, as a perfect illustration acts like a stroke of wit, and Maine's conversational hits may have seemed keen simply because they shone with light. A crystal will often give you the same sharp line of light that will flash to you from the edge of a sword's blade. But we are not concerned with that. There is enough in this picture of the young tutor to make it evident that the boy was, as always, father to the man. "Those who were intimate with him during these years," says another who knew him then, "will not easily forget his face and figure marked with the delicacy of weak health, but full to overflowing with sensitive nervous energy—his discursive brilliancy of imagination and intellect—his clear-cut style and precise accuracy of expression—and his absolute power of concentrating himself on the subject immediately before him. His mind was so graceful that strangers might have overlooked its strength, while the buoyancy of his enthusiasm was never beyond the control of the most critical judgment. . . . It was hard to drag him away from his rooms and his books, even for the ordinary minimum of constitutional exercise, though his spirits and

width of interest made him at all times a joyous companion."
⟨(Life, 7)⟩ Here was no 'dig,' who loved a book because he liked
to sit still and save himself the trouble of thinking, but a youth
to whom books were quick, not stuffing him, but setting his faculties in the way to satisfy themselves. It was reported of him many
years afterwards that he could pluck all the heart out of a thick
volume while another man was reading a hundred pages, ⟨(Life,
28)⟩—and no doubt he liked it, not because it was a book and
thick, but because it had a heart in it. It is in such a way and at
such a time that a mind fit for mastery learns how to use books.

Maine married in 1847, the year he was chosen Regius Professor of Civil Law,—married his cousin, Miss Jane Maine. His
marriage led him to look for wider fields of employment, and by
1850 he had qualified for and been called to the Bar. He soon
found practice of his profession go hard with his health, however,
and turned more and more away from it, to write for the more
serious public prints and exercise his high gifts as a lecturer.
Like Walter Bagehot, he had first tried his hand as a writer for
the public upon an exposition of the character and purposes of
Louis Napoleon, condemning from the outset the unconstitutional
aims which Bagehot was afterwards to justify. Bagehot tried to
look at the whole matter from a French point of view; Maine
looked at it always as an English constitutionalist and could find
no tolerant word for the imperial charlatan, who was just then
calling himself "President." So long, he said, as the French com-
monweal "moves steadily forward, to strike it down or trip it up,
at the cost of turning into gall the best and wholesomest blood
in the whole of France, would be a great piece of foolishness no
less than a great crime." ⟨(Life, 13)⟩ He showed his political sympathies at home by hating Mr. Disreali very heartily. "Already you
are manifesting considerable aptitude for the policy which has
conducted your leader to eminence," he says to Disraeli's followers
in 1849, with a biting sneer,—"already the Jacobinical colouring
of your language and argument shows that you are not indisposed
to alternate Conservative commonplace with Revolutionary verse
and radical prose. All you have to learn is the art of diverting attention while you shift your views, the unintelligible gabble of the
thimble-rigger as he changes his peas. When you have mastered
this accomplishment, the rest is quite simple." There is here good
partisan vigour. The strokes are direct and palpable, and show the
true zest of the political journalist. In 1852, two years after his
call to the Bar, Mr. Maine was appointed Reader in Roman Law
and Jurisprudence to the Inns of Court, and began courses of
public lectures in that beautiful hall of the Middle Temple in

which Twelfth Night' was first acted, which were to lead him to
the chief work of his life. But the serious studies of his lecture-
ship did not draw him away from his writing for the public journals. In 1855 the *Saturday Review* was established, with an extraordinary staff of writers—among them the accomplished gentleman who is now the Earl of Salisbury, Sir William Harcourt, Sir
James Stephen, Goldwin Smith, Walter Bagehot, Professor Owen,
and Henry Maine. Maine did no less than the rest of this brilliant
company to give immediate prestige to the *Saturday Review*. Mr.
Bagehot used to declare his nerves much too delicate to take the
direct impact of the *Spectator*. Its contents were much too pun-
gent and sanguine to be received without due preparation and
"he always got his wife to 'break' it to him" at breakfast; and some
of the rest of us have felt much the same way about the *Saturday
Review*. Not that it had kept the spanking pace given it by these
men when they were young; it grew dense in substance, rather, as
it grew old, and had finally to be taken in about the proportion
of one part to ten parts of water. Maine turned his hand to almost
every kind of writing to quicken its pages, and for six years made
it his business to enrich it with every matter of thought he could
contribute. At the very outset of his service as lecturer at the Inns
of Court he had been stricken with an illness which all but cost
him his life; but he came out of it with undaunted spirits and
energies not a whit dulled,—his thoughts burning within him like
flame within an alabaster vessel. Those who heard him read his
lectures were struck by the musical power of his voice, and by
the unimpeded flow of his sentences, running clear as crystal;
and those who conversed with him marvelled at the ease, the
lucidity, the telling force of his talk. "It was singularly bright,
alert, and decided," one of these reports; "you could not walk a
couple of hundred yards with him without hearing something that
interested you, and he had the enviable power of raising every
subject that was started into a higher atmosphere. In later life,"
we are told, "he became much more silent, and did not seem to
put his intelligence as quickly alongside that of the person to
whom he was talking"; ⟨(Life, 14)⟩ but it was in this time of high
tension and quick play of mind that he did the work which has
since held the attention of the world; for in 1861, at the age of
thirty-nine, he published his now celebrated volume on "Ancient
Law," his first book and unquestionably his greatest. It was the
condensed and perfected substance of his lectures at the Inns of
Court. It was in one sense not an original work: it was not
founded on original research; its author had broken no new
ground and made no discoveries. He had simply taken the best

historians of Roman Law,—great German scholars chiefly,—had united and vivified, extended and illustrated their conclusions in his own comprehensive way, had drawn, with that singularly firm hand of his, the long lines that connected antique states of mind with unquestioned but otherwise inexplicable modern principles of law, had made obscure things luminous and released a great body of cloistered learning into the world, where common students read and plod and seek to understand. What Bagehot says of Sydney Smith we may apply to Maine: "he had no fangs for recondite research." "No man of our time did so much for the revival of the study of Roman Law," said a close friend and intimate of Maine's after his death; "but it is greatly to be doubted whether he had any special familiarity with the Pandects or the Code." ⟨(Life, 80)⟩ "He had a power of seeing the general in the particular," says the same friend, "which we do not think has been equalled in literary history. His works are full of generalizations which are as remarkable for their clearness and sobriety as for their intrinsic probability, and which are reached, not by any very elaborate study of detailed evidence, but by a kind of intuition." ⟨(Life, 81)⟩ Men who tear the heart out of a thick volume while a slow and careful man reads a hundred pages, are not the men to pause over details with a nice scrutiny: they go eagerly on in search of the defining borders of the large land of detail.

Persons who suppose that Maine's "Ancient Law" is merely a text-book for lawyers will be very much and very delightfully surprised if they will but take it down from the shelf and read it,—as much surprised as young law students are who plunge into Blackstone because they must, and find to their astonishment that those deep waters are not a little refreshing, and the law, after all, no dismal science. The book has the dignity, the spirit, the clear and freshened air, the untechnical dress and manner of the world, which belong to the writing of cultured gentlemen who know the touch that makes literature. It is hard to explain, apart from a reading of the book itself, what it is that gives this quality of distinction and charm to "Ancient Law." You cannot easily illustrate it by quotations from the book, unless you quote a whole chapter, for Maine was no coiner of phrases, as I have said, and one passage is much like another,—no one page of the volume contains its method condensed, its art displayed in little. Take the following passage as a sample. It is the opening passage of Chapter V. He has been showing, with admirable breadth and adequacy, how Grotius and the other great originators of International Law founded their thought upon a so-called Law of Nature, which they had borrowed or inherited from the Roman law writers, who had taken it from the Stoics, to serve as an explanation for the common notions of justice which they called the *jus gentium*, the Stoics having used it as a part of their fanciful and wholly unverifiable theory of the universe. This is the way in which he proceeds:

"The necessity of submitting the subject of jurisprudence to scientific treatment has never been entirely lost sight of in modern times, and the essays which the consciousness of this necessity has produced have proceeded from minds of various calibre, but there is not much presumption, I think, in asserting that what has hitherto stood in the place of a science has for the most part been a set of guesses, those very guesses of the Roman lawyers which were examined in the two preceding chapters. A series of explicit statements recognizing and adopting these conjectural theories of a natural state, and of a system of principles congenial to it, has been continued with but brief interruption from the days of their inventors to our own. They appear in the annotations of the Glossators who founded modern jurisprudence, and in the writings of the scholastic jurists who succeeded them. They are visible in the dogmas of the Canonists. They are thrust into prominence by those civilians of marvellous erudition, who flourished at the revival of ancient letters. Grotius and his successors invested them not less with brilliancy and plausibility than with practical importance. They may be read in the introductory chapters of our own Blackstone, who has transcribed them textually from Burlamaqui, and wherever the manuals published in the present day for the guidance of the student or the practitioner begin with any discussion of the first principles of law, it always resolves itself into a restatement of the Roman hypothesis. It is however from the disguises with which these conjectures sometimes clothe themselves, quite as much as from their native form, that we gain an adequate idea of the subtlety with which they mix themselves in human thought. The Lockeian theory of the origin of Law in a Social Compact scarcely conceals its Roman derivation, and indeed is only the dress by which the ancient views were rendered more attractive to a particular generation of the moderns; but on the other hand the theory of Hobbes on the same subject was purposely devised to repudiate the reality of a law of nature as conceived by the Romans and their disciples. Yet these two theories, which long divided the reflecting politicians of England into hostile camps, resemble each other strictly in their fundamental assumption of a non-historic, unverifiable condition of the race. Their authors differed as to the characteristics of the præ-social state, and as to the nature of the abnormal action by which men lifted themselves out of it into that social organization with which alone we are acquainted, but they agreed in thinking that a great chasm separated man in his primitive condition from man in society and this notion we cannot doubt that they borrowed, consciously or unconsciously, from the Romans." ⟨(107-111)⟩[3] And so he goes on. I have read you two pages: I could not stop sooner,—there was no stopping place, and, stopping where I have stopped, I have simply waded out of the flowing stream,—there was no turn or eddy in it there.

I do not know how well this passage will serve to illustrate Maine's manner of writing to those who have read or heard no more. No doubt the most typical and admirable parts of the book are those which constitute the warp and woof of the sustained passages of reasoning which are the body of every chapter; but no part of them can easily or fairly be detached. Paragraphs like that I have quoted at any rate exemplify his manner, show his scope, give an idea of his tone, and furnish ground enough for comment. The London *Times*, in speaking of Maine's great work soon after his death, says of it: "The style was so lucid, the reasoning was so clear and cogent, the illustrative matter was so aptly chosen, the analogies were so dexterously handled, the survey was so broad, the grasp of principles was so firm, the whole fabric of the argument was articulated in so masterly a fashion, that the reader was easily tempted to suppose that 'Ancient Law' must have been as easy to write as it was fascinating to read." ⟨(*Times*, Feby 6, 1888)⟩ But Maine was not a rapid or an easy writer, we are told (and the article was evidently written by some friend who spoke from personal knowledge); it was a matter of infinite pains with him to rear the symmetrical structures he has left us in his published works. But when the work was done he "took the scaffolding away," gathered up his tools, cleared the ground, and left no trace of daily labour. There are no footnotes, there is no discussion of the books and materials out of which he took the finely fitted pieces of his structure; no seams or joints show, no traces of the tool: the work stands single, self-consistent, and complete as if it were a fine unassisted piece of creation. Everything he wrote reads like the utterance of "a very superior person," who speaks always out of his own knowledge, observes from a high coigne of vantage, and concludes the matter with an authoritative judgment. And so you get the feeling that he had no predecessors and fears no successors. I do not say this in disparagement of this

[3] *Ancient Law* (New York, 1885).

great writer: it seems to me necessary to say it simply by way of exigesis,—the manner is there, and we shall not understand Maine unless we reckon with it. It is partly, perhaps chiefly, due to the absence of footnotes and references. He seems to have covered all this wide field without assistance from other authors and to feel the need of no support of extraneous authority in any statement. He seems to have found it all out himself. "Starting with a little fact here and a venerable tradition there," as one of his critics has said, ⟨(*Athenaeum*, Feb. '88)⟩ "he lays a foundation with these, and proceeds to build up an edifice from stage to stage, till those who do not watch the process very closely imagine a great deal proved which, in reality, is highly plausible conjecture," with the result that "much that the author himself puts forward as only theory has been assumed to be settled doctrine." You get much the same impression in reading Mommsen's History of Rome. Here, too, you are without references, and a bold master of statement confidently builds up the great story of Rome before your eyes, age by age, the earliest times as definitely as the latest, with the air of one who remembers rather than with the caution of one who has heard and been led to infer, until at last you are fairly awed, and wonder whether the master will ever graciously vouchsafe to us any hint of his sources of information.

But it is more than the mere absence of footnotes: it is also the tone,—the tone of perfect confidence. Maine's books are one and all books of generalization,—of the sort of generalization which sweeps together the details of centuries into a single statement and interpretation. Maine is seldom in fact daring or beyond the evidence in his broad judgments: they were come at, you shall find, if you will take the pains to test them, by slow consideration and a careful elimination of the elements of error: they are sober, too, and without flavour of invention or of radical fancy. They spring always from the reason, never from the literary imagination. There is the air of a scientific calm and dispassionateness about them. But, for all that, they are so confidently spoken, they range over such spaces of time and inference, look so far abroad upon the fortunes and policies of men and nations, have such a spacious way of thought about them, and are set to so high a tune of stately diction that they quite overwhelm us with a sense of their importance not only but of the importance of their author also. "A man of the calibre of Montesquieu and De Tocqueville," the *Times* calls him. "He brought," it says, "to the study of law, politics, and institutions an intelligence as penetrating as theirs, a grasp of mind as comprehensive, a judgment as sober and impartial, and a method incomparably more searching and fruitful,"

—a style, it might have added, less personal, more cosmic,—as if it were conceived by some general intelligence. And this, let it be said at once, is Maine's greatness. It would be easy to show that he got practically all of his material of "Ancient Law" at second hand; it would doubtless be possible to prove that he had no gift for investigation, and possessed, though a man of the widest reading, no real erudition. His power lay in the art and mystery of divination. It has been said that he did nothing more than interpret for English lawyers and students of institutions the work of the great students of comparative jurisprudence in Germany; but this is not a judgment that can be held by those who are sensible of the effects which lie beyond detail. Without interpretation detail is dead, and Maine was a master of interpretation. Interpretation does not merely give details significance,—it adds something of its own, and shows that, at any rate in divination, the whole is greater than the sum of the parts. It is fact enhanced and vitalized by thought. It is the face of learning quickened and made eloquent by the suffused colour, the swift play of light in the eye, the subtle change of line about the mouth that bring the spirit forth which dwells within. It is, to change the figure, a guide to the high places from which the details of the plain may be seen massed and in proportion not only but made more significant also in their relations than they are in themselves,—*added* to by the touch of perspective. This is the highest function of learning.

It is this, no doubt, which gives one the sense of exhilaration he gets in reading Maine: we are moving in high spaces and command always a great outlook. And yet we are not in the air: there is no uneasy sense of having our feet off the ground. There is in every generalization that Maine makes a reassuring *implication* of detail,—just as there is in a towering mass of crag and mountain: we know somehow that the fine, aspiring lines are carried by granite and rooted in the centre of the solid globe. There is in such writing more than a sense of elevation, however. There is also a sense of movement,—the steady drawing on a great theme,— a movement strong, regular, smooth, inevitable, like that of a great river, sweeping from view to view, but never turning upon its course, never doubting of its direction, unimpeded, noiseless, more powerful than swift. This large and general power was characteristic of Maine in all that he did. The year after the publication of "Ancient Law" he was offered and accepted the post of law member in the Council of the Governor General of India, he removed to India, and the next seven years of his life were spent in a deep absorption in the affairs of that great dependency which has drawn to its administration so much of the best genius of the English race. He showed in Council the same gifts that made him a great writer,—those singular gifts of generalization which are, after all, in their last analysis executive in kind. "His method, his writings, and his speeches at the Indian Council Board," said Sir Alfred Lyall, ⟨(Life, 27)⟩ "have had a strong and lasting effect upon all subsequent ways of dealing with matters pertaining to India, whether in science or practical politics. He possessed an extraordinary power of appreciating unfamiliar facts and apparently irrational beliefs, of extracting their essence and the principle of their vitality, of separating what still has life and use from what is harmful or obsolete, and of stating the result of the whole operation in some clear and convincing sentence." "The local expert," he adds, almost with a smile, "the local expert, who, after years of labour in the field of observation, found himself with certain indefinite impressions of the meaning or outcome of his collected facts, often found the whole issue of the inquiry exactly and conclusively stated in one of Maine's lucid generalizations." ⟨(28)⟩ It is odd to learn, after hearing of the mass of difficult work he crowded into those seven years in India, that Maine was sometimes privately charged with indolence and idleness by his colleagues: and yet the charge carries with it a certain interesting significance. To those whose idea of labour is, to be forever poring upon a task, forever plodding from record to record, from memorandum to memorandum, he must of course have seemed idle. For all he loved reading and preferred his books to a walk abroad, his was not a mind for searching and sorting and annotating. It was a mind, rather, for brooding, and did its work with no outward show of being busy. No man bustles at thinking. The greater sorts of flight are made without noisy beat of wing.

Maine's appointment in 1862 to be Law Member of the Governor General's Council in India determined the rest of his career: from that time till the end of his life in 1888 his chief energies were given to the great and arduous business of governing India. A writer in the *Spectator* ⟨(Feb. 11, '88)⟩ declares him to have been "for seven years the avowed, and for twenty-six years the actual, English law-maker" for that troublesome dependency, and ascribes to him nearly three hundred successful statutes. He left India in 1869, and upon his return to England accepted, in 1870, the position of Corpus Professor of Jurisprudence at Oxford,—a position specially created that he might occupy it; but in the Autumn of the next year, 1871, he was appointed to a seat in the Council of the Secretary of State for India, and returned to the work for which he had so singularly fitted himself. He continued

to lecture at Oxford for seven or eight years, speaking every year
to an eager and steadily increasing company of serious students
in the quiet little hall of Corpus Christi College, and the fruits of
his work appeared from time to time in that series of interesting
volumes which we now always read along with "Ancient Law,"
as expanded gloss and commentary: "Village Communities, East
and West," published in 1871, "The Early History of Institutions,"
published in 1875, and "Early Law and Custom," published in
1883. These all grew out of his Oxford lectures, or out of articles
which he had contributed to the Reviews, and are rich with the
knowledge he had taken from India and from the later students
of institutions in the West. "Every man," he says in an interesting
passage to be found in his "Village Communities,["] "every man is
under a temptation to overrate the importance of the subjects
which have more than others occupied his own mind, but it certainly seems to me that two kinds of knowledge are indispensable, if the study of historical and philosophical jurisprudence
are to be carried very far in England; knowledge of India and
knowledge of Roman Law—of India, because it is the great reposi-
tory of verifiable phenomena of ancient usage and ancient juridical thought; of Roman Law, because, viewed in the whole
course of its development, it connects these ancient usages and
this ancient juridical thought with the legal ideas of our own
day." Ignorance of India he thought "more discreditable to Englishmen than ignorance of Roman Law, and at the same time
more intelligible in them. It is more discreditable," he said, "because it requires no very intimate acquaintance with contemporary foreign opinion to recognize the abiding truth of De Tocqueville's remark that the conquest and government of India are
really *the* achievements in the history of a people which it is the
fashion abroad to consider unromantic. The ignorance is moreover unintelligible, because knowledge on the subject is extremely
plentiful and extremely accessible, since English society is full of
men who have made it the study of a life pursued with an ardour
of public spirit which would be exceptional even in the field of
British domestic politics." ⟨⟨quoted, Life, 38, 39⟩⟩ It is evident
from the strong pulse that beats in these sentences that a new
spirit and a new and absorbing interest has come into the writer's
mind because of his actual contact with the life of the East.
It colours henceforth every part of his thought. "If there were an
ideal Toryism," he writes, in the midst of the general election of
1885, "I should probably be a Tory; but I should not find it easy
to say which party I should wish to win now. The truth is, India
and the India Office make one judge public men by standards

which have little to do with political opinion." (quoted in *Times*)
It was in 1885 that his volume on "Popular Government" showed
us how far India and the India Office had formed his opinions.
No doubt he was by constitution and temperament a Tory,—most
men of delicate health and cautious thought must be. Now and
again some invalid touched with genius gets the air of the sea
and the quick currents of the out-of-doors world into his blood,
as Robert Louis Stevenson did; but men like Maine dull their
blood while they are young by close, confining study, and no subsequent experience can take them out of the atmosphere of rooms
and books. "Popular Government" is the only book in which
Maine leaves his accustomed fields of study to make practical
test of his opinions in the field of politics,—which is, after all, an
out-of-door, and not an in-door, world. The book abounds in good
things. Its examination of the abstract doctrines which underlie
democracy is in his best manner,—every sentence of it tells. The
style is pointed, too, and animated beyond his wont,—hurried here
and there into a quick pace by force of feeling,—by ardour against
an adversary. He finds, besides, with his unerring instinct for the
heart of a question, just where the whole theory and practice of
democracy shows the elements that will make it last or fail. "After
making all due qualifications," he says, ⟨(p. 87)⟩ "I do not deny
to Democracies some portion of the advantage which so masculine a thinker as Bentham claimed for them. But, putting this
advantage at the highest, it is more than compensated by one
great disadvantage. Of all the forms of government, Democracy is
by far the most difficult. Little as the governing multitude is conscious of this difficulty, prone as the masses are to aggravate it
by their avidity for taking more and more powers into their direct
management, it is a fact which experience has placed beyond all
dispute. It is the difficulty of democratic government that mainly
accounts for its ephemeral duration." Unquestionably this is true,
and is the central truth of the whole matter. He is right, too, beyond gainsaying when he says that ⟨(p. 89)⟩ "the fact that what
is called the will of the people really consists in their adopting the
opinion of one person or a few persons admits of a very convincing illustration from experience." The ruling multitude will
only form an opinion by following the opinion of somebody—it
may be, of a great party leader—it may be of a small local politician—it may be, of an organized association—it may be, of an
impersonal newspaper." ⟨(92)⟩ But he is wrong,—and the error is
very radical,—in supposing that democracy really rests on a
theory and is *nothing but* "a form of government." It is a form of
character, where it is successful,—a form of national character;

and is based, not upon a theory, but upon the steady evolutions of experience. Mr. Morley was not just in describing the book as a rattling political pamphlet,—though he did say some fine things about it. His review of it brought forth, among other things, that fine remark of his, that any human institution will look black if held up against the light that shines in Utopia. But Maine cannot in fairness be called a partisan. The real, and very astonishing, fault of the book is, that its criticism rings false to the standards he had so greatly set up in the works which gave him his high fame. He speaks of democracy in the United States as if it were only one success amidst a host of failures, and had been nullified by the lamentable experiences of France and Spain and the republics of turbulent South America. The stability of the government of the United States is, he admitted, "a political fact of the first importance; but the inferences which might be drawn from it," he said, "are much weakened, if not destroyed, by the remarkable spectacle furnished by the numerous republics set up from the Mexican border-line to the Straits of Magellan." ⟨(18)⟩ The democracy of North America,—to be found in Canada no less than in the United States,—is as natural, as normal, as inevitable a product of steady, equable, unbroken history as the Corpus Juris of Justinian; and the heady miscarriages of attempted democracy in Spanish countries is as easily and as satisfactorily explicable as the principles of contract or the history of inheritance by will. No champion of the comparative method of historical study ought to have discredited his own canons by comparing things incomparable.

⟨The⟩ style ⟨of⟩ "Popular Government" is, as I have said, much more spirited than his style elsewhere, and smacks sometimes with a very racy flavour. "The short history of the United States," he says, ⟨(p. 111.)⟩ "has established one momentous negative conclusion. When a democracy governs, it is not safe to leave unsettled any important question concerning the exercise of public powers. I might give many instances of this, but the most conclusive is the War of Secession, which was entirely owing to the omission of the 'fathers' to provide beforehand for the solution of certain Constitutional problems, lest they should stir the topic of negro slavery. It would seem that, by a wise Constitution, Democracy may be made nearly as calm as water in a great artificial reservoir; but if there is a weak point anywhere in the structure, the mighty force which it controls will burst through it and spread destruction far and near." It was perhaps his style in this book that led the writer of his memoir in the *Times* to say that "his conversation was less epigrammatic than his writings. He did not strive at epigram," he says, "and his presence and influ-ence irradiated the society in which he moved rather with a dif-fused and steady effulgence than with brilliant but evanescent flashes." This is probably spoken of the later days in which he had fallen rather silent, the effervescence of youth being quieted and the meditative habit grown strong; but it is a very questionable choice of words to call anything he ever wrote epigrammatic. We are so accustomed to dull writers, that when we find any vivid significance in what we read we are apt to attribute it to some trick or turn in the way the thing is put. Maine's sentences, in "Popular Government," as well as elsewhere and upon less lively themes, break with no sudden light, but are radiant, rather, from end to end, burning steadily and without flash. We see the whole page irradiated, find point in every sentence, and say, out of habit, that it is epigrammatic. But no one sentence carries the meaning: it is spread upon the whole page.

Honours came thick and fast upon Maine after his return from India. In the spring of 1871, the year in which he accepted a seat in the Council at the India Office, he was gazetted Knight Com-mander of the Star of India, and was henceforth Sir Henry Maine. In 1877 he was chosen Master of Trinity Hall, Cambridge, the college in which, thirty years before, he had coached youngsters in the best "dodges in translation," and had delighted a select circle of friends with his luminous talk,—and he of course gave up the Corpus Professorship at Oxford to accept it. He still kept his seat and sedulously attended to his work at the council board of the India Office, and continued to reside in London, but he made himself felt at Cambridge none the less, and let no one feel that he was neglecting the duties or letting down the social tradi-tions of the Mastership of Trinity Hall. He was offered the Perma-nent Undersecretaryship of the Home Office in 1885, and in 1886 the Chief Clerkship of the House of Commons, to succeed Sir Thomas Erskine May. No doubt, as one of his friends has sug-gested, it was well understood that Sir Henry would himself know whether he was fitted for these offices, and could be relied upon to decline them if he was not. He accepted, in 1887, the Whewell Professorship of International Law at Cambridge, but just made vacant by the retirement of Sir William Harcourt, and in the same year delivered those lectures on disputed questions of International obligation and practice now preserved in a thin vol-ume which we should be very loath to miss from our shelves. It is said that before going to India in 1862 "he had projected, and to a great extent prepared, a work on International Law, intended as a companion to" his "Ancient Law," and "conceived in the same spirit," but that "when he returned from India the manuscript of this work could not be found," and was never recovered. ⟨(*Times*)⟩ Like the true scholar he was, he took the loss very cheerfully, assured that what he could write upon the subject now would be much more full-bodied and much more abreast of the best scholarship than what he had written then; but alas! he was not to do the work he had projected after all. He died, suddenly, of apoplexy February third, 1888, at Cannes, whither he had gone, alone, expecting to recuperate, not looking for the end; and we have only his first lectures, unrevised. They are singularly finished in tone, manner, and substance, like everything he wrote, but they are only a fragment of what he meant to do.

His friends thought, when he was gone, not of the great writer whom the world had lost, but of the genial, sweet-spirited, enlightened gentleman who would never make their gatherings bright again with his presence. The general world of society and of affairs had never known Sir Henry Maine. He gave the best energies of his life to public duty,—to the administration of India; but he rendered his service at quiet council boards whose debates were of business, not of questions of politics, and did not find their way into the public prints. He had no taste for publicity, preferred the secluded groups that gathered about him in the little hall of Corpus Christi to any assembly of the people. He did not have strong popular sympathies, indeed, and disdained to attempt the general ear. He loved knowledge and was indifferent to opinion. It perhaps went along with his delicate physique and sensitive temperament that he should shrink from crowds and distrust the populace. His "quickness of apprehension, power of expression, and luminous intuition," the writer in the *Saturday Review* tells us, would perhaps have led "an uninformed observer to the conclusion that their possessor had the temperament of a political enthusiast." But "no greater mistake," he declares, "could have been made. They were associated with a temperament which was liable to err on the side of caution, regard to actual circumstances, and a total absence of any sort of enthusiasm or illusion." ⟨(quoted, Life, 8.)⟩ And certainly no man who is without any sort of enthusiasm or illusion can easily be a democrat or a politician,—for he will take democracy in the abstract, as Maine did, instead of taking it practically and in the bulk, and will lack that serviceable confidence in good average sense and sober second thought on the part of the people, which leaders have and are justified in having among a self-possessed populace accustomed to the drill and orderly action of self-government. But immediate leadership was not Maine's function. It was his suitable part in the world to clarify knowledge, to show it in its large proportions and long significance to those who could see. His mind was an exquisitely tempered instrument of judgment and interpretation. It touched knowledge with a revealing, almost with a creative, power, and as if the large relationships of fact and principle were to it the simple first elements of knowledge. He thought always so like a seer, moved always in so serene an air! His world seemed to be kept always clear of mists and clouds, as if it were blown through with steady trade-winds which brought with them, not only pure airs, but the harmonious sounds and the abiding fragrance of the great round world.[4]

Woodrow Wilson
18 February, 1898.[5]

WWhw MS. (WP, DLC).
   [4] This lecture was published, *mutatis mutandis*, as "A Lawyer with a Style," *Atlantic Monthly*, LXXXII (Sept. 1898), 363-74.
   [5] Wilson's composition date.

To Ellen Axson Wilson .

New Atlantic Hotel

My own darling, Norfolk, Va.[1] 27 February 1898

I *must* write you a few lines, just to ease my heart. It is dangerous to my peace of mind to have a *taste* of your sweet company and then go off again to myself, to the old loneliness of the past few weeks. *Now* I have nothing to do but think about you,—how infinitely sweet and captivating you are. It involves almost a *physical* pain to separate from you. I left the station with a sort of sickness yesterday. As for my heart, it is bereaved,—my mind, too, is so lonely,—ah, my darling, I am incomplete, I am incapable, I am deeply marred without *you*.

Everything is comfortable enough here. I heard a good, old-fashioned sermon this morning. I shall keep to schedule, and sail from here about six to-morrow evening,—and Tuesday night, God willing, I shall be once more in your arms.

With all my heart, Your own   Woodrow

ALS (WP, DLC).
   [1] Wilson had gone to Norfolk in order to take the boat trip from there to New York, not to give a speech.

To Edith Gittings Reid

My dear Mrs. Reid,   Norfolk, Va.   27 February, 1898

I have my suspicions that this pen is going to be recalcitrant, like most public pens, but I don't feel like postponing my letter, and am going to try its (steel) temper. I have come away very warm at the heart because of the generous hospitality Mrs. Wilson (now that she is your friend too, I will call her Ellen) and I have just been enjoying. I know what she thinks about her visit: she thinks yours the sweetest and every way the most engaging home she has seen in many a long day, and went away in love with you and Mrs. Gittings,—as wholly in love as I expected her to be. It makes me very happy to think of your meeting and your immediate friendship. To be sure, I had described you to her and her to you as best I could,—but it was not that that drew you to each other,—it came of a law of nature—the nature of all sweet and noble women. It was beautiful, as it was delightful, to see how immediately Ellen was in love with Mrs. Gittings. She seemed to feel for her at once a sort of daughter's affection, and was charmed by her brightness and sweetness from the first.

I was somehow absorbed in Mrs. Wilson's impressions. They were new, and I could see in them my own repeated. She felt about Mr. Reid and you all just as I have felt: that there was such a just mixture of heart and mind,—of right sentiment, informed judgment, and light-hearted comment,—as makes the wholesomest atmosphere to live and be friends in, and I am sure we have both come away deeply refreshed and very happy in our week's experience.

I am spending the quietest sort of Sunday here. I have just come from church,—where I heard a really excellent old-fashioned sermon,—and feel (except for the hotel) as if I had fallen once again into the slow paced southern life which seems to me the most natural of all.

Please give Mr. Reid my warmest regards,—I enjoyed being with him more than I know how to say,—and to Mrs. Gittings my love, if she will accept it; and believe me,

With the warmest gratitude and appreciation,

                    Your sincere friend,   Woodrow Wilson

ALS (WC, NjP).

To John Franklin Jameson

My dear Jameson,　　　　　　Norfolk, Va. 27th Feb'y 1898

Your letter has been following me, and I must not keep you waiting till I get home for an answer.

I am sorry to have to decline the little job you offer me.[1] I have no doubt Dunning's book is an excellent one, and I should enjoy going carefully through it. But, believe me, it is not possible. That sort of thing takes me a long time, and I always write slowly. I have tasks laid out for the rest of the year, and am not my own man. Besides, I have told I don't know how many editors that I do *no* reviewing.

You wrote me a very long time ago about some papers of Stockton's which might throw light on the authorships of the *Federalist*.[2] I looked the matter up. I found that most of Stockton's papers had been deliberately burned by one of his heirs.[3] I set Colonel Stockton[4] ton [*sic*], of the present generation, to looking amongst such matters as remain,—or, rather, the Colonel promised to put his daughters on the search, for he never does anything himself,—and it was because I could never get him beyond promises that I let the matter drop and did not write to you.

With warmest regard,

Most sincerely Yours,　Woodrow Wilson

ALS (J. F. Jameson Papers, DLC).

[1] In a missing letter, Jameson, Managing Editor of the *American Historical Review*, had asked Wilson to review William Archibald Dunning, *Essays on the Civil War and Reconstruction and Related Topics* (New York, 1898).

[2] Wilson referred to the second Richard Stockton (1764-1828). Jameson's interest in Stockton manuscripts was aroused by a controversy over the authorship of certain numbers of the *Federalist* carried on in the issues of the *American Historical Review* for April and July 1897 between Edward G. Bourne and Paul Leicester Ford. On page 684 of the July issue appeared a footnote by Bourne citing an earlier writer who alleged that he had seen, "many years ago, in the possession of the late Richard Stockton," a manuscript by Alexander Hamilton which revealed the authorship of the *Federalist* papers.

[3] Very few of the Stockton Papers have ever come to light. There is a small collection of them in the Princeton University Library, among which nothing relating to the authorship of the *Federalist* appears.

[4] Samuel Witham Stockton.

Notes for Lectures in a Course on the Elements of Politics

[March 5, 1898-April 29, 1900]

5 March, 1898

POLITICS

I.

The Subject-matter: Nature and Field of Politics.

"*Politics*" a word of *broader* significance *than* "*Political Science*" because it is a study of life and motive as well as of form and object.

"Politics ought to be adjusted, not to human reasonings, but to human nature; of which the reason is but a part, and by no means the greatest part." (*Burke*, I., 398: "The Present State of the Nation," '69.)[1]

"*Politics*" *is*, ∴ , the study of the life of States; of the genesis and operation of institutions; of the ideas, purposes, and motives of men in political society. It is *a study both of political order and of statesmanship* (not of individual policies, but of leadership and constructive action.) Machiavelli and Montesquieu the fathers of this study. Tocqueville, Burke, Bagehot, &c. &c.

The Nature and Field of the Subject indicated in the following (selected and representative) topics, taken, for the more part, from the works of *Bluntschli* and *Roscher* on "Politik."

II.

Nature and Objects of Political Society

"*Political Society*"=another name for "The State"="*A People independently organized for Law within a definite Territory*"; and the objects of Political Society are those objects which can be attained *by means of Law*, and organic action (e.g. in foreign affs.).

We are to study Political Society in this course, as much as may be, *objectively*, *concretely*,—and, first of all, by looking back of modern political ideas, which have too much sophisticated the study.

Take the *several elements of The State* in their order:

(1.) *A People*; i.e. a body of persons, (of all ages, and not selected adults merely) habituated to living together, conscious of common ties and interests, instinctively united, accustomed to co-operation. Such an actual union and common life may be produced (*a*) by *expanded blood relationships*, i.e. the growth of the family; (*b*) by the driving of groups together by *external coercion*; (*c*) by *deliberate association*, in the first instance, for a common purpose, though the band thus associated must take the family habit and lose its first deliberateness of association before it can become a veritable state. (d) by *colonization*, ancient; by colonization modern.

(2). *A people Organized*, acting, i.e., not merely by instinctive accommodation and coöperation, but under a more or less elaborate discipline, i.e., under authority,—an authority which serves to keep

---

[1] *The Works of the Right Honorable Edmund Burke*, 5th edn. (12 vols., Boston, 1877). [All notes by the Editors unless otherwise specified]

individuals from any breach of the common habit or understanding. *Organized=having organs.*

(3). *A people organized for Law*, i.e. for the maintenance of definite relationships and fixed rules of action, established privileges and duties. This law may be wholly Habit, and based entirely on *Sentiment*. It is, in most stages, if not in all[,] *an attitude of mind*, compounded of reverence, fidelity, sympathy, and fear,—fear of disapproval, if not of punishment,—apprehension arising out of our consciousness that we cannot determine the way in which others will regard our acts or deal with them. *Enacted* law based for the most part on rational expediency *and* the habit of obedience.

(4.) *A people organized for law within a definite Territory.* Unlike the others, *not an invariable feature* of state life. There have been long periods of history during which distinctly marked political life existed (indeed men have never been without it) notwithstanding the fact that organized peoples did not remain fixed or stationary within definite territorial limits.

The Objects of Political Society are as various, almost, as States themselves. Each nation (as we have seen elsewhere) has its own form of political life, its own functional characteristics, produced by its own development, expressive of its own character and experience in affairs. (See notes on Public Law).[2] Two common objects there are however:

(1) *Order*, which is the primary object of all law,

(2) *Progress*, which has been the object of only a minority of politics,—but of so distinguished a minority that it may, perhaps, be accepted as at any rate the ultimate object of all political action.

What is Progress? Civilization has *two elements*:

(a) *A material element.* An assured mastery over nature: a knowledge of the laws of her operation and the discovery of ready and adequate means of taking advantage of them to facilitate human life and increase human power and comfort.

(b) *An immaterial element*: an assured and equitable social order: a stable system of government and authority, in which law is clearly developed, regularly obeyed, and, as nearly as may be, accommodated to existing needs and conditions: and an advance from generation to generation in principles of humanity, justice, and mutual helpfulness.

Vehicles of Progress:

Struggle, with its discipline;

Religion, with its ideals of duty

Education, with its enlightenment and its instruction as to means.

Law, with its application of accepted and enforceable rules.

Relation of the Masses to Progress is passive, depending upon the effect wrought by the discipline of life and the enlightenment of education and experience. There cannot be progress without the masses; but they are the material, not the effective cause, of progress. Progress works upon them, rather than by means of them.

Relation of the Individual to Progress may be active, but only so far as

2 Printed at Sept. 22, 1894, Vol. 9.

he can work upon and school the common thought, and so make institutional change practicable.

Political Society is *concerned with Progress only so far as Law*, its only instrument, *may be made an instrument* of Progress. And Law may become a vehicle of Progress only so far as struggle, religion, or education has brought to a common recognition such principles of action as may be universalized in their application, and equitably enforced in the field of actual transactions between man and man.

The objects of Political Organization, as distinguished from Law, should be

(1) *A place of definite and reasonably permanent leadership* for tested minds,—and open processes of self-selection.

(2) *Such processes of government* as will most surely and continuously *hold the attention* and *instruct the understandings* of the people.

(3) As an instrument of Liberty, Discussion, Agitation, progressive change.

III.

Modern Political Ideas:
(1) Self-Government.

We shall get our clearest idea of what the State is about by *a study* of our own *active ideals* and conceptions.

No doubt *the fundamental ideal* of modern political life is *freedom*,— but all concrete notions of freedom have been generated *under institutions of self-government*,—and that must first be examined.

Some careful thinking necessary. Is the 'self-government' of the *nation* of the same nature as the self-government of the *Commune*? We use the expression both for *primary assemblies* and for *representative parliaments*. Is self-government *compatible with non-democratic institutions*?

Local self-government came first, among the Germanic peoples; and *then*, thr. representation, came

National self-government, which must, of course, be representative.

National self-government (national *government*, indeed, whether *self*-government or not) *necessarily subordinates local* government, and relegates it to the exercise of a delegated authority merely[.] After national gov't. has been set up *local government necessarily means only self-direction within the* limits, and in the use of powers, defined or prescribed by (national) *law*. It may be limited also by large discretionary powers of *control* by central authorities.

It may conduce to clearness to *follow Bluntschli* in designating representative national government as *Self-Government* and local self-direction as *Self-Administration*.

Local Self-Administration has *taken the form* (See Bluntschli, *Politik*,[3] p. 90) of

---

[3] *Politik als Wissenschaft*, Vol. III of *Lehre vom modernen Staat* (3 vols., Stuttgart, 1875-76).

(1) delegating state functions to *unsalaried appointive officers* chosen from among the citizens of the local area, like the English *Justices of the Peace*; of

(2) associating *unsalaried elective councils* with *local professional officials*: e.g. Prefect and Prefectural Council, *Burgermeister* and *Stadtrath*; or of

(3) delegating local state functions to *officers or councils*, or officers *and* councils *constituted by the citizens themselves*, by election.

National Self-Government has taken *the form* either of

(1) *Checking and guiding* hereditary rulers and appointed officials *by means of representative assemblies* and fixed laws enacted by such assemblies and administered by an independent judiciary; or of

(2) Putting *both legislation and administration in the hands of elected representatives*.

Self-Government has *equally emphatic members*: The word *government* is quite as emphatic as the word *self* in the compound; and the conception as a whole warrants this *analysis*:

(1) *It is an organic thing*: the central organization must have a definite and stable action and a fixed interrelation of parts and functions which will mean very strong and definite government by legal, indisputable authority and force.

(2) *The local organization* is no less organically *subordinate* to the central than under other forms of government, and does *not necessarily* embrace the *principle of election*, or exclude professional executive services.

(3) Self-government is *quite compatible with non-democratic*, though it is sharply contrasted with autocratic, *institutions*.

(4) *The only invariable idea* involved (inasmuch as it has no invariable form) is *the participation*, whether by election or by appointment, *of free citizens* (as contrasted with professional officials) representing either interests (classes) or localities,— and *the radical idea* is most nearly approached when the citizen participants receive *no pay* for their services. An essential principle is, that *the lay element*, as contrasted with the hereditary or professional, *must control*, if not in the localities, in the national counsels, *in the choice of all fundamental policy*.

Bluntschli (*Politik*, p. 91) gives *this admirable summary of the essential conditions* of Self-Government:

(1) *Personal capacity* on the part of the citizens, which is largely, in politics, the result of training and experience.

(2) *Individual honour*, a cultivated and enlightened sense of public (as well as of private) duty.

(3) *Economic conditions which afford leisure* for affairs to the trained and capable and initiative classes of the community.

And there is much that is worthy of consideration in what he *adds*: "The combination of these three characteristics, training, civic virtue, and leisure is *nowhere in the world the common endowment of all classes of the people*, but belongs everywhere to only a relatively small minority of citizens. In this respect *Self-government* is

not, as many suppose, a democratic, but rather *an aristocratic*[4]
institution."

Moreover, "when public affairs demand a scientific and technical
professional training, and makes requisition upon the entire resources of a man's life, self-administration is not possible, *but renders necessary the work of professional officials."* (pp. 91-92).

28 March, 1898

IV.

Modern Political Ideas:
(2) *Freedom.*

The natural desire for freedom,—i.e. freedom from *bondage,*—whether
physical or spiritual. And yet *no freedom* can be *absolute.*

Liberty is not "scientific anarchy,"—as *little* government as possible,—
the notion of Jefferson. It is simply, *as little irritating, hurtful,
cramping,* and *humiliating restraint* as possible. No man objects to
having everything done to prepare for the running and to equalize
conditions

"Scientific anarchy" really the product of *a reaction,* not against
institutions (governing ways and understandings), but *against
tutelage,*—*vs.* a system under which there was no regular adjustment between the government and the individual, but a few persons determined the rights, fortunes, action of all.

Freedom (*the only practicable* freedom) exists as *a product of the*
most *enlightened order,* under which there is *the best all-round
adjustment of authority and individual choice,*—the least friction
bet. the will of the government and the will of the citizen.

*It consists in a reasonable accommodation between individual
right and public power,*—a properly adjusted balance between the
forces of individual character and the forces of public convenience.

What this reasonable accommodation and balance *are* can be *determined in no* absolute or abstract way. The *experience* of each nation must suggest the determination. The public convenience varies
with a thousand circumstances,—even individual motive and the
forces of individual character vary as between nation and nation,
place and place. *Proper freedom inheres in no one set of institutions.*

Who is a Free Man, in the political sense of the term? *What sort of
a nation* do we mean when we speak of *a "free people"?* Is a "free
man" one who does not have to submit to having affairs which immediately concern him determined without his being consulted?
Does the idea, i.e., *involve franchise?*

Not necessarily. There is something which whole generations
have contented themselves with in the idea (at any rate in the
fact) of *virtual representation* in political action,—which might, in
this connexion, be called virtual *consultation.*

A "free people" is a people *not subject to the arbitrary choices of
rulers,*—a people whose interests, and *whose individual rights,
somehow get regarded* with a good deal of system and without seri-

[4] "Of course, however, *that cannot be called an aristocracy* which is not a
fixed class,—and determined by something besides training, honour, and leisure."
[WW's note]

ous friction, being made known by *some* adequate method of communication,—*a people and a government in intelligent touch* with one another, accordant and coöperative.

A *"free man"* is one who *is not under tutelage*, but is upon an equality with others, as secure in his rights and as untrammelled in the exercise of them as all others in the same political community.

The Idea involves:

1) *Freedom to know* and to form and express *opinions*;
2)   ”   of *occupation* and of *movement*;
3)   ”   in *concerted action*,—insofar as these depend upon relation sustained by the individual to the government. In short, *freedom of individual and social self-development*,—as little as may be dictated or coached by governing authority.

Analysis of conditions precedent:

(1) A *clear, general, experimental understanding of fundamental individual rights*; the *adequate definition* of those rights in unmistakable terms; *and their guaranteeing, either by franchise or* by

(2) *Such an equality of conditions* and interests, either actual or potential, *as will breed close community* of feeling and identification between classes, and will, ∴ , *cause* the *leading spirits* of the nation *to act and to think*, naturally and spontaneously, *for the common weal*,—to be advocates for all classes. *Hence also*

(3) *An educated and experienced people* (not necessarily trained under pedagogues, however) *who can understand* the *general* as well as the individual welfare.

(4) A *polity that will breed*
   (a) A habit and a spirit of *civic duty*, and
   (b) *Leading characters* (rather than managing talents) *by processes of self-preparation* and self-assertion, irrespective of class.

(5) *Power*, lodged in a force drawn from the people, *to keep out foreign interference*,—*maintain a secure national independence.*

4th April, 1898

V.

Modern Political Ideas:
(3) *Equality.*

The word contains one of the great forces of modern politics. It would not be far from the exact to say that for the last century we have been working at the analysis of the mottoe of the French Revolution: *Liberty, Equality, Fraternity. Fraternity we may dismiss* without test, for it is a word of motive, of sentiment, and not of organization. *Liberty* (i.e. freedom) and *Equality are words of organization* and must be made to yield their meaning, as exactly as possible.

Liberty we have seen to be a matter of coördination and co-operation, —a matter of *guaranteeing a free play* of individual talents and capacities, by means of a political order by which each man will be made as free as his neighbour to develop his life and powers.

'*Equality*' is meant to express *the cardinal principle of Liberty*, and, understood in its true historical significance, does so safely and truly enough. It must be taken, *not as a word of fact*, but *as an expression of principle,*—the principle upon which individual energy is to be released from *artificial,* i.e. *legal or conventional, restraints.*

The word, in this true sense, lies latent in our conception of what is 'sportsmanlike,'—'*a free field and no favour,'*—wh. *does not mean* that the swift must wait for the slow, the strong yield to the weak, the skillful take care not to outdo the clumsy and inexpert, and *nobody win.*

'*Its true historical significance*' is easily discerned. The potency of 'Equality' as a rallying cry arose from the fact that it expressed the *reaction* of the latter part of the 18th century *vs.* so much as remained of that *preference of classes* which the Middle Ages had fixed upon the law of Europe. It was a demand for a 'free field,'—a *passionate* demand that there should be 'no favour.' So far as it was just, it demanded *a levelling of conditions,* not actual but legal; only in its mistaken excess did it contemplate *a levelling of individuals.* In its just intention it is a condition precedent to Liberty; in its unjust exaggeration (or, rather, misinterpretation) it is the sharp antithesis of Liberty. *Equality at the starting-point, natural inequality at the goal.*

Statesmanship and progress might have been impossible, had not *the democracy of the Roman Catholic Church* run along with and offset the exclusive class privileges of the feudal system. Here was *a perennial fountain of individual capacity*: equality *at the start* for every man in orders, of whatever origin,—and in some degree equality of educational preparation, too,—though *at the top hierarchy, the preference of the fittest,* the most able.

Note, consequently, *how the State drew administrative capacity from the Church,—depended upon democracy for talent* and service. Became *rationally hateful only when* Church offices came to be filled by political favourites, or when the Church as an *imperium* preferred its own secular and political interests to those of the individual States whose affairs her ecclesiastics were administering.

Test Questions:

1) Shall there be *equality in taxation?* Yes; but only equality to *capacity* to yield the State pecuniary support.

2) Shall there be *equality in Suffrage?* Yes; but only up to the point where all are equal in capacity to judge. This can be *only very roughly approximated*; but it clearly excludes *Referendum,* initiative choice,—future plan or progressive experiment.

3) Shall there be *equality in political service,*—the lot instead of the examination, native intelligence instead of technical education, rotation rather than expert experience? Again *the same answer,*—and the systematic selection and development of *suitable* capacity by education and training.

Development to be provoked at all hazards.

4) Shall there be *equality in the choice of leaders,*—and shall all alike be trusted to guide and select policy for the body politic? Shall *differences of calling, training, character, culture* be ignored where the function is choice and initiative in affairs? Always the same answer: *According to the capacity displayed in a free field.*

The Formula: Equality in initial rights; but *in privileges* equality based upon *fact and performance only.* Equality in duties=equality in the performance of duty. *Power proportioned to capacity*, and *duty proportioned to power. Selection for power based upon a suffrage limited in its actions to the recognition of character and capacity.*

A guiding thought:

"*Burke* first taught the world at large that politics are made of time and place; that institutions are shifting things, to be tried by and adjusted to the shifting conditions of a mutable world; that in fact politics are but a piece of business, to be determined in every case by the exact exigencies of that case,—in plain English, by *sense and circumstances.*" *W. Bagehot.*[5]

26 April 1898

VI.
Modern Political Ideas
(4) Nationality and Humanity (Internationality).

'*Nationality*' does *not* mean *the same* for the *German* that it means for the *Englishman* or the American. By '*Nation*' *the German* (using the word literally) *means* what we mean by 'Race.' By 'Nation' *we express* the idea the German has in mind when he uses the word 'Volk.' '*Nation,*' *for us, means* community of organization, of life, and of tradition; for the German it means community of origin and blood.

The '*Nationality*' *of modern politics* cannot be expressed exactly in either the English or the German meaning of the word. It is *based upon consciousness of community of origin, speech, and blood*; but it *has not easily crossed lines of governmental organization*, where the associations and traditions of political action are sharply severed.

It is no less expressed in the separation of America from England in the last century than in the coalescence of the German states in this century. It is conditioned and formed by habit, association, organization; is compounded of community in politics and environment as well as of community in blood and speech. *Race tradition*, in short, is for the most part *contained in and transmitted by political association*. It is largely dominated by habits of allegiance.

Language, however, is *incomparably the best conducting medium* for the transmission and diffusion of sympathy, and the communication and solidification of purpose. *The modern press*, properly used, an incalculably powerful instrument alike *for the creation and the breaking down* of organic tissue,—for *making or preventing coöperation.*

Only community of speech can bring about detailed community of thought and absolute unity in point of view. It is in *this detail* that we find *the chief differences* between *Nationality* and *Humanity*,—the thoughts and ideals peculiar to individual nations and the thoughts and ideals common to mankind.

What Constitutes National Character? It is noteworthy that a common national character can be imparted to a vast and heteroge-

---

[5] Wilson is quoting from the third of Bagehot's "Letters on the French Coup d'État of 1851," Forrest Morgan (ed.), *The Works of Walter Bagehot* (5 vols., Hartford, Conn., 1889), II, 394.

neous population, drawn, like our own, from almost all the races of the civilized world, *provided*

(1) *Differences of language be eliminated* and conducting *media* for thought, principle, ideal be provided;

(2) *A vital common life exist*, which will unite classes by freeing individuals; by keeping *economic channels open* upon equitable conditions to all; and by *organizing political action in the common interest* and upon a true co-operative principle;

(3) *Leadership be of the truly organizing and informing sort*, preserving and propagating and illustrating the best ideals and traditions.

(4) *A system of education* (pedagogic or other) lead the mind of each generation along substantially *the same road of knowledge and memory and training*.

National Character expresses itself in

(a) *common ideals* of conduct (and even of manners) drawn from common experiences and common conditions in meeting and observing life;

(b) a *common attitude towards institutions* and political practice;

(c) a *common attitude towards foreign systems* of government and foreign ideals of conduct.

Culture (i.e. scholarly culture), which is got by travel and intercourse amongst men and books, *tends always to denationalize*,—at any rate to take away all intensities of habit or prepossession,—*to universalize the habit of the mind*,—to produce *internationality* of thought and standard, by substituting the broadly *human* for the narrowly local sympathy and comprehension.

For Humanity is *bred of intercourse and sympathy*,—is killed by isolation and prejudice. Everything that fosters a common consciousness and enhances a sense of spiritual community amongst nations advances principles and sentiments of Humanity. Accordingly, these principles and sentiments have been enhanced.

1) *Slowly*, the centuries through, *by Christianity*,—tho. the sweep and efficacy of its influence have been broken and interrupted by national, political, and sectarian separateness, rivalry, and antipathy. *Modern missions*.

2) The *liberal, humanitarian politics* which has transformed the political world since the American and French Revolutions. "The Rights of Man."

3) The *extension and liberalization of International Law* which has accompanied the international contests of the century of revolution.

4) *The intercourse of trade*, quickened and made universal by *steam* and *electricity*—railway, post, telegraph, telephone.

5) *Colonization*: the union and utilization and civilization of the ends of the earth by the great civilizing powers of Europe.

6) *Emigration*: interchange and transfer of populations.

7 May, 1898

VII.

The Means of Government: Physical, Spiritual

Every government rests ultimately, of course, *on force*, the right and power of those who govern to compel the obedience of those who are governed. *But,* inasmuch as governors are always in a minority as compared with the multitudes who are governed, *this 'Force' is* obviously *not a simple idea,* but *needs analysis. Even in cases of military despotism* we need to inquire what it is that gives the ruler control of his *army.*

An army of rule is generally fickle enough, and *keeps its general in power only so long as he seems* to his soldiers *to serve* their collective sense of privilege and power. He must make and keep interest with them.

There is here, then, *some sense of organization. Concert* of action confers this power to rule: a sense of unity and a common object. *In the case of a military despotism* there is needed *also* an instant and continuous *command of overwhelming resources,—*the practically exclusive control of arms and discipline.

Widened to the measure of a non-military state, this means *a habit and sentiment of coöperation and coherence* gained through long processes and many vicissitudes of *ancient association* (See "Elements of Nationality," *ante*)

Preëminence in privilege and the *right to command* were no doubt, in primitive societies, *gained,* whenever the process was unforced and natural, *by those individuals whom fortune* or their own *energy* and *sagacity* had put in possession of *the best resources.* Advantage came with *personal initiative, organizing genius, sagacity in counsel, personal attractiveness,* and even *great physical strength. Men have always yielded to guidance,* in matters which demanded wisdom or initiative; *guidance has always tended to fall to those most capable; and command and obedience alike have always tended to become habitual,—*the one with a few men, preferred and trained, the other with the undistinguished mass of men.

Political power, then, acquired and created by such means, *has kept always in existence the idea and fact of government,—*an idea and a fact which have grown more and more definite and invariable in form and content as communities have grown in size and in complexity of organization, *until at last government itself seems to possess individuality, the idea of the State* as a definite entity arises, and with it *the idea of Sovereignty.*

The props and foundations of Sovereignty have been
1 *The habit and sentiment of Obedience,* which easily passes into
2 *Loyalty,—*personal devotion broadened in scope and power; based on
3 *Reverence*: made up of an association of ideas: deference to leaders who are elders, the presumptions of long standing practice, the ascription of past achievements to the force or perfection of particular institutions, the imaginative associations of mere antiquity, etc.
4 *Sense of duty,* springing out of training, privilege, &c.
5 *Fear or at least awe* on the part of the majority, produced by the continuous exercise of force by the government.
6 *Race or national feeling,* bred by rivalries, international ambitions, &c., which finds the government a means of self-expression.
7 *Ideals, produced by the long processes of national life,* and look-

ing forward to the accomplishment of certain ends (like political emancipation) through the operation of particular institutions (like the suffrage).

We must distinguish (in next lecture), *Sovereignty* (the [*] fountain and source of governmental power), *Authority* (delegation of sovereign power), *Leadership* (initiative in choice or change).

28 April, 1900

[VIII.]
Sovereignty,—Authority,—Leadership.

Sovereignty and *Authority* are words always *associated* but not, upon analysis, *synonymous*. Authority rests with individuals; but the State survives individuals and must itself be conceived the entity of which Sovereignty is an attribute.

There may be *'sovereign' authority* and *executive authority merely*;—the authority which originates law and policy and the authority which is merely delegated and administrative; *but in any case* we feel that '*Authority*' is a word which usually expresses nothing more than *the delegation to particular individuals or bodies of individuals of that power whose fountain and source is the organic will of a Community,—a State.* That organic will is Sovereignty.

Without Authority, Sovereignty would be *a mere abstraction.* There is no organization without Authority; and Authority always has been, and always must be lodged in some definite organ or organs of the State.

Hence the conception of the *lodgment in every State* of a supreme authority or power *in the hands of some particular person or body of persons*; and the habitual association of this idea of vested authority with the idea of the State. The *concepts 'Sovereignty' and 'Sovereign' always go together*, inseparable in fact and in thought. Sovereignty is Authority equipped for command and guidance.

FUNDAMENTAL IDEAS,—

1. *Sovereignty is an active principle*, a principle of *action and origination*, and not merely of superintendence or of administrative action. *The will* of the Community, of the organic State as a whole is, in the last analysis, the foundation, and in many cases the source also of Law; and that will is expressed, embodied in Sovereignty.

   "*Sovereignty is power*, the power of the Community, and, as power, *owes its existence*, not to law, but *to Fact.*" *Gareis*,[6] p. 28, sec. 10.

   Test cases: A sovereign king, such as Louis XIV.
   A sovereign People? (*Written constitutions*)

2. *Sovereignty must be conceived of*, if it is to possess any substance or vitality, not merely as an active and originative principle, but also *as the daily operative principle of government.* Hence it cannot be confounded with the *ultimate consent of the governed*,—a prerequisite condition of all rule.

---

[6] Carl Gareis, *Allgemeines Staatsrecht*, in H. Marquardsen (ed.), *Handbuch des Oeffentlichen Rechts der Gegenwart* (4 vols., Freiburg im B. and Tübingen, 1883-1906), I.

Attributes of Sovereignty (selected from Bluntschli's *Staatslehre*,[7] pp. 363, 364). "Theory of the State,"[8] 464.

(1) The sovereign power is, by its nature, the *highest in the State.*

(2) It is *subordinate to no superior* political authority.

(3) Its *authority* is *central and general*, as contradistinguished from local or partial (of a part).

(4) *It has Unity, because the State is organic*, and unity of structural power is necessary to its welfare, almost to its existence.

Definition of Sovereignty (provisional):

Sovereignty is the organic self-determination by the State of its law and policy; and the sovereign power is the highest constituted and organized power in the State entrusted with the choice of law and policy.

The scope of Sovereignty does not necessarily include the constituent act. That is a matter of "constitution": that is, of the limitation of Sovereignty.

FUNDAMENTAL QUESTIONS with regard to Sovereignty:

1. *Is Sovereignty susceptible of Limitation?*

Certainly of limitation de facto. Law of course receives its specific sanction from the law-making power in the State; but in fact its *ultimate sanction is Obedience*, and that is *a sanction outside itself,—that is, a limitation.*

If we conceive *Sovereignty as the daily active and originative principle in government*, and accept the habit of the Community in respect of obedience as the measure of its existence and efficacy, *we release it* from its imprisonment in the constituent act, and have *a conception which squares* with the ordinary operations of government in a unitary State.

2. *Is Sovereignty Divisible? Are sovereign powers distributable?*

A question of (a) *checks and balances*;

(b) of *dual* and *federal states.*

In what sense distributed *in the separation of Legislative, Executive*, and *Judicial* (i.e., *originative, administrative*, and *interpretative*) *powers?*

In what sense is it distributed, or divided *in the dual or the federal State?*

Only that organ of government whose power is at once *supreme* and *in its very nature originative* can be deemed really to possess Sovereignty. There is never in a dual or in a federal State in fact more than one such organ (the constituent act being left out of consideration); and of course among organs legislative, executive[,] judicial there is but one by its very nature originative

3. *Is Sovereignty necessary to Statehood?* This is a question affecting the member commonwealths of a dual or federal State.

Any political community whose powers are *not derivative, but original and inherent*; whose *political rights* are not also *legal duties*; and which can apply to its commands *the full sanctions of law*, is a State, even though its sphere be limited by the presiding and sovereign powers of a State, superordinated to it,

[7] *Allgemeine Statslehre*, Vol. I of *Lehre vom Modernen Stat.*
[8] The English translation (Oxford, 1885) of *ibid.*

whose powers are determined, under constitutional guarantees, by itself.

Sovereignty vs. *Dominion.*

 Sovereignty is political action and law-giving, subject to no superior.

 Dominion is political action and law-giving, independent, indeed, in the exercise of a full freedom in the choice of means, and with unqualified power to apply the sanctions of law, but within a subordinate sphere: subordinate because limited by the sphere of a superordinated State.

References: A. V. *Dicey*: "The Law of the Constitution," Lect. III, "Comparison between Parliament and Non-Sovereign Law-making Bodies."

 A. L. *Lowell*, "Essays on Government,"—"The Limits of Sovereignty."

 Sir H. S. Maine, "Early History of Institutions," Lect. XII.

 Laband, "Das Staatsrecht des Deutschen Reiches," I, 52-80 (2nd.ed.)

 Jellinek, "Gesetz und Verordnung," 201, 203.

 Wilson, "An Old Master and Other Political Essays,"—"Political Sovereignty."

 "The State," secs. 1445-1448, 1468-1471.

29 April, 1900

WWhw, WWT, and WWsh notes (WP, DLC).

From the Minutes of the Trustees of Princeton University

Princeton, N. J., March 10th, 1898.

. . . The Special Committee on University Affairs reported. The Report was approved, its recommendation adopted, and is as follows:

Report of Committee on University Affairs.

Princeton, March 10th, 1898.

The Committee on the Affairs of the University would report

 1. That owing to the prolonged absence from this country of Mr. Chas. E. Green, our Chairman, and his subsequent death,[1] this Committee has not been able to issue finally its business, and can now report progress only, and express the hope that we may be able to make a full report at the next meeting of the Board.

 2. That it recommends that Mr. George B. Stewart be appointed Chairman of this Committee.

 3. That it recommends that Mr. M. Taylor Pyne and Dr. David R. Frazer be appointed members of this Committee in place of Mr. Green, deceased, and of Mr. James W. Alexander, resigned.

Respectfully submitted,   (Signed) Geo. B. Stewart,
Chairman pro tem. . . .

Notes for a Chapel Talk

Univ. *Chapel*   Sunday, 13 March, 1898.
                                                    Hymns 305, 930[1]

Acts IV., 12: "For there is none other name under heaven given among men, whereby we must be saved."

Need of a concrete image or example instead of a [an] abstract principle or conviction to serve men for action: cries, mottoes, emblems, *names*,—the most powerful, because the most definite, of all.

It must be something great, and something outside ourselves:
"Self-reverence, self-knowledge, self-control,
These three alone lead life to sovereign power.
Yet not for power (power of herself
Would come uncalled for) but to live by law,
Acting the law we live by without fear;
And, because right is right, to follow right
Were wisdom in the scorn of circumstance." (*Œnone*)[2]

Self-development, character, prowess,—these cannot be ends in themselves. They are by-products,—arise out of self-forgetful endeavour, —are the children of live and high devotion.

This "a name above every name," and emblem of all purity and power.

WWhw MS. (WP, DLC).
[1] "Jesus, lover of my soul!" and "Lead, kindly Light!," in the *Presbyterian Hymnal* (Philadelphia, 1874), then being used in the Marquand Chapel.
[2] By Tennyson.

Stockton Axson to Ellen Axson Wilson

My dear Sister: Brooklyn, Mch 14, 1898

I am afraid you will not be greatly pleased with me for my telegram yesterday, and really I don't approve of myself very highly—particularly since reading your letter a second time and feeling more emphatically how much of a personal favor to yourself you made the request. It is true that from now till the Easter vacation I shall find it hard to spare a week-night (unless I get more ahead of my classes than I am at present) and that Thursday is my hard day. But notwithstanding this, of course, I could have arranged to spend Wednesday evening in Princeton, and I feel now that I ought to have done so. The plain reason for my declining your invitation is that I am afraid of "great folks." It has been so long since I went to a dining that in prospect of one I am worse than a very young and very silly girl who has a "coming out" party in prospect. Several times here and in Philadelphia I have manufactured excuses for not going to dinings—

but of course I will not, can not do that with you. You needn't tell me how silly it is to be this way, that you and Mr. and Mrs. Cleveland and all of you would expect from me absolutely nothing except the bearing of a gentleman. I understand all this perfectly and yet like those natural cowards whose legs will run away with them in spite of all reason and compunctions of conscience, I am just afraid. It is a pity that it should be so because I know I shall never get over it now (it is a comparatively new disease with me—I was not like this—at least not in the same exaggerated degree—a few years ago.) Being ill at ease, unnatural and all that in general company, I have taken to avoiding it—though I fear I ought not to have done so this time. I am really in a very penitent mood.

I don't remember the name of the hotel in Gloucester. Curiously enough just as I wrote those words the name did flash into my mind (and this after torturing my brain for it for five minutes yesterday!) It is the *Harbor View Hotel*[1]—the proprietor's name I never did know (a certain Miss Lottie being the only business head with whom I had any dealings.) [W. M.] Daniels will be able to tell you about other and somewhat more pleasantly situated hotels. There is one out near the point of the cape that I understood was not expensive, but I didn't learn either its name or its rates.

Mrs. Howe had a bad attack of indigestion accompanied by dizziness which lasted for some forty-eight hours, but she is better today and is sitting up a little while. With the exception of a bad headache today Madge has kept quite well.

By the way, I didn't say as I meant to, that I appreciated ever so much your desire to have me down to meet your guests.

Warm love, from

Ever affectionately yours,   S. Axson

ALS (WP, DLC).
[1] In East Gloucester, Mass. The Wilsons spent their vacation there in August 1898.

To Richard Watson Gilder

My dear Mr. Gilder,   Princeton, New Jersey, 15 March, 1898

You kindly said that the *Century* would like to have my new paper on Burke, and I take the liberty of sending it to you, under another cover.[1]

Shall I send you also my papers on Walter Bagehot and Sir Henry Maine?[2] The latter, especially, has not been written about at all for "the general public," and it seems a pity a lawyer *with a style* should be read only by special students. Both these papers are distinctively literary. They might be called studies in literary method.

Please do not think it indelicate in me to say a word about remuneration. I have of late received always at least one hundred and fifty dollars for an essay, and I should not like to fall *below par*.

I hope you are going to publish something of your own on Lincoln's style.

With warm regard,

Most sincerely Yours,   Woodrow Wilson

ALS (WC, NjP).
1 Wilson's paper finally appeared under the title of "Edmund Burke and the French Revolution" in the *Century Magazine*, LXII (Sept. 1901), 784-94. The reasons for the long delay in publication are not at all clear from the extant documents.
2 Gilder obviously declined them, for they were published as "A Wit and a Seer," *Atlantic Monthly*, LXXXII (Oct. 1898), 527-40, and "A Lawyer with a Style," *ibid*. (Sept. 1898), pp. 363-74.

From Joseph Ruggles Wilson

My precious Son—   Wilmington, N.C. March 16/98.

It is like cool water to a parched tongue to read again one of your dear loving letters. It is no exaggeration to say that you are never out of my thoughts, for the obvious reason that you are always in my heart. It looks like old days to get you away from the type-writer, and to perceive the revival of your own well-remembered caligraphy, after so long a burial.

My engagement with the church here was for 3 months—to end on 1st Sabbath in May. I am therefore about half through the allotted time, and am beginning to wish myself nearer the day of release. My reception, by all, is everything that could reasonably be desired—partakes, indeed, of something like enthusiasm: probably because it is found that my preaching is better than before. I have a good deal of pastoral service to discharge, and funerals have been unusually numerous. But on the whole I am quite glad that I came. My health is by no means perfect, nor at my age can it be expected to be.

Everybody I meet mentions your name with loving praise: a fact which, while it is gratifying to my paternal pride, is far from surprising to me. I am thankful for you with a gratitude—wordless. I am *very* glad that you are preparing a school history of the United [States]: a work that has been imperatively needed at the South, if impartial as yours is sure to be. It cannot but have a large sale.

I am grieved at little Nell's ailing—but all children seem compelled to run the gauntlet of the commoner infantile complaints; and the fittest survive.

Love unmeasured to yourself & to Ellie &c.

Your affc.   Father.

ALS (WP, DLC).

A News Report of a Presentation of "Democracy" in Stamford, Connecticut

[March 18, 1898]

IDEAL DEMOCRACY.

Eloquent Lecture by Prof. Woodrow
Wilson Last Night.

Prof. Woodrow Wilson of Princeton delivered his lecture on "Democracy" in the High School hall last night, to one of the largest audiences that attended any of the series so far. The professor, who is a bright and pleasing orator, at the very outset caught the attention of his audience, and kept it closely to the end. His lecture was a masterly piece [of] composition, but drew a picture of an ideal democracy rather than that of which men know. . . .[1]

Printed in the Stamford, Conn., *Daily Advocate*, March 18, 1898.
[1] Here follows a brief digest of "Democracy," printed at Dec. 5, 1891, Vol. 7.

From Charles William Kent

My dear Woodrow,   Charlottesville, Va., March, 19th. 1898

All the delights of our former associations flow in upon me as I open a correspondence that has for its end and aim to have you here at the University as my dear colleague. It is true I have no authority to make you any offer or hold out any offilial [official] inducement but I have the unofficial sanction of a member of the new Board of Visitors to tell you that you will be consulted about a plan that has the absolutely unanimous approval of the Board and that involves you personally and directly.[1] The University is now full of hope. In place of the destroyed buildings[2] we have new ones which seem to furnish an equipment and opportunity such as we have never had. Instead of a Board that has made itself more notorious for its habits than famous for its work we

have a new Board entirely sober and business-like, full of zeal
and intent upon furthering the interests of the University. Our
Faculty not always entirely harmonious would I believe be completely united on the proposition that if possible you should be
induced to cast in your lot with us. There is more hopefulness
and enthusiasm about the University's material future than I
have ever seen and in the Board no little of it centers in the hope
of having you here. The matter is in no sense public and will not
be made so for obvious reasons: it is therefore impossible to tell
you what others think but for myself I rejoice in the prospect even
and I do sincerely hope that you can see your way to accept whatever proposition is made you. I do not think it necessary to tell
you what the opportunities for work here are, or of the influence
the University still exerts particularly on Southern life, or of our
need of the best men for our Faculty but let me remind you of
the possibilities of your own conservative influence in quietly
averting some of the threatened consequences of our erratic
political life.[3] This is the point from which should go out sound
training in matters of public credit, public trusts, and public duties. By the way it will interest you to know that our Free-Silver
governor appointed on our Board three men who did not vote for
Bryan and that two members of the old Board who hold over are
also out of sympathy with the free-silver craze.

When the proposition comes do not consider it in "dry light,"
but let in all the softened light of sympathy with the South, love
for the University, desire to influence these bright young men,
and maybe your personal attachment for a devoted friend whose
warmth of regard makes room only for his sentiment of admiration. With kindest regards to Mrs. W.

Yrs cordially   Chas W Kent

TLS (WP, DLC) with WWhw notation on env.: "Ans. 30 March/98."
    [1] Wilson was "consulted" very soon—in the following letter.
    [2] Destroyed, that is, in the great fire of October 27, 1895. See Wilson's diary,
Aug. 20, 1897, n. 1.
    [3] Like the national Democratic party, the Virginia Democracy divided into
gold and silver wings during the 1890's. The silverites won control of the state
convention in 1896, played a significant role in Bryan's nomination by the
Democratic national convention in Chicago, and, in 1897, placed one of their
leaders, James Hoge Tyler, in the governorship.

From George Washington Miles[1]

My dear Sir,   Radford, Virginia, Mar. 21st. 1898

At a meeting of the Board of Visitors of the University of Va.
on the 17th., I was appointed Chrm. of a Committee "to inquire

into and define more clearly the duties of the Chairman of the Faculty" and "to suggest such adjustment as may be necessary to give the Professor discharging the duties of Chrm. more leisure &c."

I was also authorized to offer you a Professorship in the Law Department of the University and the Chairmanship of the Faculty. The Professorship carries a salary of $3000.00 and a dwelling, and the Chairmanship will carry an additional $1000.00[.] This action on the part of the Board was unanimous, the utmost harmony and good will prevailing. Two or three members of the Faculty have been taken into our confidence and it is their opinion that there can be but one opinion as to the wisdom of this choice.

You will note that this resolution gives us authority to "define more clearly" the duties of Chairman and I assure you, as the man is the plan with us, you can largely assist us in defining those duties. As to the special subject or subjects in the Law department on which you would lecture, that can be left largely to your wishes and favorite fields. I am sure it is generally conceded that the law department needs attractive strength added to it.

As to the permanency of this Chairmanship the sense of the Board was polled and it was unanimous that the arrangement was permanent so long as our authority extends. Five of the Board constituting a majority have just been appointed by the Governor for a four years term. Of course there is nothing permanent on earth but the intention is to get matters in the right hands so far as the Exec. office of the University is concerned and not to waste energy by useless changing. Nothing in this action however is to be construed as subordinating the importance of the separate schools or as interferring with the Professor's prerogatives as the head of his chosen school.

It is the sense of the Board that the time is ripe for a forward movement at the University of Virginia. With the beautiful new buildings just completed it is important that other matters move up also. The good-will of the University both here in Virginia and throughout the South and North is dormant, in places almost moribund, and with such a man as yourself there, with leisure to think and plan and even travel, great life and activity can be developed in this good-will and the University can take its place beside the greatest educational corporations of our country in point of wealth and numbers. We cannot help but think it ahead of them already in other respects.

Please take this matter under advisement and write me here at Radford Va. your conclusion. We desire nothing said about it until June. Perhaps I ought to add that an additional lucrative field might be found for you in joining in with Dr. Lile[2] in his Summer Law Class. At present Justice Harlan is doing this work.

I received a copy of your letter written a few weeks ago to our mutual friend Patterson and noted what you said about "the aggressive attitude of the Silver men &c."[3] I want to say that Mr. Carter Glass the editor of the Lynchburg News[,] an ardent silver paper, is a member of this Board and was an earnest advocate of your election. I read him that paragraph from your letter. There is absolutely nothing to be feared in the Silver quarter as interferring with your success or peace of mind and loyal support by the people of Virginia.

I sincerely trust you will feel like Virginia has this claim upon you.

With cordial regards,   Very Truly Yrs,   Geo. W. Miles
Chrm Com. Board.

ALS (WP, DLC) with WWhw notations on env.: "Ans. 29 March/98" and
"(1) Nature of the office
(2)   "   " my obligations here"
[1] Founder (1891) and Headmaster of St. Albans School in Radford, Va.; newspaper publisher and railroad promoter in southwestern Virginia.
[2] William Minor Lile, Professor and Dean of the Law Faculty.
[3] Wilson's letter is missing, but see EAW to WW, Feb. 17, 1898.

A News Report of a Princeton-Yale Affair

[March 26, 1898]

. . . THE YALE-PRINCETON SUPPER.

Immediately after the debate[1] a supper was given the debaters at the Princeton Inn. There were nearly one hundred present and the supper was perhaps the most successful one ever given after a debate in Princeton.

President Patton acted as toastmaster, and after a few preliminary remarks introduced Ex-President Cleveland as the first speaker. Mr. Cleveland expressed his friendship for Princeton and his regret over her defeat. In a very happy manner, he promised Yale hard struggles in the future. He also spoke of the manner in which debating increases the usefulness of the college man as a citizen.

President William L. Wilson, of Washington and Lee University and a member of Mr. Cleveland's cabinet, was the next speaker. He gave his impressions of the debate from the standpoint of a judge, and told something of early debating, political and academic, in Virginia.

Mr. Everett P. Wheeler, of New York City, another of the judges, developed the line of argument of the debate and urged independent political action.

Prof. J. F. Jameson, of Brown University, and an editor of the American Historical Review, told of the close relationships which have existed between Princeton and Brown.

President Patton then called upon Mr. [James Herron] Eckels, of Chicago, ex-comptroller of the Treasury, who made some excellent remarks along the line of thought, suggested by the debate of the evening.

Prof. William Lyons Phelps responded for Yale in a very able manner. He humorously referred to the strife over Yale's English department[2] and emphasized the value of debating to the layman as well as to the professional man.

Professor Woodrow Wilson was Princeton's representative and his few remarks were calculated to inspire Princeton's debaters to renewed effort for future success.

Mr. James W. Alexander, of the Princeton Board of Trustees, was the last speaker. As he is a frequent attendant at baseball and football games where Princeton men are contestants, he said that he felt that he should also attend her debates. In referring to the newspaper war over Yale's English department, he said that a man's *alma mater* should be so sacred to him that he would not attack her in the public prints. He voiced the sentiments of every Princeton man present when he said that Princeton was proud of her three debaters in spite of defeat.

The supper closed with the singing of Old Nassau, and cheers for Yale and Princeton. . . .

Printed in the *Daily Princetonian*, March 26, 1898.

1 The Yale team won the fourth annual Princeton-Yale debate held in Alexander Hall on March 25, 1898, defending the affirmative of the question, "Resolved, That national party lines should be disregarded in the choice of the councils and administrative officers in American cities." Grover Cleveland presided at the debate, and the judges were John Franklin Jameson, Everett Pepperell Wheeler, and William Lyne Wilson. *Daily Princetonian*, March 26, 1898.

2 Set off by a speech by Daniel Henry Chamberlain, Yale '62, former Governor of South Carolina, to the Central and Western Massachusetts Yale Alumni Association in Worcester on February 16, 1898. Attacking the teaching of English at Yale, Chamberlain said that one might graduate from that university and still "not know how to speak or write a sentence of his own tongue with decent accuracy." Chamberlain also directly attacked Henry A. Beers, Chairman of the Yale English Department. The report of Chamberlain's speech in the *New York Times*, February 17, 1898, inspired a number of letters to the Editor of that journal during February and March, some defending, some attacking the English Deparment. Chamberlain and Beers each contributed a letter to the epistolary war. See the *New York Times*, Feb. 17, 20, 21, 22, and 27; March 11, 17, 23, and 27; and April 2, 1898.

From Cornelius Cuyler Cuyler

My Dear Wilson: New York. 28 March 1898

During the past few months I have had many worries but not many that have caused me as much anxiety as something I heard this a.m. viz. that a great honor has been conferred on the class of '79, through your good self, by an offer to you of the Presidency of the University of Virginia.

To say as your classmate that I appreciate this but faintly expresses my feelings. We are all proud of you and realize how well deserved is the honor. At the same time I cannot for a moment bring myself to believe that Princeton is to be put in the position of losing your services, and I sincerely hope that you may decline the offer made you.

There is no honor too high for you in the future as far as Princeton is concerned, yet I believe it is not practicable for the Trustees to make you any definite promises at this writing. May I, as one of your admirers and friends, ask a rather direct question? Will the financial feature be likely to influence your decision? If so I would like to know it as soon as possible. I am aware of the selfsacrificing work you have rendered Princeton for 10 years past and the small recompense which up to a certain period you have received. Your loyalty has been unsurpassed and I do not think we can afford to lose you.

I do not suppose that anything I can say will swerve you if you have already made up your mind but shall hope to see you in the near future and discuss the matter fully with you.[1]

In any event I have done myself not so much a pleasure as a duty in writing you at once and fully upon this important matter.

With kind regards, I am, Dear Wilson,

                          Yours sincerely,   C C Cuyler.

ALS (WP, DLC) with WWhw notation on env.: "Ans. 29 Mar., 1898."
    [1] The documents will soon make clear the role that Cuyler played in helping to keep Wilson at Princeton.

From Edward Perkins Clark[1]

Dear Prof. Wilson: New York, March 28, 1898.

It has occurred to me that you might like to run your eye through a study of Mr. Cleveland's career which I wrote a year ago for the *National Review*,[2] a English periodical little seen in this country.

You will be glad to know that I stumbled on a great "find" during my call on Mr. Cleveland Saturday morning—a copy of the admirable reply which he sent to a "yellow journal" that had tried to use his name to advertise itself.[3] I enclose herewith the editorial page of the *Evening Post* today which contains the correspondence and Mr. Godkin's article upon it, as I am sure you will like to see the matter.[4]

Yours very sincerely,   Edward P. Clark

ALS (WP, DLC) with WWhw notation on env.: "Ans. 30 March/98."
  [1] Editorial writer for the *New York Evening Post*.
  [2] Edward P. Clark, "Mr. Cleveland," London *National Review*, XXIX (March 1897), 84-98.
  [3] William Randolph Hearst of the New York *Journal* to G. Cleveland, Feb. 27, 1898, and G. Cleveland to W. R. Hearst, Feb. 28, 1898, printed in the *New York Evening Post*, March 28, 1898.
  [4] An editorial entitled "Patriotism and Yellow Journalism," *ibid*.

To Vincent Charles Peck[1]

My dear Sir,   Princeton, New Jersey, 29 March, 1898.

Pardon me for not having replied to your letter of the twenty-first. A multitude of interruptions and engagements have prevented my writing.

My terms for lecturing I have been obliged to put at one hundred dollars and expenses. I have no engagement for the twenty-fourth of May, and should be glad to make your Commencement address if you should desire it.[2]

Very truly Yours,   Woodrow Wilson

WWTLS (WC, NjP).
  [1] Headmaster of the University School in Bridgeport, Conn.
  [2] He did give the commencement address. See the newspaper report printed at May 25, 1898.

From William Howard Perkinson[1]

Dear Sir—   [Charlottesville, Va.] Mar. 30/1898.

At a meeting held this afternoon of joint committees of the Board of Visitors, Faculty and Alumni it was decided to invite you as a distinguished alumnus and educator, to deliver the address on the occasion of the dedication of the new buildings here June 14th next.

It is needless to tell you that next to the founding and inauguration of the University, this will be the greatest event in its history.

We have arranged a most elaborate programme, and trust that you may be able to help us make it a success. Hoping to have your acceptance as soon as possible, I remain,[2]

Yrs truly,   W. H. Perkinson   Chairman Com.

ALS (WP, DLC) with WWhw notation on env.: "Ans."
 1 Professor of German and Italian at the University of Virginia.
 2 Wilson's reply is missing, but he was forced to decline because he had
earlier promised to deliver the annual literary address to the students of Vanderbilt University on June 14, about which see the news report printed at
June 15, 1898.

From George Washington Miles

My dear Doctor,   Radford, Virginia, Mar. 30th. 1898

 I received your letter[1] last evening and note the spirit in which you consider the offer of our Board and am much encouraged at the precise manner in which you weigh your prospective duties. Your topographical survey of the field of work tendered you leads me to hope that you will enter it, because, so far as the data required at my hands is concerned, I can return most favorable answers.

 Now, replying to your first question regarding the income of the University and its material resources, I can say that the University is not poor. Neither is it rich for that matter, but with its present number of students its annual income is $130,000. It gets an annual income from the State of Va. of $45,000. Five or six of its chairs are endowed with $50,000 each. It will receive from the Austin bequest[2] $600,000.00 upon the death of a lady who is now 45 yrs. old.

 As to your second question about carrying the increase of the endowment upon your mind I should say that that is not what the Board expects or desires. Our idea of a Chairman and of a Professor is not the idea of a Financial Agent. We think, however, that with each good man added to the University's officers it will be that much easier to attract the munificence of the rich and public-spirited. That is about as far as your connection with the endowment is contemplated by the Board. The Board expects large gifts to come to the University more in the future than in the past. Already there are stirrings in this direction. I am sure every Professor there can help in this but chiefly through the high merit and intellectual atmosphere of the place. It is the Board's business to plan for the increase of the endowment and it expects to take that up through agencies distinct from the Chairman.

 Now as to the Legislative Committees, that has been exaggerated. The University is secure in the love and support of this State. Even the Readjuster Legislature of 1879-80 under the leadership of Mahone, whose son had been expelled from the University a short while before, fostered the University and actually increased its appropriation. I should rather have the pros-

pect of this annual $45,000 than $1[,]000,000 of 4½ per cent
Bonds with the exception of Government bonds. Look at the
Johns Hopkins for instance.

Your question as to the ideal of the Visitors as to training undergraduates or crowning the work of other schools is far-reach-
ing but to answer categorically I feel sure I voice the Board's
ideal when I say that where there is a conflict between the two
ideas, the advanced and finishing work must have "the right of
way" and be fostered and planned for first. My own idea is that
the University can easily grow and be nurtured along both lines.
But its chief "raison d'être" is in the finishing work.

Again, as to the hours of teaching, we want you at the University of Va. If you think best to lecture two hours, four hours, six
hours a week, it is all right with the Board. That is largely in your
hands.

The Board expects to give you a a [sic] short-hand secretary.
That was discussed at our meeting. This is the age of the private-
secretary. If you can find a Daniel Lamont[3] to bring to the discharge of these duties with you, all right.

You can certainly keep inviolate your office-hours and coming
to the other phase of the question which I think is with you a vital
one, leisure for your literary labors, I think the Board feels that
any work done by the University Professors and especially by its
Chairman in this line will reflect honor upon the University and
make its lecture courses that much more attractive to students.
We should rejoice at your success in this direction. You can rely
upon the sympathy and interest of the Board in such plans and
aspirations.

In conclusion it has occurred to me that if you could spend
Sat. the 9th of April in Richmond, Va. being an Easter Holiday,
I could have the Sub-Committee, Mr. Bryan, Mr. Harman[4] and
I, to meet you there and have full and free conference with you.
You could from there return by way of the University.

    With cordial regards,

                Very Truly Yrs,   Geo. W. Miles.

ALS (WP, DLC).

    1 It is missing.

    2 The bequest of Samuel W. Austin to the University of Virginia in 1886
amounted, actually, to some $435,000. The lady mentioned was Austin's daugh-
ter. Philip A. Bruce, *History of the University of Virginia, 1819-1919* (5 vols.,
New York, 1920-22), IV, 249, 375-76, and V, 232.

    3 Who had first gained a national reputation as private secretary to President
Cleveland from 1885 to 1889. He served as Secretary of War in Cleveland's second
administration.

    4 Joseph Bryan and Daniel Harmon.

To Charles William Kent

My dear Charlie,   Princeton, New Jersey, 30 March, 1898.

Thank you most heartily for your kind letter of the nineteenth. It did me good to the bottom of my heart.

It was almost immediately followed by one from Mr. George W. Miles, offering me the Chairmanship of the Faculty in such form as to make it, apparently, a sort of informal prezidency [presidency] of the University. You may be sure the whole thing has made a very deep impression on me. I shall not discuss it now; for before I make up my mind what my duty is in the matter I think I shall have to come down to Charlottesville and look the situation over, and talk of many things with you and my other more immediate friends.

The real question in my mind is this: will my acceptance of this offer end my literary career? If it will, I do not think that I can or ought to accept it. To do so would be to throw away twenty years of diligent preparation and 'prentice work for the substantial part of my literary work, which is still ahead of me.

That question aside, I need not say that my affection for the University would lead me to make almost any sacrifice for her service. I feel this as great an opportunity, very likely, as will ever open to me. I am profoundly grateful that I should have been thought of for so great a function, and I shall not cease to be grateful. I am touched too very deeply by the cordial welcome which I foresee from your letter, on the part of the men who would be my colleagues. Let me see that it will not cut my life in two and destroy the effort of one half of it, and the way will seem very clear in most respects, for all my love is so rooted here also.

Hoping to see you before very long,

       As ever,   Faithfully Yours,   Woodrow Wilson

Remember me, in the warmest messages of regard, to Mrs. Kent. Mrs. Wilson joins me in hearty greetings.

WWTLS (Tucker-Harrison-Smith Coll., ViU).

From the Minutes of the Princeton Faculty

          5 5′ P.M., Wednesday, March 30, 1898.

. . . Resolved That a Committee of four (4) be appointed to confer with the Commencement Committee of the Board of Trustees in reference to the Alumni Dinner. Professors Ormond, Wilson, Hunt & Hibben were appointed the Committee. . . .[1]

[1] For their report, see the Princeton Faculty Minutes printed at April 27, 1898.

From Cyrus Hall McCormick

My dear Woodrow: Chicago, Mar. 31, 1898.

It is needless to say that your letter of the 27th[1] fills me with disappointment. I appreciate your writing me as a friend and I will keep the matter upon that line rather than as a trustee, but in fact any views I hold upon the subject would be equally applicable to my personal feeling for you or to my position as a trustee.

The position to which you have been invited is no doubt a flattering one. From many standpoints it will have attractions for you, but let me tell you frankly and forcibly that the position would not confer upon you nearly as much as you would confer upon it. You have made a signal success of the work in life that you have mapped out for yourself, and up to the present time there has not been a break in the chain of successes which have brought you to your present eminent position, but the place to which you are invited is largely an experiment. Confessedly a large share of the work is administrative, and for this it does not seem to me you are as well qualified as for the special work which you are now engaged in. Remember that President Scheurmann[2] was a rising man in philosophy until he took the presidency of Cornell College. Since then he has been obliged to sacrifice the progress in his special work for that of conducting a large business enterprise. Many men feel that the head of a University should be a signal success as a business man, whatever his qualifications on other lines, and without the least derogation of your abilities in these directions, it must be said that you would have no time left for original work along the lines of work which I know are very near and dear to you.

I cannot write today as fully as I like, being pressed with many other matters, but will say at once that I believe, after full investigation and consideration, you will not find any advantage in leaving Princeton for this call.

As to the matter of the department of history, I have with you many regrets, but the horizon of the future cannot be shut in nor clouded by my disappointment over the present incident, and I feel that the same might in a sense be true with you.

I will write you further in a day or two, but did not wish to lose a mail before giving you my first impressions.

With kind regards to Mrs. Wilson, I am,

Faithfully your friend,   Cyrus H. M. Cormick.

TLS (WP, DLC).

¹ It is missing, but C. H. McCormick to WW, April 2, 1898, quotes key portions of it.

² Jacob Gould Schurman, President of Cornell University.

A News Item About a Lecture at Mount Holyoke College

[April 1898]

COLLEGE NOTES.

MARCH.

. . . Professor Woodrow Wilson of Princeton University lectured on Democracy.¹

Printed in the South Hadley, Mass., *Mount Holyoke*, VII (April 1898), 359.

¹ On March 9, 1898, as the entry in Wilson's diary described at Dec. 9, 1897, reveals.

From Charles William Kent

My dear Woodrow,   [Charlottesville, Va.] Apr. 1st 98.

Mrs. Kent, who has been indisposed for a week or so, begs me to write in her name as well as in my own to invite you and Mrs. Wilson to be our guests during our University Finals. I am in the secret that you have been invited to deliver the Dedicatory Address here on that occasion and I sincerely trust you can see your way to accept.

The fact that you have been asked here for more important duties is unknown to a majority of those who now strongly desire your presence at the Finals. The coincidence that you are sought for two services by two sets of University authorities ought to indicate that our eyes turn very naturally and confidently to you.

I am glad you are considering thoughtfully the invitation which in one sense means more than a presidency, for a President would have been the creation of a Board of Visitors against the wishes of a very large proportion of the Faculty and the Alumni while to have you connected with our Law Dept and as Chairman would satisfy the advocates for president and please those opposed to that office. When you come—and you must come straight to our house for our invitation for the Finals does not oppose any obstacle to an earlier visit—I think you will see that with limited lecture hours and better office facilities, which the Board would gladly furnish, your literary work need not be abandoned and I hope it would not even be retarded.

My dear fellow, I think you have been signally chosen for an honorable work and I believe you should accept.

Cordially   Chas W Kent

ALS (WP, DLC).

To George Washington Miles

My dear Mr. Miles: [Princeton, N. J., c. April 2, 1898]

Allow me to thank you most warmly for your letter of the—
[30th]. It has answered my questions in so full and satisfactory
a manner that I do not think that it will be necessary to call your
committee together as you will [have] so kindly offered to do.
Much as I should like to meet them and personally talk with them
about all the important matters involved in this question of the
changes to be made at the University, it is really unnecessary to
do so, and I am this week specially pressed for time.

It is my next business to look at the matter from the standpoint
of Princeton. I must tell you very frankly that the pressure here
is tremendous and that I do not feel at liberty to disregard it.
Princeton has within the last eighteen months conferred several
very unusual honors and privileges upon me and I of course feel
under a serious obligation to consider her interests very carefully.
Before I decide what to do I must inform and consult with the
most responsible and influential men here. I realize the risk of
this (I mean the risk of losing control of the secret) but there is
a plain compulsion of honor and friendship laid upon me in the
matter, and you may depend upon me to manage it with all possible caution and discretion. I really, in mere fidelity to men who
have deeply trusted me, have no choice but to disclose the situation, in confidence, with the utmost frankness and I am by no
means sure that when the friends of the college here understand
what is up it shall be left free to go for the changes.[1]

It would be a long story, were I to tell you of all the toils (the
very gracious toils) that have been drawn about me here. I can
of course do my own will in the matter; but I cannot be sure that
I am doing the whole creditably

[Sincerely yours,   Woodrow Wilson]

Transcript of WWshL (draft) (WP, DLC).
[1] This is an exact transcription of Wilson's shorthand, awkward though it
seems.

From Cyrus Hall McCormick

My dear Woodrow: Chicago. April 2/98.

Having reflected upon the information contained in your letter of the 27th ult., I have tried to weigh as impartially as I can,
the proposal which is urged upon you, to take charge of the Uni-

versity of Virginia, and I am glad to give you my views on the subject, based,—so far as it is possible—upon the single question of your own interests.

At the outset, let me say that I appreciate how flattering is the offer, and the terms in which it is couched are calculated to impress anyone strongly. They have not over-stated their proposal in believing that "the man is the plan" when they refer to you, and my confidence in what you could do if you undertook it, is so unbounded that I would even admit that you could make a greater success of an undertaking like that than many another who might appear to be, on first thought, equally available. But, without comparing this to your present position or future outlook at Princeton, there are several matters that you should consider carefully. In the first place, the work which you are asked to take up is "to moderate an almost revolutionary change for a great institution." Think of what that means. Not only would it mean reorganizing the machinery of the present institution, but it would be searching for new men, searching for new friends, and organizing a complete machinery for educational business. After that would come the administration, which of itself, would be exhausting and perplexing. The worry and fret over work of this kind would be far more hindering to your chief literary work than any embarrassments you have ever met with up to the present time. Again, large funds would be needed to accomplish what these people invite you to accomplish, and what you, yourself would take pride in making a success. While I do not know the financial resources of the University of Virginia, I am very doubtful whether they can gain that necessary point in revenue adequate to their present needs. If this were true, a work like collecting money for our Sesqui-Centennial fund would be play compared to the securing of any large sums for the University of Virginia.

Again, the proposed work is experimental. If you win, will the sacrifice of your ambitions in other lines be sufficiently repaid by accomplishing what you seek? If you do not win, have you not taken several steps backward in obtaining your goal? No one better than yourself, knows the high standard which you would set, and I believe that the difficulties in your path are minimized by your importunate friends, who have nothing to lose, and everything to gain by your acceptance of their offer. Does it not seem strange that an institution which twenty-five years ago was so full of promise, and had so splendid a position, not only in this country, but abroad, should during all this time be in a state of comparitive inertia? It cannot be alone that they lacked a leader, for many leaders have arisen through the South. There must be other reasons hidden deeper than the surface, which have prevented that institution from making, at least, relatively the same progress that the other institutions of the country have made. Would it not be almost unreasonable to expect you in five or ten years, to bring success out of this lack of success? I surely feel so. Aside from even these considerations, do you wish to turn aside from the ambitious literary work which you have planned for yourself, and go into an administrative field? In these days of competition along intellectual, as well as in all other lines, it is almost impossible to find in one man the gifts necessary to high intellectual flights, and the experience required for plodding with the humdrum details which constitute the work necessary to the successfuf [successful] management of a business enterprise. President Scheurmann has tried this at Cornell, and has been obliged to subordinate his intellectual work, in the strain put upon him in overcoming obstacles, and striving for the material progress of Cornell. President Harper[1] is a signal illustration of the mistake of attempting to cover both these fields, although up to the present time, with superhuman efforts he has pushed the great experiment here, so that outwardly it is a success, and at the same time, has tried to maintain his literary work. He has well nigh broken down with the undertaking, and the incompleteness of his work ia [is] apparent on all sides. Seth Low and President Elliott[2] are examples of the success to be gained by those Presidents who confine themselves largely to the administrative Departments. Now, without any reflections upon your talents for either of these departments, let me suggest that after having made so signal a success in one line, is it advisable at this juncture to change your field of work. I should say, emphatically, no.

Turning now to the other side of the picture, what could be your reason for leaving Princeton? I regret exceedingly, as you do, many of the unfortunate circumstances of the past two years in connection with the Department of History, but since you very frankly admit that you have not been alienated by these transactions, and inasmuch as I am confident that the future must hold for you on this line, a better record than the past, we may lay aside the wound which has been caused by this history as not a moving cause for your leaving Princeton. You have put it more strongly than this, in saying that it does not "directly or indirectly affect your consideration of this offer." In this connection, I am pursuaded that the door is not closed against such improvements in the Department of History as would call forth your enthusiasm, and it is by no means certain that the mistakes of yesterday will be the mistakes of tomorrow.

I have written quite confidentially to my dear friend, [Moses] Taylor Pyne, who stands for much that is highest and best in Princeton, and have asked him to talk with you about this whole matter, and you need not hestitate to speak unreservedly to him. Every one of the recent elections in the Board of Trustees is a hopeful sign, and augurs well for the broadest interests of Princeton University, and in the course of a reasonable time, I am confident that good results will be secured which will be exactly in harmony with the wishes which you and I have for Princeton's greatest advancement. No one of the younger Professors holds a more conspicuous position than you do, and no one has a brighter outlook for the future.

Speaking therefore, as a friend who is deeply concerned in your highest interest wherever that may take you, my advice is to hold on where you are, and not accept even the apparently seductive invitation which the University of Virginia is now pressing upon you.

In all that I say, I will omit entirely, the deep interest which my mother, my brothers and all our family would feel in having you remain to fill the Chair which was endowed as much on account of our personal regard for your ability, as because of our deep interest in the subject of the department, but in so important a decision as this, I would not have this personal element considered as a determining factor. Were I to write from the standpoint of my personal admiration for your present position in Princeton, and my loyalty to Princeton as an alumnus and trustee, I could fill many pages with earnest pleas for your continuance in your present position, but all this I lay aside, and repeat that my calm judgment requires me to cast the weight of my influence as against the call to the University of Virginia.

Do not feel under the necessity of acknowledging or refuting any of the points I have here suggested, in answering this letter, but weigh them carefully as you are studying the whole subject, and if you determine that your duty requires you to remain at your present post, I shall receive the word to that effect with much rejoicing.

With kind regards to Mrs. Wilson, to whose deliberate judgment and intuitive knowledge of all the circumstances surrounding this question I submit also, these suggestions, I am

Faithfully your friend,   Cyrus H. McCormick.

TLS (WP, DLC).

1 William Rainey Harper of the University of Chicago.
2 Seth Low of Columbia University and Charles William Eliot of Harvard University.

To Robert Bridges

My dear Bobby,   Princeton, 4 April, '98

I am *very* sorry to hear that your mother's health is so unsatisfactory. I trust there is better news now.

I am even more glad than usual to accept your invitation to spend the night for I have some things to talk over which it is unsatisfactory to write about. You may expect me in the middle of the afternoon.

In haste and affection,

As ever   Faithfully Yours,   Woodrow Wilson

ALS (WC, NjP).

Francis Landey Patton to Cyrus Hall McCormick
Confidential

My dear Mr. McCormick: [Princeton, N.J.] April 4th 1898

I thank you very much for your kind letter & am exceedingly sorry to learn that there is even the possibility of our losing Professor Wilson. If there is anything that can be wisely done to keep Prof. Wilson of course we should do it. I confess I do not know what can be done: and I can hardly think that Professor Wilson when he looks at the matter in any light will sever his connection with Princeton University.

It pains me however to learn that you are under the impression that Professor Wilson is in any way dissatisfied with the way matters are going at Princeton. I cannot find in any thing that is within my knowledge what might be regarded as a grievance; & I beg you to consider the matter in the plain way in which I am moved to put it before you.

1. My own attitude toward Prof. Wilson has been from the beginning one of most cordial appreciation & sincere admiration. I nominated him to his chair. I took pains to overcome the reluctant attitude of a strong minority in the Board of Trustees when he was nominated. I took the responsibility of saying that he might continue to lecture at Johns Hopkins as before. I nominated him as the orator at our sesquicentennial; I was, as you know, one of the first to suggest the endowment of his chair as the best

possible use for the contribution of your family to the sesquicentennial fund. In the Faculty & out of it, I have been & still am his admirer and friend.

2. I think that Prof Wilson has a most enviable position in Princeton. His chair is amply endowed. He draws a larger salary than any Professor who is not also an executive officer—$4,300 per annum. He drafted the plan for the work of his chair & it was on my recommendation adopted by the Trustees without modification.[1] His schedule is exactly what he asked for & certainly is not burdensome. He is in absolute control of his department & has been told that as soon as the funds of the University would permit he should have an assistant. I have asked him if there was anyone whom he would like to have in that position. He has leisure for writing which he uses. He lectures at Johns Hopkins & is absent a month or six weeks every year for that purpose.[2] He also lectures or did lecture occasionally in the New York Law School.

No other professor is as highly favored as he is.

3. I cannot see that Prof. Wilson has any grievance in respect to the department of History.

It is the policy of the University for the President to get all the aid he can from the Professors in the department wherein a vacancy exists, & after forming his judgment present it to the curriculum committee of the Trustees. I have followed this course in the department of History. I have never had any difficulty in respect to other departments. I see no reason for difficulty now. The department of History is distinct from that of Jurisprudence. There was no reason obliging me to consult Prof. Wilson any more than the Prof. of Political Economy or of Greek or Latin. But I sought Prof. Wilson's counsel. He gave me two names: Haskins & Turner. I could not take the responsibility of nominating Turner. I did nominate Haskins. He was offered $3,000 & then $3,400 & declined. My course in nominating Mr. Armstrong was not approved by Prof. Wilson. But perhaps Prof. Wilson did not know as well as I did all that there was in connection with Mr. Armstrong. I do not doubt the wisdom of Mr. Armstrong's decision. But I do not regret; on the contrary I feel very well satisfied with my own course in nominating Mr. Armstrong.

I then nominated Mr. Van Dyke.[3] I consulted with Prof. Wilson however respecting it. I believe that Van Dyke's appointment will give very general satisfaction to the Faculty & the Alumni. Personally, I am persuaded that he will prove himself a much better man for us than Haskins would have been.

We have now or shall have three men in History: Van Dyke, Frothingham, Coney:—good men all of them. We have moreover $50,000 in hand toward a chair of American History. I sent a gentleman to Prof Wilson last week, who wished to be regarded as a candidate for that chair. I shall hope for a nomination for that Chair to be recommended by Prof Wilson: I shall say directly what I have already im[plied] respecting the help I desire to have from him in filling the chair of American History. But let us consider the conditions under which we are working. If you call a man who can be had for $2,000 you must get a young man. If you undertake to give a salary of $4,000 to Turner you will exceed the income of the university by about $2,000; where is this income to be found? I am free to say that a young, promising Princetonian with a future is the man for our chair of American history? Why not? Daniels in economics, Wilson in Jurisprudence, Fine in Mathematics, Scott in Geology, West & Westcott in Latin, Winans in Greek, Baldwin in Philosophy—these are all Princeton men: they all came on salaries below the maximum. Better men are not to be had. Why shd we not find a man of our own making who will grow to be the peer of these men?

But if the Board says we must call Turner, & we must give him $4000, I shall not oppose it. I cannot conscientiously nominate Mr. Turner. I do not think that it would be wise to elect him. I fear serious loss to the University if we do. But if after discharging my conscience the Board shall see fit to elect him I shall make no opposition[.] That it seems to me is the proper spirit for me to show. But why is it not also the proper spirit for Prof. Wilson to evince? particularly in view of the fact that being a Professor he is not charged before the public with that responsibility that rests upon the President of the University?

In my feeling upon this subject I am actuated, as I know you believe, by the deepest & sincerest regard for the interests of Princeton. I happen to be the sharer of certain confidences & I know that certain very important interests will be put in jeopardy if we act in this matter in an unwise way. I do not mean that I know that we shall suffer serious loss, but that I have good reason to fear that we shall. Now I have no evidence that the good Mr. Turner will do us could compensate for this loss. I see no reason why the good that he will do us might not be done equally well by another man against whom no objection can be urged. Surely in a matter of this sort Prof. Wilson would realize that he might sacrifice his preference without any surrender of dignity or self-respect; & that in declining to elect Mr. Turner no lack of respect to Prof. Wilson is intended or implied.

4. I am most cordially disposed to do anything in my power to keep Prof. Wilson in Princeton, but I confess I do not know what could be done that has not already been done. I of course agree with you in supposing that Prof Wilson will make a great mistake if he leaves his present place for the headship of the University of Virginia. For him to go there will inevitably be for him to relinquish in great part his literary work; & it is my opinion that the best work of which he is capable is in the chair & with his pen. If however Prof. Wilson situated as he is, in a chair endowed amply; & made to suit his wishes; respected, admired & honored by all, he should nevertheless decide to go to Virginia, it must be because he feels that he can do a work in administration that will be greater & more useful than the work he is now doing. If he should reach that conclusion then deeply as I should regret it, & severe as the loss would be to Princeton I see nothing that we could do that would be likely to change his decision.

You speak of our giving Prof. Wilson more recognition. I do not know in what way we could give him more recognition. He is influential on the Faculty. He is a leading member of the discipline committee. We should be glad to have him serve on other committees if he would care to. I should be glad if he would come to see me frequently & I should be delighted to talk over matters of University policy & discuss University problems with him if he would come & see me, as I do with other members of the Faculty when they come to see me. My door is always open. The largest welcome is ready for any Professor & I am glad to hear suggestions & to confer with all who come to me. What more can be done? Professor Wilson has undisputed control of his department. He has been freely consulted in regard to the department of History. What else is there that I can do? I do not feel that I ought to go to Prof Wilson in regard to a matter of which he has not spoken to me & of which he has only confidentially spoken to you. I am sure that you will agree with me that when a Professor is seriously considering an invitation to accept an appointment in another University it is only natural to expect that he should communicate the fact to the President of the University which he is serving. And though ready to do anything in my power to prevent the acceptance of the appointment which Prof. Wilson is now considering, I cannot see that it is my duty to take the initiative by seeking Professor Wilson for the purpose of opening the discussion of the question with him.

I thank you again, Mr. McCormick for your very kind letter. I am more than pleased with the tone in which you write & I sincerely hope that your letter to Prof. Wilson will be sufficient to convince him that it is the part of wisdom for him to remain in Princeton   Very sincerely yours   Francis L. Patton

ALS (Patton Letterpress Books, University Archives, NjP).
1 See WW to F. L. Patton, June 8, 1897, and the Princeton Trustees' Minutes printed at June 14, 1897.
2 Wilson obviously had not informed Patton of the severance of his connection with The Johns Hopkins University.
3 Paul van Dyke, born Brooklyn, N.Y., on March 25, 1859. A.B., Princeton, 1881. Was graduated from Princeton Theological Seminary in 1884 and studied at the University of Berlin, 1884-85. Ordained to the Presbyterian ministry, 1887. Pastor, North Presbyterian Church, Geneva, N.Y., 1887-89. Instructor in Church History, Princeton Theological Seminary, 1889-92. Pastor, Edwards Congregational Church, Northampton, Mass., 1892-98. Professor of History, Princeton University, 1898-1913; Pyne Professor of History, 1913-28. Served as Secretary of the American University Union in Paris, 1917-19. Author of several historical works, including *Catherine de Médicis* (2 vols., New York, 1922). Brother of Henry van Dyke, Murray Professor of English Literature at Princeton, 1899-1923. Died Aug. 30, 1933.

A News Item

[April 5, 1898]

MEETING OF THE AMERICAN ACADEMY
OF POLITICAL AND SOCIAL SCIENCE.

The second annual meeting of the American Academy of Political and Social Science, of which Professor Wilson is first Vice-President, will be held this year in Philadelphia, from April 11 to April 13. The annual address will be delivered by Professor Franklin H. Giddings, of Columbia University, and minor addresses by Professors Edmund I. [J.] James, of the University of Chicago, and Samuel McCune Lindsay of the University of Pennsylvania. Profs. Daniels and Wilson of this University are council members of the organization.[1]

Printed in the *Daily Princetonian*, April 5, 1898.
1 The American Academy of Political and Social Science was founded in Philadelphia on December 14, 1889. Wilson became a member of the organization's General Advisory Council in 1890 and was elected Third Vice President in 1895, an office he held until 1905. Insofar as is known from scanty records, he was never First Vice President.

To Robert Bridges

My Dear Bobby,   [Princeton, N. J., April 6, 1898]
Cuyler has persuaded me that I can acquiesce in arrangements[1] which he has suggested, and I have about made up my

mind to think no more of going South. I will explain fully when
I see you,—next week.   Woodrow Wilson

Wednesday 3:12 P.M.

P.S. I have seen J. W. A.[2]—but after seeing C. C. and said that I
had thought and so forth—but had about concluded to give up the
idea.   W. W.

ALS (WC, NjP).
  [1] For the private supplementing of Wilson's salary. The nature of the arrangement will soon become clear from documents that follow.
  [2] James Waddel Alexander.

From George Washington Miles

My dear Sir,   Radford, Virginia, April 7th. 1898

I have your favor and note carefully what you say. I see clearly
that in this proposed debate between Princeton and the University that Princeton has all the advantages because, as Demos-
thenes says in one of his orations against Philip: Τὰ τῶν ἀπόντων
τοῖς παροῦσιν ὑπάρχει, which simply means that in this as in everything else the fellow on the ground has a big advantage. I write
now to at least put you on your guard against this. Many things
that could be said in favor of your coming to the University must
perforce be left unsaid in the cramped limits of a correspondence.

I also know that "a body in rest tends to remain in rest," especially when that *statu quo* is a pleasant and honorable one. But
I am frank to say that I do not believe that Princeton has anything now or can have anything in the future as good for you
as what we now offer you. And in using the word good I do not
use it in any but the very broadest and most useful sense.

To take it up in detail, with your coming to the University we
expect to begin an era of special effort in letting the world know
more about the place and its numerous strong and honorable
points, to restore it more to the public eye, North, East, South,
West. I do not think I am afflicted with "old Virginia brag" when
I say that to preside over the destinies of such a school as it is
now is as honorable work as the educational field possesses. And
it does not yet appear what can be made of it with a few more
men like yourself working together there. A school that had Jefferson, Madison and Monroe all on its Board of Visitors at one
time should not let any other educational corporation in America
surpass it.

Now, in the matter of compensation, I think the situation at
the University can hold its own. Mr. John B. Minor used to get

$3000 a year as salary and would make from $4000 to $5000 out of his summer Law class. Mr. Lile is making a success of the summer law class, but needs someone to help him. He also is making a great success of his Law Journal and needs an associate here. I have this from one of his intimate friends. To assist him in both of these matters would absorb but very little of your time.

But the chief thing is the leisure you require to do your literary work. I think in your feelings, at least, you have exaggerated the importance of this move as being a serious interruption. You can soon be ensconced among your books and at your desk at the University and can go serenely on your way. The Board does not expect a sudden spurt or extra effort, but the fact that you are there, added to the Law Faculty, is sufficient guarantee that the University is on the upgrade and that the sceptre is coming back to old Virginia.

Another thing that I am sure of is the fact that no more intellectual student body gathers anywhere on this Continent than the ones you would lecture to at the University. The only trouble is there are not more of them. With the greatest care exercised on the part of the Board in the filling of chairs, and with some extra intelligence in getting the University again in the public eye, I think the students will flock there as never before.

But I see I can not reach the case by letter writing. In June we have at Charlottesville quite a celebration, dedication of the New Buildings, their reception on the part of the Governor &c. I trust you will let us send out from the Board, as a fitting *finale* to that occasion, that we have brought you to the University and that henceforth that will be the scene of your life work and usefulness. That country around Charlottesville has had many great and good men in it. Certainly there can be drawn from it abundant inspiration and that is one thing we all need.

The Board believes that you are able to add greatly to the University, that you will bring some of the best life-blood of Princeton to the University, otherwise the invitation would not be extended to you. Of course we expect opposition to your leaving. I can only add in conclusion that I trust you can gently disengage yourself from the toils, be they many and gracious, and come.

With cordial regards,   Very Truly Yrs.   Geo. W. Miles

ALS (WP, DLC).

From Cornelius Cuyler Cuyler

My Dear Wilson: New York. 8 April 1898

Yours of the 7th[1] has come as a welcome message to me and I am sure it will be received as such by all who have had the pleasure of realizing the value to the University of your work and your writings.

You have now put me in position by your letter and the charming sentiments expressed therein to at once start upon the work of placing the matter in business shape. As already stated to you I do not want you to positively take any position until the details which I shall try to arrange are closed. We are too good friends to have any misunderstanding about these and I desire to carry out my part as faithfully as I know you intend to carry out yours.

One or two of your intimate friends, [Cleveland H.] Dodge, Pyne and others to whom it was proper for me to speak, were much pleased when I advised them of what I thought the result of our conversation would probably be. I shall now consult them further as well as our mutual good friend Cyrus McCormick and one or two other of your and my best friends in order to finally close the arrangements.

I shall hope to see you in Princeton next Friday night April 15th (if not sooner) at which time I understand that for some reason unknown to me my work since graduation is to be spoken of by some of my friends at a dinner[2] and I hope to be able on that occasion to advise you definitely that the matter we have discussed is finally settled and that Princeton can henceforth feel sure that for all time Woodrow Wilson belongs to her!

With kind regards, I am,

Yours faithfully   C C Cuyler

ALS (WP, DLC).
  1 It is missing.
  2 See n. 1 to the notes printed at April 15, 1898.

The First Chapter of a School History of the United States

[c. April 8, 1898][1]

BEFORE THE ENGLISH CAME.

We think the English no laggards in conquest, but they let a whole century go by after America was discovered before they bestirred themselves to take possession of it. This was not because the discovery had been made by a foreign sailor for Spain and Englishmen had not heard of it. They learned promptly

1 Wilson's composition date on the WWhw draft of this chapter in WP, DLC.

enough of the daring voyage which Christopher Columbus, the adventurous Genoese seamen [seaman], had made for their majesties Ferdinand and Isabella of Spain; and within five years Henry VII., their own monarch, had despatched John Cabot, another Genoese, out of Bristol port to do the like for England. Cabot, besides, found more than Columbus had found. Columbus had discovered only the Antilles, only the islands of the West Indies; Cabot discovered the northern coasts of the continent itself,—and the next year, 1498, came again, with his son Sebastian, to go nearly the whole length of the coast. The English knew as much as any other nation knew of what had been found beyond the sea. The trouble was, that neither the English nor the Spaniards realized what it was that Columbus and Cabot had discovered.

No one dreamed for many a long day that it was a *new* world upon which these doughty sailors had chanced in their bold voyages into unknown seas,—a whole continent of which no man in Europe had ever heard. It seemed incredible the world should have held an entire unknown continent all the long centuries through, and that no man had ever so much as guessed it. How was it big enough? Where were the eastern coasts of Asia? It was the eastern coasts of Asia Columbus had set out to find; and until his death he supposed that he had found them. He had been seeking the exceeding rich provinces of the great kingdom of Cathay, of which Marco Polo had told Europe two centuries ago, only to be thought an impudent impostor for his pains. Polo, while yet a lad, had gone a long four years' journey overland, with his father, Nicolo, and his uncle, Maffeo Polo, stout merchant adventurers of Venice, to the farthest kingdoms of Asia, in the days when the great Tartar empire of Kublai Khan stretched from Europe to the Chinese sea. There he had lived through almost twenty years, had served the great Khan, seen all his wealth, and travelled as he pleased up and down the coasts of the far sea which lay beyond, in the east. For many a day no one would credit his tales, when at last he made his long way back to Venice again, a bronzed stranger. Who had ever heard before of these ends of Asia and of a great sea beyond? Who had ever told of them except this Venetian adventurer? Here was a fine tale indeed, and only this man to vouch for it!

Europeans knew almost nothing in that day about any lands that lay outside Europe. Even learned men knew only what a few ingenious scholars like Claudius Ptolemy, the celebrated Alexandrian astronomer, had guessed distant continents to be like thirteen hundred years before. They had learned nothing since. Time out of mind, it is true, there had been trade with the far eastern countries. The Romans in their day had used drugs and spices brought from India, cotton cloths and muslins fetched from the coasts of Coromandel and Malabar, silks from China, diamonds from Bengal, carpets, silks, and embroidered stuffs, as well as rice and sugar, from Arabia and Persia. And Europe did not wholly forget these old fountains of trade when the Romans were gone. Ships out of her Mediterranean ports sought them again when the first confusion of the breaking up of the Roman empire was over; carried the crude products of the European mines and forests to Alexandria or Antioch, or to the ports of the Black Sea, and received there, in exchange, the silks and spices and gems of the East, brought by ship or caravan from India, China, and the Persian Gulf. Particularly after the Crusades had for a time checked the interfering mastery of the Turks upon the Mediterranean did this trade grow great and prosperous. Venice became first a thriving seaport and then the centre and capital of a powerful state on account of it: and Genoa, across the Gulf, waxed almost as rich and influential; for these two were the natural sea-gates through which this gainful commerce made its way into and out of the interior valleys of Europe. Not a few cities within the continent grew rich also by handling this trade as it passed,—especially the cities which lay near great interior waterways like the Rhine. It was to get at the heart of some of this trade out of the East, and make more sure of its profits, that Nicolo and Maffeo Polo had made their way into the mysterious realms of the Tartar kings, to be drawn on and on till they found themselves beyond the Great Wall of China and at last in the presence of the mighty Khan himself; and it was Nicolo Polo's son Marco who had told those tales of rich kingdoms upon far away seas which few men even in Venice were found ready to believe.

Only a few sailors and bargaining ship-masters had dealt face to face with the swarthy merchants who came with their pack camels across Syria, by way of Bagdad and Damascus, from the Persian Gulf, or from beyond the Caspian to the havens of the Black Sea; or with those other seamen who fetched cargoes through the Red Sea; and such news as these men brought with them lingered where it was first told, among the seafarers and merchants who talked together on the docks or in the shops of Venice and Genoa and Marsailles and Barcelona, whither the strange trade came. Talk like this made its way very slowly to the ears of learned men, and seemed to them of little value, even when they deemed it credible at all,—a mass of idle rumour. Men knew the names of many an eastern coast or kingdom, but no one had any clear idea of how they lay, with what boundaries or with what neighbours, how large they were, or which way and how far their coasts ran. There was a vague notion that a great continent lay to the south of the African coasts of the Mediterranean, out of which ivory came and many a strange thing; but Ptolemy had supposed that this continent spread itself in solid mass to the eastward, surrounding the Indian Ocean on the south and joining itself to Asia. Others guessed that it was throughout all its breadth from west to east a separate body of land, cut off from Asia not only but from the African lands of the Mediterranean as well by a great sea of which the Indian Ocean was only a part.

Beyond the Pillars of Hercules, the gates of the Mediterranean in the west, who could say what there might be,—besides Britain and Ireland upon Europe's northern coasts, and the little groups of islands, the Azores and the Canaries, which had been found off the coasts of Africa? Of the South and East many things had been told and guessed, but of the West nothing,—except a line or two here and there in the writings of some ancient seer or poet, in which he had seemed to dream for a moment of a continent outside the Pillars. Strabo, the Roman geographer, reported that Eratosthenes, the Greek, had said two hundred years before Christ that India might be reached by going straight westward from the shores of Spain, and had even guessed it quite possible that within the temperate zone the great sea might hold "two or even more habitable earths." Seneca had prophesied a far age in which the "bonds of ocean" should be loosed and new worlds discovered in the midst of the sea. But the world had little heeded these things at any time and had now all but forgotten them. A mystery which daunted every man's fancy hung over the vast Atlantic, and England was at the back of the world. The face of Europe was towards the Mediterranean, and England hung upon her skirts in an unknown and dreadful sea. Greenland and Iceland there were, indeed. The bold northern races had peopled them, and ships passed sometimes to and fro between their shores and the ports at the north. But straight out in the tossing Atlantic,— who could say what would be found there, were any one foolhardy enough to attempt a voyage without knowing for what coast or haven he was steering?

No doubt, if you would go but far enough, the coasts of Asia were there,—who could say how far away?—if, indeed, the earth was really a globe. It had been deemed such ever since Aristotle by those who believed in astronomy and mathematics; but not many could understand how, by what was observed in the skies, by what was known of the lines of the land and sea, or by what was reckoned on paper, men who sat and pored over books and charts could possibly assure you that the earth was round like a ball, that Asia was upside down on the other side of it, and that you could reach the east by sailing west. A practical sailor might be excused for shrugging his shoulders and declaring that he must learn these things from men who had seen and made trial of them, and not from scholars who did, he knew not what, to find them out, and who certainly had never sailed a ship or braved a voyage. And so most people who were unlearned, and even some who could read and who knew what the learned said, preferred to believe that the earth was flat, and washed upon every side by a sea, it might be without bounds.

Columbus, more bold and more believeing than the rest, dared, nevertheless, to credit and to act upon what no man knew. Men of Genoa, like himself, were less daunted by the sea and by thought of unknown lands than other men were. Adventure was their familiar habit and occupation. Columbus, moreover, had fed his thought as few other seamen had with the writings of learned geographers, with charts, with the hints of travellers, and with the guesses of poets. His own hope was greatly quickened; and the tempting prizes to be won by a successful venture at finding the East in the West turned his hopes into purposes. He knew he should win glory second to no man's could he but find a straight and open waterway to Cathay,—to say nothing of the great gain he should pocket in the quick trade he should make available, or of the blessings of the Church should he unlock new lands to the Gospel. It was quite imperative that new and direct routes should be found into the East, if Europe was not to lose her trade in drugs and spices and silks and gems; for the Turks had at last closed the ways that lay eastward out of the Mediterranean. Since 1453 they had been firmly seated at Constantinople, at the portals of the Black Sea, and all the Mediterranean had become unsafe for Christian vessels. It was this conquering advance that had sent Portuguese sailors down the western coasts of Africa to find a way round about by the south to India and the eastern seas. Ever since 1415 Portuguese captains had been pushing further and further southward beyond the Canaries, Madeira, and the Azores; but no voyage had as yet carried them to the end of the seemingly interminable continent, and it had already become clear enough that the new route they sought would be intolerably long when they found it. It was quite likely, if the geographers whom Columbus consulted were right, that Japan (Cipango, they called it) lay not more than three thousand miles due west from the Canaries, with no continent like Africa thrust in the way; and Columbus determined to put this short route to the trial, at whatever hazard. The world has shown no finer example of masterful courage. This stout-hearted Genoese sailor, full of a reasonable hope, trusting and believing though he had not seen, confident and undaunted and yet not rash, proved himself, that notable year 1492, one of the world's greatest men.

And he actually did find land very near where he had expected to find it. There were no rich cities upon the coast he reached, such as Cathay was said to hold, and the native people covered their swarthy skins with scant garments and lived like mere savages. No treasure was found, save a few trinkets of gold and some curious woods out of the virgin forests. But Columbus knew not what it was he had found if it was not part of great India; and so the new lands were confidently dubbed the West Indies, and their inhabitants Indians. It was hoped to find, another time, the populous coasts and the rich particular provinces of which Marco Polo had told so many things that were pleasing to believe. Voyage after voyage was made to the new coasts, however, and nothing was found that seemed like the civilization of Asia until South America was hit upon. Three several times did Columbus himself return to the work of discovery,—disappointing work it now turned out to be,—and the second time (1498), going much further southward than before, came upon the northern coasts of South America, entered the mighty stream of the Orinoco, and concluded that this must also be an outlying shore of Asia,—unless, indeed, it were a detached continent, cut off by some strait or narrow sea. But in 1502 he failed to find any such strait when he sought it in the seas lying within Cuba to the southward, and the lands he had found seemed to him to be one and all parts of the single vast continent whose eastern shores he had risked so much to find.

Meanwhile the persistent seamen of Portugal had at last found their way round about the southern end of Africa. In 1498, the year Columbus found the mouth of the Orinoco, Vasco da Gama passed round the great cape which he called the Cape of Good Hope, and actually pressed onward, as Portuguese seamen had so long planned to do, to the coasts of Malabar. It turned out, as explorer followed explorer, that South America stretched farther, much farther, eastward into the Atlantic than any Asiatic land the geographers had yet heard of,—so far, indeed, that mariners bound upon the southward voyage round about Africa might sometimes find themselves driven upon its coasts, if the storms that crossed their path blew for very long at a time from out the east. It seemed unlikely that there could be any part of Asia thereabouts, and so it was concluded that this at any rate was a New World. And yet it, and not the northern continent which lay where Asia should lie, contained kingdoms old and rich with treasure such as all had thought to find in India and Cathay,— the populous and ancient kingdoms of Mexico and Peru. The one Cortez conquered and despoiled (1519-1521), the other, Pizarro (1531-1532); and all the world turned its eyes southward at news of the abundant booty. Great fleets of galleons began to pass to and fro between Spain and the conquered provinces, carrying gold and every precious thing. It was then that Englishmen found their sea legs. They had not much frequented the seas hitherto, except for fish upon their own coasts, the great ocean in which their home lay having been till now unknown and dangerous. But sight of Spain's booty made them bold,—particularly the men of the southern ports in Somerset and Devon, which seemed to lie near the scenes of adventure and which had bred hardy fishermen time out of mind; and Hawkins and Drake came to be the names upon every one's lips where stories of the sea were told.

The century was well advanced, nevertheless, before the English began to make any show of real power on the ocean, and Spain had meanwhile spread her conquests and her settlements far and wide on the southern continent and within the Gulf of Mexico. South America had been certainly found to be in fact a new world. In 1513 Balboa had crossed the Isthmus from a Spanish settlement on the Gulf, and, climbing a hill in the west, had

> "stared at the Pacific,—while all his men
> Looked at each other with a wild surmise,—
> Silent upon a peak in Darien."

Here was a great sea in the West! Was Asia beyond? In 1519 Ferdinand Magellan set out to find what was at the far south of the New World, passed round about the long continent through the straits to which his name was afterwards given, and sailed into the calm ocean to which he gave the name Pacific. His own life he lost, at the Phillipine Islands, which he discovered; but one of his captains pressed onward, and made its way homeward by way of the Cape of Good Hope,—thus completing the first voyage round the world. Other mariners followed Magellan soon enough, and the kingdom which Pizarro conquered ten years later was a kingdom of the Pacific, on the farther coasts of the new continent. The actual position and real character of the New World in the south were becoming clearer and clearer with every voyage and every conquest.

There [these] voyages into the Pacific by slow degrees made it evident, moreover, as they were extended further and further to the northward, that the northern coasts also, which lay on the other side of the lands which the Cabots and their successors had discovered in the north Atlantic, in the latitudes where India and Cathay were reckoned to lie, were in fact separated from Asia by all the vast width of the same sea, and that the ancient geographers, whom Columbus had believed, had left the breadth of these northern lands and the whole expanse of the Pacific out of their calculations,—that Columbus himself would have had to sail many a weary hundred untold leagues, in addition to those he had counted on, and yet not made land, had not this unknown continent and its islands lain in his path. It was not easy to know how wide these new masses of land were,—they were narrow enough where Balboa and his son had crossed,—and the world was too much engrossed with conquest and spoil in South America to think much as yet of the forested depths of the wild lands in the north. Seamen skirted its coasts, of course, put into its wide bays and rivers, and followed some of its broader streams a little way within the land; and armed expeditions were sent now and again into its forests to explore parts of the interior,— but always with the same result. There were no open ways but the rivers, no inhabitants but savages and wild beasts; and there was no hoarded treasure anywhere.

It was only Frenchmen and Spaniards who made any attempts upon the interior as yet; and they had no thought of clearing away the forests or of making a beginning at self-sustaining settlements. They wished only to find and conquer settlements already established, and to set up a trade in wares for which they could find a market in Europe. A few settlements were attempted, it is true, in Florida, and upon the great St. Lawrence in the north; but rather as trading posts than as self-maintaining colonies. Almost the only thing that looked permanent at the end of the century was the cod fisheries on the Banks of Newfoundland. It was there Europe now got fish for Fridays, her fast days. Newfoundland had become a regular fishing and trading post as early as the year 1504,—within seven years, that is, after it was discovered by John Cabot,—and by 1570, we are told, quite fifty vessels went every year from English ports to take part in the fisheries,—from France almost three times as many. Hundreds of crews were to be found in St. Johns harbour, in the season, drying their catch and sunning their nets. The Atlantic was at least very often crossed nowadays. Its routes were well known, both at the north and at the south. North America was at least easy enough to get at when Europe should know what use to make of it.

The whole of the first century of exploration and discovery in America was spent before the delusions about it were in any considerable degree cleared away. It took the whole of that hundred years of slow voyages and hazardous adventure to get rid of the notions which had come from thinking America a part of Asia. No doubt the Spaniards, and after them the French, found out a great deal that they took no pains to publish, wishing to keep the new lands for themselves and let no rival nation into any valuable secret. But the English had little thought, the while, of anything but prying into what the Spaniards had found out, and preying at every chance, like veritable buccaneers, upon the rich commerce with which Spanish galleons had filled the seas. Practical, hard-headed men though they were, it was the end of the century before they began to comprehend what there was to be done and made use of in America; and even then they had the same vague notions that everywhere prevailed about the interior and the extent of the continent. They knew only its coasts here and there.

In fact, as they were to find out by quite two centuries more of persistent exploration and effort, the interior of the great northern continent was league upon league in extent,—incredibly vast and impressive; back-boned with seemingly interminable mountain ranges; set thick with vast, tangled forests that had stood upon it, it might be, since the first ages of the world; studded here and there with shining lakes which oftentimes, in the north, hid their further banks below the horizon, like the ocean itself; beyond the forests and the lakes, spread flatly out in limitless prairies, themselves vast and level as the sea. Life there was everywhere upon it, but always wild, whether it were the life of men or the life of beasts.

The most savage of the red men who lived within the continent Europeans were to know little of for many a long day, for they lived upon the far western coasts beyond the towering mountain ranges on the other side of the plains, by the vast Pacific, or in the distant north behind Hudson's Bay, and only wayfaring mariners who beat up and down upon the faraway sea or Jesuit missionaries out of the French settlements by the lakes were likely to encounter them. The Indians of the eastern coasts, though savage enough, had ordered tribes and fixed homes; tilled the ground for maize and for many a palateable vetetable [vegetable], and for tobacco for their pipes; made rude weapons and tools for the simple uses of their lives, for hunting and tilling and for war; and seemed to have made a beginning at being civilized. Incessant wars of tribe against tribe held them back from doing more than make a beginning, made them restless, vindictive, subtile, heartless. They had a few dogs, for use in the chase, or for food when the chase yielded them nothing to eat,—but no other domestic animals: no horses or cows, no goats or sheep or pigr [pigs] even, to serve them in the draught, or for food when game failed.

Far back, in the southern recesses of the continent, where the Sierra Madre mountains rear their mass and pass down through the great neck of land that broadens at last into South America, there were other tribes, indeed, more civilized than any in the east,—tribes which knew how to bring water by long sluices out of the distant hills to irrigate their parched fields on the plains; which built stout fortresses of sun-burnt brick or of hewn stone, perched high upon the side of some hugh [huge] cliff within a deep river cañon, or towering, storey upon storey, like a castellated hive within walls, upon the more open plain, and teeming with a population many thousand strong; which knew how to work in bronze as well as in stone; wrote records, in hieroglyphic, upon bark and even upon a sort of paper; wove both garments and basket ware very dexterously; and had temples and an ordered priesthood. It was men of this interesting sort that Cortez found in Mexico and despoiled,—the Aztecs; it was a still more interesting people whom Pizarro found in Peru,—whose fine cotton and woolen cloths constituted no small part of his rich booty. But in the northern continent there were no powerful confederacies or enriched kingdoms like those of the Aztecs and the Incas. There were only a few humbler tribes like the Moquis and the Zunis, whose descendants still linger in Arizona and New Mexico; and these, being hid away, as it were in a corner, settlers and explorers in the east were to know little or nothing about until they had almost ceased to care about Indians at all, except as a singular people who must be studied ere they died out, in order to complete our record of primitive life among men. The Spaniards very early heard of these lonely tribes at the north of Mexico, and believed extravagant stories about their populous cities,—which they supposed as rich as those of Mexico and Peru, though they were in fact only simple fortresses built to ward off the attacks of the fierce Apaches at the north. It cost the Spaniards many a good life thrown away in armed expeditions to find out how little there was in these simple 'cities' that they need care to take. They frankly admitted that they had found nothing for all their marching but "mighty plains and sandy heaths, smooth and wearisome and bare of wood," with only "crook-backed oxen" (as they called the buffaloes) for inhabitants.

We know these things very familiarly now, but no man knew anything then of the continent and its inhabitants but such partial news as was brought by explorers who had tried the interior and been compelled to turn back, knowing only enough to tantalize the imagination and draw other brave men on to attempt the same thing, and fail in the same way,—or from the adventurous voyagers who more and more frequented the coasts. It was known by the end of the first century of experiment only that North America was, practically, a virgin continent,—at any rate, at every point where it could be got at and examined. This fact alone, however, was sufficient to give the English an advantage in its use and occupation. They had not been ready, when the great game of conquest and seizure began in South America, to compete with the Spaniards; for they had not ships or sailors enough and could not yet match strength in such undertakings with the great nation of the South. They could only harass her and make a beginning at breaking in upon her commerce. But the whole face of affairs had rapidly changed as that eventful century went by; and, in the end, their practical sagacity, their dogged purpose, and their masterful way of doing things for themselves, without waiting for any government to assist them, thrust the English inevitably to the front and gave them the best parts of the coveted continent. They were the first to comprehend the real character of the new land in the north; and they were the first to set themselves to take possession of it in the only practicable way.

Of [At] the opening of that busy hundred years of discovery and preparation Spain was no doubt the greatest power in Europe. Her king was also Archduke of Austria, heir of the House of Burgundy and therefore hereditary lord of the Netherlands, king of Naples and Sicily, and Emperor of Germany,—Charles V., the greatest prince in all Europe. Spain's shadow, while he reigned, covered the whole face of affairs. But the end of the century saw a very different state of things,—and what happened in Europe was sure to determine what should take place in America. The hugh [huge] piecemeal empire of Charles the Fifth had no real unity and did not hold together. By scattering her forces too ambitiously and staking her supremacy on too many things, Spain steadily lost, the century through, both in power and in prestige. Throughout the thirty-seven years of his troubled reign (1518-1556) Charles fought in vain to win back the lost possessions of Burgundy from France and to keep Germany from going to pieces because of the religious differences that had been bred by the hot movement of the Reformation; and when he gave the struggle up, by abdicating and retiring to a monastery in 1556, Spain lost her connection with the German Empire, whose power had meant so much for her while Charles was king. Then, in 1568, the Netherlands revolted, and it proved impossible by any expenditure of blood or treasure to reduce them permanently to submission again. England openly sent aid to the men of the Low Countries; but Spain sent her "invincible armada" to chastise her only to see her vast ships driven, scattered and crippled, through the Channel by the smart little craft Drake and Hawkins and Howard brought out of the ports of Devon and Dorset against them. They were beaten helplessly northward, too, by pitiless sea weather, to be thrown away at last in hopeless wreckage on the Hebrides. Incessant wars which she was obliged to keep up the century through utterly sapped the Spanish strength, though she still clung desperately to what she had. She was really beaten before the century was out.

Meanwhile, England had become a sea power, and France had compacted her strength. In 1562 the great civil war with the Huguenots broke out in France, to last for twenty years; in 1572 she stained her annals with the awful massacres of St. Bartholomew's Day; and the fatal strife ended with the expulsion of the Huguenots from her territories by which France sent the most industrious, frugal, ingenious, and spirited people of her middle classes to England and America. But she did not then realize what she had lost; and at the end of the century she seemed stronger and readier for aggressive action than ever before. Germany was still engrossed with the bitter political quarrels that sprang out of the religious controversies of the Reformation. Some of her states had espoused the Protestant faith of the great Luther, some remained Catholic in faith and allegiance, and passion was fast drawing them on to the dreadful struggle of the Thirty Years' War (1618-1648). France and England, it turned out, were to be free to compete on equal terms for the occupation and use of North America. Spain's power was hopelessly impaired, and Germany, besides being shut off from the Atlantic, was deeply preoccupied. The Dutch were to be more formidable rivals than either, after they had made sure of shaking off Spain for good and all. Her seamen were to win a fame for skill, prowess, and constancy which even the English could not justly boast of having excelled.

When the French and English actually met as rivals in the novel enterprise that should determine the future of America not only but of the rest of the world also, it very soon became evident which were the more fit for the difficult and singular undertaking. The settlement and use of a virgin continent was a new thing in the world, so far as anybody could remember,—and only experiment could show the best way of accomplishing it. France had as strong a government as that of England. Indeed, the weak Stuart kings came to the throne of England, in the place of the strong Tudors, at the very moment when the work of taking possession of America was about to begin in earnest. France used her powerful government and sent colonies out in official fleets, determined to maintain them as long as necessary after they reached America at the public expense. The English government took no direct part in the matter, but let individual Englishmen establish colonies for themselves and maintain them at their own cost,—just as she had let Drake and Hawkins fit out their own fleets and prey upon the Spanish commerce and rob the Spanish settlements in America on their own private account and at their own risk. England had become a commercial and maritime nation during the century now closing; but not by any direct assistance from her government. The government had not even kept pirates and privateers out of the English ports, but had left merchantmen to arm themselves and beat off the thieves at their own charges. Every man was left to act on his own resources, and the most the government did was to keep its hands off and ask no man any inconvenient questions about his voyages or his business. Even the fleet that beat the Spaniards in the Channel was a volunteer fleet. The English colonies were not nursed and coddled, as the French were. The men who founded them had to attend to them as to their private business. Weak men could not succeed at that cost. The same masterful spirits that had built up a profitable commerce without aid, without odds asked or given, undertook this new enterprise also,—for their own gain, benefit, comfort, or freedom,—sometimes out of mere love of change and adventure; and they proved, of course, much harder men to beat or discourage than the nursed and subsidized colonists the French government sent out. Stout-hearted, determined men, who expected to take [care] of themselves and knew how to do it, were much better fitted for the rough work of colonizing a new continent than the dependent protégés of a distant government,—and it did not take very long to make that fact evident.

At last the quiet age came in which the wilderness was to be taken possession of in a businesslike fashion. The nations which coveted North America had ceased to

"fly to India for gold,
Ransack the ocean for oriet [orient] pearl,
And search all corners of the new-found world
For pleasant fruits and princely delicates,"

and had come into the sober humour which was to make them fit to found colonies within the ancient forests that stood untouched upon the new coasts. A few mistakes, made as the century of discovery was closing, made them the more careful what they were about. Among the first to attempt the establishment of settlements had been Sir Humphrey Gilbert and his half-brother Walter Ralegh, gentlemen of Devon,—that stirring county which had always been close neighbour to the sea, its air full of the ocean's breath, and its men used to the rough and dangerous ways of adventure. Gilbert and Ralegh had been bred to books at Oxford, but they had lived their lives among seamen, had been witnesses to many a moving fortune, and knew all the sea tales that came and went at Plymouth. In 1583 Sir Humphrey himself took ship for America and lost his life on the strange coasts, seeking a harbour. In 1584, the next year, Ralegh sent two ships out to take the southern course to America and find a place for a settlement. His captains hit upon Roanoke Island, on the coasts of the Carolinas, and came back to tell him that it was a most pleasant land, full of every rich growth of vine and fruit, and its people "gentle, loving, and faithful, and such as live after the manner of the golden age." Ralegh was still dreaming of finding some El Dorado, where gold abounded. Instead, therefore, of sending out families to make permanent homes for themselves and capable workmen and good stores such as would make the task practicable, [he] sent out only a force of men who were left to explore and cast about to find something, instead of building shelter for themselves and tilling the soil for crops, and who had presently to be taken home again. Another year, Ralegh sent real settlers out, with women and families. But these soon got upon ill terms with the Indians, who very early proved anything but "loving and faithful"; they continued, too, to rely upon getting supplies from England, and did not know how to provide for themselves in the wilderness; and when at last search was made for them by the supply ships which came, too late, out of Devon, they were nowhere to be found. Their fate has remained a mystery to this day.

By that time the fateful year 1588 had come. The Spanish

armade came in its might against England. The attention and energy of Ralegh, as well as of every other Devon man, was imperatively drawn off from colonization to the duty of serving England at home. The settlement of America had to wait until another generation of Englishmen should be free to undertake it, in another temper and with other aims.

WWT MS. (WP, DLC).

A News Item

[April 9, 1898]

Professor Woodrow Wilson delivered a lecture[1] in Orange Music Hall, Thursday evening [April 7], under the auspices of the Womans' Club of Orange [New Jersey].

Printed in the *Princeton Press*, April 9, 1898.
  1 Wilson's list of appointments for 1898 in the diary described at Dec. 9, 1897, indicates that he gave his lecture, "Political Liberty."

From James Hoge Tyler

Commonwealth of Virginia. Governor's Office
Dear Sir: Richmond, Va. April, 9th, 1898.

I am in the confidence of the University of Virginia Board in their efforts to bring you to the University. I want to write just a line to express to you my interest in this matter, and my wish that you may accept the important and honorable trust offered you. The past of the University is truly grand, but the future should hold even better things in store for her. I think you can materially contribute to this future.

Very truly yours,   J Hoge Tyler

Personal

TLS (WP, DLC).

From Archibald Williams Patterson

My Dear Wilson,   Richmond, Va., 4/11/98.

I have been wanting to drop you a line for some time past, but was prevented by pressing engagements at the office, and unusual claims upon me at home.

Miles sent me a short note from the University while the Board was in session, stating that our scheme had received the approval of his associates. Subsequently, in a few moments conversation with him as he passed through this city, he further informed me that he was chairman of a committee appointed to carry out the plan. I am immensely gratified at the prospect. And now that the Visitors, after so great tribulation, have got together on the policy and the man, I trust there will be little difficulty upon your part in responding favorably to their call. That the change would involve some present sacrifice for you—a certain derange[ment] of important work, and delay in the completion of some cherished enterprise, I have no doubt. I am equally satisfied, however, that it is your first duty to assume the office now tendered you. This proposition might be demonstrated, if necessary. But as a native of Virginia and an alumnus of her proud University, your own predilections should be a sufficient argument.

Deeply as I am concerned about the future of the University, I should not urge you to this course if I believed your own usefulness or fame would suffer thereby. So far from entertaining such an opinion, I feel convinced that you would have a most honorable and distinguished career, winning fresh laurels for yourself and giving to the University that prestige which she needs above everything else.

I beg also that, in considering this question, you will not allow any feeling of modesty to stand in the way. Your misgivings are natural enough, but other people can judge of your fitness for this place far better than you can. If your friends and the authorities whose province it is to act in the premises, think you are the right man, their judgment should prevail.

I was at the University not long since. You would hardly know the old place. It is greatly changed for the better. The new buildings are both artistic and imposing in appearance, their arrangement is excellent, and the appointments promise to be in keeping with the rest. Having taken on a more attractive physical aspect, I thought of our alma mater as being likewise inspired with a new life under your administration. It would be a pity to spoil this pleasing vision.

From what Miles tells me, the Board is in a mood to give you pretty much anything you ask for. I am anxious to see a satisfactory agreement between it and yourself. If I can assist in any way, please command me.

Many thanks for the kind words of sympathy contained in your last letter. Mrs. Patterson has been quite unwell ever since, but is now out of bed and slowly regaining her strength.

With best wishes for you and yours, I remain,

Very sincerely,   A. W. Patterson.

TLS (WP, DLC).

From Cyrus Hall McCormick

My dear Woodrow: Chicago, April 13/98.

Your letter of the 7th[1] brought me great pleasure. Not only personally do I feel delighted at your decision, but as a Princetonian, I believe that your remaining means much for the interests of our Alma Mater, to which we are all loyal. Whatever may be said as to the needs of the University of Virginia, the fact remains that Princeton cannot afford to lose you, and I am sure that your decision must have been reached in large part, from the desire you have to help us all in building up and completing the splendid structure of Princeton University, whose foundations are already so well laid in the enthusiasm and loyalty of its alumni, and the ability of its faculty.

With warmest regards, I am

Very sincerely your friend, Cyrus H. McCormick.

TLS (WP, DLC).
[1] It is missing.

Notes for Remarks at a Testimonial Dinner

15 April, 1898

Cornelius C. Cuyler Complimentary dinner[1]

Natural fact.

Hard (with my feeling of identification,) to look critically at C.— he has for so many years seemed to me simply *a beneficent fact of nature*.

Action—efficient cause.

The word that comes uppermost in my mind is the word *action*— he is a sort of "efficient cause" in everything in which he has a part.

Organic efficiency.

'Seventy-nine has been prolific in efficient men,—C. represents its *organic* efficiency, its capacity for the init[i]ative which is at once social and individual.

Business—responsible ministers.

This the time of alumni *power* (as *vs.* sentiment) and C. represents, as 'Seventy-nine would have it represented, the practical, hard-headed, businesslike devotion that means power.

Responsible ministers.

Isham parliaments[2]

Comradeship *and* independence.

No man more loyally accepts than C. does the idea of responsibility and comradeship,—and yet the freedom, the individuality, the independent initiative are all there, in an uncommon degree.

WWhw MS. (WP, DLC).
¹ Held in the Princeton Inn on April 15, 1898, in recognition of Cuyler's services to Princeton University. A loving cup was presented to him.
² A reference to the dinners given annually to the members of the Class of 1879 by William B. Isham, Jr., of New York. See Alexander J. Kerr, "The Isham Dinners," *Fifty Years of the Class of 'Seventy-Nine, Princeton* (Princeton, 1931), pp. 199-206.

Cyrus Hall McCormick to Cornelius Cuyler Cuyler

[Chicago] April 18, 1898.

Letter of fifteenth received. Our family gladly contribute five hundred on behalf of our interests.¹   C. McC.

T tel. (C. H. McCormick Letterpress Books, WHi).
¹ See C. C. Cuyler to C. H. McCormick, Dec. 6, 1899, Vol. 11, for evidence that McCormick was referring to the fund that Cuyler was raising to supplement Wilson's salary.

From Cornelius Cuyler Cuyler

My Dear Wilson: New York. 18 April 1898

Allow me first in writing to thank you for the very kind sentiments expressed by you at Friday night's dinner. I really felt part of the time as if I ought to be in my coffin as the eulogies were hard for a living man to listen to.

Now to come down to everyday matter of fact life again I want to write you in rê the question we have discussed of late. There is a strong feeling on the part of McCormick that now the matter of your staying at Princeton is settled, you should call on Dr. Patton and tell him of the honor sought to be conferred on you by Virginia, of your varying sentiments during the past few weeks as to the duty of accepting or remaining where you are, and as much more of the matter as you feel inclined. McCormick makes so strong a point of this particular phase of the question that I hope you may see your way clear to complying therewith.

In any formal agreement entered into between yourself and the guarantors of the fund it is thought best that the period named should be five years and that at the end of that time the matter be taken up anew, as conditions may in the meantime change very greatly not only as regards the circumstances of the men responsible for the fund but also in the chair held by you.

On hearing from you as to the foregoing I shall have the thing put in legal shape at once, sending you one copy of the agreement and keeping the other for the Trustee of the fund whoever he may be, and thus end satisfactorily what threatened to prove a great misfortune for Princeton.

I do not want you to feel that at the end of 5 years any difficulty is anticipated in the way of a renewal. With such friends as McCormick, Pyne, Dodge and the writer you can rely on justice being shown you. It is only that they cannot well bind themselves for a longer time at the start and are merely taking care of themselves in case of death or financial reverses and other possible contingencies.

Trusting to hear that such an arrangement as outlined will meet your views,

I am, Dear Wilson,   Yours sincerely,   C C Cuyler

ALS (WP, DLC) with WWhw notation on env.: "Ans. 19 April/98."

From Louis Clark Vanuxem

My dear Woodrow: Philadelphia   April 18, 1898.

Don't forget your promise to return to me Col. Biddle's book.[1] Exoress [Express] it to me, at once, please.

Write me what Saturday you can visit me at Chestnut Hill, and remain there until Monday morning at least. My Mother wishes when the date is fixed to write to you[r] wife and ask her to be her guest also. I hope that we can have the pleasure of entertaining you both in the very near future.

Yours sincerely,   L. C. Vanuxem

TLS (WP, DLC) with WWhw notation on env.: "Storthing."
[1] See L. C. Vanuxem to WW, Jan. 7, 1897, n. 3.

From Sidney Webb

My dear Sir,   [Washington] 19 Apl/98

Mrs. Winthrop of Washington has kindly given Mrs. Webb & myself the enclosed letter to you.[1] My old acquaintance with and great admiration for your work on "Congressional Government" has been stimulated anew by a fortnight's inspection of of [sic] Congress as it is; and both Mrs. Webb and I would greatly value the chance of a talk with you upon the development of the governmental machinery since your book was written. We leave Philadelphia next Monday morning, 25th inst, and we had intended to go straight to New York, not realising that you were at Princeton, & thus on the way. If we could count on the pleasure of seeing you at Princeton anytime in the middle of the day on Monday, we should be glad to arrange to "stop over," if this is practicable—or we would stay the night at Princeton if this was our only chance of seeing you.

In studying for the last few years the working of Democratic institutions among English Trade Unions and Cooperative Associations, we have often had your description of the United States in mind; and now that we see that government at work as you described it, we are all the more anxious to have some talk with you upon certain phases of its procedure.[2]

Yours very truly   Sidney Webb

ALS (WP, DLC); hw itinerary at top of letter omitted.
[1] The enclosure is missing.
[2] For an account of their visit with Wilson, see the extract from the Diary of Beatrice Webb printed at April 25, 1898.

From Cornelius Cuyler Cuyler

My Dear Wilson: New York. 20 April 1898

I have your favor of 19th[1] in which, as throughout this whole transaction, you exhibit that charming confidence in your friends which goes far toward making life a pleasure. I will now take up the 5 year arrangement with the other men and will try to promptly put same in such shape as will be mutually satisfactory.

Again assuring you of the intense gratification I have experienced in being able to do my share toward securing the much desired result, I am Dear Wilson,

Yours sincerely   C C Cuyler.

ALS (WP, DLC).
[1] It is missing.

To Charles William Kent

My dear Charlie,   Princeton, New Jersey, 22 April, 1898.

Under ordinary circumstances I, of course, would not have let your last letter lie so long unanswered; but I felt that I must decide the question of my coming to the University before I could know what to say. I pray I may never have such another question to decide. It has torn my heart sadly to come to a conclusion about it, and now that the conclusion is fixed, I find myself left sad and unsatisfied. Not unsatisfied as to what I should do, but unsatisfied that I cannot serve both Princeton and the University.

It is hard to put into a few sentences the reasons why I have decided that I must stay at Princeton. It is a case of *must*. Almost every instinct of my nature, and almost every affection drew me towards the State and the institution I love with so deep a love and loyalty, and the impulse was all but irresistible. The Board of Visitors offered me, I very well know, what will probably turn out to be the highest honour of my life-time; and they called me to a place and to dear friends whom it would be a life-long pleasure to serve. You may be sure the reasons for declining were imperative.

And they were. It would not be possible within the limits of any letter to tell you just what bonds the Princeton trustees and alumni have drawn about me first and last,—not legal bonds, but moral,—but the simple fact is that they have so bound me that I felt constrained to yield to their protests or deem myself for the rest of my life a mere ingrate. They have heaped honours and privileges upon me in a most extraordinary way, within the last eighteen months, not only without solicitation but without hint or expectation on my part, of course; and now when they tell me, with evident sincerity, and even with a sort of passionate earnestness uncommon enough in this part of the world, that my loss would mean not only the temporary embarrassment but possibly the lasting impairment of the University, I know nothing that an honourable man can do but yield and stay.

I am not so foolish as to suppose that my loss would really have any such effect as they suppose. I am too sane, I hope, not to see the truth about that matter. But while they *think* as they do now, the loss would be most demoralizing, and I am under too many obligations to them to put them at such a disadvantage as this state of mind would entail, were I to leave. Moreover, I dearly love this noble institution with its high and great traditions. I cannot injure it.

I am giving you many subtle things merely in the crude, my dear fellow. I have been fairly taken off my feet by both the words and the actions of my friends and Princeton's hereabouts since they knew of my call, and my very serious consideration of it. I am translating for you now a multitude of impressions and experiences into a few phrases. And I am doing so to claim your sympathy. I have been drawn two ways at once; and, in obeying what has seemed to me the unmistakable dictate of conscience, I have satisfied neither my ambitions nor my affections.

And so I am writing with a sort of chastened feeling, and want nothing so much as words of sympathy and appreciation from my friends to whom I have been obliged to say No.

Has Heath Dabney been in the confidence of the Board in this matter? Mr. Miles seemed to lay a good deal of emphasis on keeping the thing private and within a narrow circle, and I should not like to speak of it at the University where the members of the Board had not themselves been beforehand with me. But if Heath knows of the matter, I should like very much to write to him about it.

Give my warmest regards to Mrs. Kent, and to all her family. I greatly appreciate her kind invitation to stay with you at Commencement and in case I should visit the University sooner. No doubt it is for the best, as relieving all parties of a little embarrassment, that I could not accept the invitation to speak at the opening of the new buildings; and my visit must be postponed until another time.

Believe me, my dear Charlie, if a little older and soberer than before this question came to disturb me, still, as ever the companion of the old days and

Faithfuly Yours,   Woodrow Wilson

WWTLS (Tucker-Harrison-Smith Coll., ViU).

Cyrus Hall McCormick to Cornelius Cuyler Cuyler

My dear C. C.—   Chicago, April 22/98.

Your letters of the 18th and 19th are before me, and I am delighted to learn of the pleasant time that you had at the dinner. . . .

Your information as to the progress you are making with the Woodrow Wilson fund is most agreeable. You have finished up this matter to the "Queen's taste" (not the Queen of Spain). I have no doubt, with $2,000. already pledged, that you will secure the $400. without much difficulty. . . . I have a most delightful letter from Woodrow, which shows that he is in fine spirits and very happy over the solution of the whole matter. He says he will go and see Dr. Patton, now that all is settled, and I very much hope this will be the occasion of cementing a closer bond of sympathy between these two big men. . . .

With kind regards, I am

Yours sincerely,   Cyrus H. McCormick

TLS (C. H. McCormick Letterpress Books, WHi).

From the Diary of Beatrice Webb

[c. April 25, 1898]

. . . Two nights at Bryn Mawr, luxurious women's college, day at Prince-Town charmingly situated university. Long talk with Professor Woodrow Wilson ⟨the most attractive and ablest American writer we have met⟩ about recent developments in "Congressional Government." Attractive-minded man—somewhat like a young John Morley—literary in language, but with a peculiarly un-American insight into the *actual* working of institutions as distinguished from their nominal constitution.[1] Stated that the complete subordination of the House to its Committees, and of the Committees to the Chairmen, and of the Chairmen to the Speaker and his two assistants (Committee of Rules) was comparatively new. He said that he asked [Speaker] Reed "where he was going to?" Reed said he did not know: that he just did what seemed to him most convenient at the moment. Wilson declared that Reed's rollicking sense of humour often led him to let the House mis-behave itself so long as it did not interfere with his plans. Wilson deplores the recent charters of American cities. "The old illusion of the American people was faith in mass meetings, in the capacity of the mass meeting to conduct the work of government. To-day they rush to the other extreme and stake all on One Man." He believes that in the end they will accept representative institutions. I doubt it!

Bound hw diary (British Library of Political and Economic Science, London School of Economics).

[1] Mrs. Webb again compared Wilson to John Morley in a letter to Kate Courtney, April 29, 1898: "W. Wilson is much the most intellectual man we have met—has none of the *literalness* of most Americans—resembles a young and alert John Morley in appearance and temperament." Quoted in David A. Shannon (ed.), *Beatrice Webb's American Diary 1898* (Madison, Wisc., 1963), p. 49, n. 2.

From George Washington Miles

Dear Dr. Wilson,   Radford, Virginia, April 25th. 1898

I have your favor and deeply regret that you reached the conclusion that you did. The new Board at the University made you the center of a forward movement there that must needs receive a very severe back-set from your decision. You do not know how sorely we needed you.

As I said to you over the phone, we were not able to make plain to you how much depended upon your action in the matter. I am loth to give it up.

I think we have shown our appreciation of your true abilities so I do not discount them at all when I say that you did not quite look out over and beyond those Princeton surroundings. Perhaps it proved you all the better man that you did not. I feel very much oppressed by your decision and trust that I may yet someday see you lecturing in the University of Virginia. Nothing would have refreshed our hopes and energies in the South after our thirty-three years of poverty and struggle more than to have seen such a man as yourself returning back Southward to take the headship of its greatest institution of learning in your own native Virginia.

That taken in conjunction with those beautiful new buildings would have warmed the heart of avarice itself and, just as men love to deposit in a strong bank, so wealth and prestige would have flowed in upon the University. We have many good and strong men that we can secure for the Chairmanship and the lecture room at the University, but you and you alone peculiarly and completely solved the problem now before us. I deeply regret that some one of us did not go in person to Princeton and talk this whole matter over with you pro and con.

I have felt all the while like a matter of this importance ought not to have been left to correspondence. I do not know that it would have made any difference in your final decision but at least we might have helped you beat back the home pressure. You recall that I requested of you to give us an opportunity to remove any difficulty that might arise, but this sense of obligation to Princeton is something inaccessible from our side. I can only take your decision as final however reluctant I am to do so, but even yet I desire to express the hope that you may use the next twelve months in disengaging yourself from your debts of gratitude and in shaping up your work so as to yet be part of the University's organic life.

I thank you heartily for the free and full manner in which you let me into the processes by which you reached your conclusion and express to you my appreciation of your sense of justice to all concerned.

With cordial regards,

Very Truly Yours   Geo. W. Miles

ALS (WP, DLC).

From Cornelius Cuyler Cuyler

My Dear Wilson: New York. 26 April 1898

Will you kindly sign the original and duplicate of the enclosed copies of agreement, returning same to me at your earliest opportunity, as I wish to have the subscribers to the fund affix their signatures as soon as practicable. After that I shall take great pleasure in sending you one copy and retaining the other myself.[1]

The matter is now definitely closed on the basis of $2400 per annum for five years and I want to say that while there is nothing in the agreement tending to show that after five years it is to be renewed nevertheless it is clearly understood by all the large subscribers that this is to be carefully considered by them at that time. In any event however my counsel as Trustee informs me that it is better to have the form of agreement drawn as per the enclosed and I hope this will prove satisfactory to your good self.

Trusting to receive the documents back from you at an early date,

I am, with kind regards,

Yours faithfully,   C C Cuyler.

ALS (WP, DLC).
[1] The agreement is printed as an Enclosure with C. C. Cuyler to WW, May 16, 1898.

From Cyrus Hall McCormick

My dear Woodrow: Chicago, April 27/98.

Your letter of the 19th is received, and has done me a world of good. I realize as fully as you do, the delicacy of your position in going to Dr. Patton before this matter was put upon the present happy basis on which it now stands. I am delighted, however, that the affair has resulted so that you can go to Dr. Patton, and confer with him with the fullest confidence, and I am glad that you are going now to confer with him. I trust that this may be only the beginning of many opportunities for cementing between you and Dr. Patton, not only the pleasant relationship of President and Professor, but also the cordial friendship which is so delightful where it naturally exists between two such important men as you and Dr. Patton.

You may be sure that I will do all I can to make your work in Princeton agreeable to you in every way.

I am getting on rapidly, and have already adopted crutches which I shall depend upon for several weeks to come.

With warmest regards, I am

Very sincerely yours,   Cyrus H. McCormick

TLS (WP, DLC).

From the Minutes of the Princeton Faculty

5 5′ P.M., Wednesday, April 27th, 1898.

. . . The Committee in reference to any changes as to The Alumni Dinner at Commencement reported that at a conference with the Commencement Committee (appointed by the Trustees) in reference to any changes deemed advisable in the present method of conducting the Annual Dinner of the Alumni Association of Nassau Hall the following Recommendations were adopted by the Commencement Committee:

1st. That the number of Speakers be limited to four, besides the President of the University, and that these be chosen on account of their eminence and ability, and that they be not necessarily Alumni of the University.

2nd. That the speeches be limited to a maximum length of fifteen minutes.

3rd. That a Committee of two be appointed to select these Speakers, one from the Faculty and one from the Trustees.

This report was accepted and ordered to be recorded. . . .

Francis Landey Patton to John James McCook

My dear Col. McCook: [Princeton, N.J.] April 28 1898

Referring to our conversation in Washington respecting the overtures made to Prof Wilson by the U of Va I write now to say that Prof Wilson called on me day before yesterday & told me all about it & also said that he had definitely decided to stay in Princeton. The invitation had great attractions for him & I am not surprised at that. But I am heart[il]y glad that he has decided to remain with us, and I think it safe to say that he is not likely now to be easily led to leave us. He also said that he had not spoken to me while the matter was pending because he realised that there was nothing that the Trustees could do to help him in the settlement of the question.

I had felt, as you know, somewhat disturbed by Prof Wilson's reticence & I told him that I had heard of the call but felt that it would have been intrusive for me to go to him & tell him how earnestly I hoped he would stay.

His silence I now understand & it grew out of his own high sense of the proprieties of the situation. . . .

Very sincerely yrs   Francis L. Patton

ALS (Patton Letterpress Books, University Archives, NjP).

From Joseph Ruggles Wilson

My precious Woodrow—   Wilmington, N. C., April 29, 1898

I write to say that I expect to leave Wilmington on Monday the 3rd of May, and make my way circuitously towards N. Orleans,[1] trying to take in Josie[2] by the way.

I have company (which by the way I have constantly) and must close at once.

Love to dear Ellie   Lovingly   your Father

ALS (WP, DLC).
[1] The General Assembly of the southern Presbyterian Church met in the First Presbyterian Church of New Orleans, May 19-27, 1898.
[2] Joseph R. Wilson, Jr.

From Cornelius Cuyler Cuyler, with Enclosure

My Dear Wilson: New York. 16 May 1898

It affords me much pleasure to enclose you herein the agreement to which it has been my good fortune to secure the signatures. This closes the matter most satisfactorily and if you will kindly acknowledge receipt of the document I shall be greatly obliged. Meantime with kind regards, I am,

Yours faithfully,   C C Cuyler

ALS (WP, DLC).

E N C L O S U R E

AGREEMENT made this 30th day of April, 1898, between WOODROW WILSON, of the first part, and CYRUS H. McCormick, MOSES TAYLOR PYNE, PERCY R. PYNE, CORNELIUS C. CUYLER, CLEVELAND H. DODGE, JOHN L. CADWALADER, JUNIUS SPENCER MORGAN and ROLLIN H. LYNDE, of the second part:

WHEREAS, the party of the first part, occupant of the Chair of Political Science in Princeton University, is in receipt of a proposition from another institution involving advantages which, notwithstanding his attachment for said University, he has felt that he could not ignore; and

WHEREAS, the parties of the second part, alumni of said University, are most desirous that the party of the first part there remain and to assure that end are willing to guarantee to the party of the first part, in addition to his official salary at said University, a further compensation for a period of five years, beginning with the college year 1898-9;

NOW, THEREFORE, the parties hereto, in consideration of the mutual covenants hereinafter expressed by each to be kept and performed, agree as follows:

FIRST: The party of the first part agrees with the parties of the second part, that for the period of five years beginning with the college year 1898-9, he will not sever his connection with Princeton University in order to accept a call to any other institution of learning; and that he will not during that time give any such course of lectures at any other institution of learning as will interrupt or interfere with the regular duties of instruction at Princeton University.

SECOND: The parties of the second part agree, each for himself and not for any other that for a period of five years, beginning with the college year 1898-9, they will on or before the first day of January in each college year, pay to and for the use of the party of the first part the sums set opposite their respective signatures.[1]

Such payments shall for convenience be remitted by the parties of the second part to Cornelius C. Cuyler at 44 Pine Street, in the City of New York, for the purpose of transmission to said party of the first part.

This agreement shall bind as well the heirs, executors and administrators of the parties of the second part.

IN WITNESS WHEREOF, the parties have hereunto set their hands and seals the day and year first above written.

Woodrow Wilson

Cyrus H. McCormick
C. C. Cuyler
Cleveland H. Dodge
John L. Cadwalader
J. S. Morgan
Rollin H. Lynde
M. Taylor Pyne
Percy R. Pyne

T MS. S (WP, DLC).
[1] The sums are missing from this copy, but the total giving provided, actually, for an annual payment to Wilson of $2,500, as C. C. Cuyler to WW, Dec. 23, 1898, Vol. 11, divulges.

Notes for a Letter to Cornelius Cuyler Cuyler

[c. May 17, 1898]

these arrangements will release my powers for "quiet hours, continuous thought, uninterrupted labour" thought I might have to change my work to gain time to do my best—systematically

the privilege and duty of serving Princeton becomes also an opportunity to make the most of myself instead of scattering my powers.

WWhw MS. (WP, DLC).

To John Bassett Moore[1]

My dear Mr. Moore,   Princeton, New Jersey, 17 May, 1898.

A young friend of mine, Mr. Henry B. Armes, who lives in Washington, and whose father was until very recently Assistant District Attorney, tells me that he is about to seek employment in the State Department and has asked me to write to you, to say what I can in his behalf. I do so very cheerfully.

Mr. Armes graduated here in 1896. He was not only an excellent student but he also won our thorough respect in every way. I feel quite sure that my colleagues would give him as thorough an endorsement as I can; and that they would all be glad if a place could be found for him. He desires nothing more than a foothold in the Department,—a subordinate appointment, if any such be available. His special training is in the law, and I think he won special distinction as a law student.[2] Certainly no mistake would be made in giving him a chance. He has the making of a first-class public servant in him.

I do not often or willingly write recommendations; but this young fellow seems every way so genuine and deserving that I have not had the heart to decline him.[3]

I have not troubled you with a letter of congratulation on your appointment to the Assistant Secretaryship of State; but I have rejoiced in it as all your friends have, and as I have no doubt every enlightened patriot has also. I would fain believe that such an appointment was the beginning of more ideal things in the public service.

With warm regard,

Very cordially Yours,   Woodrow Wilson

WWTLS (J. B. Moore Papers, DLC).

[1] Assistant Secretary of State, April-September 1898.

[2] Armes received his LL.B. from the Law School of Columbian (now George Washington) University in 1899.

[3] Not until 1902 did Armes secure a position in the State Department. He went to work for the Southern Railroad upon his graduation from law school.

From Archibald Williams Patterson

My Dear Wilson,   Richmond, Va., 5/19/98.

Your letter came just before I left this city on a business trip to the far south, from whence I returned last week.

I greatly appreciate the pains you took to explain and justify your decision touching the University question; and while the announcement of this decision caused me deep regret and sore disappointment the reasons assigned are so potent that I am constrained to acknowledge the prop[r]iety of your course. I can well understand the struggle through which you passed in reaching such a conclusion:—the conflict between natural impulse and the sense of obligation, between the promptings of sentiment and the ties of gratitude, between love for the mother Commonwealth and attachment to the Alma Mater—and you have my sympathy in the "season of deep distress" for which I feel in some sort responsible. It is gratifying to me, however, to know that although the result is a set-back for those who had this matter most at heart, yet the impression which you made upon every one connected therewith has been most favorable. Miles dropped into my office recently, and in speaking of his failure to accomplish the desired object, gave unstinted praise to you for the honesty and candor which had characterized your intercourse with the Committee. I am sure there is not a member of the Board who does not approve the motives which influenced your action, or whose regard for you has suffered any diminution. Indeed, it seems more apparent than ever that you were just the man for the place, your own opinion to the contrary notwithstanding. Let us hope that the time may come when existing causes of separation will be removed, and you can serve the land of your birth without any compunctions of conscience, at least; but if we have to wait until Princeton is willing to give you up, and northern friends no longer protest against the change, I fear there will be a very small remnant of your life left for us, though your days were as many as those of Methuselah.

I am greatly interested in the literary undertaking upon which you are at work. I suspect it is in the field of history, if, indeed, you did not tell me so last summer. No more important subject can engage the attention of the thoughtful student, and much remains to be done along this line on behalf of our own country. Please accept the assurance of my best wishes for your continued success and happiness.

Mrs. Patterson requests me to thank you for your kind remembrance of her, and to say that she hopes to see you and Mrs. Wilson in Richmond next fall.[1]

Sincerely, your friend,   A. W. Patterson

TLS (WP, DLC).
[1] That is, when Wilson was to lecture at Richmond College. See EAW to WW, Feb. 9, 1898, n. 4.

A News Report of a Religious Talk

[May 20, 1898]

MEETING OF THE PHILADELPHIAN
SOCIETY.

Professor Woodrow Wilson was the speaker in Murray Hall last evening. Professor Wilson in the first place called attention to the frequent comparison in the New Testament between the Christian and the soldier. Endurance belongs not only to the soldier but to every occupation in life. No man reaches an end without travelling a hard path, for every endeavor carries with it hardness. From endeavor one must proceed to action. The Christian is to carry the war into the enemy's country. Then from action to circumspection. It goes further here, departing from the military idea that the soldier must obey his captain, who in his turn is subordinate to others. No man that warreth entangleth himself with the things of this life. The Christian soldier must look out for himself. His conscience must tell him what to do. Only those men who can fill themselves with the spirit of Christianity are able to meet troubles calmly.

Our Christian religion is the most independent and robust of all religions, because it puts every man upon his own initiative and responsibility. Then, too, it is the most tender and unselfish of religions, for no one who is a true lover of Christ thinks first of himself. The men who are thinking of their country and their God are the best fighters.

In conclusion Professor Wilson said, "Let the Christian endure hardness and avoid entanglements and then he will have a strong robust religion with which to meet every hardship and trial which may come to him."[1]

Printed in the *Daily Princetonian*, May 20, 1898.
[1] There is a WWhw outline for this talk dated May 19, 1898, in WP, DLC. Wilson used II Timothy 2:3, 4 as his text.

A Newspaper Report of a Commencement Address

[May 25, 1898]

UNIVERSITY SCHOOL.

Able Lecture by Woodrow Wilson
at Commencement.

A large audience composed of the representative people of this city attended the commencement exercises of the University school[1] in Warner hall[2] last evening. The speaker of the evening, Woodrow Wilson, Ph.D., LL.D., of Princeton University, proved very interesting in his address, "Leaders of Men."

The stage was artistically decorated with potted palms and plants of the tropical variety. Besides these the stage was set off with two large American flags at the rear of the stage, between which hung the shield of the school with the letters T. U. S. in gilt upon it. The balcony and supporting pillars were also decorated. . . .

Charles Sherwood[3] then arose to introduce the speaker but he stated that Mr. Wilson hardly needed any introduction to a Bridgeport audience as he had appeared before a number of them in the Contemporary club[4] about four years ago, when his address was spoken of in the highest manner possible.[5]

As Mr. Wilson arose to speak he was greeted with loud applause. He spoke in a pleasing style, using only the choicest language, and expressing himself very clearly and distinctly, making the address a most enjoyable treat to those who were fortunate enough to have been present.

In speaking of the leaders of men Mr. Wilson said that the book was often quite as quickening a trumpet as any made of brass and sounded in the field. The men who act, however, stand nearer to the most of men than do the men who write. The men of learning may be back of the leaders but they are not the leaders. He spoke of several men whose words and thoughts lead the world to-day, but in their own day other men were the leaders of the people. The masses must have their ideas very absolutely put, and are much readier to accept a half truth which is well put, than a whole truth which has many sides of thought.

In speaking of Gladstone Mr. Wilson said that the grand old man was not so decisive in the house of commons as Palmerston or Peel had been before him. His honesty was such that he had to admit what good he could see on the other side. The party likes to be led by a very absolute opinion, and will not admit that there is any reason on the other side. The true leaders are those who act, and people will follow only those whose words are very absolutely put. The general mass of men like to be led by men strong in deeds, and the literary man influences only a few. If, however, there are those who read the works of great men, the knowledge is diffused gradually, and finally leavens the whole mass.[6]

At the close of the address the applause was nearly deafening, the speaker having given one of the best literary treats which has been heard in this city for some time. . . .

While in this city Mr. Wilson was the guest of Mr. and Mrs. George C. Edwards.[7]

Printed in the *Bridgeport*, Conn., *Evening Post*, May 25, 1898.
[1] The University School of Bridgeport, Conn., founded 1892. Vincent Charles Peck was the Headmaster.
[2] In the Y.M.C.A. Building at 259 Main St.
[3] A Bridgeport lawyer.
[4] Organized in 1894 to present speakers and entertainers.
[5] No newspaper report of Wilson's earlier address in Bridgeport can be found. However, the records of the Contemporary Club reveal that he delivered his address, "Political Liberty," at the second meeting of that organization, most probably on October 22, 1894. Philip Hawley Smith to A. S. Link, May 1, 1969.
[6] The text of "Leaders of Men" is printed at June 17, 1890, Vol. 6.
[7] Edwards was president of the Holmes and Edwards Silver Co., the Bridgeport Chain Co., and the Miller Wire Spring Co.

A Final Examination

May 25, 1898.

PRINCETON UNIVERSITY.

EXAMINATION IN THE ELEMENTS OF POLITICS.

1. Analyze the four several elements of the following definition: "A State is a people organized for law within a definite territory."

2. What is Seeley's[1] general classification of States, and to what sort of a State does he apply the adjective 'inorganic'?

3. What is Seeley's analysis of the meaning of Liberty? Upon what conditions and circumstances does he conceive Liberty to depend in the development and government of States?

4. What was taken, in the lectures, as the meaning of the words, "a free people"? What is Freedom and what are the conditions precedent to its safe establishment and exercise?

5. What is a Nation, in the English sense,—as contradistinguished from a Race? How does national character express itself?

6. What does Seeley regard as the apparent, and what as the real, difference between despotism and government by assembly?

7. Explain and comment upon the following sentence from Seeley: "I deny, then, that between the unitary State and the federation or federal State there is any fundamental difference in

kind; I deny that the one is composite in any sense in which the other is simple."

8. What is Seeley's analysis of Self-government? What does he say of the "invention" and influence of representation; and what of the rights of the numerical majority in government?

"I pledge my honor as a gentleman that, during this examination, I have neither given nor received assistance."

Printed examination (WP, DLC).
1 John Robert Seeley, *Introduction to Political Science* (London and New York, 1896), the textbook for this course.

From the Minutes of the Princeton Faculty

5 5′ P.M., Wednesday, May 25th, 1898.

. . . Professors W. Wilson, Daniels & Perry were appointed a Committee to select the Question for the Lynde Debate. . . .¹

1 About the Lynde Debate, see Wilson's diary, June 23, 1876, n. 1, Vol. 1. The question set in 1898 was "Resolved, That the United States should permanently occupy and govern the Philippine Islands." The winners in the debate on June 14, 1898, were Ivy Ledbetter Lee, affirmative, first prize; Matthew Lowrie, negative, second prize; and Robert Livingston Beecher, affirmative, third prize.

From Frederick Stanley Root¹

Dear Sir: New York, May 27, 1898.

THE AMERICAN SOCIAL SCIENCE ASSOCIATION, one of the oldest scientific and literary societies in this country,² by resolution of its Council, on December 17th, 1897, empowered a Committee to select one hundred names of men most prominent throughout the country in Literature, Science and the Arts: nomination by this Committee to render such persons eligible to membership in that Assoc[i]ation.

Whether this group of one hundred men shall remain as a separate section of the Association or shall incorporate themselves under some such name as The National Institute of Arts, Science and Letters, will be determined at a meeting of the proposed body, to be held simultaneously with that of the American Social Science Association in September next.³

The American Social Science Association is now organized in five sections. It has been the parent of several of our most successful educational and sociological organizations, and is willing to assist in the formation of a body of the character now contemplated, in the belief that it can thus aid in doing an effective service to the general cause of American literature and science.

In order to avoid, as far as possible, the influence of personal preferences in the selection of members, the list has been prepared in conjunction with the Council of the Association by a Committee of fifteen, in the composition of which special care has been exercised to secure men familiar with the leaders throughout the country in Art, Science and Letters.

The principal object of the proposed organization is to bring together as a corporate body those individuals who are recognized by the country at large as representative men in their respective branches and to promote social intercourse among its members.

An annual meeting will be held (probably at Saratoga,) at the close of August or in the first part of September in conjunction with the regular meeting of the American Social Science Association.

Further accessions to membership in this body will be determined by its own action after organization.

Your name has been proposed by the Committee of fifteen and accepted by the Council of the American Social Science Association, and you are cordially invited to become a member of the new body. Your acceptance of the election hereby tendered will be signified by sending the enclosed blank to the Secretary of the American Social Science Association, and you will be duly notified of further progress in the scheme of organization.

The dues will not exceed five dollars a year.

It is particularly requested that you will give an immediate answer to the Secretary.[4]

Fredk. Stanley Root,   General Secretary.

Proposed by Charles Dudley Warner
Sec. by Wm. D. Howells & F. Marion Crawford

Printed letter signed with hw additions (WP, DLC) with WWhw notation on env.: "Ans. 28 May '98." Encs.: engraved invitation to membership in the American Social Science Association, dated May 27, 1898, and printed list of proposed members.

[1] Author, former Congregational clergyman, and, at this time, General Secretary of the American Social Science Association.

[2] Founded in 1865 and modeled after similar societies of recent origin in Europe, it had two principal objectives: "to gather all the information within reach, both at home and abroad, with regard to Social Science in all its branches; and second, to diffuse this information throughout and beyond our country." "Introductory Note," *Journal of Social Science*, 1 (June 1869), 3, and Henry Villard, "Historical Sketch of Social Science," *ibid.*, pp. 5-10.

[3] The group selected by the committee was elected to the Social Science Association at the annual meeting of 1898 and later that same year organized the National Institute of Arts and Letters for the "furtherance of the interests of literature and the fine arts."

[4] Wilson's reply is missing, but he returned an affirmative response and was elected to the Social Science Association and the National Institute of Arts and Letters in 1898.

From Joseph Ruggles Wilson

My precious Woodrow,   N. Orleans, May 29, 1898

I have been quite sick—am better, much—expect to leave for Richmond, 30th. My address there will be 113 East Franklin St. I have resigned my Clerkship[1] you will be glad to learn and my successor (Dr. W. A. Alexander of Clarksville, Tenn.,[2] a capital man) will at once take hold of affairs so as to relieve me of care. Thus I may get to Princeton earlier than I had at first supposed. But as the Smith girls[3] are going, there may not be room should they stay as long as they expect to do. I have seen them, and think very highly of both.

Love to dearest Ellie & the children,

Your affectionate, but weak,   Father

ALS (WP, DLC).

[1] That is, his position as Stated Clerk of the General Assembly of the Presbyterian Church in the United States, which he had held since 1865.

[2] The Rev. Dr. William Addison Alexander, Professor of Bible Literature at Southwestern Presbyterian University in Clarksville, Tenn.

[3] Lucy Marshall and Mary Randolph Smith of New Orleans.

An Outline of a Speech[1]

PATRIOTISM

Princeton, 30 May, '98.)   (Outline

The WORD.   The TIME.

A SENTIMENT? ENERGY of CHARACTER beyond SELF-INTEREST.

A sentiment *NOT of TASTE, but of DEVOTION,* involving *DUTIES based on the NATURE of the OBJECT.*

Object of NATIONAL LIFE, CHARACTER.—*ONLY THIS WORLD—*
    (flame to flame) (Thought to thought)

Days of *ACHIEVEMENT, DAYS OF PEACE.—VISION—*

Let your minds take fire by CONTACT
    (1) We must "remain *a nation yet,* the rulers and the ruled" "organized for law."
    (2) "Some *sense of duty*";
    (3) "Something of a *faith*";
    (4) "Some *reverence for the laws* ourselves have made";
    (5) "Some *patient force to change* them when we will";
    (6) "Some *civic manhood* firm against the crowd."

An *INTELLECTUAL and DEBATING POLITY.* We should be
    Studious of the life of the nation.
    Studious of the *conditions of practical success* in politics
    Fearless in criticism; but *fearful of radical change.*
    Partisans of the right.
    Unclouded by books,—unduped by men.
    Lovers and followers of good men.

WWT MS. (WP, DLC).
    1 The following document gives an account of this affair.

A Newspaper Report of a Speech

[June 4, 1898]

PROFESSOR WOODROW WILSON IN ALEXANDER HALL,
MONDAY EVENING.

It has been a custom, more or less closely observed, to wind
up Decoration Day in town with a public oration or address. This
year the custom was not omitted. Professor Woodrow Wilson was
selected, and kindly consented, to deliver an oration on "Patriotism." This was done in Alexander Hall of the University. It was
not under the auspices of the veterans, the Grand Army of the
Republic, but of a cognate body, "The Princeton Battle Monument
Association."1 Professor H. C. Cameron, its President, presided.
There was present a very good audience, though it did not look
like a large body, the reason being the vast size of the house,
which has been constructed for special emergencies. But it was
much larger than can ever be gathered in Princeton except on
very extraordinary occasions.

It was a graceful act in Professor Wilson to accept the invitation to deliver this oration. It was not a commemoration of the
war for the Union, though delivered on Decoration Day, but a
laudation of patriotism, in its broadest sense and extent. If anything, it commemorated rather therefore the War of Independence, the spirit of '76. The oration had no political drift, but was
the utterance of a sentiment, native to every man, and which
ought to be a culture. There was a calm, lucid, forcible, chaste
and elegant presentation of the subject in hand. It was full of wit
and wisdom, and carried the audience. Professor Wilson is a fine
writer and speaker, and is always heard with pleasure. He does
not write his discourses, nor did he, on Monday evening, that we
saw, use a scrap of paper with notes, to keep him in the line of
thought and delivery; yet the address was flawless from beginning to end. We could wish to read it and that all our citizens had
heard it. Had it been written out, we should have been glad to
have obtained a copy for publication. No synopsis that we could
give from simple hearing would be satisfactory, else we would
give one. We will only add it was full of striking thoughts, well
expressed, gems of sentiment, wisdom and wise policy.

Professor Cameron opened the meeting with a patriotic address, such as few are able to give, and then introduced the
speaker, who was vociferously received then and at the end. Dr.

Cameron's remarks, too, were well timed and given with free utterance. The whole of the exercises were closed by the audience, led by the organ singing "My Country 'Tis of Thee."

Printed in the *Princeton Press*, June 4, 1898.
    [1] Incorporated on February 4, 1887, for the purpose of erecting a suitable monument to the Battle of Princeton. Progress was slow, and not until October 1907 was a site obtained at the intersection of Bayard Lane and Nassau Street. At this point, the Princeton Battle Monument Association disbanded, and its work was carried forward by a Princeton Battle Monument Commission consisting of representatives from Princeton and the State of New Jersey. A monument by Frederick MacMonnies was dedicated by President Harding on June 9, 1922.

To Gellert Alleman[1]

My dear Mr. Alleman,   Princeton, 8 June, 1898

Pardon my delay in replying to your letter of May 29. The fact is, that I know of only one good account of the working of our honour system, and, amidst the rush of small tasks that crowd the end of the college year, I did not have time to look its whereabouts up. I now know that it appeared in *Harper's Weekly* in the first number for June, 1895.[2] The account is thoroughly trustworthy and candid.

Our satisfaction with the system and its operation is entire and enthusiastic. It has worked a sort of regeneration, and it has never since its establishment been for a moment discredited or in danger of missing success. But its establishment should not be "by authority." It ought to come from the students.

In haste,   With warmest regard,   Woodrow Wilson

ALS (WC, NjP).
    [1] Instructor in Chemistry at the University of Maine.
    [2] "Student Honor in Examinations at Princeton," *Harper's Weekly*, XXXIX (June 1, 1895), 509-10.

From Walter Hines Page

My dear Mr. Wilson: [Cambridge, Mass.] June 8, 1898

I take the liberty to trouble you to give me your opinion, if you will, whether an edition of Bagehot would, as you look at it, be a practicable publishing enterprise. I have said nothing about it officially to our people here, but the subject has been coming up at times in my mind. My recollection is that no edition of him has ever been published in the United States except the edition that was put forth some years ago by an insurance company in Hartford,[1] and I do not know that this was ever put upon the market, or whether it was merely a sort of private enterprise. How much is Bagehot read or likely to be read in future, and how large a part of him may fairly be considered live literature? I have no right to take your time to answer such professional questions as these, but in view of the disappointments that you have given me concerning Atlantic articles, I feel a certain necessity to get even with you in other ways.

And I will trouble you with one other question, if I may. Where are you going to spend the summer? Of course you will plan for your own discomfiture by answering such a question, but I will put it and see how generous and self-sacrificing you really are.

With all good wishes

Very sincerely yours,　Walter H. Page

TLS (Houghton Mifflin Letterpress Books, MH).
[1] A citation to this edition appears in n. 1 to "Walter Bagehot.—A Lecture," printed at Feb. 24, 1898.

From the Minutes of the Trustees of Princeton University

Princeton, N. J., June 13th, 1898.

. . . The Special Committee on University Affairs reported. The Report was accepted, approved, its recommendations adopted, and is as follows:

Report of Committee on University Affairs.

To the Board of Trustees of Princeton University.

In December, 1896, a Special Committee was appointed by you to make investigation of the several departments of the University, with a view of reporting to the Board such suggestions as might be of general advantage to the institution, and more especially to report a plan of re-organization of the School of Science, if it should seem desirable.

Mr. Charles E. Green, Mr. James W. Alexander, Mr. McCarter, Mr. McCook, Dr. Craven, Dr. Dixon and Dr. Stewart were appointed that Committee.[1]

At the meeting of the Board held on June 11th, 1897, that Committee made a written report of progress which was received and approved by the Board. The Committee was continued with the addition to its number of the President of the University.[2]

During the subsequent months the Chairman, Mr. Green, on account of the prolonged illness and resulting death of his son, was not able to call the Committee together. The great loss this University sustained in the death of Mr. Green deprived this Committee of its Chairman. At the meeting of the Board in

[1] See the Princeton Trustees' Minutes printed at Dec. 10, 1896. This is the only time that Thomas Nesbit McCarter has been mentioned as a member of this committee.
[2] *ibid.*, printed at June 14, 1897.

March last, Mr. Alexander was allowed to resign from the Committee; Mr. Pyne and Dr. Frazer were added to the Committee, and Dr. Stewart was appointed Chairman.[3]

Since then the Committee has prosecuted its work with diligence and thoroughness. Six meetings, each of several hours duration, have been given to the consideration of the important matters committed to us. Individual members of the Committee, chief of whom is the President of the University, have given much thought and time outside of the Committee meetings to these matters.

We are of the opinion that few, if any, of the general or detailed affairs of this University have escaped the attention of your Committee, and we are happy to report to you today our unanimous conclusions.

A year ago this Committee sent to the Faculty a series of questions, touching matters in which the Committee desired information from that body. The questions addressed to the Professors were eleven and are as follows:

Dear Sir: June 10th, 1897.

Will you kindly reply to the following questions, by the 25th, and address them to Trenton, N. J.

I. What topics are taught in your department? Give names of your assistants. Are their methods and work satisfactory?

II. How many hours a week do you give instruction? How many by lecture? How many by recitation?

III. What text books, if any, do you use?

IV. Give nature and number of written exercises, if any, required by you during the year.

V. Do you give any instruction to students other than that given in the recitation room? Specify its nature.

VI. What laboratory work, if any, have you with students?

VII. Are the studies in your department properly coordinated with others? What changes, if any, should be made?

VIII. Should required studies be increased? Should the number of electives be increased or reduced?

IX. Do students come to you properly prepared? If not, what is the nature of the defect? What remedy have you to suggest?

X. What suggestions have you to make for the improvement of your department?

XI. Have you published any book or article in any form during the past year? Give title or titles.

Yours truly,   Charles E. Green, Chairman.

[3] *ibid.*, printed at March 10, 1898.

Those addressed to the Instructors were seven and are as follows:

Dear Sir: June 10th, 1897.

Will you kindly reply to the following questions, by the 25th inst., and address them to Trenton, N. J.

    I. What topic do you teach?

    II. How many hours a week do you give instruction?

    III. If unable to meet your classes, do you endeavor to have another instructor meet them?

    IV. What text books do you use?

    V. Give nature and number of written exercises, if any, required by you during the year.

    VI. Do you give any instruction to students other than that given in the recitation room? Specify its nature.

    VII. What laboratory work, if any, have you with students?

        Yours truly,   Charles E. Green, Chairman.

We have carefully and in detail considered the fifty three replies, many of them being voluminous, which we received to these questions. These replies and an abstract of the replies which has been made, accompany this report as a part thereof.

It is almost impossible to make accurate generalizations from this material, but some broad, general remarks may not be without their value.

1. It appears that our curriculum embraces a wide range of subjects; classified into several great departments, and with few exceptions properly arranged and co-ordinated. Most of our Professors are permitted to devote themselves to particular departments, and thus have opportunity to specialize.

2. It appears that our Faculty is not overburdened with a heavy schedule of class-room work. The average number of hours per week for each professor seems, from the replies received, to be about ten, while some Professors have as few as two and others as high as sixteen.

The methods of the various Professors differ widely: Some using the lecture system exclusively; some almost exclusively using the oral recitation; while the majority rely on a combination of the oral recitation and lecture, or lecture with written recitations or quizzes. The proportion of lectures to oral recitations seems to be about as one to two. It appears that the professors are uniformly wise in adapting their method to their subject.

3. There is a large number of required text books in use, and

a still larger number of reference and collateral reading books in the lists furnished the students by the Professors.

4. Few of the Professors are giving instruction outside of the class-room for compensation, but many of them seem to be ready to render, and actually do render, extra help to those students who need or who seek it from them.

5. Our laboratories are all full and some are overcrowded with students working under the personal direction of the Professors or their assistants.

6. The literary activity of the Professors greatly varies. Some have published much, some nothing at all. All that has been published seems to have been of high order of excellence, and to have brought credit to the writer and to the University.

The policy of the University is to make the schedule of each Professor sufficiently light to admit of private study, investigation, and writing, and your Committee commends those Professors who have availed themselves of the opportunity thus accorded them, and ventures to express the hope that all of our Faculty may be diligent in these directions.

7. The information obtained from personal interviews and investigations, and from other answers in writing to the foregoing inquiries is embraced in the following classification:

Administration, Discipline, Curriculum, Academic Faculty,
Scientific Faculty, and Needs of the University.
We will consider these in their order:

I. Administration.

In its report to the Board made June 11th, 1897, the Committee used the following language:

"The Committee are clearly of the opinion that one of the most pressing needs of the institution at this time is a University Secretary. His office should, in a measure, correspond to the confidential clerk of a great business house. The University has become a great business concern. It cannot longer proceed with the old fashioned methods unchanged. Such an officer should aid in the organization of the President's and Dean's offices. He should be thoroughly acquainted with the general workings of the institution, conduct the general correspondence and be prepared to give such information as is authorized to be made public, or that patrons or intending patrons may desire and are entitled to have. He should be an alumnus; of business capacity and habit, of established loyalty to trust, prompt, courteous, and of good address, and should have a general acquaintance with the alumni. He should of course be entirely acceptable to the President."

This matter has received further consideration by your Committee, and while it is of the same opinion as a year ago, yet it is clear that the funds of the University will not now justify the expense necessary to secure a competent person to fill this position.

We therefore recommend that for this reason no appointment be made at present.[4]

In our former report we referred to the subject of Deans in the following language:

"In the matter of Administration, the general opinion prevails that the system of Deans should be adopted.

"On this head it is enough to say, that even if the Committee were practically a unit in its favor—which they are not—there seem to be serious difficulties in the way of appointing any of the Professors now in the service of the University as Deans of the Academic and Scientific Faculties; and even if men of high and unquestionable qualifications for these offices were known to your Committee and could be procured, there are absolutely no funds available to pay their salaries.

"The Committee, however, is seriously considering this question, and it may be that upon further light and reflection the Committee will recommend the appointment of Deans."

Your Committee has given the matter the further consideration then promised, and for the reasons then given your Committee does not deem it best to recommend the system of Deans.

But for the better disposition of Faculty business and a step which may possibly lead to this system, we recommend that in order to secure a more efficient administration of the affairs of the University, the Faculty of the University be divided into two Sub-Faculties, to be known respectively as the Academic Faculty and the School of Science Faculty; the former being composed of those Professors and Assistant Professors whose duties pertain mainly to the Academic Department, and the latter being composed of those Professors and Assistant Professors whose duties pertain mainly to the School of Science; that the President, or in his absence the Dean, shall preside over each Sub-Faculty; that the proceedings of the two Sub-Faculties be reported regularly to the Faculty of the University at its stated meetings; that in all ordinary cases the action of the Sub-Faculties in respect to the admission, standing, and discipline of students be final and the

---

[4] As has been noted earlier, a Secretary of the University was not appointed until 1901.

University Faculty shall deal mainly with questions pertaining to the general policy of the University.[5]

It is also recommended that the President prepare for the Curriculum Committee a list of the Professors and Assistant Professors, who, in his judgment, should constitute the new Sub-Faculties referred to in the foregoing recommendation.

It is believed that this arrangement will materially improve the administration of the University and accomplish much, if not all, that is aimed at in the suggestion respecting the appointment of Deans.

Your Committee is further of the opinion that the Board has not assigned that importance to the Committee of the Faculty appointed to meet the Board at each of its meetings, that its dignity and the possibilities of its usefulness as one of the bonds of union between the two bodies warrant.

We therefore recommend that the By-Laws of the Board be revised to the effect that in the general order of the docket of each stated meeting it be provided that immediately after the presentation of the President's and Dean's reports a Committee of the Faculty may appear and present the written and oral communications that the Faculty may have committed to it for the Board.

II. Discipline

Your Committee has had several matters connected with the Discipline of the University under its consideration. The administration of discipline over an under-graduate body of eleven hundred students presents grave, perplexing, and intricate problems. It is the last place for doctrinaires and martinets to exploit their views and gifts. Many considerations must always weigh in the solution of these problems, and a righteous expediency must be consulted.

Your Committee has heard various criticisms of the discipline of the University, and has not failed to give heed to all; so far as the time at its disposal would admit.

It is believed that the re-organization already effected in the Committees of the Faculty of the School of Science has removed the ground for most of these criticisms, and that the re-organization of the University Faculty proposed in this report will remove still further occasion for criticism.

The delightful social features of Commencement have in recent years seriously encroached upon the time allotted to the literary exercises to the great detriment of the latter. Your Committee deems this worthy of the consideration of this Board. We understand that an attempt is to be made at this Commencement to correct this abuse. It is to be hoped that the effort will succeed. If it does not, other measures should be tried until the abuse is corrected.

The Registrar's office is overcrowded with work and is inadequately equipped for a speedy and satisfactory disposition of it.

We, therefore, recommend that if the funds of the University allow, the sum of Five Hundred ($500) Dollars be added to the budget to compensate the present clerk to the Registrar for the whole of his time, and to enable the Registrar to employ occasionally additional help.

Your Committee had its attention called to the subject of club-life, but owing to the lack of time necessary to properly consider a subject having so many important bearings upon the life of the University, and to the difference in point of view respecting it existing in the Committee, we are unable to make any recommendations on this subject. But we are of the opinion that it demands thoughtful consideration, and firm and wise disposition, by this Board.

An important part of the discipline, which ordinarily would have come to the attention of your Committee is the subject of Temperance. While recognizing the importance of this matter, your Committee also recognizes the fact that the Board recently appointed a Special Committee to consider it and its report was passed upon at the late December meeting. We, therefore, have no recommendation to make.

III. *Curriculum*

There have been various criticisms in respect to the School of Science and these have all been carefully considered. In the first place it is to be remembered that there has been a steady advance in the entrance requirements until now it is safe to say that little, if any, more could be asked for in that respect.

The curriculum of the B. S. Department is undergoing revision, and it is believed the changes contemplated in the Freshman and Sophomore years will greatly improve the efficiency of the course leading to the B. S. degree, and meet the most obvious criticisms to which the curriculum has been exposed.

It has also been suggested that the course for the C.E. degree ought to be a two year's postgraduate course. This suggestion has been most carefully considered and your Committee has been convinced that it would be unwise to undertake so radical a change as this. They believe, however, that improvements looking toward the increase of professional courses in the Junior and Senior years and the removal of some of the general culture courses from the Junior year to the Sophomore year ought to be made. These changes are already under consideration, and it is expected that a revised curriculum of the C.E. Department will be presented to the Trustees at its present meeting.

The attention of your Committee has been called to the great advantage that would accrue to the students in the C.E. course if there could be provided a Summer School in Geodesy. The Professors and Instructors in this department have been consulted and they think that the establishment of such a school is desirable and feasible. By its establishment some of the work now put into the Academic year could be removed and thus leave room in the curriculum for other, and at present neglected, subjects; and, further, opportunity would be given for out-door work during the most favorable season for it; and, still further, the long vacation would be utilized to some extent, for the professional training of the C.E's.

We, therefore, recommend that the Board authorize the establishment of a Summer School in Geodesy and refer the matter to the President and Faculty for the arrangement of the necessary details.

The attention of the Committee has been called by several of the Faculty to the importance of changing the elective unit from two, which it is now, to three: That is to say, the basis on which electives are assigned their place of importance in the curriculum and in determining the grade of the students, is that of two hours per week. Those Professors, whose electives cover large and important departments, feel that this allottment of time is inadequate and strongly urge that it be increased by the addition of one hour per week. As against this suggestion, it is with great force urged that two hours per week is ample time for many of the less important electives.

Your Committee has given the matter careful consideration and believe that by combining certain co-ordinate related electives, this objection could be removed and the three hours unit be established, and thus secure to the important electives the time which they in reality need, without giving undue value to minor electives.

We would recommend that this matter be referred to the Faculty with a request that they give the subject careful consideration and report to the Board.

The attention of the Committee has also been called to the

fact that the students tend to fall off in their attention to study during the Junior and Senior years; and the question as to what can be done to remedy this condition of affairs has been considered.

It is true that the lecture system, which prevails in the Junior and Senior years, has a tendency to relieve the students from the necessity of daily application to study. It is admitted too that students have facility in discovering the courses of lectures which involve the least expenditure of strength on their part. Nor must it be forgotten that the increasing fascination of undergraduate life, with its club-houses and its various athletic, social, and musical organizations, have a tendency to divide the attention of the students and diminish their interest in serious intellectual work. It is difficult to see how these tendencies can be counteracted. On the other hand, however, it must be borne in mind that the curriculum of Princeton University contemplates a rigid course of required work in the Freshman and Sophomore years, that in the Junior year six out of fifteen hours of the curriculum are occupied in required work on serious and difficult subjects. And further, that in both Junior and Senior years it will be found that students who choose some easy subjects also choose some difficult ones; so that the condition of things is really not so bad as it at first appears.

It will be found too, that in Senior year especially, many of the students who are choosing subjects in which they can pass examination with but little study are in many cases doing this in order that they may have more uninterrupted time for private collateral reading upon the subjects in which they have the deepest interest and which lie nearest to their life work.

It must be admitted, however, that there is, and in all probability there will always be a class of men in the University who are incorrigibly indolent and who will endeavor to secure their degree with the least possible outlay of effort. The University needs a decided intellectual quickening; without this, improvements in the curriculum, no matter how admirable they may be, will have but little effect.

To be more specific, however, there are two classes of student who should be thought of. In the first place this question is how to get more work done by the class of men who are dull, indifferent, indolent—in fact the lower half of the class. It is possible that it may be best to limit the right to take an elective course of study to those who earn it in their Freshman and Sophomore years. In other words, it may be a question whether for the ordinary pass-man there should not be a prescribed curriculum running through to the end of the Senior year. This is only a suggestion, and it may be found that there would be greater objection to it than is now made to the present system.

In the second place it is very important that some plan should be devised to secure a larger amount of work and a better quality of it from our better students; that is for those who under our present system are candidates for general or special honors. According to our present plan the same paper is set the pass-man and the honor man. It is the fact that one gets a higher grade "first group" on the paper that constitutes him an honor man.

We have, moreover, two systems that are working side by side. We have the old system whereby general honors are assigned on the basis of a computation of grades through one's entire curriculum. There will always be those who will prefer to strive after what is called general excellence rather than devote themselves exclusively to a special group of homogeneous studies. Moreover, the ambition to take general honors will very naturally lead a man, if he has one hard subject like Mathematics, to take a number of easy studies as his electives in which he can secure a first group with very little difficulty; a day or two of devotion to a syllabus being, it is said, sufficient in some cases.

If now we turn to the catalogue we shall find that last year the special honors reported are one in Philosophy; two in History, Jurisprudence and Politics; three in Classics; two in Modern Languages; one in English; two in Mathematics; three in Physical Science; showing that only a very small percentage of the class crave, under present conditions, the distinction of special honors. And yet, there can hardly be room for question that our success in fostering the intellectual life and in turning out a high type of students must depend very largely upon the ability to induce men at the beginning of their Junior year to give themselves to advanced study in some department.

In order to do this, it would be well to institute certain Honor Schools; seven would be sufficient: 1. Philosophy; 2. Jurisprudence, Politics, Political Economy; 3. History, Art, Archaeology; 4. Ancient Languages; 5. Modern Languages; 6. Mathematics and Physical Science; 7. Natural Science. It might be well to require from the members of these schools a smaller amount of time per week for lectures than is required by other men, say ten hours instead of fifteen.

It would be best probably, that their whole schedule time should be given to subjects strictly within the purview of their honor subjects, except, of course, that in the Junior year they should not be excused from the required studies (occupying six hours of that year).

These honor schools would, of course, cover a definite area of instruction in each case and the Professors and Instructors in each school would therefore be definitely known. It would be possible for each school to publish annually its own scheme of lectures, and in this way high class students might be drawn to Princeton in the Junior and Senior year for the special attractions that might be offered them in these schools.

Moreover, it would be found that a body of forty or fifty men in the Junior and Senior years distributed among several honor schools, would form the nucleus of intellectual effort which, because of its visibility and definiteness, would have a marked effect upon the general intellectual tone of the University. Moreover, the men in these schools would be in much closer relations with the Professors in the schools to which they belong, and thus a new and most important bond would be created between the teaching and the student body.

We recommend that the President be requested to elaborate this scheme and present the same at an early meeting of the Board.[6]

IV. *Academic Faculty*

Your Committee has carefully considered the work and efficiency of the several Professors and Instructors in this Faculty, and desire to bear testimony to the uniformly high character and faithful service of these honored servants of the University. We cannot ignore the fact that in the course of time, and that perhaps a short time, it will be necessary for some of our most faithful Professors to be relieved of a portion, or all, of their work. We have no recommendations to make at present concerning these.

We would recommend that the resignation of Prof. Duffield, which was presented to this Board at its meeting in June, 1893, and was then laid upon the table, be now taken from the table and be accepted, with expression of grateful appreciation of the long and valuable service Prof. Duffield has rendered this University and of our high personal regard for him.

We would recommend that Prof. Duffield be made Professor emeritus of Mathematics, at a salary of $1700, and that he be requested to continue to administer the charitable funds of the University, for which he shall receive the sum of $300 per an-

---

[6] Patton never responded to this recommendation.

num. This action is to take effect at the beginning of the next Academic year.

We recommend that beginning with the next Academic year the salary of Dr. Cameron be $2000 instead of $2500.

V. *Scientific Faculty*

Your Committee gave the same careful consideration to the Faculty of the School of Science that it did to the Academic Faculty. As already stated in this report, the re-organization of this Faculty has removed the ground for most of the criticisms made respecting the School of Science, and it is hoped that the remaining occasion for criticism will entirely disappear upon the adoption of the contemplated changes in the curriculum. We have discovered uniform fidelity and ability in the Faculty of this school.

We have had under very careful consideration the suggestion that the students in the B. S. course should have required Latin throughout the Freshman year, and the new curriculum for that course contemplates this modification. This change, and the subsequent addition to the Faculty of an Instructor in Latin, meet the approval of your Committee,

The Mathematic Department has been greatly strengthened by the addition of Dr. Lovett,[7] who has proved himself to be a remarkably strong addition to the Faculty. The C.E. students in Mathematics are under his exclusive instruction. It will be necessary to increase Dr. Lovett's salary by $1000 at the beginning of the next Academic year.

Prof. Guyot Cameron[8] was promised upon his coming to Princeton, that at the beginning of the next Academic year his salary should be increased in the sum of $500.

[7] Edgar Odell Lovett, born Shreve, Ohio, April 14, 1871. A.B., Bethany College, 1890; M.A., Ph.D., University of Virginia, 1895; Ph.D., University of Leipzig, 1896. Professor of Mathematics, West Kentucky College, 1890-92; Instructor in Astronomy, University of Virginia, 1892-95; Lecturer in Mathematics at the University of Virginia and the University of Chicago, 1897. Instructor in Mathematics, Princeton, 1897-98; Assistant Professor of Mathematics, 1898-1900; Professor of Mathematics, 1900-1905; Professor of Astronomy, 1905-1908. First President of Rice Institute (now Rice University), 1908-46. Contributed numerous articles on geometry, mechanics, and mathematical astronomy to American and European journals. Died Aug. 13, 1957.

[8] Arnold Guyot Cameron, born Princeton, N. J., March 4, 1864, the son of Prof. Henry Clay Cameron. A.B., Princeton, 1886; A.M., 1888; Ph.D., 1891. Professor of French and German, Miami University, 1888-91; Assistant Professor of French, Sheffield Scientific School of Yale University, 1891-97. Professor of French, Princeton, 1897-1900; Woodhull Professor of French, 1900-1905. After leaving Princeton University in 1905 he was active as a writer and editor and served on the staff of the *Wall Street Journal*, 1912-16. Wrote many articles on economics and international affairs and was the author of several textbooks in modern languages. Died July 29, 1947.

Prof. Loomis, Mr. Phillips, and Mr. Sylvester[9] all deserve, and should receive, increase of salary. Mr. Carter,[10] Instructor in French, has resigned, and his work can, without serious difficulty, be assigned to the remaining Instructors in that department.

As the budget of the School of Science shows a very considerable deficiency, it was necessary for your Committee to reduce this deficiency as much as possible by resorting to what is always a painful, though in this case, a necessary duty, of reducing salaries.

We, therefore, recommend that Prof. Rockwood's salary be reduced in the sum of $900; Prof. Huss'[11] salary in the sum of $500; Mr. Brooks'[12] in the sum of $200.

We recommend further, that the services of an Instructor in French be dispensed with, and that the budget be thus relieved of $800. These reductions relieve the budget of the School of Science in the sum of $2,400.

We would recommend that if the funds of the School of Science admit, that $1,000 be devoted to securing an Instructor in Latin; that Prof. Lovett's salary be increased $1000; Prof. Loomis's salary by $300; Prof. Phillips' salary $300; Prof. Cameron's salary $500; and Mr. Sylvester's salary $150; a total addition to the budget of the School of Science of $3,250.

VI. *Needs of the University*

Your Committee carefully considered the general affairs of the University with reference to its needs, and had before it several suggestions for strengthening the various departments of the Institution. We have duly weighed these suggestions, and, as our conclusions touching this part of our duty, we offer the following recommendations:

1. We are impressed with the necessity of equipping our Physical Department. There ought to be a full complement of Professors and Instructors and adequate Laboratory facilities. To secure this, an endowment of $500,000 is needed.

2. It is the judgment of your Committee that an earnest effort should be made to adequately endow the department of History and the department of Economics. To accomplish this even in a very imperfect way, $100,000 is needed in each department.

[9] Elmer Howard Loomis, Assistant Professor of Physics; Alexander Hamilton Phillips, Instructor in Mineralogy; and Charles Frederick Silvester, Preparator in Anatomy.

[10] Benjamin Franklin Carter, who in fact stayed on another year as Instructor in French.

[11] Hermann Carl Otto Huss, Professor of Modern Languages and Literature.

[12] John Milton Brooks, Instructor in Mathematics.

3. We would recommend that as soon as the funds of the Institution will admit, the department of Jurisprudence and Politics ought to be developed and strengthened by the creation of a chair in Politics; or at least by granting an assistant in this department.

4. Many of the members of the School of Science Faculty called the attention of your Committee to the need for a Professor of Architecture. We have all the necessary equipment for giving instruction in co-ordinate branches, and the only thing that prevents us from giving a course in Architecture, and so retaining a considerable number of students who now go to other institutions to study Architecture, is a Professorship in this department. We cordially approve the suggestion of these Professors and recommend that such a Professorship be created when the necessary funds are secured.

5. There is imperative need for more Fellowships. The department in [of] English, one of the most important in our curriculum, has no Fellowship. And the Classical Department has had a Fellowship, which, in the past, has been dependent upon such occasional gifts as came to it from time to time. Both of these departments should have at least two Fellowships, and we recommend, that at as early a date as possible, endowments be sought for two Fellowships in English and two in Classics, of which the Classical Fellowships are the more important.

There is at present one Fellowship in Modern Languages which is divided equally between French and German. In the judgment of your Committee it is desirable that there should be another Fellowship in Modern Languages, and one of the two should be devoted to German and one to the Romance Languages. We recommend that endowments be sought for these Fellowships.

6. In order to develop our higher University work and to secure graduate students, it is necessary for us to have graduate Fellowships. There should be at least six of these Fellowships endowed as early as possible. We recommend that endowments for these be sought.

7. Several of the Professors have called the attention of your Committee to the conspicuous deficiencies in the Library in their several departments. This we regard as a matter of importance, and we would, therefore, recommend to the Board that the friends of the University be advised that our Library is in need of endowment in several departments of literature.

8. Your Committee would call the attention of the Board to the several "seminar" rooms, which at present are not available, because of lack of funds for their proper furnishing and equipment. This lack should be supplied at an early date, that the

splendid accommodations which we now have for "seminar" work may be utilized.

9. Your Committee was impressed with the excellent work which Prof. Westcott is doing in connection with the Sophomore class at an annual cost of about $500, and would suggest to the Board that this work deserves encouragement.

10. We would recommend that the attention of the Committee on Grounds & Buildings be called to the necessity for more recitation rooms, and would suggest that the need may be temporarily met at a small cost to the University by the division of some of the larger existing recitation rooms.

In concluding our report, we deem it proper to say that we have practically exhausted the various matters committed to our consideration, and have discharged, to the best of our ability, the duty assigned us. We asked to be discharged. Respectfully submitted,

Princeton, June 13th, 1898.   By order of the Committee
                     (Signed)   Geo. B. Stewart, Chairman.

After the adoption of the foregoing Report, it was

Resolved, That the Report of the Committee be printed as a private document for confidential use.

Ellen Axson Wilson to Albert Shaw

Princeton, New Jersey June 14, 1898.

Plan impossible[1] because of Mr. Wilson's absence in south. Will be away ten days.   E. A. Wilson.

TC tel. (in possession of Virginia Shaw English).
[1] See A. Shaw to WW, June 13, 1898, printed as an Enclosure with EAW to WW, June 17, 1898.

A News Report

[June 14, 1898]

WOODSON WILSON
In the City and Will Deliver
His Address This Evening.

Prof. Woodson Wilson, of Princeton University, who will this evening deliver the annual literary address before the students of Vanderbilt University, has arrived in the city, and is the guest of Dean W. F. Tillett, of the Theological Department.[1]

Prof. Wilson was out when a Banner reporter called to see him this morning, but it is understood he will remain in Nashville no longer than to-morrow evening.

To-day at 2 o'clock Prof. Wilson met a number of invited guests at a dinner in his honor, given by Dean and Mrs. Tillett. Judge and Mrs. Robert Ewing, relatives of Prof. Wilson, will entertain him at dinner this evening.

A scholar of such renown and popularity as Prof. Wilson is received with much pleasure in university circles, and the Vanderbilt society is happy over the presence of their distinguished guest. The address will be delivered in the university chapel at 8 o'clock this evening.

Printed in the *Nashville Banner*, June 14, 1898.
1 Wilbur Fisk Tillett, Professor of Systematic Theology, Dean of the Theological Faculty, and Vice-Chancellor, Vanderbilt University.

A News Report of Wilson's Delivery of "Democracy"

[June 15, 1898]

PROF. WILSON SPEAKS
Delivers Annual Address Before
Literary Societies of
Vanderbilt University.
ON DEMOCRATIC GOVERNMENTS
Democracy Defined in a Scholarly Address—
Commencement Exercises Take Place This Morning
at the University.

The audience that gathered last night in the chapel of Vanderbilt University to hear the address before the literary societies by Prof. Woodrow Wilson, of Princeton University, was large and cultured. Not a seat was available when Prof. Wilson began his address.

It was a scholarly address and was heard with interest by the audience. Chancellor [James Hampton] Kirkland introduced Prof. Wilson as one whom all Vanderbilt students knew from the study of his text books and his "Life of Washington." . . .1

Printed in the *Nashville American*, June 15, 1898.
1 Here follows a paraphrase of "Democracy," printed at Dec. 5, 1891, Vol. 7.

From Ellen Axson Wilson

My own darling   Princeton June 15 [1898]

I am feeling very remorseful that I have not managed to write you before—in spite of the distractions and demands upon me!

I fully expected to write Monday night and again last night. But on Monday night I was with the girls at the orchestra concert on the campus[1] until half past ten, and last night we had four visitors until the same hour. I ought to have written after that, but was so dead tired after the heat and fatigues of the day that it really seemed impossible. Today it is much cooler—a really charming commencement day, and everything went off beautifully this morning. I am thankful Sister[2] has such a fine day for her trip to the city. She went to the *dance* last night,—also Lucy and Mary![3] George, who you know, intended to go alone, persuaded them to go with him for an hour just to see what it looked like. They all enjoyed it very much. George in his Paris dress suit looked like a prince sure enough! We spend this evening too on the campus of course, and after that for *rest!*—and time I trust for decent letters to my darling.

We are all perfectly well. How I hope the cool change has extended to Tenn. I miss you, and think of you every moment, dear, —and oh *how* I *love* you my treasure, deeply, tenderly, passionately, altogether!   Your little wife,   Eileen.

Much love to all.

ALS (WC, NjP).
  [1] This was a "promenade concert" by "the military band from Annapolis" on the lawn in front of Nassau Hall on Monday evening, June 13, 1898.
  [2] Annie Wilson Howe.
  [3] Lucy and Mary Smith, who were visiting the Wilsons.

From William Preston Johnston[1]

Dear Sir,   New Orleans, June 16th 1898

I have the honor to inform you that the Board of Administrators of Tulane University have authorized me to confer on you the Degree of Doctor of Laws, at our Commencement on June 30th.

I beg leave to say to you that this is not intended as an idle compliment, but with a full recognition of the able and most excellent work you have done for American scholarship in letters, history and political science. The only other recipient of a doctor's degree at this Commencement will be Mr Thomas Nelson Page.

I would be glad to hear from you of your acceptance of our degree; and, if it is convenient and agreeable to you, that you will be my guest on this occasion.[2]

With the felicitations of our authorities, and the highest personal esteem,

        I am Sincerely Yours   Wm Preston Johnston

ALS (WP, DLC).
  [1] President of Tulane University.
  [2] See WW to W. P. Johnston, June 27, 1898.

Two Letters to Ellen Axson Wilson

My own darling,   Clarksville [Tenn.] 16 June, 1898

This is the only paper at hand at this moment, and I *must* use *some*thing to write on. It has made me very unhappy to have to wait so long without writing. But in Nashville I was literally allowed not five minutes leisure, or five minutes by myself. It was Company or Commencement exercises *all the while*. My address was received as favourably as I could wish—everybody seemed enthusiastic about it, genuinely to my surprise, and I was immensely relieved. I saw cousin Hattie[1] two or three times. On Tuesday morning [June 14] I paid them a little visit and saw them *all*. On Tuesday afternoon I took a meal with them. On Tuesday evening they came out (i.e. Cousin Robert, Cousin Hattie, Hoyt, and May)[2] to hear my address. On Wednesday afternoon I made them another call just before leaving, and saw cousin Hattie, Hoyt, Lil.,[3] and another of the boys,—a delightful little chap who went to the station with me to show me the way. Josie[4] came down to hear me speak and spent yesterday (Wednesday) in Nashville. I *had* to stay to the graduating exercises in the morning, and we came up here in the evening. We left Nashville at 5:10 in the afternoon, and *such* a time as we had getting here! About half-way between Nashville and Guthrie (where we change for Clarksville) our engine broke the connecting rod between the driving wheels on one side,—an accident which nearly wrecked the cab of the locomotive and narrowly missed injuring the engineer very seriously. We had to stop and work at the engine for quite an hour and a half. Finally a freight engine came to our assistance from the nearest village—three miles away; we were pulled in to its station, and transferred to another, much later, train. Of course we missed connection at Guthrie; had to wait till one o'clock to be brought to Clarksville; found no conveyances at the Clarksville station; walked a mile and a half in a pitch-dark town; and got to the house at two o'clock A.M.: Add *breakfast at 7* and you have the *data* for determining how like an owl I feel at this moment. But I am quite well, passionately in love with you,—send the warmest and most affectionate messages to all; and am wide enough awake to feel in every fibre of me how entirely I am

                                    Your own   Woodrow

[1] Harriet Hoyt Ewing.

2 Mr. and Mrs. Robert Ewing and two of their children, Hoyt and May.
3 Lillian, another of the Ewings' children.
4 Joseph R. Wilson, Jr.

My own darling,   Clarksville, Tenn., 17 June, 1898

I am a good deal rested now, after a real night's sleep and a good deal of loafing. True, I have been away from home five whole days and have had no letter from my dear one, and it's hard to get the body rested when the heart is heavy; but I know how busy my sweet little wife is and keep my spirits going tolerably well.

There was not much besides my little visits to cousin Hattie's house to make my recollections of Nashville very lively or engaging. The people I could have enjoyed most I saw for but a moment or two, among those who crowded about me after my address. For the rest, I had to use much discourse with Methodist bishops galore, and I was not stimulated. Prof. and Mrs. Tillett, with whom I stayed, were as kind as they could be, but they were *not* interesting, poor souls! It seemed incredible they could have been born in North Carolina! They were New Englanders every inch. The tones of their voices were New England tones,—and the tones of their minds,—and it made me feel queer and uncomfortable in this latitude! I wonder if it can be Methodism that does this?

Ah, my Eileen, how I love you and pine for you, my solace and inspiration! I am wholly and passionately

Your own   Woodrow

Love to *all*. I am perfectly well.

ALS (WP, DLC).

From Ellen Axson Wilson, with Enclosure

My own darling,   Princeton, June 17, 1898.

Visitors, a great batch of calls which had to be made with Sister Annie,—her whole list all in one day!—and many other distractions, entirely prevented my writing yesterday.

I write now in very great haste as Sister leaves this afternoon.

I enclose in this Longman's check. It is nice that they send a hundred, is it not?[1] Sister A. has also deposited today the hundred dollars she borrowed.

I enclose Mr. Shaw's interesting letter—please keep it for me,

—which of course I answered by telegraph,—saying you could not write the article.

I had yesterday a letter from Stock.[2] He is very much worried because he hasn't the money to send Madge South[3] and thinks it must be given up until the Xmas holidays, though it seems to him very important for her to go *now*. I have thought of a plan which will make it quite possible, and that is for her to go in August to Sister Annie in Va.[4] instead of coming all the way back to Boston.[5] Sister Annie is *delighted* at the idea, and it will be pleasant for Madge; George will be there, also the Flynn girls.[6] The cost of ticket from here to East Gloster & back plus the difference in board between Mass. & Va. for the six weeks is $36.00, which will take her to Athens and give her $10.00 extra for "incidentals." It will need a similar sum to bring her back to the Va. springs,—from whence she would go direct to Balt.[7]—and I should like to offer to advance it until the fall. Have you any objection? I know you might have to borrow it yourself! But it seems important. If you think it practicable will you please telegraph me, dear? She is anxious to go at once if she goes at all before all her young friends leave Athens;—and *I* should like her to leave before your return, because I will have no room for her then!

Please excuse this frightful scrawl—desperate haste.

I love you darling beyond measure, I am in every heart-beat,

Your own   Eileen.

ALS (WC, NjP).
  [1] For Wilson's revision of *Division and Reunion*.
  [2] S. Axson to EAW, June 15, 1898, ALS (WP, DLC).
  [3] That is, to send their sister to Athens, Ga., to visit their aunt, Louisa Hoyt Brown.
  [4] Annie Wilson Howe planned to vacation at Dagger's Springs in Virginia.
  [5] To join the Wilsons at East Gloucester, Mass.
  [6] The daughters of the Rev. Dr. John William Flinn, Chaplain and Professor of Philosophy at South Carolina College.
  [7] To the Woman's College of Baltimore (now Goucher College), to which she would transfer from Adelphi Academy.

ENCLOSURE

From Albert Shaw

My Dear Wilson: New York. June 13, 1898.

Please do not say no until you have read this letter to the end. I want you to write for the Review of Reviews a short article of say three or four thousand words on The Hero of Santiago. The person to whom I refer is not Admiral Cervera, but young Hobson. The kind of article I want is not a painfully genealogical one, nor yet a piece of thrilling rhetoric on the Merrimac exploit.[1]

Our people in the office can easily make you up at once a bundle of newspaper biographies and clippings which would, I think, supply all the data you could well use as regards Hobson's career. Just the sort of article I want is the sort I think you would naturally and easily write. You will possibly remember a paragraph that appeared one day last week on the editorial page of the *Evening Post*, in which certain moral and intellectual qualities in Hobson's career were brought to the front and favorably suggested.[2] War is a very bad business of course, even when "our cause it is just," but there is something in Hobson, that seems to have a lesson for the young men of the country. It is both an inspiring lesson and also a reassuring and an encouraging one. At this moment there are some thousands of young fellows graduating from our colleges and universities and stepping into the world of action. Notwithstanding the newspaper jibes at the self-complacent assurance of the annual crop of young graduates, my own opinion is that the great majority of them are rather timid and self-distrustful. Hobson seems to have been at Annapolis the quiet retiring student of the particularly conscientious sort. His subsequent career was that of the studious scholarly fellow who used his brains to the best possible purpose. The chief wealth of this country must always lie in its supply of young men of fine personal qualities, whose patriotism has some of the kind of stuff in it that you talked about before Mrs. Abbe's society[3] and before the Quill Club in New York some months ago.[4] As against a lot of men who are just now using political pulls of every sort to get army commissions or army contracts, and who hope this war will, without much risk to themselves, bring them personal advantages, it is a very reassuring thing to find that the country possesses men like Hobson, who can calmly face death in the line of his duty to his country without making any fuss, and apparently without any thought of seeking anything for himself. I am immensely glad that Hobson was a Southerner, because I believe it will do the whole country good to have a chance to recognize in him the fact that the South somehow does produce a lot of these thoroughbred lads, who have the qualities that make the real gentleman, and who have no superiors in any country, because they are thoroughly fine men.

We want to use this article in our July number.[5] We ought to have it within three or four days. We will pay you from $50 to $75 for it, according to its length, or more if you say so. It is an article that I think you would make easily and with a certain feeling. It seems to me that it would be a good thing somehow to give it the tone of a word spoken to our world of young Americans, particularly of the student type and element. I feel strongly that it does not make much difference what our external policies are, that is to say, whether we annex this or that island, or do not annex, but it is a matter of the most vital importance that we should produce young men of the Hobson quality. We can administer territory, or do anything else that may fall to us as a task, if we have Hobsons enough to draw upon. Of course you are tired just finishing up your school year, but on the other hand you will not have relaxed yet, for I know you can hardly have begun to think fairly of vacations.

With heartiest good wishes, as ever,

Sincerely yours,   Albert Shaw.

P.S.—Please telegraph me at our expense, and mention in telegram whether you want us to send the clippings.

TLS (WP, DLC).
    1 During the blockade of Cuba, Rear Admiral William T. Sampson, commander of the North Atlantic Squadron, conceived a plan to lock the Spanish fleet in Santiago harbor by sinking a large collier, *Merrimac*, in the narrow part of the harbor entrance. Under the command of Lt. Richmond Pearson Hobson of Alabama, the vessel, carrying ten torpedoes for scuttling, sailed into the channel during the early morning of June 3, 1898. Intense shellfire prevented completion of the plan, and the collier was sunk before it could swing broadside at the intended location. Hobson and his crew, unable to escape in a lifeboat, took to the water and were picked up by the Spanish. The exploit gained much attention in the press, and Hobson and his men, subsequently released, were widely feted.
    2 "The Exploit at Santiago," New York *Evening Post*, June 6, 1898.
    3 The City History Club. See the news report of Wilson's speech printed at Dec. 11, 1897.
    4 See the news report printed at Dec. 15, 1897.
    5 An article on Hobson did appear in this issue: William Hayes Ward, "Lieutenant Hobson," New York *Review of Reviews*, xviii (July 1898), 36-41.

To Ellen Axson Wilson

My own darling,   Clarksville, 18 June, 1898

My heart has been greatly lightened to-day by the arrival of your first letter. A separation without constant letters is always more than my spirits can bear. Not your love only but your constant attentions too seem as essential to me as the air itself. My dependence upon you almost frightens me sometimes, my sweet, incomparable little wife.

I have found the dear ones here very sweet and they have made me feel very much at home; but nothing in any degree takes the place of what you give me, and I would be just as uneasy in our own sweet home itself if you were absent from it. Josie is absent all morning and all afternoon at his office, and I do not see much of him. Kate is busy most of the time about the house, for she keeps but one servant and does *all* of her own housework. Little

Alice is ubiquitous and is an attractive little tot,—very bright and funny; but she is not good company *all* the time, and I have spent a good deal of my time correcting proof[1] (to get the decks clear before you send me more) and writing business letters. I have had calls from several gentlemen: Dr. Price and Prof. Fogartie of the University[2] (I knew Fogartie at Davidson College),[3] old Mr. Kennedy,[4] and Mr. Owen (who lived opposite father's when we were here). I shall hear Fogartie preach to-morrow. Dr. Lupton[5] has just resigned the pastorate. Give my warm love to all,— and remember that, for me, the world centres about you. I love you more than I shall ever be able to say or to show: in all my life I am   Your own   Woodrow

ALS (WP, DLC).
  [1] Of the revised edition of *The State*.
  [2] Rev. Dr. Robert Price, Professor of General and Ecclesiastical History, and the Rev. Dr. James Edward Fogartie, Professor of Philosophy, Southwestern Presbyterian University.
  [3] Fogartie was a senior when Wilson was a freshman at Davidson College.
  [4] D. N. Kennedy, Secretary of the Board of Directors of Southwestern Presbyterian University and a close friend of Joseph Ruggles Wilson.
  [5] Rev. Dr. Jonah W. Lupton, pastor of the Clarksville Presbyterian Church, 1872-98.

From Ellen Axson Wilson

My own darling,   [Princeton, N.J.] June 18, 1898

Your first letter has just come, to my great delight;—of course I understood perfectly why you could not write earlier. Am so glad they appreciated "Democracy"; and that Josie had the opportunity to hear it. I can guess how much such intelligent people as Cousin Hattie and Mr. Ewing were delighted.

What a journey you had, to be sure! too bad. But *why* the seven o'clock breakfast? If necessity drove poor Josie to it, you at least might have been spared.

We are all quite well except that Nellie has a little cold from the cool change,—which I *hope* has reached Tenn. Sister Annie & party got off in very good condition yesterday;—little Annie *much* improved.

I enclose Mr. Wilder's characteristic letter![1] I suppose he alludes in the last sentence to Mr. Halsey and Mr. Davis being D. D.'d.[2]

Madge is just going down town on an errand and I am making haste to finish this so that it may get out of town before we are "bottled up" for Sunday. Am very busy making her dress.

Oh how I love you my darling! how I miss you! It is very good to think that the first week ends today, and that *a* week from to-day at the latest I will be in your arms. As ever

Yours devotedly   Eileen.

ALS (WC, NjP).
¹ The letter from William Royal Wilder, secretary of the Class of 1879, is missing.
² Abram Woodruff Halsey and John D. Davis, members of the Class of 1879, both received honorary degrees at the Princeton commencement.

Two Letters to Ellen Axson Wilson

My own darling,   Clarksville, Tenn., 19 June, 1898

Your second letter, with a lot of proof and letters, came to-day. It is *such* a comfort to be in communication again, even if it does mean a deal of letter writing to people I do *not* love as well as to the one I love better than anybody or any*thing* else in the world.

I have planned to leave here, darling, on Thursday morning, the 23rd., speak that evening in Hodgensville,¹ start again early the next morning, and reach Philadelphia on Saturday, the 25th, between twelve and one. If the train is on time, I ought to reach home either at about three or between five and six,*—before* the last train of the afternoon! It is a deep pleasure to be with these dear ones here, and I hate to make so brief a stay; but, ah! how impatient it makes me to even so much as pause on a journey which leads homeward to you!

I have had quite enough to do since I reached here. I read all the proof I brought with me, and answered the letters I brought away, as I told you yesterday, and it has proved a capital way of keeping off home-sickness. Kate is a dear girl, but she is not ex-actly an interesting companion, having neither ideas nor charms out of the common, and I should be hard put to it to kill *much* time with her. Her older sister, Addie, seems most interesting,— the Margaret Miller² of the place, apparently, constantly busy in good works among the poor; and a good talker besides, read in good books, and interested, intelligently interested, in ideas and ideals[.] She seems to have had the time and the taste for think-ing which her prettier sisters lacked, without having any less of sweetness and womanly grace. I think you would find her as at-tractive as I do,—and you know how seldom a woman who is not pretty attracts me. Perhaps a southern woman manages it by dint of grace and sweetness.

My friend Fogartie disappointed me sadly in the pulpit this morning. It was sound doctrine he preached, but the sound overwhelmed the doctrine. He preached like a Methodist rather than like a Presbyterian,—and I cannot take pleasure even in sober sentences rendered in the manner of a big bass drum[.] I told Fogartie afterwards that 'I was glad to have heard him,'—I *am* glad that it's *over*. I met several old acquaintances after service and stayed to hear the choir practice for this evening while a fierce thunder storm raged outside. I was quite inducted into the habits of the place and of the weather.

We have had several thunder storms since I arrived in these parts. I reached Nashville in one. They have lightened the heavy air often enough to make the weather very tolerable. I have suffered very little from the heat so far. I am quite well.

I am rather sorry to have missed the chance to write that article on Lieutenant Hobson. I could (and would) have done it *con amore*. I agree with almost every word of Shaw's excellent letter, and the object he had in view attracts me deeply, as I need scarcely tell you.

Give Miss Lucy and Miss Mary my warm love and tell them I hope they are not going to Morristown the moment I get back to Princeton.

Love unspeakable to my dear ones,—and for your sweet, incomparable self, the whole heart of

Your own   Woodrow

* Probably at 4:11.

1 The Editors have been unable to find any news report of this speech at Lincoln's birthplace.

2 Margaret ("Maggie") Miller of 38 Washington St., Princeton, daughter of the late Rev. John Miller.

My own darling,   Clarksville, 20 June, 1898

Things are going here equably and without noteworthy incident. Last night the several pastors of the churches here said good-bye to Dr. Lupton in a service, at the Presbyterian church, which was really touching and beautiful as a demonstration of inter-denominational good fellowship and a manly expression of admiration and an ardour for the advancement of Christian ideals all along the line. It must have been deeply comforting to Dr. Lupton to discover of a sudden and at the very last how much people of all creeds have trusted and silently admired him. There was some excellent choir music (chiefly by Wilsons). Josie played a violin solo excellently well and with fine feeling, it seemed to me. I was glad to be present,—and longed, as I do whenever anything seems to me to have anything really beautiful and inspiriting in it, for *you*, to whom all such things seem by nature to belong, as being *like yourself*. You stand for me as a sort of standard of what is beautiful and good, and I cannot pay anything a higher compliment than by feeling that *you* would have enjoyed it! That means that it has in it something *suitable to your nature*. You cannot enjoy anything irresponsibly, as I enjoy so many things; and I do not always wish you with me *for your own sake*. I sometimes wish for you selfishly and simply for my own sake. But by every sign I know that I am

Your own   Woodrow

Much love to all

ALS (WP, DLC).

To Albert Shaw

My dear Shaw,   Clarksville, Tennessee. 20 June, 1898.

Mrs. Wilson has already answered your letter about Hobson by telegraph, and of course my absence from home put it out of the question for me to do what you wanted. But she has forwarded the letter to me here, and I want to thank you for it. The trust you put in me in such matters gratifies me more than I can say. Moreover, I subscribe to every word of your letter, and wish with all my heart I could have written as you wished me to of that splendid fellow. Thank you for thinking of me in such a connection, and believe me

With real affection,

Most sincerely yours,   Woodrow Wilson.

TCL (in possession of Virginia Shaw English).

From Walter Hines Page

My dear Mr. Wilson,   [Cambridge, Mass.] June 20, [189]8

It was a great pleasure to receive your letter in which you were kind enough to tell me about Bagehot. One of the many pleasures that I am promising myself this summer is to take up these books and see if there be any practical way to further his fame.

I am still more interested in what you say about your purpose to spend August and part of September in this neighborhood, and one of the penalties that you will have to pay will be to give at least a few hours to me.

By all means send along "A Lawyer with a Style."[1]

Very truly yours,   Walter H. Page

TLS (Houghton Mifflin Letterpress Books, MH).
1 Printed at Feb. 25, 1898.

To Ellen Axson Wilson

My own darling,   Clarksville, Tenn., 21 June, 1898

It is astonishing how time drags when it is a weight holding me back from you! I am having a good time here,—have absolutely nothing to complain of except separation from you, and everything to enjoy and be glad of in my association with these dear ones whom I so love; but generally when I am away from you I am either moving from place to place or busy about engrossing professional work, while here I have a formidable amount of leisure in which to think of you, while Josie is at his office and Kate busy about her household duties. It is painful to love anyone as much as I love you, my Eileen, my darling,—and I don't mean to write about it very much, if you please.

I have been interesting myself in renewing a few old acquaintances here, and comparing former with present appearances. That house on Madison St. whose delicious green colour, behind the cool tones of the trees, we used so much to admire[1] is now a cold gray! That harmony was an accident, after all!

Do you remember the charming little beauty who played the chief rôle in the comic opera in which Dode[2] took part? She has not changed a hair! She has been married quite ten years and has a son who comes up to her (not very high) shoulder, and her husband (as young looking, almost, as she) is a deacon in the church; but it was a delight to see them come into church on Sunday,—as young, as debonnair, as evidently interested in and pleased the one with the other, as a bride and groom,—and the youngster by their side as bright and pleased as they! I wanted mightily to kiss her and tell her how charming she was!

But, for all that, there is one little woman incomparable beside them all, and I am   Her own   Woodrow.

ALS (WP, DLC).
1 When they spent the summer of 1886 with Wilson's parents in Clarksville.
2 His brother, Joseph.

Two Letters from Ellen Axson Wilson

[Princeton, N.J.]

My own darling,   Tuesday morning [June 21, 1898]

It is ten o'clock and I must write a few lines for the 10.30 collection since it may *possibly* reach you before you leave on Thursday morning. Your letter of the 19th just at hand; also one from Father saying he will be here Sat. afternoon "between six & seven." Could have written earlier had not Bob Stirling[1] been in to make a farewell call. He and Ed are both talking of going to Daggers the latter part of the summer. Madge is going to Athens on Friday if she is well enough,—has a very bad cold just now. Oh dear! here is the plumber calling for me!—and Mr. [Andrew F.] West has just been announced too!

I love you dear with all my heart and soul,—I am always and altogether,   Your own   Eileen.

[1] Robert Fulton Sterling, Princeton, 1897, a student at Princeton Theological Seminary.

My own darling,   Princeton June [21, 1898]

Your two sweet letters, of Friday and Saturday have reached me, to my very great comfort. Also the kind telegram.[1] I shall arrange to send Madge South on Friday I think, if she is well; she has rather a bad cold just now. I am very busy finishing her summer sewing; and to do that and at the same time give attention to my guests and the callers who are coming in unusual numbers is so engaging my time and distracting my attention, that I have a most unhappy feeling of neglecting my darling in the matter of letter-writing. But oh how constantly I think of you! It seems to me I never wanted you so much, or felt my heart so melt within me at thought of you, my darling, *my darling*! I am simply abashed sometimes at thought of my own happiness; it seems almost too good to be true. Why should *I* have so much more than anyone else? Suppose it should turn out a dream!—all a mere woman's dream of a perfect lover and an ideal life. Are you sure, dear, that you are really a "hold-me-fast"—Woodrow?

We are all quite well except Mary and Madge who have colds. Cooper[2] is here for the day—to Madge's intense discomfort. Dear love to all.   Your devoted little wife   Eileen.

ALS (WC, NjP).
[1] This telegram, which was probably about Ellen's advance to Margaret Axson, is missing.
[2] Cooper Hoyt, son of the Rev. Dr. Thomas Alexander Hoyt.

From Alexander Witherspoon[1]

My Dear Prof. Wilson: New York, June 21/98.

It was my full intent and wish to call and say "good-bye" to you before leaving Princeton last week as an undergraduate, and

I hope you will accept this note for the will if not for the deed. Let me thank you very cordially for the instruction and pleasure derived in your courses, and also for your kindness to me personally in all our relations. With very kind regards, I am, as ever,

Your true friend,   Alexander Witherspoon.

ALS (WP, DLC) with WWhw notation on env.: "Ans."
[1] Of the Class of 1898, from Louisville, Ky. He became permanently invalided soon after his graduation and died on March 20, 1914.

From Robert Ewing

My Dear Woodrow,   Nashville, Tenn. June 22, 1898

I tried hard last Wednesday afternoon to get to the house in time to bid you goodbye, but on the eve of our departure, things crowded on me so, that I found it impossible. Let me now say though that your few hours with us gave the most genuine pleasure and that some of the thoughts, expressed towards the close of your address, gave me new courage. It is not the first time that words of yours have inspired me. How I wish we could see more of you & yours! If that ship of ours would but come in! She must be in charge of some slow-hiding, dastardly Spaniard who will let the cargo spoil—at least for this generation. Give my kindest regards to your dear wife and love to the little ones.

Very Sincerely   R. Ewing

ALS (WP, DLC) with WWhw notation on env.: "Ans."

To William Preston Johnston

My dear Sir,   Princeton, New Jersey, 27 June, 1898

My telegram[1] has already in part explained my delay in answering your important letter of June 16th. I was away from home, for a stay of a couple of weeks, when it came, and was moving from place to place. Although promptly forwarded to me, therefore, it failed to find me, and has followed me home again. I trust the mishap has caused you no serious inconvenience.

The contents of your letter,—and particularly, let me say, the very cordial terms of kind appreciation in which it is couched,— have given me the deepest gratification. That Tulane University, one of the leading institutions of the South which I love so well, should offer me her highest honorary degree affords me a pleasure and a source of pride of which I cannot speak too warmly; and I should wish, in accepting it, to express in the heartiest

possible manner my gratitude and happiness at being so honoured. I wish it were possible for me to be present at your Commencement; but, since it is not, I trust that you will utter for me
the appreciation I would like to utter in proper person.[2]

    With cordial regard,

                Most sincerely Yours,   Woodrow Wilson

ALS (Johnston Papers, LNHT).
  [1] It is missing.
  [2] Wilson acknowledged receipt of his diploma in WW to W. O. Rogers, Sept.
20, 1898, Vol. 11.

From Annie Wilson Howe

My darling Brother,   Daggers Springs [Va.] July 7th 1898

    I hope you do not think that I have forgotten the twenty five
dollars I owe you. I deposited the one hundred to your credit in
Princeton Bank, as I suppose Ellie told you. Now I find that I will
have to have another hundred because some payments from
Columbia are delayed. Please, dear, borrow it from the Bank for
four months, or three will do. Do not send me any of your own.
If there is any reason why you do not like to borrow it, please be
perfectly frank about it, and I will get the amount from Columbia.

    It is very warm here. Dr. Flinn is very anxious for us all to go
to Roaring Gap [N.C.] for a few weeks to get some "*real* mountain
air" before we go back to the city, and if we can have our return
tickets changed so that we can go back by Lynchburg instead of
the other way it will cost us very little to get there from here—not
more than we would make up on the board. It would cost us
thirteen dollars a month less than we pay here.

    Now, dear, will you ask the agent if it would be possible to do
that. We went from Charlottesville, through Staunton to Clifton
Forge. Our tickets are from Hot Springs to Princeton. We want to
return by way of Lynchburg.

    Madge could join us at Roaring Gap more easily than she could
come here—and the board is twenty dollars there. The climate is
much more bracing. It would not cost Ed. any more to go there
either, because the small difference in price of ticket would not
more than cover the difference in board. I want to find out about
the tickets at once, so that if we *can* go I can tell Madge all about
it in time. So please ask the agent if we can exchange the portion of our ticket which takes us from Hot Springs to Charlottesville for one by way of Lynchburg. Both routes are over the C. &
O. I think.

    I hope dear father is still with you, and that he is feeling quite like himself now. I wish I could go with him to Saratoga—I cannot bear to think of his going alone. Has he any plans for the winter?

I am sorry to trouble you this way, dear, but it seems impossible to avoid it this time.

Did Ellie receive my letter?[1] I will write to father in a day or two. Warmest love to dear Ellie and to father. Love to the Smiths if they are in Princeton. In haste and with a heart full of love

Your sister, Annie

ALS (WP, DLC).
[1] It is missing.

To Lyon Gardiner Tyler

My dear Dr. Tyler,   Princeton, New Jersey, 11 July, 1898

I find I am lacking vol. II. of the William and Mary Quarterly. If it is still to be had, will you not kindly have it sent to me, with the bill, whether the same as or a little more than the regular subscription price.

I have just had the pleasure of revising the pages in my little volume, "Division and Reunion" in which I spoke of President Tyler's administration, and I hope I have entirely corrected the injustice which I unintentionally did him in the text as first written.[1] I should have liked to rewrite the whole narrative there; but I was obliged, by the economy of the publishers, to change the plates as little as possible, and had to confine myself—very unsatisfactorily—to altering sentences here and there,—and that without changing their length! Still I hope the original wrong is undone, and wish to thank you for calling my attention to it.

With much regard,

Sincerely Yours, Woodrow Wilson

ALS (Tyler Family Papers, ViW).
[1] See L. G. Tyler to WW, July 23, 1897, n. 1.

From Walter Hines Page

Dear Mr. Wilson,   [Cambridge, Mass.] July 13, 1898

"A Lawyer with a Style" is one of your very best essays I think, and the Atlantic will be very proud to publish it in its September number.[1] It has been sent to the printer, and proof and copy will go to you in due time.

I have taken the liberty to omit the passage that you quote from Maine,[2] because your reader will take your word for your statements about his style, and being a reader, and not a hearer, he can take Maine down from his bookshelves and sample him at will to verify all your criticism. I have taken this liberty for the additional and special reason that you show on your manuscript that you made this selection for reading aloud; for you say just after you quote the passage, "Now I have *read* you two pages."

It seems to me that the omission of this evidently oral part of the essay would not mar it for printing, but of course it is left out subject to your approval. If when you receive the copy and the proof you wish to restore it, you have simply to send it back with the proof, indicating where it is to go in, and your wishes shall be carried out to the very letter. I cannot help saying, however, that I hope that you will not do so.[3]

I look forward with very great pleasure to seeing you when you come up this way.   Very truly yours,   Walter H. Page

P.S. I want a paper quickly done & want it bad on Mahan's book[4] —not a review but a general article on the Mahan point of view & doctrine with an application (over[5]

TLS (Houghton Mifflin Letterpress Books, MH).
  [1] "A Lawyer with a Style," *Atlantic Monthly*, LXXXII (Sept. 1898), 363-74.
  [2] In the text (printed at Feb. 25, 1898), Page deleted from "Take the following passage as a sample" through "I do not know how well this passage will serve to illustrate Maine's manner of writing to those who have read or heard no more."
  [3] Wilson accepted Page's emendation.
  [4] It was probably Alfred T. Mahan, *The Interest of America in Sea Power, Present and Future* (Boston, 1898). Wilson did not write the article.
  [5] The verso of this page was not pressed.

To Robert Randolph Henderson

My dear Bob,   Princeton, New Jersey, 16 July, 1898.

This is indeed a delightful scheme you propose; and you may be sure I do not know how to say No.[1]

I am so tied up with other people, over whom I have no control, in the matter of my summer plans, that I shall not be free to move as I please until September; but, if you can make up your party to begin some time during the week which begins September 4, I can be with you and shall come right gladly. Even early the next week I could manage it, though that would be coming uncomfortably close to the opening of college.

How jolly it will be, and how heartily I am obliged to you for the invitation! It will be the finest kind of rejuvenating preparation for the winter's work.

With warmest messages from us all,

Affectionately Yours,   Woodrow Wilson

WWTLS (WC, NjP).

¹ Henderson's letter is missing, but he had invited Wilson to visit him in Cumberland, Md., and said that he would invite certain other members of the Class of 1879 once a date agreeable to Wilson had been set.

From Mary Salome Cutler Fairchild¹

Dear sir: Albany, N. Y.   18 Jl '98

We appreciate deeply your interest in our work² and your willingness to help should it not consume too much time. We have divided the large subject which in the library classification which we are using is called sociology, taking out statistics, political science, education and customs. The large subject, with these exceptions, will be in charge of a committee of five as follows: F. M. Crunden, librarian St Louis public library, Prof. J. W. Jenks, Cornell, Prof. [F. H.] Giddings, Columbia, Prof. [A. W.] Small, Chicago university and John G. Brooks of Boston. Mr Crunden and Prof. Jenks have already accepted. The committee on education (already accepted) is Dr Nicholas Murray Butler of Columbia, Pres. Eliot of Harvard and Prof. [Charles] DeGarmo of Cornell. We have for statistics one man, Prof. Richmond Mayo Smith of Columbia. We had placed you alone as the committee on political science. We would send you either this summer or in September, as you prefer, a check list of books published during that period and would forward to you at the seashore, if you wish, books that you wish to examine there. Since you are alone on this subcommittee, there would be no correspondence involved unless from difference of opinion as to the classification of a few books. I have given you the names of the committee on sociology, statistics and education, thinking you might be interested to know who were working on allied subjects. You will understand that we will attend to the proper classification and cataloguing of the books. You will only need to check entries on the lists sent you and to add others if the check list fails to include some which you think belong there. Trusting that this arrangement will reduce the amount of work required on your part to a minimum, and that this minimum is so small that you will feel justified in cooperating with us,

Very sincerely yours   Salome Cutler Fairchild

TLS (WP, DLC) with WWhw notation on env.: "Ans. 22 July, '98."

¹ Vice-Director of the New York State Library School, Albany, 1889-1905.

² Mrs. Fairchild had asked Wilson to participate in the selection of books for the American Library Association's projected catalogue of recommended books for public and private libraries. Much of the work was done in the 1890's by the New York State Library and its library school, both of which were under the directorship of Melvil Dewey. A preliminary list of 5,000 titles was

published in 1893 in conjunction with the A.L.A.'s exhibit at the World's Columbian Exposition in Chicago. The completed work appeared in 1904 under the
auspices of the Library of Congress as Melvil Dewey (ed.), *A.L.A. Catalogue: 8000
Volumes for a Popular Library, with Notes* (Washington, 1904). There is a
copy of this volume in the Wilson Library, DLC, which would seem to indicate
that Wilson cooperated in the undertaking.

A Memorandum

[c. Aug. 1, 1898]

WHAT OUGHT WE TO DO?

A brief season of war has deeply changed our thought, and has
altered, it may be permanently, the conditions of our national
life. We shall be wise to assess the change calmly, if it be indeed
inevitable, and to examine ourselves, what it is we intend and
by what means we hope to accomplish it. We have passed, it
would seem, the parting of the ways: interest and prudence
alike turn our thought to the new country we have entered.

We did not enter upon a war of conquest. We had neither
dreamed of nor desired victories at the ends of the earth and the
spoils of war had not entered in our ca[l]culations. It was for us
a war begun without calculations, upon an impulse of humane
indignation and pity,—because we saw at our very doors a government unmindful of justice or of mercy, contemptuous in its every
practice of the principles we professed to live for, oppressive and
yet not efficient or fit to rule, spoiling men and thwarting
the very bounties of nature in fair islands which it had pillaged
and not used. Its character seemed of a sudden revealed to us,
by an act of assassination. We did not know, we could hardly believe, that its authoritative masters had ordered or done the mad
and brutal thing that wrecked our battle ship and sent her un-
suspecting crew unwarned out of the world; but we did know of
what sort the men were to whom Spain was wont to entrust
power in Cuba; we somehow felt sure that, although it might be
that no man whom Spain had honoured had conceived or done this
dastardly thing, it was nevertheless suitable to the place and its
associations of unjust might and sinister intrigue; it helped us
to know what Cuba was, what her people had seen and endured.
It brought us on the instant to look point blank upon the place
and all that it held, and one look direct was enough. Hitherto
we had heard; now we saw.

It may be that we were a trifle too hasty in some of the things
that followed. No doubt it would have been handsomer to hold
to a somewhat more deliberate pace in negotiation; as if we really
expected it to change the whole course of affairs; and certainly

it would have been more prudent to muster, drill, and equip an army before plunging into war. But very likely history will judge us leniently in these details, if it find us sincere in purpose and just in the motives that led us to take up arms. And, when all is said, were we really hasty? Had we not long been coming to this mind? There was haste only at the end of the journey. Even Mr. Cleveland, calm and masterful beyond other men in moments of crisis, had told Spain very plainly that our time of doubt was near its end; that she must right herself in Cuba very promptly or else look to have us intervene and ourselves dictate a settlement. She cannot have been surprised by what followed; and even our manners in the business were as good as need be when rough work is to be done.

Whatever our judgments or scruples in these matters, the thing is done; cannot be undone; and our future must spring out of it. The processes of our modern life are swift: we cannot stay them by regrets. Only those nations shall approve themselves masterful and fit to act either for themselves or others in such a time which show themselves capable of thinking on the run and amidst the whirl of events. If a nation have the habit of thought, that habit will tell then, and show itself a sort of instinct of steadiness and wisdom. It is for such moments a nation gets itself in training while peace holds and the elements of its life are at rest. It will not run with its head over its shoulder; it will choose its way and make the pace. No doubt the war pleases the jingoes; but any war would please them, and this war was undertaken, not because war is pleasing, but because this particular war was just, and indeed inevitable; and we have not made ourselves a nation of jingoes by undertaking it. It need make no difference to us, moreover, whether we end it in a way to please the jingoes or not. And yet, when it is ended, we shall not be where we were when it began. We cannot return to the point whence we set out. The scenes, the stage itself upon which we act, are changed. We have left the continent which has hitherto been our only field of action and have gone out upon the seas, where the nations are rivals and we cannot live or act apart.

We had forgot what our sailors could do. We have diligently trained them, men and officers, against the time when their grim work should begin, and the lads every year sent to Annapolis have found it a stern school of duty, fit to make them love their profession and to confirm them in the temper of mastery born in them with their blood. We have studied shipbuilding, too, and have put our sailors in charge of fearful engines of warfare constructed after modern models and made perfect in mechanical outfit by the busy inventive genius of their own officers. We have done this as quietly and with as little apparent thought of war as if battle ships and armoured cruisers were but intended as specimens of our handiwork or as yachts for their officers' travels. We had little notion how hard youngsters like Hobson studied; how long men like Dewey could remember the lessons Farragut taught, what it meant to give a man like Wainwright leave to use cannon from the decks of a yacht.[1] It is these quiet gentlemen, for whom we seemed to be providing, first an education, and then only food and uniform and tours to foreign ports, who have now changed the world for us! Their terrible efficiency has given us Manila and has made Cuba and Porto Rico untenable by Spain. Moreover, they have strangely quickened our blood. The work of war seems ennobled when done as they do it,—with a manifest earnest passion for service, but with no love of slaughter,—with a great pity, rather, for those whom they destroy,—like the christian gentlemen we would have them be

The world into which they have brought us is a very modern world. It is not like any other the nations have lived in. In it civilization has become aggressive, and we are made aware that choices are about to be made as vital as those which determined the settlement and control of North America. The question is not, Shall the vital nations of Europe take possession of the territories of those which are less vital and divide the kingdoms of Africa and Asia? The question is now, Which nations shall possess the world? England, Russia, Germany, France, these are the rivals in the new spoliation:—perhaps only England, Germany, and Russia, for France cannot keep the same course for two months together. Her cabinets are not free to make up their minds. Of a sudden we stand in the midst of these. *What ought we do*? It is not simply a question of expediency: the question of expediency is itself infinitely hard to settle. It is a question also of moral obligation. What *ought* we to do?

WWhw MS. (WP, DLC).

[1] Commander Richard Wainwright, executive officer of the battleship *Maine* when she blew up in Havana harbor. Wainwright later commanded *Gloucester*, formerly the yacht of J. Pierpont Morgan, a small, frail vessel with an inadequate battery. Under his command, *Gloucester* took part in the battle of Santiago on July 3, 1898, attacking two Spanish destroyers, each the superior of *Gloucester*, sinking one and causing the other to run ashore. Congress advanced Wainwright ten numbers in rank for his exploit.

To Daniel Moreau Barringer[1]

Harbor View Hotel,

My dear Barringer,   East Gloucester, Mass., 3 Aug. 1898

Yes, the books[2] reached me promptly, and it gratified me very keenly that you should wish me to have them. It was thoughtful and kind of you to send them, my dear fellow, and I have not written to acknowledge their receipt because I knew that you were on a tour around the world and did not know where to reach you. I shall value them not a little.

I am delighted to hear that you are going to bring Mrs. Barringer[3] to Princeton, and hope it will be when we are at home. Mrs. Wilson will be as delighted as I shall be.

I know you must be happy, and, for my part, I feel that you have a right to be. We shall look forward with the greatest pleasure to seeing you both.

With affection,   Faithfully Yours,   Woodrow Wilson

We shall return home about the middle of September.

ALS (WC, NjP).
[1] Born Raleigh, N.C., May 25, 1860. A.B., College of New Jersey, 1879; A.M., 1882; LL.B., University of Pennsylvania, 1882. Practiced law, 1882-89. Deciding to go into geology and mining, he took special courses in geology at Harvard in 1889 and in chemistry and mineralogy at the University of Virginia in 1890. From that time on he was a mining engineer and geologist and president and director of several mining companies. Died Nov. 30, 1929.
[2] Daniel Moreau Barringer, *A Description of Minerals of Commercial Value. A Practical Reference-Book* (New York, 1897), and Daniel Moreau Barringer and John S. Adams, *The Law of Mines and Mining in the United States* (Boston, 1897).
[3] Barringer had married Margaret Bennett on October 20, 1897.

To John Albert Potter[1]

My dear Mr. Potter,   East Gloucester, Mass., 6 August, 1898

I am sorry to have been obliged to delay my answer to your letter so long; but I must ask you to excuse the delay as in fact unavoidable.

I would suggest as a very stimulating subject for a thesis the following, and hope that you will be able to take it up: *The Arguments for and against a Codification of English law or of the law of an American State.*[2]

With much regard,

Very sincerely Yours,   Woodrow Wilson

ALS (in possession of John A. Potter, Jr.).
[1] Princeton '96, at this time teaching at Irving Institute in Tarrytown, N. Y.
[2] If Potter had plans to do graduate work, he soon abandoned them. He taught at Irving Institute until 1899, at J. A. Browning's School in New York, 1899-1903, and at Carpenter's School in New York while he was a student at the New York Law School, 1903-1905. He began the practice of law in New York in 1905.

From Harper and Brothers

Dear Sir: New York City   Aug 27, 1898

Your letter of the 7th inst was duly received.[1]

We have waited to hear from the artist who drew the illustration of "Congress Hall," before writing you concerning it. The artist only remembers that he got his authority from an old volume which was sent him, and the head of the art department at that time is now dead, and we cannot trace the book from which the drawing was made. Can you conveniently indicate some picture from which a new drawing can be made, if it should be deemed of sufficient importance that we should have a new view of the building, at that period?

We are considering the matter of a popular edition of "George Washington," and shall write you shortly concerning it.

Our idea, however, is rather to print from the present plates on smaller and lighter paper, and to make the retail price much lower.[2]

We return Mr. Riter's letter enclosed herewith.

Very truly yours   Harper & Brothers.   per a.

ALS (WP, DLC) with WWhw notations on env.: "Ans. 30 Aug., '98" and "G. Washington."

[1] Wilson's letter is missing. He had written after receiving Frank M. Riter to WW, Aug. 2, 1898, TLS (WP, DLC). Riter, director of the Department of Public Safety of Philadelphia, pointed out that the cut of Congress Hall, 1790-1800, in *George Washington*, facing page 282, was from a print made in 1813 or afterward.

[2] Harper and Brothers brought out an inexpensive popular edition of *George Washington* in 1900.

From Ellen Axson Wilson

My own darling,   Princeton   Sept 8/98

The telegram reached me yesterday and was a great comfort.[1] Am so glad you are well and happy;—am glad Mr. Lee could be of your number too. Five[2] is enough to be quite a jolly party,—it delights me to think what a good time you are having.

We are all perfectly well and happy, though it certainly was dreary to reach home without my darling. It took all flavour out of the home-coming—for me at least. The children were as usual wild with glee over everything. Puff and Bunnie[3] we found duly installed and in excellent condition. Puff charmed the children by her evident delight in their arrival.

The place looks lovely and beautifully taken care of; both Mrs. Ricketts & the Hunts testify to the extraordinary faithfulness of Richard.[4] The house too was in perfect order, so that I have really had nothing to do but unpack. We have been chiefly occupied in going out enjoying the glorious autumn weather, seeing our friends, and reading "Mansfield Park,"[5]—that is the girls read and I embroider. Everyone says the weather all the summer has been something frightful, culminating in the last almost intolerable week. This delicious change came with that storm just an hour before our arrival. I cannot be thankful enough for your sake that we were led to go to a really cool place this summer and to stay as long as we did. Really no one can talk of anything but the awful heat; and it seems to have been general everywhere —"summer resorts" included—in this part of the world. I write in great haste to get this off by the early mail. Your sweet letter[6] has come since I began to write. With love beyond all words I am as ever, darling,   Your devoted little wife,   Eileen.

ALS (WC, NjP).
  [1] This telegram, telling about Wilson's safe arrival at Cumberland, Md., to visit Robert R. Henderson, is missing.
  [2] Robert Bridges, William Brewster Lee, Wilson, Hiram Woods, Jr., and their host, Robert R. Henderson, all members of the Class of 1879.
  [3] Cats.
  [4] A watchman and yardman.
  [5] By Jane Austen.
  [6] This letter, probably written in Baltimore on September 7, is missing.

Four Letters to Ellen Axson Wilson

My own darling,   Cumberland, Md.,   9 Sept., 1898

Our journey was without unusual incident of any sort. We spent a pleasant night in Baltimore; left there at 10:12 yesterday (Thursday) morning, and reached here yesterday afternoon at 3:12. I had no idea Cumberland was so far away from Baltimore! We came by the B. & O. through Washington and were (I should judge by the R. R. map) nearly half-way to Pittsburgh when we got here!

We saw Mitchell[1] for a little while on Thursday evening at the hotel. Bridges reached Balto. about 5 in the afternoon and left word at Charlie's house when I would arrive and where he was to look us up, and he was promptly on hand when I got there. Bob. saw the new *Mrs.* Mitchell[2] when he went to look Charlie up, and reports her bright, cheery, and handsome,—altogether attractive. Charlie does not seem to have been bidden hither. We did not like to ask at either end. Probably Bob. H. felt that he had room for only four of us; though the rooms of this beautiful house are big enough for twice as many. There does not seem to be a bed-room in the establishment smaller than ours at home.

We found Woods already here and Lee arrived an hour or two after we did. It is the jolly, boyish set you would expect, and the time is likely to go merrily. I am afraid there will be no getting home before Wednesday,—so much has been put on our programme.

Mrs. Henderson is most attractive and the home every way delightful. I am perfectly well. My fall on the platform did not give me even a moment's inconvenience. Love to all. My heart overflows for my darling, and I am altogether

Your own   Woodrow

¹ Dr. Charles W. Mitchell of Baltimore, Princeton '79.
² Mitchell married Florence M. Crowe on July 14, 1898.

My own darling,   Cumberland, Md., 10th September 1898

The time goes smoothly,—as well for me as possible with no letter from home. Bridges and Lee are golf devotees and much of their time goes to that sport. This morning I went over the course with them as a spectator and found it as interesting as a spectator usually does. It really seems worth playing; but it does not follow that I shall conclude to play it.¹

Cumberland is well up in the hills, not to say the mountains (it is the site of the Fort Cumberland built on Wills' Creek in Washington's time, at the first passes of the mountains) and the views are as fine as the air. It is a manufacturing place, but is not big enough to foul the air in any hopeless fashion & any respectable breeze will clear the smoke away and disclose the truly lovely outlook. Bob. has a fine team of horses and has taken us on several drives which have revealed the region at its best, and we are all charmed with it. The weather has been charming. The temperature went down with a rush the very day we came, and we have had, both nights, to sleep under two blankets. I have a big room all to myself and a delightful bed and have slept like a top. I am very well indeed, and not doing too much. Jno. Wilson of '92 lives next door and to-night we are to dine with him, to meet the five or six Princeton graduates of the town. I am afraid it is certain that we cannot get away until Wednesday morning. Don't let the girls² go before I get back. Give them my love; kiss the children all around and think of me as with unspeakable longing

Your own   Woodrow

¹ The first evidence that Wilson had taken up golf comes from the announcement in the *Daily Princetonian*, April 12, 1899, that Wilson would participate in the Spring Handicap Golf Tournament on April 12, with a handicap of sixteen.
² Lucy and Mary Smith.

My own darling,   Cumberland, Md.,   11 September, 1898

Your first letter reached me this morning (Sunday) and was more welcome than I can say. I was too anxious for it to let myself dwell on the matter at all. I am *so* glad that you are all well and that home seems sweet. My darling seems to exclude herself from the enjoyment, and to ascribe it all to the children. You are not blue, are you, sweetheart? Did you find everything all right, and are you not happy?

I shall get away as early as decent on Wednesday morning, and shall try to arrange a schedule by which I shall reach home that night; but it *may* not be possible to get to Princeton before Thursday morning,—so don't be disappointed.

John Wilson's little dinner last night was a great success. The crowd was thoroughly congenial, the things to eat were savoury and excellent, the talk was lively and entertaining, and the evening passed gaily. After dinner we went for about half an hour to the birth-day party of an old gentleman who was eighty-two years old, and saw the most diverting party of elderly men solemnly absorbing punch and saying never a word. Our coming in seemed to add the necessary zest of young blood and things went more merrily after that. You would have admired the art with which I pretended to drink the punch and participate in the toasts, without drinking a drop, in order not to dampen the jovial spirit of the occasion!

I am writing in the midst of conversation and interruption; but my heart is full always of you, no matter what the time or the matter in hand. Ah, my darling, I am never happy away from from you. I am always and altogether

Your own   Woodrow

Love to "the girls" and the darling chicks. Regards to Fraülein C.[1] I am quite well.   W.

1 The German governess, Clara Böhm.

My own darling,   Cumberland, Md. 12 September, 1898

Sunday was a day of comparative rest—church in the morning, naps in the afternoon, callers in the evening. To-day Bridges and Lee and Woods have gone about 20 miles up the road to the "South Branch" of the Potomac to fish for black bass, getting up at five o'clock to catch a train. I feel sadly out of sport, being unable to play golf or fish with flies. I must qualify in one or the other sport in order not to seem a mere book-man—a mere theorist in life—a mere man of letters.

We made an interesting discovery at breakfast this morning, Bob H. and I. He too is descended from the FitzRandolphs of New Jersey,—just how, i.e. by what particular line or lines, he will tell me when he finds his chart of the tree. He thinks it traces to, or near to, the giver of the college land.[1] He sends his warmest regards to you, and hopes you and he will turn out to be cousins.[2] You certainly could not have a nobler or more lovable fellow for kinsman,—and I sincerely hope it will turn out that the lines run together.

There is nothing particular on hand for me to-day, but this evening there is to be a reception here at Bob's—the only affair in wh. "the gang" is concerned to which ladies are bidden. To-morrow we dine with the Governor (Lowndes),[3] who resides here and is to have a man's dinner.

I've caught a slight cold in the head, as a consequence of the extraordinary change of weather, but it amounts to very little, and I am quite well. I love you with all my heart and want you, even in the midst of pleasure, more than I can ever say. My chief pleasure is always from you, and I am altogether

Your own   Woodrow

Love in full measure to all.

ALS (WP, DLC).

[1] Nathaniel Fitz Randolph deeded four and one half acres of land to the trustees of the College of New Jersey on January 26, 1753, and this tract became the original campus of the college.

[2] As this remark indicates, there was a lively tradition in the Wilson family that Mrs. Wilson was descended from Nathaniel Fitz Randolph. See Eleanor Wilson McAdoo (ed.), *The Priceless Gift* (New York, 1962), p. 218. The Editors have been unable to verify the tradition.

[3] Governor Lloyd Lowndes of Maryland.

INDEX

NOTE ON THE INDEX

THE alphabetically arranged analytical table of contents at the front of the volume eliminates duplication, in both contents and index, of references to certain documents, such as letters. Letters are listed in the contents alphabetically by name, and chronologically within each name by page. The subject matter of all letters is, of course, indexed. The Editorial Notes and Wilson's writings are listed in the contents chronologically by page. In addition, the subject matter of both categories is indexed. The index covers all references to books and articles mentioned in text or notes. Footnotes are indexed. Page references to footnotes which place a comma between the page number and "n" cite both text and footnote, thus: "624,n3." On the other hand absence of the comma indicates reference to the footnote only, thus: "55n2"—the page number denoting where the footnote appears. The letter "n" without a following digit signifies an unnumbered descriptive-location note.

An asterisk before an index reference designates identification or other particular information. Re-identification and repetitive annotation have been minimized to encourage use of these starred references. Where the identification appears in an earlier volume, it is indicated thus: "*1:212,n3." Therefore a page reference standing without a preceding volume number is invariably a reference to the present volume. The index supplies the fullest known forms of names, and, for the Wilson and Axson families, relationships as far down as cousins. Persons referred to in the text by nicknames or shortened forms of names can be identified by reference to entries for these forms of the names.

A sampling of the opinions and comments of Wilson and Ellen Axson Wilson covers their more personal views, while broad, general headings in the main body of the index cover impersonal subjects. Occasionally opinions expressed by a correspondent are indexed where these appear to supplement or to reflect views expressed by Wilson or by Ellen Axson Wilson in documents which are missing.

INDEX

WOODROW WILSON

AND ELLEN AXSON WILSON

APPEARANCE

BIOGRAPHY

FAMILY LIFE AND DOMESTIC AFFAIRS

Woodrow Wilson, cont.

HEALTH

THE JOHNS HOPKINS UNIVERSITY

NEW YORK LAW SCHOOL

OPINIONS AND COMMENTS